Pen and Ink Witchcraft

Pen and Ink Witchcraft

TREATIES AND TREATY MAKING IN
AMERICAN INDIAN HISTORY

Colin G. Calloway

OXFORD
UNIVERSITY PRESS

Oxford University Press is a department of the University of Oxford.
It furthers the University's objective of excellence in research, scholarship,
and education by publishing worldwide.

Oxford   New York
Auckland   Cape Town   Dar es Salaam   Hong Kong   Karachi
Kuala Lumpur   Madrid   Melbourne   Mexico City   Nairobi
New Delhi   Shanghai   Taipei   Toronto

With offices in
Argentina   Austria   Brazil   Chile   Czech Republic   France   Greece
Guatemala   Hungary   Italy   Japan   Poland   Portugal   Singapore
South Korea   Switzerland   Thailand   Turkey   Ukraine   Vietnam

Oxford is a registered trademark of Oxford University Press in the UK and certain other
countries.

Published in the United States of America by
Oxford University Press
198 Madison Avenue, New York, NY 10016

Calloway, Colin G. (Colin Gordon), 1953-
  Pen and ink witchcraft : treaties and treaty making in American Indian history /
Colin G. Calloway.
      pages cm
  Includes bibliographical references and index.
  ISBN 978-0-19-991730-3 (alk. paper)
  1. Indians of North America—Treaties. I. Title.
  KF8205.C35 2013
  346.7301'3-dc23
                                    2012045536
ISBN 978-0-19-991730-3

9 8 7 6 5 4 3 2 1
Printed in the United States of America
on acid-free paper

"that *pen and ink witch-craft*, which they can make speak things we never intended, or had any idea of, even an hundred years hence; just as they please."—the Ottawa chief Egushawa in council on the banks of the Ottawa River, 1791

"Nations that deserve the Title of Treaty breakers, that are not to be bound by the most solemn Covenants, but break the chain of Friendship, will soon fall into Contempt."—Governor James Glen of South Carolina to the Six Nations, 1755

To Marcia, Graeme, and Meg

{ CONTENTS }

Acknowledgments and a Note on Terminology   xi

Introduction   1

1. **Treaty Making in Colonial America:
   The Many Languages of Indian Diplomacy   12**

2. **Fort Stanwix, 1768: Shifting Boundaries   49**

3. **Treaty Making, American-Style   96**

4. **New Echota, 1835: Implementing Removal   121**

5. **Treaty Making in the West   164**

6. **Medicine Lodge, 1867: Containment on the Plains   182**

   Conclusion: The Death and Rebirth of Indian Treaties   226

Appendix: The Treaties   245
Notes   285
Bibliography   335
Index   351

{ ACKNOWLEDGMENTS AND
A NOTE ON TERMINOLOGY }

Anyone doing Indian history has to take account of Indian treaties. I began reading them nearly forty years ago, as a graduate student poring over the manuscript records of innumerable Indian councils in the British Museum and the Public Records Office (now the National Archives) in London. But many scholars have thought about treaties, . . . talked about them, and written about them long before I took on this project. In addition to those whom I have cited in the notes and bibliography, an incomplete list of individuals I remember talking with, listening to, and learning from over the years must include N. Bruce Duthu, the late William N. Fenton and the late Francis Jennings, Laurence M. Hauptman, Frederick E. Hoxie, Francis Paul Prucha, K. Tsianina Lomawaima, Heidi Kiiwetinepinesiik Stark, the late Helen Hornbeck Tanner, Dale Turner, Jace Weaver, and David Wilkins. They and other friends and scholars fueled my interest in Indian treaties at one time or another even if they didn't know it, although they bear no responsibility for this book.

A few had more direct influence. William Campbell and I found ourselves studying the Treaty of Fort Stanwix at about the same time; for Bill it was the core of his dissertation—now his first book—and for me it was a story that had to be told in the book I was envisioning. I am grateful to Bill for sharing his manuscript with me and for reading my chapter on Stanwix. I am indebted to Theda Perdue for reading and commenting on the chapter on New Echota. Not for the first time (and I'm sure not for the last) I called on my good friend and colleague Bruce Duthu to cast his expert eye over what I had to say about treaties in modern America. I would not have found Howling Wolf's drawing of the Medicine Lodge treaty council without Joyce M. Szabo, and Sharon Muhlfeld first provided me, many years ago, with the original reference for the pen and ink witchcraft quotation. Ned Blackhawk and a second, anonymous, reviewer carefully read the manuscript for Oxford University Press and provided thoughtful comments and insightful suggestions that helped me to bring out the story more effectively.

In completing the research for this book, I benefited enormously from the assistance of good staff members at the Baker/Berry Library and Rauner Library of Dartmouth College; at the National Archives at College Park, Maryland; and at the Manuscripts and Archives Division of the New York Public Library. For assistance in acquiring illustrations and sometimes other materials, I am grateful to Josh Shaw at Rauner Library; Bridgeman Art Library International–New York; Chicago History Museum; Washington State Historical Society; Library and Archives, Canada; Pennsylvania Historical Society; New-York Historical Society; New York State Library; Oklahoma Historical Society; University of Oklahoma Western History Collections; History Colorado (the Colorado Historical Society); and the National Anthropological Archives and Human Studies Film Archives of the Smithsonian Institution.

As in all my writing and teaching, I use the terms "Native American" and "Indian" interchangeably. I also use "tribe" and "nation" interchangeably when describing Native American tribal nations, and I do not mean to suggest that they are either less than or the same as nation-states. I recognize that the tribal names that appear in historic records and later histories often reflect other people's names for the nations in question, not the names the people used to identify themselves, and sometimes not the preferred names today. However, though respectful to the peoples involved, replacing anglicized names with the tribes' own names causes other problems. Many readers might recognize Haudenosaunee as a more appropriate term for the Iroquois, and some might recognize Kanien'kehaka as Mohawk, but applying this practice consistently to every Indian nation mentioned in the book would confront readers with a bewildering array of unfamiliar terms. For this reason, I suspect, Taiaiake Alfred replaces Mohawk with Kanien'kehaka as the appropriate name for his own nation, but he continues to use anglicized names like Sioux, Cheyenne, and Cherokee when referring to other people.[1] Rather than privileging just a few tribes with their own names, I have opted for consistency, using the anglicized names more familiar to most readers, except in cases like Dakota and Lakota, which are not only commonly recognized but also specify particular divisions of the Sioux.

Pen and Ink Witchcraft

{ Introduction }

In the summer of 1701, 1,300 Indians descended on Montreal, a town with slightly more than one thousand inhabitants. The Indians came from nearly forty separate nations, from as far away as Acadia in the East and the Mississippi in the West. Many of them traveled months to get there. A dozen years earlier, a huge Iroquois war party had destroyed the nearby settlement of La Chine, killing or capturing one hundred people. But the Indians who flocked to Montreal in 1701 came to talk, not to fight.

The Great Peace of Montreal, as it came to be known, was an international summit meeting, the culmination of years of negotiations. After decades of recurrent conflict with the French and their Native allies, the Five Nations that composed the Iroquois League—the Mohawks, Oneidas, Onondagas, Cayugas, and Senecas—faced a demographic crisis. War and disease had scythed their populations, and they needed peace.[1] So did the French and the Indian nations who allied with them. An Onondaga chief named Teganissorens had begun exploring paths to peace after a French army destroyed three Mohawk towns in 1693, and his shuttle diplomacy between Onondaga, Albany, and Quebec had slowly built momentum. For almost three weeks in the summer of 1701 Montreal was the stage for a brand of political theater that played out time and again in North America over the course of three centuries as Europeans and Indians engaged in rituals of diplomacy, exchanged lengthy speeches in formal councils, and hammered out deals in private meetings.[2] In between the negotiations, Montreal resembled a Bruegel painting, brimming with human activity, as delegates came and went, visiting, feasting, wandering the streets, looking in stores, and trading goods and stories. Indian men, women, and children, speaking dozens of different languages and wearing distinctive hairstyles, body tattoos, and clothing, found themselves rubbing shoulders with French soldiers and colonists, donning French hats and coats, and sampling French food. In the final peace treaty signed on August 4, the various nations agreed to bury the hatchet, consider each other friends, and recognize the French governor as the mediator in disputes. The western tribes allowed the Iroquois to share hunting territories north of Lake Ontario and west of Detroit, and the Iroquois agreed to allow France's Indian allies access to trade at Albany. Iroquois delegates in Albany also made a new alliance with the English. The Iroquois secured a pivotal position in the international relations of eastern North America and essentially embarked on a new foreign policy, assuming a neutral role in the escalating conflict between Britain and France. It was always an imperfect neutrality—Mohawks regularly fought alongside the English, and Senecas often sided with the French—but it enabled the Iroquois to recover from the crippling losses of the previous century and to sustain their position as the major Native power in the Northeast in the next century.[3]

Not all Indian treaty councils were as big, dramatic, or far-reaching in their influence as the Great Peace of Montreal. But some were, and all of these meetings were human and cultural encounters that were hugely important to both the Indian people who participated in them and those who did not participate but whose lives were nonetheless affected by those who did and the documents they signed.

Narratives of American history emphasize the bloody series of wars with indigenous peoples that marked European colonization of North America and the westward expansion of the United States. But colonization and expansion were also marked by a series of treaties with Indian peoples. Wars and treaties—violence and law—worked hand in hand in taking America from the Indians. Although Indians sold land to individual colonists or groups of colonists, governments tried to curb the practice and treaties became the primary instruments by which an Indian continent passed into non-Indian hands, and tribal homelands were transformed into real estate. Treaties functioned as stepping-stones of empire. They enabled colonists to establish a foothold on the continent, colonies to expand their domains, and the United States to march westward, one chunk of territory after another. In treaty after treaty, Indian people were coerced, deceived, manipulated, and misled into giving up their lands in return for pittances and promises that more often than not proved empty. In treaty after treaty, Europeans and Americans produced documents that they utilized to justify, codify, and perpetuate their acquisition and occupation of America. When the imperial or federal government tried to protect Indians and their lands from fraud and dispossession, colonial and state governments, land companies, and speculators often undermined their efforts, making treaties and land deals of their own. Indian leaders understood that the words spoken in treaty councils, translated, transmitted to writing, and recorded on paper had the power to take away their lands and their rights. They called the process "pen and ink witchcraft."[4]

Indians participated in the pen and witchcraft process by putting pen to paper, signing their agreements usually by marking an *x* next to or below their names. As the Ojibwe/Dakota scholar Scott Lyons explains, "An x-mark is a sign of consent in a context of coercion; it is the agreement one makes when there seems to be little choice in the matter. To the extent that little choice isn't quite the same thing as no choice, it signifies Indian agency."[5] Nevertheless, the notion that Indian negotiators were invariably naïve, gullible, and befuddled by legal language or drink does not gibe with the evidence regarding Indian presence and participation that emerges from the records of treaty negotiations. Confronted by duplicitous dealings, divide-and-rule tactics, the arrogance of power, and threats of starvation and destruction, Indians frequently spoke out forcefully, matched their colonizing counterparts in diplomatic savvy, and shaped the outcome of negotiations as they tried, literally, to hold their ground. Sometimes they employed negotiations and treaties to preserve their lands and postpone dispossession. Confronted by hard choices, Indian delegates often knew exactly what they were doing and what the consequences of their decisions were likely to be. And after the treaties were made, they remembered what they had done, protested against abuses of the treaties they had made, lobbied hard to have treaties honored or overturned, and, finally, fought for their treaty rights in the "courts of the conqueror."[6] Early treaties that revolved around trade and required Indian cooperation were more often agreements between equals than were later treaties that revolved around land and required Indian dispossession. When the Mohawks opened their territory to Dutch traders early in the seventeenth century, they negotiated a pact of peace and friendship. The metaphor for the relationship was embodied in the *Gus-Wen-Tah* or *Kaswentha,* a two-row wampum belt: a background of white beads linked the Mohawks and Dutch in peace, while parallel rows of purple beads represented them traveling the same river side by side but each group in its own boat, forever separate and equal as autonomous nations.[7] As time went on, power relations became increasingly lopsided. The contradictions, flagrant abuses, and hypocrisies in treaty making became glaringly apparent when the United States adapted and applied processes and procedures developed in the colonial era to fuel national expansion with the rapid acquisition of Native lands. Tracing the evolution, application, abolition, and resurgence of treaties illuminates shifts in power, changing attitudes about the place of Indian people in American society, and contested ideas about indigenous rights in a modern constitutional democracy. Treaties are a barometer of Indian-white relations in North America.

Europeans claimed America by the right of discovery. Rights of discovery, Europeans agreed, gave them first claim against other Europeans, although, of course, they frequently and fiercely contested each other's claims. They established claims to territory by planting standards, making speeches, and acting out other rituals of possession, often in the presence of bemused Native people they had assembled to bear witness to the event.[8] At Sault Ste. Marie in 1671, for instance, amid music and pageantry and with four Jesuit priests and delegates from fourteen Indian nations in attendance, the French announced that Louis XIV was taking possession of the entire Mississippi Valley, an area the size of the Indian subcontinent. It was a fiction, of course—France lacked any real power in the area and depended on a network of Indian alliances and recurrent local rituals to build and sustain its western empire—but the purpose of the ceremony was to exclude the English rather than to establish an actual French presence.[9] European powers invoked the doctrine of discovery to claim that Christian nations that discovered new lands gained property rights over such lands and could assert sovereignty over the indigenous people living there. Europeans justified taking the lands of indigenous people according to their own colonizing rule of law, which was grounded in medieval discourses of conquest, and they felt free to transfer their claims to other powers without consulting the territory's indigenous inhabitants.[10]

In the colonial era, Indians made treaties with the French, Dutch, Spaniards, British, and various British colonies. Roger Williams declared in 1630 that Europeans could justly occupy lands in America "only by purchasing those lands from their rightful owners, the Indians" (an opinion that got him into hot water with the authorities in Massachusetts Bay Colony), but individuals and groups who purchased land from Indian people in private transactions and deeds often employed fraudulent practices. They threatened violence, designated "chiefs" to act for the tribe, plied Natives with alcohol, forged signatures, mistranslated terms, misrepresented boundaries, and often furnished shoddy trade goods in exchange for the lands they acquired. Colonial governments struggled to regulate or prohibit any private purchases and the question of whether individuals had the right to buy Indian lands remained a recurrent issue. Events in the 1760s initiated a new era of treaty relations that brought to the fore tensions—between local interests and imperial or national authority, as well as between Indians and white settlers—that characterized treaty making and treaty maintenance for generations to follow. At the end of the so-called French and Indian Wars in 1763, France relinquished its North American territory, handing over everything east of the Mississippi to Britain and its possessions west of the Mississippi to Spain. Confronted with a vast new empire to administer, the British colonial government tried to control the process of acquiring Indian land by establishing formal treaties between Indian tribes and the Crown's representatives as the legal means of doing so. Twenty years and a revolution later, Britain ceded all its territory south of the Great Lakes, east of the Mississippi, and north of Florida to the United States, and the government of this new nation set about obtaining full title to the territory in much the same way. The federal government claimed the sole right to acquire Indian lands, which became part of the public domain, and it then re-sold land to American citizens. Transactions carried out by land companies and individual speculators, sometimes in defiance of imperial or federal laws and regulations, were sometimes designated as "treaties," but formal treaties between sovereigns were the legal basis for acquiring most Indian land in America.[11]

Twenty years after the United States acquired the region between the Atlantic and the Mississippi from Britain, it bought the Louisiana Territory—stretching roughly from the Mississippi to the Rocky Mountains—from Napoleon Bonaparte, who had acquired it back from Spain with a proviso that he would not sell it to a third party. The next year, Thomas Jefferson dispatched Meriwether Lewis and William Clark on an expedition to the Pacific, during which they proclaimed the United States the new sovereign in the West, and in subsequent decades the United States obtained full title to land in the West by making treaties with the Indian nations that lived there. What European powers conveyed to one another or to the United States was not the land itself, but the preemptive right to negotiate with the indigenous people for title to that land. In *Johnson v. McIntosh* in 1823, the United States Supreme Court affirmed American inheritance of rights of discovery from Britain and deployed the doctrine of discovery to legitimize national expansion: Native people retained a limited right to occupy the land, but they could sell it to only the United States. In other words, the Indians were little more than tenants. The doctrine of discovery proved to be "a perfect instrument of empire" for the United States, justifying acquisition of the American continent in accordance with the colonizing rule of law derived from Europe.[12] Transferring paper claims to territory into actual ownership of land required taking possession by purchase, war, treaty, or some combination of the three.

Between the American Revolution and 1871, when Congress ended Indian treaty making, Indians made more than four hundred treaties with the United States. About 370 were ratified; many others were not. They also made treaties with some individual states. During the Civil War, twenty-one tribes in Indian Territory negotiated nine treaties at four locations with the Indian commissioner for the Confederate states. Some Indian nations made treaties with Spain and Mexico; First Nations tribes made seventeen treaties with the Canadian government; one tribe (the Pomo Indians of northern California in 1817) made a treaty with Russia; in 1847 the Comanches made a treaty with a German settlement in Texas.[13] Some tribes made treaties with each other, such as the oral peace pacts in the Comanche-Ute treaty of 1786 or the Great Peace of 1840 between the Kiowas and Cheyennes.[14] Some tribes signed no treaties, some just one, and some signed many. The Potawatomis held the record at twenty-six with the United States but the Cherokees made a total of some thirty-eight treaties with colonial, state, and federal governments, as well as a couple with Spain and the Republic of Texas. Some treaties were done in a day, but many treaty councils went on for several weeks. The 1794 treaty council at Canandaigua between the Iroquois and the United States lasted two months. Some treaties involved one tribe; others many. Some were made with only the imperial or federal government; others involved several colonies or states as well. Most treaties involved at least the formalities of establishing or reaffirming peace and friendship, and most but not all involved ceding lands. Although treaty making was infused with power relations and the power shifted dramatically away from the Indian participants over time, treaties, by their nature, remained formal agreements between sovereigns.

Sensing a market for these historical documents, Benjamin Franklin printed the proceedings of thirteen Indian treaties and then sold them in England.[15] Treaties have been available in print ever since; more recently they have become accessible in electronic compilations as well as on numerous websites.[16] Not surprisingly, lawyers have been most concerned with the terms of the treaties. Others have examined the political and historical as well as the legal dimensions of Indian treaties and, more recently, the process of treaty making and the different philosophies that Indians and Europeans brought to that process.[17] While I, too, examine the terms of treaties (and reproduce their original wording in the appendix), I focus on the treaty negotiations as much as on the outcomes of those negotiations, on the individuals who participated as well as the agreements they reached, and on what became of those individuals in the aftermath—and sometimes as a result—of the treaties they made. Before treaties were documents that shaped American history they were events shaped by individuals. Each treaty had its own story and its own cast of characters and involved particular maneuverings and competing ambitions. Treaties were made out of cultural encounters and human dramas, where people representing different societies and ways of life faced each other in a public contest of words rather than weapons, and where power struggles took place as two distinct civilizations and their idea systems collided.[18]

Viewed from a long perspective of continental domination, the hundreds of Indian treaties look like well-ordered steps in the inevitable march of empire. But it would be wrong to assume that all treaties involved powerful and duplicitous whites browbeating and cheating powerless and clueless Indians. Not all treaties included cessions of Indian land, and many early treaties between colonies and tribes were held primarily to establish, sustain, or renew good relations that were important to both parties. Indians who attended treaties were sometimes concerned with opening or maintaining trade, resolving disputes, or averting conflict rather than selling or protecting their land. As in other encounters, they often found ways to derive advantage from their dealings with colonizing powers. For example, some chiefs used treaties as opportunities to display and enhance their status and to secure gifts that bolstered their own standing and support when distributed among their followers.

The power dynamics usually and increasingly stacked the odds against the Indian participants, and sometimes the United States dictated treaties to Indians in an exercise of raw power. But earlier negotiations usually followed Indian protocol and forms and were sometimes conducted on Indian terms, and Indians usually played a part in determining at least some of a treaty's final language. Often, Indian participants did not fully understand what was going on; sometimes they understood better than their white counterparts. At times, Indian diplomats played off rival colonial powers, invoked colonial power to browbeat Native rivals, sold the lands of other tribes, and even on occasion sold land out from under their own people. At other times they exerted their oratorical and diplomatic skills in desperate efforts to preserve a way of life in the face of devastating changes. Sometimes, weighing their options and weighing the odds, they chose to accept change as their best chance of survival. A traveler and botanist, John Bartram, who in 1743 visited Onondaga, the central council fire of the League, described the Iroquois as "a subtile, prudent, and judicious people in their councils."[19] They had to be. Indians often learned from hard experience how to hold their own during hard bargaining.[20]

Treaties are stories within the larger story of American expansion and Indian dispossession, and the story of each treaty contains many other stories. Treaties generally pitted Indians against whites in the contest for America's resources and the American future, but the colorful cast of characters who assembled at treaty councils followed various paths to get there and brought different experiences and agendas, diverse cultural perspectives, and common human failings. Sometimes a handful of Indians, authorized delegates or not, signed treaties, maybe in a government office or a tavern; at other times Indians assembled at treaty grounds by the hundreds or even thousands. Treaty commissioners often brought with them an entourage of clerks, interpreters, suppliers, and soldiers. Depending on the location of the treaty councils, dozens or even hundreds of spectators and hangers-on could turn out to watch.

Tribes, nations, and colonies did not speak with a united voice. Individuals and groups within groups often had tangential motives for attending the treaties, and competing personalities, agendas, fears, and egos complicated the plot. Individuals often engaged in personal diplomacy prior to or on the sidelines of treaty councils. Treaties were stages for political theater. Even on occasions where the issues had already been settled in battle, in preliminary talks, or in private meetings, treaty councils offered a public ceremony in which to assert sovereignty, revisit past injustices, proclaim the legitimacy of claims, or make a name for oneself. With a sense of the occasion and of their own importance, speakers sometimes engaged in posturing and grandstanding. While the leading actors held forth in public, other players also had key roles, performed behind the scenes, and sometimes deviated from the script. Participants acted for the best or in their own interests but they could not know for sure what the consequences of their actions would be. Sometimes, like nations blundering into war, they made decisions with unforeseeable consequences simply to avoid making other decisions whose consequences were clear and unacceptable. Sometimes the cultural gulf between speakers meant that they talked past each other; sometimes participants left treaty councils dissatisfied, unsure what had happened, or with very different understandings of what had happened. Their lives intersected for a moment of intense cultural and diplomatic encounter and were affected, and in some cases shortened, by the actions they took and the agreements they made.

More than eighty years ago, the scholar Lawrence Wroth made the case for regarding Indian treaties as the first real American literature, containing "the quick stuff of an epic fermentation" and in which "one reads the passion, the greed, and the love of life of hard-living men brought into close relationship without parallel conditions in the history of either race to guide its conduct." Wroth wished he had read Indian treaties in school as the literature of colonial America, instead of the dull writings of Puritan ministers.[21] James Merrell, a historian, agrees: "Councils are compelling theatre, a lively stage on which the peoples of early America acted out the contest for the continent."[22]

Treaty making and treaty relations changed over time as multiple Indian nations negotiated with changing Euro-American governments in very different circumstances. *Pen and Ink Witchcraft* begins with the protocols, practices, and precedents of Indian diplomacy in colonial America but then focuses on a century of shifting treaty relationships that is crucial to understanding not just American Indian history but also the history of America. In 1768 the Treaty of Fort Stanwix culminated imperial efforts to create and maintain a boundary line separating Indians and whites; in 1871 Congress ended treaty making with Indian tribes and assumed that individual Indians would soon be swallowed up within American society. I trace a transition from treaty making in the colonial era to treaty making in the new nation, and from treaty making with the goal of removing Indians to treaty making with the intent of confining and transforming Indians. The core of this book contains the stories behind the Treaty of Fort Stanwix, the Treaty of New Echota in 1835, and the Treaty of Medicine Lodge in 1867. Of course, many other treaties qualify as events of major importance: the Peace of Montreal in 1701, the Treaty of Lancaster in 1744, the Treaty of Fort Pitt in 1778, the Treaty of Greenville in 1795, and the Treaties of Fort Laramie in 1851 and 1868, to name a few, were dramatic in their content and enduring in their consequences. Like the treaties featured here, they shaped the course of Indian relations and American history in what they did and what they failed to do, in the intentions they made clear and the changes they signified, and in the legacies they left. Yet each of the three treaties

I concentrate on represents a distinct phase in treaty relations and in the acquisition of Native American land.

Growing hostilities between Indians and colonists after the middle of the eighteenth century, and the bloodletting during and after the French and Indian War, destroyed many previous patterns of coexistence, generated new levels of race hatred, and increased requests on both sides for boundary lines that would separate Indians and whites, even though these people often disagreed about the meanings of boundaries as well as about their placement. The Treaty of Fort Stanwix in New York established a new boundary line between Indian and white lands in a world where Indian and white people mingled, but in doing so this division contributed to escalating racial violence and eventually to the revolution that destroyed that world. In creating this treaty, Sir William Johnson and George Croghan, two Irish traders who became Indian agents and land speculators, exceeded their authority, shifted an imperial boundary westward, pulled off a massive land deal, and did very well for themselves. The Iroquois secured imperial endorsement of their claims to dominance over lands and people they did not dominate. But much of the land the Iroquois gave up belonged to someone else, and the consequences for Johnson and Croghan and for the Iroquois proved dire. Ultimately neither the Iroquois nor the British were able to preserve their former authority in the region.

The Indian Removal Act of 1830 stands as a landmark in federal Indian policy, but the process of Indian removal involved negotiations among the federal government, the states, various tribes, and factions within tribes, and it generated and deepened divisions within the tribes. The Treaty of New Echota implemented removal of the Cherokees from the Southeast and from a world where, said the United States, there was no longer a place for Indians, no matter how "civilized" they might have become. A handful of prominent Cherokees, including Elias Boudinot, a former editor of the bilingual newspaper *The Cherokee Phoenix*, and Major Ridge and his son John, bowed to what they saw as the inevitable by ceding tribal lands to the United States and setting their people on a dreadful march into exile along the Trail of Tears. They signed the treaty knowing that the penalty for doing so under Cherokee law was death; four years later they died at Cherokee hands in the Indian Territory to which they had been exiled and the schisms that formed around the treaty continued to divide Cherokee society through the Civil War. The Treaty of New Echota stands as the most glaring example of American determination to implement by treaty the policy of removing Indians from the eastern United States to the open spaces beyond the Mississippi, and it is an enduring indictment of a nation that trampled its own treaties in order to carry out ethnic cleansing.

As the United States expanded west across the Great Plains after the Civil War it sought to implement a policy of confining Plains Indians to reservations

where they would abandon their mobile hunting lifestyle and adopt a sedentary life as farmers. The Treaty of Medicine Lodge established reservations as
crucibles of change where Indians would learn to adapt to a new world and
prepare for absorption, and ultimate disappearance, within American society.
During the treaty council, an event covered by a young reporter named Henry
M. Stanley (famous later in life for his "Doctor Livingston, I presume" greeting
in "darkest Africa"), the Kiowa chiefs Satank and Satanta argued for a vision
of a future on the southern Plains that their American counterparts knew was
impossible and they affixed their names to a peace that could bring no peace. In
the violence that followed, both died self-induced deaths. Further breaches of
the treaty led, a quarter century later, to one of the most momentous Supreme
Court decisions in American Indian history.

These three meetings—in the colonial Northeast, in the early national
South, and on the Great Plains as American expansion geared for its final push
across the West—signpost the story of Indian relations and nation building in
this country. These three stories stand on their own as dramatic human and
cultural encounters with far-reaching repercussions; together they represent the
workings and evolution of the treaty-making process and the role of treaties in
wresting America from its original inhabitants.

Individually and collectively, the men who made these treaties shaped the
course of American history. Negotiating in pressure-cauldron situations, they
tried to find the words to advance or stem, or just divert and delay, tides of historical change. Their efforts were sometimes sordid, often heroic, but too often
tragic and futile. When the dust of conquest and colonialism settled, Indians
were left with little land and with treaties that often seemed to be not worth
the paper they were written on. But Indian and non-Indian treaty makers left a
documentary record unlike any other, and far from being dry and dusty documents or "ancient history," Indian treaties have life and power. They are foun-
dational documents in the nation's history, alongside "sacred texts" like the
Declaration of Independence and the Constitution, and, like them, they are
open to interpretation by subsequent generations.

Treaties hold pledges made long ago and sometimes long deferred. During
a visit to Canada in May 2012 Britain's Prince Charles met with several First
Nations leaders in Toronto who showed him a replica of the Treaty of Niagara
covenant chain wampum belt their ancestors had given to Sir William Johnson
in 1764. They explained its meaning, and Grand Council Chief Mahdabee took
the opportunity "to remind him that England is not off the hook yet," that
Canada and Britain are still bound by the obligations made there. In the United
States, each year the federal government continues to expend $4,500 for treaty
cloth to be delivered to the Iroquois as required by the Treaty of Canandaigua
in 1794. Although the government broke the treaty when it built the Kinzua

Dam in 1965 and flooded ten thousand acres of Seneca land, and although $4,500 now buys small quantities of muslin instead of yards of expensive cotton cloth, the Iroquois still hold the government to its obligation as evidence that the treaty remains in effect, defining their relationship with the United States and demonstrating a clear expression of their sovereignty.[23] Although treaty making in the United States officially ended in 1871, nearly four hundred Indian treaties remain the law of the land today and Indians are the only group in the country that has treaties. Treaties continue to define the status of tribes as sovereign entities; determine rights to hunting, fishing, and other resources; shape dealings with state and federal governments; and provide the basis for much litigation and lobbying. Indians in modern America have not forgotten the treaties their ancestors made and they tend to protest the disregard and breaking of those treaties and the negation of their treaty rights, rather than the treaties themselves. Ironically, protests against treaties more often come from non-Indians who claim that these dusty old documents have no relevance in the modern world and that they give Indians special rights and unfair advantages. Treaties document, sometimes with disturbing clarity, how America in its youth dealt with the first Americans; the pledges that these treaties still contain challenge America in its maturity to do better as its citizens continue to work out the meanings and implementations of treaties in the twenty-first century.[24]

Treaty Making in Colonial America
THE MANY LANGUAGES OF INDIAN DIPLOMACY

"Whosoever has any affairs to transact with Indians must know their forms and in some measure comply with them," said Sir William Johnson. As Britain's superintendent of Indian affairs in the North, Johnson built his career doing just that.[1] Treaty making in colonial America was a learning process for Indians and Europeans alike. Europeans brought their established and elaborate diplomatic protocols for making treaties with other nations in Europe to North America. Indians had equally well-established and elaborate protocols for dealing with other Native nations in North America, and they drew European empires and colonists into their existing systems of diplomacy and exchange. Europeans learned to operate with the languages, rituals, and rhythms of Indian diplomacy as a necessity to doing business in Indian country, but at the same time they introduced their own diplomatic procedures and shifted the balance of power away from Indians. European and Native American traditions and practices melded to produce a new, uniquely American form of cross-cultural diplomacy. But it was never a perfect mix and was replete with opportunities for misunderstanding, deceit, and abuse.

Diplomacy was nothing new in North America. Long before Europeans arrived, Indian people demarcated and maintained territorial borders and negotiated multicultural frontiers.[2] Reaching across barriers of language, distance, and culture, they operated and traveled trade networks, built and sustained alliances, conducted foreign policies, and concluded international agreements. They developed rituals of respect and reciprocity that allowed, indeed required, them to resolve conflicts, establish mutual trust, and come together in peace. "Trade & Peace we take to be one thing," said the Iroquois.[3] Dealing with other peoples as trade partners required making alliances and turning strangers who were potential enemies into friends and even relatives. Native peoples extended or replicated kinship (anthropologists call it "fictive kinship") to include people with whom they were not related by birth or marriage, bringing them into their community by adoption, alliance, and ritual. Forging and renewing relationships of cooperation, coexistence, and kinship with others was essential to survival in the pre-contact multitribal world. It became even more essential in the violent and chaotic world generated by European invasion and colonialism, where war and disease upset balances of power and when alliances offered viable alternatives to endless cycles of bloodshed in escalating competition for diminishing resources. In the seventeenth century, European colonies were fragile and often rendered vulnerable by supply problems. Like Native Americans, the colonists struggled to survive "in a world in which international or cultural isolation could easily lead to extermination," and like Native Americans—and like European colonists in other parts of the globe— they sought and made intercultural alliances and trade to protect and enhance their positions. European diplomatic encounters with Indians occurred at the edges of a world of multiple Indian-to-Indian social, political, and exchange relationships that fanned out across the continent and brought the newcomers into existing nation-to-nation networks.[4] The diplomatic landscape of colonial America was a kaleidoscope of shifting relationships where different Indian communities, nations, and confederacies pursued their own foreign policies, just as European nations, empires, and rival colonies pushed their own agendas. Relations with any one group could affect relations with others.

Few in number at first, and evidently inept in their new environment, the English settlers at Jamestown cannot have seemed much of a threat to the peoples of the powerful Powhatan chiefdom, some thirty tribes extending across most of eastern Virginia. The Indians supplied corn to the colonists and the paramount chief, Powhatan, seems to have tried to incorporate the English into his domain. John Smith, the leader of the colonists, recalled several years later how he was captured by the Indians in December 1607 and saved from execution when Powhatan's daughter, Pocahontas, threw her body across his "at the minute of my execution." If (and it's a big "if"—in Smith's accounts of his adventures, beautiful women save him from dire peril not once but three times) the events occurred as Smith described them, Pocahontas was most likely performing a prescribed role in a standard ritual by which Powhatan could adopt Smith and make him a *werowance*, or subordinate chieftain. She continued to play an important role as a mediator between the Powhatans and the English during the rest of her brief life.[5]

Similar diplomatic misunderstanding occurred in New England where Governor William Bradford of Plymouth Colony and the Wampanoag sachem Massasoit made a treaty of peace and friendship in 1621. Massasoit likely understood the agreement as forming an alliance that would bolster him in a power struggle with the neighboring Narragansetts. The English, on the other hand, regarded the treaty as a formal submission by the Wampanoag sachem to King James and an acknowledgment of English sovereignty.[6] The English were quick to proclaim dominance over Indians. At the Treaty of Hartford in 1638 they proclaimed the Pequot tribe extinguished. But Indians balked: Narragansetts asserted their independence from and equality with the New England colonies by "going over their heads" and making "a voluntary and free submission" to King Charles I in 1644, and Indians elsewhere in New England regularly refuted English assertions of sovereignty.[7]

Early European diplomatic encounters with Indians occurred in areas and eras where Indians held the power. Would-be imperialists had to adjust to local and kinship politics and to make a place for themselves within a network of fluid relationships, held together by various languages, rituals, and patterns of behavior. First the French and then the British had to come to terms with the reality that to succeed in Indian country they must behave as Indians thought friends and allies should, and to conciliate more often than command.[8] Indians extended to newcomers from Europe the same metaphors and mechanisms for peace that they employed among themselves. "What happened in the hinterland called colonial North America," wrote the historian Dorothy Jones, "was the development of a multilateral, multicultural diplomacy unlike the diplomatic tradition of any single participant but partaking of them all." This hybrid diplomacy combined legal documentation of agreements and ritualized renewals of human relationships. Indian chiefs, perhaps wearing uniform coats, three-cornered hats, and medals given to them by European allies, negotiated with colonial emissaries who had learned to smoke the calumet pipe and speak on beaded wampum belts, while their words were translated by interpreters, who might be white men tattooed, painted, and dressed like the Indians with whom they lived.[9]

Treaty making for Indians involved extending relationships and establishing sacred obligations, and they went about it all with solemn purpose following time-honored procedures. Edmond Atkin, a Charlestown merchant in the Indian trade who became Britain's southern Indian superintendent, remarked in his report of 1755 that "in their publick Treaties no People on earth are more open, explicit, and Direct. Nor are they excelled by any in the observance of them." George Croghan, a trader and Indian agent not known for an overabundance of scruples and principles in his dealings, acknowledged that Indians "to their Honour" never "attempted to dissolve a Contract, justly and plainly, made with them."[10] "It must not be supposed that these treaty conferences were in any sense haphazard in character, in any degree less ceremonious than meetings for a similar purpose between the high contracting parties to European agreements," the historian Lawrence Wroth wrote many years ago; and Indians who engaged in treaty making compelled Europeans to observe ancient protocols "that reached back through centuries of ceremonial observance.[11] These rituals and metaphors held significant symbolism and precise meanings. Indians and Europeans who endeavored to deal with each other across cultural gulfs had to negotiate a collision and confluence of worldviews; consequently, the texts of their treaty conferences "can be deciphered now only with careful scrutiny and an informed appreciation of cross-cultural interaction."[12]

Reaching Across Cultures

Indians generally preferred to hold treaties in their own country and away from disease-infested colonial cities. One of the major architects of the Great Peace at Montreal, a Huron chief known as Kondiaronk (or the Rat), died during an epidemic (probably influenza) at the treaty, and the Iroquois complained that they lost many men every time a delegation went to Philadelphia. "The evil Spirits that Dwell among the White People are against us and kill us," they said.[13] But it was not uncommon to see Indian delegates walking the streets of Quebec, Montreal, Albany, Philadelphia, Williamsburg, Charlestown, St. Augustine, San Antonio, Santa Fe, and other colonial capitals. On occasion, they also traveled to Paris or London, conducting diplomacy in a strange new world, although such visits often constituted "a kind of crude theater, drained of the dialogue and intensity that marked intercultural negotiations in America."[14] When Indian delegates came to town, the host governments wined and dined and tried to impress them with their power and wealth. Creek delegates in Charlestown in July 1763 were treated to a river cruise with musical entertainment.[15] Indian visitors to London saw the sights, attended the theater, and visited royal palaces, although the filth and poverty they saw in the streets shocked them as much as the power and wealth impressed them.

Rather than assemble in Indian villages or colonial capitals, however, treaty delegates often met at frontier locations distant from both, which meant that Indian communities and colonial governments might not learn until much later what had transpired at the treaty. Once a treaty council was announced, messengers went to Indian villages, summoning the tribes to attend. It took time for the participants to assemble, especially when delegates came from various and sometimes distant nations. Indians often marked their arrival at the treaty site with a ceremonial entrance. James Thacher, a surgeon with the American army during the Revolution, walking in the woods one morning prior to a conference being attended by two hundred Iroquois men and women, saw them "occupied in dressing and ornamenting themselves for the ceremony; painting their faces, adjusting their hair, putting jewels into their ears, noses, &c." Several of the young men and girls wore "little bells about their feet, to make a jingle when dancing." When the proceedings began, the Indians filed in and "arranged themselves, by sitting on the ground in a circle, the men on one side, the women on the other, leaving a vacancy for our commissioners, who were seated on chairs." In the intervals between talks, the Indians danced around the fire in the center of the circle and, taking each commissioner one at a time by the hand, danced with them around the circle.[16]

The Iroquois were so influential and played the game of Indian-European diplomacy so well that Iroquois forms, conventions, and terminology pervaded the diplomacy of northeastern North America. At the opening of an Iroquois council, a speaker greeted the participants and metaphorically wiped their eyes, cleansed their ears, and cleared their throats so that they might see, hear, and speak without impediment, a ritual of condolence that dated back to the legendary founding of their league when Deganawidah the Peacemaker assuaged the grief and torment of Hiawatha. The condolence ceremony typically began by greeting messengers "at the wood's edge," as they emerged from the forest to the clearing around the village. Then strings of wampum—shells or later glass beads—were presented, with the speaker telling the stories spoken by the wampum, accompanied by songs, to remove past grievances, resentments, and grief. These rituals created or renewed connections of peace and goodwill between the council participants, who put aside bad memories and negative feelings in order to meet with open hearts and minds.[17] The condolence ceremony marked the beginning of any Iroquois negotiation with Europeans, and abbreviated versions of the ceremony marked the opening of many councils with other northern Indians, even when no Iroquois were present.[18] A condolence council was not a one-time, once-and-for-all affair; in an increasingly volatile world, people met recurrently to settle differences, mend allegiances, and assuage anger and grief. In the Southeast, colonial officials dealing with the Creeks and their neighbors could similarly expect to partake of a ceremonial and purgative black drink before talks got under way.[19]

European treaty makers had to learn to tolerate such time-consuming indigenous rituals and deliberative processes that involved frequent adjournments. "The Indians adhere so closely to their Tedious Ceremonies that I am sensible you must have had a most fatiguing time of it," Governor Robert Hunter Morris of Pennsylvania sympathized with William Johnson after one treaty.[20] For the Indians, those "tedious ceremonies" sanctified the proceedings and established relationships of trust that were the very "sinews of diplomacy." Without the proper rituals, "a treaty simply was not a treaty."[21] Peace for Indians meant more than just an absence of conflict or an end to fighting; it was a state of being and a state of mind that carried moral obligations.[22]

As the anthropologist Raymond DeMallie explains in regards to treaty negotiations on the Great Plains, "If the council as a diplomatic forum was commonly understood by both whites and Indians, the concept of the treaty was not." For Indians, the council was an end in itself. What mattered was coming together in peace, ritually smoking a pipe, establishing trust, speaking the truth, and exchanging words. Indians generally reached decisions by consensus so all opinions and points of view had to be discussed. "Until that occurred, no decision was made, and once it was reached, no vote was necessary." For whites, the council and its associated rituals were preliminaries to the real business at hand: drawing up and signing a written treaty. Indians, who "had already sworn themselves to the truth," regarded signing the treaty as redundant, but they recognized that it was an important ritual for white men.[23]

European diplomats in Indian country had to deal with systems of government that were quite different from their own centralized and hierarchical structures and which made negotiations tedious and treaties tentative. Colonial powers generally appointed commissioners to treat with the Indians and they expected Indian leaders to make agreements that were binding on their people. Indian orators often spoke on behalf of their people, but representation at treaty councils was fuller and decision making more fluid than Europeans were accustomed to. Governor Cadwallader Colden of New York, writing of the Iroquois in the 1720s, said, "Each Nation is an absolute Republick by its self, govern'd in all Publick Affairs of War and Peace by the Sachems or Old Men, whose Authority and Power is gain'd by and consists wholly in the Opinion the rest of the Nation have of their Wisdom and Integrity. They never execute their Resolutions by Compulsion or Force upon any of their People."[24] A trader named John Long said, "The Iroquois laugh when you talk to them of obedience to kings....Each individual is sovereign in his own mind."[25] Southern Indians felt the same way, according to the trader James Adair: "The power of the chiefs is an empty sound. They can only persuade or dissuade the people," and everyone "to a man" voiced opinions.[26] In such political systems, leaders relied on the power of their words to achieve consensus, not the authority of their office to enforce obedience.

To complicate things further, the Indian delegates who appeared at treaties, and whom colonists courted and cultivated, were often the men who possessed the ritual knowledge and oratorical skills necessary for public speaking rather than the political leaders, who might remain silent while these front men did the talking. "Chief" was a term that embraced a variety of people in a variety of leadership roles. Europeans and Americans "not only misunderstood the origin and exercise of chiefly power but also failed to understand the nuances of how this authority was held, transferred, and wielded differently through Native American societies." They expected and pressured chiefs to be more authoritarian than their societies allowed, which in many cases undermined consensus and caused divisions. But Indian leaders rarely made decisions on their own and regularly consulted with their constituencies, which meant bringing large numbers of people with them to the treaty grounds or securing the consent of people back in the villages to any agreements they made. Speakers at treaty councils frequently made a point of explaining whom they spoke for and asserting that they acted with the support of the other chiefs, the warriors, and the women.[27]

Although men typically negotiated and concluded the treaties, women traditionally exercised important diplomatic roles in some Native societies. A Quaker who expressed surprise at seeing an old woman speak in a council near the Susquehanna River in 1706 was told "that some women were wiser than some men, and that they had not done anything for many years without the council of this ancient, grave woman." Gendered language pervaded the discourse of diplomacy and women served as a metaphor for peaceful intentions throughout the eastern woodlands. The Delawares were often called, and called themselves, "a nation of women" because of the tribe's historic role as intertribal mediators.[28] Women continued to feature in the diplomacy of colonial early America. They signed their names to land deeds and petitions.[29] They functioned as peace emissaries and mediators in the Texas borderlands as well as in the northeastern woodlands.[30] They accompanied delegations to treaty councils and wove wampum belts. At the treaty grounds, they erected and took down lodges, kept an eye on the children, and cooked food. Sometimes, the women sat on one side of the circle as the treaty talks proceeded and they doubtless exerted more influence on negotiations than the official transcripts of the treaties recorded. In matrilineal societies only women could adopt outsiders as fictive kin—which they did by ritual embrace—establishing bonds of kinship as a prerequisite to engaging in diplomacy.[31] And private relationships and intermarriage between Indian women and European men often provided a basis for public and diplomatic relations.[32] Often, women had their say back in the villages *before* the male delegates departed for the treaty grounds or in the evening during breaks in the negotiations. What women said to their husbands or sons did not usually make it into the written records of treaty proceedings but, as the Arapaho chief Little Raven explained at Medicine Lodge, a treaty could not be made without their participation.[33]

Europeans were troubled by the influence and independence that Indian women displayed in public meetings (as well as in their private lives), and they tried to limit female involvement in political processes. In addition, Europeans were primarily interested in Indians as allies or enemies in war and as partners and customers in the fur and deerskin trades; consequently they expected to deal with men, the warriors and hunters, not women, who were peacemakers and farmers. The Iroquois came to employ "women" as a pejorative term to describe the Delawares as militarily weak and politically powerless.[34] Sir William

Johnson married Mary or Molly Brant, who became an influential clan mother, and he was well aware of the influence women exercised in Iroquois society. (In 1758, for example, he heeded the entreaties of Mohawk women, and others, not to attend the League council at Onondaga.) But he downplayed the role of women in Iroquois diplomacy and tried to deal exclusively with men (in part, no doubt, to try and reduce the numbers of people running up expenses at treaty councils).[35] Iroquois women turned up for a treaty at Johnson Hall in April 1762 despite Sir William's request that they stay away. The Oneida chief Conoghquieson explained (as if Johnson did not know), "it was always the Custom for them to be present on Such Occasions (being of Much Estimation Amongst Us, in that we proceed from them, and they provide our Warriors with Provisions when they go abroad)."[36]

Gifts of Meaning

Doing business in Indian country involved giving and receiving gifts. The first governor of New France gave presents to the Iroquois, explained a Jesuit priest, "according to the custom of the country, in which the term 'present' is called 'the word,' in order to make clear that it is the present which speaks more forcibly than the lips."[37] Gifts—in the form of wampum, feathers, medals, items of clothing, knives, ammunition, blankets, tobacco, food, rum, horses on the Plains, and a host of other articles—were essential lubricants of Indian diplomacy, although the objects themselves, and giving and receiving them, often held different meanings for Indians and Europeans. To Indians, gifts signified greetings, generosity, and goodwill; they helped to establish and reaffirm reciprocal relations, and they served to amplify a request, underscore a point, and seal an agreement. Gifts established obligations; hence the importance of generosity as an attribute of leadership in Native societies. Indians requested gifts from their allies, sometimes pleading poverty or hunger, and they expected their allies to request gifts from them: mutual dependence underscored the need for alliance; refusing to give or receive gifts indicated a lack of mutual reliance and potential hostility. Accepting a gift meant accepting the message that accompanied it, the agreement it signified, or the undertaking it symbolized.[38]

In January 1621 the Narragansett sachem Canonicus sent Governor William Bradford of Plymouth Colony a gift of a snakeskin stuffed full of arrows. Bradford's interpreter told him it represented a threat and a challenge, and the governor read it to mean that the Narragansetts were the dominant power in the region to which the English had better submit. To accept the gift would have been to acknowledge Narragansett dominance; instead, Bradford added bullets and gunpowder to the snakeskin and sent it back to Canonicus. Canonicus was no more willing to submit than Bradford and "hee would not once touch the powder and shot, or suffer it to stay in his house or Country," and the snakeskin bundle "at length came whole back againe."[39]

Alliances that were not built on the trust of gifts given and received were always fragile and would usually founder. In 1752, Miami Indians sent the governor of Virginia the gift of a scalp and a wampum belt "to confirm what we say and assure you that we will ever continue true Friends and Allies to our Brothers, the English."[40] Sending gifts, especially of tobacco, was a way to open communication, invite people to meet, and "break the ice." "Sit down with them and command tobacco for them so that they may smoke as is their custom," Don Tomás Vélez Capuchín advised his successor as governor of New Mexico in 1754 as the best way to receive visiting Comanche chiefs and initiate diplomatic proceedings with them.[41]

Gifts were given in public council and in private meetings, to assemblages, and to individuals as "marks of distinction." Sir William Johnson often recognized individual chiefs with medals, laced coats, and hats. After a conference at Fort Johnson in the summer of 1756, he gave departing Onondaga chiefs "a Handsome private Present in cloathing and money and a quantity of Corn for their families who were in great want."[42] Such largesse cemented personal and national alliances, bolstered Johnson's individual standing among the Iroquois, and strengthened Britain's position in Indian country at a time of escalating competition with the French. It also allowed Johnson to exert increasing influence in Iroquois politics and chief making.[43]

Competition with the French also allowed Indians to leverage more and higher-quality presents from the English. Warriors from the Ohio country asked for better weapons during King George's War (1744–48) because "the French have hard Heads, and…we have nothing strong enough to break them." At the beginning of the French and Indian War (1754–63), the Oneida chief Scarouady told the English "You think You perfectly well understand the Management of Indian Affairs, but I must tell You that it is not so, and that the French are more politick than you. They never employ an Indian on any Business but they give him fine Cloathes besides other Presents, and this makes the Indians their hearty Friends, and do any Thing for them. If they invite the Indians to Quebec, they all return with laced Cloathes on, and boast of the generous Treatment of the French Governor."[44] Scarouady was not making things up: the French did indulge their Indian allies. The Marquis de Montcalm and the Marquis de Vaudreuil held a conference at Montreal in 1756 with forty Iroquois ambassadors and delegates from other nations to try and secure their neutrality or allegiance against the English. As the conference wound down at the end of December, the Iroquois "asked to remain until the morrow, New Year's day, because they had been told that on that day the Pale faces kissed each other and that liquor was furnished." The cost of hosting the Iroquois for an extra day would have been dwarfed by the total expenses for the conference, which were large enough to merit explanation and justification in the record of the conference: "The Ambassadors, their women and children, have been fitted out entire and entertained at the King's expense from the moment of their arrival to that of their departure. They had also been furnished with supplies and provisions for their journey, and the civil and war chiefs have received special presents. These expenses are unavoidable. The neutrality of those Nations is one of the greatest advantages we could obtain over the English."[45] The invoice of goods given by the English to the Indians at a relatively small "private conference" held at Easton, Pennsylvania, in 1758, a critical point in the contest for Indian allegiance, included some 30 different kinds of cloth, 100 blankets, 5 laced coats, 160 matchcoats, more than 400 shirts, 33 painted looking glasses, 50 pairs of shoes, knives, handkerchiefs, hats, ivory combs, buttons, thread, stockings, handkerchiefs, garters, and tobacco boxes.[46] This was nothing compared to the cost of food and gifts for the three thousand Indians who ten years later assembled for three weeks at the Treaty of Fort Stanwix.

Medals constituted a particularly important and common form of distinction. The Spanish, French, and English all presented medals to Indian chiefs (or to designate chiefs) and used them to interfere in tribal politics. The Spaniards recognized three levels of leaders—great medal chiefs, small medal chiefs, and chiefs, usually war captains, who merited the gorgets commonly worn by European officers. (Originally designed as armor to protect the throat, gorgets by the eighteenth century were small crescent-shaped plates primarily designed as ceremonial wear.) A formal presentation of such medals signified allegiance to the nation presenting them and conveyed status on the recipient. For Indians who wore them, the medals and gorget may have signified a pledge of their allegiance to a European ally but they also signified access to the sources of power Europeans represented (trade goods and weapons) and, like shell gorgets, may have carried spiritual power. Choctaws called medals *tali hullo*, a "sacred piece of stone." When the British replaced the French after 1763 and Spain took over possession of Louisiana many Choctaw chiefs turned in their French medals and requested replacements, so that colonial recognition of their leadership might continue unbroken.[47] When the governor of New Mexico, Juan Bautista de Anza, negotiated peace with the Comanches in 1786 he tried to make Ecueracapa (Leather Shirt or Iron Coat) head chief of all the Comanches (something that would have made little sense to the various independent Comanche bands); to that end, he formally presented him "with his Majesty's medal" and a complete uniform to better display it.[48]

Colonial governments frequently complained about the cost of gifts and William Johnson's rivals, in particular General Jeffery Amherst, the British commander-in-chief, criticized his extravagance. When Britain emerged victorious but facing financial ruin at the end of the French and Indian War, Amherst decided to dispense with the expensive practice of cultivating Indians' allegiance by giving them gifts. "I Cannot See any Reason for Supplying the Indians with Provisions," he wrote to Johnson, "for I am Convinced that they will never think of providing for their Families by hunting, if they can Support them by begging Provisions from Us." Johnson retorted that Amherst's stinginess would alienate the Indians and compromise the safety of British garrisons in Indian country and he was right. By giving gifts, the British could appease the spirits of warriors who had fallen in the war, demonstrate that they spoke from the heart when they assured Indians of their good intentions, and show that the King of England was prepared to take the place of the French king as a benevolent father. Gifts could restore relationships and turn enemies into friends. Withholding gifts had the opposite effect. Amherst saw his policy of retrenchment as an appropriate response to a changed situation and a financial crisis; Indians saw it as tantamount to a declaration of war.[49]

The Power of Words

Indian diplomacy, of course, involved exchanging words as well as gifts. In societies where leaders persuaded rather than commanded, speakers were renowned for their oratory. A Jesuit missionary named Pierre Biard described the Montagnais in 1616 as "the greatest speech-makers on earth. Nothing is done without speeches." Fellow Jesuit Paul Le Jeune said, "All the authority of their chief is in his tongue's end; for he is powerful in so far as he is eloquent."[50]

Europeans and Native Americans at the earliest stages of contact employed concrete terms as the easiest means of communication. Translating abstractions was always problematic.[51] "Metaphor is largely in use among these Peoples," wrote Father Le Jeune about the Hurons in 1636. "Unless you accustom yourself to it, you will understand nothing in their councils, where they speak almost entirely in metaphors."[52] Metaphors like "speak with forked tongue" and "bury the hatchet" have entered popular culture as figures of speech, but these now stereotypical expressions do little justice to the image-rich language of Indian orators who planted trees of peace; opened and maintained white paths of peace by removing thorns, clearing obstacles, and keeping them straight; polished chains of friendship to keep them free of rust; wiped away tears; rekindled fires; dispelled clouds; warned against listening to "bad Birds that whistle Evil things in our Ears"; cast weapons into bottomless pits; turned aside anger; softened hard hearts; distinguished between a peace "made from the Teeth outwards" and one that came from the heart; and even, on occasion, asserted dominance over a rival tribe by assuming a second penis![53]

Indians conducted diplomacy by the stories they told as well as by the arguments they made and points they negotiated. Orators used storytelling to convey their meanings, to draw listeners into their vision of the world, and "to invoke the imaginative capacity in others to see themselves as connected in a world of human solidarity."[54] They used body language, poise, posture, and gestures for dramatic effect; Father Barthélemy Vimont saw an Iroquois orator employ "a thousand gestures, as if he had collected the waves and caused a calm, from Quebec to the Iroquois country."[55]

Canasatego, an Onondaga who figured in many mid-eighteenth-century treaties, was famous for his oratory. He was also famous for his hard drinking and some observers thought him a braggart rather than a statesman, but time and again he impressed with his dignified bearing, his speech making, and his astuteness. Canasatego headed the Iroquois delegation at the Treaty of Lancaster in 1744, where he politely, but with tongue in cheek, declined Virginia's offer to educate Iroquois children: "we thank you for your Invitation; but our Customs differing from yours, you will be so good as to excuse us," an answer that, in the longer and more elaborate version Benjamin Franklin printed, became a telling indictment of colonial pretensions to cultural superiority. Canasatego is also famous for advising the individual colonies to follow the model of the Iroquois League and form a union. He did so, coincidentally, on the fourth of July.[56]

"The conference," Lawrence Wroth explained, "was not a debate: it consisted in the delivery of set speeches by either side in response to the proposals made by the other at the preceding session. Speaking only after deliberation in tribal council, and expressing the common opinion, the Indian had few ill-considered words to regret when the conference was ended."[57] A speaker delivered his talk, punctuated, in the northeast, by presenting strings of wampum to reinforce his points, and made sure, everywhere, to pause for one or more interpreters to translate his words. The audience sat in silence while he spoke. A speaker from the other side recapitulated what had been said, to ensure that everyone understood, but would not usually respond until his group had had an opportunity to consider and agree on their answer. Composed in advance, like those of their white counterparts, Indian speeches were more often "tribal or band position statements," rather than spontaneous flights of oratory. Objections or questions were rarely answered when they were raised; more often they were dealt with in later speeches after an opportunity for deliberation.[58] The pace was slow, deliberate, and frequently frustrating for time- and cost-conscious Europeans who were anxious to take care of business. Lieutenant Colonel Tench Tilghman, secretary of the Indian commissioners appointed by the Continental Congress to treat with the Six Nations at German Flatts, New York, in the summer of 1775, found that multiple translations and lengthy recapitulations of speeches made for "dull entertainment."[59]

Many tribes and confederacies had their own metaphors to describe their alliances and relationships, but it was the Iroquois Chain of Friendship or Covenant Chain that became almost the standard term.[60] The Iroquois regarded the Covenant Chain as one of many chains by which they were linked—allied—to other Native and colonial peoples by regularly renewed relationships of friendship and reciprocity; the British preferred to see it as an exclusive alliance between themselves and the Iroquois, through which they also gained access to and exerted influence over other Indian nations. Either way, the Covenant Chain was a multinational alliance in which "no member gave up its sovereignty" and decisions were made by consultation and treaty.[61] When the Crown and the New York Assembly cut allowances for Indian affairs after King George's War, the Mohawk chief Hendrick publicly and symbolically broke the Covenant Chain during a conference in 1753, precipitating a crisis in British-Iroquois relations. With conflict looming against France in the Ohio Valley, the English government could ill afford to alienate the Iroquois and hurried to mend fences, reconstituting the Covenant Chain at the Albany Congress the following year.[62]

For the Iroquois, diplomatic relations with outsiders involved "an extension of the same principles that governed social relations within Iroquois families and communities."[63] In societies built around kinship, kinship ties were the sinews of diplomacy and kinship terms were more than just a form of address. They constituted a system of establishing the rights and obligations of the parties vis-à-vis one another and they conveyed real messages. Employing the language of Indian diplomacy, Europeans often stood as "fathers" to their Indian "children"; coming from a patriarchal and patrilineal society, they naturally assumed that the father figure represented authority and wisdom in dealing with Indian children. Indians addressed colonial officials as "father," but the term had rather different connotations in matrilineal societies where the most important adult male in a child's life was the mother's brother, not the biological father. Indians who addressed Europeans as fathers expected them to act like indulgent and protective Indian fathers who gave gifts, not orders; who observed rituals, not rules; and who counseled proper conduct instead of invoking paternal authority. Indians would sometimes remind colonial officials that they were their brothers, not their fathers. "Brother" clearly conveyed equal status, but the qualifiers "older" or "younger" brother gave the relationship a slightly different cast. The Mohawks, Onondagas, and Senecas were the elder brothers in the Iroquois League; the Oneidas, Cayugas, and Tuscaroras were younger brothers. The elder brother(s) in a diplomatic relationship might enjoy seniority and greater influence but would also likely have particular obligations to protect the younger brother(s).[64] Europeans had not only to learn the meanings of kin metaphors as applied in their own dealings with Indians but they also had to learn that kinship relations often had different meanings in Indian societies and that different nations applied different kin metaphors in dealing with one another. Hendrick Aupaumut, who acted as a Mahican emissary to the western nations, said his people called the Delawares grandfathers; the Shawnees younger brothers; and the Miamis, Ottawas, Ojibwes, and Potawatomis grandchildren. John Norton, an adopted Mohawk of Scots-Cherokee descent, said the Ojibwes called the Delawares grandfathers; the Delawares called the Iroquois and Hurons uncles; and other tribes called the Iroquois and Hurons elder brothers. The Cherokees also called the Delawares grandfathers but called the Iroquois elder brothers. The Creeks and Chickasaws called the Cherokees elder brothers, but the Choctaws called the Cherokees uncles.[65]

Indians frequently bestowed names and titles on Europeans, titles that often stayed with the office. The Iroquois called the governor of New France *Onontio* (meaning "Great Mountain," a translation of the name of the first governor, Chevalier de Montmagny); the governor of Pennsylvania was *Onas* (meaning feather or quill, their translation of and play on William Penn's name); the governor of New York was called *Corlaer*, after Arent van Curler who had negotiated a treaty between the Dutch and the Mohawks in 1643; and the governor of Virginia was *Assaraquoa* or *Assaryquoa,* signifying a sword or long knife. The names passed from one governor to the next in the same way that the names of the Iroquois League chiefs were passed down from generation to generation.[66] Indians also gave names, sometimes their own, to individual colonists.

The Language of Wampum and the Ritual of Pipes

Wampum belts and calumet pipes were essential to diplomacy in Indian country. They turned treaties into sacred commitments. Indian messengers running forest trails carrying wampum belts and tribal delegations bearing calumet pipes of peace were more common than war parties on raids. "When a nation is desirous of negotiating a peace they send ambassadors, two or three in number, with a string of wampum denoting their desire," said Jacob Jemison, a Dartmouth-educated Seneca, in the 1820s; and, as the Delaware chief Teedyuscung explained, "Messengers of Peace pass free amongst all Nations, and should they meet with 10,000 Warriors, they are not hurt by them." A Moravian missionary, John Heckewelder, maintained that Indians traditionally protected peace messengers and ambassadors as a sacred obligation, and they attributed deviations from the custom to white men who "paid no regard them-selves to the sacred character of messengers."[67]

In the eastern woodlands, words meant little unless accompanied by wam-pum. From the Algonquian word *wampumpeag*, wampum was originally made from shells: white from whelks and purple from quahog shells, supplied primar-ily from beds along Narragansett Bay and Long Island Sound, and drilled and strung on fiber or thread or woven into rectangular belts. A traveler described Indians making wampum on Staten Island in 1760:

> It is made of the clam shell; a shell consisting within of two colors, purple and white, and in form not unlike a thick oyster shell. The process of manufacture is very simple. It is first chipped to a proper size, which is that of a small oblong parallelepiped, then drilled, and afterward ground to a round smooth surface, and polished. The purple wampum is much more valuable than the white, a very small part of the shell being of that color.[68]

Shells were supplemented and eventually supplanted by glass beads, usually manufactured in Italy and supplied by European traders, but they fulfilled the same functions.

Indians used wampum as gifts, jewelry, and trade items, and it served as currency for a time in coin-poor colonies. Dutch authorities banned the bak-ing and selling of white bread and cakes because the common medium for small-scale exchange in New Netherland was strings of wampum, and Indians, who had greater quantities of wampum than the colonists, were getting better bread than good Christians.[69]

Other gifts might serve to confirm speeches and demonstrate agreement, but exchanging wampum belts became the standard at treaty conferences.[70] European negotiators had to learn "the language of beads" because "Without Wampum Nothing is to be Done."[71] Messages were not credible unless they were accompanied by wampum. In 1707, as the English continued their efforts to recover Eunice Williams, who had been abducted and adopted by Mohawks from Kahnawake in the famous raid on Deerfield, Massachusetts, in 1704, New York's commissioners of Indian affairs gave a sachem from Canada "three small belts of wampum to Releace mr. williams ye minister of dear feild his Doughter from ye Indians if She be possible to be gotte, for money or Els to give an Indian girle for ye Same."[72] (Despite the appropriate wampum embassy, it did not happen: Eunice Williams married a Mohawk and, apart from fleeting visits to New England, lived at Kahnawake for almost eighty years.)

Without wampum, words might come only from the mouth, not from the heart. Governor William Shirley of Massachusetts gave Penobscot and Norridgwock chiefs a belt of wampum "as a Token of the Sincerity of my Heart, in what I have said to you." He need not have explained: as a Mohawk told Sir William Johnson, Indians understood that "Our words are of no weight unless accompanyed with Wampum."[73] In other words, if a speaker failed to present wampum, he was "just talking," perhaps floating a trial balloon or indulging in diplomatic hyperbole or double talk that carried no obligation.[74] On a rare occasion when Iroquois delegates at a conference with the governor of New York had no wampum with them, they took pains to reassure him "that what we relate is the truth."[75]

Communication that depended on wampum was sometimes delayed by its absence. Prior to the Treaty of Logstown in 1752, the Indian council there sent the commissioners from Virginia a string of wampum "to let them know they were glad to hear of their being on the Road" and to ensure them safe passage. "The Commissioners not having any Wampum strung, without which Answers cou'd not be returned, acquainted the Indians that they wou'd answer their Speeches in the Afternoon." Once the commissioners reached Logstown and negotiations began, they had their wampum belts strung, ready to do business, and matched the Indians string for string: "That what we have said may have the deeper impression on you & have its full force we present you with this Belt of Wampum."[76]

Wampum served as aids to memory and storytelling as well as being ritualized gifts and records of agreements. An Indian speaker would often lay out a batch of wampum strings or belts in front of him and then pick up each belt in turn as he spoke, punctuating each point or paragraph with a wampum string; women who accompanied treaty delegations were kept busy stringing belts for the speakers' prepared talks. A treaty council at Carlisle, Pennsylvania, in 1753 was delayed, an Indian explained to the waiting audience, because the Indian delegates had "mislaid some Strings, which has put their Speeches into Disorder; these they will rectify, and speak to you in the Afternoon." It was almost as if the Indians had misplaced the notes for a speech.[77] John Heckewelder said that it was customary when a speaker was about halfway through his speech to turn the belt on which he was speaking, "as with us on taking a glance at the pages of a book or pamphlet while reading; and a good speaker will be able to point out the exact place on a belt which is to answer to each particular sentence, the same as we can point out a passage in a book."[78] (See figure 1.1.)

Strings and belts of wampum contained messages, affirmed messages, and emphasized the significance—and truth—of messages.[79] Wampum was "a coded remembrancer of sacred traditions and political negotiations."[80] A Dutchman traveling in Mohawk country in 1680 described how Indians employed wampum and collective memory to preserve records of their treaties. Each speaker held a wampum string (or "counter") until he had made his point; when both

FIGURE 1.1 **Nicolas Vincent Isawanhonhi, chief of the Hurons of Lorette.** *The chief is pictured speaking on a wampum belt he presented to King George IV in England in 1825. Although his clothing is from the nineteenth century, the belt dates back to colonial times. (Library and Archives Canada, C-038948)*

sides were satisfied, the wampum was marked and put away; the process was repeated for each point until the whole agreement or contract was reached:

> Then they add up their counters, representing so many articles and the specific meaning which each signifies. As they can neither read nor write, they are gifted with powerful memory; and as it is done so solemnly, they consider it absolutely unbreakable. And because they cannot leave it to their posterity in written form, after the conclusion of the matter all the

children who have the ability to understand and to remember it are called together, and then they are told by their fathers, sachems or chiefs how they entered into such a contract with these parties. Then the markers are counted out to them, showing that the contract consists in so many articles and explaining the significance given to the markers and the story of how it was done. Thus they acquire understanding of each article in particular. Then these children are commanded to remember this treaty and to plant each article in particular in their memory, and they and their children [are commanded] to preserve it faithfully so that they may not become treaty-breakers, which is an abomination to them. Then all these shells or counters are bound together with a string in such a manner, signifying such a treaty or contract with such a nation. After they have been bound together, the bundle is put in a bag and hung up in the house of the sachem or chief where it is carefully preserved.[81]

In the summer of 1743, Conrad Weiser, a German farmer turned frontier interpreter, traveled to the council seat of the Six Nations at Onondaga, accompanied by John Bartram, a Quaker and botanist from Philadelphia, and a Welsh mapmaker and surveyor named Lewis Evans. Weiser's mission was to prevent a backcountry skirmish between colonists and an Iroquois hunting party from turning into an all-out war. Weiser first met the Onondaga speaker Canasatego "in the Bushes to have a private Discourse" and "explained my Instructions to him, and show'd him the Wampum." The council assembled and after "a deal of Ceremonies"—reciting the origins of the Iroquois League, greeting delegates who had traveled from afar, giving thanks for the opportunity to meet—called for Onas (Pennsylvania) and Assaryquoa (Virginia) to speak. Weiser asked Canasatego to speak for him, handing him a belt of wampum to "document" each statement. "Brethren, the united Nations, these Strings of Wampum serve to dispel the Dark Cloud that overshadowed Us for some Time, that the Sun May shine again and we may be able to see one another with Pleasure." The wampum belts were hung from a horizontal pole set up across the council house about six feet from the ground "that all the council might see them, and here have the matters in remembrance, in confirmation of which they were delivered." After a meal, the Iroquois delegates responded to each statement Weiser had made, and they presented wampum, string for string, belt for belt: "Brother Assaryquoa, this String of Wampum serves to return you our Thanks for dispelling the dark Cloud that overshadow'd Us from some Time. Let the Sun shine again, let us look upon one another with Pleasure and Joy." With harmony restored, Weiser and his companions carried away wampum belts "as our tokens of peace and friendship."[82]

At the Montreal conference in 1756, the French, Iroquois, and other Indians exchanged numerous wampum belts, which must have been bewildering for anyone not accustomed to this form of communication. A note attached to the account of the conference explained:

> These Belts and Strings of wampum are the universal agent among Indians, serving as money, jewelry, ornaments, annals, and for registers; 'tis the bond of nations and individuals; an inviolable and sacred pledge which guarantees messages, promises and treaties. As writing is not in use among them, they make a local memoir by means of these belts, each of which signifies a particular affair, or a circumstance of affairs. The Chiefs of the villages are the depositories of them, and communicate them to the young people, who thus learn the history and engagements of their Nation.[83]

John Heckewelder said that the chiefs were "very careful in preserving for their own information, and that of future generations, all important deliberations and treaties made at any time between them and other nations." To ensure that such information passed intact across the generations, they assembled once or twice a year at chosen locations in the woods, laid out all the records of treaties (whether wampum or written), and had a speaker who had been trained in the business recite the contents of the belts one by one. Consequently, Delawares in the 1700s could "relate very minutely" what had passed between William Penn and their forefathers at their first meeting and at every transaction since with the governors of Pennsylvania.[84]

Color, design, and length symbolized a belt's content and message. Belts might be of one color or of a combination of purple and white beads strung to form graphic patterns. Straight lines connecting squares or diamonds represented paths or alliances between nations and council fires. White beads represented life, peace, and well-being; purple or "black" beads represented death, war, and mourning.[85] Southeastern Indians venerated white wampum beads as tokens of peace and friendship after they adopted wampum during the eighteenth century.[86] White feathers served a similar purpose. Staffs with eagle feathers attached were "white wings of peace," and waving or holding white eagle tail feathers over the head of a visiting diplomat was deemed "the strongest pledge of good faith."[87] A delegation of seven Cherokees in London in 1730 made a treaty and then laid feathers on the table. "This is our way of talking which is the same to us as your letters in the Book are to you," they explained. "And to you Beloved Men we deliver these feathers in confirmation of all we have said and of our Agreement to your Articles."[88] White deerskins—presented as gifts or sat upon at peace talks—also symbolized peace and friendship.[89]

At the outbreak of the Revolution, a delegation of northern Indians traveled south to the Cherokee town of Chota in present-day eastern Tennessee. At a meeting in the council house, the Mohawk delegate produced a belt of white and purple wampum and "he supposed there was not a man present that could not read his talk." The Ottawa delegate produced a white belt with purple figures, indicating the desire to form a lasting friendship between the tribes. The Shawnee delegate offered them a nine-foot wampum belt "strewn with vermilion" as a call to war against the Americans. Cherokee warriors accepted the call by laying hold of the belt.[90]

Belts often carried more intricate messages. To invoke the memory of the treaty made at Albany in 1754, remind the British of the promises of friendship and support they had made there, and reassert their status as allies, an Onondaga chief at Johnson Hall in 1763 produced a large wampum belt

> whereon was wrought in white Wampum the figures of Six Men towards one End, as representing the Six Nations, towards the other End, the figure of Nine men to represent the Nine Governments who assembled at Albany; . . . between both was a Heart Signifying the Union and friendship then Settled between them. At the Top were the letters G R made of White Wampum, and under that the full length of the Belt was a white line, which they were told was a long board to Serve as a Pillow, whereon their and our Heads were to rest.[91]

Presenting wampum confirmed and "documented" the words that were spoken. Among the Iroquois, said Jacob Jemison, "the only ceremony attending the conclusion of a peace is the delivery of the wampum belt, which is used to signify their contract."[92] In fact, in negotiations with the governors of New York, Virginia, and Maryland in the seventeenth century, the Iroquois also sang a song "after thar maner being thar method of a new Covenant." The singing confirmed the agreement and committed the hearers to remember it. As the Mohawk speaker said to the governors, "Let me drive it into you with a song."[93]

Taking, or touching, the belt indicated acceptance of the message, and agreement usually entailed a reciprocal gift of wampum to seal the agreement, as it were. Rejecting, returning, or refusing to touch a belt meant the message was not acceptable. Dramatically casting belts aside could convey other messages as well. In 1691, in conference with the governor of New York, the Iroquois said they had rejected as "venomous and detestable" a French wampum belt offering peace "and did spew it out and renounce it . . . and left the belt upon the ground in the Court house yard." Three years later, Count Frontenac "kicked away" three Iroquois belts proposing a truce with the English "and by this mark of contempt and haughtiness, indicated to the proudest nation throughout this New World his indifference for peace." Five years after that, when a sachem at Onondaga asked for five belts sent by the governor of Canada, "one of the Young Indians threw them to the Sachim with an angry countenance"; when the belts did not quite reach him "another Indian most disdainfully kick'd them forward to the Indian that demanded them." Wyandot, Mississauga, and Ottawa delegates at Fort Duquesne in 1758 each, in turn, kicked back to the French commander a wampum belt inviting them to take up the hatchet.[94] Whether or not these offers were actually dismissed with the vehemence described, the meaning of such rejections was clear.

Sir William Johnson mastered the art of wampum diplomacy with the help of good teachers. At a treaty conference at Fort Johnson in 1756, the speaker for the Six Nations "took up a large belt, which the general gave, with an emblem of the six nations joined hand in hand with us," and addressing Johnson as "Brother Warraghiyagey," said: "Look with attention on this belt, and remember the solemn and mutual engagements we entered into, when you first took upon you the management of our affairs; be assured, we look upon them as sacred, and shall, on our parts, punctually perform them as long as we are a people." He then took up another large belt that had been given by the governor of New York years before, asked the English to remember the promises that were made at that time, and promised that the Iroquois would do the same, "though we have no records but our memories."[95]

According to John Long, who spent twenty years in Indian country, when Johnson held a treaty with the Indians the wampum belts were generally several rows wide, black (or purple) on each side and white in the middle "to express peace, and that the path between them was fair and open." In the center of the belt was the figure of a diamond made of white wampum, representing a council fire. Johnson took the belt by one end, while the Indian chief held the other. If the chief had anything to say, he moved his finger along the white streak; if Sir William had anything to communicate, he touched the diamond in the middle. Long explained that "these belts are also the records of former transactions, and, being worked in particular forms, are easily deciphered by the Indians, and referred to in every treaty with the white people. When a string or belt of wampum is returned, it is a proof that the proposed treaty is not accepted and the negotiation is at an end."[96]

Wampum spread throughout the eastern woodlands, but the calumet (from the French word for reed), commonly called the peace pipe, became a key artifact of diplomacy from the St. Lawrence Valley, down the Mississippi, and out to the Rocky Mountains. Jacques Marquette, a Jesuit Father, said there was "nothing more mysterious or respected" among Indians than the calumet. "It seems to be the God of peace and of war, the Arbiter of life and death." Indians used the calumet "to put an end to Their disputes, to strengthen Their alliances, and to speak to Strangers."[97] French and Métis traders contributed to the spread of the calumet and French, English, and American traders and officials "found that learning the ritual language of pipes" was indispensible for conducting business in Indian country.[98]

Bearers of calumet pipes decorated the stems with feathers of different colors and sometimes with wampum. A British captain, Robert Carver, who spent three years traveling through the Great Lakes and upper Mississippi, described the pipe of peace or calumet as about four feet long; the bowl was made of "red marble" (by which he meant catlinite), and the stem "of a light wood, curiously painted with hieroglyphicks in various colours and adorned with the feathers of the most beautiful birds." Each nation decorated their pipes in a different way "and they can tell at first sight to what band it belongs. It is used as an introduction to all treaties, and great ceremony attends the use of it on these occasions."[99]

Ritually smoking the pipe opened communications, solemnized proceedings, and established friendships; it was a necessary prelude to negotiations and trading relationships. Western Indians at a conference in Albany in 1723 explained to the New York commissioners and the Iroquois in attendance: "When one brother comes to visit an other it is the common practice among us to smoke a pipe in Peace and reveal our Secrets." They asked "that according to our Custom we may each take a Whiff out of a Calumet Pipe in token of Peace and Friendship"; smoking their calumet pipe, they said, was "a sufficient proof to us of your friendship."[100] Pennsylvania Governor William Denny puffed on a pipe and passed it to the disgruntled Delaware chief Teedyuscung at a council in Philadelphia in 1758 with the words or at least the wishful thinking that "We have found by experience that whatever Nations smoked out of it two or three hearty Whiffs, the Clouds that were between us always dispersed."[101] Smoking together and pointing the pipe in the four directions, and above and below, was a sacred action that opened the channels of communication and bound the smokers in a collective commitment to speak the truth. The smoke metaphorically carried their words upward and bound the speakers in a covenant with the Great Spirit.[102] The calumet was "the symbol of peace," said John Long, and Indians held it "in such estimation that a violation of any treaty where it has been introduced would, in their opinion, be attended with the greatest misfortunes."[103] Council participants might also retire from negotiations to smoke their pipes and reflect on what had been said and consider their response. In a world of escalating violence and disorder, the calumet made peace, reason, understanding, and trust possible.

The calumet ceremony, in which Indians smoked and danced to welcome newcomers, transformed strangers into kin and enemies into friends; it opened the way for good relations and was a prerequisite for negotiations. When Robert Cavalier, Sieur de La Salle, entered the villages of the Quapaws in Arkansas in 1682, the Indians greeted the Frenchman with a calumet dance, a feast, and an exchange of gifts, to establish ritual ties and to give status within their social system.[104] Mesquakie or Fox Indians seem to have taken the calumet ceremony to Abenakis and the Iroquois adopted it in the form of the Eagle Dance.[105]

Jacob Jemison told Governor Lewis Cass in the 1820s that "No pipes are used among the Six Nations."[106] That may have been the case traditionally but the calumet began to appear in Iroquois diplomacy in the eighteenth century. In the spring of 1710 New York commissioners at Onondaga found three Ottawa emissaries there, singing. "They had long Stone Pipes in their hands & under the Pipes hung Feathers as big as Eagles Wings." The commissioners filled their pipes and the assembled parties smoked to demonstrate friendship. In 1735, sachems from Kahnawake, who had traveled to Albany to reconcile differences between the Iroquois in Canada and the Six Nations in New York, opened the meeting "by offering the Calumet or Pipe of Peace to all the Commissioners who according to the Indian custom take each a Whif [sic]." At the chiefs' request, the commissioners sent the pipe to Onondaga to be stored there along with the wampum "as a Memorial to Posterity of this Solemn Treaty." Twenty years later, the Iroquois seemed well versed in the ritual of the pipe: when Sir William Johnson gave them a large pipe in 1756 "to be a constant memorial of the important advice you have given us, when you are dead and gone, and to smoke out of it, at our public meeting-place, where we jointly and maturely reflect upon our engagements" the Onondaga Red Head assured him, "we shall hang it up in our council-chamber, and make proper use of it upon all occasions."[107]

Indians carried calumets as passports guaranteeing safe conduct through other nations' territories. Nicholas Perrot said the calumet stopped vengeful warriors in their path and compelled them to receive peace delegates who carried it. "It is, in one word, the calumet that has authority to confirm everything, and which renders solemn oaths binding."[108] In 1721, a Chickasaw chief who had traveled all the way from the Mississippi entered the council chamber in Williamsburg in company with some Cherokee chiefs; "they entered singing, according to their Custom; And the Great Man of the Chickasaws carrying in his hand a Calamett of Peace."[109] On their way to the Treaty of Logstown in 1752, the commissioners from Virginia were met by a party of Delawares on horseback about three miles from Shenapin's town on the Ohio. "The Indians having filled and lighted their long Pipes or Calumets, first smoak'd and then handed them to the Commissioners and others in their Company, who all smoak'd. After the Ceremony had been repeated two or three Times, the Chief of the Indians made a short Speech to welcome the Commissioners, which being answered, they all mounted and the Indians led the Way" to the village.[110] When Alejandro O'Reilly arrived as the governor of Spanish Louisiana in 1769, nine Indian chiefs went to New Orleans to smoke and establish peaceful relations. Each chief presented O'Reilly with his burning pipe and held it while the governor smoked, which "His Excellency did as he was not ignorant of its significance."[111]

The Oglala Lakota holy man Black Elk explained that when the pipe was smoked, a three-fold peace was established. There was peace between individuals and peace between nations but first and most important was the peace in men's souls that came with understanding their relationship to the universe and all its Powers; "the others are but a reflection of this." There could be no peace between nations until there was peace within men's souls.[112]

Writing and Memory

As Europeans and Americans learned the art of wampum and calumet diplomacy, they expected Indians to reciprocate by learning their customs. "We understand that by an ancient Custom observ'd by your Ancestors, the Delivery and Acceptance of the Calumet Pipe are the Ceremonies which render valid, and bind fast your Alliances," Pennsylvania commissioners told Miamis who had come to Lancaster in 1748. "We must now tell you what our Usages are on these Occasions. The *English* when they consent to take any Nation into their Alliance, draw up a Compact in Writing, which is faithfully interpreted to the contracting Parties, and when maturely consider'd, and clearly and fully understood by each Side, their assent is declar'd in the most publick Manner, and the Stipulation render'd authentick by sealing the Instrument with Seals, whereupon are engraven their Families Arms, writing their Names, and publishing it as their Act and Deed." This was how the English ratified treaties and other nations had drawn up documents like this when they first made alliances with the English. The Miamis would be expected to do the same.[113]

It was not always easy. "I cannot write as you and your beloved Men do," a Cherokee chief named Skiagusta told Governor Glen of South Carolina in council. "My Toungue is my Pen and my Mouth my Paper. When I look upon Writing I am as if I were blind and in the Dark."[114] Understanding this, Europeans asserted the superiority of writing as a method of recording. "Writing," Virginian commissioners lectured Iroquois delegates at the Treaty of Lancaster in 1744, "is more certain than your Memory. That is the way the white people have of preserving Transactions of every kind and transmitting them down to their Children's Children for ever; and all Disputes among them are settled by this faithfull kind of Evidence, and must be the Rule between the Great King and you."[115]

Indian people valued the spoken word, the gifts or wampum exchanged, and the oral tradition that preserved memory more than they did the written word by which Europeans recorded history. They assured Europeans that, although they did not commit transactions to writing, "we nevertheless have Methods of transmitting from Father to Son an account of all these things, whereby you will find the Remembrance of them is faithfully preserved."[116] Iroquois delegates assured the governor of Pennsylvania in 1721 that they remembered well the agreements their ancestors had made with William Penn, because "though they cannot write, yet they retain every thing said in their Councils with all the Nations they treat with, and preserve it as carefully in their memories as if it was committed in our method to Writing."[117] Non-Indians frequently were impressed by Indian methods of recall. "It is amazing with what exactness these people recollect all that has been said to them," marveled Tench Tilghman, in council with the Six Nations. "The speech which we delivered took up nine or ten pages of folio Paper, when they came to answer they did not omit a single head and on most of them repeated our own words, for it is a Custom with them to recapitulate what you have said to them and then give their Answer. They are thorough bred politicians!"[118]

The distinctions between oral and written culture can be exaggerated.[119] Indians inscribed messages, information, and symbols on bark, trees, rocks, and paper, and they recorded information in wampum.[120] They recognized writing as a parallel form of record keeping and as a parallel kind of ritual: sometimes they sent a letter along with wampum belts, although the English worried that if the letter fell into French hands they would "make the Indians believe quite the Contrary what the Letter mentions."[121] Indians presumably had similar worries about their belts being misinterpreted to Englishmen who were illiterate in reading wampum. Many Indians acquired an appreciation of the "power of print" and some learned to read and write; they understood that literacy could serve them as a weapon in the fight for cultural and political survival as well as it served the English and Americans as an instrument for dispossession.[122]

It is often said that the spoken word and oral tradition, and the wampum belts that contained them, were alive, compared to the dry, dead documents of Europeans. But Indians who distrusted writing as "pen and ink witchcraft" did so precisely because they understood that written words had power and life, or at least that documents could take on a life of their own. Indians who signed treaties, affixed their marks, or "touched the pen" usually did so to affirm what they had said or to indicate their agreement to *what they had been told* the treaty document said. Canasatego referred disparagingly to "the Pen-and-Ink Work that is going on at the Table (pointing to the Secretary)" at Lancaster because Indians knew from experience that written words could come back to bite them.[123] Indians sometimes requested, preserved, and referenced duplicate copies of treaties and agreements written by colonial scribes, just as they preserved the wampum belts of other nations they dealt with.[124] A delegation of Esopus Indians from the Hudson Valley meeting Sir William Johnson in 1769 brought with them the transcript of a treaty they had made with the governor of New York more than one hundred years before, and which they periodically renewed, although the document was falling to pieces.[125]

The written records of treaty conferences did not necessarily provide an accurate account of what was said, how it was said, or what was meant. Between the words emanating from a speaker's mouth and the words appearing on paper, several hands intruded, multiple agendas could exert an influence, errors occurred, and numerous shadings could, and often did, occur.[126] Scribes, clerks, and secretaries became regular figures at treaty conferences, producing an invaluable collection of written sources. They also played a significant role in shaping the written record of the conferences. In theory, their job was to preserve in English a verbatim account of multilingual negotiations translated by an interpreter. In practice, that almost never happened. Scribes struggled to keep up, rested their hands, let their attention wander, grew bored, misheard things, ignored asides spoken between individuals, omitted words and phrases, glossed over or condensed lengthy passages, or even put their pens down and sat back while Indian speakers went into lengthy orations or recapitulated earlier speeches. Once the conference was over, scribes sat down to make "fair copies" from their drafts for the official record, initiating another round of editing, in which they "corrected" the minutes; omitted, inserted, and changed words; and altered the tone and shifted the emphasis of conversations, sometimes in the interests of efficiency and style, sometimes with the deliberate intention of giving a particular slant to the proceedings.[127] Sometimes, what was left out could be as damaging as what was included. Charles Thomson, a Philadelphia schoolmaster who served as a clerk at the Treaty of Easton in 1758, wrote a tract blaming Indian support for the French on Pennsylvania's record of unscrupulous treaty practices, but he acknowledged that the paper trail evidencing such practices was thin:

> It is true, as the *Indians* have no Writings, nor Records among them, save their Memories and Belts of Wampum, we can only have Recourse to the Minutes taken, and Records kept, by one Party, nay, oftentimes, by those who, if any advantage was taken of the *Indians*, must have been concerned in it, and consequently would not care, by minuting every Thing truly, to perpetuate their own Disgrace.[128]

Indians often found wanting the documentary record of the treaties they had attended. Loron Sauguaarum, a Penobscot who participated in negotiations with the English at the Treaty of Casco Bay in 1727, denounced the written terms of the treaty. "These writings appear to contain things that are not," he said, and he proceeded to provide an article-by article correction of the record, refuting English assumptions and assertions regarding Indian land, sovereignty, and war guilt. "What I tell you now is the truth," he concluded. "If, then, any one should produce any writing that makes me speak otherwise, pay no attention to it, for I know not what I am made to say in another language, but I know well what I say in my own."[129]

The Delaware chief Teedyuscung had plenty of experience with the power of writing and spent much of his life battling the theft by treaty of Delaware lands.[130] Between 1630 and 1767, the Delaware, or Lenni Lenape, Indians of New Jersey and Pennsylvania signed nearly eight hundred deeds of land to colonists (see figure 1.2). In 1734, Thomas Penn, son of William, the first governor and proprietor of Pennsylvania, claimed to have found a copy of a deed made in 1686 in which certain Delaware chiefs granted his father and his father's heirs lands "as far as a man can go in a day and a half," and from there to the Delaware River and down its course. Thomas Penn and his associates persuaded a number of Delaware chiefs to agree to measuring out the lands.

FIGURE 1.2 **William Penn's Treaty with the Indians in November 1683, 1771–72 (oil on canvas) by Benjamin West (1738–1820).** *Benjamin West's later idealized painting of William Penn's Treaty with the Delawares under an elm tree at Shackamaxon in 1683 reflects an earlier era of treaty making and peaceful relations in Pennsylvania. Indian treaties in eighteenth-century Pennsylvania more often seemed to involve fraud and land theft than peace and friendship. (Pennsylvania Academy of the Fine Arts, Philadelphia/The Bridgeman Art Library)*

Instead of dispatching a man to walk the woods, the Pennsylvanians cleared a path and sent a relay team of three runners speeding along it. By the time the third runner collapsed in exhaustion at noon on the second day, they had covered about sixty-five miles. This infamous "Walking Purchase" deprived the Delawares of their last lands in the upper Delaware and Lehigh valleys.[131] They protested but to no avail and the governor of Pennsylvania called in Canasatego and the Iroquois to help silence their complaints. Teedyuscung was still fuming over it in November 1756 when he met the Pennsylvania authorities in a treaty conference at Easton, at the confluence of the Lehigh and Delaware rivers. Teedyuscung was a formidable presence—Richard Peters described him as "near 50 years old, a Lusty rawboned Man haughty and very desirous of Respect and Command. He can drink 3 quarts or a Gallon of Rum a day without being Drunk"—and not afraid to speak his mind. "The Times are not now as they were in the Days of our Grandfathers," Teedyuscung said, "then it was Peace, but now War and Distress," and he presented wampum belts of condolence to remove tears of mourning and heal past wounds. But old wounds still festered. "This very Ground that is under me (striking it with his Foot) was my Land and Inheritance and is taken from me by Fraud," he declared. Governor William Denny responded that part of the problem was that, in Indian society, memory of land sales sometimes died with those who made the sale, "and as you do not understand Writings and Records, it may be hard for me to satisfy you of the Truth. Though my Predecessors dealt ever so uprigthly."[132]

Teedyuscung understood only too well. He knew what consequences a change of words could have. "Somebody must have wrote wrong, and that makes the Land all bloody," he said.[133] He knew English, but he had his own interpreter, John Pumpshire. He was concerned that everything he said and everything that was said to him "be taken down aright; some speak in the Dark; do not let us do so; let all be clear and known. What is the Reason the Governor holds Councils so close in his Hands, and by Candle Light?" The governor insisted that he held his council in the open and had no secrets, but the following year Teedyuscung requested that he be provided with his own clerk to record the minutes of meetings "along with the Governor's Clerk." The colonists balked at his request—having Indians read what was written was one thing; involving them in the recording process was another matter—but Teedyuscung got his clerk: the Quaker Charles Thomson, a former schoolteacher who wrote *An Enquiry into the Causes of the Alienation of the Delaware and Shawanese Indians* and who later became secretary of the Continental Congress.[134] George Croghan thought Quaker commissioners must have put Teedyuscung up to it. He objected when Teedyuscung had a speech drawn up in writing "and desired his clerke [*sic*] to read it off as a lawyer would put in a plea before the bar" and insisted Teedyuscung deliver the speech himself. It was, he reported to Sir William Johnson "very extraordinary and the most unprecedented procedure ever known at an Indian treaty."[135] Indians understood the power of writing but they understood that it lay predominantly in white hands. "We have often seen (and you know it to be true)," Iroquois deputies told William Johnson in 1769, "that the White people by the help of their paper (which we don't understand) claim Lands from Us very unjustly and carry them off."[136]

The written records of treaties covered the public conferences in which statements, and wampum, were presented and considered. They did not usually record meetings "in the bushes" or "the Debates, Arguments and discourses at the private Conferences where the principal Subjects are first Agitated and determined upon."[137] Private meetings between treaty commissioners and Indian leaders sometimes flag shady deals, but working things out in private before agreements were formally concluded in public was standard practice in both Native American and European diplomacy.[138]

Interpreters and Go-Betweens

Someone had to translate the exchange of words, wampum belts, gifts, and rituals across cultures. Translation, and the imposition of language that distorted Native meanings and did violence to indigenous worldviews, was central to European colonization and imperialism in the Americas, and it was critical to the process and purpose of treaty making.[139] Many Indians learned to speak French, Spanish, and English, of course, but as John Heckewelder observed, "even if an Indian understands English he prefers communicating to a white man through an interpreter."[140] And an interpreter might mishear, misunderstand, misremember, mistranslate, or misrepresent what was said.[141]

Interpreters obviously played a key role in treaty negotiations. The French sent young boys to live in Indian villages as a way of creating a pool of interpreters. Jacques Cartier in 1541 left boys among the Indians to learn their language; Samuel de Champlain sent boys to the Hurons and Algonquins in 1610–11, and the French continued the practice in Louisiana into the eighteenth century.[142] Most interpreters in the seventeenth century were Indians, but despite the fact that more and more Indians learned English, interpreters during the eighteenth century were usually non-Indians: professional interpreters like Conrad Weiser, George Croghan, and Andrew Montour, and agents, missionaries, traders, and captives who had learned Indian languages and Indian ways. A good interpreter had to do more than translate speeches. He, and occasionally she, needed to understand and advise on the protocols of intercultural diplomacy, know the names of the chiefs, have their fingers on the pulse of tribal and intertribal politics, provide guidance on the tone and content of speeches and messages, operate as cultural intermediaries behind the scenes, participate in private meetings, understand the language and handling of wampum belts, edit speeches for fluency and efficiency, and exercise judgment about what *not* to translate in order to avoid misunderstandings, head off a potential breakdown of the talks, or obscure shady deals from public view.[143] "It surely dos [*sic*] not require any detail of Reasoning to evince how very important the Capacity & Integrity of an Interpreter is to the public," wrote New York's secretary of Indian affairs in 1738, although he had serious doubts about the abilities of the current one.[144]

Conrad Weiser "practically made a career of the Indian business." Born in Germany in 1696, Weiser settled with his family in southeastern New York. He was adopted by the Mohawks, developed a facility in Iroquoian languages, and became an interpreter. After moving to Pennsylvania, he played a pivotal role as a negotiator and intermediary in tribal relations with the colonial governments of Pennsylvania, Maryland, and Virginia. Weiser understood that effective translation required more than knowing Indian words; it was necessary, he said, "to converse with the Indians and study their Genius."[145] At the Treaty of Lancaster, wrote Witham Marshe, a young Scotsman serving as secretary to the Maryland commissioners, "Our interpreter, Mr. Weiser desired us, whilst we were here, not to talk much of the Indians, nor laugh at their dress, or make any remarks on their behaviour: if we did, it would be very much resented by them, and might cause some differences to arise betwixt the white people and them. Besides," added Marshe, "most of them understood English, though they will not speak it when they are in treaty."[146] When Weiser died in 1760, Iroquois delegates in council with Pennsylvanians condoled the passing of a great man, who was one half Indian "and one half an *Englishman*." They were "at a great Loss, and sit in Darkness, as well as you," they said, "as since his Death we cannot so well understand one another."[147]

Interpreters and cultural mediators did not just operate between two sides with two clearly defined agendas; effective brokers drew on their connections and expertise to negotiate their way through "a kaleidoscope of local and supralocal leaders working at cross-purposes, struggles and alliances among competing interest groups, and tangled family ties" to help produce agreements that everyone could accept as promoting or protecting their interests.[148] At the Treaty of Logstown, where the Indians confirmed the earlier deed made at Lancaster, the Virginian commissioners dispatched their interpreter, Andrew Montour, "to confer with his Brethren, the other Sachems, in private, on the Subject, to urge the Necessity of such a Settlement & the great Advantage it wou'd be to them, as to their Trade or their Security."[149] Struggling to make headway building Indian alliances in the Ohio country on the eve of the French and Indian War, a young George Washington regretted not having the benefit of Andrew Montour's expertise. "Montour would be of singular use to me here at this present, in conversing with the Indians," he wrote to Virginia Governor Robert Dinwiddie in June 1754: "for want of a better acquaintance with their Customs I am often at a loss how to behave and should be reliev'd from many anxious fear's [sic] of offending them if Montour was here to assist me." In fact, Dinwoodie had already sent Montour, armed with wampum belts, to assist Washington in his Indian diplomacy.[150]

Treaty councils might require teams of interpreters speaking several different languages. Conferences in Albany in the seventeenth century often involved several Iroquoian and Algonquian languages as well as Dutch and English; conferences in Pennsylvania in the eighteenth century might involve Iroquoian and Algonquian and German and English (with Quakers or Moravians acting as mediators).[151] In 1748, in order for the Oneida chief Shickellamy to converse with a German visitor, another colonist translated the German's words into Mahican; a Mahican woman translated into Shawnee for her husband, who then translated into Oneida for Shickellamy. The reply then made its way back along the translation chain.[152]

Few interpreters could handle more than a couple of languages and the challenges of translating across several languages and across cultures and worldviews taxed even the best of them. Cadwallader Colden knew from his dealings with the Iroquois that "our Interpreters may not have done Justice to the Indian Eloquence." Indian orators used "many Metaphors in their Discourse, which interpreted by an hesitating Tongue, may appear mean, and strike our Imagination faintly, but under the Pen of a skilful Interpreter may strongly move our Passions by their lively Images." He had heard Indian speakers move their audience "with much Vivacity and Elocution," only to have an interpreter "explain the whole by one single Sentence," satisfied with communicating "the Sense, in as few words as it could be exprest."[153] The areas where translation was difficult most clearly reveal the differences in ideological systems.[154]

Interpreters could influence the outcome of treaty negotiations and sometimes exerted that influence to help themselves. Some interpreters did well in the Indian business, coming away from treaties with land given by Indians in "grateful recognition" of their services. After Conrad Weiser's death, Tachendorus (also called John Shickellamy, son of the Oneida chief) called him "one of the greatest thieves in the World for Lands."[155] James Dean, a white boy who grew up at Onoquaga and received a free education at Dartmouth College in the 1770s in return for his skills in Iroquois languages, later used those skills to make a small fortune interpreting at treaties in which the federal and state governments and private land companies separated the Oneidas from millions of acres of land.[156] Individuals of mixed heritage and uncertain or multiple identities were well suited to fulfilling the roles of culture broker and translator that were essential on the diplomatic frontiers of early America but they were rarely trusted.

Land, Liquor, and Captives

It is easy to assume that while Indians were masters of oratory and the rituals of the council fire, they were babes in the woods when it came to dealing with Europeans on land and politics. Certainly Indians sometimes claimed to be naïve in such matters, but they were quick learners from hard experience. "We know our Lands are now become more valuable," Canasatego explained in a meeting at Philadelphia in July 1742. "The white People think we do not know their Value; but we are sensible that the Land is everlasting, and the few Goods we receive for it are soon worn out and gone."[157] Men like Teedyuscung and Canasatego regularly called colonial governments on their record in acquiring Indian land, citing chapter and verse. Unwitting colonial representatives might find themselves in trouble if they had not done their homework or if they failed to keep up with Indian diplomats who led them into a maze of intertribal relations or bogged them down in intercolonial controversies and contention over land.

Oratory could conceal bluff and bluster and a treaty council was a good place to elevate a claim by voicing an assertion for the record. So, at the Treaty of Lancaster in 1744, when delegates from Maryland expressed doubts about the validity of Iroquois claims to land within their colony, Canasatego brushed aside any such reservations with "an oratorical barrage":

> Brother, the *Governor* of Maryland,
> When you mentioned the Affair of the Land Yesterday, you went back to old Times, and told us, you had been in Possession of the Province of Maryland above One Hundred Years, but what is a Hundred Years, in Comparison of the Length of Time since our Claim began? Since we came out of the Ground? For we must tell you, that long before a Hundred Years, our Ancestors came out of this vey Ground, and their Children have remained here ever since. You came out of the Ground in a Country that lies beyond the Seas; there you may have a just Claim, but here you must allow us to be your elder Brethren, and the Lands to belong to us long before you knew any thing of them.

Canasatego reinterpreted Iroquois history to suit his purposes. Iroquois claims to aboriginal occupancy of Maryland were dubious at best, but by placing the Iroquois in the position of indigenous inhabitants and relegating the colonists to the status of recent arrivals Canasatego effectively undermined Maryland's objections.[158]

But it was not enough to stave off a massive cession of Indian lands. Canasatego and the other Iroquois left Lancaster "well pleased," believing that they had ceded their claims to the Shenandoah Valley on Virginia's western border. But Virginia's original royal charter granted the colony land "from sea to sea." As the Treaty of Lancaster was written, the Iroquois actually ceded a huge chunk of America, including the Ohio Valley and all the way to the Pacific! In 1747 a group of influential individuals, including two brothers of George Washington, formed the Ohio Company of Virginia to lay claim to lands within the Lancaster cession and the next year the Crown granted them two hundred thousand acres near the headwaters of the Ohio River.[159] The English and the French saw the Ohio Valley as the key to controlling the continent and Virginian ambitions and French imperial agendas clashed there, igniting the so-called French and Indian War that became the global conflict known as the Seven Years' War. Canasatego had good reason to fear pen and ink work.

Treaties that involved land sales also involved different relationships to land and conflicting concepts of occupation and property. Europeans and Americans saw land in economic terms, a commodity to be surveyed and measured, bought and sold; property to be bounded, fenced, and owned. Indians, who "shared a pervasive understanding that a particular place belonged to a particular people only to the extent that the people belonged to the place," had different notions about how it could be sold and owned, if at all.[160] Indians who signed deeds sometimes thought they were sharing the right to use the land, not conveying exclusive ownership. Sometimes they "sold" land and were later shocked to find themselves excluded from it by fences, or treated as trespassers when they returned to old hunting territories; sometimes they sold the same lands several times over. They soon learned that when colonists bought land they insisted they acquired exclusive title once and for all. The Mohawk chief Hendrick clearly understood how the different conceptions of land ownership worked to the disadvantage of the Indians. When Pennsylvanians offered to buy Iroquois lands west of the Susquehanna at the Albany Congress in 1754, Hendrick replied:

> We are willing to sell You this Large Tract of Land for your People to live upon, but We desire this may be considered as Part of our Agreement that when We are all dead and gone your Grandchildren may not say to our Grandchildren, that your Forefathers sold the Land to our Forefathers, and therefore be gone off them. This is wrong. Let us be all as Brethren as well after as before of giving you Deeds for Land. After We have sold our Land We in a little time have nothing to shew for it; but it is not so

with You, Your Grandchildren will get something from it as long as the World stands; our Grandchildren will have no advantage from it; They will say We were Fools for selling so much Land for so small a matter and curse us.

Colonists may have given lip service to such requests while a land sale was being negotiated but paid scant attention to them after the transaction was completed.[161]

The Iroquois also famously sold the British on the idea that they exercised dominion over the tribes of the Ohio Valley (the British seized on it to promote their own imperial agenda) and on more than one occasion they sold the British land that belonged to other tribes.[162] When they did so at the Treaty of Fort Stanwix, they were indeed cursed "for selling so much Land for so small a matter."

Where spoken and written words failed, alcohol often proved effective in inducing Indians to relinquish their land. Alcohol was an instrument of market capitalism and colonial control, prevalent in the fur and deerskin trades as a means of stimulating overhunting and devastating in its effects in Indian communities.[163] Alcohol lubricated many a land deed and flowed freely at treaty councils. Colonial commissioners and Indian delegates drank rounds of toasts to each other, to colonial governors, to the king. Indians were given wine, rum, punch, and tobacco during adjournments in negotiations. The record of one treaty council, in Philadelphia in 1743, noted simply: "Here the Conversation drop'd; and after another Glass of Wine, the Indians resumed the Discourse." Indian delegates often negotiated while under the influence and "Wine and other Liquors" were regularly dispensed at the end of conferences "according to the Indian Custom."[164]

But Indians and colonists alike knew the dangers of drink. Negotiations sometimes were delayed or disrupted because Indian delegates turned up drunk or hungover.[165] Conrad Weiser and George Croghan often dispensed liquor and drank with Indians during negotiations but when many of the Ohio Indians with whom they were negotiating in the summer of 1748 got drunk, they staved an eight-gallon cask belonging to a trader who had "had brought near 30 Gallons of Whiskey to the Town." Thomas Lord Fairfax, Virginia's commissioner for dealing with the Iroquois and their allies at Winchester in 1753, gave the Indian delegates five gallons of rum but prohibited local tavern keepers from serving liquor to the Indians while they were in town.[166]

Indians took their own measures to restrict the liquor trade and to exercise restraint. In 1725–26, Iroquois delegates went to Albany to complain about rum sales and sent the New York commissioners a wampum belt "as a Solemn Token that they desired there might be an Absolute Prohibition of bringing rum in their Country."[167] The delegates at the Treaty of Lancaster in 1744, noted

Witham Marshe, "were very sober men . . . and sundry times refused drinking in a moderate way." Whenever Indians made treaties or sold land, he said, "they take care to abstain from intoxicating drink, for fear of being over-reached; but when they have finished their business, then some of them will drink without measure."[168] Even the hard-drinking Teedyuscung "earnestly desired that a Stop might be put to the sending excessive Quantitys of Rum Into the Indian Country, and that at Treaties especially particular care might be taken to prevent Indians getting it."[169] Unfortunately, such measured abstinence was not always the case. Plying Indians with alcohol and then getting them to put their marks on deeds of sale was common practice, and many chiefs under the influence acquiesced in treaties that robbed their people of thousands of acres of land. During a conference with William Johnson in 1755, the Oneida speaker Conoghquieson pointed an accusing finger at the trader John Henry Lydius and said: "That man sitting there . . . is a Devil and has stole our Lands, he takes Indians slyly by the Blanket one at a time, and when they are drunk puts some money in their Bosoms, and perswades them to sign deeds for our lands upon the Susquehanna, which we will not ratify nor suffer to be settled by any means."[170]

Once negotiations were finished, the treaty was drawn up (if it had not been drawn up in advance) and signatures affixed. Indian signatures could take a number of forms. Indians who were literate signed their names; more often they made their mark by their name or, as the phrase went on the Plains, "touched the pen." In many cases in the eastern woodlands, Indians signed by drawing pictographs of their clan totems—bear, beaver, deer, turtle, eagle, hawk—that conveyed individual and collective identity. Sometimes these pictographs appear upside down on the treaty—because the document was slid across the table from a commissioner or scribe for the Indians to sign. Such pictographs might better be understood as the equivalent of wax seals rather than individual signatures on European documents. Just as seals could not be duplicated on the facsimile copies of treaties that were made, so totems were often omitted or imperfectly copied from those drawn on the original document, and they were rarely reproduced on printed copies of treaties. Distortions and removals of totemic signatures frequently obscure the identity and affiliation of Indian signatories.[171]

After the treaty was signed, presents—often displayed but withheld as an inducement to signing—were distributed, usually to the chiefs who would then redistribute them among their people. The Indians would depart with their payment and the commissioners would leave with their treaty. Then, increasingly, the surveyors and settlers moved in.

After a treaty involving a land transaction, the new boundary lines had to be delineated on the ground as well as on the maps. Those boundaries often ignored and cut across kinship connections and patterns of shared land use between tribes.[172] Sometimes, Indians drew their own maps of their country and the territory they ceded. Sometimes they accompanied surveyors as they "marked the land" by etching symbols on rocks and blazing hatchet marks on trees. Sometimes Indians marked the new boundary themselves to warn off trespassers.[173] Long before the poet Robert Frost, Indians understood the relationship between good fences and good neighbors, even if whites rarely respected Indian "fences."

Some treaties involved delivering up people as well as, or instead of, land. Indians often returned captives as peace initiatives and gave captives to forge friendships, cement alliances, and end bloodshed. In 1762 Abenakis gave Sir William Johnson a Panis Indian slave to be sent together with two wampum belts to the Stockbridge Indians to atone for a killing and to make peace. The gift of a captive, notes the historian Brett Rushforth, "even more powerfully than wampum or the calumet, signified the opposite of warfare, the giving rather than the taking of life." In New France, where Indian slavery was omnipresent, the French quickly adopted such practices and made exchanging captives a key component of their Indian diplomacy.[174]

As captive taking escalated in the mid-eighteenth century, English colonists increasingly made the return of captives a condition of peace treaties. "You must bring here with you also all the Prisoners you have taken during these Disturbances," Governor Robert Hunter Morris told Teedyuscung and the Delaware chiefs at the Easton council in July 1756. "I must insist on this, as an Evidence of your Sincerity to make a lasting Peace, for, without it, though Peace may be made from the Teeth outwards, yet while you retain our Flesh and Blood in Slavery, it cannot be expected we can be Friends with you, or that a Peace can come from our Hearts." But Indians were often reluctant to return captives they had adopted and chiefs had limited ability or desire to compel people to give up relatives. They also balked at the idea that they should return captives *before* peace was established. "Such an unreasonable demand," they told the Moravian missionary Christian Frederick Post, "makes us appear as if we wanted brains." Sometimes returning captives was a relatively straightforward process and Indians handed over people who were only too eager to be liberated. In other cases, captives who had been adopted into Indian communities and had become accustomed to Indian ways of life were reluctant to be freed and their new families were reluctant to let them go. Colonel Henry Bouquet made a peace treaty in 1764 that required the Delawares and Shawnees to turn over all captives taken during the French and Indian War and Pontiac's War. The Indians complied, reluctantly. They reminded Bouquet that the captives had been "tied to us by Adoption.... We have taken as much care of these Prisoners, as if they were [our] flesh and blood." They wanted to make sure that

Bouquet would treat them "tender, and kindly, which will be a means of inducing them to live contentedly with you." Many of the captives resisted liberation and regarded their new "freedom" as captivity. The children parted from their Indian families in tears, and even some of the adult captives had to be bound by the English to prevent them from running off and rejoining the Indians.[175] In the South, treaties often stipulated that Indians must return runaway slaves who had taken refuge with Indian nations.

Even when treaties were conducted in good faith and resulted in mutually satisfying terms, they were subject to modification or even rejection by people who had not been present when the agreement was made. Indian leaders pointed out, and whites complained, that they lacked authority to make binding commitments for all their people, who had to be convinced before they would accept a treaty. Iroquois delegates at a meeting in Albany in 1714 told the governor of New York that they could not answer his proposals point by point but would convey them to "the ears of our people when we get home to our country and shall make it our business to imprint them into their minds and hearts."[176] In 1756 a delegation of Upper Creeks led by the chief Gun Merchant negotiated and signed a treaty with the English in Charlestown, South Carolina, but when they returned home the Creeks refused to accept it, "thereby reducing the treaty text to worthless paper." Creek headmen told Governor William Lyttleton that Gun Merchant "has not the Consent of one Man in the Nation."[177]

Complaints about inadequate representation reflected how treaty making changed during the colonial era. Initially treaties were forums in which Indians and Europeans met to establish or renew peace, alliance, and trade; settle disputes; and perhaps exchange land for gifts. Increasingly, treaties became almost entirely about land, and for Europeans, as the Treaty of Stanwix would show, sealing the deal was often more important than who was there to seal it.

Fort Stanwix, 1768

SHIFTING BOUNDARIES

The Treaty of Fort Stanwix, held at present-day Rome, New York, in 1768 was the biggest Indian treaty council and the biggest land cession in colonial America. For two weeks, three thousand Indians talked, ate, and drank with Crown agents; delegates from New York, New Jersey, Pennsylvania, and Virginia; merchants; various interested parties; and assorted hangers-on. When it was over, the British gave the Indians twenty boatloads of goods and £10,000 in cash; the Indians gave the British millions of acres of land in the Ohio Valley that they claimed but did not occupy.[1] Ostensibly carried out to ensure an orderly movement of a boundary line dividing Indians and colonists, the Treaty of Stanwix instead turned the ceded lands into a racial killing ground, dismantled the world that both sets of signatories hoped to preserve, and rendered the Ohio River a battle line that Indians fought to defend and whites to breach for almost thirty years.

Searching for a Boundary

After the Peace of Montreal in 1701, the Iroquois negotiated the treacherous waters of international, intercolonial, and intertribal competition by playing off rival powers and asserting their primacy in intertribal affairs at colonial conferences. By offering each colonial power the possibility of allegiance but never totally committing to such allegiance, they maintained their independence from European control while simultaneously maintaining access to European goods.[2] By claiming sovereignty over peoples who inhabited lands where their war parties had ranged in the seventeenth century, Iroquois leaders created a mythology of conquest and domination that the British bought into and that allowed the Six Nations to negotiate away other peoples' lands in their dealings with the British colonies. At the Treaty of Lancaster in 1744, for example, Iroquois delegates ceded title to a vast territory in the interior, lands occupied by other Indian nations. They would do the same thing at Fort Stanwix, but that would be the last time.

The Iroquois held a preeminent position in British-Indian relations, and the Mohawks in particular enjoyed a privileged role, in large part due to their relations with Sir William Johnson (see figure 2.1). Johnson had migrated from Ireland and settled in the Mohawk Valley in 1738. Starting out as an Indian trader, he developed close ties with the Mohawk community at Canajoharie, became a prosperous merchant and landlord, and expanded his trading ties westward. He presided over an Anglo-Irish-Iroquois household and took readily to Indian ways. As early as 1746, he rode into a treaty conference in Albany "dressed and painted after the Manner of an Indian War Captain." He participated in Indian dances and sang Indian war songs. He married an indentured German servant girl named Catherine Weisenberg and had three children with her, but he also slept with Indian women and when Catherine died he took

FIGURE 2.1 **Sir William Johnson.** *Copy after a lost portrait painted by Thomas McIlworth at Johnson Hall in 1763. (Collection of the New-York Historical Society)*

sixteen-year-old Mary or Molly Brant as his common-law wife. Johnson developed a close friendship with the Mohawk sachem Hendrick, who helped him gain acceptance in Iroquois communities and attendance at council meetings. Like Johnson, Hendrick knew how to operate on a multicultural frontier: he accepted Christianity, dealt regularly with colonial officials and, in Timothy Shannon's phrase, "dressed for success" on the frontier, melding indigenous and European styles of clothing.[3] Supported by large sums of Crown money, Johnson, in Cadwallader Colden's judgment, "made a greater figure and gained more influence among the Indians, than any person before him." Governor George Clinton of New York believed no one on the continent could hold the Iroquois allegiance "so much as this gentleman." It was clearly a mutually beneficial relationship: "you have been A Great Good Standing tree amongst us a long time," the Mohawks told Johnson.[4]

Johnson resigned from public office in 1751 when British-Iroquois relations hit a low point but he had made himself indispensable to the British and to the Iroquois and his star continued to rise. Hendrick was killed at the Battle of Lake George with the French in 1755 but Johnson's action in the same engagement saved the day and earned him a baronetcy. With the support of Iroquois leaders who wrote letters to the Crown recommending him for the position, William Johnson was appointed superintendent of Indian affairs north of the Ohio. (A Scotsman, John Stuart, was appointed in the South.) One thousand Indians assembled in conference at Fort Johnson in the summer of 1755 and from that point onward Johnson seemed to be engaged in an endless stream of meetings, councils, and negotiations to restore and keep bright the Covenant Chain. He cultivated personal alliances with Iroquois chiefs, bolstered the standing of chiefs with whom he was allied, exerted influence in the appointment of chiefs, and did not hesitate to circumvent the sachems and deal directly with war chiefs when the empire needed Iroquois warriors. He built a network of connections and his marriage to Molly Brant took him into the kinship networks of Iroquois society. He understood, as he told the Iroquois, "your Women are of no small consequence in relation to public affairs," and he took account of them in his conduct of business. However, he also manipulated Iroquois gender relations and tried to exclude women when he felt their presence hindered or complicated the business at hand. Molly evidently did not: according to contemporaries, "she was of great use to Sir William in his Treaties" and "often persuaded the obstinate chiefs into a compliance with the proposals for peace, or sale of lands." "He knew that Women govern the Politics of savages as well as the refined part of the World and therefore always kept up a good understanding with the brown Ladies," Tench Tilghman wrote in his journal the year after Johnson's death.[5] Sir William sent Molly's younger brother, Joseph, to school in Connecticut to study under the Congregationalist minister Eleazar Wheelock, the future founder of Dartmouth College, and Joseph became both Johnson's protégé and an important ally. The British increasingly looked to Johnson to conduct the Crown's Indian affairs, and Johnson artfully advanced British interests and his own standing among the Iroquois. He lavishly bestowed gifts, food, and even cash, demonstrating that the king, and he himself, was a true father, and binding the Iroquois to the empire with ties of economic dependence and reciprocal obligation.

He made his home in the Mohawk Valley, which was the favored site for intertribal meetings and the diplomatic hub for British-Indian relations, trumping Albany and Onondaga. He built his first estate, Mount Johnson, on the north bank of the Mohawk. Ten years later, he moved a few miles downriver to a larger, stone-built house that became known as Fort Johnson. In 1763, with the French defeated and future prospects looking bright, he built a new mansion, Johnson Hall. Johnson's homes reflected his increasing fortunes and Britain's growing empire. They were also places where peoples and cultures mingled. He employed Dutch, German, and Irish workers; had African American slaves; and attracted Highland Scots as tenants on his estates. And Indians were there constantly. He hosted, lodged, fed, and entertained Indian visitors, and he complained to his superiors that Indians ate him out of house and home. He and Molly had eight children together. Johnson donned Indian attire and hosted feasts of bear meat; Molly donned European clothes and served tea in porcelain crockery.[6]

Johnson described himself to the Iroquois as "one Half *Indian* and one Half *English*."[7] He learned Iroquois ways, adopted Iroquois customs, and loved Iroquois women, but in truth he had no intention of becoming Iroquois. He went native to the extent that doing so promoted his own and his empire's interests. The trader John Long related a story, one of several versions, that though likely apocryphal, illustrates how Johnson exploited his knowledge of Indian ways. During a council meeting with a party of Mohawks, a chief (identified as Hendrick in other versions) told Johnson that he had dreamed the night before that Sir William had given him a fine laced coat, and he believed it was the same one he was wearing. "Well, then," said Sir William, observing Indian custom, "you must have it," and pulling off his coat, he handed it to the chief. The next time they met in council, Johnson told the chief that he, too, "had dreamed a very surprising dream": the chief "had given him a tract of land on the Mohawk River to build a house on and make a settlement, extending about nine miles in length along the banks." The chief smiled and said that "if he really dreamed it he should have it; but that he would never dream again with him."[8]

Johnson built his career on Iroquois trade and friendship. He regarded a well-regulated Indian trade as vital to the prosperity and security of Britain's

North American empire, and he thought the Iroquois were "the only barrier against our troublesome Neighbours the French."[9] He used his position to promote the transfer of Iroquois land to the Crown, to private purchasers, and to himself. He portrayed himself to William Pitt as "a man who was willing to Sacrifice his own ease, & business to the public Welfare,"[10] but he linked his own fortunes to those of the empire and the Iroquois and he was adept at serving the king and himself. By the 1750s, Johnson was "the most famous American in the British Empire," far surpassing men like Benjamin Franklin and George Washington, whose historical reputations rose as Johnson's world, and the Iroquois power on which it rested, fell apart.[11]

Iroquois skills in intercultural diplomacy and representing themselves to the British as the dominant voice in Indian country, together with Johnson's skill in building his power base and managing the Iroquois role in his vision of empire, combined to create a mystique of Iroquois influence: "What Johnson was for British policy, the Iroquois League was assumed to be for Indian policy." Britain's propensity for dealing with other Indians via the Iroquois meant that other tribes often had to deal with the British through the Iroquois and by attending multitribal gatherings at Johnson Hall.[12] But Britain's total defeat of France after more than half a century of recurrent conflict in North America meant the Iroquois were no longer able to play off European rivals. They must now deal only with King George and his representatives, or, more accurately, with his main representative: Sir William Johnson.

Even before the Peace of Paris in 1763 officially ended the great Anglo-French conflict, colonists were encroaching on eastern Iroquois lands in growing numbers. "We have sometime past heard that our Brethren the English were wanting to get more Lands from us," said an Oneida chief named Conoghquieson. The Iroquois had sold their English brothers land as long as they had any to spare but they no longer had enough left for hunting; they would not consider further cessions until all that land was fully settled, and any future land deals would have to be made with the consent of all the Six Nations. "We have had our lands from the beginning of the World, and we love them as we do our lives," said Conoghquieson. He handed Johnson a six-row wampum belt to keep at his home so "that when any person shall be desirous of purchasing any more you may shew them thereby, that the six Nations are all determined not to part with more of their Lands on any account whatsoever."[13] Conoghquieson (also spelled Kanaghwaes, Kanaghqweasea, and Kanongweniyah, and meaning "standing ears of corn") appears to have been one of the fifty league chiefs. Johnson already knew him. He was present in 1755 when the Oneida chief was ceremonially "raised up" in the place of his deceased predecessor and given the same name.[14] Three years later Conoghquieson asked Johnson to put a stop to "the selling of any Strong Liquors to our People" because it "disturbs us in our

Meetings & Consulations where the drunken People come in quarelling" and it caused many deaths.[15] Despite his strong voice in defense of *Iroquois* lands, Conoghquieson would continue to talk with Johnson about selling *Indian* lands. Their conversations would culminate with the Treaty of Fort Stanwix.

The Iroquois strategy of claiming, and sometimes selling, other peoples' lands reduced their influence among the western tribes at a time when the focus of British-Indian relations was shifting westward, undermining the League's once-pivotal position. Indian peoples who had migrated into the Ohio country earlier in the eighteenth century—not just the Delawares and Shawnees but also western Iroquois who became known as the Mingos—increasingly asserted their independence from the Confederacy.[16] The British had assured Ohio Indians that their lands would be protected when the Seven Years' War was won, and the surrender terms at Montreal in 1760 stated that France's Indian allies were to "be maintained in the Lands they inhabit."[17] The victorious King George III had it "much at heart to conciliate the Affection of the Indian Nations, by every Act of strict Justice, and by affording them His Royal Protection from any Incroachment on the Lands they have reserved to themselves, for their hunting Grounds, & for their own Support & Habitation."[18]

The king had to afford his protection sooner than he expected. The Peace of Paris in 1763 redrew the map of North America. More American territory changed hands than at any other treaty before or since. France handed over to Britain Canada and its claims east of the Mississippi. Louisiana went to Spain, mainly to keep it out of the hands of the British. Britain now had to try and govern its hugely expanded empire in North America, regulate the frontier, and deal with powerful Indian nations formerly allied with the French. British garrisons occupied French outposts and many British officers treated the Indians as a defeated people. Alarmed by the presence of British garrisons and offended by the absence of British gifts, Indians took action even before the war was officially over. As early as 1761 the Seneca chief Guyasuta (or Kayusuta) carried a red wampum belt to Detroit and "under the nose of the British commandant" exhorted the Indians in the region to take up arms against the redcoats. In 1763, Guyasuta, the Ottawa Pontiac, and other war chiefs of the Ohio Valley and Great Lakes tribes launched assaults that destroyed every British fort west of the Appalachians except for those at Detroit, Niagara, and Fort Pitt. The Senecas inflicted a bloody defeat on a British convoy at Devil's Hole near Fort Niagara. Once the fighting was over, Sir William Johnson demanded that the Senecas cede the Niagara portage route to the Crown as reparation.[19] General Amherst advocated using germ warfare and when Indian emissaries came to Fort Pitt a trader named William Trent confided in his journal that the British "gave them two Blankets and an Handkerchief out of the Small Pox Hospital. I hope it will have the desired effect."[20] Backcountry settlers fled east to escape

Indian raiding parties and Indian hating escalated: in December, Scotch-Irish frontiersmen in Pennsylvania known as the Paxton Boys slaughtered peaceful Conestoga Indians and marched on Philadelphia to vent frustration at their colonial government's failure to defend the frontier.[21]

The imperial response to the Indians' war of independence triggered a series of unanticipated events that culminated in another war of independence a dozen years later.[22] The government hoped to bring peace and order to the frontier by separating Indians and Europeans. In October 1763 King George signed a proclamation establishing the Appalachian Mountains as the boundary between British settlement and Indian lands. The Royal Proclamation also stipulated "that no private Person do presume to make any Purchase from the said Indians of any Lands reserved to the said Indians within those parts of our Colonies where We have thought proper to allow Settlement." Only Crown representatives acting in formal council with Indian nations could negotiate land transfers, and only licensed traders would be permitted to operate in Indian country. By such measures, the government sought to prevent "all just Cause of Discontent, and Uneasiness" among the Indians in the future.[23] In the winter after the proclamation was issued, Indian delegates carrying copies of the document and strings of wampum traveled Indian country from Nova Scotia to the Mississippi, summoning the tribes to meet Sir William Johnson in council at Niagara. "At this Treaty," Johnson informed General Gage, "we should tye them down according to their own forms of which they take the most notice, for Example by Exchanging a very large belt with some remarkable & intelligible figures thereon, expressive of the occasion which should be always shewn at public Meetings, to remind them of their promises; and that we should Exchange Articles with the Signatures of the Chiefs of every Tribe." At Niagara, in the summer of 1764, Sir William read the terms of the proclamation to two thousand Indians from two dozen nations, and they sealed the agreement with an exchange of gifts and wampum.[24] In Canada, the principles and protections established by the proclamation made it "the single most important document in the history of treaty-making,"[25] and it is recognized in section 25 of the Canadian Charter of Rights and Freedoms, the first part of the Constitution Act of 1982. In the area that became the United States, it produced a rather different outcome.

The proclamation attempted to bring order by running a line through a morass of competing, intersecting, and overlapping colonial, tribal, and individual claims. Many non-Indians already lived west of the mountains (and many Indians still lived east of them) and it failed to keep colonists off Indian lands. Four years after the proclamation, Indians complained that settlers were making "more incroachments on their Country, than ever they had before."[26] By concentrating land purchasing in the hands of the government, the proclamation transformed the land market. Squatters could ignore the proclamation; land speculators could not: their ability to make profits in the West depended on being able to convey clear title to the lands in which they invested and now they could not buy and sell western lands legally. The new measures "infuriated Virginia land speculators" who saw tyranny in the Crown's attempt to monopolize granting and acquiring land and in Britain's interference with their freedom to make a fortune. In their eyes, a new British and Indian barrier had replaced the old French and Indian barrier.[27]

But the imperial government had no intention of permanently halting the westward expansion of the colonies; the boundary line was a device for regulating and not eliminating frontier expansion. Eventually the line would be abolished as old colonies grew and new ones were created. Once the barrier was moved west, deeds of Indian land could be converted into clear title. Between 1763 and 1768, under the authority of superintendents Sir William Johnson and John Stuart, Britain and the various tribes negotiated a series of agreements that attempted to define a new boundary line.[28]

Johnson, like Stuart, believed strongly in regulating the frontier and he supported the proclamation line as a blueprint for peace in British North America, although he never expected that it should be permanent or restrict his own land-dealing activities. In November 1763 he recommended that the Board of Trade establish a boundary "beyond which no settlement should be made, until the whole Six Nations should think proper of selling part thereof." He recommended himself as the person to carry it out. "I am certain, I can at any time hereafter perswade them to cede to His Majesty more land, if it may be found wanting from encrease of people," he said. If such a boundary was needed, Johnson stood ready to "make the Indians acquainted therewith, and settle the same in such manner, as may prove most to their satisfaction, and the good of the public."[29] In Johnson's view a clearly defined boundary, moved periodically by "fair purchase" of land from the Indians, in treaties that he orchestrated and carried out with the Iroquois, would permit peaceful imperial expansion.[30]

To help implement and maintain the proclamation line, the Board of Trade in 1764 circulated among colonial governors and Indian superintendents a plan for the future management of Indian affairs. Imperial officials, rather than the individual colonies, were to be responsible for conducting Indian relations. Johnson had advocated such a move for years, urging that his department should function as an independent administrative branch, reporting only to the imperial government. The Indian department, not the army or the colonies, should control Indian affairs; the superintendents should call Indian councils, conduct political relations with the tribes, and exercise jurisdiction over Indian country and the traders who did business there.[31]

In Johnson's world the Indian department was a personal and, almost literally, a family affair. Johnson and three other men effectively managed Indian affairs north of the Ohio. The Deputy Superintendent for the Indians of Ohio and Pennsylvania was George Croghan, an Irish emigré like Johnson and of the same age. He married the daughter of a Mohawk chief named Nickus in 1757 and his Mohawk daughter, Catherine (in matrilineal Mohawk society, the child of the mother was Mohawk, no matter the identity of the father), later married Joseph Brant, the brother of Sir William's wife, Molly. Deputy agent Guy Johnson was Sir William's nephew and son-in-law: he married one of Johnson's daughters by Catherine Weisenberg. In 1768 the Deputy Superintendant for Canadian Indians was Daniel Claus, a German emigré who had accumulated a wealth of experience in Indian affairs and knowledge of Mohawk, and he married Johnson's other daughter by Catherine Weisenberg. With these three close associates Johnson dominated British-Indian relations north of the Ohio.

Croghan was almost a replica on the Ohio and Pennsylvania frontier of what Johnson was on the New York frontier. "No colonial fur trader earned greater respect from Indians, or traveled farther on that respect," notes James Merrell, and "no one was more enamored of Indian lands." The historian Alan Taylor describes Croghan as "the most avid, indeed manic," land speculator in colonial North America.[32] Croghan migrated from Ireland in 1741 and worked as a trader in western Pennsylvania and in the Ohio Valley from about 1745 to 1754. In 1749 three Iroquois chiefs granted him some two hundred thousand acres of land around the Forks of the Ohio (a gift the Iroquois would confirm in 1768). Croghan said it was in recognition of his services but a huge quantity of goods changed hands as well. In 1753 Scarouady, the Oneida chief and "Half King" representing the Ohio Six Nations, named Croghan to speak for the Indians in their dealings with the governor of Pennsylvania. Croghan was with General Edward Braddock and George Washington at the rout of Braddock's army on the Monongahela in 1755, and he accompanied General John Forbes at the capture of Fort Duquesne (rechristened Fort Pitt) in 1758. Appointed Deputy Superintendent for the Ohio and Pennsylvania Indians in 1756, he operated primarily out of Fort Pitt, regulating the Indian trade there, traveling extensively in the West, and exerting his influence to undermine French-Indian alliances.[33] No one exerted greater influence on affairs in the West. Johnson relied on the old trader's knowledge of Indian affairs and Croghan occasionally interpreted for him.

Croghan was not known for his honesty and integrity. He was a heavy drinker and on one occasion he suffered from such a severe case of venereal disease that he took to wearing a Scottish kilt to ease his discomfort.[34] He was easygoing and generous, but, in the words of one biographer, he was "a born actor, a master of the poker face," "devious and dangerously speculative." He knew how to talk people into loaning him money but he "did not keep his promises; he was not candid; he misrepresented; he lied."[35] He was notorious in government circles for his lavish expenditures on Indian presents.[36] He was also up to his neck in land speculations in the West and he needed to have the proclamation line moved to make his land purchases "legal." The proclamation offered a land bounty to each soldier who had served in the French and Indian War. The highest amount offered to any officer was five thousand acres, but Croghan sent a memorial to the Board of Trade in 1765 asking for a grant of twenty thousand acres in New York as a reward for his services; he received a grant of ten thousand acres but in 1768 submitted another memorial for the additional ten thousand acres, which were granted.[37] In addition, he sought compensation for losses that his trading operations had suffered in the Indian wars. Croghan "almost always positioned imperial assignments to act as vehicles to settle personal debts and speculate in trade and land." After 1763, his future "depended on the careful readjustment of the Indian boundary."[38]

Like Johnson, Croghan had kinship ties in Iroquois society through his Mohawk wife and also had kinship ties to many of the men who had their eyes on Indian land. His brother-in-law, the Pennsylvania merchant William Trent, was on hand when smallpox blankets were given to Indians visiting Fort Pitt; his half-brother, Edward Ward, built the original Virginia fort at the forks of the Ohio; his nephew William Croghan married the sister of an Indian fighter named George Rogers Clark who would later serve as a US treaty commissioner; his cousins Thomas Smallwood and William Powell were leading merchants of early Pittsburgh.

Croghan and Trent "figured conspicuously" among a group of traders who had lost merchandise during the Indian wars. Samuel Wharton, a merchant from Philadelphia (figure 2.2), in partnership with John Baynton, George Morgan, and Croghan, had attempted to gain control of the Indian trade of the Ohio Valley but Pontiac's War brought the company to the brink of bankruptcy. Wharton, "characteristically, enlarged his ambitions in the face of adversity." He directed Trent, his agent, to buy up the claims of other traders for the losses they had incurred between 1754 and 1763. Then, calling themselves "the suffering traders," Wharton and his fellow merchants sought compensation for their losses.[39]

They tried first to obtain reimbursement from the British Treasury and, after a meeting at the Indian Queen Tavern in Philadelphia, chose Croghan to go to England to represent their claims. Croghan's trip was financed by a company headquartered in Burlington, New Jersey, and headed by William Franklin, the governor of New Jersey and illegitimate son of Benjamin Franklin. Croghan carried letters of introduction from Baynton, Wharton, and Morgan. He set sail from Philadelphia in December 1763, was shipwrecked off the coast of France,

SAMUEL WHARTON.

FIGURE 2.2 **Samuel Wharton.** *From a woodcut of a miniature painted in England.*
(The Historical Society of Pennsylvania)

but reached London early in 1764. After waiting for three months, he declared
he was "sick of London" and ready for home: "there has been Nothing Don
Sence I Came to London by the Grate ones butt Squebeling & fighting See who
will keep in power," he wrote to Johnson; "it will Larn Me to be Contented on
a Litle farm in America if I Can gett one when I go back." Back in America,
the memory of that lesson quickly faded. Finding that direct payment of their
claims for compensation would require a special act of Parliament, the suffering traders tried instead to get a compensatory grant of land from the Indians
when the boundary negotiations began. In February 1765 they presented their
claims to Sir William who promised to do the group "an essential Piece of
Service" when he next met with the Indians to renegotiate the boundary line.[40]

Johnson and Croghan made themselves indispensable in the negotiations.
Promoting the notion that many of the western tribes were dependents of the
Iroquois, Johnson "felt that the intended partition of much of North America
could be worked out exclusively between himself, as the King's representative, and the Iroquois, as the owners of the land."[41] Croghan was the pivotal
link in the West, "the man who could go among the western Indians, sit down
with them, and discuss indemnity to the merchants as well as the Indian-white
boundary."[42] With his finger in land schemes that had to fall on the eastern side
of the new boundary, he was not above using his position to try and whip up
fears of an Indian war to help speed up the government's plans for moving the
boundary westward.[43]

In April and May 1765, Johnson held a conference with some nine hundred Indians—Six Nations and Delawares—at Johnson Hall and broached the

subject of working out a new boundary. The Onondaga speaker responded that they thought it was "very necessary, provided the White People will abide by it." Having been cheated so often in the past, they were suspicious. "We were always ready to give, but the English don't deal fairly with us, they are more cunning than we are, they get our names upon paper very fast, and we often don't know what it is for." Croghan, not long returned from London, conducted negotiations with the western nations at Fort Pitt. In July, Shawnee, Delaware, and Iroquois delegates convened at Johnson Hall and agreed to the terms that had been worked out in principle in the spring meetings.[44] These were preliminary agreements without official authorization, but if implemented they would transfer vast amounts of territory to colonial hands, most of it from non-Iroquois nations who, in Johnson's view, deserved to pay for their part in the recent wars. Johnson next sent Croghan to initiate peace talks with the nations of the Wabash and the Illinois country. It was a perilous journey and Croghan's mission almost ended in disaster when a war party of Kickapoos and Mascoutens attacked them, and killed and wounded several people, including three of the Shawnee delegates accompanying Croghan as escorts. Croghan himself took a hatchet blow to the head ("but my Scull being pretty thick," he later joked to Johnson, "the hatchet would not enter") and was taken captive. But once the Kickapoos realized they had killed Shawnees and might bring down vengeance on their heads, they hastened to make amends and allowed Croghan's party to proceed.[45]

The government in London faced mounting difficulties administering its new American empire and dealing with its existing colonies; it was three years before Johnson received the instructions he was waiting for to renegotiate the boundary. Johnson, Croghan, and the traders mounted an intensive lobbying campaign to convince the home government that a new boundary was vital to avert an Indian war and that the tribes were willing to grant land. Both Johnson and Croghan wrote to the Board of Trade, and Croghan and Governor Franklin enlisted the support of Benjamin Franklin, Pennsylvania's agent in London. Croghan told Benjamin Franklin that the Shawnees, Delawares, and other Indians who had robbed and killed traders had informed him "they were *not only very willing but anxious, to make a* REPARATION to the representatives of the unhappy Sufferers" but they had no way of doing it "except by a *Surrender of a part of their Country*, which they would *most chearfully* do, and especially of that part, which lies on this side of the River Ohio (on the back part of Virginia) as it is now, of no use to them, for Hunting Ground." Baynton, Wharton, and Morgan made sure Benjamin Franklin understood the connection between the boundary line and the land grant: Johnson had done them "an essential piece of service" by getting the Indians to grant part of the land encompassed by the new boundary when the treaty was held, but unless the government authorized a new boundary, the Indians "cannot give us the Land." Benjamin Franklin never set foot west of the Appalachian Mountains but he wanted to see the West populated with British Protestants rather than French Catholics, just as he would later want it settled by American citizens rather than British subjects. He lost no time in bringing the boundary issue to the government's attention.[46] By Christmas 1766, Samuel Wharton who, in addition to his claim as a "suffering trader" had land schemes in the Illinois country, told William Franklin that he expected to be "Ere long, a *Considerable* Proprietor of Terra Firma."[47]

Meanwhile, Baynton, Wharton, and Morgan kept the pressure on Johnson: "We really blush, to be so free," they wrote, but a letter from the superintendent to the Earl of Shelburne now could be just what was needed to secure confirmation of the land grant—"the great & long sighed for Object"—to the poor traders.[48] In the fall of 1767 William Trent sent Benjamin Franklin a list of the traders' losses. Croghan and Wharton each wrote to Franklin urging prompt action on the boundary line: an Indian war was imminent unless the government seized the moment to establish a boundary, they claimed, and the Indians had already agreed to it in principle. "Indians, you well know Sir," wrote Wharton, "are not always in a Temper to dispose of a large Part of their Country. What a Pity is it Therefore, That so fair an Opportunity should be lost, When the Crown might for a small Consideration purchase Land sufficient for Us to settle or hunt On, And at the same Time remove the present unfavorable Disposition of The Natives, by fixing a *Line* between Them And Us, beyond Which, No Englishman should presume to settle or hunt!"[49] Franklin duly pushed the matter in London, over dinner with Lord Shelburne and on the following morning with Lord Clare of the Board of Trade.[50] Croghan, meanwhile, was on the road again in his capacity of deputy superintendent: leaving Fort Pitt in mid-October, he reached Detroit a month later and held council with the Great Lakes tribes; by December 9 he was back at Fort Pitt where he held a council with the Shawnees, Senecas, and Delawares.[51]

Pennsylvania had its eyes on the Wyoming Valley lands along the Susquehanna River. It was contested ground. The Susquehanna Company, a joint-stock company formed in 1753 by Connecticut land speculators, believed that Connecticut's colonial charter, which granted sea-to-sea land rights, entitled the province to the valley. The eastern Delaware chief Teedyuscung had protested English settlement in the area. He declared "he did not unders[tan]d what the White People meant by settling in their Country unless they intended to steal it from them," and he warned off colonial settlers and speculators he found on the land. The Crown feared the colonists' intrusions would provoke "all the horrors and Calamities of an Indian war," and orders were issued to desist. But the Susquehanna Company "were Determined to Settle Immediately on the Land, to the Amount of a Thousand families and Upwards." Iroquois, Delawares, and Pennsylvanians all watched with growing alarm as settlers from Connecticut pushed into the Susquehanna Valley. Then, in April 1763, as Teedyuscung lay sleeping in the town of Wyoming on the north branch of the Susquehanna (near present-day Wilkes-Barre), someone set his log cabin on fire. The sixty-three-year-old chief, a veteran of many battles and treaties, was burned to death. Within weeks, colonists from New England, most of them people Teedyuscung had chased away the previous fall, were building cabins and planting fields in the Wyoming Valley. Iroquois delegates complained to the Connecticut Assembly in Hartford. Teedyuscung's son, Captain Bull, went to Philadelphia to protest. Then, after drunken militiamen murdered his cousin, a baptized Delaware named Zacharias, along with his wife and child, Captain Bull took his revenge, killing twenty-six Wyoming settlers.[52]

Thomas Penn, the elder proprietor and oldest surviving son of William Penn (and one of the men behind the infamous "Walking Purchase" in 1737), now saw a chance to settle the issue. He wrote to William Johnson in December 1767, urging him to get from the Indians as much land for "us" as he could between the west branch of the Susquehanna and Delaware rivers. To "prevent the possibility of the people from Connecticut giving us any more trouble there," Sir William should get the Iroquois to agree that "when they incline to sell the rest, they will sell it only to us."[53] Pennsylvania's interests would be well represented at the Fort Stanwix treaty and the Iroquois looked favorably on Pennsylvania representatives who acknowledged Iroquois authority over the disputed lands.

Benjamin Franklin's lobbying and the warnings of impending bloodshed in the West paid off. Convinced that a new boundary was necessary "to prevent the fatal consequences of an Indian War," the Lords of Trade advised Shelburne to send immediate orders to Johnson to negotiate the final settlement of the line. They cautioned, however, that the new line should extend no lower down the Ohio than the Kanawha River; going any farther might furnish colonists with a pretext for settling land that, though claimed by the Six Nations, was occupied by the Cherokees as part of their hunting territory.[54] Shelburne, too, thought the new boundary "essential for the Preservation of Peace and Harmony," and he instructed Johnson in December 1767 "to convey the proper Intelligence to the different Tribes of Indians concerned, that they may be ready to co-operate with you in bringing it to a Conclusion."[55] Johnson was already on it. In November he had sent an Onondaga with a large string of wampum to let the Six Nations know "that I intended a General Meeting with them Some time in ye. Spring."[56] The wampum belt not only summoned the tribes but also informed them of the agenda for the conference. He followed up with a series of meetings with various groups and sent additional wampum through the Ohio Valley. On January 5, 1768, in one of his last actions in office, Shelburne authorized Johnson to negotiate a new boundary line.[57]

By then, the government had dropped its plan for imperial management of Indian affairs. Political unrest following passage of the Stamp Act and the need to reduce the cost of imperial administration rendered the plan impractical. Shelburne concluded by the summer of 1767 that management of the Indian trade should be returned to the colonies and the following spring the Board of Trade recommended that imperial regulation of Indian affairs be abandoned. But at least Johnson finally had official permission to negotiate a new boundary. According to the historian Peter Marshall, Johnson accepted the decline of his official authority and "turned to the advancement of his private interests."[58] But at Fort Stanwix he managed to promote an imperial as well as a personal agenda.

In January 1768, Lord Hillsborough was appointed to a newly created cabinet-level position, secretary of state for the colonies. Benjamin Franklin was quick to press the boundary issue with the new secretary and Hillsborough confirmed Shelburne's instructions to Johnson to carry the boundary line to the Great Kanawha in western Virginia.[59] The Lords of Trade recommended to George III "that this boundary line should as speedily as possible be ratified by your Majesty's Authority" and that the superintendents be "impowered to make Treaties in your Majesty's name with the Indians for that purpose." Johnson had secured preliminary Indian agreement three years earlier to the boundary being extended some seven hundred miles lower down the Ohio to the mouth of the Cherokee or Tennessee River, but his instructions, and an accompanying map, made it clear that the Kanawha River was to be the western boundary. The boundary was to begin at Owego on the New York–Pennsylvania border, run south along the Susquehanna River to Shamokin, along the west branch of the Susquehanna to Kittaning, and then southwest along the Ohio to the mouth of the Kanawha. There the northern line negotiated by Johnson would join up with one being negotiated by John Stuart with the Cherokees in the South.[60]

Negotiating the new boundary required getting the Iroquois and Cherokees to settle their differences. The "Great Warriors' Path," the traditional war trail between the Iroquois and the Cherokees, ran through the territory that colonial officials hoped to acquire by pushing the line westward. Attakullakulla, known to the British as Little Carpenter because of his ability to fashion diplomatic agreements, the Great Warrior Oconostota, and other Cherokee delegates sailed for New York in November 1767. After attending a performance of *Richard III* (Attakullakulla was getting to be a regular theatergoer—he had attended performances at Sadlers' Wells and the Theatre Royal when he visited London with a Cherokee delegation in his youth),[61] they set off for Johnson

Hall, arriving at the end of December. The Iroquois delegates did not arrive until March. Bad roads and deep snow delayed them; besides, said Thomas King, the Oneidas' speaker, making peace with their old enemies the Cherokees was such a weighty issue that they had taken a long time to discuss it before coming to the meeting. The Cherokees presented wampum belts to each of the Six Nations, and "a Belt and a Calumet with an Eagles tail" to Johnson, "that he may always keep it so that any of our friends resorting hither may smoak out of the Pipe, and See that we have been about Peace." They also brought a belt from the Cherokee women for the Iroquois women, as "they must feel Mothers pains for those killed in War, and be desirous to prevent it." The Iroquois and Cherokees "buryed the Axe and opened the Road."[62]

Johnson assured the Iroquois at the conference that a boundary line to preserve their hunting grounds would soon be settled. The eastern Iroquois were glad to hear it. They had enjoyed relatively harmonious relationships of coexistence and exchange with colonists on their eastern frontier for much of the eighteenth century,[63] but the pressure on Mohawk and Oneida lands had increased alarmingly since the end of the French and Indian War. "We and our dependants have been for some time like Giddy People not knowing what to do," Conoghquieson told Johnson. "Wherever we turned about we saw our Blood." When they went hunting they found the country covered with fences, the trees cut down, and the animals driven away. If the British were unable to protect the Mohawks' land, keep their own settlers away from the Ohio, "and keep the Road open making Pennsylvania and Virginia quiet," the Iroquois would "get tired of looking to you, and turn our faces another way."[64] The stage was set and the issues were clear for the great council to be held at Fort Stanwix: if Johnson hoped to shift the boundary to the west he must protect Iroquois lands in the east. Sir William made a point of cultivating men like Conoghquieson. "I have always made use of a few approved Chiefs of the several Nations, whose fidelity I have had occasion to test on many occasions for above twenty years past, who have never yet deceived me," Johnson confided to Shelburne in August 1767.[65] He was not likely to switch strategy a year later at Fort Stanwix when the stakes were so high.

The meeting between the Iroquois and Cherokees in March "was held in the open Air at a severe season," and Sir William caught a cold. The next month, on his doctor's advice, he took a trip to the seaside in Connecticut, "having for some time laboured under a violent disorder of the Bowels, as well as severe pains from his old Wound, with both of which he has been much afflicted for some Years past." (He would make return trips to the sea for his health in years to come.)[66] But his mind was on the upcoming treaty, and interested parties sought him out in Connecticut. Meanwhile, Croghan met with one thousand Indians, primarily western Senecas, Delawares, and Shawnees, at Fort Pitt in

April and May, to settle differences and restore the chain of friendship. The Ohio Indians were worried by the presence of British forts and the encroachments of British settlers. Nimwha, a Shawnee chief, said they were "uneasy to see that you think yourselves Masters of this Country, because you have taken it from the *French*, who you know had no Right to it, as it is the Property of us *Indians*." Croghan responded that after the British defeated the French and opened a road into the Ohio country, the Six Nations agreed to it, "and we thought the Six Nations had a Right so to do, as we always understood that they were the original Proprietors of this Country."[67] Croghan was placing on record the justification for purchasing that same country from other people who "had no right to it" less than six months later.

In Johnson's absence on the coast, Guy Johnson presided over a three-week council at Johnson Hall in June where the Mohawks voiced concerns about encroachments on their land, especially by claimants to the Kayaderosseras patent, some four hundred thousand acres of land west of the Hudson and north of the Mohawk River originally patented more than sixty years before but which, the Iroquois speaker at Albany in 1754 said, "upon inquiry among our old men, we cannot find was ever sold."[68] When Sir William got home, he negotiated a settlement of the contested area, confirming a substantially reduced area of the patent: for $5,000 the Mohawks agreed to "give up all pretensions to this Tract." In return, the Mohawk chief Abraham made clear, they expected Johnson "to procure some good Strong writing, as a security for the Land we live upon, that we may no more be disturbed." Johnson assured them he would "endeavor to the utmost of his power to have their Lands secured to them, and their Posterity, in the most effectual manner."[69] The agenda and much of the content for the upcoming treaty was in place well before the participants gathered at Fort Stanwix in the fall.

The Great Giveaway

Fort Stanwix sat at the Oneida Carrying Place or the Oneida Carry, the critical portage between Wood Creek and the Mohawk River that in turn linked the Great Lakes and the Hudson. It took several months for everyone to assemble. Sir William thought it "best for me to Conclude the affair on behalf of the Crown for the whole," but he had to inform the various colonial governments concerned in the upcoming treaty, consult them "on such points as may effect them," and invite them to send commissioners to ratify the agreement. He invited Delawares and Shawnees because their proximity to Virginia and Pennsylvania meant they could be troublesome and "makes their perfect Agreement necessary." But they had fought against the British in the French and Indian War and Pontiac's War and Johnson included them as interested parties and dependants of the Six Nations, "not as Owners of the Land." He made it clear that he intended to deal with the Six Nations as spokesmen for all the tribes.[70]

The treaty proceedings were scheduled to begin at Fort Stanwix on September 20 but the Indians drifted in slowly—the Seneca contingent was detained by the death of a chief and the necessary ceremonies of condolence—so the start of the conference was delayed by more than a month. Given the Senecas' role in Pontiac's War, it was important that they be there. While the Indians who were already at Fort Stanwix waited, complained Johnson, they consumed enormous quantities of food.[71]

As soon as Samuel Wharton heard that Johnson had received royal instructions to settle the boundary, he and William Trent, the attorney for the "suffering traders," set off for Mohawk country. Trent, Croghan, William Franklin, and Baynton, Wharton, and Morgan had organized the Indiana Company to consolidate their claims. Johnson's ill health delayed things and Wharton and Trent stayed with him at Johnson Hall, using the time to promote their cause with the Indians for "a Reimbursement for the Losses, which we and others had sustained, by the Depredation of the *Shawanese* and *Delawares* in the year 1763."[72] Johnson left home on September 15 and traveled by boat up the Mohawk River, accompanied by William Franklin and "other Gentlemen," probably Trent and Wharton. They arrived at Fort Stanwix the day before the conference was due to start, and Trent and Wharton promptly handed Johnson and some of the Iroquois chiefs "an account of the Traders losses in 1763, together with their Powers of Attorney for obtaining a retribution of lands, pursuant to an article of the Treaty of peace in 1765."[73] Twenty boatloads of goods made their way upriver, intended as presents for the anticipated cession of land to the king. Johnson represented New York as well as the Crown. His three deputies, George Croghan, Daniel Claus, and Guy Johnson, were present.[74] Croghan had been preparing for the big event for months and now, in the words of one biographer, he was "by far the most active of the speculators who busied themselves in making last minute purchases from the Indians before the Crown obtained title to the ceded area"; in the words of another, he "was busy looking after the interests of the empire, the Penns, the traders, and himself."[75] In addition to serving as the deputy superintendent for the Indians of Pennsylvania and the Ohio Valley, Croghan also represented the "suffering traders"; he, Trent, and Wharton drew up a deed ceding to the king to be held in trust for the traders about 2.5 million acres bounded by the southern boundary of Pennsylvania, the Ohio, the Little Kanawha, and the Monongahela.[76]

Dr. Thomas Walker and Colonel Andrew Lewis, the commissioners from Virginia, had learned on August 18 that the treaty conference was to begin on September 1. Both had financial interests in the claims of the Loyal Land Company. Walker, the company's agent for more than forty years, "had his finger in every official land activity in Virginia in the second half of the eighteenth century." He had explored and surveyed parts of southeastern Kentucky eighteen years before and had given the Cumberland Gap its name (one of a number of sites named in honor of William, Duke of Cumberland—Butcher Cumberland to the Highland Scots—who had defeated the Jacobite clans at Culloden in 1746). Walker had acquired property when he married a widowed cousin of George Washington and he had become the guardian of Thomas Jefferson when the boy's father, his friend, neighbor, and fellow surveyor Peter Jefferson, died in 1757. Lewis, a member of the Virginia House of Burgesses and a surveyor in western Virginia, was also a major player in the Greenbrier Company of land speculators. Like George Washington and other Virginian veterans of the French and Indian War, he had a claim to lands based on bounties that Governor Dinwiddie had promised. Walker and Lewis hurried to Johnson Hall and arrived on August 27, only to be told by Johnson that the Indians would not assemble until September 20. They stayed "at a dirty Tavern near the Hall till the 14th from thence proceeded to Fort Stanwix where we arrived on the 17th and waited for the *Indians* till the 12th of October." It was then decided that Lewis should leave to attend John Stuart's treaty with the Cherokees scheduled to begin at Hard Labor, nine hundred miles away. (In the event, for a variety of reasons, no Virginian representatives attended the Cherokee treaty.) Walker later claimed that he merely witnessed the treaty at Fort Stanwix but, representing the interests of Washington, Jefferson, and other Virginians speculating in lands beyond the Blue Ridge Mountains, he doubtless arrived early to speak with Johnson in private and advance those interests without making a public record of it. In doing so, noted the late Iroquoian scholar William Fenton, he was not departing from council protocol, but simply exploiting a well-established Iroquois negotiating device.[77]

Lieutenant Governor John Penn and the commissioners from Pennsylvania, Richard Peters and James Tilghman, arrived on September 21, although Penn had to return to Philadelphia before negotiations got under way. Penn and Peters were experienced in the business of acquiring land by treaty: they had both figured prominently as the Penn family's agents at the Albany Congress in 1754 where they executed a land deed.[78] Peters, an Anglican clergyman, provincial secretary, and sometime business partner of George Croghan, once called Croghan a "vile Rascal."[79] It took one to know one. The son of a well-to-do family, Peters had attended the Westminster School in London. While there, he married a serving maid and his parents whisked him off to Leyden for several years to escape the disgrace and the clutches of the "impossible and vulgar person" who had "ensnared" their teenage son. Returning to London, he read law at the inner Temple and then was ordained in the Church of England. He married the daughter of the Earl of Derby but just as she was about to give birth to their child, his first wife turned up. Once again, Peters fled the country, this time to Philadelphia to make a new start.[80] There he became Thomas Penn's adviser and rose within the government of Pennsylvania. He had "a talent for deception," was "equally at home in saving souls and making fortunes," and wasted no time in getting into the Indian land business.[81] As secretary, Peters spent years tampering with the written records of treaty conferences to undermine Delaware sovereignty and separate the Delawares from their land.[82] Chief Justice Frederick Smith of New Jersey also attended, as did "Sundry Gents" from different colonies.

At the beginning of October 800 Indians had arrived; by the 22nd there were 2,200, with more expected the next day; eventually more than 3,000 attended, "the greatest Number of Indians, That ever met at any Treaty in America."[83] The great majority were men from the Six Nations. Women regularly attended treaty conferences but this was harvest time in Iroquois villages. Moreover, Johnson, whether to keep down expenses or to ensure the absence of a group that might balk at the huge land cession he was planning, had sent word to Iroquois headmen not to bring women to the treaty "as business is best carried on when none but fit men go about it."[84] The Iroquois delegates included the Mohawk warrior and orator Abraham or Little Abraham (his Mohawk name was variously recorded as Tayorheasere, Teyarhasere, Tyorhansera, Tigoransera, and Teirhenshsere). Conoghquieson, the chief sachem of Old Oneida, and Tagawaron from Kanonwalohale represented the Oneidas. Bunt and Diaquanda or Teyohaquende, a "chief Warrior and Sachim" and a close ally and friend of Sir William, spoke for the Onondagas. With fences still to mend with Johnson, the Senecas sent the old Genesee chief Guastrax and the noted war chief Sayenqueragtha (or Old Smoke), who had been with Johnson at the capture of Fort Niagara in 1759. Now in his sixties he was still a commanding figure, over six feet tall, and, said the Seneca chief Blacksnake, he towered "far above his fellows" in intellect.[85] A handful of Shawnees and Delawares attended, more as observers than as active participants. Amid the throng of governors, Indian agents, land speculators, colonial commissioners, traders, interpreters, missionaries, and hundreds of Iroquois, they were "lost in the crowd."[86] Killbuck and Turtle's Heart represented the Delawares. Turtle's Heart had met the trader William Trent before. He was one of the two Indians who came to parlay at Fort Pitt in 1763 and had been given blankets from the smallpox hospital. Evidently, Turtle's Heart survived Trent's germ warfare (many others did not); perhaps he had had smallpox before.

Guy Johnson served as the secretary and Andrew Montour, John Butler, and Philip Philips acted as interpreters. Sir William could get by in Mohawk but a formal multinational council such as this demanded the multilingual skills of an experienced interpreter like Montour who, in addition to being fluent in French and English, spoke Mohawk, Oneida, Wyandot, Delaware, Miami, and Shawnee. Montour had developed a pivotal role as well as an ambiguous identity as a cultural broker on the eighteenth-century frontier. The son of a famous Oneida-French woman, Madam Montour, he had grown up among the Oneidas in New York and the Delawares and Shawnees on the Susquehanna River. Also known by his Indian names Sattelihu or Eghnisera, Montour favored elaborate European clothing while wearing Indian facial paint, applied with bear's grease, and ear ornaments. He worked as an agent and interpreter for Pennsylvania from 1742 to 1756 and was commissioned to raise a company of scouts for George Washington's campaign into Ohio country in 1754. Richard Peters called him "a dull stupid Creature, in great Esteem with the Indians." The Ohio Iroquois made him a chief councilor in 1752, which meant he could "transact any publick Business in behalf of us, the Six Nations." At the Treaty of Logstown that year the Seneca Half King, Tanagharison, handed Eghnisera a ten-row wampum belt to remind him "that you are one of our own People." They were pleased to have him there as an interpreter, "for we are sure our Business will go on well & Justice be done on both Sides," but he should remember that he had done "a great Deal of Business among us" before Pennsylvania and Virginia employed him: "you are not Interpreter only; for you are one of our Council, have an equal Right with us to all these Lands." In 1756 Montour transferred to the northern department of Indian affairs and the service of William Johnson; from 1766 to 1772 he served as a post interpreter at Fort Pitt. He had a turbulent life, marked by recurrent problems with alcohol, indebtedness, and failed marriages. His contemporaries never quite figured him out or trusted him—was he Indian or white, loyal to Britain or in the employ of the French?—but they relied on him to negotiate and interpret the complex cultural landscape of his world.[87]

John Butler was born in Connecticut and moved to the Mohawk with his family when his father, an officer in the British army, was posted to Fort Hunter. He was a trader at Fort Oswego from 1745 to 1755, served as an Indian agent, saw action in the French and Indian War, and worked as an interpreter for William Johnson. Like Johnson, he accumulated considerable landholdings in the Mohawk Valley, some twenty-six thousand acres, making him the second wealthiest man in the valley after Sir William.[88] Philip Philips, a "Dutchman," had been captured by Kahnawake Mohawks at age fourteen in 1747 during King George's War, and he had refused to return with other released captives at the end of the war. He had participated in an Indian attack on George Croghan's trading party in 1753.[89]

Most of the negotiations at Fort Stanwix were conducted privately. Johnson complained afterward that he was in poor health and worn out by sitting "whole nights generally in the open woods in private conferences with the leading men." These private meetings "where most points are discussed & settled" did not usually make it into the record; "if they had it would have been too Voluminous," said Johnson.[90] Private meetings always raised suspicions of shady dealing, and often with good reason, but "talk in the bushes"—to arrange an agenda, discuss an issue, or hash out a disagreement prior to more formal negotiation in open council—was not unusual. The real business often took place behind the scenes.[91]

On Monday, October 24, Johnson opened the formal negotiations. Speaking through the Mohawk chief Abraham, he welcomed the Indians "to this place where I have kindled a Council Fire for affairs of importance." He and the delegates from Virginia and Pennsylvania had waited a month to see them. "I hope therefore that you are now come fully prepared and with Hearts well inclined to the great business for which we are convened, and in order to prepare you the better for these purposes, I do now, agreeable to the antient custom established by our Forefathers, proceed to the ceremony of Condolence usual on these occasions." He then duly presented strings of wampum to wipe away tears, clear throats, and open ears and hearts. He gave a wampum belt to rekindle their council fires, another to bid them assemble, and another to dispel darkness. He took "the clearest water" to cleanse their insides, advised the sachems to consult with their war chiefs and the war chiefs to listen to their sachems, and urged the different nations to be unanimous. Also, "as there are but two Council Fires for your confederacy, the one at my house and the other at Onondaga, I must desire that you will always be ready to attend either of them, when called upon, by which means business will I hope, always be attended & properly carried on for our mutual Interest." Johnson punctuated each statement with the presentation of a wampum belt and the Indians "gave the Yo-hah at the proper places." With the proper rituals completed, the council adjourned until the following day.[92]

Conoghquieson opened proceedings the next day, giving his own name to Governor Franklin, as he was the only one of the several governors on whom the Iroquois had not yet bestowed a ceremonial name. Then Conoghquieson thanked Johnson for his adherence to the ancient rituals, "repeated all that Sir William had said," and thanked him for each statement and belt, giving belt for belt in response. That done, the council adjourned again until the next day.[93] As William Fenton noted, Johnson "had learned that adhering to Iroquois customary ways was the sure way to get what he wanted out of a council. Others of his contemporaries who found Indian ceremony tedious and who bridled at the waste of time accomplished far less."[94]

On Wednesday Conoghquieson got to his feet and announced that, not being satisfied with his giving his own name to Franklin, the Six Nations now bestowed on the governor the name Saorghweyoghsta, or Doer of Justice, in recognition of New Jersey having recently imposed the death penalty on some Indian killers. (In fact, the chiefs may have not wanted to give him the name of one of the league's founders.)[95] Sir William moved the proceedings along, producing a fifteen-row wampum belt with human figures at each end, representing their alliance, and he renewed and confirmed the Covenant Chain, "rubbing off any rust which it may have contracted that it might appear bright to all Nations as a proof of our love and Friendship." Then he got down to business. Three years before, the Indians had agreed in principle to settling a boundary and they and he both knew only too well that until such a firm and clear line was established trespass and trouble would continue. "After long deliberation on some means for your relief, and for preventing future disputes concerning Lands," the great and good king of England had ordered Johnson to fix a boundary line and give the Indians "handsome proof of his Generosity proportiond to the nature and extent of what Lands shall fall to him." According to Wharton, "in order that all the different Tribes might clearly understand his Speech," Johnson "departed from the Usual Method of *treating* with Them and had it translated into the Mohock Tongue by an Indian, who spoke and wrote, both English and Mohock excellently well." Abraham repeated what Sir William had said, thanked him for saying it, and called for an adjournment so that they could give this "weighty affair" their "most serious consideration."[96]

On Thursday, September 27, Johnson's Onondaga ally Diaquanda and eighty-six other Indians came to Sir William's quarters "to pay him the usual compliments." Johnson returned the compliments and "ordered them paint, Pipes, Tobacco & a dram around and dismissed them." On Friday, the weather turning cold, he "clothed the old chiefs of every Nation for which they returned many thanks."[97] The Indians continued discussing the boundary issue among themselves until four in the afternoon, and then they informed Johnson that they were ready to speak with him. They acknowledged that a firm line between the Indians and the English would be to everyone's advantage. Experience had taught them "we cannot have any great dependence on the white People, and that they will forget their agreements for the sake of our Lands," but Johnson had done much to assure them that things could be different this time and they moved from debating the concept of a boundary to discussing the details. In particular, they worried that their northern towns would lay open if the line stopped at Owego on the Susquehanna River, the northern point of the boundary negotiated in 1765. What was the point of drawing a line between Iroquois country and Pennsylvania and Virginia "whilst the way to our Towns lay open?" They needed to extend the line northward to close off the Finger Lakes region from colonial settlers. Johnson was ready for this issue. He invited the chiefs of each nation back to his quarters, saying, "I have prepared a Map on which the Country is drawn large & plain which will enable us both to judge better of these matters."[98]

Johnson's instructions were to fix the boundary line at the Kanawha River, where it would meet the southern line negotiated by John Stuart with the Cherokees. The Iroquois speaker, probably Conoghquieson, reminded Johnson that the Tennessee River, not the Kanhawha, marked the proper limit to their lands. The Six Nations had "a very good & clear Title to the Lands as far as the Cherokee River," and they expected Britain to recognize it. The understanding was clear: by accepting a land grant from the Iroquois reaching as far as the Tennessee River, Britain would implicitly recognize Iroquois dominance over the region. There were few surprises at Fort Stanwix. Johnson and his associates had been laying the groundwork for years and he knew what the Iroquois would be willing to grant. Even if he did not orchestrate Conoghquieson's assertion and offer, Johnson was ready to act on it. To accept such an offer would require Johnson to disobey his orders from London, but how could he do otherwise?[99]

The Iroquois were more concerned about land closer to home. They had been generous in the past and had given white people lands from which they had "often had bad Returns," but they intended to be as generous as they could be now "without ruining our Children." The country from Owego to Oswego was full of Iroquois towns and villages and "we can not be expected to part with what lies at our Doors, besides your people are come already too close to us." Like Joseph Brant's village of Conajoharie, Abraham's village lay on the wrong side of the proclamation line and the proposed Stanwix line and stood to be engulfed by colonial settlements. They suggested instead a boundary that would run from the Delaware to the upper Mohawk River and across to Lake George. Johnson replied that the king had no intention of disturbing them on the lands where they lived but countered with the suggestion that the line run as far as Lake Ontario. The Indians withdrew, taking the map with them, to discuss the matter among themselves. That night "Sir William had a private conference with the Cheifs [sic] of the most Influence with whom he made use of every argument to bring matters to an agreeable issue."[100]

The Indians debated in council all Saturday morning and then said they needed more time and hoped to give their answer on Monday. Johnson agreed to wait but made clear "that he was really become very impatient through the delays which was given to the business, that the security of their Lands depended upon their dispatch and the freedom of the Cession." That night, belts arrived from the Shawnees carrying news that French and Spanish agents were stirring up trouble among the Ohio nations and telling them the English planned to drive them from their homelands. The western Indians were on the verge of going to war against the English but were waiting to hear the outcome of the negotiations at Fort Stanwix. Concerned about the prospect of pushing the Ohio Indians to war, Conoghquieson, Tagawaron, Tyearuruante, and Abraham the next morning told Johnson "they would not part with any Lands to the Westward of Oriscany or down towards Wioming or the Great Island, as they reserved that part of the Country for their Dependants." Sir William responded to the four chiefs with "a long and warm speech." The Crown had spent a lot of time and money negotiating the boundary line and "if they rejected this opportunity now offered them and drew the Line so as to interfere with Grants, or approach almost to our settlements, he could not see that any thing more effectual could thereafter be proposed for preventing encroachments." In other words, this is your best offer: think again. "After these and many other arguments, & further explaining the several courses laid down on the draft, they agreed to take the Map back to their Council Hutt for farther consideration, promising to use their Interest with the rest for a more favorable Line." Sir William assured them "they should be particularly rewarded for their services or endeavours to shew the Indians the reasonableness of the requisition." That night, Tagawaron returned the map to Sir William. He said the Indians were still debating the issue. Johnson promptly went to work and "had many other private conferences which occupied a great part of the night."[101]

The Oneidas took a lot of work. They made up nearly five hundred of the three thousand Indians in attendance, which meant that almost one-third of the Oneida population was present, and, Tagawaron told Johnson, they were "much divided in opinion." The sachems were expected to function as peacemakers and they also saw the treaty as a way to obtain goods and maintain their influence among the young warriors, but the warriors were intent on preserving their hunting territories and their access to the Carrying Place between Wood Creek and the Mohawk where they could earn money as porters.[102] Johnson said "the greatest trouble and difficulty I met with was to bring the Oneidas to allow the line to run any farther West than Oriskane Creek" and that the negotiations on that question "engaged all my interest three Days & almost 3 nights," more than all the rest of the line.[103] At nine o'clock on Sunday evening, October 30, six Oneida chiefs came to see Johnson in private and proposed running the line from the Susquehanna north to Fort Newport on Wood Creek. Johnson rejected it because the crucial portage would be left in Indian hands. He offered the Oneidas an additional $500 and promised each of the chiefs "a handsome present" if they could persuade the nation to give up the Carrying Place, but the Oneidas would not budge. The next morning the chiefs returned to tell Johnson "that their people positively refused to agree to any other Line than they had proposed the last night"; game was growing scarce and they needed to keep the Carrying Place so that they could supplement their declining income from hunting by transporting traders' goods. Johnson refused to accept their decision and some of the other chiefs by this time were pressing the Oneidas to close the deal. The Oneida chiefs "withdrew to consult further upon it," and returned soon after with their final offer: for $600 "over and besides the several Fees which were given in private," they would share the Carrying Place and accept a line ending slightly farther west at Canada Creek, a tributary of the Mohawk. "Sir William finding it best not to urge this matter farther told them that he acquiesced for the present leaving it to be confirmed or rejected by His Majesty."[104] Conoghquieson returned that night to tell Johnson the Indians were ready to present their final resolves: they insisted on the Cherokee River as their western limit and they would agree to make a cession to Pennsylvania on payment of $10,000.[105]

The Rev. Eleazar Wheelock had sent two missionaries to the treaty to lobby for setting aside some land for the new college he hoped to build "in the heart of the Indian country." Johnson had initially supported the missionary work of the Congregationalist minister and had recruited students for his Charity School in Lebanon, Connecticut. One of Wheelock's students, Rev. Samuel Kirkland, was the resident missionary among the Oneidas. But Johnson, an Anglican, grew cold to Wheelock and withdrew his support for the work. Johnson blamed the missionaries for encouraging the Oneidas to oppose extending the boundary to the north or west, in order to "reserve those Lands for the purposes of Religion," and to refuse selling land along the Susquehanna, where Wheelock also had his eyes on a grant for his college. "The Arguments they made use of in private amongst the Inds. Their misrepresentations of our Religion, & the Extraordinary private Instructions of Mr. Wheelock of wch I am accidentally possessed would shew them in a very odd Light," Johnson wrote later.[106] (Unsuccessful in his efforts to secure lands in the Susquehanna, Wheelock built his new school, Dartmouth College, in the upper Connecticut Valley in New Hampshire.)

The general congress reconvened on Tuesday, November 1. The Iroquois speaker reviewed the history of relations with the English and, presenting a wampum belt to Johnson, pledged to keep the Covenant Chain "so long as you shall preserve it strong & bright on your part." After "sundry Meetings amongst ourselves and with you," the Iroquois had reached a final resolution, on the understanding that this would be the final line, that there would be no more demands for land, and that none of the colonies or colonists should attempt to breach it "under color of any old Deeds, or other pretences whatsoever for in many of these things we have been imposed on." The boundaries they agreed to would

> begin on the Ohio at the mouth of the Cherokee River which is now our just right, and from thence we give up on the South side of Ohio to Kittanning above Fort Pitt, from thence a direct Line to the nearest

Fork of the West Branch of Susquehanna thence through the Allegany Mountains along the south side of the said West Branch till we come opposite to the mouth of the Creek called Tiadaghton thence across the West Branch & along the East side of that Creek and along the ridge of Burnets Hills to a Creek called Awandae thence down the same to the East Branch of the Susquehanna, and across the same and up the East side of that River to Oswegy, from thence Eastward to Delaware River, and up that River to opposite where Trinaderha falls into Susquehanna, thence to Trinaderha and up the West side thereof and its West Branches to the Head thereof thence by a straight Line to the mouth of Canada Creek where it emptys itself into Wood Creek at the end of the long carrying place beyond Fort Stanwix, and this we declare to be our final Resolves and we expect that the conditions of this our Grant will be observed.

Another wampum belt handed to Johnson encoded the message. The Indians were to retain the right to hunt in the ceded territory "as they have no other means of subsistence," but white people were restricted from hunting on the Indian side of the line "to prevent contensions." Two Mohawk towns and the Oneida town of Oriske lay east of the new line and were to remain as enclaves of Indian country. Handing Johnson another belt, they addressed the King of England on behalf of the Six Nations, Shawnees, Delawares, "and all other our Friends, Allies, & Dependants." They were giving him "a great and valuable Country, and we know that what we shall now get for it must be far short of its value." They did so on condition that the relationship forged at Fort Stanwix be maintained into the future and that the king should not forget his commitments or allow the chain to rust.[107]

The Mohawks, whose villages in the Mohawk Valley fell within the area opened to colonial settlement, insisted that the lands they occupied "be considered as their sole property and at their disposal both now, and as long as the sun shines," and that any grants or agreements they had made be considered as "Independent of this Boundary." In other words, they could sell their lands if they saw fit. The final deed stipulated that "the Lands occupied by the Mohawks around their villages...may effectually remain to them and to their posterity."[108]

The Iroquois agreed to the massive cession of lands to Pennsylvania. In doing so, they supported Pennsylvania's claims to land south of the Ohio contested by Virginia, and the Wyoming Valley, finally, was bought for the Penns. No commissioners from Connecticut were present to protest the sale and argue their claims. Johnson, Croghan, and the Iroquois had strategized to exclude John Henry Lydius, a well-known land speculator and smuggler, and the Indians rejected his claims as invalid. But they made a private agreement and signed a deed granting the "suffering traders" land around the Forks of the Ohio in compensation for their losses in the war: "in order to shew that we love justice, we expect the Traders who suffered by some of our dependants in the wars five years ago, may have a grant for the Lands we now give them down Ohio, as a satisfaction for their losses." The traders received almost 2.5 million acres, about one-quarter of the current state of West Virginia. In addition, said the Iroquois, "as our friend M[r] Croghan long ago got a Deed for Lands from us, which may now be taken into M[r] Penns Lands, should it so happen, we request that it may be considered and get as much from the King somewhere else, as he fairly bought it." In addition to his share in the suffering traders' grant, Croghan thus received reaffirmation of the earlier grant of two hundred thousand acres on the Ohio that "conveniently" fell within the new cession. He had also bought up deeds to 127,000 acres of land in the weeks leading up to the treaty. The Iroquois granted Sir William two hundred thousand acres in New York. Having "given enough to shew our Love for the King and make his people easy," they expected the Crown to permit no old claims or new encroachments.[109]

Sir William thanked them for their words and the council adjourned. Heavy rain prevented a meeting the next day, but Johnson kept busy presenting gifts of clothing to chiefs and preparing papers. He made a final effort to persuade the Mohawks to extend the boundary beyond Wood Creek but the Mohawks stuck to their guns. After another day spent preparing speeches and drawing up the deed of cession, the parties reconvened on Friday, November 4, to conclude the treaty.[110] After conducting a condolence ceremony for the death of an Oneida chief, Johnson assured the Indians that their speech to the king would be forwarded along with the rest of the proceedings and that the boundary was intended to last; however, "should it be found necessary by His Majesty or yourselves to make any future additions or alterations he will treat with you by those who have management of your affairs." Finally, on that last day, Johnson turned to the Shawnees and Delawares. Having brought the Senecas back into the British orbit after years of rocky relations, he now treated their erstwhile allies with disdain and effectively discredited them as participants in the treaty. He told them he knew they had been talking with England's enemies and warned them not to listen to mischief makers; the British had conquered Canada and driven the French out of their country and would always have it in their power to defeat any future French efforts. He instructed the Shawnees and Delawares to remember their agreements with the English, observe the peace with the Cherokees, "& pay due regard to the Boundary Line now made." If they made no disturbances on the frontiers and kept "the Roads & Waters open and free," they would "enjoy the benefits of Peace & Commerce, the esteem of the King of Great Britain & the friendship of all his subjects." He handed them a wampum belt and told them to "remember & often repeat my words."

Johnson wanted the Ohio nations united under the leadership of the Six Nations, not scattered and following their own paths. Because the government was transferring management of the Indian trade to the individual colonies, he called on the governor of New Jersey and the various commissioners "to enact the most effectual Laws for the due observance of this Line & the preventing all future intrusions." All that remained then, said Johnson, was for the Indians to execute a deed of cession to the king and for him to deliver to the Indians the presents and money he had promised.[111]

The next morning, when the Indians filed into the fort, the presents and money were laid out on the parade ground for all to see. Wharton said it was "the greatest Quantity of Indian Goods, and Dollars, I ever saw on such an occasion" and that the presents were arranged so that they "circumscribed" Johnson, Governor Franklin, and the commissioners on three sides. The Indians' spokesman repeated what Johnson had said the day before and thanked him for his words and advice. The deeds to the king, the proprietors of Pennsylvania, and the traders were then laid on the table and signed. Six chiefs, one for each of the Six Nations, affixed their signatures to the final deed: Abraham for the Mohawks, Conoghquieson for the Oneidas, Sequarusera for the Tuscaroras, Bunt for the Onondagas, Tegaia for the Cayugas, and Gaustrax for the Senecas. No Shawnees or Delawares were included, and there was not any statement indicating that they had agreed to the largest cession of Indian land in colonial America. The chiefs of each nation then "received the Cash which was piled on a Table for that purpose" and spent the rest of the day dividing the goods among their people. Governor Franklin and the other commissioners wasted no time and headed for home that afternoon. Johnson and the Indians left the next day, Sunday.[112]

The treaty extended the boundary line almost four hundred miles farther west than Johnson's instructions from London stipulated, embracing most of Kentucky and West Virginia (see figure 2.3). Asserting their right to the Tennessee River and their authority to act for "the Shawanoes, Delawares, Mingoes of Ohio and other Dependent Tribes," the Iroquois delegates had signed away thousands of square miles of other peoples' lands. The grant of lands as reparations to Philadelphia merchants—the Indiana grant—lay north and east of the Kanawha, the authorized boundary. South and west of the Kanawha lay "the whole Cumberland-Tennessee-Kentucky region so productive of future difficulties."[113] As the historian Timothy Shannon says, "The handprints of private land speculators, including Johnson's own, were all over these cessions." In return for £10,000 in cash and trade goods, and a measure of protection for their own lands, the Iroquois sold Shawnee hunting grounds "to agents whose official credentials barely disguised their private interests."[114] Yet at Stanwix, Crown purposes, private speculations, and Iroquois interests were

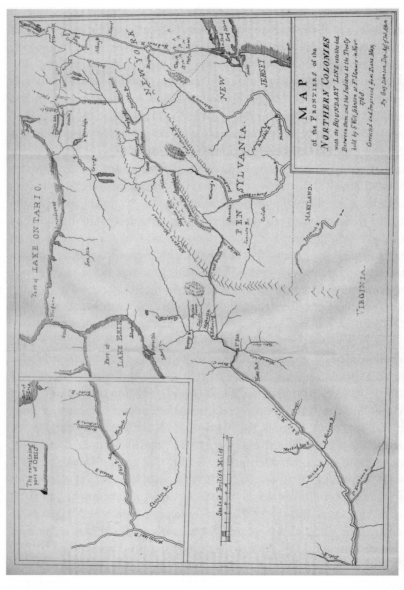

FIGURE 2.3 **Guy Johnson's map of the boundary line established at the Treaty of Fort Stanwix.** *(A Map of the Frontiers of the Northern Colonies with the Boundary Line established between them and the Indians at the Treaty held by Sir Will Johnson at Ft Stanwix in Novr. 1768. DRCHNY, 8, opp. 136; Courtesy Dartmouth College)*

not at odds; they were just not quite in line. The total cost came to £13,156, 14 shillings, and one penny: £10,460 7s. 3d in cash; £2,328. 5s. 0d. in gifts, and £758. 4s. 5d. in provisions, with additional expenses for travel, messengers, making wampum belts at the treaty, and so on.[115] The Ohio Indians were allotted just £27 worth of trade goods.

In the name of George III, Johnson bought from the Iroquois "a vast expense of the American West which the Crown had specifically ordered him not to buy."[116] In Johnson's mind, imperial and personal interests were easily conflated: he and the Crown both got what they wanted at Fort Stanwix. An Indian war was averted, the traders were compensated, the boundary line was run, and both the empire and its chief agent came away with lots of land. It appeared that the authority of the Crown and its superintendent over the regulation of the boundary was reaffirmed. When he got home from the treaty, Johnson wrote to Governor Penn that "after a Great Struggle & more difficulty that can be conceived by those who were not Eye Witnesses I have at length in the Settlement of the boundary Line procured for you a very advantageous cession."[117] Richard Peters promised on his return to Philadelphia to give the governor a full account of Johnson's "attention to his interest & the prudence & zeal with which you transacted that part of the business in which he was concerned."[118] Samuel Wharton was delighted with the treaty. "I can assure you," he wrote Benjamin Franklin, "To the Honour of Sir William and Mr. Croghan that no Treaty was ever Conducted with more Judgement and Candour and none I am convinced, ever finished with more solid satisfaction on the part of the Natives, than this did....There is now the fairest prospect, that these Colonies have ever had since the Year 1749, to perpetuate the Blessings of an Indian peace to their Posterity and of rendering our Commerce with the Natives much more beneficial to the Mother Country, than it Ever has been." The Indians had given up their rights to a huge amount of territory for a "very *small* Sum," and the king's ministers should confirm the treaty, and its compensation to the traders, without delay. Once the cession was confirmed, continued Wharton with an eye to the future, settlers could occupy the Ohio and the interior parts of Virginia, Maryland, Pennsylvania, and New York and no longer be threatened by Indian attacks: "In case of a Rupture, the War can be readily and at a little expence carried into the Indian Villages and They thereby be compelled to seek a retreat, To the Westward of the great Lakes."[119]

The Iroquois got what they wanted as well. In the words of William Fenton who spent his life studying Iroquois history and culture, from an Iroquois perspective, "the Fort Stanwix treaty was the greatest giveaway in history." They were in no position to defend what they claimed, their power was declining as that of the English increased, and their influence among the Ohio nations was in decline.[120] But at Fort Stanwix, for a moment, the Iroquois reaffirmed their dominance over the western nations and regained their standing with the British. They diverted the swelling tide of British settlement away from Iroquoia onto lands that they claimed but which other people inhabited, and for a hefty sum they gave up a tenuous claim to an area they could no longer control, if indeed they ever had. The Iroquois traded land for time and it was someone else's land.

Johnson and the Iroquois both saw in the treaty an opportunity to bolster their authority—Johnson as the Crown's man-on-the-spot dealing with Indians and negotiating the expansion of the empire, and the Iroquois as the key players in Britain's relations with a wider Indian world. The treaty also gave Johnson and others an opportunity to advance their individual interests. The interests of the Crown's agent, colonial speculators, and eastern Iroquois headmen converged in an agreement to hand over the country south of the Ohio—and the Ohio Indians paid the price.[121] But Johnson and the Iroquois would also pay a heavy price for their immediate gains. The treaty did not maintain Sir William's influence; it did not maintain Iroquois influence, and it did not bring peace. In fact, the British-Iroquois deal at Fort Stanwix produced disastrous consequences for British-Iroquois dominance in North America.

The Struggles for the Stanwix Cession

The treaty was immediately controversial. General Thomas Gage, the British commander in North America, feared that pushing the boundary to the Tennessee River would cause trouble with the southern Indians: "for whatever Pretensions the Six Nations May have to the Territorys claimed by them on that Side, if our Provinces should ever pretend a Right to those Lands in Consequence of this Cession of the Six Nations, it seems most probable that a Quarrell will ensue with the Southern Nations, who by no Means admit of these Claims of the Six Nations."[122] Johnson assured him that the Tennessee River boundary would "have no Ill Effect, what I have done is only vesting the Claim of the Northeren [sic] Indians (which would always hang over that Country) in the Crown," and the Cherokees had not objected. Had he not moved the boundary west, the Virginians would have pushed into the area anyway.[123] Gage remained skeptical: the Cherokees might not have openly denied the Six Nations' claim to those lands but they did not openly acknowledge it either. "And if by Virtue of the Claim of the Six Nations Made over to Us, we should in Consequence possess those Lands, the Cherokees would look upon such a step with a Jealous and evil Eye, and that would sooner or later occasion Hostilities between us." Gage had little faith in boundaries anyway: They were only effective if they were strictly enforced and the frontier people were "too Numerous, too Lawless and Licentious ever to be restrained."[124] Johnson agreed that the frontier inhabitants would inevitably push west but felt that it was better that they dispossess the Cherokees than the northern tribes "who are more capable of Shewing their Resentment & more inclined to do so."[125]

At the Treaty of Hard Labor in October 1768, John Stuart and the Cherokees confirmed a new boundary approved by the Board of Trade.[126] Starting at Fort Chiswell, the terminal point of a boundary negotiated between Governor William Tryon of North Carolina and the Cherokees the year before, the treaty continued the boundary to the Ohio at the mouth of the Kanawha River. The treaty completed the Virginia section of the boundary although no Virginian representatives attended. In November, Stuart negotiated a boundary treaty with the Creeks at Augusta in Georgia.[127] But the unauthorized Stanwix cession of lands beyond the Kanawha threw the southern boundary issue into confusion. Virginians petitioned for an extension of the southern boundary to bring it into line with the Stanwix boundary, and the governor of Virginia, Lord Botetort, promptly dispatched Andrew Lewis and Thomas Walker to Stuart to negotiate a new boundary with the Cherokees.[128] At the Treaty of Lochaber in October 1770 one thousand Cherokees agreed to shift the boundary farther west, so that it ran from the mouth of the Kanawha to the Holston River. "We never had such Talks formerly but now all our Talks are about Lands," the Cherokee chief Attakullakulla reflected ruefully. Surveyors running the line in the summer of 1771 deviated from the agreement, and the next year John Donelson secured a new deal from Attakullakulla that moved the boundary west to the Kentucky River. The new line still did not meet up with the Stanwix line or give Virginians all they wanted but it did secure for Virginia an additional ten million acres in what is today eastern Kentucky and West Virginia.[129] Now the southern treaties confused the boundary issue in the North. Surely Botetort had no authority to grant lands beyond the Appalachians in defiance of the Proclamation of 1763, William Franklin wrote his father. "It also seems improbable to me, that the Crown should, thro' Lord Botetort, give the Virginians Leave to purchase of the southern Indians the very Land which the Crown had before purchased of the Six Nations."[130]

The Treaty at Fort Stanwix marked the end of an era in Virginian-Iroquois relations. For almost a century, Virginian colonists had relied on alliance with the Iroquois for security against the French and to build their own power. As the colony grew, boundary lines with the Iroquois were negotiated in 1684, 1722, and at the Treaty of Lancaster in 1744. Fort Stanwix was the last time colonial Virginians and Six Nations chiefs met in council. After 1768, Virginians regarded the Iroquois as "simply another Indian group that impeded the speedy settlement of western lands."[131]

Lord Hillsborough was furious that Johnson had ignored his instructions in order to extend the boundary west, thereby undermining the agreements Stuart had reached with the southern tribes.[132] The Board of Trade looked into the matter and reprimanded Johnson for ignoring his orders and allowing "the claims and interests of private persons to mix themselves in this Negotiation."[133] Johnson acknowledged in correspondence with William Franklin that his friendship with the suffering traders might have caused him "to espouse their cause," but he had only done what the government had already approved and he had "acted on the most equitable as well as disinterested principles."[134]

In any case, the Iroquois grant to the traders was worthless without confirmation by the imperial government. Having achieved their goals in America, Samuel Wharton and William Trent sailed for England early in 1769 to head off rivals with competing claims and "have the final Stroke given to the Grant." They carried letters of introduction to well-placed people, and they relied on Benjamin Franklin for guidance and advice. Wharton spent years in London, cultivating friends in high places and promoting his schemes. "He has acquired better connections here, than any American that I know of, ever did," wrote one business associate. In Peter Marshall's assessment, he was "energetic, persuasive and above all unscrupulous." The original group of Philadelphia merchants expanded to include British politicians and speculators, and the claim for reparations for losses in the Indian trade became absorbed into a much larger project that reached the highest levels of government. The suffering traders joined forces with the Ohio Company and formed a new consortium known as the Grand Ohio Company or the Walpole Associates (Benjamin Franklin involved the British politicians Thomas and Richard Walpole). The company first petitioned the Privy Council for a grant of 2,400,000 acres to be carved out of the lands ceded to the Crown at Fort Stanwix. The Privy Council referred the petition to the Board of Trade; after a five-month delay the board approved it in December 1769. By that time, the company was scheming to develop a new western colony in the ceded lands south of Ohio, and it petitioned for a grant of twenty million acres within the Stanwix cession that would have swallowed up the Indiana grant. They initially called the proposed colony "Pittsylvania" in honor of William Pitt but, hoping to win royal support, changed the name to Vandalia, in honor of Queen Charlotte, who was reputed to be descended from Vandals. Hillsborough attempted to obstruct the project but Wharton and Franklin won over influential people. The Lords of the Treasury approved the twenty-million-acre grant in 1770; the Privy Council approved the Vandalia proposal in 1772, and Hillsborough fell from power to be replaced by the Earl of Dartmouth. But Vandalia never became a reality. Opposition from rival interest groups—Virginian speculators with eyes on the same lands also had connections in London—continued to delay progress and the Quebec Act of 1774 placed supervision of western territory in the hands of the governor-general of Canada, leaving the speculators involved in the Grand Ohio Company and the Vandalia project empty-handed. Relations between Wharton and the Franklins strained and then broke. When Benjamin Franklin left England in 1775 "eleven years of lobbying for various land-speculating ventures had netted him absolutely nothing." Then the Revolution changed everything and Wharton's and Croghan's schemes "were among the first casualties of the war."[135]

Croghan had hoped that the Treaty at Fort Stanwix would secure his fortune and his future, and he leveraged loans on the basis of land granted to him and the suffering traders. But his plans soon ran into trouble. Laid up by a severe attack of gout and a dislocated foot in the summer of 1769, he traveled by wagon to Johnson Hall when he heard that the government was unlikely to confirm the private transactions Johnson had written into the treaty.[136] The following February he was confined to his bed; an acquaintance described him as "a Poor Soul" who did "nothing but pray and talk about the Sufferings of the Inner Man," and occasionally sighed in regret "about the Tricks of his Youth."[137] In the spring, fearing an Indian war was imminent, Croghan hurried to Fort Pitt to try and sell off the merchandise and buildings he owned there, presumably to someone less aware of the impending catastrophe. He then set up a private land office in Pittsburgh, selling land titles to anyone who would buy them, liquidating his claims as quickly as possible to try and pay off his debts.[138]

One of the individuals interested in making a purchase was George Washington. Washington had told a friend, the fellow land speculator and agent William Crawford, in 1767 that he regarded the proclamation line of 1763 as no more than "a temporary expedient to quiet the Minds of the Indians & [one that] must fall of course in a few years especially when those Indians are consenting to our Occupying the Lands." Anyone who missed "the present opportunity of hunting out good Lands & in some Measure Marking & distinguishing them for their own (in order to keep others from settling them)" would never get another chance. Through Crawford, Washington consulted Croghan about purchasing fifteen thousand acres. He also considered buying Croghan's interest in the Walpole Company but finally decided it was too shaky. Washington did acquire, by grants, some of the lands claimed by Croghan, and he later had to resort to litigation to reinforce his rights to the land.[139] The government's procrastination and ultimate rejection of the Vandalia scheme sent Croghan deeper into debt.

The Mason-Dixon line had separated Pennsylvania from Maryland and Virginia but the western end of the line remained undetermined. The Treaty of Fort Stanwix also left Pennsylvania's western boundary undetermined and Pennsylvania and Virginia contested a large area. In which colony, for example, did Fort Pitt fall? Pennsylvania took the position that the Stanwix treaty put the ceded lands at its disposal and immediately began surveying and settling lands in the area. Virginia insisted that the ceded territory lay within its borders. The Virginia governor Lord Dunmore's chief agent in the region was Dr. John Connolly, who occupied Fort Pitt after British regulars abandoned it in 1772, and he renamed it Fort Dunmore. Connolly was George Croghan's nephew.

According to the historian Dorothy Jones, the Treaty of Fort Stanwix "closed the book on one era of treaty-making in early America and opened it on another." Before Stanwix, treaties dealt with issues of trade, war and peace, alliances and relationships, and criminal jurisdiction, and they sometimes, but not always, transferred Indian lands into colonial hands. After Stanwix, treaties as conferences of accommodation disintegrated; more and more often, they became instruments for transferring land and as methods to separate Indians and Europeans.[140] As Timothy Shannon puts it, the "simple equation of land for loot" established at Fort Stanwix "provided the template" by which the United States conducted its diplomacy with Indian nations in years to come, demanding land cessions in exchange for annuities of cash or goods that the Indians needed to sustain themselves as they were confined to small, unproductive reservations.[141]

The Fort Stanwix treaty also accelerated a movement toward private land acquisition. The boundary that was meant to bring peace and order to the frontier in fact created conditions for conflict and confusion in which "the step from treaties as a public instrument of cession to treaties as a private instrument of cession was a very short step, and one easily taken."[142] Shifting inter-tribal power and politics, shifting British imperial policy, and unrelenting white expansion created chaos in the early 1770s. British actions in the wake of the treaty made things worse and contributed to the collapse of their empire in the Ohio Valley. When the government ordered Fort Pitt and Fort Chartres abandoned in 1771 as a measure of economy, it removed the British army as "a restraining power" in the region. At the same time, by failing to provide for limited land development beyond the proclamation line and by stalling indefinitely in giving approval to various proprietary schemes, "the ministry guaranteed that impatient, unscrupulous, or opportunistic adventurers would take the lead in western development and compound the confusions and conflicts that were already developing over western lands."[143]

The Stanwix cession unleashed an invasion of Indian country. In Virginia, veterans of the French and Indian War, with Washington at the forefront, asked the Executive Council for the land bounties they had been promised. Influential Virginians lobbied the Privy Council for rights to Kentucky and other lands that Virginia claimed by charter but which the suffering traders claimed were theirs. Samuel Wharton wrote a lengthy tract arguing that the territory west of the Alleghanies "never belonged to Virginia." (He also argued that Indians had "an indefensible right freely to sell, and grant to any person whatsoever"—in other words the land grants to private individuals at Fort Stanwix were valid. As the law professor Blake Watson notes, those who defended the property rights of Indians were often those who were most eager to buy their lands.)[144] The Penns opened their portion to settlement in April 1769 and received 2,790 applications for three-hundred-acre lots on the first day. Croghan reckoned between four and five thousand families crossed the mountains in 1769, and all spring and summer the next year the roads were "lined with wagons moving to the Ohio." Alexander McKee, an agent in the Shawnee towns, reported that the flood of white settlers and surveyors in the country around Fort Pitt and down the Ohio "has set all their Warriors in a rage."[145] The Delaware chief Killbuck told the governors of Pennsylvania, Maryland, and Virginia that since the Stanwix treaty "great Numbers more of your People have come Over the Great Mountains and settled throughout this Country." They were "very fond of our Rich Land," constantly quarreling among themselves about land, and had had some violent quarrels with the Indians. Unless the governors found a way to control their people, the Indians would not be able to restrain their young men; "the black Clouds begin to gather fast in this Country," Killbuck warned. The western Indians frequently heard of English meetings with the Six Nations and Cherokees "which gives us cause to think you are forming some bad designs against us Indians who Live between the Ohio and the Lakes."[146]

Even the Iroquois did not get the respite or benefit they hoped the treaty would bring them. Crops failed in 1769 and many Iroquois had to use the money they received at Fort Stanwix to buy provisions from colonial settlers to make it through the winter and spring.[147] In July 1770, at a conference both Abraham and Conoghquieson attended, Johnson confirmed the treaty and the Iroquois reaffirmed their right to cede the western lands. But, Abraham reprimanded Johnson, "at the treaty of Fort Stanwix you then told us, as you had done before, that we should pass our time in peace, and travel in security, that Trade should flourish & goods abound; that they should be sold us cheap, & that care should be taken to prevent any persons from imposing on us." Things had not worked out that way. "It is now worse than it was before."[148] Two years later, the Mohawks reminded Johnson that they had made the "great cession of Territory" to the king in expectation that their villages east of the line would be protected but now their lands were again under pressure from the people of Albany.[149] The Iroquois position would soon deteriorate further.

The harder the British and the Iroquois tried to maintain their influence and authority in the West, the faster it declined. Iroquois adherence to the British as a way of preserving their power among the western nations actually reduced it, as those nations became increasingly resentful of the British-Iroquois alliance.

In selling their neighbors' lands and protecting their own, the Iroquois forfeited their leadership role among the western tribes; in failing to protect the western tribes' lands, the British forfeited their role as fathers. The Ohio nations denounced the treaty as a deal concocted between the British and the Iroquois to steal their lands. The Six Nations had given up their hunting grounds to the English without asking for their consent, they said, and "had Shamefully taken all the Money and Goods to themselves and not Shared any part thereof with them." They called the Six Nations "slaves of the white people." Young warriors said it was better to die like men than be kicked about like dogs.[150]

Shawnee resentment of the Iroquois predated 1768 and ran deeper than the Fort Stanwix cession—they had voiced defiance of the Six Nations at Fort Pitt the spring before—but the treaty brought things to a head. The Shawnees became increasingly vocal and began to build a coalition of Indian nations that was independent of both the Iroquois and the British and opposed to the Stanwix cession. The Shawnee chief Red Hawk said the Six Nations had no more "right to sell the Country than we have." The Shawnees had acknowledged the Iroquois as their elder brothers and listened to them while their advice was good, he said, but "their power extends no further with us." Shawnee emissaries carrying wampum belts traveled north to the Great Lakes and south to Creek country and delegates from southern and western tribes gathered at "a very large Council House" that the Shawnees built on the banks of the Scioto River.[151] "The scheme of the Shawnese to form a confederacy of all the Western and Southern nations is a notable piece of policy," General Gage warned John Stuart, "for nothing less would enable them to withstand the Six Nations and their allies against whom they have been much exasperated on account of the boundary treaty held at Fort Stanwix."[152] As Shawnee emissaries reached out to Cherokees, Stuart informed his deputies that the Shawnees "are at the head of the Western confederacy which is formed upon the principle of maintaining their property in the lands obtained from the Six Nations at Fort Stanwix and prevent their being settled by white people."[153] Hillsborough became increasingly convinced of "the fatal Policy" of deviating from the proclamation line and feared the outbreak of a general Indian war.[154]

The Shawnees also protested against the Cherokees selling lands in Kentucky that they regarded as their hunting grounds. The boundary lines that were agreed upon by the Iroquois and the Cherokees converged on the Ohio River. In the words of the late historian Wilbur Jacobs, the lines "silhouetted a huge geographical arrowhead directed to the heartland of America."[155] Whites entered the arrowhead confident that their invasion was legal; Shawnees who had never relinquished the land treated them as trespassers. Daniel Boone was one of the first intruders. In 1769 with half a dozen men, he crossed from North Carolina through the Cumberland Gap and spent the summer hunting in the game-filled forests of northern Kentucky. The Shawnees caught them, confiscated their furs and guns, and sent them home. Boone sneaked back into Kentucky the next spring, and in 1773, he sold his farm in North Carolina and led five families and forty single men through Cumberland Gap. A war party of Cherokees and Shawnees ambushed them and killed six people, including Boone's eldest son, James. Boone's party retreated but regrouped and returned two years later.[156]

Kentucky became a battleground where two worlds and worldviews collided. Backcountry settlers hunted, supplementing their crops and livestock, and adopted Indian hunting techniques, but they did not adopt Indian hunting values. They felt no kinship with animals; they ignored rituals that Indians believed were necessary to harvest plant and animal life and keep the world in balance, and they slaughtered game wastefully. Indians fought to preserve their hunting territories; invading settlers fought to transform them into fields and pastures. They felled trees with fire and axes, fenced and plowed fields, brought in pigs and cattle, and tried to hold the land they seized as private property. They changed the landscape and many of its meanings. Colonists called the Indians savages; Shawnees called the invaders who disrupted the balance of their world "crazy people [who] want to shove us off our land entirely."[157]

And the crazy people kept coming. Pioneers from Virginia, North Carolina, and Maryland followed in Boone's footsteps. "You told us that we should have no more Disturbance or trouble about our Lands after the Boundary line was run. But trouble still continues with us," the Cherokee chief Oconostota complained. "We think the Virginia People don't hear your talks nor mind, nor do they seem to care for King George's talks over the great Water."[158] The country around Pittsburgh was "in great Confusion," said Croghan, "on account of the Governour & Council of Virginia granting patents to Col. Washington for 200,000 acres of Land on Ohio & the Great Kanahwa," and the Indians were alarmed to see surveyors and colonists heading downriver "to Settle a Country wh[ich] they were Informed by the Kings Messages was not to be settled." If reports of sixty thousand people settled between Pittsburgh and the mouth of the Ohio by the end of 1773 were true, wrote Croghan, "the policy of ye People in England delaying ye Grant of ye New Colony in order to prevent Emigration answers not their purpose."[159] As Johnson explained to the Earl of Dartmouth, "These settlers generally set out with a general Prejudice against all Indians and the young Indian Warriors or Hunters are too often inclined to retaliate."[160] Shawnees who found "the Woods covered with White People" and surveyors marking the land said they "had many disagreeable Dreams" about it that winter.[161] "Being Sure the White People intended to take all our Country from us, and that very soon," the Shawnees urged other tribes to be ready to "defend it to the last Drop of blood."[162]

The British employed divide-and-conquer tactics to dismantle the coalition the Shawnees were building: "we must either agree to permit these people to Cut each other's Throats or risk their discharging their fury on Our Traders & defenceless Frontiers," Johnson wrote to Hillsborough. Johnson worked on the Iroquois, Stuart on the Cherokees, and Croghan among the western tribes, to keep them out of the impending conflict. Shawnee delegates who tried to rally the tribes met rebuffs. In one instance the Iroquois threw the Shawnees' wampum belt back at them.[163]

Croghan kept borrowing money to buy Indian land and kept hoping for word from London that the government had approved his purchases. But the world in which he had lived and operated for years was coming to an end as fast as that of the Shawnees. In 1772, Croghan buried his old friend Andrew Montour, who had been murdered by a Seneca. In the historian Patrick Griffin's words, Croghan and the Indians who attended Montour's funeral near Fort Pitt "were remembering more than a man. They were paying homage to a moment now passed on the frontier and to a process of cultural accommodation that underscored the viability of the imperial plan." That plan was dead, authority west of the line was collapsing, and Croghan's influence was evaporating. He resigned his post as deputy, "hoping to make as much money as he could before his world dissolved."[164]

In the final weeks of his life Sir William Johnson also saw the treaty he had maneuvered and the world he had created coming apart.[165] The land ceded at Fort Stanwix, he assured Lord Dartmouth in late June, "was secured by the plainest & best natural boundaries, and the Indians freely agreed to make it more ample that our people should have no pretext of narrow limits, and the remainder might be rendered the more secure to themselves & their posterity." But now squatters were pushing beyond the boundaries. He expected soon to hear they had even crossed the Ohio "wherever the lands invite them; for the body of these people are under no restraint, they perceive that they are in places of security, and pay as little regard to Government, as they do title for their possessions." Atrocities like the murder of the Mingo chief Logan's family by frontier thugs (an event made infamous when Thomas Jefferson included Logan's alleged lament in his *Notes on the State of Virginia*) threatened to spark fresh wars. And there was little hope of establishing order in the West until better order was restored in the East.[166]

As Johnson was writing, parties of Iroquois gathered at Johnson Hall to discuss "the critical state of Indian Affairs." Conoghquieson opened the meeting on Saturday, July 9, 1774. Serihowane, a Seneca, got down to the business at hand:

> Brother, we are sorry to observe to you that your People are as ungovernable, or rather more so, than ours. You must remember that it was most solemnly, and publicly settled, and agreed to at the General Congress

held at Fort Stanwix in 1768... that the Line then pointed out and fixed between the Whites and Indians should forever after be looked upon as a barrier between us, and that the White People were not to go beyond it. It seems, Brother, that your People entirely disregard, and despise the settlement agreed upon by their Superiors and us; for we find that they, notwithstanding that settlement, are come in vast numbers to the Ohio, and gave our people to understand that they wou'd settle wherever they pleas'd. If this is the case we must look upon every engagement you made with us as void and of no effect.

The conference adjourned for the rest of the weekend. On Monday Johnson responded that the Crown would take steps to keep colonists off Indian lands but the Iroquois must do their part and keep the Shawnees in check. Then, fatigued from his exertions, he ordered pipes, tobacco, and some liquor for the Indians, and he retired to give them time to consider. Two hours later Sir William Johnson was dead.[167]

Conoghquieson conducted the condolence ceremony at Johnson's funeral. He handed Guy Johnson a black and white wampum belt, exhorting him to follow in his uncle's footsteps and take over the conduct of their affairs. Abraham repeated that if the British could not prevent their settlers from breaching the Stanwix line, it "must end in troubles."[168] The chiefs returned to Johnson Hall in September to hold a formal condolence ceremony and invest Guy Johnson as superintendent with a new name. Several chiefs who had been with Sir William at the Fort Stanwix treaty but not at the council where he died— Bunt, Diaquanda, and Sayenqueraghta—conveyed their sympathies and assured Guy Johnson of their support.[169] In December, the Iroquois again reminded Guy Johnson that they had given up so much land at Fort Stanwix in expectation that the king would hold the line and they hoped that would not be forgotten, "for we remember it still, and you have it all in writing."[170]

The Treaty of Fort Stanwix bulged the 1763 proclamation line to the west; it did not demolish or revoke it. Although the line did little to restrain colonial settlers, land speculators in Virginia and elsewhere still chomped at the bit, frustrated in their investments unless they could obtain clear title. The British government denied Virginia's bid for Kentucky, and Indian resistance to the cession made things worse. As a result, writes Woody Holton, "the total yield of the Virginia land rush set off by the Fort Stanwix treaty was a pile of rejected land petitions and worthless surveys." Lack of clear title infuriated Virginia gentry like George Washington, Patrick Henry, and Thomas Jefferson who had received preliminary grants to millions of acres. They would have to find other ways to acquire the Indians' lands.[171]

In the spring of 1774 Virginia went to war against the Shawnees.[172] There was, said Croghan in August, "too great a Spirit in the frontier people for killing

Indians." He requested thirty thousand white wampum beads and twenty thousand black beads in order to help preserve the friendship of the Delawares and Six Nations and prevent a general Indian war.[173] Isolated by British diplomatic strategy, the Shawnees fought virtually alone. While James Murray, Governor Dunmore, led one army down the Ohio from Fort Pitt, Andrew Lewis, who had represented the claims of Virginian officers at Fort Stanwix, led another down the Kanawha River. Chief Cornstalk and the Shawnees attacked Lewis at Point Pleasant, where the Kanawha joins the Ohio. Charles Lewis, the general's brother, died in the daylong firefight that ensued but the Shawnees were outnumbered and outgunned and forced from the field.[174] Cornstalk made peace with Dunmore, and the Shawnees conceded their lands south of the Ohio. Dr. Thomas Walker, who represented Virginia at the treaties at Fort Stanwix and Lochaber, was present at this treaty as well.

As Dorothy Jones noted, Dunmore's War might "better be called the War of the Stanwix Cession." The Shawnees protested first against the land ceded north and east of the Kanawha and they fought against Virginia to try and keep white settlers out of that region. After they were defeated and compelled to accept that cession, they and their western allies fought to keep whites out of the unauthorized part of the Fort Stanwix cession, the lands south and west of the Kanawha in Kentucky and Tennessee that became the famous "dark and troubled ground" of frontier history.[175] The fighting over the Stanwix cession merged into the fighting of the American Revolution.

When the Revolution broke out, many Indians in the Ohio country hoped to stay out of the conflict. But they understood that it was a war over their land as well as a war for American independence and their best option was to side with the British, who had offered at least token protection for Indian lands, rather than with the Americans who were hell-bent on taking them. Shawnee chiefs told the Virginians in July 1775 "we are often inclined to believe there is no resting place for us and that your Intentions were [sic] to deprive us entirely of our whole Country."[176]

More than six hundred Indians showed up at Fort Pitt in the fall of 1776 to meet with the American commissioners for Indian affairs, one of whom, once again, was Thomas Walker. George Morgan, now an Indian agent for the United States, was on hand. The Americans assured the Indians their lands would not be touched as long as they held fast the chain of friendship. Both sides pledged themselves to peace, although a Seneca chief named Round Face reminded the commissioners, "You know the Boundary lately established at Fort Stanwix—You then told us if any of your people should presume to set their Feet over the Line, they should be cut off." The commissioners assured the Indians that "no white people will be suffered to pass the Line settled at Fort Stanwix, for although that agreement was made with the King yet as we are satisfied with it, we shall take care that it is complied with." Nevertheless, Cornstalk had Morgan write down his speech and send it to the Congress in Philadelphia. American land thefts struck at the core of Shawnee life, and "all our lands are covered by the white people," he said. Referring to the lands south and west of the Kanawha—the lands Johnson was *not* authorized to buy—he declared: "We never sold you our Lands which you now possess on the Ohio between the Great Kenhawa and the Cherokee River, and which you are settling without ever asking our leave, or obtaining our consent....That was our hunting Country and you have taken it from us. This is what sits heavy upon our Hearts and on the Hearts of all Nations, and it is impossible for us to think as we ought to whilst we are thus oppressed."[177]

The next year Cornstalk visited the American garrison at Fort Randolph on the Kanawha River, at the site where he had fought the Virginians exactly three years earlier. He was taken hostage, held in the fort, and later murdered by American militia.[178] Meanwhile, the Delaware chief White Eyes publicly threw off the subordinate status the Iroquois had assigned his people and negotiated a defensive alliance with the United States at Fort Pitt in September 1778.[179] But American militia murdered White Eyes. By 1779 most Shawnees and Delawares joined the British alliance. Shawnee war parties and Kentucky militia raided back and forth across the Ohio River, burning villages and taking scalps in a vicious conflict along the boundary set at Fort Stanwix.

Cherokees also fought to preserve the disputed lands. No matter how much land Cherokees gave up, the colonists kept coming; Cherokees said they could "see the smoke of the Virginians from their doors." In March 1775, at the Treaty of Sycamore Shoals in Tennessee, Judge Richard Henderson and a group of North Carolina land speculators known as the Transylvania Land Company induced Attakullakulla, the principal headman Oconostota, and the Raven of Chota to sell twenty-seven thousand square miles of land between the Kentucky and Cumberland rivers—most of modern Kentucky—in exchange for a cabin full of trade goods. The chiefs later claimed that Henderson had deceived them as to what they were signing. A young chief named Dragging Canoe reputedly stormed from the treaty council in disgust, vowing to make the ceded lands "dark and bloody." He told the British "that he had no hand in making these Bargains but blamed some of their Old Men who he said were too old to hunt and who by their poverty had been induced to sell their land but that for his part he had a great many young fellows that would support him and that they were determined to have their land."[180]

In April 1776 a Shawnee chief and a delegation of fourteen northern Indians traveled to Cherokee country. In the council house at the town of Chota the Shawnee produced a nine-foot wampum belt, painted red as a sign of war. He recited the grievances of the Shawnees and other nations, particularly their cruel treatment at the hands of the Virginians. The Indians once held the whole country; now they barely had enough ground to stand on. "Better to die like men than to dwindle away by inches," he declared. The older Cherokee chiefs, who had seen war and tasted defeat, sat silent, but Dragging Canoe led the warriors in accepting the war belt. Cherokee war parties attacked the colonists who encroached on their lands but armies from Virginia, Georgia, and the Carolinas immediately retaliated, burned Cherokee villages and crops, and then dictated peace terms that took more Cherokee land. Rather than surrender, Dragging Canoe led his warriors deep into present-day Tennessee and continued the fight from the Chickamauga River and Lookout Mountain. Chickamauga Cherokees made common cause with militant Shawnees.[181]

The Revolution ended many careers, alliances, and hopes that had rested on the Fort Stanwix treaty. Delegates from the Six Nations and the Continental Congress met at Albany in the summer of 1775 to remind each other of their peaceful intentions. Abraham and Conoghquieson were both there.[182] The Fort Stanwix treaty had left the Oneidas on the border of the new boundary and they faced hard choices when the Revolution broke out. The British had endeavored to regulate white encroachment on their lands, but they had failed to stop it and the Oneidas knew that if they displayed British sympathies their American neighbors would be sure to seize their lands and the Carrying Place they had negotiated so hard to keep at Fort Stanwix. Conoghquieson blamed the missionary Samuel Kirkland for meddling in Oneida affairs and dividing the tribe (which he did) but most Oneidas supported the Americans.[183] But the Revolution swept away the Fort Stanwix treaty provisions that protected Mohawk and Oneida land; in their place, it brought frontier violence and racial conflict.

Joseph Brant sided with the Crown and the Mohawks were driven from their homeland. Guy Johnson and his followers fled to Canada. American troops occupied and trashed Johnson Hall, the center of the world that Sir William had constructed and dominated with the help of his Iroquois friends and allies. John Butler, who had interpreted at Fort Stanwix, also fled to Canada with his sons Thomas and Walter, although his wife and other children were imprisoned by the rebels and he did not see them again until an exchange was arranged in 1780. Dispatched to Niagara to manage the Indian department there, Butler orchestrated raids on the American frontier and organized a corps of rangers to serve with the Indians, fighting alongside Joseph Brant and the aging Seneca war chief Sayenqueraghta. His property in New York was confiscated and he tried to recoup his losses through various means—monopolizing trade at Niagara during the war, speculating in Indian lands and other shady ventures in Upper Canada after the war—which got him investigated by the British colonial government but brought little success. He continued to serve as deputy superintendent of Indian affairs and, despite growing infirmities, attended the Sandusky conference between the Indians and Americans in 1793, his last public act. At Butler's funeral in 1796 Brant described him as "the last that remained of those that acted with that great man the late Sir William Johnson, whose steps he followed and our Loss is the greater, as there are none remaining who understand our manners and customs as well as he did."[184]

Sayenqueraghta remained firm in his allegiance to the British. The rebels, he declared, "wish for nothing more, than to extirpate us from the Earth, that they may possess our Lands, the desire of attaining which we are convinced is the Cause of the present War between the King and his disobedient Children." He led Seneca war parties harassing Fort Stanwix, now in American hands, and fought with Butler in the bloody Battle of Oriskany in the woods near the fort in 1777. Seneca villages bore the brunt of the American invasion of Iroquoia in 1779, when General John Sullivan's army burned forty towns, destroyed an estimated 160,000 bushels of corn, and systematically wasted fields and orchards. Left without food and shelter as one of the harshest winters on record gripped upstate New York, many Senecas accompanied Sayenqueraghta to the British garrison at Fort Niagara, where he continued to exercise a prominent role in the refugee community that grew up there and in British-Iroquois relations. In 1780 he moved with his family and followers to Buffalo Creek in New York, where he died six years later.[185]

The Mohawk chief Abraham pursued a precarious and perilous neutrality and stayed behind when most of his people went to Canada. In the winter of 1779–80 he and another Mohawk named Crine, together with two Oneida leaders, Good Peter and Skenandon, set out through the snow to Niagara, carrying letters and hoping to arrange an exchange of prisoners. They met with a cold reception. The British and their Iroquois allies at Niagara regarded them as traitors. Sayenqueraghta, who had negotiated alongside Abraham at Fort Stanwix, drank to the health of the other Indians, "omitting the four Rebels as a Mark of his Contempt." Guy Johnson threw the emissaries into the fort's dungeon, where they languished in cramped confinement for several months. By the time Johnson agreed to release them, Abraham was dead.[186]

Richard Peters did not have time to profit from the Revolution; he died six days after the Declaration of Independence was signed.[187] The Revolution ended the Penn family's control of Pennsylvania. John Penn was the last colonial governor of Pennsylvania. He pursued a careful policy of neutrality and managed to hold on to his private lands but the Pennsylvania Assembly divested the proprietorship of twenty-four million acres.

Unlike many of his associates, Croghan sided with the Patriots and became chairman of the Pittsburgh Committee of Correspondence. But he kept in contact with Loyalists as well as Patriots as he struggled to make his speculations pay off. He was a natural candidate for Indian agent at Pittsburgh, but the post went first to Richard Butler and then to George Morgan, who had little time for Croghan. Accused of being a Loyalist, Croghan had to move from Pittsburgh to Lancaster. There, still struggling with debts and with most of his remaining lands heavily mortgaged, he lived his old age in poverty. He died on the last day of August 1782. After his death more lands were sold to settle debts. Croghan Hall, his home for much of his life near the growing city of Pittsburgh, was lost through mortgage foreclosure. A man who had spent most of his life speculating in Indian lands died essentially landless.[188]

Andrew Lewis was appointed brigadier general in the Continental Army and he attended the United States treaty with the Delawares at Fort Pitt in 1778. He resigned his commission owing to ill health and died in 1781. Thomas Walker fared rather better. In 1775 he bought more than a million acres from George Croghan,[189] and by the time he died in 1794 he was one of the richest men in Albemarle County, Virginia.

Samuel Wharton was in London when the Revolution broke out, still working to secure the Crown's approval for the land grant. When some of his letters to rebels were made public, he was forced to flee to France. Returning to America in 1780 he took an oath of allegiance to the American cause. In 1782 and 1783 he was a delegate to the Continental Congress where he seems to have worked quietly but unsuccessfully to secure recognition for his western landholdings. After the Revolution, Pennsylvania, New York, and Delaware ceded their western land claims to the federal government; Virginia ceded its claims to lands north of the Ohio but retained its claims south of the river. Congress passed the Northwest Ordinance in 1787 governing the territory north of the Ohio, and Virginia refused to confirm private purchases. Wharton's claims came to nothing.

Unlike his father, William Franklin remained loyal to the Crown. He continued to serve as governor of New Jersey until 1776 when he was arrested and imprisoned on the orders of the Provincial Congress of New Jersey. He was released in a prisoner exchange in 1778 and continued to be active in the Loyalist community. He joined other Loyalists leaving for England in 1782. He met his father once more, during Benjamin's trip to England in 1785, but in his will Franklin senior left him only some land in Nova Scotia, explaining, "The part he acted against me in the late war, which is of public notoriety, will account for my leaving him no more of an estate he endeavored to deprive me of."[190] William died in London in 1813.

By the terms of the Peace of Paris in 1783 Britain recognized American independence and handed over to the new United States all lands south of the Great Lakes, east of the Mississippi, and north of Florida. The Indians who inhabited this territory were neither included nor consulted and were left to make their own terms with the victorious Americans. Britain's Indian allies were outraged. They were "thunderstruck" when they heard that British diplomats had sold them out to the Americans: "the peacemakers and our Enemies have talked away our Lands at a Rum Drinking," declared a Cherokee chief named Little Turkey. They were not defeated subjects of King George; they were independent nations still fighting to defend their territorial boundaries as set by colonial treaties to which at least some of them had agreed. "These people," Governor Frederick Haldimand of Canada wrote to Lord North in November 1783, "have as enlightened Ideas of the nature & Obligations of Treaties as the most Civilized Nations have, and know that no Infringement of the treaty in 1768...Can be binding upon them without their Express Concurrence and Consent." Indians saw the treaty as an act of betrayal "that Christians only were Capable of doing." The British responded lamely that they had only ceded the right of preemption to Indian lands.[191] For Indians the fighting did not end in 1783; it merged into a longer war to halt American expansion at the Ohio River—the boundary established at Fort Stanwix.

Treaty Making, American-Style

The outbreak of the Revolution and the uncertainties it created generated fever-ish diplomatic activity as Indian nations explored their options and reshuffled alliances and relationships. Indian messengers carrying wampum belts ran for-est trails from Indian village to Indian village as well as to Albany, Detroit, and Fort Pitt. Employing the rhetoric, metaphors, and rituals of wampum diplomacy, the Americans competed with the British to secure the support, or at least the neutrality, of Indian tribes, and they negotiated treaties that emphasized alliance and friendship. Major General Philip Schuyler, together with other commissioners appointed by the Continental Congress and commis-sioners appointed by the government of New York, held a series of treaties with the Iroquois.[1] Operating out of Fort Pitt, George Morgan, who as a trader and junior partner in Baynton, Wharton, and Morgan had built connections in the Ohio Indian country, held councils with the Six Nations, Shawnees, Delawares, and Wyandots.[2]

Beginning with the Declaration of Independence, the United States endeav-ored to stake its place as a new nation by establishing relations with the nations of Europe and entering the system of treaties and diplomatic customs by which supposedly civilized nations dealt with each other. At the same time, the United States established relations with the Native nations of the American continent, which required conforming to the system of treaties and diplomatic customs that Indians had developed with colonial powers, although its participation in these treaties involved performance of protocol more often than commitment to substance.[3] The United States' first formal recorded treaty with an Indian nation was held at Fort Pitt in 1778. US commissioners and Delaware delegates led by White Eyes exchanged pledges of perpetual peace and friendship on a wampum belt depicting the thirteen states and the Delaware nation holding the chain of friendship. The United States guaranteed the Delawares' territorial rights as defined in previous treaties and even laid out the possibility that other tribes that were friendly to the United States might join the alliance and "form a state whereof the Delaware nation shall be the head, and have representation in Congress." But the final version of the treaty committed the Delawares to an offensive and defensive alliance, allowed American troops free passage through Delaware country, and permitted US soldiers to build forts there. The Delawares complained that the American commissioners "put a War Belt & Tomahawk in the hands of said Delaware Nation & induced some of their Chiefs to sign certain Writings" that contained "declarations & engagements they never intended to make." They returned the war belt and tomahawk. The speaker for the Delaware Council said he had "looked over the Articles of the treaty again & find that they are wrote down false, & as I did not understand the Interpreter what he spoke I could not contradict his Interpretation, but now I will speak the truth plain & tell you what I spoke." George Morgan, who was not present at the treaty, said the Delawares had "a very wicked false Interpreter," and he denounced the treaty as "villainously conducted." He subsequently submitted his resignation to Congress "as Policy may require a certain conduct toward the Indians which Col. Morgan is not capable of."[4] The peace and friendship pledged at Fort Pitt did not last long. White Eyes died in November, murdered by American militia. William Crawford, a friend and business associate (read: fellow land speculator) of George Washington and who had attended the treaty, died four years later, ritually tortured to death by Delaware warriors exacting vengeance for the slaughter of their relatives. Needless to say, nothing came of Delaware representation in Congress. Between the treaty with the Delawares in 1778, and 1871, when Congress terminated treaty making, the United States ratified and passed into law about 370 treaties. The conduct and consequences of the first US treaty did not bode well for those that followed.

In 1783 Indians were massively affected by a treaty in which they took no part: the lands Britain ceded to the United States at the Peace of Paris were Indian lands. For the Americans those lands were both a natural resource and the economic engine of the new nation. Acquiring and selling the lands would provide homes for citizens, fill the empty treasury, and ensure the growth and survival of the young republic. Western lands, said Richard Henry Lee, abounded with "all those primary and essential materials for human industry to work upon, in order to produce the comfort and happiness of mankind."[5] In other words, the new nation would build on Indian homelands and also transform them into productive commodities. That meant uprooting Native people, severing their ties to places where generations of ancestors had lived and died, and restricting and then eradicating mobile patterns of subsistence that had sustained Indian societies from time immemorial. "Our lands are our life and our breath," a Creek chief named Hallowing King explained. "If we part with them, we part with our life."[6] In the terms Richard Henry Lee and Hallowing

King understood the contest for land, the future of the American nation and the survival of Indians as Indians were incompatible. Treaties had developed as an American blend of Indian and European diplomacies in which the participants met to establish or renew peace, alliance, and trade; settle disputes; and exchange land for gifts; now treaties were instruments for transferring Indian land to American ownership and treaty negotiations became life-and-death struggles.

Following British precedent, the Confederation Congress planned initially to establish a boundary line that could be renegotiated and moved westward as Indians retreated before the advancing tide of American settlement. But the US government was no better able than the imperial government to maintain such a boundary and was not the only player in the game. Individual states also made their own treaties with Indians, often in defiance of federal wishes, and sometimes they challenged the authority of the federal government to conduct Indian affairs. Between 1783 and 1786 twenty-one major treaties were held but the Confederation Congress negotiated only six of them. Spain made four; Britain, one; individual states, seven; and private interest groups made three. "Nowhere along the seaboard or in the backcountry on either side of the Ohio River was there a clear-cut center of authority, white or red," writes the historian Dorothy Jones.[7] The northern states and Virginia ceded their claims to land north of the Ohio to the federal government, but south of the Ohio Virginia retained its claims to Kentucky, North Carolina did not cede Tennessee until 1789, and Georgia claimed Alabama and Mississippi until 1802. In the North and South, private companies and land speculators also tried to get in on the act; in fact, Congress worked with private land companies to try and settle the territory northwest of the Ohio in a systematic and orderly way. Like the Indian confederations that formed to resist the insatiable American assault on tribal lands, the American confederation was subject to internal divisions and tensions. Meanwhile, the British in Canada and Spaniards in Florida watched from the wings and maintained their own alliances among the tribes as a potential buffer against an aggressive new republic.

US negotiators continued to adhere to forms of intercultural diplomacy as they had been developed and fine-tuned in countless councils in colonial America and as practiced in the treaty system that Britain had operated. The first secretary of war, Henry Knox, saw no point in "waging war for an object which may be obtained by a treaty" and argued that "the independent nations and tribes of Indians ought to be considered as foreign nations, not as the subjects of any particular state."[8] American treaty commissioners smoked peace pipes, spoke on wampum, and gave gifts. The federal government also built on European precedents in bringing Indian delegations to the nation's capital, where they toured the sights, sat for portraits, and sometimes met the president.[9] American commissioners had no qualms about employing "fathers and children" terminology in their dealings with Indians; however, rather than a kinship metaphor indicating reciprocal relations it increasingly served as a way to infantilize Indians and emphasize their dependence on the Great Father for protection, guidance, and subsistence. The United States continued colonial practice and issued medals to Indians. These medals bore a likeness of the president on the obverse (with the exception of John Adams, every president from Washington to Benjamin Harrison issued one) and were known as peace medals because of the clasped hands of friendship embossed on the reverse. Without medals, Thomas McKenney, the head of the Indian Office, explained in 1829, "any plan of operations among the Indians, be it what it may, is essentially enfeebled." The Indians esteemed them as "tokens of Friendship," "badges of power," and "trophies of renown" and regarded the receipt of medals as an "ancient right." But as the balance of power shifted dramatically to the United States, peace medals increasingly became tokens of "good behavior" rather than symbols of allegiance.[10] Indian oratory continued to find a receptive audience in the early years of the Republic and examples of Indian eloquence appeared in print, but increasingly they were sentimentalized as befit a tragic people who were assumed to be dying out.[11]

The power dynamics that had produced the intercultural diplomacy of the colonial era were changing. Americans were eager to expand and impatient with long-winded protocols that allowed all parties ample time for reflection and discussion. As American power increased, respect for Indian customs and concerns diminished and long-standing practices and rituals of reciprocity eroded. More and more often, treaties were conducted on American terms and by American schedules. Treaties established boundaries but the boundaries became ever more permeable and impermanent. Henry Knox admitted that breaches of treaties were the main cause of Indian wars. Unless the federal government restrained its citizens, the Indians could "have no faith in such imbecile promises, and the lawless whites will ridicule a government which shall, on paper only, make Indian treaties, and regulate Indian boundaries."[12]

Few Americans shared Knox's concerns that the United States deal honorably with the Indian nations and maintain the traditions of wampum diplomacy. James Duane, a congressional delegate from New York and chairman of the committee on Indian affairs, urged his state to dispense with wampum and abandon "the disgraceful system of pensioning, courting and flattering them as great and mighty nations." "The Stile by which the Indians are to be addressed is of Moment also," he wrote. "They are used to be[ing] called Brethren, Sachems and Warriors of the Six Nations. I hope it will never be repeated. It is sufficient to make them sensible that they are spoken to[,] without complementing 20 or 30 Mohawks as a nation and a few more Tusceroes and Onondagoes as distinct nations." They were defeated dependants and should be treated as such.[13]

The United States approached its first post-Revolution treaties with the assumption that they had already acquired the Indians' lands by right of conquest. General Philip Schulyer told the Six Nations they were deceived if they thought that Britain had made provision for them in the Peace of Paris: "the treaty does not contain a single stipulation for the Indians," he said. "They are not so much as mentioned." The Indians had chosen the wrong side and had lost. "We are now Masters of this Island, and can dispose of the Lands as we think proper or most convenient to ourselves," Schulyer declared. The government would make peace with the Indians but in doing so would establish "lines of property" that would be "convenient to the respective tribes, and commensurate to the public wants." Because the United States had pledged grants of land to veterans of the Revolutionary War but "the public finances do not admit of any considerable expenditure to extinguish the Indian claims," the Indians would be required to give up land as atonement for their participation and barbarities in the war.[14] American commissioners replaced elaborate speeches and wampum rituals with blunt talk and forceful demands. Treaties, they said, consisted of the United States granting peace to Indians and *giving back* to the tribes those lands it did not immediately require. Asserting its rights of conquest, the United States assumed it could abolish the boundary line of 1768, and it demanded hefty cessions of territory from the Indians as the penalty for fighting on the wrong side in the Revolutionary War.[15]

US commissioners Richard Butler, Arthur Lee, and Oliver Wolcott held a second treaty at Fort Stanwix with the Six Nations in October 1784. In fact, they hurried to Fort Stanwix to participate in a treaty that New York had already initiated and the conference involved multiple negotiations between representatives from Congress, New York, Pennsylvania, and the Six Nations. The Seneca chief Cornplanter and the other Iroquois delegates argued for the Ohio River boundary but the American commissioners would not hear of it: most of the lands had been ceded in the treaty at the same place eighteen years before. Divided and bitter, intimidated by the presence of American troops, and cowed by the American demand for hostages, the Iroquois ceded all land west of the western boundary of Pennsylvania. The tone of negotiations at the treaties in 1768 and 1784 could not have been more different.[16] The Iroquois delegates met with scorn when they returned home and Cornplanter feared for his life. Seven years later in Philadelphia, Cornplanter and his fellow Seneca chiefs Half Town and Big Tree met President Washington, "the Great Councillor of the Thirteen Fires" (whom they also knew as "the town destroyer" after his scorched-earth policies in Iroquois country during the Revolution), and delivered a lengthy complaint about injustices and deceptions in the Fort Stanwix treaty of 1784. "You have compelled us to do that which has made us ashamed," they said. And they were not convinced by Washington's assurances of future protection for their lands: "Father: Your speech, written on the great paper, is to us like the first light of the morning to a sick man, whose pulse beats too strongly in his temples, and prevents him from sleep. He sees it, and rejoices, but he is not cured."[17]

The Treaty of Fort Stanwix promised to protect the lands of the Oneidas and Tuscaroras who had supported the Americans during the war. But New York was anxious to extinguish Indian title to western lands before other states advanced rival claims. At the Treaty of Fort Herkimer in 1785, Governor Clinton of New York bought a large tract of land along the New York–Pennsylvania border from the Oneidas, pushing the 1768 Fort Stanwix treaty line west to the Chenango River. Good Peter, the Oneida chief, at first refused to part with so much territory but the commissioners kept up the pressure, lobbying and dividing the Oneidas in private evening meetings until eventually they caved. "We have several times spoke, and sometimes near each other," said Good Peter. "It often happens that in the Course of a Night People's Minds get altered."[18] In a series of shady deals, New York State representatives and rapacious land company agents proceeded to gobble up Oneida, Onondaga, Cayuga, and Seneca lands, sometimes over protests by the Iroquois that they believed they were leasing the lands, not selling them. Iroquois diplomatic rituals traditionally served to bring people together with good minds, and their council protocols usually allowed time for consideration and consensus building. "Possess your Minds in Peace, that we decline making an Answer at present," an Oneida sachem named Oneyanha (or Beech Tree) told the New York commissioners. "A good Mind is necessary in deliberating on Things of Importance." But New Yorkers in a hurry to get their hands on Oneida lands did not possess peaceful minds, and they pressured and divided the Oneidas. "Our minds," said Good Peter, "were much agitated, and drawn various ways."[19]

The Indians having their women along may have limited such agitation and distraction. At a treaty council held at Denniston's Tavern in Albany in February 1789, "female Governesses [clan mothers] and other Women" accompanied the Iroquois chiefs and warriors. The Indians told the New York commissioners why they were there: "Our Ancestors considered it a great Transgression to reject the Council of their Women, particularly the female Governesses. Our Ancestors considered them Mistresses of the Soil. Our Ancestors said who bring us forth, who cultivate our Lands, who kindle our Fires and boil our Pots, but the Women. Our Women say, they think their Uncles had of late lost the Power of Thinking, and were about sinking their Territory." In other words, the women were not happy with the land cessions made by the men. On this occasion, the men had "much Conversation with our Sisters" before any agreement was made. "It is an acknowledged Truth that our Sisters are the principal

Inhabitants of the Earth," Good Peter explained to the governor. "The Earth from whence spring the Articles necessary to sustain Life is theirs, and it is thereupon necessary we should hearken to their Advise."[20] But women were not immune to the pressures and tactics applied to acquire Oneida lands and they were unable to stem the tide of dispossession. As New Yorkers secured the land by treaty and chicanery, Samuel Kirkland, who had a hand in many of the deals, reported that it became commonplace for Indians to say "cheat like a white man."[21]

The United States dictated treaties by right of conquest to most of the Ohio tribes. At Fort McIntosh, at the confluence of the Ohio and Beaver rivers (present-day Beaver, Pennsylvania), the treaty commissioners Butler, Lee, and George Rogers Clark addressed the Indians "in a high tone" and told them they were a conquered people. Because the English king had made no provision for the tribes, they were "therefore left to obtain peace from the U. States, & to be received under their government and protection, upon such conditions as seem proper to Congress, the Great Council of the U. States." The commissioners brushed aside the Indians' objections that these lands had been handed down to them by their ancestors and that they still regarded them as their own: "The detail of these claims and title may appear to be of consequence among your-selves. But to us & to the business of the Council Fire to which we have called you, they have no relation; *because* we claim the country by conquest; and are to *give* not to *receive*."[22] The commissioners demanded southern and eastern Ohio as the price of peace.

A year later, 150 Shawnee men and 80 women of the Mekoche or Maquachake division—traditionally responsible for matters of mediation and peacemaking—arrived at Fort Finney at the mouth of the Great Miami River. "Painted and dressed in the most elegant manner," they entered the grounds of the fort "in very regular order; the chiefs in front, beating a drum, with young warriors dancing a peculiar dance for such occasions." The two head dancers each carried the stem of a pipe painted and decorated with wampum and bald eagle feathers as symbols of peace. Behind the warriors came the women and children. The Indians sang, the Indians and Americans each fired a salute, and the American commissioners entered the council house and took their seats. Then the Indians filed in; the men "entered at the west door, the chiefs on our left, the warriors on our right and round on the east end until they joined the chiefs; the old chief beating the drum, and the young men dancing and waving the feathers over us, whilst the others were seated; this done, the women entered at the east door, and took their seats on the east end, with great form." The Shawnee speaker rose to address the commissioners and urged them to be of good mind; then, holding a string of wampum, he ritually cleared their ears, wiped their eyes, and "removed all sorrow from [their] hearts."[23]

But the American commissioners had little patience with such protocols and were in no mood for conciliation. Richard Butler had been a trader among the Shawnees, spoke their language, and had two children by a Shawnee woman, but he had fought against the Shawnees in 1764. This was also his third treaty council in three years and it was time to wrap things up. Clark had made a name for himself as an Indian fighter during the Revolution; he had led assaults on Shawnee villages in 1780 and 1782 and operated on the assumption that the only thing Indians understood or respected was force. His idea of Indian diplomacy was to hold out a red or black wampum belt in his right hand and a white one in his left and say, "Hear is a Blody [*sic*] Belt and a white one take which one you please."[24] Samuel Parsons, a Harvard graduate, Connecticut lawyer, and former officer in the Continental Army, was intent on opening Indian country to veterans—or to men like himself who bought up the veterans' land bounties at a fraction of their value. The Americans demanded that the Shawnees cede all land east of the Great Miami and give hostages as a guarantee of compliance. The Shawnees protested: "God gave us this country, we do not understand measuring out the lands, it is all ours." They insisted on the Ohio River as the boundary and refused to give hostages. When the Shawnee speaker offered the wampum belt on which he spoke, the American commissioners refused to accept it. Butler picked up the belt "and dashed it on the table." Clark pushed it off the table with his cane and ground it into the dirt with his boot. The Americans then withdrew "and threw down a black and white string" of wampum, symbolizing the choice between war and peace, promising destruction for the Shawnees' women and children if they failed to comply. The Mekoche chief Moluntha urged his people to reconsider. When the council reconvened the Shawnees gave the commissioners a white belt and begged them to have pity on the women and children. They then grudgingly accepted the American terms and ceded their tribal lands east of the Great Miami, which meant they gave up most of southern and eastern Ohio.[25] But the Mekoches did not necessarily speak for the rest of the Shawnees and the treaty did little to restrain Kentucky militia who had become accustomed to crossing the Ohio and attacking Shawnee villages during the Revolution. Before the year was out, Moluntha's village lay in ruins and the old chief lay dead, a Kentuckian's axe in his skull and his fingers still clutching a copy of the treaty he had persuaded his people to sign.

The national assault on Indian homelands got under way more slowly in the South. The southern states posed a more immediate threat than Congress. The United States signed its first treaties with the major southeastern tribes at Hopewell in northwestern South Carolina. US commissioners Benjamin Hawkins, Andrew Pickens, Joseph Martin, and Lachlan McIntosh met with nine hundred Cherokees in November 1785 and then gathered with Choctaw and Chickasaw delegates in January 1786. The Indians produced their British medals and commissions and asked for American ones in exchange. Corn Tassel, the chief of Chota, reminded the Americans that the Indians were the first inhabitants of the land and the white people were now living on it as their friends. "From the beginning of the first friendship between the white and red people, beads were given as an emblem thereof: and these are the beads I give to the commissioners of the United States, as a confirmation of our friendship." The Americans wanted to reaffirm tribal boundaries, but even so Tassel seemed to lose land. He drew a map detailing Cherokee territorial claims, reviewed the treaties they had made, and dismissed the Henderson treaty of 1775 as fraudulent. "I know that Richard Henderson says he purchased the lands at Kentucky and as far south as Cumberland, but he is a rogue and a liar, and if he was here I would tell him so." Henderson had asked only for some grazing land on the Kentucky River; he must have concocted the deed and added the chiefs' names himself. But the commissioners would not budge:

> You know Colonel Henderson, Attacullacula, Oconostoto, are all dead; what you say may be true; but here is one of Henderson's deeds, which points out the line, as you have done, nearly til it strikes Cumberland, thence it runs down the waters of the same to the Ohio, thence up the said river as it meanders to the beginning. Your memory may fail you; this is on record, and will remain forever. The parties being dead, and so much time elapsed since the date of the deed, and the country being settled on the faith of the deed, puts it out of our power to do anything respecting it; you must therefore be content with it, as if you had actually sold it, and proceed to point out your claim exclusive of this land.

Reluctantly, Tassel agreed to "say nothing more about Kentucky, although it is justly ours." The US commissioners read the treaty out loud and the Cherokees then signed it. Georgia and North Carolina had not ceded their western lands to the federal government, and their commissioners and agents who were present immediately lodged a written protest against the treaty as "a manifest and direct attempt to violate the retained sovereignty and legislative right" of their states. The agent for North Carolina was William Blount, whose reputation for land grabbing earned him the name the "dirt king" among the Indians.[26] In the face of state opposition, the federal government lacked the power to honor the boundaries it had reaffirmed. "We have held several treaties with the Americans, when Bounds was always fixt and fair promises always made that the white people Should not come over," Tassel complained three years later, "but we always find that after a treaty they Settle much faster than before."[27]

Choctaw delegates arrived at Hopewell the day after Christmas in 1785 after a seventy-seven-day journey from their Mississippi homeland. In addition to the physical difficulties and dangers they encountered, the delegates also likely traveled at a deliberate and ritualistic peace, as befitted a mission that was both diplomatic and spiritual. They did not go there to give up their land or their sovereignty; they went to talk about trade, establish peaceful relations, and instruct the American commissioners about Choctaw ways of conducting diplomacy.[28] The Americans were not particularly interested in learning Indian protocol. They were interested in Indian land, although they did not yet have the power to coerce compliance with their demands.

As the tribes recovered from the shock of the Peace of Paris, resistance stiffened. Indians who were not present at the treaties dictated by the United States denounced those who were and refused to accept the terms. As 1786 drew to a close, delegates from the Iroquois, Shawnees, Delawares, Hurons, Ojibwes, Potawatomis, Ottawas, Piankeshaws, Weas, Miamis, and Cherokees gathered in council near Detroit and adopted a united stance. In a forceful message to Congress they declared that the previous treaties were invalid and that they would only recognize land cessions "made in the most public manner" and approved by the united tribes.[29]

Faced with the prospect of an all-out war with still-formidable Indian nations, Congress had little choice but to retreat from its high-handed policy of dictating treaties by right of conquest. Knox recommended returning to the British practice of purchasing Indian lands in open council, and the Northwest Ordinance, passed by Congress in 1787, proclaimed that the United States would observe "the utmost good faith" in its dealings with Indian people and that their lands would not be taken from them without their consent or would be invaded except in "just and lawful wars authorized by Congress." But Congress did not retreat very far. The ordinance also laid out a blueprint for national expansion: the Northwest Territory was to be divided into districts that, after passing through territorial status, would become states. Ohio, Indiana, Illinois, Michigan, and Wisconsin eventually entered the Union as states carved from the Northwest Territory. The same year, prepared to purchase Indian claims to lands that had been ceded in the treaties at Forts Stanwix, McIntosh, and Finney, Congress authorized and financed Arthur St. Clair, the newly appointed governor of the Northwest Territory, to convene the tribes in a general council and get them to confirm the land cessions. He was to establish peace with the tribes but not depart from the earlier treaties "unless a change of boundary beneficial to the United States" could be obtained. And while purchasing Indian land was not the primary goal of the treaty, he was not to "neglect any opportunity that may offer of extinguishing the Indian rights to the westward, as far as the river Mississippi." About two hundred Indians met St. Clair at Fort Harmar near present-day Marietta, Ohio, in December 1788. But they demanded the Ohio River be restored as the boundary, making the negotiations "both tedious and troublesome" for St. Clair. He resorted to the haughty language employed by American commissioners in earlier treaties, telling the Indians that Britain had ceded their lands and that the United States was generous in its restraint. He eventually browbeat the delegates into signing. The two treaties signed on January 1789 were, yet again, essentially dictated treaties.[30]

Most of the Indians stayed away from Fort Harmar. They had already had their fill of American treaty making. An Ottawa war chief named Gushgushagwa, Augooshaway, or Egushawa reviewed and denounced the Americans' diplomatic tactics to his Indian listeners a couple of years later. The United States had invaded their country, built forts, assembled the rum-loving Indians, told them a long story about how having conquered the English they had conquered the lands of all the Indians, and then presented them with papers to sign. The Americans had said that their papers, writings, belts, and messages were proof of their desire for peace, but "they were not presented with the dignity which the importance of the subject required, or comformably to the wise customs of our ancestors, but flung at you with threats." Egushawa reminded his audience how the Virginian commissioner at Fort Finney had picked up the Shawnee wampum belt and "threw it off, *contemptuously*, with his cane!" A few Indians from various tribes attended the Fort Harmar treaty, "although their chiefs forbad them; knowing well that our elder brethren would require more of that *pen and ink witch-craft*, which they can make speak things we never intended, or had any idea of, even an hundred years hence; just as they please." The Americans professed to want peace but they were the aggressors, said Egushawa: "notwithstanding their pen and ink work," they attempted "to make dogs of all the nations who have listened to them."[31] Indian resistance, in large measure, was a protest against the treaty-making tactics of the Americans.

As the young nation consolidated its government it established the machinery and basic policies by which it conducted relations and negotiated treaties with the Indian tribes. The US Constitution, adopted in 1789, affirmed federal control over Indian affairs. Article 1 gave Congress the power to regulate commerce with the Indian tribes, and Article 2 authorized the president to make treaties, subject to ratification by a two-thirds majority in the Senate. The secretary of war was responsible for supervising the negotiation of Indian treaties. The president appointed commissioners to carry out negotiations on his behalf, and the commissioners and the Indian leaders signed the treaty. Not all treaties were ratified and Congress modified others—cutting the amount of annuity payments to the Indians, for instance. The revised version of a treaty then had to be taken back to the tribes for acceptance. By the time that happened, things could be very different in Indian country, leaders could have changed, and the original signers would have acquired a rather jaundiced view of American pledges and promises. Once a treaty was ratified, the president signed it. From the initial negotiation to proclamation could take several years.[32]

In 1790 Congress passed the Indian Trade and Intercourse Act. Traders required licenses to operate in Indian country, and transfers of Indian land required congressional approval. The Trade and Intercourse Act was renewed periodically until 1834. In words that must have sounded reminiscent of British assurances after the Proclamation of 1763, George Washington told the Iroquois "the General Government only has the Power to treat with the Indian Nations, and any Treaty formed and held without its Authority will not be binding. Here, then, is the Security for the Remainder of your Lands. No State, nor Person, can purchase your Lands, unless at a general treaty, held under the Authority of the United States."[33]

But frontier settlers, squatters, and speculators seldom shared their government's concern for orderly expansion and individual states, that were often resentful of attempts by the federal government to restrict their rights, sometimes made treaties that never received congressional approval. Like the British imperial administration in 1763, the US government found that proclaiming order on a distant frontier was a far cry from being able to enforce it and restrain its citizens as they flooded Indian lands. Many Federalist leaders were concerned with restoring social order on the frontier in the wake of the bloody Revolutionary War and they wanted to exert the government's authority to ensure a well-ordered national expansion. In that, they shared some common goals with Indian civil or village chiefs; both groups of leaders sought to establish trade and boundaries and to avoid war. But Indian and Federalist leaders also shared similar challenges. Civil chiefs influenced, persuaded, and acted as a check on warriors, but they did not control them. As battle lines hardened, Indian warriors and Indian-hating frontiersmen turned away from the moderate policies of their "civil" leaders. Warriors denounced tactics of accommodation and forged new multitribal resistance movements; frontiersmen denounced leaders who seemed to pander to Indians while American settlers' cabins burned. American citizens embraced the vision of a rapidly expanding agrarian republic and American policies justified taking Indian land by eradicating Indian cultures and hunting economies.[34]

Not everything that went into an Indian treaty appeared in the Constitution. Sometimes the United States resorted to bribes to get the results they wanted. In 1790, Alexander McGillivray led a delegation of Creek chiefs to New York where they signed a treaty in which they ceded most of their lands in Georgia to the United States and the United States guaranteed Creek territorial boundaries. Secret articles in the treaty gave the head chief an annual salary of $1,200 and salaries of $100 each to lesser chiefs.[35] Creek complaints about inadequate representation in the treaties they made with the United States increased, and secret articles became more common.[36] After the Treaty of Holston in July 1791, negotiated with William Blount, governor of the Territory south of the Ohio River and ex-officio superintendent of Indian affairs, Cherokees complained that Blount pressured them into selling land and that the federal negotiators inserted clauses without their knowledge and bribed the interpreter to tell them that the land being ceded was smaller than it actually was and that the payment would be double the amount that was written in the treaty.[37] After their experience with Blount, the Cherokee chief Bloody Fellow asked the secretary of war to "Tell General Washington that the Carolina people ought not to be appointed to hold talks with the Indians, as they always ask for our lands."[38] As Georgia continued to encroach on Creek and Cherokee lands, Creek chiefs in the 1790s worried that if they parted with any more land "at last the white people will not suffer us to keep as much as will be sufficient to bury our dead" and that before long the whites would take "every fork of a creek where there is a little good land ... and every stream of water, where there is a fish to be found."[39]

Despite the bombast of its treaty commissioners, the United States still lacked the military power to crush Indian resistance. The Indian confederacy that formed north of the Ohio repulsed General Josiah Harmar's expedition in 1790 and then, in November 1791, the confederacy shattered an army led by St. Clair, inflicting some nine hundred casualties and effectively destroying the only army the infant republic possessed. It was the biggest single defeat ever inflicted by Indians on the United States and it took the new nation three years to reverse the outcome. With its army reduced to a shambles, the government opted to negotiate, or at least to stall and break down the tribes' united stance while it rebuilt its army. In the summer of 1792, it sent peace feelers via an Iroquois delegation headed by the noted Seneca orator Red Jacket. Almost one thousand Indians from the confederated nations assembled in council on the Auglaize River to hear the Americans' offer. Although Joseph Brant, the Iroquois, and some other groups favored compromise, the western tribes stood firm on maintaining the Ohio River boundary that had been established in 1768. A Shawnee chief named Painted Pole demanded that Red Jacket "speak from your heart and not from your mouth," and, picking up the strings of wampum on which Red Jacket had spoken, he threw them at the feet of the Seneca delegation. The Shawnees had been fighting for the Ohio River boundary for more than twenty years and they would accept no other boundary. The fighting had taken its toll on the authority of their civil chiefs: war leaders sat in front of civil chiefs during the councils and the Mahican emissary Hendrick Aupaumut reported that it was now the Shawnee "custom that the Chief Warriors should be foremost in doing business."[40]

The following year in an abortive peace council at Sandusky in northwestern Ohio matters were not helped by the fact that Simon Girty was interpreting.

Girty, who had been captured by Indians at fourteen and then liberated at the end of the French and Indian War, had built a career in a conflicted ethnic and national borderland on his dual identity, his multilingual skills, and his knowledge of Indian and white cultures. During the Revolution he went over to the British and worked in the Crown's Indian Department, incurring the wrath of Americans who hated him as a renegade who had betrayed both his country and his race. Girty continued to side with the Indians and the British after the Revolution. At one Indian council, according to Secretary of War Henry Knox, "no other white person was admitted but Simon Girty, whom they considered as one of themselves." The Sandusky peace talks had barely gotten under way when a Wyandot chief, with Girty interpreting, told the American commissioners that the Indian delegates would convey their words to their warriors but that the commissioners might as well go home. As the council was breaking up, someone pointed out that the speech had been misinterpreted. Girty modified his translation to say instead that the commissioners should wait for the Indians to consult and give their answer. Girty had earlier vowed "that he would raise hell to prevent peace."[41]

The Indians at Sandusky suggested to the commissioners, rather tongue-in-cheek, that the United States take all the money it was offering the Indians for their lands and all the money expended in raising and paying armies, and divide it among the poor settlers who had been "in continual trouble ever since they cross the Ohio," so they would happily go back to where they came from. The commissioners were not amused. The Indians also rejected the premises on which the United States claimed their land:

> We never made any agreement with the King, nor with any other nation, that we would give to either the exclusive right of purchasing our lands; and we declare to you, that we consider ourselves free to make any bargain or cession of lands, whenever and to whomever we please. If the white people, as you say, made a treaty that none of them but the King should purchase of us, and that he has given that right to the United States, it is an affair which concerns you and him, and not us: we have never parted with such a power.

The federal government rejected (and the Supreme Court in *Johnson v. McIntosh* later explicitly denied) the Indians' assertion that they could sell their lands to whomever they pleased, and the commissioners at Sandusky were adamant: "it is impossible to make the river Ohio the boundary, between your people and the people of the United States." The Indians were equally adamant: "Look back, and review the lands from whence we have been driven to this spot," they said; "We can retreat no further." With negotiations at an impasse, the commissioners departed. The Indians had only themselves to blame for the continuing war, they reported. As the commissioners withdrew, General Anthony Wayne advanced with his rebuilt American army.[42] In August 1794 Wayne defeated the confederated tribes at the Battle of Fallen Timbers.

Word of the battle reached US treaty commissioner Colonel Timothy Pickering and the Iroquois at Canandaigua. Pickering, a veteran of the Revolutionary War, had been assigned a double task: keep the Six Nations, especially the Senecas, from joining the western confederacy, and obtain unconditional surrender of any Iroquois claims to land in the Ohio Valley. He had been educated at Harvard, but he learned about doing business in Indian country from Red Jacket, who had matched him in two previous meetings and lectured him on proper council protocol.[43] More than 1,500 Iroquois, including Red Jacket, Cornplanter, Handsome Lake, and other prominent leaders, gathered at Canandaigua in the fall of 1794. At the invitation of both President Washington and the Iroquois, four Quakers attended the treaty as observers, and three of them kept journals, in which they recorded both Iroquois and American perspectives on the proceedings. The treaty dragged on for almost two months with frequent delays and adjournments. Red Jacket conveyed the sentiments of the Iroquois women, who insisted that their voices be heard because "it was they who made the Men, [and] altho' they did not sit in council, yet that they were acquainted from time to time with the transactions at the Treaties." At one point, irritated that Pickering was busy writing down what he was saying, Red Jacket stopped and "would not proceed until he looked him in the face." The Quakers William Savery and James Emlen both commented on the need for patience. "It is to no purpose to say you are tired of waiting," explained Savery, "they will only tell you very calmly, Brother, you have your way of doing business, and we have ours; we desire you would sit easy on your seats. Patience then becomes our only remedy." Emlen reflected: "Perhaps no people are greater masters of their time, hence in their public transactions we often complain of their being tedious, not considering that they & we estimate time with very diff[eren]t. judgm[en]ts—we are very apt to condemn any natural practices that differ from our own but it requires a greater conquest over prejudices & more penetration than I am Master of clearly to say that we are the happier people."[44]

Pickering was there to appease the Iroquois. He told them his principal purpose was "to heal the wounds which have been given by disposing of your lands, and to point out the way in which you can avoid future strife." The Oneidas had seen their homeland shrink from five or six million acres to one-quarter of a million acres and the recurrent land losses divided their nation. "Brother," one said, "you requested that we would lay before you the whole cause of our difference: *I repeat, that is our land.*"[45] An Oneida chief named Onondiyo (or Captain John) "had much to say about the many deceptions which had been practiced upon them by the white people; observing that however good and honest white men might be in other matters, they were all deceivers when they wanted to buy Indian lands; and that the advantages of learning which they possessed made them capable of doing much good and much evil." The Iroquois were particularly incensed by the intimidation and deception at Fort Stanwix ten years earlier, although Pickering explained to the Quakers that the lands they ceded constituted just compensation for siding with Britain during the Revolutionary War. "He instanced the case of an individual who had committed a trespass on another; the law determines that the trespasser shall suffer either in person or in property, and this law is just. Such," added Savery, "is the reasoning of conquerors."[46]

Pickering acknowledged that some white people had imposed on the Indians, exploiting their ignorance in computing the value of their lands, plying them with alcohol, and getting them to sign papers that had not been properly interpreted. Sometimes the interpreters deliberately deceived; sometimes their interpretations were not exact because Indian languages lacked the words to express the terms used in treaties, which even few white people understood. "You ought never to set your hands to a paper unless the interpreters first say, in the presence of the Great Spirit, that they have faithfully interpreted every word," Pickering advised. "If this were done, brothers, such papers would contain but a few words; and the fewer words the less danger of you being deceived. But I must not enlarge on these matters." For Pickering, the best way for the Iroquois "to avoid future strife" was to adopt white ways so they could match whitemen and to become literate so they could avoid being cheated.[47]

But the short-term goal was to keep the Iroquois out of the war that was winding down in the West. When the Treaty of Canandaigua was finally signed, the United States confirmed Oneida, Cayuga, and Onondaga lands in New York; restored lands to the Senecas; and promised never to disturb them "in the free use and enjoyment thereof." Fifty sachems signed the treaty.[48] Three weeks later, Pickering signed a second treaty with the Oneidas, awarding them, and their Stockbridge and Tuscarora allies, compensation for their services to the United States during the Revolution. Washington recognized Pickering's peace-keeping diplomacy by promoting him to replace Henry Knox as secretary of war, but Philip Schulyer and other powerful New Yorkers continued to erode the Iroquois homeland in defiance of federal law and federal treaties.[49]

In August 1795, the western Indians assembled at Greenville to make peace with Wayne (see figure 3.1). Wayne opened the councils in customary fashion—"I have cleared the ground of all brush and rubbish, and opened roads to the east, to the west, to the north, and to the south, that all nations may come in safety and ease to meet me," he announced. He stated that he adhered to the protocol of the calumet and wampum belt "to evince that my mind and heart

FIGURE 3.1 **"Indian Treaty of Greenville,"** Ohio, 1795. *Artist unknown; believed to be Officer of General Wayne's staff. (Chicago History Museum [ICHi-64806])*

are always the same."[50] The American officers and commissioners maintained a façade of civility in dealing with the Indians and the Indians still attempted to establish social obligations with the Americans.[51] New Corn, a Potawatomi chief, asked Wayne to replace the Indians' old medals, which they had received from their former British allies, with General Washington's medals. They had "thrown off the British" and henceforward would regard the Americans as their only true friends. "The Great Spirit has made me a great chief, and endowed me with great power," said New Corn. "The heavens and earth are my heart, the rising sun my mouth." He knew that other people had made and broken treaties but he was "too honorable and too brave a man to be guilty of such unworthy conduct." The Great Spirit heard what he said and he dared not tell a lie. He asked Wayne, "the Great Wind," not to deceive the Indians as the French, British, and Spaniards had done but to keep his promises. "My friend," he concluded, "I am old, but I shall never die. I shall always live in my children, and children's children." And he handed Wayne a string of wampum.[52]

But lofty rhetoric and respectful relationships could not mask the marked shift in power: Wayne effectively dictated the terms and presented the Indians with a prepared treaty for signing. Sixty-nine chiefs, including Little Turtle of the Miamis, and Black Hoof and Blue Jacket of the Shawnees who had fought to defend the Ohio boundary since before the Revolution, acknowledged that the fight was lost and ceded most of Ohio to the United States. Egushawa, who had denounced treaties as "pen and ink witchcraft," signed this one.[53] The war for the boundary established at Fort Stanwix in 1768 was finally over.

Even as Little Turtle and Wayne negotiated a new boundary between Indians and whites, the individual who stood beside them translating their words reflected the porous nature of such boundaries. William Wells had been captured by the Miamis as a boy, married Little Turtle's daughter, and apparently "went Indian." He participated in raids against frontier settlements, helped lure travelers on the Ohio River into ambushes, and had fought against both Harmar and St. Clair. Then he left the Miamis, enlisted as a scout in Wayne's army in the Fallen Timbers campaign, and was at the treaty as one of the team of interpreters. Seventeen years later, Wells would escort the garrison and families as they evacuated Fort Dearborn (present-day Chicago) at the beginning of the War of 1812. Dressed as an Indian with his face painted black as was the Miami custom when confronting certain death, Wells was killed by attacking Potawatomi warriors, who cut off his head and tore out his heart.[54]

The Greenville boundary was no more effective in checking American expansion than the Proclamation Line of 1763 or the Fort Stanwix boundary had been. "Scarcely anything short of a Chinese Wall, or a line of Troops will restrain Land Jobbers, and the Incroachment of Settlers, upon the Indian Territory," said George Washington.[55] Treaties increased dramatically in number and frequency—more than two hundred between 1795 and 1840 and sometimes every couple of years with the same tribes. Just three years after the Treaty of Canaidaigua, Red Jacket, Cornplanter, and other Seneca chiefs agreed to the Treaty of Big Tree, which ceded millions of acres of land west of the Genesee River and effectively reduced the Seneca homeland to eleven parcels. Red Jacket received a cash payment for his compliance. Although he later took a strong stand against further reductions of Seneca land, many Senecas remember him for the land-sale treaties he signed and depict him as "as a man condemned by the Creator to push a dirt-filled wheelbarrow up a hill for eternity."[56] Treaty making became land marketing, and some Indians were active participants; they sold off chunks of tribal land to finance consumption of new goods and pay off old debts, and some used treaties as a way to enter the land market and make money on the one valuable commodity they possessed.[57]

Treaties were the key instruments in the recurrent dispossession of Indians as the United States pushed steadily westward. In the winter of 1802–3, President Thomas Jefferson told Delaware and Shawnee delegates in Washington that he would "pay the most sacred regard to existing treaties between your respective nations and ours, and protect your whole territories against all intrusions that may be attempted by white people." At the same time, Jefferson was implementing plans to deprive the Indians of their lands. Jefferson and others easily solved the dilemma of how to deal honorably with Indians (as they said they would) while at the same time taking their lands (as they knew they must); they determined that having too much land was a disincentive for Indians to become "civilized." Ignoring the role of agriculture in Eastern Woodland societies, Jefferson argued that Indians would continue to hunt rather than settle down as farmers unless their options were restricted. Taking their lands forced Indians into a settled, agricultural, and "civilized" way of life and was therefore, in the long run, good for them. As Indians took up farming, Jefferson wrote in 1803 to William Henry Harrison, the governor of Indiana Territory, "they will perceive how useless to them are their extensive forests, and will be willing to pare them off from time to time in exchange for necessaries for their farms and families." To promote this process "we shall push our trading houses, and be glad to see the good and influential individuals run into debt, because we observe that when these debts get beyond what the individuals can pay, they become willing to lop them off by a cession of lands." In this way, American settlements would gradually surround the Indians "and they will in time either incorporate with us as citizens of the United States, or remove beyond the Mississippi." The process of dispossession could be comfortably accomplished within Jefferson's philosophy of minimal government. The government could do little to regulate the frontier and protect Indian lands, which meant that the Indians would fight for their land. The government would then have no choice but to invade Indian country, suppress the uprising, and dictate treaties in which defeated Indians signed away land. The stage was then set for the process to repeat itself. Jefferson's strategy for acquiring Indian lands resulted in some thirty treaties with a dozen or so tribal groups and the cession of almost two hundred thousand square miles of Indian territory in nine states. Jefferson regretted that Indians seemed doomed to extinction, but he had little compunction about taking away their lands.[58]

Traders were willing participants in Jefferson's strategy. The Scottish traders William Panton and John Forbes, who continued to dominate Indian trade in the Southeast after the Revolution, knew all about leveraging Indian debts to secure Indian lands—they'd been doing it for years—and readily collaborated with the United States. They bought at discount the debts individual hunters owed small traders and then aggregated them into one lump sum. By 1803, the southeastern tribes owed John Forbes and Company $192,526 (the Creeks alone owed $113,000). The United States compelled the Creeks to cede millions of acres, in exchange for which it paid off some of the traders' debts. In 1805, the traders exerted their influence among the Choctaws, Chickasaws, Cherokees, and Upper Creeks to help secure the cession of almost eight million acres.

The United States paid the tribes a total of $380,000 in money and goods, of which more than $77,000 went to Forbes and Company to settle the Indians' debts. Eventually, the company recouped all but a little under $7,000 of the original debt. In this way, "thousands of small, face-to-face exchanges between traders and hunters were transmuted by a multinational company and an expanding nation-state into massive land cessions that affected an entire people."[59] At the Treaty of Mount Dexter in 1805, for instance, Choctaws ceded more than four million acres of land in southern Mississippi and southwestern Alabama to the United States for $50,500. Of that amount, $48,000 went to pay off their debts to traders. The remaining $2,500 went to the interpreter, John Pitchlynn, "to compensate him for certain losses sustained in the Chaktaw country, and as a grateful testimonial of the nation's esteem." (Pitchlynn, who had interpreted in the Choctaws' first treaty with the United States twenty years earlier, was long recognized as a "friend to the United States" who could exert influence over the tribe.) The Choctaws were left with $3,000 a year in trade goods.[60] Such arrangements became common in US treaty making and trader-creditors became regular attendees at treaty councils.

United States commissioners in the first decade of the nineteenth century held treaties with individual tribes, or groups from several tribes, and pressured them into exchanging land for cash, annuities, or trade goods. These tactics yielded millions of acres of land in Ohio, Indiana, Michigan, and Illinois. The Treaty of St. Louis in 1804 stood out as infamous even by the treaty-making standards of the time. Sauk and Fox (Mesquakie) delegates signed away a huge swath of tribal lands for $1,000. The Sauk war chief Black Hawk denounced the treaty and said the delegates were "drunk the greater part of the time they were in St. Louis." A dozen years later he unwittingly confirmed the deal: "Here, for the first time, I touched the goose quill to the treaty," he recalled in later life, "not knowing, however, that by that act, I consented to give away my village. Had that been explained to me, I should have opposed it, and never would have signed their treaty." As far as Black Hawk was concerned, he could not have sold the land even if he had wanted to: "my reason teaches me that land cannot be sold. The Great Spirit gave it to his children to live upon, and cultivate, as far as is necessary for their subsistence; and so long as they occupy and cultivate it, they have the right to the soil....Nothing can be sold, but such things as can be carried away."[61]

As governor of Indiana territory, William Henry Harrison built his career on advancing Jefferson's policies of national expansion and Indian dispossession.[62] He exploited divisions within and among the tribes, coercing one tribe into signing by threatening to cut a better deal with another; he bribed compliant chiefs, and he ignored or rode roughshod over the reciprocal obligations that treaty making entailed and the pledges that treaties established. At the Treaty of Fort Wayne with Delawares, Potawatomis, Miamis, and members of the Eel River tribes in September 1809, the Miamis resisted Harrison's demands and a chief named Owl insisted that the United States pay the going rate for their land—about $2 per acre. Such a price was totally unacceptable to Harrison. He withheld annuities due under previous treaties until this one was signed, and he injected alcohol into the proceedings to move negotiations along. The Miami position became untenable and in the end the United States acquired almost three million acres for less than two cents an acre. The Shawnee chief Tecumseh called it a "whiskey treaty." Harrison told the secretary of war that the treaty terms were "just to all" and he assured the Indians that the United States would always adhere to their agreements: "To do otherwise would be offensive to the great spirit and all the world would look upon them as a faithless people."[63] Harrison became president in 1840.

Indians understood how American treaty makers operated, even if they found it hard to do anything about it. Wyandots at Detroit in February 1812 sent a message to the president and Congress:

Fathers, Listen! We can assure you in sincerity and truth, how the thing is conducted at all treaties. When the United States want a particular piece of land, all our nations are assembled; a large sum of money is offered; the land is occupied probably by one nation only; nine-tenths have no actual interest in the land wanted; if the particular nation interested refuses to sell, they are generally threatened by others, who want the money or goods offered, to buy whiskey.[64]

Such treaty-making tactics fueled the cause of the Tecumseh, who denounced the American practice of making treaties with individual tribes, and added urgency to the idea that Indian land belonged to all the tribes and could be ceded only with their unanimous consent. Tecumseh's vision was to create a united and independent Indian state in what was to become the heartland of the United States. A boundary line between Indians and whites like that implemented in 1763 and reaffirmed in 1768 became a dream for Indian freedom fighters in the first decade of the nineteenth century. Tecumseh's resistance movement attracted warriors from more than thirty tribes but his vision ended with his death in battle in 1813. The men who killed him, and according to some accounts stripped the skin from his body, were Kentuckians, who had grown up on the dark and bloody grounds opened up by the Treaty of Fort Stanwix in 1768.

In the South, Upper Creek towns tended to favor adopting a militant stance in dealing with the United States; Lower Creek towns tended to advocate peace and accommodation. Conflicts within the Creek confederacy spilled over into attacks on American settlers, and the United States responded with swift military action against the militant Creeks or "Red Sticks." In the Creek War of 1813–14 General Andrew Jackson led a series of devastating campaigns that culminated in the slaughter of some eight hundred Creek warriors at the Battle of Tohopeka, or Horseshoe Bend, on the Tallapoosa River in present-day Alabama in March 1814. About five hundred Cherokees and one hundred Lower Creeks helped Jackson win his victory. But Jackson paid no attention to former allies as he drove to acquire Indian land. At the Treaty of Fort Jackson in 1814, the future president met with thirty-five pro-American Creek chiefs and exacted retribution and "just indemnity" for the expenses of the war. As Jackson made clear to the secretary of war, this was not to be a negotiated peace: "The Commissioners appointed to make a treaty with the Creeks will have little to do but assign them their proper limits. Those of the friendly party, who have associated with me, will be easily satisfied; and the remainder of the hostile party, pleased that their lives were spared them, will thankfully accept, as a bounteous donation, any district which may be allowed them for their future settlement." The first article of the treaty began with the words "The United States demand." Jackson took twenty-three million acres in Georgia and Alabama, the biggest single land cession in southeastern Indian history, and most of it from "friendly" Creeks who had helped him win his victories.[65] Meanwhile, the end of the War of 1812 effectively removed Great Britain as an ally of Indian nations in the Southeast. The way was open for the United States and the expanding cotton kingdom to advance across the Old Southwest. Nations like the Choctaws who in the past had successfully played off rival colonial powers now had to deal only with the United States; Indians who had formerly traded deerskins now found increasingly that Americans wanted only their lands. They took those lands in treaty after treaty, but increasingly the federal government, and Jackson in particular, resorted to force rather than "the old norms of negotiation." As Leonard Sadosky notes, "The forms remained the same, but the realities of power behind them were very different."[66]

As the cotton kingdom and its slave labor force expanded across the South, treaties generated more and more cessions of Indian land. Southern cotton fed the mills of northern England and New England, and southeastern lands were too valuable to be left in Indian hands. Americans increasingly demanded the occupation of all Indian lands. In 1803 American emissaries in Paris had purchased the Louisiana Territory—some 827,000 square miles of territory between the Mississippi and the Rocky Mountains for a mere $15 million— and the United States doubled its size overnight. Many Americans saw the West as barren and virtually empty, useless for American farmers but good enough for Indian hunters. Removing Indians from the East was now a practical possibility. American treaty makers began pressuring Indian people to cede their lands in exchange for new lands west of the Mississippi. As American

pressures and market forces undermined traditional social and economic structures, Indians seemed to face a choice between destitution and removal, and
many Indians chose the latter. In 1817, Cherokees gave up two large tracts of
land in Georgia and North Carolina in exchange for land in Arkansas. In 1820,
Andrew Jackson bullied and threatened Choctaw chiefs into making a treaty
at Doak's Stand, ceding lands in Mississippi and accepting lands in the West
in return. Ten years later, at the Treaty of Dancing Rabbit Creek, US commissioners told the Choctaws that if they refused to move west, they would be
made subject to Mississippi state law and lose their existence as a tribe. Some
Choctaws remained in Mississippi but most headed west.

In 1825 the Creek chief William McIntosh and a handful of minor chiefs
signed the Treaty of Indian Springs, giving up all remaining Creek lands in
Georgia between the Flint and Chattahoochee rivers. In return the United States
paid $400,000 to "the emigrating nation," of which $200,000 went directly to
McIntosh and the treaty signers. McIntosh had led the pro-American faction
of the Lower Creeks in the Creek War, fought alongside Andrew Jackson at
the Battle of Horseshoe Bend, and signed the Treaty of Fort Jackson that confiscated two-thirds of *all* Creek land. McIntosh grew wealthy through a series
of shady land deals, and he engineered further cessions of Creek lands into
American hands. In addition to the Treaty of Fort Jackson, he signed treaties
with the Americans in 1805, in 1818, and twice in 1821. He overreached in the
Treaty of Indian Springs, which blatantly flouted a recent tribal law that made
selling tribal lands a capital offense. Despite protests from the Creeks against
such "base treachery," abundant evidence of fraud, and a warning from the
Indian agent that ratification might "produce a horrid state of things among
these unfortunate Indians," the Senate ratified the treaty. Creek warriors acting on the orders of the Creek National Council assassinated McIntosh for
treason.[67]

Removal treaties secured millions of acres in the North as well. Charles
Latrobe, a traveling Englishman of Huguenot descent (and later the first lieu-
tenant-governor of Victoria in Australia), stopped off at Chicago in the fall of
1833 while a treaty was being negotiated with the Potawatomis. Latrobe found
the "little mushroom town" "crowded to excess." Six thousand Indians camped
on the prairie around the town. Gaudily dressed and painted warriors were
accompanied by wives, children, ponies, and dogs; groups of older chiefs sat
around smoking and talking; local merchants dispensed their wares; and whiskey flowed freely. In addition to "emigrants and land speculators as numerous
as the sand," there were

> horse-dealers, and horse-stealers, rogues of every description, white,
> black, brown, and red—half-breeds, quarter breeds, and men of no breed
> at all;—dealers in pigs, poultry, and potatoes;—men pursuing Indian

claims, . . . creditors of the tribes, or of particular Indians, who know that they have no chance of getting their money, if they do not get it from the Government agents;—sharpers of every degree; pedlars, grog-sellers; Indian agents and Indian traders of every description, and Contractors to supply the Pottawattomies with food. The little village was in uproar from morning to night, and from night to morning.

Latrobe saw casks of whiskey "for sale under the very nose of the Commissioners" and drunken Indians everywhere. "Who will believe that any act, however formally executed by the chiefs, is valid, as long as it is known that whiskey was one of the parties to the treaty"? Watching the proceedings, Latrobe concluded "that the business of arranging the terms of an Indian Treaty, whatever it might have been two hundred years ago, . . . now lies chiefly between the various traders, agents, creditors, and half-breeds of the tribes" on whom the chiefs had become dependent and the government agents. The Potawatomis signed the treaty and gave up the last of their lands on the Great Lakes, some five million acres in present-day northern Illinois and Wisconsin, in exchange for an equal quantity on the Missouri and $1 million in removal expenses and support, part of which, $175,000 to be precise, went to paying off debts to traders and other creditors.[68]

Amid such chaos and confusion, Indian homelands became American real estate. Pressured by American demands and divided by American tactics, Ojibwe, Potawatomi, and Ottawa leaders signed away thousands of acres of land around the Great Lakes in the 1820s and 1830s. The Potawatomis held the unfortunate record: they signed a treaty each year from 1826 to 1829, two treaties in 1832, the Chicago treaty in 1833, four treaties in 1834, nine in 1836 (!), and another in 1837.[69] The pressure on the Iroquois also continued in the nineteenth century as politicians, transportation interests, and land speculators conspired to divest them of their lands, and canals, railroads, the massive influx of settlers, and the rapid growth of cities transformed Iroquoia. In 1826, under pressure from the Ogden Land Company, the federal government made a treaty with the Senecas, which the US Senate never ratified, taking thousands of acres. A dozen years later, sixteen Seneca chiefs signed another treaty at Buffalo Creek, "one of the major frauds in American Indian history," but nonetheless ratified by the Senate. Coerced by threats, bribery, and alcohol, they agreed to sell their remaining lands in New York to the Ogden Land Company, to give up their four reservations, and to move to Kansas. Commissioner Ransom H. Gillet induced more chiefs to sign their agreement after the treaty council.[70]

Despite the bribes, whiskey, intimidation, and divide-and-conquer tactics, Indians did not succumb easily or go quietly. Time and again in treaty negotiations they cited chapter and verse from earlier treaties and requested redress for agreements not met and payments not made.[71] In 1820, a chief named Sassaba kicked away the gifts of tobacco that American officials placed on the ground before the Ojibwe delegation, by the same action rejecting the Americans' request for a land cession.[72] Ojibwe, Potawatomi, and Ottawa leaders learned that the United States could not be trusted to honor its treaty commitments; they became acquainted with American business and financial practices and in subsequent meetings often kept American treaty commissioners on the defensive with pointed questions about long-overdue payments. They spoke out against boundaries and land cessions; they resisted attempts to divide their nations, and at the same time frustrated efforts to consolidate or conflate different bands into a single polity capable of making comprehensive land cessions; they articulated their nationhood on their own terms, stressing kinship and alliances, and pointed to the autonomy of individual bands who had multiple and overlapping claims to the lands being negotiated.[73] At the Treaty of Dancing Rabbit Creek, seven Choctaw elder women sat in the center of a circle comprising some sixty Choctaw councilmen, the US commissioners, and other persons involved in the negotiations. The women freely expressed their opinions and one of them threatened to cut open with a butcher knife a Choctaw man who agreed to sell the Choctaws' land and move west. The US commissioners chose to make no mention of the presence or participation of the Choctaw women in their formal record of the treaty.[74]

And the Senecas fought a "heroic battle" against the fraudulent Treaty of Buffalo Creek of 1838. Even while he was still a student at Dartmouth College, Seneca Maris Bryant Pierce helped wage a campaign to have the treaty overturned. He gave speeches, wrote a letter to President Van Buren, organized petitions to the Senate, and traveled to Washington as part of a delegation to present their case to the secretary of war. Despite the protests, the Senate ratified and the president proclaimed the treaty, but the Senecas kept up their efforts to renegotiate it. An amended treaty, signed in 1842, fell far short of meeting their expectations, but it did preserve a foothold in their homeland. The Senecas regained the Allegany and Cattaraugus reservations but not Buffalo Creek and Tonawanda (although the Tonawanda Senecas were "allowed" to buy back a small portion of their reservation in 1857).[75]

And the Cherokees turned their fight against removal into a national debate in print, in Congress, and in the Supreme Court.

New Echota, 1835

IMPLEMENTING REMOVAL

In the 1830s, the Cherokee Indians of Georgia, Tennessee, and North Carolina became the focus of a national debate and the test case in a number of interrelated issues: Would the United States honor its Indian treaties—described in the Constitution as the supreme law of the land? Did Indians' treaty rights trump state rights? What was the status of an Indian nation within state boundaries? Was there indeed a place for Indian people in American society? For many Americans, Native and white alike, these questions were vital to the future growth and moral character of the young nation. The Treaty of New Echota provided the answers. Four days after Christmas in 1835, in an action illegal under Cherokee law, twenty Cherokees signed away the tribal homeland in exchange for $5 million and lands in the West. Ratified by the Senate and signed by the president in clear defiance of the will of the majority of Cherokee people, the Treaty of New Echota raised a storm of protest among Americans as well as Cherokees but it gave the United States justification to relocate the Cherokees beyond the Mississippi. As many as four thousand Cherokees died on the resulting Trail of Tears. The key signers, as they knew they might, perished at the hands of fellow Cherokees. The Treaty of New Echota plunged the Cherokee Nation into enduring internal conflict and stands as an enduring indictment of a nation that broke treaties and trust to implement a policy of ethnic cleansing.

Renaissance to Removal

The Cherokees had had plenty of experience with treaties, both fair and fraudulent. From their first treaty with South Carolina in 1721 to the Treaty of New Echota in 1835, the eastern Cherokees negotiated thirty-eight treaties with Britain, colonial governments, states, and the United States and "refused almost yearly to negotiate other agreements."[1] By 1835 Cherokee territory was a fraction of what it had once been (see figure 4.1).

Despite escalating pressure on their lands, the Cherokees experienced a renaissance after the devastation of the American Revolution. They rebuilt their economy, remodeled their society, and sustained their national identity and sovereignty in a world increasingly dominated by Americans. Many Cherokee males made the transition from hunting to agriculture; some had prosperous farmsteads; some owned plantations and slaves.[2] Many Cherokees displayed more of the attributes of supposedly "civilized" society than did the American frontiersmen who were so eager to occupy their lands. A census conducted in 1825 showed that Cherokees owned 33 gristmills, 13 sawmills, one powder mill, 69 blacksmith shops, two tanyards, 762 looms, 2,486 spinning wheels, 172 wagons, 2,923 plows, 7,683 horses, 22,531 cattle, 46,732 pigs, and 2,566 sheep. The

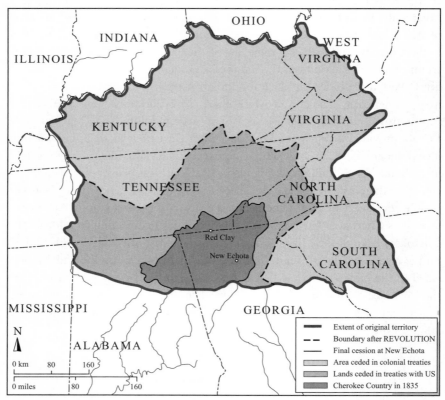

FIGURE 4.1 **The Cherokee Homeland by 1835.** *(Adapted from James Mooney, Nineteenth Annual Report of the Bureau of American Ethnology, 1897–98 [Washington, D.C.: Government Printing Office, 1900], plate 2, and Francis Paul Prucha, Atlas of American Indian Affairs [Lincoln: University of Nebraska Press, 1990], map 23)*

Cherokees seemed to be doing everything the United States required of them to take their place in the new nation as a self-supporting republic of farmers.

In fact, Cherokee society was a mixture of change and tradition, and the new developments also created fracture lines—younger Cherokees generally favored more rapid acculturation than did the older generations; wealthy Cherokees participated in the market economy, spoke English, and "got ahead," whereas the majority of Cherokees retained an economy based on subsistence, kinship, and communal sharing. As more southeastern Indians became slaveholders, many Cherokees adopted increasingly racial attitudes toward Africans that conflicted with traditional notions of kinship. James Vann, a Cherokee chief, established a plantation and a manor and by 1809 owned more than one hundred slaves, which not only made him probably the wealthiest man in the Cherokee Nation but also placed him among the elite of southern planters. Vann bought and sold slaves and by all accounts treated them as harshly as any white slaveowner. Following the black codes in most southern states, the Cherokee Council in the 1820s began to adopt a code of laws to regulate black slaves.[3]

Cherokees who adopted American ways did not necessarily abandon Cherokee ways and values. Born at Hiwassee in Tennessee in 1771, the chief known as The Ridge (an abbreviation of the translation of his Cherokee name Kahmungdaclageh, "the Man Who Walks on the Mountaintop or Ridge") had fought against Americans as a teenager, but by the first decade of the nineteenth century he was taking up the life of a small southern planter (see figure 4.2). He also rose in influence as a member of the Cherokee National Council and took the lead in defending what remained of the Cherokee homeland. In August 1807, Ridge was one of three men appointed to carry out the execution of Doublehead, an overbearing chief who had grown rich selling Cherokee lands and accepting American bribes. He had received cash and lands from the Americans for his role in brokering two treaties in 1805. Ridge shot Doublehead through the jaw, and the assassins finished him off with knives and tomahawks.[4] Soon after, Ridge was appointed to the Lighthorse Guard, two six-man companies charged with "riding the judicial circuit" to enforce the laws of the Cherokee nation as "the judges, jurors, and executioners of justice."[5] In the Creek War of 1813–14, Ridge fought alongside Andrew Jackson's forces, as did fellow Cherokees John Ross and Stand Watie. At the Battle of Horseshoe Bend, Ridge and the Cherokees led the encircling movement that trapped the Creek warriors after Jackson's forces had breached their defenses.[6] Ridge kept his military rank of major after the war but Jackson paid no attention to former allies as he drove to acquire Indian land.

Some Cherokees had begun moving west voluntarily as early as the 1790s and the trickle continued. In face of growing pressures, however, Cherokees who remained in the East adopted a harder line on land sales. In 1809, the

FIGURE 4.2 **Major Ridge.** *(From History of the Indian tribes of North America, with biographical sketches and anecdotes of the principal chiefs. Embellished with one hundred and twenty portraits, from the Indian Gallery in the Department of War, at Washington, by Thomas L. McKenney and James Hall, 3 vols. [Philadelphia: J. T. Bowen, 1848–50], Dartmouth College, Rauner Library)*

Cherokee National Council established a thirteen-member national committee to manage the Nation's affairs; the next year the council declared that Cherokees who had emigrated to the West were guilty of treason and had forfeited their citizenship. In 1817 the Cherokees drew up "Articles of Government," a written constitution providing for election and terms of membership for the national committee. Major Ridge joined sixty-six other chiefs in signing a remonstrance against the policy of Indian removals. Dealing with colonial males who expected to deal only with men and whose interests focused on war and trade had given Cherokee women a less direct voice in the Nation's affairs than they had exercised in the early eighteenth century, but they, too, were adamant that there be no more land sales: "keep your hands off of paper talks," they advised the National Council. Jackson managed to push through land cession treaties in 1817 and 1819, which provided for equivalent amounts of land for those Cherokees who had migrated to Arkansas, but there were no more land sales after that. By the 1820s, Ridge and the Cherokees were committed to selling "not one more foot of land."[7]

Major Ridge served with Jackson again—in 1818 he led a company of seventy-two Cherokees in Jackson's Seminole campaign, technically an invasion of Spanish Florida[8]—but he continued to resist the American assault on tribal lands. In 1823 John Ross exposed the venal Creek chief William McIntosh for offering the Cherokees bribes to sell their lands. Ridge, as speaker of the council, denounced his former comrade-in-arms and "cast him behind my back." Two years later, when the Creek National Council condemned McIntosh to death for the Treaty of Indian Springs, Ridge approved of the execution.[9]

Indian agents Amos Kendall and Samuel C. Stambaugh, who knew Major Ridge and took his side in the conflicts that were to divide the Cherokee Nation, described him as "a man of great bravery, strong intellect, and, though uneducated, clearly comprehending the interests of his people, and zealously devoted to them."[10] Ridge knew that providing the next generation with the education he lacked would be the key to Cherokee survival. He and his wife, Sehoya, also called Susanna Wickett, had four children (another baby died). In 1810, Nancy, the eldest, and the second child, seven-year-old John, enrolled in the Moravian mission school at Springplace where John remained until he turned eleven. After a stint with a private tutor, in 1817 Ridge enrolled John and Nancy in the Brainerd mission of the Boston-based American Board of Commissioners for Foreign Missions (ABCFM). The Rev. Elias Cornelius selected John (figure 4.3) and his cousin Galagina or Buck Watie (figure 4.4) to attend the Foreign Mission School in Cornwall, Connecticut, a school established by the ABCFM to educate young men from indigenous cultures around the world so they could return them to their people as preachers, translators, teachers, and health workers. In the fall of 1818 the two young Cherokees set off for New England. Buck Watie adopted the name of Elias Boudinot, the president of the American Bible Society and former member of the Continental Congress, who sponsored him during his first year at the school.[11] (Buck's younger brother, on the other hand, dropped his Christian name, Isaac, in favor of his Cherokee name, Dagdoga, "He Stands," and thereafter became known as Stand Watie.) Suffering from recurrent ill health because of a scrofulous hip, John was cared for in the home of the school steward and by the steward's daughter, Sarah Bird Northrup. At one point, John's health reached such a critical point that his father rode north

JOHN RIDGE.

A CHEROKEE

Lith.d Col.d & Published by J.T. Bowen, Philad.a

FIGURE 4.3 **John Ridge.** *(From History of the Indian tribes of North America, with biographical sketches and anecdotes of the principal chiefs. Embellished with one hundred and twenty portraits, from the Indian Gallery in the Department of War, at Washington, by Thomas L. McKenney and James Hall, 3 vols. [Philadelphia: J. T. Bowen, 1848–50], Dartmouth College, Rauner Library)*

to see him. "With his instinct for the proper impression, he hired for the last lap of his journey a coach-and-four, 'the most splendid carriage...that ever entered the town'" and during his two-week stay he cut a striking figure in his white-topped boots and gold-braided military uniform.[12]

Impressed as they were with the Cherokees, however, the citizens of Cornwall shared the prejudices of their time. Both Ridge and Boudinot fell in love with white girls. In January 1824 Ridge married Sarah Bird Northrup; two years later, Boudinot married Harriet Ruggles Gold. The racist outrage in the community

FIGURE 4.4 **Buck Watie, a.k.a. Elias Boudinot.** *(Research Division of the Oklahoma Historical Society)*

was so extreme—a mob burned Boudinot and Harriet in effigy on the village green—that the ABCFM closed the school in 1826.[13] Giving speeches in cities throughout the eastern United States to raise money for a printing press, Boudinot spread the word among church groups and other interested parties that the Cherokees were a "rapidly improving...industrious and intelligent people." They had two choices: "they must either become civilized and happy, or sharing the fate of many kindred nations, become extinct."[14] But the events at Cornwall altered Boudinot's thinking: the Cherokees must develop their own "civilized" institutions, but they would do so to preserve their Cherokee identity and strengthen the Cherokee Nation, no longer with the expectation that they would earn an equal place in American society.[15]

The Ridges, father and son, built themselves fine homes that reflected their growing prosperity and their position as members of the Cherokee elite. At Ridge's Ferry on the Oostanaula River, in what is today Rome, Georgia, Major Ridge built a two-story "elegant painted mansion with porches on each side as the fashion of the country is." The house had eight rooms, four brick fireplaces, two verandas, a balcony with a glass door opening on to it, and thirty glass windows with blinds and shutters. "The arched triple window at the turn of the staircase looked out on a line of poplars." There were two log kitchens near the back door, stables, sheds, cribs, a smokehouse, and cabins for Ridge's thirty slaves. At the height of his prosperity, Ridge's estate contained 280 acres of fields, in which he grew corn, cotton, tobacco, wheat, oats, indigo, and potatoes. His orchards contained more than 1,100 peach trees, more than 400 apple trees, and various other fruit trees. There was a vineyard, a nursery, and a garden with ornamental shrubs. Livestock included cows and pigs. Contemporaries reckoned that "his farm was in a higher state of cultivation and his buildings better than those of any other person in that region, the whites not excepted." In addition to the income from his ferry—estimated at $1,200 a year—Ridge was a silent partner in a nearby trading post.[16] John Ridge became one of the first lawyers in the Cherokee Nation and also did well. His two-story house and plantation were not as large as his father's but his estate was nonetheless that of a prosperous gentleman, with fields, orchards, stables, smokehouses, and slaves.[17]

In the 1820s the Cherokees acquired a written language, based on the syllabary developed over a dozen years by Sequoyah (a.k.a. George Gist, c. 1770–1843). In Sequoyah's phonetic system each symbol represented a vowel or a consonant plus vowel, with the exception of a character representing /s/. It was easily learned and literacy in written Cherokee spread quickly. People began using the new writing for personal correspondence, record keeping and accounting, notebooks containing medicinal texts, and even translated parts of the Bible, and political leaders began to produce government documents in Cherokee.[18]

In 1827 the Cherokees drew up a written constitution and code of laws and restructured their tribal government into a constitutional republic modeled after that of the United States, with an independent judiciary, a supreme court, a principal chief, and a two-house legislature.[19] They divided their country into eight electoral districts; elected a first and second principal chief every four years; and elected representatives to the legislature every two years. The elected council made laws, established a police force and treasury, and created a court system to adjudicate civil and criminal cases. The constitution declared the Cherokees' sovereignty and their right to remain undisturbed in their homeland "solemnly guaranteed and reserved forever to the Cherokee Nation by the Treaties concluded with the United States." Those treaties and the laws of the United States made in pursuance of treaties guaranteed Cherokee rights and protected them against intruders. "Our only request is, that these treaties may be fulfilled, and these laws executed." Elias Boudinot printed the constitution in the first issue of the *Cherokee Phoenix*, which rolled off the presses in February 1828.

The *Phoenix*, much of it published in both English and Cherokee, was the first Indian newspaper and a significant weapon in the Cherokees' public relations campaign. As editor, Boudinot managed the business of the paper; wrote articles and a weekly editorial that he translated into Cherokee; printed laws and public documents of the Cherokee Nation; and selected, translated, and reprinted news items from other papers, along with "miscellaneous articles, calculated to promote Literature, Civilization, and Religion among the Cherokees." At the same time, he worked with the missionary Samuel Worcester to produce a fifty-page hymnal, the first Cherokee book published, and to prepare a Cherokee edition of the gospel of St. Matthew.[20] The Cherokees' written language, printing press, and literacy (according to the Cherokee census of 1835, 18 percent of Cherokees could read English and 43 percent could read Cherokee) put them "at the center of a print culture debate over the legal status of Native nations residing in the United States."[21] As the threat of removal and assault on their sovereignty increased, the Cherokees kept up a lobbying campaign in Washington and in print, keeping in the public eye their achievements, rights, and sufferings at the hands of Georgia. They attributed their progress to their treaties with the United States and then held up those treaties as a test of national honor and morality.[22]

The Ridges, Boudinot, and John Ross were united in their opposition to the policy of Indian removal. In the tribal elections held in October of 1828, the Cherokees elected John Ross principal chief by an overwhelming majority; Major Ridge, as speaker of the council, was his main advisor. Ross (figure 4.5) was thirty-eight, the grandson of a Scots Loyalist, and seven-eighths Scottish in ancestry. That mattered little in matrilineal Cherokee society where his maternal line was Cherokee but it would provide fuel for enemies who tried to discredit his leadership during the furor over removal.[23] Mindful of the role played by men like William McIntosh in selling tribal lands, in the autumn of 1829 the National Council reenacted an old law establishing the death penalty for anyone who sold Cherokee land without the council's approval. According to some accounts, Major Ridge proposed the idea; the Ridges, Ross, and Boudinot all strongly supported the law.[24]

Unfortunately for the Cherokees, a month after Ross was elected principal chief Andrew Jackson was elected president of the United States, and Jackson was the most forceful advocate of Indian removal that had yet entered the

FIGURE 4.5 **John Ross.** *(From History of the Indian tribes of North America, with biographical sketches and anecdotes of the principal chiefs. Embellished with one hundred and twenty portraits, from the Indian Gallery in the Department of War, at Washington, by Thomas L. McKenney and James Hall, 3 vols. [Philadelphia: J. T. Bowen, 1848–50], Dartmouth College, Rauner Library)*

White House. Thomas Jefferson, a student of the Enlightenment, had believed in the essential unity of the human race and regarded Indians as culturally inferior but capable of improvement. Jackson, and an increasing number of Americans in his day, believed in a hierarchy of races that left Indians permanently apart and inferior. Whatever they achieved, they were still Indians. Their cultural resilience and resistance proved they were incapable of changing with the times. The Cherokees and their supporters presented themselves as a modernizing Indian nation, with sovereign rights that the United States was bound to respect by the terms of its own treaties. Jackson and Lewis Cass, the governor of Michigan Territory who became Jackson's secretary of war in 1830, presented the Cherokees as timeless savages, whose treaties did not have the same standing as treaties with other nations, and who must make way for civilized white people who would put their land to good use.[25]

Publication of the Cherokee Constitution, hailed in the North, spurred Georgia into action. Like other settler societies elsewhere in the world Georgia in the 1820s and 1830s sought to expand its sovereignty by subordinating the Native people within its territorial boundaries and asserting local control over the process of dispossessing them of their land. The Georgia Assembly adopted a resolution, which was to go into effect in June 1830, extending state jurisdiction over Cherokee country. The Cherokee Nation was divided into counties administered by local governments and presided over by state courts and "hundreds of Cherokee Indians found their way into Georgia's courts."[26] Georgia demanded that the federal government carry out its obligations under the Compact of 1802 and begin negotiations to compel the Cherokees to cede those lands. "The lands in question belong to Georgia," the Assembly declared. "She *must* and *will* have them."[27] Georgia carried out a systematic campaign of harassment and intimidation, culminating in an assault on Cherokee government. After gold was discovered in Cherokee country in 1829, several thousand prospectors flooded in to pan the streams. Elias Boudinot laid out the issue clearly in the pages of the *Cherokee Phoenix* in January 1829: "The State of Georgia has taken a strong stand against us, and the United States must either defend us in our rights, or leave us to our foe. In the former case, the General Government will redeem her pledge solemnly given in treaties. In the latter, she will violate her promise of protection, and we cannot, in future, depend consistently, upon any guarantee made by her to us, either here or beyond the Mississippi."[28] John Ross placed the matter before Congress (and "before the world") as "a question of great magnitude": could a state usurp "the most sacred rights and privileges of a weak, defenceless, and innocent nation of people, who are in perfect peace with the United States, and to whom the faith of the United States is solemnly pledged to protect and defend them against the encroachments of their citizens"?[29] Boudinot, Ross, and Major Ridge were adamant that the Cherokees were opposed to removal and nothing could "induce them ever to enter into a treaty on the subject."[30] In January 1830 Major Ridge led a troop of the Light Horse, dressed and painted as if for war, in expelling squatters near the Georgia-Alabama border, an action that Georgia newspapers seized on for its propaganda value.[31]

Jeremiah Evarts, the secretary of the ABCFM, spent the last two years of his life (he died in May 1831) leading a moral crusade and orchestrating a petition campaign against removal. Writing under the name William Penn (the first governor of Pennsylvania was known for respecting Indian treaties), Evarts, in a series of widely circulated essays, reviewed the Cherokees' sixteen treaties, "ratified with the same solemnity, as treaties between the United States and the powers of Europe," to show they had been guaranteed title to the soil and sovereignty over their territory "till they voluntarily surrender their country; such an act on their part being the only way in which their title can be *legitimately* extinguished, so long as treaties are the supreme law of the land." To implement removal would demonstrate to the world that "the great and boasting Republic of the United States of North America *incurred the guilt of violating treaties.*" Removal, said Evarts, was more than just a political question: "It relates to the great questions of the law of nations, and to fundamental principles of right and wrong. It implicates the reputation of our country throughout the civilized world; and will bear witness against the rulers and the people who sanction it, so long as the record of these transactions shall be preserved." To implement removal would be a national calamity.[32] Edward Everett, a representative from Massachusetts and later president of Harvard, agreed: apart from the injustice to countless Indians, removal was an assault on Indian treaties, on the treaty-making authority of Congress, and on the Constitution itself. It threatened the reputation of the nation in international affairs and threatened the union. It was, he said, "the greatest question that ever came before Congress, short of the question of peace and war."[33]

Nevertheless, in May 1830, after extensive debate and a close vote in both houses, Congress passed the Indian Removal Act, authorizing the president to negotiate treaties of removal with all Indian tribes living east of the Mississippi. The Senate passed the bill by 28 votes to 19; the House of Representatives by 102 to 97. The voting involved political and moral issues and did not break down along pro- and anti-Indian lines so much as along regional and party lines. Some who voted against the bill did so out of opposition to Jackson rather than sympathy for the Indians; some who voted in favor of the bill did so in reluctant conviction that removal represented the Indians' best, and perhaps only, chance of survival. Davy Crockett, the renowned Indian fighter from Tennessee, voted against the bill, arguing that it violated the treaty clause of the Constitution—a stand that cost him his seat in the House. Daniel Webster worked with Senator Henry Clay of Kentucky and other anti-Jacksonians against the bill, but he was more interested in impugning Jackson than in championing Indians. Like many politicians and businessmen who took up the Cherokee cause in the South, Webster profited by investing in lands obtained from Indians in the North. The act authorized the president to make removal treaties, but those treaties still had to be approved by a two-thirds majority in the Senate, where Webster vigorously opposed their ratification.[34] In Jackson's view, negotiating treaties with the tribes was absurd now that the power lay so emphatically with the United States; Indians should be treated as subjects, not as sovereign nations.

The government and its Indian agents presented removal as the benign policy of a generous father. The Cherokees would be well advised to accept it but they could choose to stay where they were: "There will be employed no force any way, but the force of reason." At the same time, Jackson was adamant that while the federal government would try to keep intruders out of Cherokee country, it would not and could not interfere with a state exercising its sovereignty and its laws over the Indians within is borders.[35] As soon as the Indian Removal Act became law, surveyors and squatters entered Cherokee country and Georgia stepped up its campaign of harassment. Beginning June 1, Georgia extended its laws over Cherokee lands; nullified the Cherokees' constitution, laws, and court system; and prohibited Cherokee assemblies, including meetings of the National Council. Cherokees were forbidden to speak out against removal, to testify in court, or even to dig for gold on their own land. As far as Georgia was concerned, the Cherokee Nation had ceased to exist. Georgia created a police force—-the Georgia Guard—to patrol Cherokee country and handed out Cherokee lands to Georgian citizens in a state lottery.[36]

The Cherokee delegation in Washington reminded the government of its past assurances. Thomas Jefferson had told them that "*all our proceedings* towards you shall be directed by *justice* and *a sacred regard to our treaties*" and that the United States would never wish to buy their land "except when you are *perfectly willing* to sell." Even Andrew Jackson just the past spring had said "that he would protect them in their territorial possessions."[37] In a letter that later received wide circulation in Cherokee country, Henry Clay reaffirmed that, according to the principles that had governed US Indian policies:

> the Cherokee Nation has the right to establish its own form of Government, and to alter and amend it from time to time, according to its own sense of its own wants; to live under its own laws; to be exempt from the operations of the laws of the U. States, or of any individual state; to claim the protection of the U. States, and quietly to possess and enjoy its lands subject to no other limitation than that, when sold, they can only be sold to the U. States.

Jackson, said Clay, had announced a policy hostile to these principles "and thereby encouraged Georgia to usurp powers of legislation over the Cherokee Nation which she does not of right possess."[38]

John Ross hired former attorney general William Wirt and other lawyers to represent his people's interests. Wirt filed a series of test cases. He first obtained a writ of error from Supreme Court Justice John Marshall to stay the execution of a Cherokee named George Corn Tassel. A Georgia court had sentenced

Corn Tassel to death for killing another Indian, a crime the Cherokees and their supporters argued should fall under Indian jurisdiction because it occurred in Cherokee country. In a special session, the Georgia legislature voted to defy the writ, and Corn Tassel was hanged. "The conduct of the Georgia Legislature is indeed surprising," wrote Elias Boudinot in a passage prophetic of future events; "they...authorize their governor to hoist the flag of rebellion against the United States! If such proceedings are sanctioned by the majority of the people of the U. States, the Union is but a tottering fabric which will soon fall and crumble into atoms."[39]

Three days before Tassel's execution Wirt filed suit against Georgia before the Supreme Court of the United States. The Cherokees were the first Indian nation to bring a case in the highest court. In *Cherokee Nation v. Georgia,* the Court found that it lacked original jurisdiction, but Chief Justice John Marshall tried to define the status of the Cherokees—and by extension all Indian tribes—within the United States. The Cherokees, he said, were "a domestic, dependent nation," who had retained some aspects of their sovereignty through treaties. He likened the Indians' relationship to the government to that between a ward and a guardian. However, without a strong show of federal power to enforce United States laws protecting tribal sovereignty, the Cherokees remained vulnerable to Georgia's assaults.

The Cherokees succeeded in getting their case into the Supreme Court the next year via a United States citizen. In March 1831, the Georgia Guard arrested nine missionaries for preaching in Cherokee country without having taken an oath of obedience to the laws of Georgia. Seven of the missionaries took the oath or left the state, but two, Samuel Worcester and Elijah Butler, refused to do either and were sentenced to four years of hard labor. Worcester and Butler petitioned the Supreme Court, which accepted the case. As US citizens, there could be no question regarding their standing. As in *Cherokee Nation,* Georgia refused to appear. In March 1832, Chief Justice Marshall, seventy-five years old and in poor health, rendered the verdict in *Worcester v. Georgia.* In a 6–1 decision the court found Worcester's arrest was illegal. Georgia had no authority to execute its laws within an Indian nation protected under the treaty clause of the United States Constitution:

> The constitution, by declaring treaties already made, as well as those to be made, to be the supreme law of the land, has adopted and sanctioned the previous treaties with the Indian nations, and consequently admits their rank among those powers who are capable of making treaties. The words "treaty" and "nation" are words of our own language, selected in our diplomatic and legislative proceedings, by ourselves, having each a definite and well understood meaning. We have applied them to Indians, as we have applied them to the other nations of the earth. They are applied to all in the same sense.

The Cherokee Nation was "a distinct community, occupying its own territory...in which the law of Georgia can have no right to enter but with the assent of the Cherokees." The Georgia law under which the missionaries were arrested was "void, as repugnant to the Constitution, treaties, and laws of the United States."[40] The Cherokee delegation in Washington and their supporters greeted the decision with jubilation.

Their elation was short-lived. It quickly became clear that Jackson was not going to enforce the decision. The case reaffirmed the supremacy of the federal government in dealing with Indians, which only redoubled Georgia's efforts to drive the Cherokees into making a federal treaty. Now more than ever was the time to stick together, Ross said; a treaty with the United States could not take place "if our people continue to remain firm & to be united in the support of our common interests."[41] But divisions soon appeared. Ross and John Ridge returned to Washington to join the Cherokee delegation there. Ridge secured an audience at the White House and asked the president point-blank "whether the power of the United States would be exerted to execute the decision and put down the legislation of Georgia." Jackson replied equally bluntly that it would not. He urged Ridge "to go home and advise his people that their only hope of relief was in abandoning their country and removing to the West." The interview seems to have been a turning point for John Ridge. "From that moment," wrote Indian agents Samuel Stambaugh and Amos Kendall, "he was convinced that the only alternative to save his people from moral and physical death was to make the best terms they could with the government, and remove out of the limits of the States."[42]

Secretary of War Lewis Cass called the Cherokee delegation to his office and offered them a removal treaty. Meanwhile, the Cherokees' white friends were giving the same advice. David Greene of the ABCFM, the Cherokees' long-time allies and advocates, wrote John Ridge on May 3, 1832: "It makes me weep to think of it," he said. "But if your friends in Congress think that all further effort in your behalf will be useless...then, for aught I can see, you must make the best terms you can, & go."[43] Twelve days later, the Cherokee delegation left for home.

In the fall of 1832, Georgia held another lottery to distribute Cherokee land among its citizens. Andrew Jackson's victory over Henry Clay at the polls in November dashed any hopes that a change of administration might bring a change of policy.

"I have signed my death warrant"

Whether they bowed to the inevitable or saw an opportunity to advance themselves, the Ridges now took the position that the Cherokees' best hope—indeed their only hope—was to try and negotiate terms for removal. Ridge finally entered the Presbyterian Church and accepted baptism in 1832.[44] Elias Boudinot by this time also believed there was no alternative to removal. He explained his change of heart and his change of policy as patriotism: his intention was still the preservation of the Cherokee Nation but it was clear that if the people stayed where they were they would be destroyed. Better to give up the homeland than to see the people perish. So long as the people survived, the nation could survive, but now it could do so only in the West.[45]

A pro-removal group known as the Treaty Party began to coalesce around the Ridges and Boudinot. There was more to their action than a realization that the Cherokees had no choice. Cherokees who joined the Treaty Party tended to be better off economically than the majority of Cherokees but were not as well-to-do as the elite; those who took the lead, with the exception of Major and John Ridge, did not hold elective office, and a number had been defeated in their bids for tribal office. Invoking the rhetoric of Jacksonian Democrats, the historian Theda Perdue characterized the Treaty Party as members of "a rising middle class." Like Jackson and his followers they were moving up but they wanted more and felt a privileged elite was holding them back. Not surprisingly, Jackson cultivated this group to divide the Cherokee Nation, undermine its elected leadership, and ignore the will of the Cherokee majority. For the Treaty Party the removal crisis was also an opportunity to usurp political authority and to secure concessions for themselves by taking the lead in negotiating a treaty with the United States. For John Ridge, the crisis demanded leadership by John Ridge, not John Ross.[46]

Ross and the majority remained firmly against removal. They did not subscribe to Boudinot's vision of a civilized Cherokee Nation that could survive and even prosper separated from their homeland. The West was not a land of opportunity to Cherokees; moving west meant heading in the direction of death. Lines quickly hardened between former allies. In 1832 the Cherokee Council met at Red Clay, just over the Tennessee border, rather than at New Echota (Georgia law criminalized Cherokee meetings within the state's borders). Ross tried unsuccessfully to prevent public discussion of the treaty Cass had offered. In view of the crisis, the council decided not to hold national elections and passed a resolution continuing the same chiefs and officeholders in their positions. John Ridge believed he was better qualified than Ross and believed Ross was behind the move. Stressing the need to present a united front, Ross also opposed printing anything in the *Phoenix* that diverged from the antiremoval stance. Boudinot resigned: "Were I to continue as Editor," he informed Ross, "I should feel myself in a most peculiar and delicate position."[47] The council subsequently expelled the Ridges and other members who favored removal. Boudinot and the Ridges accused Ross of despotism but Ross can be seen as acting in accordance with traditional consensus politics, which required dissenters to withdraw and maintain their silence so that the community could present a united front.[48]

The Ridges and Boudinots saw themselves as patriots, giving up land so that the people might survive but "a man who will forsake his country...in time of adversity," declared Ross in August 1833, "is no more than a traitor and should be viewed—and shunned as such."[49] That month General R. G. Dunlap of Tennessee who had, he said, "conversed freely" with both John Ridge and John Ross, wrote to Jackson, "I do sincerely believe that the ultimate views of both these men are the same in regard to the final destiny of their nation," but each was "catching at everything to weaken the other, and gain or keep the ascendancy, for the furtherance of their ends."[50]

Governor Wilson Lumpkin of Georgia, hardly a disinterested observer, weighed in on the side of Ridge. Convinced that removal was the only way to protect his state's sovereign right to govern its own territory, Lumpkin dismissed the opponents of removal as "a few of the interested half-breeds" and self-serving white politicians, and he impugned Ross as a descendant of Scots Tories who had fought on the wrong side in the Revolution. Ross was well educated and gentlemanly in his manners but compared with John Ridge and Elias Boudinot, he was "a mere *pygmy*." Ridge, said Lumpkin, was "one of nature's great men, who looks beyond the present moment and seeks the good of his people with an eye to their posterity...and, therefore, hazards life and everything dear to him as a man, to effect a great public object of deep and lasting interest to his native race, the Cherokees."[51] Ross on the other hand governed the Cherokees "in the most absolute manner" and had deluded them into believing there was an alternative to removal. There was not. Georgia was determined to enforce its laws "throughout what is still called the Cherokee Country. If reason and considerations of interest should fail to sustain the execution of our laws, other and stronger measures must and will be resorted to," Lumpkin warned. "It is extreme folly and wholly fallacious for the Cherokees to entertain the shadow of a hope that the Federal Government will ever attempt, in the slightest degree, to overturn the laws of Georgia in regard to the soil or population within the chartered limits of the State."[52]

As Georgia intensified efforts to undermine the political and economic bases of Cherokee society, Ross and the Cherokee delegation found themselves competing with the Ridge faction for attention in Washington. Sitting in Brown's Hotel, where many Indian delegations to the capital stayed in these years, Ross and his delegation wrote letters to President Jackson, reminding him of their political rights "which have been recognized and established by the laws and treaties of the United States."[53] In May 1834, fifty Cherokees from the Coosawatie district sent Lewis Cass a protest against the delegation of Major Ridge, Boudinot, Andrew Ross, and James Starr, denying that Ridge and Boudinot had any authority.[54] In June, Ross's brother Andrew agreed to a humiliating removal treaty in Washington, ceding all Cherokee land east of the Mississippi for an annuity of $25,000 for twenty-four years.[55] John Ross responded by offering to sell most of the Cherokees' Georgia land in return for a dozen years of federal protection while the Cherokees "amalgamated" into American society, with a view to becoming US citizens. Boudinot and the Ridges totally rejected Ross's proposal, the Senate rejected Andrew Ross's treaty as lacking official Cherokee sanction, and Secretary of War Lewis Cass rejected anything "short of an entire removal."[56] At a council held at Red Clay in August 1834, Cherokee Tom Foreman denounced Major Ridge and charges were brought against the Ridges and David Vann. John Ridge stood up to defend his father's conduct but there were murmurs of "Let's kill them."[57] At the annual council in October, Ross and the others who controlled the proceedings declined to prosecute the impeachment charge against the Ridges and Vann but neither would they withdraw it. The Ridges and Vann rode off before the council adjourned, and they convened their own council at Running Water near Boudinot's home at the end of November.[58]

There were two Cherokee delegations in Washington but the Ridge delegation had the inside track with the administration. Ross and his fellow delegates wrote Cass an impassioned letter in the middle of January 1835: "The property, the peace, and the existence of the Cherokee people, are in jeopardy," they said, "and nothing but the timely interposition of the General Government can save them." They asked that the president extend his "protecting arm . . . to arrest this unconstitutional and fatal course of Georgia." They sent similar appeals to Congress and the president. They were asking the fox to guard the henhouse: Georgians were not about to be stopped and Jackson had no intention of trying to stop them.[59] Perhaps in desperation by this point, Ross made Cass another offer—to sell the eastern Cherokees' lands for $20 million, hoping to move his people to Texas and buy and build a new homeland in territory claimed by Mexico.[60] But the government knew it could get a better deal. The Ridge delegation in January 1835 submitted a memorial to Congress from those Cherokees who were willing to migrate. Indian nations could not survive east of the Mississippi, they said, because the United States "has refused to fulfill its faith pledged to us in the treaties." The Cherokees were at a crisis in their history and faced the choice between remaining "in a state of vassalage to the States" and migrating to the West. Although many within the Treaty Party had already "amalgamated," they now apparently found the prospect of "*amalgamation* with our oppressors," as suggested by Ross, "too horrid for a serious contemplation." The only way to preserve the nation and its sovereignty was to transplant it.[61] The Ridge delegates were under no illusions but they were ready and willing to negotiate a removal treaty.

Jackson appointed John F. Schermerhorn to make the treaty. An evangelical minister in the Dutch Reformed Church from New York, Schermerhorn had traveled among the western Indians as a missionary and was convinced that removing Indians beyond the Mississippi and away from whites was a "benevolent enterprise," essential to their survival and their "moral and religious improvement."[62] He corresponded with Jackson and Cass, conveying his views on Indian removal and informing them of his availability for the new position of Indian commissioner in the West. With the ABCFM and many other church groups opposed to removal, Jackson was eager to enlist clergymen on his side and appointed Schermerhorn as commissioner in October 1832. Schermerhorn left Schenectady, New York, with his wife and eight children and headed for Fort Gibson on the Arkansas River, in what is now Oklahoma.[63] He quickly built a track record negotiating removal treaties. He negotiated treaties with the Senecas and Shawnees of Lewistown in Ohio in December 1832, with the western Cherokees and Creeks at Fort Gibson in February 1833, with the Seminoles in March, and with the Quapaws in May.[64] In June he urged Potawatomis in Indiana to move west; in August he joined the treaty commissioners negotiating a removal treaty with the Seneca in upstate New York. Called away to assist at the Treaty of Chicago with the Potawatomis in September, he sent a talk to the Six Nations council at Onondaga, portraying himself as a friend to the Iroquois and urging them to remove.[65]

Schermerhorn arrived in Chicago to find that George Porter, the governor of Michigan Territory and superintendent of Indian affairs, and the other treaty commissioners had made little headway in getting the Indians to give up their lands west of Lake Michigan and agree to removal. The Potawatomis had been bombarded with treaties in recent years and "had utterly refused for several days to sell any of their lands." The day after he arrived, by his own account, Schermerhorn held a private interview with two of the principal chiefs conducting negotiations: Sauganash, better known as Billy Caldwell, was the son of an Irish officer and a Potawatomi woman; Chechebinquey, also called Alexander Robinson, was son of a Scottish trader and an Ottawa woman. Both chiefs frequently mediated and interpreted at treaty councils. Schermerhorn met with them during an adjournment of several days in the negotiations. The journal of the treaty proceedings does not record what transpired at the meeting, but by the time the journal picked up again the commissioners had the treaty ready for the Potawatomis to sign. Caldwell and Robinson each received $10,000, although Governor Porter denied it was a bribe. The treaty stipulated "four hundred dollars a year to be paid to Billy Caldwell, and three hundred dollars a year, to be paid to Alexander Robinson, for life, in addition to the annuities already granted to them." Charges of bribery and fraud held up the treaty's ratification, and before the Senate finally gave its approval it reduced the amounts paid to Caldwell and Robinson, which were "so large as to induce a well-founded presumption that they have, by some means, acquired an influence over the Indians which they have been disposed to use to an unreasonable extent for their individual benefit."[66]

Having taken care of the Potawatomi resistance, Schermerhorn departed to do the same with the Miamis in October. But he met his match in the person of the old Miami head chief Jean-Baptiste Richardville, a successful merchant, consummate politician, and savvy negotiator. Schermerhorn was authorized to offer the Miamis up to 50 cents an acre; Richardville scoffed at the offer and the treaty failed. "It was a public treaty," Schermerhorn explained significantly, "and not a private negotiation as I recommended." (The next year Richardville offered to sell some Miami land for $5 per acre and he subsequently accepted removal treaties.)[67] As commissioner in the West, Schermerhorn in 1834 dealt with resettling the Shawnees and Senecas of Lewiston and with claims stemming from a treaty with the western Cherokees in 1828. As he urged eastern Cherokees to relocate with promises of peace and prosperity he was well aware that western Cherokees felt aggrieved to be inundated by emigrants who had not shared the hardships they had suffered when they had moved west.[68]

Such was the man and such were the methods Andrew Jackson called upon to secure a removal treaty with the Cherokees. Cherokees nicknamed Schermerhorn the Devil's Horn. In February 1835 Cass instructed Schermerhorn to meet with the Ridge delegation and draw up a preliminary treaty, which the delegates would sign and then take home for ratification by the Cherokees. Schermerhorn and Ridge reached a tentative agreement and in March they wrote a secret treaty that offered the Cherokees $5 million "for the cession of their entire claims east of the Mississippi river." Jackson issued a proclamation to the Cherokees admonishing them to think of their future and their children; their condition was deteriorating rapidly, things were only going to get worse, and they must delude themselves no longer. If only they had listened to Jackson years ago, they could now be enjoying peace and prosperity in the West.[69]

John Ridge left Washington in March, telling Cass that the Cherokees who had once been unanimously opposed to a treaty were now ready to accept it; only Ross and his followers stood in the way. "Sir," he wrote, invoking his full-blood identity, "I am an Indian, and understand the character of my countrymen. The common Indians are not to blame, and have only been misled by the avaricious half-breeds of the Ross party."[70] Ridge, who had called Andrew Jackson a chicken snake in 1832, had apparently had a significant change of heart: he named his new son Andrew Jackson Ridge.[71] Federal emigration agent Benjamin Franklin Currey believed that Ross exercised "a secret & powerful influence over the destinies of his people" and warned the chief that the president would hold him and his council responsible if anything happened to the members of the treaty party.[72] There was little protection for Ross. He returned to his home at Coosa to find it occupied by people who had "won it" in the lottery. He resettled his family across the Tennessee border at Red Clay.[73]

Schermerhorn followed Ridge back home and, together with Currey, they began selling the treaty to the Cherokees. In the words of the author, poet, and playwright John Howard Payne (best known for writing the song "Home Sweet Home"), "The President sends a Treaty with a letter to explain it. He then sends Mr. Schermerhorn to re-explain the explained Treaty. The end of it is, the Treaty is so much explained that it is explained away." Payne arrived in Cherokee country later in the year and the National Council invited him to write a history of the Cherokees in the hope it would help educate the public about the Cherokee cause. Payne and Schermerhorn had attended the same school. (Schermerhorn was an upperclassman when Payne entered Union College in Schenectady; Schermerhorn graduated; Payne dropped out after two or three years when his father went bankrupt, and began an acting career.) But they were diametrically opposed on the Cherokee issue.[74]

In July Schermerhorn and Currey called a meeting of Cherokees at Running Water. Ross and his supporters at first urged people to stay away but then attended, along with some four thousand Cherokees. Schermerhorn mounted a platform and "began his speech of three hours and twenty minutes, counted anxiously by the watch," noted Payne. Once the Cherokees removed to Indian Territory, said Schermerhorn, they could look forward "to the day when your several tribes of Indians shall there be organized into a territorial government, with the rights and privileges of American citizens; and that the time will yet come, when an Indian State will be added to our Federal Union: and which, though the last, will be the brightest star and fairest stripe upon the banner of our nation, and fill up the measure of our country's glory." But they should make no mistake and, he had told this to Ross, this was their last and only hope: "if you reject these propositions for a treaty, and come to no final agreement with the commissioners now appointed to treat with you, [the president] will enter into no further negotiation with you, during his administration." If they rejected "the very liberal and generous offers" now being made they risked losing the sympathies of even their friends. There was no use trying to delay things any longer; time was running out: "You cannot mistake the policy of Georgia. She is determined to get rid of her Indian population, and she will soon legislate you out of the country, by granting your possessions to her own citizens, who claim the fee of your lands. And then where will you go?" Payne's account of the council phrased the offer more bluntly than Schermerhorn's report did: "'Take this money,' said the Reverend Commissioner, 'for if you do not, the bordering States will forthwith turn the screw upon you tighter & tighter, till you are ground to powder.'" Agent Return J. Meigs, who attended the meeting, said the

Cherokees listened with attention and interest as Schermerhorn explained the terms of the treaty and the Rev. Jesse Bushyhead faithfully interpreted them. Schermerhorn entreated Ross and Ridge to settle their differences and head a joint committee representing the Cherokees in the treaty discussions.[75] But Schermerhorn told the commissioner of Indian affairs that he would have to deal with one or the other party. "I wish to see neither Ross nor Ridge injured," he explained, "but if a treaty can be carried only by putting down one and exalting the other, I should not long hesitate to make my election."[76]

In August 1835, fearing Ross would use the printing press of the *Cherokee Phoenix* to publish antiremoval propaganda, Stand Watie secured the assistance of the Georgia Guard in confiscating it and restoring it to the Ridge-Watie-Boudinot faction.[77] Governor Lumpkin considered it "a perfect *farce*" for the government "to pretend any longer to consider or treat these unfortunate remnants of a once mighty race as independent nations of people, capable of entering into treaty stipulations *as such*." During his administration, the Cherokee part of Georgia had been transformed from a howling wilderness into a cultivated country settled by thousands of civilized people. "Having effected all this without a treaty, why should Georgia, upon selfish considerations, care about a treaty?" As far as Georgia was concerned, he declared, "I feel entirely indifferent whether the Cherokees ever enter into a treaty or not. I no longer look to the Federal Government, or its agents, to relieve Georgia from her Cherokee perplexity." However, since a treaty was on the table, every effort should be made to overcome the opposition of the Ross faction and induce the Cherokees to take it. "Starvation and destruction await them if they wait much longer in their present abodes."[78]

John Ridge and Schermerhorn presented their treaty to the Cherokee Council at Red Clay in October. John Ross led the opposition. Cherokees were outraged, John Ridge's life was threatened, and opposition was so overwhelming that he and Boudinot joined the majority in voting against it. But Schermerhorn refused Ross's requests to return with him to Washington and told the elected chief of the Cherokees that he would not be received there. He circulated a printed notice, which Boudinot translated into Cherokee, urging the Cherokees to think it over and meet again at New Echota in December for further discussion. The notice also contained a warning that all who failed to show up would be considered to "give their assent and sanction to whatever is done at the council."[79]

Benjamin Currey warned of "the evil consequences likely to attend the departure of a delegation from the Eastern Cherokees for Washington at this juncture in time." In November the Georgia Guard crossed the border into Tennessee, arrested Payne and Ross, and confiscated Payne's papers. Payne and Ross were held for two weeks at the old Moravian mission at Springplace.

Payne was accused of being an abolitionist and a French spy, and Ross of impeding the census that was being carried out in Cherokee country, but no official charges were brought. Immediately after his release, Ross hurried to Washington. Payne returned to New York but continued to work for the antiremoval cause, assisting the Ross delegation in Washington and helping to write petitions.[80]

In his annual report, in November 1835, Commissioner of Indian Affairs Elbert Herring stated there had been no letup in efforts to induce the Cherokees to move west of the Mississippi "in conformity with the policy adopted by the Government in favor of the Indians." He attributed "the disinclination of a large portion of the nation to emigrate, and avail themselves of the obvious benefit in the contemplated change" to "bad advisement, and the intolerant control of chiefs adverse to the measure."[81] Major Ridge, Elias Boudinot, and other members of the Treaty Party wrote to Andrew Jackson on December 1 "to express our entire confidence in your full determination to secure justice to the poor Indians."[82] In the absence of the principal chief and the majority opposition, and while a Cherokee delegation authorized to negotiate a treaty was away in Washington, Schermerhorn went ahead and made his treaty with the members of the minority Treaty Party.

The treaty council convened as scheduled on December 21. Most Cherokees saw no need to attend. Many lived in Tennessee and did not face the immediate threat confronting their relatives in Georgia. Others had already voiced their rejection of the treaty at Red Clay. A long preamble to the treaty justified dealing with only part of the tribe: the Cherokees had been given notice that the meeting was to be held at New Echota and that those who did not attend would be assumed to give their approval. Only eighty-six Cherokee men turned up at New Echota, together with several hundred women and children; Schermerhorn characterized them as "the most intelligent and best informed among them."[83] Women, who had participated in eighteenth-century treaties and remonstrated against earlier removal efforts, took no part in the treaty proceedings here.[84] According to one Ross supporter, Schermerhorn addressed the Cherokees "in his usual style, only a little more so." The treaty makers met in the council house but Currey's reading of the proposed treaty was interrupted when the roof caught fire. "Whether this fearful blaze was emblematical of the indignation of Heaven at the unlawful proceedings within, or of the fiery trial of our people, the Lord only knows," wrote one witness.[85]

Major Ridge addressed the assembled Cherokees as a Cherokee patriot and reluctant advocate of removal. The Cherokee title to the land was far older and derived from a far higher authority than what the Georgians claimed.

> Yet they are strong and we are weak. We are few, they are many. We cannot remain here in safety and comfort . . . an unbending, iron necessity

tells us we must leave them. I would willingly die to preserve them, but any forcible effort to keep them will cost us our lands, our lives, and the lives of our children. There is but one path of safety, one road to future existence as a Nation. That path is open before you. Make a treaty of cession. Give up these lands and go over beyond the Great Father of Waters.

Boudinot reiterated the necessity of the treaty, even though he knew that by signing it "I take my life in my hand."[86]

The Cherokees appointed a twenty-man committee, headed by Major Ridge and Boudinot, and including John Gunter, Andrew Ross, and Archilla Smith, to negotiate with Schermerhorn and consider the terms of the treaty.[87] The final treaty contains a lengthy self-serving prelude justifying the treaty and the actions of the signers: the Cherokees are not being driven out by violence and injustice, they are moving west to reunite their nation and secure a permanent homeland. Instead of collaborators in a treaty depriving their people of their homeland, the Treaty Party presented themselves as the responsible government; they, not the obstinate and short-sighted Ross, were the ones willing to make the hard choices that had to be made if the people were to survive.[88]

The treaty contained twenty articles. Basically, the Cherokees ceded ten million acres of land in the East for $5 million in cash plus money for investment; in other words just over 50 cents an acre. In return, they received lands in the West and assurances that at "no future time without their consent" would those lands "be included within the territorial limits or jurisdiction of any state or Territory." Cherokees agreed to keep peace and not wage war against their neighbors and the United States promised to prevent trespass onto Cherokee land. In addition, the Cherokees were entitled to send a delegate to the House of Representatives "whenever Congress shall make provision for the same." (The treaty contained a provision for reservation lands for those Cherokees who wanted to stay in the East, but Jackson objected, insisting "that the whole Cherokee people should remove together and establish themselves in the country provided for them west of the Mississippi river." So, supplementary articles, agreed to by Ridge and other signers of the original treaty on March 1, 1836, declared this provision null and void and authorized an extra $600,000 in payment for the Cherokees' lands.)[89]

Reverend James Trott, a Methodist missionary, called the treaty the "*Christmas trick* at New Echota."[90] However, as the Cherokee scholar Daniel Heath Justice acknowledges (somewhat reluctantly, having himself always been "a Ross man"), the treaty is not just a manifestation of American deceit and Treaty Party betrayal; it is "a much more complicated document of resistance, particularly in its concerns about the People's ultimate survival." The Treaty Party used the document to assert their own legitimacy as leaders of the Cherokee Nation and also to include provisions for rebuilding the nation in the West, by outlining the Cherokees' new territories, asserting their rights of self-determination, making provision for a possible diplomatic delegate to the House of Representatives, and securing schools, teachers, farmers, and mechanics, and funds to educate and support orphan children. Schermerhorn and co-commissioner Governor William Carroll were only concerned with getting a removal treaty, but the Cherokee signers were concerned with the independence and future survival of the Cherokee Nation, albeit with themselves at the head.[91]

On December 29 those present voted on the treaty: seventy-nine approved, seven opposed. The members of the negotiating committee signed the treaty. Major Ridge's name appears first. In their report and regulations of Indian treaty making submitted to the Senate in 1829, Lewis Cass and William Clark had noted that "he who signs first, incurs a heavy responsibility; and it requires no ordinary degree of resolution in the man, who thus, in the presence of his countrymen, leads the way in sanctioning a measure which many may regret after the presents are expended and the excitement of the moment has subsided."[92] Never did that responsibility weigh more heavily than on Major Ridge. As the seventy-year-old chief made his mark on the treaty, he was reputed to have said, "I have signed my death warrant."[93] For years to come, many Cherokees called it "Ridge's Treaty."[94] The illegal council adjourned on December 30 "after distributing among the Cherokees a blanket each, which had been brought to the council ground for the accommodation of the Cherokee people at that inclement season."[95]

Elated, Schermerhorn scribbled a quick letter to Cass the same day: "The meeting was large and respectable, and everything conducted in that open and fair manner, that there will be no difficulty in its ratification," he said. "Ross, after this treaty, is prostrate. The power of the nation is taken from him, as well as the money, and the treaty will give general satisfaction."[96]

The Ridge party gave their approval to sending the treaty to the Senate. John Ridge and Stand Watie (figure 4.6), who were in Washington when the treaty was made, added their support, impugning at the same time the "constituted authority" of the Cherokee Nation as "a few men, at the head of whom is John Ross, who is nearly a white man in color and feelings."[97]

Despite the Ridges' insistence that they acted only for the good of the Cherokee people and to preserve the Cherokee Nation, the National Council at Red Clay declared the treaty null and void, denouncing it as "a fraud upon the Government of the United States, and an act of oppression on the Cherokee people."[98] Stunned to hear that a treaty had been made while they were away in Washington, John Ross and his delegation bombarded the president, the secretary of war, Congress, influential individuals, and the public at large with

FIGURE 4.6 **Stand Watie.** *(Western History Collections, University of Oklahoma Libraries, Phillips 1459)*

protests and appeals for justice. Ross could not believe that the United States government would countenance "the Christmas trick" if it knew the truth. The Cherokees had been faithful allies of the United States and had made advances in agriculture, education, literacy, government, and all civilized pursuits; what wrong had they committed to merit such treatment? "Before the civilized world, and in the presence of Almighty God," they declared, "the instrument entered into at New Echota, purporting to be a treaty, is deceptive to the world, and a fraud upon the Cherokee people." If the Cherokees had ceased to exist by state legislation as a nation or tribe, then the president and senate could not make a treaty with them; if they had not, then no treaty could be made for them without their consent and against their will. If treaties were to be made and enforced "wanting the assent of one of the pretended parties, what security would there be for any nation or tribe to retain confidence in the United States?" In the case of the New Echota treaty, the assent of the Cherokee Nation had been "expressly denied." A handful of chiefs, "seduced and prompted by officers of the United States Government," had assumed powers that had not been conferred by the people and had negotiated a treaty "over the heads and remonstrances of the nation. Is there to be found in the annals of history, a parallel case to this?"[99]

Assistant Principal Chief George Lowery secured more than fourteen thousand signatures to a petition against the treaty.[100] Schermerhorn and the Treaty Party dismissed Ross Party protests as the efforts of a self-serving minority and contended that the numbers on the petitions were inflated and that there were irregularities in the way the signatures were obtained.[101] Citizens from towns throughout the northern states sent petitions and protests to Congress, and even Congress had misgivings—the debates over the treaty lasted almost two months. In the House, John Quincy Adams called it "an eternal disgrace upon the country."[102] Adams had his own anti-Jackson axe to grind, of course, but it was a view widely shared. Missionary Rev. Cephas Washburn believed "a tremendous responsibility rests upon our government for that transaction. By that treaty, a foul stain is fixed upon our national escutcheon, which is now indelible. No subsequent act can wash it away. It will not be washed away in all time, nor all eternity."[103] Missionary Daniel Butrick, formerly a close friend of John and Major Ridge, now denounced the action of the treaty signers as "not only a political crime but a Christian sin."[104]

Petitions were not likely to carry much weight with a government that had deliberately chosen to deal with the Treaty Party rather than the legitimate Cherokee leadership. When the treaty finally reached the Senate, the vote on ratification did not divide along the same sectional lines as had the debates and was as much to do with the expansion of the Cotton Kingdom and slavery as about the rights of the Cherokees. On May 23, 1836, the Senate approved the treaty by just one vote more than the two-thirds majority required for ratification. Senator Hart Benton of Missouri said that the votes of the free state senators secured for the South a treaty that would convert "Indian soil to slave soil."[105] Jackson proclaimed the treaty the same day. The clock on Cherokee removal was ticking. They had two years in which to be gone.

The emigration agent, Benjamin Currey, did not live to see the Cherokees emigrate; he died in December 1836 "after a serious and painful illness of several weeks."[106] Stand Watie and Elias Boudinot lost their wives in the same year. In April, while Watie was in Washington, his wife Betsey died in childbirth (the child died, too).[107] Harriet Gold Boudinot died in August. Within the year, Elias Boudinot married Delight Sargent, a missionary. She accompanied him and his six children when they migrated west.[108]

The Treaty Party leaders claimed that most Cherokees received the treaty with relief and gratitude, even, said Boudinot, "with cheerfulness." Major and John Ridge told the president: "We have been hailed by the poor Cherokees as their deliverers from Ross's domination. So far all is well." But all was not well: the Cherokees were being fleeced and abused by the Georgians, and the Ridges implored Jackson to send regular troops "to protect our people as they depart for the West."[109]

By supporting Georgia in its unlawful actions against the Cherokees and demanding removal the government disregarded promises it had made in every treaty with the Cherokees since 1785.[110] But it was determined to carry out this one to the letter. On the president's instructions, Brigadier General John Wool, commander of the army in Cherokee country, issued a proclamation at Red Clay in September 1836, announcing that no alteration would be made in the treaty "and that the same, in all its terms and conditions, will be faithfully and fully executed." Another proclamation from General Nathaniel Smith, who replaced Currey as superintendent of Cherokee removal, issued in late December 1837 and published in the *Athens Courier* warned the Cherokees that they now had only five months left. It was time to stop listening to Ross and fooling themselves. "The treaty will be executed, without change or alteration, and another day beyond the time named, cannot or will not be allowed you." The president had refused any further discussion or correspondence with Ross in regard to the treaty and further delay risked bringing "evils" and "horrors" on the Cherokees and their families. It was time for the Cherokees to get moving or suffer the consequences.[111]

In 1836 Jackson called Wilson Lumpkin out of retirement to serve with Tennessee governor William Carroll as commissioner for settling all Cherokee claims under the terms of the treaty. By his own estimation Lumpkin "had contributed more than any one man in bringing this Treaty into existence." He thought it "exceedingly liberal and advantageous in all its provisions to the Cherokee people," and the sooner it was implemented the better. The fact that most Cherokees opposed it caused him little concern: "In truth, nineteen-twentieths of the Cherokees are too ignorant and depraved to entitle their opinions to any weight or consideration whatever." He made it clear to the Cherokees that he was there to execute the treaty, not negotiate a new one, and he urged a strong military presence to eliminate any possibility of trouble. "The intelligent and wealthy" Cherokees were busy settling their affairs, "getting all the money they can under the treaty, and looking exclusively to their own interest, with the most perfect indifference to the interests of the great body of their people." For eighteen months, Lumpkin tried to push ahead with adjudicating thousands of claims arising from the treaty.[112]

After he resigned to take up his seat in the US Senate "much fraud and corruption found their way" into the commissioner's office. For twelve years, first in the House of Representatives, then as governor, then as commissioner, and finally as senator, Lumpkin made it his policy "never to cease my efforts while an Indian remained in Georgia" and he continued to push for speedy implementation of removal on the floor of the Senate. As far as Lumpkin was concerned, Indian treaties were a farce and should be abandoned, leaving the federal and state governments to legislate directly for Indians "in the same manner that we legislate for minors and orphans, and other persons who are incompetent to take charge of their own rights."[113]

Meanwhile John Ross worked tirelessly to have the treaty abrogated or amended, denouncing it as an illegal act carried out by greedy and self-interested traitors. Lumpkin considered Ross "the master spirit of opposition," a "wary politician" who committed no overt act but whose presence and influence stiffened resistance to removal among the mass of Cherokees. Colonel William Lindsay of the Second Artillery, the commanding officer in the western district of Cherokee country, saw things rather differently. Lindsay told Secretary of War Joel Poinsett that the vast majority of Cherokees would be willing to consider a fair treaty but would never move under the fraudulent one made at New Echota except under force. Many vowed to die rather than leave. Lindsay did not hold Ross responsible for the resistance; Ross was "the slave, rather than the leader of his nation," and his real position was "mysterious." Whereas Lumpkin warned that Ross's ambition risked destroying the Cherokees, Lindsay thought Ross "a man of enlarged mind and consummate judgement" who fully understood the consequences of war with the United States and stood in the way of bloodshed, a difficult task given "the exasperated state of party feeling prevailing through the Cherokee nation."[114]

The Treaty Party maintained that they had achieved the best deal possible under the circumstances. Unable to claim legitimate leadership on traditional grounds of consensus or mandate of the community, Ridge and Boudinot instead took the position that an intelligent leadership had a moral responsibility to act for the good of the ignorant and misinformed majority. In a "Reply to Ross," which was published with accompanying documents in 1837 and became public record as a Senate document, Boudinot accused Ross of intransigence, misleading the people, and prolonging their suffering. "If one hundred persons are ignorant of their true situation, and are so completely blinded as not to see the destruction that awaits them," wrote Boudinot, "we can see strong reasons to justify the action of a minority of fifty persons—to do what the majority *would do* if they understood their condition—to save a *nation* from political thralldom and moral degradation." Exile was far better than submitting to the laws of the states "and thus becoming witnesses of the ruin and degradation of the Cherokee people." In another country and under different circumstances, there was a chance for the Cherokee Nation to survive and rebuild.[115]

Ross and the Cherokee delegation continued to look for justice in Washington. How would "the faithful historian" view the government's sorry record in this affair? they asked Congress. "In the name of the whole Cherokee people we protest this unhallowed and unauthorized and unacknowledged compact. We deny its binding force. We recognize none of its stipulations." They presented the new president, Martin Van Buren, with an account of the fraudulent treaty and implored him to investigate. "Our fate is in your hands—may the God of truth tear away every disguise and concealment from our case—may the God of justice guide your determination and the God of mercy stay the hand of our brother uplifted for our destruction."[116] In February 1838, 15,665 Cherokee people signed another petition protesting the treaty and begging relief from "the appalling circumstances in which we are placed by the operation of that perfidious compact." In April Ross and the delegation submitted it to Congress. The Cherokees' last hope against the coming storm lay in appealing to the justice of the US government: "Will you sustain the hopes we have rested on the public faith, the honor, the justice, of your mighty empire? We commit our cause to your favor and protection. And your memorialists, as in duty bound, will ever pray."[117] They reached in vain for the conscience of America.

As the deadline for removal approached, many officers and officials in Cherokee country feared bloodshed and saw Ross as the best person to prevent it. The removal commissioner Nathaniel Smith, who had known Ross for twenty-seven years, echoed Colonel Lindsay's appraisal that he was "an honest man and a slave to his people." Georgia governor George Gilmer hoped that once Ross and the Cherokee delegation lost all hope of delaying the treaty and returned home, they might be induced to help convince the Cherokees that their interest and safety required moving West and would "undertake to effect their voluntary removal in their own way."[118]

About nine hundred Cherokees had migrated west in the spring of 1834. Measles and cholera killed eighty-one people before they reached Arkansas. The members of the Treaty Party began their migration early in 1837. A group of about 600 went first; Major Ridge, Stand Watie, and 466 people departed in early March, and another 365 set out in October. The third detachment suffered from bad weather and sickness, and fifteen people, mostly children, died en route.[119] Pointing to the emigration of the first six hundred, Lumpkin invoked the efficacy of the same divide-and-conquer tactics that had secured the treaty. "This policy of making prudent advances to the wealthy and intelligent has gone far to remove all opposition to the treaty among the most influential class," he wrote to the commissioner of Indian affairs. "The great body of the intelligent, who have been numbered with the opponents of the treaty have become recipients under the treaty, and consequently their tone and temper in relation to that instrument have been wholly changed."[120] Major Ridge rebuilt his home and estate on Honey Creek in the northeastern part of the new Cherokee lands, near the border of Arkansas and Missouri and near where the relocated Senecas lived. He and John formed a partnership in late 1837 and opened a large general store. There would be plenty of displaced Cherokees to supply once the exodus from the East got under way.[121]

Back in Georgia, the deadline for voluntary removal expired in May 1838. On May 10 General Winfield Scott issued an address to the Cherokee people, informing then that time was just about up and that he had been sent "with a powerful army" to compel their removal in accordance with the treaty. He and his soldiers intended "to execute our painful duty in mercy." As federal troops began rounding up the Cherokees and placing them in stockades ready for relocation, Scott sent Secretary of War Poinsett encouraging reports of progress. Things were moving ahead with little interference from whites "and with all practicable kindness & mercy on the part of the troops." In Scott's mind, removal was inevitable, the Treaty of New Echota simply its instrument: "The decree of Fate," he wrote, "more than the paper called a Treaty, requires that it should be completed without delay."[122]

Huddled in internment camps, the Cherokees would succumb to removal but they would not accept the Treaty of New Echota. Scott reported that many of them "obstinately refused to receive clothing & blankets, both of which were much needed—fearing to do anything which might be construed into an acknowledgment of the treaty."[123] In late July, the Cherokee National Committee and Council met at Aquohee Camp in eastern Tennessee and passed a series of resolutions necessitated by the fact that "the whole population of the Cherokee Nation have been captured by order of the President of the United States, in order to [effect] their transportation from the land of their fathers to the west of the river Mississippi, in execution of the alleged stipulations of an instrument purporting to be a treaty made at New Echota in 1835 but against the validity of which the Cherokees have earnestly protested." They authorized Ross and other leaders to work with General Scott and direct "the whole business of the emigration of our people"; they reasserted their rights of sovereignty and self-government as recognized in their treaties with the United States, and they denounced the Treaty of New Echota and called on the United States to renegotiate it in good faith with the proper representatives of the Cherokee people. They were being removed by fraud and force but they were emigrating "in their national capacity" and had not given up their claims to their homeland, their institutions, or their pre-Echota treaty rights. Ross assumed the role of Superintendent of Removal and Subsistence. Scott was happy to work with the Cherokee leadership—despite his upbeat reports, like many other US officers and officials he regarded Ross's assistance as important to stave off bloodshed.[124]

Opposition from Ross was not the only thing holding up removal; there were problems with the logistics and planning. The panic of 1837 had hamstrung the efforts of commissioners to settle claims, and periodic wavering on the part of the Van Buren administration perpetuated hopes that the deadline might be extended.[125] Removal under the terms of the treaty involved more than simply herding people west. Article 8 stipulated that once the Cherokees reached their new homes the United States would support them with rations for one year or $33.33 each "if they prefer it."[126] The challenges of dealing with Cherokee claims, assessing the value of improvements, and trying to ascertain how many Cherokees preferred cash rather than subsistence caused headaches for the officials responsible for implementing removal under the terms of a treaty noted, according to Hon. Joseph L. Williams, for its ambiguity, verbiage, and complexity. "If Mr. Schermerhorn deliberately *designed* and contrived its precise structure, to involve difficulty and defy construction," he wrote the secretary of war, "then is his *ingenuity* most complete and incontestable; but, if perspicuity was honestly his aim, then his folly and stupidity deserve to be patented."[127]

John Ross managed to get Congress to increase the total allowed for removal to $6,647,067. Ross and his removal committee organized the people into thirteen detachments of about one thousand each and recorded every financial transaction associated with the process. The funds for removal had been estimated at $30 per person. The actual costs for those who had already migrated came closer to $60 each. Delayed by drought, fleeced by traders and turnpike keepers, and traveling through snow, the emigrants in Ross's parties ran up expenses that exceeded $100 per person. The expenses exhausted the funds set aside for removal and cut into the funds provided for per capita distribution to the tune of about $500,000, approximately 10 percent of the total amount awarded by the treaty. Controversy over these costs raged for years: Ross campaigned to get more money from the government to help meet the costs; his opponents accused him of lining his own pockets.[128]

Ross had led his people in prayer as they began their march west. The hardships of the early migrants paled in comparison with the horrors and death toll experienced by those who underwent forced removal. John G. Burnett, a private in the Second Tennessee Volunteers, recalled that "men working in the fields were arrested and driven to the stockades. Women were dragged from their homes by soldiers whose language they could not understand. Children were separated from their parents and driven into the stockades." He saw Cherokees driven at bayonet point and loaded into wagons "like cattle or sheep." He watched them struggle through rain and snow and along "a trail of death," saw twenty-two die in one night of pneumonia, and was on guard duty the night that Quatie, John Ross's wife of twenty-five years, died. More than half a century later, he was still haunted by the memory of "six-hundred and forty-five wagons lumbering over the frozen ground with their Cargo of suffering humanity" and "the four-thousand silent graves that mark the trail." In Burnett's view, it was a national act of murder. "At this time," he wrote in

1890, "we are too near the removal of the Cherokees for our young people to fully understand the enormity of the crime that was committed against a helpless race, truth is the facts are being concealed from the young people of today. School children of today do not know that we are living on lands that were taken from a helpless race at the bayonet point to satisfy the white man's greed for gold." He expected future generations to condemn the act.[129]

John Ridge, however, blamed Ross for much of the suffering: "If Ross had told them the truth in time," they would have had chance to sell off "their furniture, their horses, their cattle, hogs, and sheep, and their growing corn."[130] Elijah Butler, the missionary who had gone to jail with Samuel Worcester, disagreed and charged "all the suffering and all the difficulties of the Cherokee people...to the accounts of Messrs. Ridge and Boudinot."[131]

According to War Department statistics, 1838 was the high-water year for removal of eastern Indians to the west of the Mississippi: of the 73,860 people relocated in the eight years after the Indian Removal Act, 25,139 went in 1838.[132] While Cherokees made their way along the Trail of Tears as a result of his work at New Echota, John Schermerhorn was busy closer to home in New York, negotiating another fraudulent removal treaty, this one at Buffalo Creek with the Senecas, although the government withdrew his commission before the treaty was completed in 1838. He also orchestrated the removal of Brothertown and Stockbridge Indians. Originally from New England, these Indians had built new Christian communities in Oneida country after the Revolution, only to be removed first to Indiana and then to Wisconsin. Schermerhorn tried to bully them into yet another removal to Kansas. As he had shown at New Echota, the Indians' Christianity, "civilization," and record of friendship with the United States counted for nothing: he saw all Indians as a race who could not live side by side with whites and who stood in the way of American progress.[133] In his time as Indian commissioner, Schermerhorn participated in negotiations with twenty different tribes. In 1841 the Dutch Reformed Church appointed him missionary to establish a new congregation in Indiana. He died in 1851 at the age of sixty-five.[134]

Cherokee Civil Wars

Things did not improve for the Cherokees after they arrived in Indian Territory. Under the Treaty of New Echota the US government was to provide rations for a year, but widespread fraud among officials and contractors resulted in insufficient rations of poor quality reaching the Cherokees.[135] The treaty also stipulated that, after the costs of removal had been deducted from the $5 million owed the Cherokees for the sale of their eastern homeland, the remaining amount was to be divided on a per capita basis. Did that mean all the Cherokees, or only those who were forced west against their will, as John Ross argued? The chief of the western Cherokees, John Brown, and assistant chiefs John Rodgers and John Looney argued that their people were entitled to a share of the money because they were being asked to share their lands with the roughly fourteen thousand Cherokees who survived the Trail of Tears. In one of its last acts before removal, the Cherokee National Council had passed a resolution declaring that the government and constitution of the Cherokee Nation would be transferred intact to the West. The Old Settlers, as the three thousand or so western Cherokees were known, had their own government and had no intention of letting it become submerged in the newly imported government of the Cherokee majority. The two thousand Cherokees associated with the Treaty Party were also understandably nervous about a government dominated by Ross and the National Party. The several groups met at Takatoka in June 1839 to discuss how to rebuild the Cherokee government but at the end of the council some 100 to 150 National Party members met secretly and drew up a list of men they believed should suffer the death penalty for signing the Treaty of New Echota in violation of the Cherokee law that Major Ridge had supported and John Ridge had put into writing ten years before. Both Ridges, Elias Boudinot, Stand Watie, and others were named. Three men from the clan of each of the accused were asked to sit in judgment and, in each case, they condemned the accused to die. Numbered slips of paper were drawn from a hat; those who drew a paper marked with an X were designated the executioners.[136]

Early on the morning of June 22, 1839, two dozen men surrounded the home of John Ridge. Three of them entered the house, dragged Ridge from his bed and into the yard where they stabbed him twenty-three times, and then beat him to death in front of his screaming wife and children. Ridge's twelve-year-old son, John Rollin, said later that the killing "darkened my mind with an eternal shadow"; he carried the image, and the desire for revenge, the rest of his life. Another group went to Elias Boudinot's house and requested medicine from the nearby mission of Samuel Worcester. As Boudinot led them to the mission they stabbed him in the back with their bowie knives and split his skull with repeated tomahawk blows. Major Ridge was shot from his horse on his way "to visit a sick negro belonging to his family." Someone—Samuel Worcester, or a Choctaw riding Worcester's horse, or a carpenter sent by Delight Boudinot— got warning to Stand Watie, who fled to safety. Watie, who now became the recognized leader of the Treaty Party, blamed Ross and swore to avenge the killings. Ross's son, Allen, claimed his father knew nothing about the killings. Delight Boudinot sent warning to Ross that Watie was after his life; Cherokees from the National Party mounted an armed guard around the chief's house, and Ross asked Brigadier General Matthew Arbuckle, the US military commander of the area stationed at Fort Gibson, to intervene and prevent the spilling of innocent blood.[137]

Men who had worked with the victims to dispossess the Cherokees were outraged at the murders. John Schermerhorn wrote a public tribute to John Ridge, defending his conduct in making the Treaty of New Echota. Ridge, Boudinot, and their friends "knew they were running a dreadful risk" in signing the treaty in defiance of a law Ridge himself had drawn up, but they "had counted the cost and deliberately made up their minds, if need be, to offer up their lives as a sacrifice . . . to save their country from a war of extermination and ruin." Unlike Ross, said Schermerhorn, Ridge and his friends acted from pure and patriotic motives. At their last meeting, in New York the previous April, Ridge had told Schermerhorn: "I may yet some day die by the hand of some poor infatuated Indian, deluded by the counsels of Ross and his minions, but we have this to console us, we shall have suffered and died in a good cause." In the hands of the architect of the Treaty of New Echota, Ridge and his associates became martyrs, not traitors, elevating Schermerhorn's treaty from a sordid land grab to a noble cause.[138] Governor Lumpkin likewise extolled the members of the Treaty Party as men of vision who had led their people to happiness and prosperity in the West, only to fall victim to "that most *horrid, appalling, deepest* of all mid-night crimes" (although the murders were carried out in daylight). "The best half of the intelligence, virtue and patriotism of the Cherokee people has been basely murdered, to gratify the revenge and ambition of John Ross," he wrote. Suddenly concerned about the nation's honor, Lumpkin thought it "a crying sin against the United States" that the murderers had not been punished "as justice and law demanded."[139]

News of the murders produced predictions of "fatal consequences" and civil war within the Cherokee Nation.[140] General Arbuckle compiled a list of those believed responsible for the killings and asked Ross to hand them over. He also advocated military intervention to settle the difficulties.[141] Ross and his chiefs denied responsibility for the assassinations and asked why the Cherokees were being singled out for attention, when the law of retaliation still functioned in many tribes. Ross, who had requested that Arbuckle intervene with federal troops when his life was in danger, now protested against Arbuckle's interference in Cherokee affairs and asked what right the United States had to deprive the Cherokee Nation of its sovereign right to exercise its legitimate authority over acts committed by one Cherokee against another. *If* it was true that Ridge and Boudinot "were killed by the orders of the constituted authorities of the nation, their lives were forfeited under an existing law of the nation," a law Ridge himself had voted. The Ross party cited the terms of the Treaty of New Echota, the treaty they rejected, as evidence of their right to self-government and the United States' obligation to keep peace with all the Cherokees, not just the minority.[142]

In 1839, various branches of the Cherokee Nation reassembled in Indian Territory. Several hundred Cherokees had settled in eastern Texas in the winter of 1819–20, welcomed by the Mexican government as a buffer against expanding American settlement. Their position became tenuous after Texas won its independence in 1836, and it grew increasingly perilous under Governor Mirabeau Lamar's policies of ethnic cleansing. In July 1839 the Republic of Texas drove out the Cherokees; their chief Duwali or Bowles was killed at the Battle of Neches River, and the survivors fled to Indian Territory where they rejoined their relatives.[143]

That same month, nearly two thousand Cherokees—Old Settlers, eastern Cherokees, and Texas Cherokees—gathered in a meeting at the Illinois Camp Ground at Tahlequah. Declaring themselves a general convention of the Cherokee Nation, they drafted documents for a new government. The National Party adopted a resolution pardoning those who had carried out the executions and outlawing anyone who advocated vengeance on the executioners. Some Old Settlers signed an act of union with the National Party and the Tahlequah council ratified a new Constitution of the United Cherokee Nation and elected Ross principal chief. But most Old Settlers joined the Treaty Party in its opposition to Ross.[144]

At the same time as the Cherokees and other emigrant tribes wrestled with their internal schisms, they had to deal with the Indian peoples of the southern plains and prairies who regarded them as intruders. Tahlequah became the scene of multinational Indian councils where the Cherokees and their neighbors attempted to establish peaceful relations and bring peace and order to Indian Territory by the practiced methods of Indian diplomacy and alliance building. Four thousand Indians from twenty-two nations attended the grand council at Tahlequah in June 1843. Cherokee, Creek, Delaware, Shawnee, Wyandot delegates reaching out to Osages, Iowas, Pawnees, and other western tribes employed the diplomatic traditions they had brought with them from the East, relying on "wampum, kinship, ritual, and council fires to help organize life in their new environment." But the intertribal and intratribal divisions stemming from removal proved insurmountable.[145]

After the deaths of the primary signatories of the Treaty of New Echota, the story of that treaty revolves around the man who most steadfastly resisted it. Year after year John Ross wrote page after page—to the secretary of war, Congress, successive presidents, and various individuals—on Cherokee rights, Cherokee history, Cherokee treaties, and Cherokee political status. He pushed the government to honor or even improve the terms of the treaty at the same time as he continued to deny the validity of the treaty. Sometimes he was in

Washington six months a year. At first the government refused to recognize him, and continued to deal with Treaty Party delegates. In April 1840, General Arbuckle informed a delegation of Old Settler and Emigrant Cherokees at Fort Gibson that, despairing of the Cherokees being able to settle their differences themselves, the United States insisted that the Old Settlers hold one-third of the offices in the new Cherokee government, and Secretary of War Poinsett ordered that John Ross and William Coodey be removed from office. The Cherokee Council immediately denounced such measures as an assault on the Cherokee Nation's rights of elective government and "destructive to the principles of a republican Government."[146]

But the 1840 elections brought a Whig administration to power, and President Harrison (soon replaced by John Tyler) and the new secretary of war, John Bell, gave Ross a much warmer reception. Again invoking the written assurances that Jefferson had given the Cherokees forty years before, Ross reminded Bell that the Cherokee Nation sought "nothing more than the performance of such promises as this parchment embodies, and as have been so often reiterated, not only before, but since; and in the solemn form of treaties."[147] For a while Ross was hopeful that his efforts to renegotiate the New Echota treaty might bear fruit, but by the time he wrote his annual message to the Cherokee Nation in November 1842 it was clear that no renegotiation was likely.[148]

Meanwhile the violence emanating from the treaty continued and escalated. In 1840 Archilla Smith, who had signed the treaty, stabbed John McIntosh to death in an argument. He was arrested and put on trial in Cherokee court in Tahlequah. Stand Watie defended him but Smith was found guilty. Watie drew up a petition for pardon, Ross denied it, and Smith was hanged.[149] In May 1842, according to the Treaty Party, an armed group "set out upon the unhallowed purpose of murdering the aged widow of fallen Major Ridge."[150] That same month Stand Watie encountered James Foreman, one of the men accused of assassinating the treaty signers, in a grocery store. There was an altercation, and Watie threw his drink into Foreman's face. As Foreman reached to pick up a board, Watie stabbed him with his bowie knife and then fired his pistol at him but missed. Foreman died shortly afterward. Watie stood trial in the state of Arkansas the next year but was acquitted on grounds of self-defense.[151] Meanwhile, Watie gained a wife and lost his father: in September 1842, he married Sarah Caroline Bell (they had three sons: Saladin Ridge, Comiskey, and Solon Watica, and two daughters, Ninnie Josephine and Charlotte Jacqueline); his father died later that year.[152]

In 1843, Isaac Bushyhead was murdered and David Vann seriously wounded, by George and Jacob West and others. Elijah Hicks was also attacked. The sons of James Starr, who had been condemned to death with Boudinot and the Ridges, murdered a Cherokee family and burned their home.[153] John Rollin

Ridge, away at school in Great Barrington, Massachusetts, wrote his uncle, Stand Watie, telling him he would always be pleased to hear of the deaths of those who had murdered his relatives.[154] Eighteen forty-five brought another round of killings. On November 2, a party of pro-removal Cherokees including Thomas, Ellis, and Washington Star, Ellis Rider, and Ellis West, murdered two Cherokees "and mangled their bodies in the most horrible manner." Someone burned the home of Ross's daughter, Jane, and attempted to kill her husband, Return J. Meigs (a grandson of the Indian agent of the same name). A week later, a mob killed James Starr and Ellis Starr; five days after that Stand Watie's brother Thomas was tomahawked, shot, and stabbed to death.[155] Watie gathered guns and men and vowed to avenge his brother. Robberies, murders, and revenge killings spread fear through Cherokee country, and alarmed whites in Arkansas urged the government to take action.

The civil war in Cherokee country was accompanied by a war of words in delegations by all three parties to Washington and memorials to Congress, and fees to Washington lawyers, all of which fueled "the flame of discord in the Cherokee nation."[156] The Old Settler party complained to Congress that the Treaty of New Echota ignored the prior treaty rights of the western Cherokees, sending the eastern Cherokees to live on their lands without asking their consent or paying compensation. Whereas the Treaty Party had moved west and settled under laws of the existing Cherokee community in Arkansas, Ross and his followers thought of themselves "not as ordinary emigrants, but as a *nation* moving, carrying with them sovereignty, a constitution, laws, usages, and all the officers of an organized community.... They determined, by bloodshed and revolution, at once to overthrow the established government, and take all power over our territory and our people into their own hands." The relationship of the three Cherokee parties to the Treaty of New Echota presented "a spectacle": "The treaty party, who were recognized east as competent to cede away a territory and extinguish a nation, are not considered west worthy to be protected when living, or avenged when dead." Ross and his chiefs, "who were not recognized east as clothed with authority to prevent the execution of the treaty," were now recognized as the Cherokee Nation and received all its benefits, even though they rejected the treaty. And the western Cherokees, who were not party to the treaty, were left to "protest against its assumptions and its consequences."[157]

Indian agents Stambaugh and Kendall were outraged at the turn of events in the ten years since New Echota. "Look now at the condition of those whom the United States had encouraged to make a treaty with them, and had a hundred times promised to protect," they wrote the secretary of war. "*Their first men were murdered, and all the rest of them outlawed, for no other offence than signing that treaty!*" Not one of the assassins had been brought to justice. The government had abandoned the Treaty Party "to the tender mercies of John Ross" who, "with scarcely enough Cherokee blood in his veins to mark him as of Indian descent," had deluded the majority of the Cherokees into thinking "that he is true to the aboriginal race, while his full-blooded rivals are traitors to their country and their kindred." Ross was truly "an extraordinary man." He had resisted removal to the last, causing untold suffering, and then had gotten himself put in charge of the removal arrangements. "Thus strengthened for mischief, upon his arrival on the Arkansas, he destroyed his rivals, overturned the existing government, established his power through blood and usurpation; and in all this he has been tolerated by the United States." Ruled by avarice, they contended, Ross "comes to Washington every year, spending in luxury and pleasure the funds of the nation, under pretence of settling their difficulties; but never makes a proposition which tends to their settlement."[158] Ross meanwhile, in the summer of 1844 courted, largely by correspondence, and married a new wife, a Quaker named Mary Stapler.[159]

A change of administration changed the situation in Washington again. The new government was not likely to renegotiate the Treaty of New Echota. Ross and Watie were both in Washington in the spring of 1846, Ross still pushing for a new treaty, but in Cherokee country the violence continued. A letter to Watie from John Rollin Ridge, then studying law in Fayetteville, Arkansas, contained a telling line: "No very important transactions have happened since your departure, except the killing of five or six Indians of the Ross party." A few days later, he wrote again, asking his uncle to get him a bowie knife.[160] Ross portrayed Watie and his "lawless band of armed men" as a threat to the Cherokee government and the safety of Cherokee people and asked President James Polk to order them dispersed.[161] Doubting that the different Cherokee parties could ever again live together in peace, Polk in April 1846 proposed dividing the Cherokee Nation among the various factions.[162] The House Committee on Indian Affairs supported the president's recommendation and a bill was introduced seeking legislation to divide the Cherokee Nation. The bill did not pass but it pressured the groups to make peace. Ross read the president's message "with equal grief and astonishment."[163] He had fought for years *against* the Treaty of New Echota and *for* the sovereignty and unity of the Cherokee Nation; now he had no choice but to compromise or see the nation permanently divided. By the terms of a treaty, signed on August 6, 1846, Ross agreed to accept and work with the Treaty of New Echota. He also agreed to include the Old Settlers and members of the Treaty Party in the per capita distribution of the land sale. In return the Old Settlers relinquished their claim to be sole owners of the new homeland and in effect yielded government of the nation to the National Party. The treaty stipulated that there should be a general amnesty for all crimes committed by the rival groups during the previous seven years. Ross and Stand

Watie shook hands when they signed the treaty. The Senate ratified it the next day.[164]

The feuds and vendettas subsided and the Cherokees directed their energies to rebuilding their nation. As principal chief, Ross worked assiduously "to squeeze every possible cent" owed to the Cherokees by the Treaty of New Echota. After 1846, the nation's annual operating expenses were met essentially from the income of a trust fund of $500,800 established under the treaty. The $35,000 to $45,000 the fund generated each year was insufficient to pay for government buildings, salaries, police, courts, delegations to Washington, the tribal newspaper, and the nation's schools. Ross argued that the government had no right to deduct the costs of removal from the $5 million it paid for the Cherokee homeland; that Cherokees who had resisted removal and the treaty of New Echota should be fully compensated for the losses they suffered; that the government still owed the nation some of the expenses incurred in carrying out removal, and that it should pay the Cherokees interest at 5 percent on all unpaid sums. For Ross, securing these additional monies was vital to rebuilding the Cherokee Nation. But the War Department resisted his demands and when the federal accounting office tallied up all the amounts subtracted for the costs of removal, compensation for spoliations, and remunerations for lost improvements, it determined that of the original $5 million only $627, 603.95 remained for per capita payments. Ross fought on, despite the fact that the government's attention was focused on the War with Mexico, and lawyers' bills further depleted the Cherokees' finances. Finally, in 1852, the government agreed that removal costs should not be deducted from the $5 million paid for the Cherokees' land, that almost $1 million was owed the Cherokees for removal expenses, and that 5 percent interest should be added to these sums when they were paid. When the per capita payments were finally made to the members of the Ross and Treaty parties, each Cherokee received $92.79. Years later, after Ross was dead, Congress reconsidered the issues he had raised and decided that the government owed the Cherokees an additional $961,368.[165]

Slowly, the Cherokee economy began to recover. Stand Watie developed a law practice and merchandise business. But the Treaty of 1846 did not heal the deep divisions between the Ross and Ridge parties.[166] Some members of the Watie-Boudinot family went to California during the gold rush, including John Rollin Ridge. In 1849, in a dispute over a horse, John Rollin shot and killed a Ross sympathizer named David Knell. John Rollin's mother and family wanted him to "leave the nation forever, and have nothing more to do with it." He fled across the Missouri border and made his way to California the next year, leaving his wife and daughter to follow. From California, he wrote to Stand Watie: "There is a deep-seated principle of revenge in me which will never be satisfied until it reaches its object." But he also wrote other things. He became a journalist, poet, and author. (His fictionalized story, *The Life and Adventures of Joaquin Murieta, The Celebrated California Bandit* [1854] was the first novel by a Native American, the first written in California, and the basis of later Zorro stories.) He never returned to Cherokee country.[167]

The old removal-era divisions flared again with the outbreak of the Civil War.[168] The Confederacy sent General Albert Pike, its commissioner of Indian affairs, to negotiate treaties of alliance with the tribes in Indian Territory. Ross favored neutrality. The month after Confederate guns fired on Fort Sumter, he issued a proclamation to the Cherokee people "reminding them of the obligations arising under their Treaties with the United States and urging them to the faithful observance of said Treaties, by the maintenance of Peace and friendship towards the People of all the States." He then wrote to Albert Pike respectfully declining the invitation to enter into a treaty with the Confederate States of America.[169] Stand Watie, on the other hand, raised a regiment for the Confederacy. His second son, fifteen-year-old Saladin, joined the Confederate army to serve alongside him.

Ross and the Cherokee Nation soon changed their tune. So long as there was hope that the differences could be resolved, he explained, neutrality was the proper course for the Cherokee people. But the withdrawal of federal troops from frontier posts and early Confederate victories indicated that the Union would not survive, leaving the Cherokees with no choice: "Our Geographical position and domestic institutions [i.e., slavery] allied us to the South." In October, the Cherokee Nation made a treaty with Pike. The Confederacy assumed all the treaty obligations due the Cherokees from the United States and the Cherokee changed their political relations "from the United to the Confederate States."[170] The Cherokees raised a second mounted regiment, commanded by John Drew.

But the Union forces returned in 1862. Watie remained steadfast in his allegiance to the Confederacy but Drew's regiment defected to the Union side after the North's victory at the three-day battle of Pea Ridge in March. "Now the Cherokee schism was wider," notes the historian Laurence Hauptman in his study of Native Americans in the Civil War, "between blue and gray as well as Indian and Indian." In the summer, Union forces marched on Tahlequah and captured Ross. He was paroled after making a proclamation of loyalty to the United States, and he spent the rest of the war in Washington and Philadelphia trying to mend fences with the United States. In his absence the Cherokee National Council elected Watie principal chief of the Cherokee Nation (South). Watie's forces not only conducted hit-and-run raids against Union troops and supply lines but also raided within the Cherokee Nation, plundering and sometimes killing Ross followers.[171] In 1863 the Ross party abrogated the alliance with the Confederacy, declared their allegiance to the

United States, and abolished slavery. Ross cited the Treaty of New Echota to justify the brief Confederate alliance. By the sixth article the United States had agreed to "protect the Cherokee Nation from domestic strife and foreign enemies." Ross had resisted earlier intrusions on the basis of this provision as an infringement on Cherokee sovereignty; now he cited the United States' failure to provide the promised protection in 1861 as leaving the Cherokees "utterly powerless" in the face of the rebel invasion and with no choice but to make a Confederate treaty.[172]

In effect there were now two Cherokee nations: the Northern Cherokees led by Ross and the Southern Cherokees led by Watie. Watie burned John Ross's home at Park Hill during the war. Three of Ross's sons served in the war, and James died in a prison camp in 1864. Ross's wife, Mary, died of lung congestion in Philadelphia in July 1865.[173] Watie's nephew Elias Cornelius Boudinot was sent as a delegate to the Confederate Congress, in accordance with the Cherokee-Confederate treaty. The war years took a toll on Watie's family. Watie's wife, Sarah, took refuge in Texas. Their third son, Comiskey, died in the spring of 1863. Two months later, Sarah heard that Saladin had killed a prisoner. She wrote Watie that she found herself "almost dead sometimes thinking about it. I am afraid that Saladin will never value human life as he ought." Sarah suffered from poor health and depression. She had lived with the internal Cherokee conflicts so long that she said she would like to live "a short time in peace just to see how it would be." Watie was appointed commander of the Confederate Indian Cavalry Brigade in 1864; in June 1865, he was the last Confederate general to surrender.[174]

The Civil War in Cherokee country, and the resurgent civil war within the Cherokee Nation, was disastrous. Population fell from twenty-one thousand to fifteen thousand; thousands of Cherokees were refugees; one-third of married women were widows and one-quarter of Cherokee children were orphans; and Cherokees lost three hundred thousand head of cattle in raids by Union and Confederate forces.[175] Then, at the Treaty of Fort Smith in September 1865, the United States imposed terms on the Cherokees. The Cherokee delegation to the multitribal council was made up of two factions: one representing Ross's Northern group, the other Watie's Southern followers. The five US commissioners (who included the Seneca General Ely S. Parker, who served as General Grant's military secretary during the war, and Major General W. S. Harney, who would figure prominently in negotiations at Medicine Lodge two years later) treated the Cherokee delegations as one. Cherokees had supported the Confederacy; consequently, the Cherokee Nation had forfeited all treaty rights with the United States. In the summer of 1866, the Northern and Southern Cherokees each sent a delegation to Washington to negotiate a final peace treaty, each hoping to be recognized as the legitimate Cherokee nation. John

Rollin Ridge traveled to Washington to join Stand and Saladin Watie and Elias C. Boudinot as a member of a Southern Cherokee delegation. Finding that the United States recognized Ross and the Northern Cherokees, Watie and the Southern Cherokees sought to have Cherokee country divided into two nations but lost their bid. A new treaty was drawn up between the Cherokees and the United States, declaring null and void the Cherokee treaty with the Confederacy, prohibiting slavery, and establishing railroad rights of way through Cherokee country. In addition, the United States asserted the right to settle other Indians in the Cherokee Nation and took possession of Cherokee lands in Kansas and the Cherokee Strip. The Senate ratified the treaty on August 11, 1866.

John Ross died in Washington ten days before the treaty was ratified. John Rollin Ridge returned to California where he died in September 1867. Saladin died in February 1868 at age twenty-one; Watica died of pneumonia while away at school in April 1869.[176] Stand Watie, a delegate at the Okmulgee council in 1870, died at Honey Creek, in September 9, 1871.[177] Both his daughters died, unmarried, in 1875. Sarah Watie lived another eight years. A widow who had buried all five of her children, she never got the chance "to see how it would be" to live in peace.

Because the emigrant tribes who allied with the Confederacy forfeited all their treaty rights with the United States, the government was free to disregard removal-era guarantees that the Indians would enjoy undisturbed possession of their new lands. In the next couple of years, some tribes would be required to give up substantial lands in the western part of Indian Territory—to provide reservations for the Southern Arapahos, Southern Cheyennes, Kiowas, Comanches, and Plains Apaches established under the terms of the Treaty of Medicine Lodge.

Treaty Making in the West

In 1804 Meriwether Lewis and William Clark, the brother of George Rogers Clark, departed St. Louis on a two-year odyssey to the Pacific and back with "the Corps of Discovery." They went to explore the newly acquired Louisiana Territory and beyond and to proclaim American sovereignty over a world where Native people held the power. "In all your intercourse with the natives," Jefferson instructed Lewis, "treat them in the most friendly and conciliatory manner which their own conduct will permit."[1] Lewis and Clark had both been at the Treaty of Greenville in 1795, and, although the young nation's muscle flexing was never far beneath the surface during their western expedition, they generally followed tried and tested protocols of Indian diplomacy in order to make their way through Indian country, just as they relied on Indian guides, Indian knowledge, and Indian assistance to get them where they were going. Their expedition marked the beginning of a diplomatic and colonial relationship between the United States and the Indian nations west of the Mississippi that would generate dozens of treaties. As the eminent scholar of Indian law Felix Cohen observed, the United States paid Napoleon Bonaparte $15 million for the transfer of political authority over the Louisiana Territory, and then proceeded to pay the Indian tribes—the actual owners of the ceded territory—more than twenty times that amount as it took possession of the land in treaty after treaty.[2] American diplomacy west of the Mississippi replicated what had happened in the East. When Indians held the power, Americans adhered to Native American protocols; when the balance of power shifted irrevocably away from Indians, the United States continued to observe some of the forms of treaty making but subordinated them to the function of its treaties: to remove Indians from the land and obliterate their way of life.

Lewis and Clark entered a complicated diplomatic landscape in which initiating an alliance with one Indian nation could jeopardize relations with another. For more than a century, Indian tribes on the Great Plains and beyond had waged escalating contests for horses, guns, and hunting territories; at the same time, they engaged in increasing diplomatic activity to create, maintain, and renew alliances and exchange networks that were vital to obtaining and defending access to horses, guns, and hunting territories.[3] Intertribal diplomacy catered for the suspension of hostilities in the interests of exchange. Alliances were part of the strategies necessary to deal with changing situations; the ebb and flow of power on the Plains sometimes made it expedient to make peace with yesterday's enemies in order to confront a more serious threat today. When Europeans arrived, some Indian people incorporated the outsiders into their kinship systems and exchange networks, but the onus was on the Europeans to adjust to Indian ways when they dealt with the nations who held the upper hand and, to a large extent, determined which Europeans entered and operated in their country.

At the end of the seventeenth century, both France and Spain had imperial aspirations in Texas. The French saw it as an area into which they could extend the network of Indian trade and alliances they had already established in the Mississippi Valley. For Spain, Texas represented a northern periphery of a great American empire, a vast borderland that might help thwart French intrusions and protect more valuable holdings to the south, particularly the silver mines of Mexico. French and Spaniards both courted the allegiance of the Caddos in what is now eastern Texas and Louisiana. Caddo power and numbers had plummeted since the first Spanish expedition wandered through their country in 1542: epidemic diseases had cut their population dramatically, perhaps from as many as two hundred thousand to as few as ten thousand, and as farmers they faced increasing pressure from mounted and mobile enemies. Nevertheless, they were strategically located, and far-reaching trade routes ran in and out of their villages. Accustomed to making pacts of friendship with other tribes, they extended their network of trade and alliance to include Europeans, who might provide merchandise and military assistance against their enemies. Caddos smoked the calumet pipe with the newcomers, gave them gifts, and offered them their women. Europeans frequently misinterpreted this as evidence of Indians' promiscuity—Caddo women often functioned as diplomatic mediators.[4]

Indian power in the interior of the continent continued to limit European ambitions and compel European diplomatic responses throughout the eighteenth century. The Osages dominated the region between the Arkansas and Red rivers for much of the century. They exploited their trade with the French to expand their power over rival tribes and dictated the terms on which Europeans entered their domain. Spaniards and French alike treated them with healthy respect and courted their friendship.[5] Meanwhile Spain confronted a new and growing power on the southern Plains, one produced and propelled by the horses the Spaniards themselves had introduced. Comanches and Utes moved out of the foothills of the Rockies and advanced onto the rich grasslands of the southern Plains, where they consolidated their position as horse-and-buffalo Indians. They captured and enslaved women and children from other tribes, incorporated other peoples into their society, and built exchange networks that enabled them to dominate trade between New Mexico and French Louisiana. By mid-century, the Comanches were the dominant power on the southern Plains. They raided deep into Texas, New Mexico, and Spain's other northern provinces, carrying off captives and livestock and draining the limited resources Spain could afford for frontier defense.[6] Confronted by Ute, Comanche, and Apache nomads who proved more than a match for heavily equipped Spanish soldiers in thinly spread garrisons, Spaniards came to rely on Pueblo and O'odham allies and on diplomacy to defend their provinces.[7]

When Tomás Vélez Cachupín became the governor of New Mexico in 1749, he inherited a colony beset by Indian enemies. Lacking the manpower and resources to maintain a constant war effort, Vélez Cachupín turned to diplomacy to secure the protection his province needed. After he defeated a large Comanche war party in 1751, he made peace, sitting down and smoking with the Comanche chiefs who visited trade fairs at the Pueblo towns. By the time he left office, he had made peace with the Utes, Navajos, and Apaches as well. He left his successor advice on how to preserve that peace with the tribes, especially the Comanches, and why it was necessary to do so. Spain had been too quick to respond with force and had alienated Indians whose friendship might have been secured by trade and diplomacy, he said. "There is not a nation among the numerous ones which live around this government in which a kind word does not have more effect than the execution of the sword."[8] The peace did not hold, and when Vélez Cachupín became governor a second time in 1762 he found the Comanches on the brink of war with New Mexico. Quickly following his own advice, he dispatched six captive Comanche women as emissaries, inviting the Comanches to Santa Fe for peace talks. A month later a Comanche delegation rode in, armed with French guns and ammunition. Vélez Cachupín reestablished peace with them and sent them away well fed and loaded with presents and bundles of tobacco "so that, in the councils of their chiefs, principal men, and elders, they might smoke and consider well their resolution in regard to my purposes."[9]

Despite Vélez Cachupín's advice and efforts, Spanish-Comanche relations continued to be marred by hostilities. In 1779, Governor Juan Bautista de Anza defeated and killed the Comanche chief Cuerno Verde (Green Horn). Realizing that the years of fighting could have been avoided if Spain had always treated the Comanches "with gentleness and justice," Anza quickly moved to restore peace.[10] Following Native diplomatic protocols that involved exchanging gifts and sending Comanche women as mediators, Spaniards and Comanches made peace in Texas in 1785 and in New Mexico early the next year at Santa Fe.[11] The Utes, alarmed at the prospect of peace between their Spanish allies and the Comanches, sent delegates to Santa Fe to observe the Comanche-Spanish peace and then made peace themselves with the Comanches. After the requisite pipe ceremonialism, gifts of horses, and probably an exchange of captives, the Utes and Comanches became reconciled after more than a quarter century of conflict and concluded a peace agreement in February 1786, sanctifying the pact "according to their manner, their chiefs and the individuals mutually exchanging clothes in the presence of the governor."[12]

Horses that transformed the balance of powers on the southern Plains spread northward, following and expanding networks of exchange, kinship, and alliance. Apaches traded horses to Pueblos; Kiowas and Kiowa-Apaches traded them to Caddos; Wichitas and Pawnees traded them to Osages; Comanches and Utes traded them to Shoshonis. Shoshonis, Flatheads, and Nez Perces traded them to Crows and to Blackfeet. Blackfeet traded them to Assiniboines. Crows, Kiowas, Arapahos, Cheyennes, and others brought horses to the villages of the Mandans, Hidatsas, and Arikaras. The Lakotas, the western Sioux, obtained horses at the Arikara villages and traded them to their eastern Yankton and Dakota relatives. Indian hunters living on the Plains who for years had traveled to the Missouri River trading centers to exchange meat and leather for corn, tobacco, and other crops grown there now went to obtain manufactured goods and guns as well. Bands of Crows and Cheyennes brought horses and meat to the villages, traded for guns and goods, and then headed back to the Plains where they traded those guns and goods to more distant neighbors. Crow traders often traveled to a rendezvous with the Shoshonis in southwestern Wyoming; the Shoshonis in turn traded with the Nez Perces, Flatheads, and other groups in the mountains. Many of those groups were in contact in turn with Native traders at the Dalles, the great salmon fishing site on the Columbia River. The Native traders also connected with European and American maritime traders on the Pacific Coast. When Indian peoples traded, they smoked, made or renewed alliances, and intermarried. The huge web of trading networks that spanned the West was held together by ritual, kinship, and sacred pledges as well as by shared economic needs and opportunities.

Lewis and Clark traveled across parts of this web, but they could neither see its full extent nor fully appreciate how it was built. They were rather like the blind man feeling the elephant. Leaving St. Louis in June 1804 and heading up the Missouri River, they had to learn to navigate the turbulent waters of inter- and intratribal politics. They tested their Indian diplomacy among the Otos, Omahas, and Missouris, once-powerful tribes badly reduced by disease. Meeting and smoking in council after council, the American captains announced the new era of peace and prosperity that would surely come to the Indians now that their land "belonged" to the Great Father in Washington. They gave gifts, flags, and medals to Indian chiefs, sometimes distinguishing between chiefs of different rank by giving medals of different grade.[13] Lewis and Clark understood that giving tobacco served "as a calling card for Europeans and Americans seeking entrée into Indian societies," and they dispensed twists of tobacco and other gifts among the tribes they met. But their reluctance to give gifts to the Brulé Sioux almost caused them to come to blows.[14]

The Sioux bands on the Missouri were accustomed to levying tribute from St. Louis traders and were not about to allow the American strangers to pass upriver to other tribes without exacting a share of their cargo. Clark called them "the pirates of the Missouri." Determined to show that the United States would not be bullied, the Americans refused to concede. There was a tense scene in which each side stood to arms. "I felt my Self warm & Spoke in verry [sic] positive terms," wrote Lewis with characteristic understatement. Only the presence of Indian women and children and a measured conciliation on the part of the Brulé chief Black Buffalo averted conflict. The Americans tossed the Indians some tobacco as a token tribute and Black Buffalo allowed them to proceed. It was touch-and-go. The Brulés followed the Americans for a while and offered them women, which Lewis and Clark rejected (or at least they said they did in their journals), interpreting the offer as evidence of immorality rather than an effort to establish relations of peace and trust.[15] The first serious test of American diplomacy in the West initiated a pattern of hostility between the Sioux and the United States that would endure through the century.

For Lewis and Clark flags symbolized Indian loyalty and recognition of US sovereignty. But when they gave a Brulé chief a flag he displayed it alongside two Spanish flags. He was either building multiple alliances or just collecting flags. Clearly, the flags meant something different to Indians. Farther upriver at the Mandan villages, Lewis and Clark found that traders from Canada had given the Indians British medals and flags. They protested to the traders and told the chiefs "to impress it on the minds of their nations that those Simbells were not to be recved by any from them, without they wished incur the displeasure of their Great American Father."[16] Jean Baptiste Truteau, a St. Louis fur trader who presented Spanish medals, flags, and commissions to Arikara and Cheyenne chiefs in the 1790s, noted that the Indians carefully preserved these objects in wrapping and when they took them out "smoked" them, smudging them with burning sweetgrass.[17]

Lewis and Clark participated in the smoking rituals of the peoples they met, recognized how important pipe rituals were in establishing friendship, and incorporated the rituals into their own diplomatic repertoire. When they met Shoshonis in the foothills of the Rockies in the summer of 1805, Lewis "had the pipe lit and gave them smoke; they seated themselves in a circle around us and pulled off their mockersons before they would receive or smoke the pipe. This is a custom among them as I afterwards learned indicative of a sacred obligation of sincerity in their profession of friendship given by the act of receiving and smoking the pipe of a stranger." Lewis and Clark became "fluent in the language of the pipe." They brought back from their journey more pipes than any other category of object, not because they "collected" them but because Native people had given them the pipes as powerful diplomatic gifts in order to establish formal relations between the Indian nations and the United States.[18]

The language of pipes was especially important where the language of humans failed, which it often did as the Americans made their way through various language groups. In western Montana, for instance, Lewis and Clark attempted to open relations between the United States and the Flathead or Salish Indians. The captains gave their speech in English; one of their men translated it into French; the expedition's interpreter Toussaint Charbonneau translated it into Hidatsa; his Shoshoni wife, Sakakawea, who had lived among the Hidatsa, translated it into Shoshoni; and finally a Shoshoni boy who was living with the Flatheads translated it into Salish.[19]

On their return home, a Mandan Indian chief named Sheheke accompanied Lewis and Clark as an ambassador to the nation's capital, embarking on his own voyage of discovery.[20] Throughout the rest of the century the federal government followed European precedents and brought Indian delegations from the West to Washington, D.C. The Indian delegates usually received a tour of the sights and military installations, were outfitted with suits of clothing, and also sat for portraits or, later, had their photographs taken. Sometimes they negotiated treaties in Washington with the commissioner of Indian affairs. Sometimes, like Sheheke, they met the president.[21]

The Indian diplomacy of Lewis and Clark did not end with their expedition. Jefferson appointed Lewis as territorial governor of upper Louisiana, and he appointed Clark as the principal Indian agent for the tribes west of the Mississippi, except for the Osages, where Pierre Chouteau served as agent. Clark drew up his first formal Indian treaty in September 1808 with the Osages. Perhaps anxious to impress the government in his new position, he coerced Osage chiefs to sign a treaty that ceded fifty thousand square miles of land (about half of present-day Missouri and Arkansas). Governor Lewis tweaked the treaty and had Choteau present it to the Osages for approval, repeating Clark's thinly veiled threats that they must sign it if they wished to remain at peace with the United States and continue to receive American trade. In later years Clark reflected that the Osage treaty "was the hardest treaty on the Indians he ever made and that if he was to be damned hereafter it would be for making that treaty."[22]

Lewis was highly strung, driven, and subject to fits of depression that worried his few friends. In 1809 he committed suicide. Clark was easygoing, dependable, pragmatic, and levelheaded. In 1813, Madison appointed him as the governor of Missouri Territory. In addition to his former duties as Indian agent, Clark was now responsible for all tribes in the Louisiana Purchase north of the state of Louisiana. American treaty commissioners in the upper Mississippi region after the War of 1812 were primarily concerned with establishing peace with tribes who had been allied to the British, regulating Indian trade, and extending American sovereignty, rather than obtaining land cessions. Clark served as commissioner for twenty-five treaties during his tenure as governor, many of them signed at the great treaty council held at Portage des Sioux near the confluence of the Missouri, Mississippi, and Illinois rivers in 1815.

In 1822 President Monroe appointed Clark to be the superintendent of Indian affairs in St. Louis, with responsibility for a vast array of tribes on the upper Mississippi and Missouri. At the Treaty of Prairie du Chien in 1825, Clark and Lewis Cass, an arch-advocate of Indian removal, negotiated over sixteen days with one thousand Sioux, Sauk and Fox, Menominee, Iowa, Winnebago, and some Ottawa, Potawotami, and Ojibwe Indians to safeguard trade and settlement in the region west of the Great Lakes by reducing conflict and establishing boundaries between the tribes. Clark and Cass associated intertribal warfare with a lack of well-defined territorial boundaries, but peace in Indian country depended on maintaining or mending relationships between people rather than drawing lines to separate them.[23] Meanwhile, Brigadier General Henry Atkinson and Clark's Indian agent, Benjamin Fallon, accompanied by almost five hundred troops as a demonstration of American power, retraced the route followed by Lewis and Clark in order to establish treaty relations with the nations of the upper Missouri. In the summer and fall of 1825 they met with the Arikaras, Mandans, various bands of Sioux, Cheyennes, Crows, Otos and Missouris, Pawnees, and Omahas. They presented them with identical pre-written treaties in which the tribes acknowledged the sovereignty of the United States, placed themselves under American protection and criminal jurisdiction, and agreed to American trade regulations. The Indians took the trade goods Atkinson and Fallon offered and signed the treaties.[24]

Increasingly, as Americans intensified the pressures on Indian peoples to remove from their coveted homelands in the East, Clark applied his expertise and experience to supervising the exodus of displaced peoples and negotiating a string of treaties with the Osages (again), Kansas, Pawnees, Poncas, and other prairie tribes, acquiring title to their lands in preparation for the influx of exiles. In some cases, he negotiated removal treaties with tribes who had removed before. He presided over the transfer of millions of acres of Indian lands and signed thirty-seven separate treaties with Indian nations, about one-tenth of all the Indian treaties the United States had made. "No government official signed more treaties than Clark," concludes one scholar of his Indian diplomacy.[25]

Clark's diplomacy had faltered when he encountered the Brulé Sioux in 1804, but he learned well the business of doing business in Indian country. In 1829, he and Cass drew up regulations and guidelines for dealing with Natives. "When they assemble to deliberate upon their public affairs, they are pure democracies, in which every one claims an equal right to speak and vote," they noted. "The public deliberations, however, are usually conducted by the elderly men, but the young men or warriors exercise the real controlling influence. No measure can safely be adopted, without their concurrence." That was the reason, said Cass and Clark, "why so many signatures are usually appended to our Indian treaties."[26]

Confronted with the invasion of Indians from the East and the increasing presence of Americans, Indians on the prairies and Plains implemented new diplomatic initiatives and adjusted their foreign policies as they jostled for position and competed for trade networks and hunting territories in contests for diminishing resources. The Crows, increasingly besieged in their southern Montana homelands by more powerful enemies, generally maintained amicable relations with the Nez Perces and Flatheads to their west, who supplied them with horses, but they found their major ally in the new and growing power on the Plains. For Atkinson and Fallon, the treaty they made with the Crows in 1825 established American supremacy; for the Crows, it initiated an alliance that would help them survive their struggles against the Lakotas and Cheyennes.[27]

The Cheyennes, too, forged new alliances. They allied with the Arapahos and the Lakotas but Cheyennes who migrated south of the Platte River clashed increasingly with Comanches, Kiowas, and Plains Apaches who dominated the southern Plains and sometimes ranged north of the Arkansas River to hunt. But pressed by eastern Indians and Texans in the south, the Kiowas and Comanches did not need to be fighting Cheyennes in the Arkansas Valley. After some tentative peace feelers between the tribes, the Cheyennes and Arapahos and the Comanches, Kiowas, and Apaches agreed to meet on the Arkansas River near Bent's Fort. "There we will make a strong friendship which shall last forever," declared the Kiowa chief Little Mountain. "We will give you horses, and you shall give us presents." The Cheyennes camped north of the river, and the Kiowas stayed on the south bank. They agreed to share the upper Arkansas Valley and engaged in an elaborate ritual exchange of gifts that not only signaled and confirmed the peace but also established the trade in desired items that made the new alliance economically beneficial to both parties. The horse-rich Kiowas gave horses; the Kiowa chief Satank was said to give away 250 head. The Cheyennes, middlemen between the central Plains and the great trade rendezvous at the Mandan, Hidatsa, and Arikara villages on the upper Missouri, gave guns and manufactured goods. The Cheyennes needed more horses, both for themselves and for trade for more goods. They called the site of the peace agreement "Giving Presents to One Another Across the River." As Little Mountain had foretold, the Great Peace of 1840 lasted forever.[28]

Peace with tribes to their north freed the Comanches, Kiowas, and Apaches to escalate their incursions south of the Rio Grande. Their attacks drove away settlers, left whole areas devastated, generated political instability, and rendered Mexico's northern provinces ripe for conquest by American armies in the war of 1846–48.[29] The Kiowas and Comanches had waged a life-and-death struggle with Texans since Governor Mirabeau B. Lamar initiated a policy of Indian extermination in the late 1830s.[30] But after New Mexico and Texas were incorporated into the United States in the 1840s, the US government determined to stamp out attacks on what were now American citizens and American property.

At the Treaty of Guadalupe Hidalgo in 1848, the United States took from Mexico more than half a million square miles of territory, including present-day California, most of Arizona and New Mexico, Nevada, Utah, and part of Colorado, and it secured Mexican recognition of the independence and annexation of Texas. Invoking their Manifest Destiny (a term coined in 1845) to occupy the continent, Americans were determined to extend the blessings of Anglo-Saxon civilization to the inferior races inhabiting the West.[31] That meant dispossessing and radically changing the lifestyles of thousands of Natives over huge stretches of the continent. According to the historian Francis Paul Prucha, "the government conceived of no way to deal with the new problems except by the traditional method of formal treaties."[32]

Removal treaties promised Indian exiles new homes in the West that would be theirs forever. The Indian Trade and Intercourse Act of 1834 designated "Indian country" as a permanent reserve stretching the length of the eastern Plains from the headwaters of the Missouri River to the Red River in Texas, where indigenous and immigrant Indian peoples would inhabit lands American settlers did not yet need and where traders and other non-Indians could enter only with government permission. But the government's idea of a safe haven where Indians could lead better lives was illusory from the start and inhabitants of Indian country were immediately under pressure. The acquisition of valuable new territories in the Far West sent emigrants teeming to the gold fields of California and the rich valleys of Oregon, and the government needed to ensure their safe passage and to establish transportation links across Indian lands. The old policy of removing Indians before an advancing tide of white settlement and maintaining a boundary separating Indians and whites was no longer feasible; curbing westward migration was neither feasible nor desirable. Instead of constituting "a permanent Indian frontier," Indian country in the West was to be broken up into a series of separate reservations. Indian people would relocate to reservations to minimize conflict with whites and undergo the transformation to a new way of life that was their only alternative to extinction.[33]

The Indian Office, later known as the Bureau of Indian Affairs, was established in 1824 to consolidate the administration of Indian relations. In 1832, Congress authorized the president to appoint, with Senate approval, a commissioner of Indian affairs who operated under the direction of the secretary of war. To deal with the increase in Indian relations that came with the massive increase in territory, President Polk asked Congress for more Indian agents. Congress did not grant the request but in 1849 it transferred the management of Indian affairs from the War Department to the newly created Department of the Interior, on the assumption that the civilian branch would do better than the military in promoting the work of civilizing Indians. The Indian Office exercised growing influence in shaping Indian policy and administering the reservations. The United States continued to make treaties—more than one hundred between 1850 and 1868—but the outcome of those treaties was never in doubt. Power trumped protocol as American commissioners secured agreements that established boundaries, removed obstacles to American expansion, and opened Indian lands to logging, mining, farming, and ranching. Treaties whose sole purpose was to take away Indian land and eradicate Indian ways of life bore little resemblance to colonial-era councils that had begun with Natives and Europeans negotiating cultural thickets and building alliances through ritual exchange and kinship ties.

In California, beginning in 1850, US commissioners negotiated eighteen almost identical treaties, setting aside an estimated 11,700 square miles for reservations, mostly in the foothills. In January 1851, the treaty commissioners published an address to the people of California in the *Daily Alta California* newspaper. With Indian people being pushed to extinction, the commissioners advocated a policy of moderation:

> As there is now *no further west* to which they can be removed, the General Government and the people of California appear to have left but one alternative in relation to these remnants of once numerous and powerful tribes. *viz: extermination* or *domestication*. As the latter includes all proper measures for their protection and gradual improvement, and secures to the people of the State an element greatly needed in the development of its resources, viz: cheap labor—it is the one which we deem the part of wisdom to adopt.[34]

But the state legislature opposed reserving potentially valuable lands for the exclusive occupancy of Indians and removing Americans who were already settled on those lands. President Fillmore submitted the treaties to the Senate in 1852, but the Senate refused to ratify any of them. The senators held their debate and vote in executive session and imposed an injunction of secrecy on the original documents that was not removed until 1905, so their arguments do not appear in a published Senate document and if a transcript of the executive session was made it seems not to have survived, but the costs of establishing the reservations and the value of the lands in question were clearly major concerns that killed the treaties. It is difficult to argue with the assessment of archaeologist and professor of anthropology Robert Heizer more than forty years ago that the whole thing was "a farce, from beginning to end." In other parts of the country, the president stated in his annual message to Congress in December, the government set apart particular lands for the exclusive occupation of the Indians and they acknowledged and respected their rights to those lands. But in California the government did not recognize the exclusive right of the Indians to any part of the country. "They are, therefore, mere tenants at sufferance, and liable to be driven from place to place at the pleasure of the whites." Not until several decades later did the government establish small reservations (rancherías) for California Indians who survived the gold rush and the genocidal Indian policies that followed in its wake.[35]

Indians attacked wagon trains in twentieth-century Hollywood, but rarely on the nineteenth-century Great Plains.[36] Nevertheless, migrants on the overland trails to California and Oregon generated tensions and in 1849 they brought cholera. To head off conflicts the government attempted to assemble the southern Plains tribes in the spring of 1850 for a treaty to ensure the safety of the emigrant roads, but Comanche medicine men told their people to stay away from the whites until the cholera epidemic died out, and the negotiations were postponed until 1851 at Fort Laramie and 1853 at Fort Atkinson.[37]

In its treaties with the Dakota or Eastern Sioux at Traverse des Sioux and Mendota in 1851, the United States required the Sisseton, Wahpeton, Mdwekanton, and Wahpekute bands to "cede, sell, and relinquish" their lands in the state of Iowa and the Territory of Minnesota, in all about twenty-four million acres.[38] But out on the Plains what the United States wanted that year was to establish peace and to secure free passage for its westward-moving citizens. Once again, it tried to do so by imposing boundary lines on a complex intertribal landscape where relationships overlapped, alliances fluctuated, and borderlands were shared as well as contested. At the government's request, the Indian agent and former mountain man Thomas "Broken Hand" Fitzpatrick convened more than ten thousand Plains Indians in a huge multitribal tepee encampment at Horse Creek near Fort Laramie, Wyoming, a post established to safeguard the California and Oregon trails. The famous mountain man Jim Bridger brought a Shoshoni delegation. The Crows made a dramatic arrival "in a solid column, singing their national melody" and impressing one news reporter as "much the finest delegation of Indians we have yet seen." Many of the tribes had long histories of conflict but for three weeks in September they met, smoked, talked, socialized, and held dances and horse races. Fitzpatrick and David D. Mitchell, the superintendent of Indian affairs at St. Louis, met the Indians in council, adhered to Native custom by smoking the pipe, and drew up a map delineating tribal territories, while the Belgian Jesuit missionary Pierre-Jean De Smet, well known among the tribes, worked to promote goodwill. With representatives from the Sioux, Cheyennes, Arapahos, Crows, Shoshonis, Gros Ventres, Assiniboines, Mandans, Hidatsas, and Arikaras, the conference involved western Algonquian, Siouan, Shoshonean, Caddoan, English, and Plains sign languages, and the interpreters—Bridger, De Smet, Robert Meldrum for the Crows, former mountain man and frontier guide John Simpson Smith for the Cheyennes, C. Campbell for the Sioux, H. Culbertson for the Assiniboines and Gros Ventres, François L'Etalie for the Arikaras, and John Pizelle for the Arapahos—were kept busy. The Sioux resented efforts to impose boundaries –"You have split the country and I do not like it," said an Oglala chief named Black Hawk—and resisted the idea of creating chiefs with whom the government could deal, but they consented to "touch the pen" along with the other tribes. The Treaty of Fort Laramie defined the territorial boundaries of the various tribes, who agreed to live in peace with the United States and each other and recognized the right of the United States to build roads and posts in their country. In return, the commissioners distributed a wagon train full of presents and the United States pledged to protect the Indians from depredations by whites and to pay the tribes $50,000 per year for fifty years in "provisions, merchandise, domestic animals, and agricultural implements."[39] The government requested no land at Fort Laramie, but the boundaries established there could be redrawn in subsequent treaties, thereby breaking up the Indian reserve into separate and ever-diminishing individual reservations. As the historian Jeffrey Ostler concludes, the Treaty of Fort Laramie was "merely a temporary convenience of a relentlessly expansionist nation-state."[40]

After the treaty, Fitzpatrick, Mitchell, De Smet, and John Simpson Smith accompanied a delegation of chiefs down the Missouri by steamboat to St. Louis and then to Washington where they met President Fillmore.[41] But the good feelings from Horse Creek soon evaporated. The Miniconjou Sioux chief Lone Horn, who as a young man had been instrumental in making peace with the Cheyennes in 1840, now worked hard to maintain this peace with the Crows and the truce held for half a dozen years. "Given the volatile politics of a Sioux camp," comments the historian Kingsley Bray, "Lone Horn's achievement in engineering and maintaining the Crow peace between peoples who had been implacable enemies for generations evinces a political acumen, a breadth of vision, and diplomatic skill rare among any people in any age." But the northern bands—the Hunkpapa and Blackfoot Sioux—would have nothing to do with the peace and their war parties were soon pressing hard again into Crow country.[42] Congress altered the terms of the treaty, reducing the government's commitment to pay the signatory tribes $50,000 a year from fifty years to ten, with an additional five years to be paid at the discretion of the president. In 1854, in a bungled dispute over a stray or stolen cow, a rash lieutenant named John Grattan and his men were killed in a Brulé village. Conquering Bear (a.k.a. Frightening Bear), whom Mitchell had selected at Fort Laramie as a chief to represent the Sioux, died in the melee.[43] General William Harney destroyed another Brulé village at Ash Hollow, Nebraska, in retaliation.

In 1853, Senator Stephen Douglas of Illinois called for the removal of "the Indian barrier" and the extension of territorial governments as the necessary first step in protecting American possessions along the Pacific Coast, prompting a debate that led to passage of the Kansas-Nebraska Act in 1854 that opened the territories to settlement. It also reopened the divisive and ultimately explosive issue of slavery in the territories, effectively nullifying the Compromise of 1820 and the Compromise of 1850 and leaving the inhabitants to decide for themselves whether the territories should be free or slaveholding. Between 1854 and 1860, more than one hundred thousand non-Indians entered Kansas Territory.[44]

On the southern Plains, at the Treaty of Fort Atkinson in 1853, the Kiowas, Comanches, and Plains Apaches agreed to peace among themselves and with the United States and to allow Americans free passage and across their territories. The Treaty of Fort Wise in 1861 restricted the Cheyennes and Arapahos to the plains of eastern Colorado, south of the Arkansas River. In 1863, Samuel Colley, an agent on the Upper Arkansas, took a delegation of fourteen southern Plains chiefs (and two women) to Washington, D.C. Several of the delegates— Lone Wolf of the Kiowas, Paruasemena or Ten Bears of the Yamparika band of Comanches, and Poor Bear of the Plains Apaches, as well as interpreter John Simpson Smith—would figure prominently in the Treaty of Medicine Lodge four years later. The Indians toured the capital, attended a play, and met President Lincoln in the East Room of the White House, where the throng of onlookers included the secretaries of state, treasury, navy, and interior, as well as visiting ministers from England, France, Prussia, and Brazil. Lincoln assured the Indians of his government's peaceful intentions but reminded them with a smile that no father could get his children to do exactly as he wished.[45]

John Simpson Smith was married to a Cheyenne woman and in November 1864 he was back from Washington and living with her in a village of Southern Cheyennes and Arapahos on the banks of Sand Creek near Fort Lyon, where the Indians had camped supposedly under the protection of the US Army.

Smith and his son Jack were eating breakfast when Colonel John Chivington and a regiment of Colorado Volunteers attacked the village. John Smith survived the ensuing slaughter, as did the Cheyenne chief, Black Kettle, and his wife, who sustained nine gunshot wounds. Jack was murdered after the massacre. The treacherous nature of the attack, the wanton slaughter of women and children, and the gruesome mutilation of the bodies prompted a congressional investigation and inflamed the Plains.[46]

In the Pacific Northwest, Congress in 1853 divided Oregon Territory into Oregon and Washington territories. The new superintendent of Indian affairs in Oregon, Joel Palmer, negotiated a series of treaties with Oregon tribes.[47] In Washington, anxious to clear the way for construction of the Northern Pacific Railroad through his territory, Governor Isaac Stevens acted as superintendent of Indian affairs as well. Between Christmas 1854 and January 1856, he negotiated, many would say dictated, ten treaties with multiple tribes in what would become Idaho and western Montana as well as Washington State. He acquired some seventy million acres by "confederating" multiple tribes onto shared reservations where they were expected to learn to live like Americans. To expedite matters, Stevens and his associates drafted the treaties in advance of the treaty councils and the texts, except in their descriptions of the lands to be ceded, were nearly identical. "This is a great day for you and for us," Stevens announced to the Nisqually, Puyallup, and other Indians who assembled for his first treaty at Medicine Creek at the mouth of the Nisqually River on Christmas Day, 1854. "You are about to be paid for your lands, and the Great Father has sent me today to treat with you concerning the payment." The Indians ceded 2.5 million acres and retained 3,840 acres. The story was the same at the other treaties in the Puget Sound Basin as the small tribes gave up most of their land, but they did retain "the right of taking fish, at all usual and accustomed grounds and stations...in common with all citizens of the Territory." Stevens's high-handed, threatening, and deceitful treaty-making tactics, combined with continuing encroachments by American miners and settlers, sparked outbreaks of violent resistance, which Stevens promptly and ruthlessly suppressed. The Nisqually chief, Leschi, was tried by a kangaroo court and hanged for his part in the fighting.[48]

Stevens faced stiffer opposition from the larger tribes east of the Cascade Mountains. The Cayuses, Wallawallas, Umatillas, Yakamas, and Nez Perces who met with Stevens and Palmer in the Walla Walla Valley in May 1855 were in no mood to be browbeaten. Lieutenant Lawrence Kip, a young officer who was with the military escort, described the dramatic arrival of the Nez Perces, some 2,500 "wild horsemen in single file, clashing their shields, singing, and beating their drums as they marched past us. Then they formed a circle and dashed around us, while our little group stood there, the centre of their wild evolutions" (see figure 5.1). By the time all the tribes arrived, about five thousand Indians were gathered in the valley, and there was much feasting and horse racing. The Nez Perces had been friendly to Americans since Lewis and Clark had stumbled starving into their country, and in 1831 four Nez Perces had journeyed to St. Louis to see William Clark and learn about Christianity. Now, noted Kip, they held prayers in their lodges every morning and evening, and several times on Sunday.[49]

When the council got under way, Stevens and Palmer sat in front of an arbor facing the Indians who sat in the open air in concentric semicircles, "the chiefs in the front ranks, in order of their dignity, while the background was filled with women and children." Several scribes sat at a table taking notes of everything that was said and, Kip learned later, "two or three of the half civilized Nez Perces, who could write, were keeping a minute account of all that transpired at these meetings."[50] Stevens and Palmer had to work hard before their inflated promises, threats, and behind-the-scenes maneuvering took effect. Monitoring what had been going on west of the mountains, the Yakama head chief Kamiakin had worked to stiffen resistance among the tribes, and he demonstrated his distrust of the commissioners and their treaty making by refusing Stevens's gift of tobacco. The Nez Perce chief Lawyer, a Christian so-called for his ability to talk, voiced his approval of the treaty, but the other

FIGURE 5.1 *Arrival of the Nez Perce Indians at the meeting for the Walla Walla Treaty, May 1855, by Gustav Sohon. (Washington State Historical Society, Tacoma)*

tribes were hostile to it and Kamiakin kept silent. Then on Saturday, June 9, seventy-year-old Looking Glass, the second Nez Perce chief who had been away hunting when the council began, spoke so strongly against the treaty that not only the Nez Perces but all the other tribes refused to sign it. Kip assumed the commissioners would have to "bring some cogent arguments to bear upon Looking Glass." The Nez Perces spent all Sunday in council among themselves, and Lawyer and a group of Indians visited the commissioners before breakfast on Monday. At 10 a.m. Stevens opened the council with a short speech and then asked the chiefs to come forward and sign the papers. "This they all did without the least opposition," wrote Kip. "What he has been doing with Looking Glass since last Saturday, we cannot imagine, but we suppose savage nature in the wilderness is the same as civilized nature was in England in Walpole's day, and 'every man has his price.'"[51] William Cameron McKay, a secretary and interpreter, was present when Kamiakin signed the Yakama treaty. When the Indians hesitated, Stevens told them that if they did not sign the treaty they would "walk in blood knee deep." Kamiakin made a cross on the paper. "When he returned to his seat, his lips were covered with blood, having bitten them in suppressed rage." "Thus ended in the most satisfactory manner this great council," McKay wrote in his journal. The Indians ceded about forty-five thousand square miles at Walla Walla.[52] The same year, gold was discovered on the newly created Yakama reservation. When Kamiakin led the tribes in a united resistance against trespassing miners, tensions exploded in the so-called Yakama War.

After Walla Walla, Stevens met with 1,200 Salish (Flathead), Pend d'Oreilles, and Kutenais at the Hell Gate Council near Missoula in western Montana. There, in the summation of the Jesuit historian Robert Ignatius Burns, he demonstrated his customary "patronizing impatience" for a "lesser race whose problems intruded upon his policies and career."[53] Accompanied by delegates from the western tribes, he then pushed on across the Continental Divide to Fort Benton where he met the Blackfeet in a large multitribal gathering of fifty-nine chiefs from ten different tribes, although it is often called Lame Bull's Treaty, after the Piegan chief whose name appears first on the document. Unlike Stevens's previous treaties, the purpose of the Blackfoot peace council was not to impose land cessions or remove people to reservations but to establish intertribal peace and obtain consent to building "roads of every description" through the region. In the Walla Walla and Hell Gate treaties Stevens had recognized the right of tribes from west of the Rockies to continue crossing the mountains from their newly established reservations to hunt buffalo on the northern plains; now he designated a common hunting ground centered on the headwaters of the Missouri and the Yellowstone and secured Blackfoot agreement to share it in peace with the tribes from beyond the mountains. In return, the Blackfeet would receive $20,000 in annuities for ten years and an additional $15,000 for the same period in farming instruction and education. A contentious council with the Spokane, Coeur d'Alene, and Colville Indians that failed to produce a treaty wrapped up Stevens's rapid-fire diplomatic grand tour through Northwest Indian country.[54] Construction of the Northern Pacific Railroad began in 1870 and eventually it snaked across Montana, Idaho, Washington, and Oregon. Stevens did not live to see it; he died while fighting in the Civil War. But the so-called Indian problem Stevens faced—removing Indians to make way for railroads and settlers—remained.

Congress passed the Pacific Railroad Act of July 1862 as a war measure designed to help preserve California and the West for the Union. The act provided government bonds and land subsidies to encourage and assist the Union Pacific and Central Pacific Railroad companies in constructing a line between the Missouri River and the Pacific. It also charged that the United States must "extinguish as rapidly as may be the Indian titles to all lands falling under the operation of this act." Subsequent railroad acts increased the incentives. The Pacific Railroad Act of 1864 doubled the amount of land granted so that the railroad companies received 12,800 acres of land in checkerboard sections along both sides of the railway line for every mile of track they built. The railroad companies attracted emigrants (and sold their lands to them) which also increased the value of the lands retained by the government for sale. The "public land" that the government awarded to the railroad companies in vast quantities was Indian land.[55] Thomas Jefferson had envisioned the United States as a republic of self-sufficient yeoman farmers but the thousands of immigrants who poured into eastern cities became mill and factory workers dependent on food from elsewhere. The West would feed the labor force of the industrial revolution. Texas cattlemen found a way out of the postwar depression by driving herds north to meet the railheads and shipping their cattle east. The government needed to remove Indians to make way for railroads that were vital to the nation's growth and unity, and to replace herds of buffalo with herds of cattle to feed the nation's workers.

The task of reuniting and reconstructing the nation after the war required remaking the West as well as remaking the South, incorporating Indians as well as former slaves, which, as western historian Elliott West notes, meant "giving freedom to slaves and taking it away from Indians." No sooner had the United States settled "the negro question" and fought a bloody war over the black race, declared Senator John B. Henderson of Missouri, chairman of the Senate Committee of Indian Affairs, than "it seems, we must have another war over the red man."[56] The question of the hour for men like Henderson was what to do about the Indians given the harsh realities of American expansion and the inevitable outcome of the historic struggle between barbarism and civilization. "We have reached a point in our national history," wrote Commissioner of Indian Affairs Nathaniel G. Taylor in 1867, when "there are but two alternatives left to us as to what shall be the future of the Indian, namely swift extermination by the sword, and famine, or preservation by gradual concentration on territorial reserves, and civilization." Located "in the way of our toiling and enterprising population," the Plains tribes would be submerged and buried unless they were confined and "civilized."[57] Instead of being removed from place to place and pushed to the brink of extinction, the Indians must be assigned to reservations where they would give up living as buffalo-hunting nomads and become sedentary farmers on their own land. And they had better do it soon. They did not have many options.

Medicine Lodge, 1867

CONTAINMENT ON THE PLAINS

In October 1867, the United States Peace Commission negotiated three treaties in one—with the Kiowas and Comanches, with the Plains Apaches, and with the Southern Cheyennes and Southern Arapahos—at the confluence of Elm Creek and Medicine Lodge Creek in Kansas. The Treaty of Medicine Lodge was a major event in shaping and implementing the nation's Indian policy in the aftermath of the Civil War. Pressured by humanitarian concerns that the Indians faced extinction, and by the staggering financial costs of a protracted Indian war, the Peace Commission sought to bring peace and civilization to the Plains. The goal of the Treaty of Medicine Lodge, in the view of the commissioners who negotiated it, was to settle the southern Plains Indians in Indian Territory alongside the Cherokees and other tribes "preparatory to declaring them citizens of the U. States, and the establishment of a government over them."[1]

The policy of confining Indians to reservations and "civilizing them" was not new, but the Treaty of Medicine Lodge laid out a blueprint for transforming Indians and set out the agenda with unprecedented clarity and new urgency. More than ever before, reservations were to function as crucibles of change. Indians would be assigned a reservation that would serve as "a permanent home" where no whites could enter without the tribe's approval; they would be furnished with the tools and skills to survive in American society, and they signed their agreement to embark on a new path. As a prerequisite to this new start, the Peace Commission sought to end the bloody clashes between Americans and Native Americans on the Plains and end the way of life the Indians were fighting to preserve. Indian speakers at Medicine Lodge repeatedly voiced their reluctance and refusal to give up the life they loved but the treaty was predicated on the certainty that the destruction of the economy and culture of the southern tribes was imminent and inevitable. Indians had to move on to reservations to survive.[2]

A Peace Commission for the Plains

The Plains were on fire in 1867. After the Sand Creek massacre in November 1864, Cheyenne warriors flocked to the camps of the militant Dog Soldiers, the elite military society, in the Smoky Hill region of northern Kansas and southern Nebraska. They carried out raids in Kansas, Nebraska, and Colorado, and attacked railroads and wagon routes across the central Plains, although Black Kettle moved his band of some seventy lodges south of the Arkansas and joined the Southern Arapahos, Kiowas, and Comanches.[3]

Attempts to end the violence proved futile. In October 1865 US commissioners met some of the southern Plains tribes at the Treaty of the Little Arkansas, near present-day Wichita. The shadow of Sand Creek hung over the talks. "There is something very strong for us," said the Arapaho chief, Little Raven: "that fool band of soldiers that cleaned out our lodges and killed our women and children." The commissioners showed the Indians the government's investigations in "a book and papers that contain all the proceedings of the Sand Creek affair," and the treaty included an apology and reparations for "the gross and wanton outrages perpetrated." The treaty also assigned a new reservation on the border of Kansas and the Indian Territory to the Cheyennes and Arapahos, although they were free to range between the Platte and Arkansas rivers until the United States had extinguished the title claims of other Indians, especially the Cherokees and Osages, to the reservation area. The treaty promised annuities for forty years, and special grants of land were made to leading chiefs. In return, the Cheyennes and Arapahos present relinquished claims to all other land, including their hunting territories in western Kansas, thereby accepting a substantial reduction of the territory designated for them at Fort Laramie in 1851. The Plains Apaches agreed to be party to the treaty. In a separate treaty, the Kiowas and Comanches were assigned a large reservation stretching across the Texas and Oklahoma Panhandles and part of west Texas, with freedom to range south of the Arkansas River until title to the reservation area was settled. The chiefs agreed to refrain from attacking transportation routes and settlements and to return white captives. Black Kettle stressed that he could not speak for those who were not there, however, and most Cheyennes and Arapahos rejected the treaty.[4]

Many of the tribal representatives would appear two years later at Medicine Lodge: Black Kettle and Little Robe of the Cheyennes; Little Raven of the Arapahos; Satank, Satanta, Teneangopte or Tonaenko, known as Kicking Bird, and Lone Wolf or Guipahko of the Kiowas; Ten Bears of the Yamparika Comanches, and Toshaway or Silver Brooch, chief of the Penetekas or "Honey Eaters," the largest Comanche band who lived on the Wichita agency and "already could be classified as reservation Indians."[5] Army generals John

B. Sanborn and William Harney, the interpreters John Simpson Smith and Margaret Wilmarth or Wilmott, the Indian superintendent Thomas Murphy, the agent Jesse Leavenworth, and the treaty commissioner William Bent also would reconvene at Medicine Lodge. Margaret Wilmott was Thomas Fitzpatrick's widow. William Bent and his brother Charles had been trading with the Plains Indians since the early 1820s. In 1833, together with Cerain St. Vrain they built Bent's Fort on the north side of the Arkansas River (at present-day La Junta, Colorado), a prominent adobe structure and the largest trading post on the Plains. William Bent married a Cheyenne named Owl Woman, daughter of the keeper of the sacred medicine arrows, with whom he had four children; after she died in 1846, he married her younger sister, Yellow Woman, with whom he had a fifth child. Senator John Henderson said Bent was "known to every man who knows anything about the Indians." At "the special request" of the Cheyennes and Arapahos, the United States at the Little Arkansas treaty granted patents for 640 acres in fee simple to certain persons, "all of whom are related to the Cheyennes or Arrapahoes by blood," including Margaret Wilmott and her children, William Bent's children and their children, and John Smith's children.[6]

The Senate ratified the Little Arkansas treaty in May 1866 but amended it so that no land in Kansas would be included in the reservation, and commissioners had to return to the southern Plains to secure tribal agreement. The Cheyennes kept Sand Creek "fresh in their memories"[7] and those who had refused to attend the treaty felt no obligation to observe the terms Black Kettle had accepted. The famous Cheyenne warrior Roman Nose agreed to listen only because the Americans were strong. "I do not believe the whites," he said. "I do not love them. If I had plenty of warriors I would drive them out of this country." When the commissioners asked Tall Bear and Bull Bear to sign the amendment papers, the two Dog Soldier chiefs smoked for a time, then got up and left without signing or replying. The Dog Soldiers continued to dominate the region between the Platte and the Arkansas. Annuities promised under the Little Arkansas treaty arrived late and were of poor quality. Construction crews pushed the Kansas Pacific Railroad westward along the Smoky Hill River but Cheyenne attacks threatened to bring work to a standstill. Settlers in Kansas were angered that the Treaty of the Little Arkansas acknowledged Indian hunting rights north of the Arkansas. Texas steadfastly resisted setting up a reservation for Kiowas and Comanches in its public domain. War on the southern Plains continued.[8] The Kiowas were as resistant as the Dog Soldiers. Agent Charles Bogy reckoned the Kiowas "probably the worst tribe, considered in all respects, on the plains."[9]

On the northern Plains, in the so-called Red Cloud War, the Lakotas, Northern Cheyennes, and Arapahos fought to close the Bozeman Trail that crossed their hunting grounds en route to the Montana gold fields. In December 1866 they inflicted a stunning defeat on the US army, annihilating Captain William Fetterman's eighty-man command.

In the spring of 1867, Major General Winfield Scott Hancock, commanding the Department of the Missouri, led an expedition to restore peace in the Smoky Hill country. With 1,500 men, including the Seventh Cavalry led by George Armstrong Custer, he marched up the Pawnee Fork of the Arkansas River, burned an abandoned Cheyenne village, and aggravated the state of affairs. The army's failure to pacify the Plains fueled a growing demand for a peaceful solution to the "Indian problem."[10]

Even before Hancock's expedition, a Joint Special Committee of Congress headed by Senator James R. Doolittle completed a two-year investigation into the causes of the Indian wars. The Doolittle report placed the blame squarely on the shoulders of whites, and this fueled growing demands for a reform of Indian policy that would implement reservation life as an urgent necessity. Congress responded in July 1867 by establishing the Indian Peace Commission, a select group of soldiers and civilians with particular interest and expertise in Indian affairs, who would conduct negotiations and implement the new policies. As the historian Jill St. Germain notes, the very creation of the commission was somewhat "irregular," in that Congress "authorized" the president to appoint a commission, an authorization he did not need because treaty making was the president's constitutional responsibility.[11]

The Peace Commission faced a formidable task and had broad authority: to assemble the chiefs of the warring tribes, to ascertain the causes of hostility, and to negotiate treaties that would "remove the causes of war; secure the frontier settlements and railroad construction; and establish a system for civilizing the tribes." The commissioners were committed to advancing American settlement but they saw clearly that unregulated expansion spawned violence and spelled doom for the Indians: "If the savage resists, civilization, with the ten commandments in one hand and the sword in the other, demands his immediate extinction." The current war against the Indians was not only expensive and ineffective but "it was dishonorable to the nation, and disgraceful to those who had originated it."[12] In the face of opposition from Indian agents, traders, settlers, speculators, and contractors who stood to lose a lucrative business if troops were withdrawn, and newspapers that inflated the rate and extent of "Indian depredations,"[13] the Peace Commission sought to achieve an Indian policy of expansion with honor that had eluded the United States since the days of the founding fathers. "We have spent two hundred years in creating the present state of things," the commissioners said in their report to President Johnson. "If we can civilize in twenty-five years it will be a vast improvement on the operations of the past."[14]

The twin goal was to establish the kind of peace that "will most likely insure civilization for the Indians and peace and safety for the whites." On both counts, that meant getting the Indians onto reservations. The commissioners intended to remove the Indians from the vicinity of the Union Pacific and Kansas Pacific railroads that were being built across their hunting territories and concentrate them in two large reservations. The Sioux and affiliated bands would be allocated land north of Nebraska; the Kiowas, Comanches, Southern Cheyennes, Southern Arapahos, and Plains Apaches would be confined to an area south of Kansas, on lands acquired from other tribes then living within the Indian Territory. "The goals of the commission could not have been clearer," says St. Germain, "nor could they have been any broader. They encompassed most of the concerns that plagued American Indian policy on the Plains—war and peace, settler and railroad security, and the compulsion to 'civilize' the Indians." Could the commission secure peace, secure American expansion, and secure a future for the Indians? If it failed to achieve peace, the United States would resort again to military action—"a sop to those in Congress and in the West who would have preferred an all-out war of extermination instead." The commissioners were given little concrete direction as to how they should achieve these goals and no fiscal restrictions or guidelines. Because conflict over footing the bill for the Peace Commission's treaties brought the treaty system to an end in 1871, this was, as St. Germain notes, "a significant oversight indeed."[15]

Watching the Peace Commissioners (figure 6.1) discuss "the long mooted and most detested Indian question," the newspaper reporter Henry Morton Stanley felt confident that if the peace effort failed it would not be for want of honest endeavor on their part: "Like philosophers, like astute geometricians do these gentlemen look the question in the face patiently and kindly," he informed his readers. Nathaniel G. Taylor chaired the commission. A rather hefty former Methodist minister and Princeton graduate, "a man of large brain, full of philanthropic ideas relative to the poor Indian," Taylor was considered "soft" on Indians in some quarters. Senator John B. Henderson was "never forgetful of Western interests; a cool head, courteous in deportment, affable to all." He frequently acted as the group's spokesman, its principal draftsman, and its liaison with the press. Samuel F. Tappan, "a gentle man of few words" and a former officer in the Colorado militia, had headed the investigation into the Sand Creek massacre. John B. Sanborn, a Civil War veteran who had attended the Treaty of the Little Arkansas, was "a garrulous, good natured and jovial gentleman, fond of good living and good company," and "pretty thoroughly posted on Indian matters."

The military members, appointed by the president, were the commander of the Division of the Missouri, General William Tecumseh Sherman; retired General William S. Harney; and Major General Alfred H. Terry, commander

FIGURE 6.1 *Members of the Peace Commission pose with an unidentified Indian woman. From left to right: Generals Terry, Harney, and Sherman; Commissioner Taylor; Samuel Tappan; and General Augur. (Smithsonian Institution, National Anthropological Archives and Human Studies Film Archives)*

of the Department of Dakota. Sherman was recalled to Washington and did not go to Medicine Lodge; Major General Christopher C. Augur, commander of the Department of the Platte, substituted for him and then became a regular member of the commission. Augur, said Stanley, was "a courtly gentleman of the old school" and "a man of rare ability." He had distinguished himself during the Civil War, was seriously wounded at Cedar Mountain, and had fought Indians in Utah and New Mexico. Harney had joined the army nearly fifty years before; in the 1830s he fought in the war against Black Hawk and the Sauks and against the Seminoles; in 1846–48 he fought in the War against Mexico, and in 1855 he attacked a Brulé Sioux village at Ash Hollow in retaliation for the so-called Grattan massacre. He had come out of retirement to serve on peace commissions. Tall and white-bearded, Harney cut an impressive figure. "When he stands erect he towers above all like Saul the chosen of Israel," Stanley wrote, and then, with less hyperbole: "Really, a goodly man, a tried soldier and a gentleman." The Lakotas remembered him rather differently from Ash Hollow and called him Winyan Wicakte, "Woman Killer." Harney and Henderson did not get along and had frequent disagreements during the course of the negotiations. Harney could be pretty irascible. According to his biographer he could be impulsive and obstinate and had a "contentious and quarrelsome nature."[16]

The six-foot-two Terry, on the other hand, was a thoughtful and likeable fellow; "gallant and genial," said Stanley. Born in Connecticut to an old New England family, Terry had graduated from Yale Law School in 1848 and served with distinction in the Civil War. After a tour of Reconstruction duty in the South he was assigned to the Plains. In 1867 Terry was still a newcomer to the Indian West, but he was to play a key role making treaties and making war for the next ten years. Examining the orders Terry gave the flamboyant and head-strong George Custer in 1876, Nathaniel Philbrick holds him largely responsible for the disaster at the Little Bighorn. He had, writes Philbrick, "a lawyer's talent for crafting documents that appeared to say one thing but were couched in language that could allow for an entirely different interpretation should circumstances require it."[17] Whether Terry developed or applied this talent as a member of the Peace Commission, the treaty documents the commission produced fit the description. Governor Samuel Crawford and Senator Edmund G. Ross of Kansas joined the commissioners prior to the negotiations at Medicine Lodge.

A press corps accompanied the Peace Commission, forerunners of twentieth-century "embedded" journalists. This was history in the making, and the nation's newspapers dispatched reporters to cover the story. Henry Morton Stanley represented the *Missouri Democrat* in St. Louis, and he also wrote for other papers. Born John Rowlands in Wales in 1841, Stanley had a childhood that "was Dickensian in its hardships." His parents were unmarried and his birth certificate recorded him as a "bastard." His father died and his mother abandoned him. Raised by his maternal grandfather until he was five, he was sent to a workhouse for the poor when the old man died. He managed to secure an elementary education and at seventeen or eighteen took a ship to the United States as a cabin boy. In New Orleans he found work and, according to his autobiography, a cotton merchant named Henry Morton Stanley adopted him, and he took his benefactor's name. He joined the Confederacy during the Civil War and was at the Battle of Shiloh, but after being imprisoned he joined the US Navy. Soon after the war, he began a career as a newspaper reporter and traveled to Turkey, where he found himself in jail again, though he apparently talked his way out of the predicament. Returning to St. Louis, he was assigned by the *Missouri Democrat* to accompany General Hancock's expedition in the spring of 1867; he covered the treaty councils on the Platte and continued to report for the paper until November 1867.[18]

Milton Reynolds, a small man with a goatee, had lived on the Kansas frontier since 1862 and had established a daily newspaper in Lawrence called the *State Journal*; he now covered the story for the *Chicago Times* and also dispatched stories to the *New York Herald*. A seasoned reporter, he provided the most comprehensive account of the Kiowa-Comanche treaty and was not afraid to take on Kansas politicians in his columns. S. F. Hall, reporting for the *Chicago Tribune*, showed interest in and empathy for the Indians. George Brown of the *Cincinnati Commercial* and H. J. Budd of the *Cincinnati Gazette* did not; they had little good to say about either the commissioners or the Indians. William Fayel reported for the St. Louis *Missouri Republican*; he spent a lot of time walking through the Indian camps, demonstrated an interest in Plains Indian life and culture, and produced the most complete account of the Cheyenne-Arapaho negotiations. A *New York Herald* reporter named Solomon T. Bulkley had covered the Civil War for the paper and had been held as a prisoner of war in Virginia for seven months. James E. Taylor was the artist for *Frank Leslie's Illustrated Newspaper*; John Howland, *Harper's Weekly* artist, had traveled in the Southwest, wore fringed buckskin leggings, carried a Navy Colt revolver, and "told funny stories." He spoke Spanish and signed on as an official member of the commission as a shorthand stenographer. The newspapermen each had their own styles, opinions, and biases, but Stanley thought them all "good souls." The reports they dispatched made Medicine Lodge one of the most thoroughly covered Indian treaties.[19]

The commissioners held their first meeting in St. Louis in August. They agreed to send runners to the tribes north and south of the Platte River to assemble at Fort Laramie, Wyoming, in September and at Fort Larned, Kansas, in October.[20] Then they traveled by steamer to Fort Leavenworth, Kansas, where they held interviews with General Hancock, the renowned Jesuit missionary Father Pierre De Smet, and Governor Samuel Crawford. Heading up the Missouri to Omaha, they set out across the High Plains toward Fort Laramie. In September 1867, the commission met with Oglala, Brulé, and Northern Cheyenne delegates in North Platte, Nebraska, but nothing was settled and negotiations were suspended, both sides agreeing to meet again at Fort Laramie in the spring. Returning to Omaha, the commissioners turned their attention to the southern Plains. They boarded the Union Pacific for Fort Harker and then traveled by military ambulance to Fort Larned.

The site and date of the Medicine Lodge council had been fixed three months beforehand. Thomas Murphy, head of the central Indian superintendency, was responsible for the arrangements. Working with Edward Wynkoop, a Cheyenne and Arapaho agent who had been the commander at Fort Lyon prior to the Sand Creek massacre and testified in the subsequent investigations, and with Jesse Leavenworth, an agent for the Kiowas, Comanches, and Southern Cheyennes, Murphy sent out runners during the summer to call the bands together for the peace talks. Most of the runners were Arapahos although the trader William Bent and his sons George and Charley also helped to spread the word among the Cheyennes.[21]

William Bent had sent his sons to school in Westport, Missouri (present-day Kansas City), and in St. Louis. When the Civil War broke out, the brothers joined the Confederate Army and served under General Sterling Price. George was captured and released on parole and by 1863 he had returned to his mother's people, just in time to be thrown into the middle of another war. He and his half brother Charley were in the village at Sand Creek when Chivington's Colorado militia, guided at gunpoint by their brother Robert, attacked. George was wounded and he and Charley fought alongside Cheyenne warriors in vengeance raids. But George married Magpie, a daughter or niece of the Cheyenne chief Black Kettle, and at Medicine Lodge, he was trying to bring the bands in to talk peace (figure 6.2).

FIGURE 6.2 **George Bent and his Cheyenne wife, Magpie, 1867.** *Magpie gave birth to a daughter on the opening day of the Medicine Lodge council. (Courtesy of History Colorado, Scan #10025735)*

The commissioners arrived at Fort Larned, eighty miles northeast of Medicine Lodge, on October 12. There they were met by several chiefs whom Murphy had asked to escort them to the council site: the Crow, Stumbling Bear, and Satanta of the Kiowas, and Little Raven, Yellow Bear, and Wolf Slave of the Arapahos.

Satanta, or White Bear (figure 6.3) was a member of an elite warrior society known as the Koietsenko, Katsienko, or Qóichégàu ("the Real/Principal Dogs" or "Sentinel Horses"); as one of only ten sash wearers in the society, he was considered one of the Kiowas' "greatest and bravest warriors."[22] Contemporaries described him as "a man of magnificent physique, being over six feet tall, well built and finely proportioned." He also had a reputation for

FIGURE 6.3 **Satanta.** *Photograph by W. S. Soule c. 1867. (Smithsonian Institution, National Anthropological Archives and Human Studies Film Archives)*

oratory and theatrics, arrogance and boastfulness, characteristics he displayed at Medicine Lodge.[23] He had built a record and a reputation as a fierce raider. On one occasion, after driving off horses from Fort Larned, Satanta sent a message to the post commander, complaining about the quality of the horses and expressing his hope that the army would provide better animals for him to steal in the future. On another, dressed in clothes he had been given at a council, he led a raid that stampeded the herd at Fort Dodge. "He had the politeness, however, to raise his plumed hat to the garrison of the fort, though he discourteously shook his coattails at them as he rode away with the captured stock."[24] He was about fifty years old in 1867. His face was painted red, he wore a blanket, and he carried a brass bugle hanging from his waist. He had met Henry Stanley the year before and now greeted him with "a gigantic bear's hug." The other members of the press "looked upon him with some awe, having heard so much of his ferocity and boldness. By his defiant and independent bearing he attracted all eyes." Stanley felt "he would certainly be a formidable enemy to encounter alone on the prairie." Satanta boasted that he had killed more white men than any other Indian on the Plains.[25] He had also declared that he wanted all military posts and troops removed from his country immediately.[26]

The reporter William Fayel was impressed with Satanta's "splendid physique" and with his reputation as a terror to frontier whites. He noted: "His head is large and massive, measuring twenty-three inches around the cranium only one inch less than that of Daniel Webster." Another correspondent reckoned the crania of Satanta and Webster were of equal size. The scenario of newspaper correspondents sitting down the infamous warrior and measuring his head is certainly bizarre, but as the historian Charles Robinson notes, it is "not unlikely considering their curiosity, the nineteenth-century fascination with physiognomy, and Satanta's vanity."[27] Satanta was loud and effusive, and one correspondent thought he was drunk. At one point he abruptly announced that he wanted to leave because "it stink too much white man here," but the commissioners informed him he had to remain and escort them to Medicine Lodge. Robinson suggests that Satanta's "bluster concealed his nervousness" in a situation he could not control. He calmed down after a few drinks.[28]

At Fort Larned, wrote Henry Stanley, "we were joined by an army of special agents, special bosses, special caterers, special bummers, each sent on special business by the Government." After a day there, the assemblage set off on the sixty-mile journey to Medicine Lodge, a huge cavalcade stretching five miles as it threaded its way across the plains. Satanta rode in the lead wagon with General Harney. Behind them trailed the other commissioners, two (later increased to four) companies of the Seventh Cavalry, a battery of artillery equipped with Gatling guns; soldiers and the regimental band of the Thirty-Eighth Infantry; news correspondents, Indians, and an entourage of aides, bureaucrats, camp attendants, teamsters, cooks, interpreters, and other camp followers: a column of 600 people, at least 165 (and perhaps as many as 211) wagons and ambulances, and 1,250 horses and mules.[29] The Seventh Cavalry was temporarily without its commander—Lieutenant Colonel George Armstrong Custer had been suspended for leaving his troops to visit his wife without authorization—and Major Joel Elliott was the officer in command. En route, the caravan encountered a buffalo herd and many in the party took the opportunity to join a hastily organized hunt. The fact that they took only the tongues from the fallen animals infuriated Satanta. "Has the white man become a child, that he should kill the buffalo for sport?" he demanded. "An unprejudiced man could not blame him for his language," one of the reporters admitted.[30]

The Peace Commission reached Medicine Lodge on October 14. Thousands of Indian ponies grazed the nearby hills and five different camp circles were already there. As the commissioners entered the valley at its northwestern end, the nearest encampment was that of the Arapahos, consisting of 171 lodges; across the stream were 250 Cheyenne lodges. The Plains Apaches were farther down the creek, with 85 lodges on the same side as the Arapahos. The Comanches were encamped in 100 lodges across the creek from the Apaches, and the 150 Kiowa lodges were at the far end. In total, about five thousand Indians eventually congregated in the area.[31]

A group of chiefs came to welcome the commissioners. One of them was Black Kettle. In October 1867, he was the only prominent Cheyenne chief advocating peace. In the wake of Sand Creek and Hancock's campaign, the Dog Soldiers and Roman Nose were calling the shots for most Cheyennes. Roman Nose stayed away from Medicine Lodge. Nervous enough about being amid so many Indians, the commissioners were especially apprehensive about the proximity, a day's ride to the south, of a large Cheyenne encampment forty miles away on the Cimarron River, who they feared might disrupt the council. Black Kettle seems to have been apprehensive about them, too (at one point, Dog Soldiers threatened to kill his horses). When the Dog Soldier chief Bull Bear visited camp, newspaper reporters recognized him as "the man of the Cheyennes." The Cheyennes were also apprehensive about the commissioners and their large entourage. "For two weeks they kept themselves at a distance, sending in small parties to discover if possible our true intentions."[32] In fact, the Cheyennes were gathered at the Cimarron for the renewal of the Sacred Arrows, their most important ceremony, which the whole tribe was summoned to attend. (Black Kettle's absence may have triggered the threats against him.)[33]

Preliminary talks began on October 15. The commissioners had set up two hospital tents, facing one another with flysheets between them and, shielded from the sun, they sat waiting for the Indians to assemble.[34] Senator Henderson was in a hurry to get down to business but Commissioner Taylor insisted on doing things according to Indian protocol, which meant being patient. The Comanches made a point of keeping everyone waiting. Taylor gave a short welcome and the various chiefs reciprocated. But intertribal rivalries threatened to end the meeting before it began. The Kiowas and Arapahos wanted to start talks immediately and threatened to leave because the Cheyennes had asked that the talks be postponed for eight days. The other tribes were suspicious that some separate agreement had been made with the Cheyennes. The chiefs assembled in a semicircle around the commissioners, who lined up at the front of the tent. The dark suits and army uniforms of the commissioners contrasted with the colorful trade blankets, breechcloths, leggings, moccasins, eagle feathers, beads, trade silver, soldier's coats, and occasional hats of the Indians. Satanta, Black Eagle, Kicking Bird, and Fishermore represented the Kiowas. Fishermore was the senior counselor; Stanley described him as "a stout Indian of ponderous proportions, and [he] speaks five languages. He is a favorite with all the tribes." Ten Bears, the Yamparika Comanche chief, scoffed: "What I say is law for the Comanches, but it takes half a dozen to speak for the Kiowas." Ten Bears said the Comanches were willing to talk when the Kiowas did. Poor Bear, speaking for the Apaches, said he would wait only four more days for the talks to begin. Eventually, the commissioners agreed to start the talks in five days. The council adjourned and rations of flour, coffee, and sugar were distributed to each tribe. Ten Bears had been to Washington and met President Lincoln: "You laid out the road once before and we traveled it," he told the commissioners.[35] Commissioner Taylor knew from Jesse Leavenworth that Ten Bears "is a very good man, and is doing more than any other to preserve peace between the Red and white man."[36] Now a worn, gray-haired old man, possibly around seventy, Ten Bears peered at the commissioners through gold-rimmed spectacles (see figure 6.4). But he was quick-witted, understood the issues at stake and, noted the historian Douglas Jones, was the only man at the council who ever managed to get Satanta to stop talking![37]

While the preliminary talks were going on, reported Stanley, "the honorable gentlemen" of the Peace Commission occupied themselves in different ways. Harney, "with head erect," watched the faces of the Indians. Sanborn "picked his teeth and laughed jollily." Tappan read reports about Hancock's destruction of the Indian village at Pawnee Creek. Henderson, "with eyeglass in hand, seemed buried in deep study." Terry "busied himself in printing alphabetical letters, and Augur whittled away with energy." Agent Leavenworth "made by-signals to old Satank." The newspaper correspondents "sat à la Turque on the ground, their pencils flying over the paper."[38]

At dusk, about eighty Cheyenne warriors arrived from the Cimarron. Painted, armed, and chanting, they rode their ponies across Medicine Lodge

FIGURE 6.4 **Ten Bears.** *Photograph by Alexander Gardner. (Smithsonian Institution, National Anthropological Archives and Human Studies Film Archives)*

Creek to the edge of the commissioners' camp. Two Dog Soldier chiefs, Gray Head and Tall Bull, dismounted and shook hands with General Harney whom they had met before, but most of the warriors remained sitting on their ponies while their chiefs conversed with the general in his tent. When they emerged, Gray Head said his men were hungry after their ride from the Cimarron and they went to Black Kettle's camp to share the rations there. Late that night, they rode back to the Cimarron.[39] Two evenings later, Gray Head and Tall Bull returned to talk with the commissioners, this time minus the escort of chanting warriors. Gray Head said his people were not hostile but after Sand Creek and Hancock's attack on the Pawnee Fork village he could not speak for other Cheyennes.[40]

In the days before the formal talks began, the commissioners took depositions on the causes of the warfare on the Plains. Wynkoop blamed the Sand Creek massacre and General Hancock's campaign. Major Henry Douglass, a former commandant at Fort Dodge, blamed Satanta.[41] The news reporters and some of the officers visited the Indian camps and some recorded descriptions of Indian life. Some of them attended a dance in the Arapaho camp.[42]

The tribes at Medicine Lodge had their own histories, rivalries, and foreign policies. The Comanches had pushed most Apache groups off the Plains in the eighteenth century. The Kiowas were longtime allies of the Comanches, and both were enemies of the Cheyennes and Arapahos until 1840 when they fashioned a peace of mutual benefit. The Indians at Medicine Lodge spoke several languages. Most spoke Comanche, a Shoshonean language that had developed into the lingua franca of the southern Plains as a result of Comanche dominance and trade networks. Few spoke Kiowa, a Tanoan language quite unlike others spoken on the Plains. An army officer who had heard Kiowa in the 1840s described it as "an entirely different language" from Comanche, "being much more deep and guttural, striking upon the ear like the sound of falling water." Cheyenne and Arapaho are related Algonquian languages but are not mutually intelligible. The Indians also used sign language. Three interpreters—George Bent, Philip McCusker, and A. A. Whitaker—signed the treaties as witnesses but there were more. They had their work cut out for them. McCusker, a former army scout with a Comanche wife, was the busiest because the speeches were often translated first into Comanche, and then from Comanche into other languages. Satanta occasionally switched from Kiowa to Comanche. McCusker may also have had a smattering of Kiowa and Kiowa-Apache, although Kiowas told the anthropologist James Mooney in the 1890s that McCusker spoke only Comanche and that a Kiowa called Bao (Cat), or Having Horns, translated his words. Richard Henry Pratt, who used McCusker as an interpreter during the Red River War, said he was "a most capable Comanche linguist" and proficient in sign language but had difficulty understanding Kiowa. McCusker earned more than the other interpreters at Medicine Lodge—$583.65—although that was not all that he asked for: General Sherman rejected his voucher for $1,565 ($5 per day for 313 days) as unreasonable.[43]

Jesse Chisholm, the part-Cherokee trader, guide, and cattle rancher, and the ubiquitous Delaware scout Black Beaver also served as interpreters. William Bent and three of his children, George, Charley, and Julia, interpreted for the Cheyennes. Charley wore a red trade blanket much like others in the Cheyenne delegation, but George dressed for the occasion and for his intermediary role, wearing a broadcloth suit, vest, cravat, and moccasins. George's wife, Magpie, gave birth to a daughter on October 19, the opening day of the council. Also present were John Simpson Smith and Ed Guerrier, who was the son of a white father and a Cheyenne mother and had attended St. Louis University. Guerrier married Julia Bent. Like the Bent brothers, Smith and Guerrier had been in the Cheyenne camp at Sand Creek, where Smith's son Jack had been murdered.[44]

The interpreter who attracted the most attention was the thirty-three-year-old daughter of a Kentucky-born trader and an Arapaho mother named Margaret or Walking Woman. She was the daughter of the trader John Poisal or Pizelle (who interpreted at the Fort Laramie Treaty in 1851) and Snake Woman (who had been taken captive from the Blackfeet as a small child and was the adopted sister of an Arapaho chief named Left Hand). In 1849, Margaret married Thomas Fitzpatrick, the first US agent to the Arapahos. They had two children. After Fitzpatrick died in 1854, leaving her well provided for, Margaret married an American from Ohio named L. J. Wilmarth or Wilmott, with whom she lived in Denver and Leavenworth, Kansas. By the time of the Medicine Lodge treaty, she had married a third time and was now Mrs. Margaret Adams. She accompanied Little Raven as the Arapaho interpreter. She caused a sensation when she showed up wearing "crimson petticoat, black cloth cloak, and a small coquettish velvet hat, decorated with a white ostrich feather."[45] According to one reporter, she usually showed up drunk. The Plains Apaches spoke an Athapaskan language. Bulkley said an Apache-speaking Arapaho translated the Apaches' speeches into Arapaho, and then Mrs. Adams translated them into English. The Indian speakers often had to pause after each sentence while their words were translated into three languages. It was a precarious chain of communication by which to convey philosophies and worldviews central to the way of life they were trying to preserve.

"I want to live and die as I was brought up"

The great council finally got under way on October 19 at ten o'clock in the morning. In a grove of elms and cottonwoods, the commissioners sat under a brush arbor facing a huge half circle of four hundred chiefs. The principal chiefs sat on logs in the front row of the half circle. The Kiowas were on the left. Satanta sat in front on an army campstool, wearing an army coat given to him by General Hancock. Immediately behind Satanta sat Satank and Kicking Bird.[46]

Unlike Satanta, Satank (Sitting Bear) was an old man of slender build. But he was a formidable presence. Satank was one of the architects of the Great Peace made with the Cheyennes in 1840 and was "the foremost warrior in a nation of warriors." As head of the Koietsenko society, he wore a broad elk-skin sash across his chest from his left shoulder and he carried a ceremonial arrow. The lower end of the sash trailed the ground; when the Kiowas went into

FIGURE 6.5 **American depiction of the Medicine Lodge treaty.** *Medicine Lodge Council, 1867. Sketched by John Howland for Harper's Weekly, November 16, 1867, p. 724. (Smithsonian Institution, National Anthropological Archives and Human Studies Film Archives)*

battle the sash wearer dismounted in front of the warriors and thrust the arrow through a hole in the sash, pinning himself to the ground. He could only retreat if freed by his warriors. Like Satanta, Satank had a fearsome reputation as a killer of whites, but on this occasion he wore a peace medal bearing a likeness of President Buchanan.[47] Unlike Satanta, he remained quiet throughout most of the talks. Kicking Bird represented the peace faction of the Kiowas. Satanta was in a power struggle with Kicking Bird's peace faction and also with Lone Wolf for control of the war faction.

The Comanches sat to the left of the Kiowas, with Ten Bears at their head and McCusker in front of them. Black Kettle and Gray Head, with the Bents sitting behind them, represented the Cheyennes. Mrs. Adams, "in a new crimson gown, specially worn for this important occasion," sat in a folding chair near Little Raven, whom Stanley characterized as a good-natured, "fat, short, asthmatic fellow." Poor Bear and the Plains Apaches were on the far right. Fishermore, "the lusty crier of the Kiowa nation," opened the council, calling in the tribes "to do right above all things"[48] (figures 6.5 and 6.6).

Commissioner Taylor called the council to order and Senator Henderson got down to business outlining their goals. There must be peace on the Plains, he said. Indians had attacked railroad construction crews and murdered settlers, but white men were far from blameless. The commissioners wanted to hear the Indians' side of the story so they could remove their causes of complaint and

FIGURE 6.6 **Indian depiction of the Medicine Lodge treaty.** *"Treaty Signing at Medicine Lodge" by Howling Wolf from a ledger book done at Fort Marion, Florida, 1876. The Cheyenne warrior-artist Howling Wolf, who was probably in Black Kettle's village at the time of the treaty, recorded the scene nine years later when he was a prisoner of war in Fort Marion. Indians encamped at the forks of the river watch the council, with the commissioners wearing hats in a grove of elm trees. (Courtesy of the New York State Library, Manuscripts and Special Collections, PRI0672–11)*

bring the war to an end. Furthermore, the government intended to civilize the Indians. The commissioners were authorized to set aside some of the "richest agricultural lands" for the Indians and furnish farming implements, cattle, sheep, and hogs; they were authorized to build churches and schools and provide teachers for their children.[49]

Satanta "became uneasy, buried his hands in the ground, and rubbed sand over them." He then shook hands with everyone and stood in the circle to speak. His heart was glad to see the commissioners and he would hide nothing from them, he said. It was the Cheyennes who had been fighting the Americans, not the Kiowas and Comanches, who had kept the peace. Then he announced: "All the land south of the Arkansas belongs to the Kiowas and Comanches, and I don't want to give away any of it. I love the land and the buffalo, and will not part with it." He said the Kiowas did not want to fight and that they had not fought since the Little Arkansas treaty, which was not the case. Indicating the commissioners, he said: "I hear a good deal of talk from these gentlemen, but they never do what they say. I don't want any of these medicine homes [i.e., churches and schools] built in the country." He wanted to see his children raised as he was and he had no intention of settling down: "I love to roam over the prairie; I feel free and happy; but when we settle down we get pale and die." When he traveled to the Arkansas River, he saw soldiers cutting down timber and killing buffalo, "and when I see it my heart feels like bursting with sorrow." "I have told you the truth," Satanta asserted. "I have no little lies about me; but I don't know how it is with the Commissioners." He then sat down and wrapped a crimson blanket around himself. According to Henry Stanley, the commissioners gave Satanta "a rather blank look."[50]

Ten Bears echoed Satanta's sentiments. The Comanches wanted to be left free to live as they had lived and to go where they pleased. They had fought to defend their lands in Texas. "I have no wisdom," Ten Bears concluded rather tongue in cheek, looking at the commissioners. "I expect to get some from you." Silver Brooch, a Paneteka Comanche who had accompanied Ten Bears to Washington and had met Lincoln, recited his people's struggle against the Texans and reminded the commissioners that following the white man's path had not helped his people much. They had been given many promises but had received little. "My band is dwindling away fast," he said. "My young men are a scoff and a by-word among the other nations. I shall wait until next spring to see if these things shall be given us; if they are not, I and my young men will return with our wild brothers to live on the prairie," perhaps a reference to the Kwahadi Comanches out on the Staked Plains who were not represented at the treaty. The old chief Poor Bear promised that his Plains Apaches would listen to the commissioners' words and "follow the straight road," but they were anxious to return south. The preliminary speeches took up most of the day. The meeting adjourned until the next morning.[51]

Before evening the commissioners drafted the treaty they intended to present to the Kiowas and Comanches. The United States had no intention of leaving them to roam the Plains, and the commissioners knew that the buffalo herds on which the tribes based their existence and their future would soon be destroyed. But in order to get them to accept the treaty and make the bitter pill of reservation life more palatable, the commissioners offered to continue the Indians' hunting rights below the Arkansas River and in the Texas Panhandle, an offer that was almost certain to spawn conflicts with American settlers who were already living in the region. The commissioners were still nervous about the Cheyennes out on the Plains. After dark a dozen Osages turned up, evidently to see what was going on. They complained about their agent, shoddy provisions, and thefts of their horses. The Osages were enemies of the Kiowas but they left without incident.[52]

The meeting reconvened on Sunday, October 20, but things did not go smoothly. Senator Henderson and General Harney had a "spat." The Indians drifted in late and some of the warriors were hungover, although the chiefs were not. It was almost noon before the proceedings got under way. The Kiowas and Comanches continued to object to schools and farms. Ten Bears spoke first: "There is one thing which is not good in your speeches; that is, building us medicine houses. We don't want any. I want to live and die as I was brought up. I love the open prairie, and I wish you would not insist on putting us on a reservation." If the Texans had been kept out of Comanche country, there might have been peace and the Comanches might have lived on a reservation, he said, but the Texans had already taken the lands where the grass grew thickest and the timber was best and now it was too late to do what the commissioners wanted. The assembled Indians voiced their approval of his words as the old man sat down. Satanta got to his feet and said everything that needed to be said had been said yesterday. But he did demand that the annuities be delivered on schedule for a change and asked for a new agent for the Comanches, in place of Jesse Leavenworth, joint agent for the Kiowas and Comanches. At some point, Satanta and Ten Bears got into a heated argument and the old Comanche said his people liked Leavenworth and did not want him removed. For a moment, it looked like the council might unravel. Nevertheless, by the end of the second day the Kiowas and Comanches agreed in principle to the idea of a reservation in what is now southwestern Oklahoma.[53]

Senator Henderson wrapped up the council with a classic expression of United States Indian policy that blended humanitarian concern, paternalism, cultural arrogance, cynicism, hypocrisy, and veiled threats. Stanley thought it so important that he copied it down verbatim:

You say you do not like the medicine houses of the whites, but you like the buffalo and the chase, and that you wish to do as your fathers did.

We say to you that the buffalo will not last forever. They are now becoming few and you must know it.

When that day comes, the Indian must change the road his father trod, or he must suffer, and probably die. We tell you that to change will make you better. We wish you to live, and we will now offer the way.

The whites are settling up all the good lands. They have come to the Arkansas River. When they come, they drive out the buffalo. If you oppose them, war must come. They are many and you are few. You may kill some of them, but others will come and take their places. And finally, many of the red men will have been killed, and the rest will have no homes. We are your best friends, and now, before all the good lands are taken by whites, we wish to set aside a part of them for your exclusive home.

The government was offering the Indians an alternative to that bleak future. They must settle down, learn to farm, send their children to school, and take their place in American society. The government would feed, clothe, and educate them, and provide a physician, a blacksmith, and a farmer to instruct them. The Indians, however, did not share the commissioners' enthusiasm for American-style civilization. Nor did they share their sense of urgency: they would hunt buffalo as long as they could and then worry about making the transition to farming. Henderson assured them they could continue to hunt buffalo south of the Arkansas River. Convinced that the Indians would not accept the treaty without such a provision, and over the objections of the military commissioners who argued that the concession would jeopardize the peace they were trying to establish, Henderson inserted a clause to that effect in the treaty. As Douglas Jones noted, this provision made the treaty "a bit ambiguous."[54] Also ambiguous was the promise of a "permanent" reservation; by their very role in the process of transforming Indians into individual property owners, reservations were designed to be impermanent.[55] The commissioners spent most of the next day explaining the terms to the Kiowas and Comanches. Henderson assured them that the purpose of the treaty was to give them more goods than they received before. "It is solely for your good and not for the good of the whites," he lied.[56]

At some point Kicking Bird, the Kiowa peace chief (figure 6.7), made clear his opinion of what the Indians were being offered, in a way that stuck in the memory of artillery officer Edward Godfrey sixty years later. At the end of his speech, the Kiowa chief remained standing, "his gaze fixed on the high silk hat in front of one of the commissioners." When the commissioner asked what he wanted, he replied, "I want that hat." Thinking he intended just to look at it, the commissioner handed it over, but Kicking Bird took it and walked away. "Later, he appeared in the immediate vicinity of the council tents arrayed in moccasins, breechclout, and the high hat. He stalked back and forth, telling the tribesmen to look at him; that he 'was walking in the white man's ways,' and using other set phrases that had been used in the council. Finally he grew tired of the burlesque, set the hat on the ground, and used it as a football until he had battered it out of shape, then stalked away."[57]

On October 21, the chiefs duly made their marks on the treaty.[58] It pledged the Kiowas and Comanches and the United States to live in peace. Individual violators of the peace, whether Indian or white, would be dealt with under US law. Annuities would be delivered to the agency every October for thirty years: each male fourteen years or older would receive a suit of good woolen clothing, "consisting of coat, pantaloons, flannel shirt, hat, and a pair of home-made socks"; each female would get one flannel skirt or cloth to make it, a pair of woolen hose, and other material; and there would be clothes for children. The secretary of the interior would be allotted $25,000 each year to spend on necessities for the Indians and Congress was prohibited from changing the amount.

FIGURE 6.7 **Kicking Bird.** *Photograph by W. S. Soule. (Smithsonian Institution, National Anthropological Archives and Human Studies Film Archives)*

The treaty outlined the boundaries of the reservation, for "the absolute and undisturbed use" of the Indians. The Kiowas and Comanches agreed to live on a reservation on lands ceded by the Choctaws and Chickasaws, between the Canadian and Red rivers, west of the ninety-eighth meridian. In effect, they gave up claims to some ninety million acres in exchange for a reservation of less than three million acres in the southwestern corner of Indian Territory, a tiny fragment of the Kiowa and Comanche range.[59] The treaty set aside 160 acres of farm land for each member of the tribes on the reservation, and it specified the buildings that would be constructed—an agency building, medical facility, school, sawmill, and buildings for a blacksmith, carpenter, miller, farmer, and engineer. Instead of living at a nearby army post, as was common practice, the Indian agent would live on the reservation. Article 6 of the treaty stipulated that heads of families who wished to farm could select 320 acres with the agent's assistance, and that tract would be taken out of the tribe's communal land and became the private property of the individual and his family. The land was not held in fee simple, but the president could give it fee simple status at his discretion. The transactions would be recorded in a land book. This provision was the core of the government's "civilization program": the Indians would give up an entire way of life and their former independence in exchange for the right to work and to own a piece of real estate.[60] Once an Indian selected land for farming he was entitled to up to $100 in seeds and farming implements for the first year and up to $25 for the next three years. Silver Brooch was the only individual mentioned in the text of the treaty. Because he was already farming in the area set aside for the reservation, the treaty authorized $750 to build a house for him and his family.

Article 7 stipulated that "in order to insure the civilization of the tribes," children aged six to sixteen would be compelled to attend school. For every thirty students the government would provide a teacher "competent to teach elementary branches of an English education." Some colonial colleges had recruited Indian students, and some earlier American treaties had included clauses providing for education, but this was a new departure: the government was now committed to making education mandatory for Indian children. Education had become "an integral part of an aggressive policy of pacification."[61]

In Article 11 the Indians relinquished all rights to permanently occupy the territory outside their reservation, but retained the right to continue hunting south of the Arkansas "so long as the buffalo may range thereon in such numbers as to justify the chase." They also agreed to stop harassing railroad construction crews, wagon trains, settlers, and army posts. Article 12 stipulated that no part of the reservation could be ceded without the consent of at least three-quarters of the adult male population. It appeared almost as an afterthought in the treaty and the Indians must have thought it sounded like a solid guarantee that they would never lose more land. The newspaper correspondents paid little attention to it,[62] but in years to come this provision—or rather the breach of it—would have major repercussions.

Beyond agreeing to peace, it is difficult to believe that the Kiowas and Comanches understood all the treaty's provisions or had them fully explained, and it is doubtful that they would have signed it had they done so. At the treaty signing Satanta repeated his sentiment that "this building of houses for us is all nonsense; we don't want you to build any for us. We would all die." He wanted all his land from the Arkansas to the Red River, and he did not want houses. Time enough to worry about settling down when the buffalo were all gone. Ten Bears said he wanted the houses built, but only if they were completed before the next summer; so many things had been promised before and not delivered. Kicking Bird asked why they needed a new treaty since they had not broken the one they made on the Arkansas two years before: "I don't see any necessity for making new treaties. You are piling more papers here, one after another. Are you ever going to get through with all this talk?"[63] Ten Kiowas and ten Comanches signed, including Satanta, Satank, Kicking Bird, Stumbling Bear, Fishermore, and Ten Bears. Then annuity goods were distributed: two thousand uniforms, two thousand blankets, tobacco, bolts of cloth, axes, knives, mirrors, needles and thread, and fifty revolvers—an event marred by the fact that three of the pistols exploded when their new owners tried to fire them. The Kiowas and Comanches loaded their ponies and headed back along the creek to their encampment.[64]

In the evening an autumn storm hit. That night a group of Cheyennes, blanketed against the wind and rain, emerged out of the dark at the commissioners' tent and asked for a conference. It was Black Kettle, together with Little Robe, Grey Beard, and White Horse from the Cimarron encampment. The Cimarron chiefs said they were ready to talk peace but they could not begin talks for four days, after they had finished their Medicine Arrow ceremony, and they wanted the Kiowas and Comanches to remain at the treaty to hear what was said. The commissioners reluctantly agreed to the delay, but only after some debate and disagreement—Senator Henderson was anxious to wrap things up and declared he was leaving for St. Louis; General Harney was determined to wait for the Cheyennes and threatened to have Henderson arrested until they arrived! No one could promise that the other Indians would stay to hear what the Cheyennes had to say. Meanwhile, Little Raven told Superintendent Murphy that the Arapahos wanted to negotiate separately from the Cheyennes, and the Plains Apaches told him they wanted to share a reservation with their Kiowa and Comanche allies. The commissioners ignored Little Raven's request but promptly met the Apache's request with an appendix to the Kiowa-Comanche treaty. The Plains Apaches agreed to confederate with the Kiowas and Comanches and live on the same reservation.[65]

Stanley summed it all up: "Much breath has been expended, and many fine poetical sentiments wasted on the prairie air. Councils have broken up time and again with eternal promises of love and friendship on both sides, many a shaking of hands and gesticulations, the meaning and the true interpretation of which is only known to the favored few." On the morning of October 22, the Kiowas and Comanches gathered to receive the treaty presents. Wagonloads of goods were distributed: blankets, army coats, cotton clothes, knives, ammunition, thousands of glass beads, and hundreds of army surplus brass bugles.[66] On a one-hundred-year pictorial calendar recorded by the Kiowa artist Silver Horn, the Treaty of Medicine Lodge is represented by a pile of trade goods placed between a Kiowa and a bearded white man in a hat and uniform coat, beneath an American flag.[67]

Kicking Bird gave Commissioner Taylor a hunting pony and some Arapahos brought General Harney a gift of buffalo meat. Some Kiowas and Comanches, anxious to reach their winter grazing ranges, took down their lodges and headed south, but others stayed for the next round of talks. In the days that followed whites and Indians visited back and forth. In the Kiowa encampment the newspaper reporters met two white women, one Irish, one German, who had been captured as children and now lived as Kiowas. Neither had any interest in leaving.[68]

Satank (see figure 6.8) had not spoken during the negotiations. On October 24 or 25, before he left for the winter hunting grounds, he rode up to the council tent, dismounted, and addressed the commissioners. It is not clear whether he spoke in Kiowa or Comanche, or who interpreted—presumably McCusker was involved—but Stanley told his readers that he took down the old man's words verbatim in shorthand. George Wills, the commission stenographer, also was there. Standing alone before the Peace Commission, holding the silver peace medal that hung around his neck, the old man said:

> It has made me very glad to meet you, who are the commissioners sent by the Great Father to see us. You have heard much talk by our chiefs, and no doubt are tired of it. Many of them have put themselves forward and filled you with their sayings. I have kept back and said nothing—not that I did not consider myself the principal chief of the Kiowa Nation, but others younger than I desired to talk, and I left it to them.
>
> Before leaving, however, as I now intend to go, I come to say that the Kiowas and Camaches [sic] have made with you a peace, and they intend to keep it. If it brings prosperity to us, we of course will like it the better. If it brings prosperity or adversity, we will not abandon it. It is our contract, and it shall stand.
>
> Our people once carried war against Texas. We thought the Great Father would not be offended for the Texans had gone out from among his people, and became his enemies. You now tell us that they have made peace and returned to the great family. The Kiowas and Camanches will seek no bloody trail in their land. They have pledged their word and that word shall last, unless the whites break their contract and invite the horrors of war. We do not break treaties. We make but few contracts, and them we remember well. The whites make so many that they are liable to forget them. The white chief seems not able to govern his braves. The Great Father seems powerless in the face of his children. He sometimes becomes angry when he sees the wrongs of his people committed on the red man, and his voice becomes loud as the roaring winds. But like the

FIGURE 6.8 **Satank, toward the end of his life.** *He wears the sash of the Koietsenko Warrior Society, and may have amputated his left little finger at the joint in mourning for the death of his son. Photograph by W. S. Soule. (Research Division of the Oklahoma Historical Society)*

wind it soon dies away and leaves the sullen calm of unheeded oppression. We hope now that a better time has come. If all would talk and then do as you have done the sun of peace would shine forever. We have warred against the white man, but never because it gave us pleasure. Before the day of oppression came, no white man came to our villages and went away hungry. It gave us more joy to share with them than it gave him to partake of our hospitality. In the far-distant past there was no suspicion among us. The world seemed large enough for both the red and the white man. Its broad plains seem now to contract, and the white man grows jealous of his red brother.

The white man once came to trade; he now comes as a soldier. He once put his trust in our friendship and wanted no shield but our fidelity. But now he builds forts and plants big guns on their walls. He once gave us arms and powder and ball, and bade us to hunt the game. We then loved him for his confidence; he now suspects our plighted faith and drives us to be his enemies; he now covers his face with the cloud of jealousy and anger, and tells us to begone, as an offended master speaks to his dog. Look at this medal I wear. By wearing this I have been made poor. Formerly, I was rich in horses and lodges—today I am the poorest of all. When you put this silver medal on my neck you made me poor.

We thank the Great Spirit that all these wrongs are now to cease and the old day of peace and friendship [is] to come again.

You came as friends. You talked as friends. You have partially heard our many complaints. To you they may have seemed trifling. To us they are everything.

You have not tried, as many have done, to make a new bargain merely to get the advantage.

You have not asked to make our annuities smaller, but unasked you have made them larger.

You have not withdrawn a single gift, but you have voluntarily provided more guarantees for our education and comfort.

When we saw these things done, we then said among ourselves, these are the men of the past. We at once gave you our hearts. You now have them. You know what is best for us. Do for us what is best. Teach us the road to travel, and we will not depart from it forever.

For your sakes the green grass shall no more be stained with the red blood of the pale-faces. Your people shall again be our people, and peace shall be between us forever. If wrong comes, we shall look to you for right and justice.

We know you will not forsake us, and tell your people also to act as you have done, to be as you have been.

I am old, but still am chief. I shall have soon to go the way of my fathers, but those who come after me will remember this day. It is now treasured up by the old, and will be carried by them to the grave, and then handed down to be kept as a sacred tradition by their children and their children's children. And now the time has come that I must go. Good-bye!

You may never see me more, but remember Satank as the white man's friend.

The old man passed down the line shaking hands with each of the commissioners, then mounted his pony and rode away. The correspondents and commissioners were moved by his words. Reporter H. J. Budd, who rarely had much good to say about Indians, wrote that he had heard plenty of oratory in Congress and in church "But never have I known true eloquence before this day." Stanley said it was the best speech they heard at Medicine Lodge, equal to any by Red Jacket or Logan, and that there was "a good deal of truth in it which strikes home." Satank closed the Kiowa treaty on a note of good feelings and hope for the future.[69]

Neither lasted long. Like the commissioners' talks, Satank's talk contained some wishful thinking and some half truths as well as hard truths. After Medicine Lodge the United States pressed on destroying the Kiowas' way of life and Satank and Satanta went back to raiding.

There could be no peace without the Cheyennes, and although the commissioners and reporters were tired of the endless proceedings and "hankered for the flesh pots of St. Louis" and the joys of city life, they waited. The Cimarron Cheyennes finally showed up on October 27. The news that they were coming spread through the camp "like wildfire." Led by the renowned Dog Soldiers ("modern Spartans, who knew how to die but not to be led captive," wrote Stanley), five hundred warriors galloped in, chanting in unison, and firing their pistols in the air—an event that caused considerable alarm in the camp even though Little Robe had given the Peace Commission advance warning. They reined their horses to an abrupt halt right in front of the commissioners, a dramatic grand entry that impressed everyone: "The Wild Chivalry of the Prairie in Force," said the *Chicago Tribune*. That evening a Cheyenne woman, who was giving gifts in celebration of the birth of her son, presented a pony to General Harney.[70]

The next day Henderson began the proceedings by explaining to the Cheyennes gathered in a semicircle before him that the Great Father had sent the commissioners to make peace. Bad men on both sides had caused bloodshed but, said the senator, "the world is big enough for both of us." He then offered the Cheyennes the same treaty the Kiowas and Comanches had agreed to: they must stop attacking railroads and settlers and settle on a reservation of their own. The government would provide the implements and livestock they needed to become farmers: "In lieu of the buffalo you must have herds of oxen and flocks of sheep and droves of hogs, like the white man." Nevertheless, so long as there were sufficient buffalo, the Cheyennes could continue to hunt south of the Arkansas River, in accordance with the terms of the Little Arkansas treaty.[71]

When Henderson had finished, the Cheyenne and Arapaho chiefs smoked and passed the pipe. Then Little Robe invited Little Raven to speak first, for the Arapahos. Somewhat surprised, Little Raven, who only a few days before had wanted a separate treaty and did not get it, now expressed his undying love for his Cheyenne friends. "The Cheyennes are like my own flesh and blood," he said, "and what they do, I am concerned in it." He said he was pleased with the idea of a reservation now that the buffalo were disappearing and hoped that whites would not encroach on it. If the whites were kept away, he promised not to interfere with the railroads. "As for myself, and men aged like me, we will be dead before the farms get to be productive, but those who come after us will enjoy them and have the benefit." He repeated his request for a separate Arapaho reservation: "This country here don't belong to me. It belongs to the Kiowas, Comanches, and Cheyennes. That country in Colorado belongs to me and I want to go there. I do not want to be mixed up with the other Indians." He asked when the annuities would be delivered, hoped the commissioners would keep their promises, and requested that honest traders be appointed. However, the Arapahos did not get their Colorado reservation.[72]

Buffalo Chief spoke for the Cheyennes. Did the whites really want peace? Henderson assured him they did. Then the Cheyennes would not molest the railroads and travelers, Buffalo Chief said. But they did not want houses or to be treated as orphans: "You think that you are doing a great deal for us by giving these presents to us, but we prefer to live as formerly. If you gave us all the goods you could give, yet we would prefer our own life. You give us presents, and then take our land; that produces war." In short, they just wanted to be left alone to live their own way of life as long as they could. When they chose to live like whites they would ask for advice; until then they would take their chances. The Cheyennes never claimed any land south of the Arkansas, said Buffalo Chief, "but that country between the Arkansas and the South Platte is ours." Almost at the end of the Treaty of Medicine Lodge, notes Douglas Jones, Buffalo Chief touched "the raw nerve that everyone had been afraid would be touched." The territory he referred to was a vast expanse of territory embracing western Kansas and part of eastern Colorado. The Cheyennes and the Kiowas and Comanches had contested it and then shared it but the United States now wanted it cleared of Indians to make way for settlers and railroads. The Cheyenne land claim could wreck the whole treaty.[73]

Little Raven stood up again and said that the Arapahos wanted Mrs. Adams as their regular interpreter and wanted an honest trader on their reservation, but the commissioners were too busy worrying about how to deal with Buffalo Chief's bombshell to pay him much heed. They didn't pay much more attention when a Cheyenne Dog Soldier named Little Man launched into a tirade against the Kiowas and Comanches.[74]

For a moment, it looked as if the commissioners might have to adjourn the meeting and draw up a new treaty: clearly the Cheyennes would not agree to the one they had prepared. But Henderson was determined to get the treaty signed that day. Huddling with Buffalo Chief and several Dog Soldier chiefs at a distance from the council, with George Bent and John Smith interpreting and mediating, the senator hammered out a quick fix. He "explained to the Indians the obnoxious treaty clause" and that they did not have to go onto the reservation immediately. Henderson assured them that they could have hunting rights north of the Arkansas as far as the South Platte as long as there were buffalo and so long as they adhered to the terms of the Little Arkansas treaty and kept ten miles away from travel routes and white settlements. Henderson knew that, at the rate Americans were settling Kansas, the Cheyennes' hunting would soon be severely restricted and the buffalo herds would not last long. But the Cheyennes bought his verbal promise and signed the treaty as it was written. Bull Bear (the head chief of the Dog Soldiers), White Horse, and Little Robe at first balked at touching the pen. (Indian leaders frequently objected to "touching the pen": they were suspicious of it, thought it unnecessary, and did not always realize that affixing their names to the treaty signified their approval of everything in it, not just to the things they themselves had said.[75]) "By dint of infinite coaxing," even the Dog Soldier chiefs were induced to fix their marks, although Bull Bear drove the pen through the paper when he signed. Little Raven led the Arapaho delegates in signing. Some Cheyennes refused to sign. Roman Nose stayed away from the council, and, perhaps most significantly, Medicine Arrows, also called Stone Forehead, the Keeper of the Sacred Arrows, would have nothing to do with the treaty. No provision authorizing the Cheyennes and Arapahos to hunt in the area between the Arkansas and the South Platte appeared in the final treaty ratified by the Senate; like the Kiowas and Comanches, they were permitted to hunt lands only *south* of the Arkansas.[76]

The terms of the Cheyenne treaty were essentially the same as those in the Kiowa and Comanche treaty, with the exception that the Cheyenne reservation was to be bounded on the north by the southern border of Kansas, on the east by the Arkansas River, and on the south and west by the Cimarron. It is difficult to believe the Cheyennes knew what they were getting into beyond agreeing to let the railroads through to secure peace. Stanley captured the essence of the Cheyenne position. They had been at war all summer and had come to Medicine Lodge at the commissioners' invitation. "They had been conquerors, and we wished for peace. They did not wish any peace, but, since we asked it they, as brave men, were willing to accord it. As a recompense for this action we might, if we chose, build them schools, but they could not occupy them. They preferred the life they led."[77] As had the Kiowas and Comanches, the Cheyennes signed a treaty containing items they had expressly opposed during the treaty talks. On October 27, their Sacred Arrow ceremonies completed, they had galloped into Medicine Lodge full of power; the next day, they apparently agreed to surrender lands they said they would not give up, agreed to move to a reservation they said they did not want, agreed to have tribal members tried in white courts, agreed to have their children educated in English, and agreed to be trained to live as sedentary farmers. Alfred Barnitz, a captain in the Seventh Cavalry who was present during the negotiations, wrote that the Cheyennes "*have no idea that* they are giving up, or that they have ever given up the country which they claim as their own, the country north of the Arkansas. The treaty all amounts to nothing, and we will have another war sooner or later with the Cheyennes, at least, and probably with the other Indians, in consequence of misunderstanding of the terms of present and previous treaties."[78] George Bent later wrote that Medicine Lodge was "the most important treaty ever signed by the Cheyenne" in that it "marked the beginning of the end" for them as free and independent warriors and hunters.[79]

The Peace Commission had been at Medicine Lodge more than two weeks. Eager to get back to St. Louis now that the treaty was signed, the commissioners had the treaty presents delivered promptly to the Cheyennes and Arapahos. The Arapahos held a dance for the commissioners that night, in another rainstorm, and the next morning the great council at Medicine Lodge broke up. The commissioners headed back east to St. Louis where they met and briefed General Sherman.[80] Reaching St. Louis after a seventy-five-hour journey, Taylor telegraphed the secretary of the interior with the good news: "Please congratulate the President and the country upon the entire success of the Indian Peace Commission thus far." Treaties of peace had been concluded with the five tribes south of the Arkansas and "everything passed off satisfactorily." The commission now turned its attention to the northern tribes.[81]

Henry Stanley agreed. When the Peace Commission began its work, war raged all across the Plains, he wrote. The commission met thousands of Indians in council "and turned their thoughts and feelings from war to peace." "Peace has been concluded with all the Southern tribes," declared Stanley. "Civilization is now on the move, and westward the Star of Empire will again resume its march, unimpeded in the great work of Progress."[82] After Medicine Lodge, Stanley's newspaper career took a decided upward swing when he joined America's most famous newspaper, the *New York Herald*. The *Herald's* editor dispatched him on an expedition to "Darkest Africa" to find the famous missionary Henry Livingstone. Stanley's success, and his greeting—"Doctor Livingstone, I presume"—won him world renown, and even a small measure of immortality. The first European to travel the full length of the Congo River, the illegitimate boy from the workhouse became one of the most famous, and controversial, British explorers of the Victorian era.[83]

Others who attended the treaty were not so fortunate. The commissioners had handed out peace medals to Satanta, Satank, Kicking Bird, and Black Eagle of the Kiowas, and to Tall Bull, Bull Bear, Little Robe, and the son of a former head chief of the Cheyennes.[84] The chiefs would not have much peace.

Medicine Lodge was the last great treaty council held on the southern Plains and it was one of the very last treaties. The Great Peace Commission was a product of dissatisfaction and demand for change in Indian affairs but it failed to satisfy the dissatisfied or to effect the necessary changes. The commission was intended to bring peace to the Plains but it brought only an appearance of peace. In order to get the Indians to agree to the terms of the treaty, the commissioners had promised them they would be able to continue the very way of life the treaty was designed to terminate. They had persuaded the chiefs to touch the pen to documents the Senate could accept as valid treaties and which "gave the stamp of legitimacy to United States efforts to concentrate the Indians and open the region to white exploitation." The Indians at Medicine Lodge accepted the peace treaty but rejected the new way of life that came with it, making conflict inevitable with the Americans who invaded their hunting lands.[85] Back in the summer General Sherman was quoted as saying that the mission of the Peace Commission was "a humbug" and that it would achieve nothing. He now ordered that hostilities cease with the tribes who had signed the Medicine Lodge treaty and that their rights to hunt south of the South Platte be respected. Sherman's goal was to clear the Natives out of the territory between the Platte and the Arkansas and he believed "it makes little difference whether they be coaxed out by Indian commissioners or killed." He now informed General Ulysses Grant that "the chief use of the Peace Commission is to kill time which will do more to settle the Indians than anything we can do."[86] The flawed peace cobbled together at Medicine Lodge quickly unraveled as American expansion drove the pace of events even faster than the commissioners' cynical schedule anticipated. As Douglas Jones points out, "October 28, 1867, was the last time the representatives of the United States ever sat at a treaty table with any of the Southern Plains tribes. The next time red and white diplomats met, terms were not offered, they were dictated."[87] Less than four years after Medicine Lodge the treaty system itself was terminated.

The Many Deaths of Medicine Lodge

Press reports of the Medicine Lodge council had been appearing in newspapers while it was going on. Once the treaty was over, the commissioners prepared an official report.[88] The press reports and the official report show essential agreement but, even before the official report was written, Major Joel Elliott, commander of the cavalry escort at Medicine Lodge and commander of the Seventh Cavalry during Custer's fifteen-month suspension, was criticizing the Peace Commission and advocating tougher measures in fighting Indians. He filed his own dissenting report and sent it to General Sherman. Elliott claimed the treaties were never interpreted to the Indians, charged the commissioners with pandering to the Indians, and complained that the negotiations "were conducted in such a manner that anyone unacquainted with the relative strengths of the two contracting parties would have imagined the Indians to have been the stronger and we the suppliants."[89]

Enoch Hoag, Indian superintendent for the central region, tried to see things from the Indians' perspective. They had relinquished "a domain large enough for an empire, comprising some 400,000 square miles, with the agreement to abandon their accustomed chase, and move to a diminished and restricted reservation in the Indian territory, and enter upon the new and untried duties of civilized life, with the assurance on the part of our government of protection in all their rights"[90] (see figure 6.9). But Congress was busy impeaching President Andrew Johnson and did not ratify the Medicine Lodge treaty until July 1868. The required appropriations were not included in that year's budget, no annuities were paid, the reservations were not established on time, and the promised rations were not delivered on schedule.[91] Congressmen argued at length about whether appropriations were pledges honoring treaties and payments for Indian lands or "handouts to a broken people" that constituted an endless drain on the Treasury. Corruption, notorious within the Indian department, further reduced the quantity and quality of the goods designated for Indians. General Sherman used the rations of food and clothing as an inducement to attract Indians to the reservations but things were in short supply. Withholding rations from people whose economies were being destroyed—in essence, keeping them on the edge of starvation—was a powerful instrument of colonial control, calculated to render formerly independent people entirely dependent on the government and its agents, but the policy pushed young men off the reservations and back into the kind of activities the government was trying to suppress. Indians complained that their families were going hungry waiting for the government to honor its pledges and some went back to raiding. At the same time, the government failed to honor its treaty commitments to keep predatory whites out of the reservations, and horse thieves preyed on the Indians' herds.[92]

Jesse Leavenworth took charge of the Kiowa, Comanche, and Apache reservation and the Kiowas settled in the Eureka Valley near their agency at Fort Cobb on the northern edge of the reservation. But they protested that the government had "no right to pen them up on this small tract of land, only about one hundred miles square, and then give half their rations of provisions in corn, feeding them as the white people do their horses and mules." The cornmeal often arrived damaged and caused diarrhea if they ate it—sometimes they did not even take the corn from the commissary, "thinking it not worth carrying home." The Comanche chief Silver Brooch said his people were supposed to receive coffee, sugar, flour, seeds, and farm implements but their agent gave

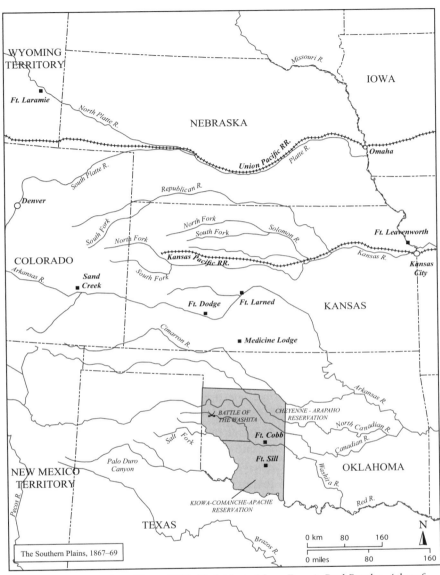

FIGURE 6.9 *The southern Plains, 1867–69. (Adapted from Francis Paul Prucha, Atlas of American Indian Affairs [Lincoln: University of Nebraska Press, 1990], 101)*

them nothing but cornmeal. Silver Brooch also asked where was the house he was promised? Kiowa men ranged west into the Texas Panhandle looking for buffalo, raided Wichita and Caddo villages for food and horses, and raided into Texas for horses and mules. The interpreter Philip McCusker intercepted one raiding party and asked why they were going to Texas and had so quickly forgotten their talk to the Peace Commission: "they told me that their Agent no longer cared for them, that he had induced them to move down into this country where they had been cheated with false promises and had given their goods and provisions away to other Indians." The Kiowas and Comanches generally were displeased with Leavenworth and complained that he "always makes away with a large share of their goods."[93]

There was more to raiding Texas than stealing mules. Kiowas, Comanches, and Plains Apaches kept the peace they had made in Kansas but quickly resumed—or simply continued—their raids into Texas, carrying off captive children as well as livestock. They drew a distinction between the two places, between Americans with whom they signed a treaty and *Tejanos* whom they had been fighting for years. They asserted "their right to roam at will in Texas, they having been driven from their hunting grounds in that State by superior force, and never having relinquished there rights thereto."[94] For a time it seemed that the US government drew a similar distinction; after all, it, too, had been fighting the former Confederate state until quite recently. The Peace Commission had been primarily concerned with affairs in Kansas and the government did not immediately regard raids south of the Red River as constituting a breach of the treaty. But Leavenworth, his "patience with them and their promises" exhausted, recommended that the Kiowa and Comanche annuities be stopped, and if the guilty parties were not delivered up for punishment, the military should "make short and sharp work of them, until they can see, hear, and feel the strong arm of the government." Leavenworth had become jittery, was constantly calling for troops, and soon left his post. But Commissioner of Indian Affairs Nathaniel Taylor agreed with him, and he questioned whether the treaty he had negotiated at Medicine Lodge should be ratified since the Kiowas and Comanches had clearly broken their treaty obligations.[95] The Kwahadi Comanches who carried out many of the raids had not attended Medicine Lodge or agreed to the treaty. United States authorities criminalized the Kiowa and Comanche raids and brought in the military to force them back onto the reservations.[96]

Tensions increased in Kansas as well. The Cheyennes and Arapahos were dissatisfied with their barren reservation and claimed they never fully understood the boundaries prescribed in the Medicine Lodge treaty.[97] Even so, the Arapaho chiefs Little Raven, Spotted Wolf, and Powder Face "came in" and expressed their desire to live in peace, as did Black Kettle's Cheyennes. But chiefs such as Roman Nose and Medicine Arrows who had not attended the Medicine Lodge treaty felt no obligation to honor its terms, fueling accusations that all Indians were treaty breakers. Cheyennes and Arapahos did not stop raiding the Kaw or Kansa Indians and the Osages; whiskey traders caused trouble in the Indian camps; and angry young warriors committed raids and killings.[98]

General Sherman intended to settle the Indians on the reservations "one way or the other." He took a hard line and was determined to punish not only the individuals who conducted raids but also the groups from which they came. "All of the Cheyennes and Arapahoes are now at war," he declared in September 1868. "Admitting that some of them have not done acts of murder, rape, &c, still they have not restrained those who have, nor have they on demand given up the criminals as they agreed to do. The treaty made at Medicine Lodge is therefore clearly broken by them." Because it would be difficult for troops "to discriminate between the well-disposed and the warlike," the peaceful bands must go to the reservation in Indian Territory and stay there. The Cheyennes and Arapahos "should receive nothing and now that they are at open war I propose to give them enough of it to satisfy them to their hearts' content," wrote Sherman. "The vital part of their tribes are committing murders and robberies from Kansas to Colorado and it is an excess of generosity on our part to be feeding and supplying the old, young and feeble, whilst their young men are at war." After the peaceful bands had been given a reasonable time to withdraw, all Indians who remained outside the reservation would be declared outlaws. Indians who wanted to hunt buffalo off the reservation could be regulated by issuing permits but, Sherman wrote, "the treaty having been clearly violated by the Indians themselves, this hunting right is entirely lost to them if we so declare it."[99] Superintendent of Indian Affairs Thomas Murphy took an equally hard line: in previous wars the Cheyennes and Arapahos had just cause for previous hostilities, but they had none now—every promise made to them at Medicine Lodge had been strictly carried out. "This time, I recommend that they be left to the tender mercies of our army until they shall be forced to sue for peace"—and that would be a peace they would keep for all time.[100]

Just one year after it had signed the treaty, the Peace Commission resolved:

That the recent outrages and depredations committed by the Indians of the plains justify the government in abrogating those clauses of the treaties made in October 1867, at "Medicine Lodge Creek," which secure to them the right to roam and hunt outside their reservations: That all said Indians should be required to remove at once to said reservations and remain within them, except that after peace shall have been restored, hunting parties may be permitted to cross their boundaries with written authority from their Agent or Superintendent.

Resolved further, that military force should be used to compel the removal into said reservations of all such Indians as may refuse to go ...[101]

Major General Philip Sheridan, the new commander of the Department of the Missouri, dispatched troops into Indian country. Roman Nose died at the Battle of Beecher's Island in September 1868. In November Sheridan launched a campaign on the Washita River, where Black Kettle's Cheyennes, Little Raven's Arapahos, and Kicking Bird's band of Kiowas were in their winter encampments. Black Kettle had survived the massacre at Sand Creek but this time there was no escape. George Custer, back in action after his suspension, divided his command and hit Black Kettle's village from four sides at dawn. Captain Louis Hamilton, who had been with the cavalry escort at Medicine Lodge, was shot off his horse as he charged through the village. Black Kettle and his wife both died in the ensuing melee. George Bent and Magpie were not in the camp—they had gone to visit Bent's relatives near Fort Lyon, a move Bent said saved them from sharing the same fate. As warriors from the other camps along the valley hastened to join the fight, Custer pulled back. He left behind a detachment of seventeen men led by Major Joel Elliott who had gone in pursuit of fleeing women and children. Elliott and his men were cut off, killed, and mutilated by Kiowa, Cheyenne, and Arapaho warriors. Some of them may have recognized Elliott from Medicine Lodge.[102] According to Edward Godfrey, Stumbling Bear had become friends with Elliott during his constant visits to the soldiers' camp at Medicine Lodge. When Godfrey saw Stumbling Bear a couple of months after the Washita, the Kiowa had cut his hair "and gave me to understand that he was in mourning for the loss of his good friend Major Elliott."[103]

Although Black Kettle was a Cheyenne, Silver Horn's Kiowa calendar marked his death that winter—depicted by a death owl perched on the handle of a black bucket or kettle: not only were there Kiowas in the village on the Washita but the killing of a chief who had worked so hard for peace at Medicine Lodge was an ominous event for all the tribes.[104] The year 1868 was a bad one for the Kiowas. A Kiowa war party carrying one of the tribe's three *taimes*—the small figurine or doll that was central to the sun dance—was badly defeated in a battle with the Utes and the sacred medicine bag was lost. Edward Wynkoop said the loss of the medicine made the Kiowas "more subdued and humbled than he has ever known them to be." Thomas Murphy suggested that the government buy the medicine from the Utes and then keep it—it would do more "than a regiment of soldiers" to keep the Kiowas in line and stop their raids into Texas.[105] In December, during a parley, George Custer had Satanta and Lone Wolf seized and put in leg irons as hostages until the rest of the Kiowas came to the agency. "They are among the worst Indians we have to deal with," Sheridan told Custer, "and have been guilty of untold murders and outrages, at the same time they were being fed and clothed by the Government. These two chiefs, Lone Wolf and Satanta, have forfeited their lives over and over again."[106] Slowly, the Kiowas came in and Lone Wolf and Satanta were eventually released—against Sheridan's better judgment; he would much rather have hanged them. As far as Sheridan was concerned, the only way for Indians to live in peace was to succumb to the reservation regime. "I do not care one cent," he told Custer to inform Cheyenne and Arapaho delegates who asked for peace, "whether they come in or stay out. If they stay out I will make war on them Winter and Summer as long as I live or until they are wiped out."[107]

Tall Bull, the Dog Soldier chief who had reluctantly signed the treaty, died fighting the cavalry and Major Frank North's Pawnee scouts at the Battle of Summit Springs in July 1869. That defeat ended the Cheyennes' occupation of the country between the Platte and Arkansas rivers. Bull Bear, who had driven the pen through the paper when he signed the treaty at Medicine Lodge, was with Roman Nose when he died and he continued the fight for several years longer but it was the Dog Soldiers' last stand. After the Cheyennes were forced onto the reservation, Bull Bear sent his son to school and endeavored to follow the new path.[108]

General Grant's inauguration as president in 1869 brought a new "Peace Policy" toward the Indian tribes of the West, at least those who accepted the reservation system. Indians were under the control and jurisdiction of their agents when they were "on their proper reservations"; Indians outside the reservation were under military jurisdiction and were considered hostile.[109] A Quaker named Lawrie Tatum took over as agent for the Kiowas and Comanches at the new agency near Fort Sill. He told the Indians that they would be protected as long as they remained on the reservation but punished if they left without permission. It was "peace on the Reservations," said Tatum, and "it was war off of them."[110] In August Grant established the Cheyenne and Arapaho reservation by executive order, changing its location. The new reservation lay between the Cimarron River and the ninety-eighth meridian in the east and the one hundredth meridian (the Texas state line) in the west, bounded by the Cherokee Outlet on the north and the Kiowa-Comanche-Apache reservation on the south. Another executive order in 1872 assigned the southwestern part of the area to the Caddos, Delawares, Wichitas, and other Indians. George Bent accepted a position as government interpreter at the Cheyenne-Arapaho agency.

In March 1870, the secretary of the interior informed the president that Indians from the Canadian border to the Mexican frontier were complaining "of what they declare to be a lack of faith on our part, in carrying out the stipulations of treaties heretofore made with them, and redeeming the promises which, as they allege, induced them to consent to the peaceable construction of railroads to the Pacific coast." The situation was acute among the tribes who signed the Medicine Lodge treaties, and only "the greatest exertions" by civil and military officers had prevented war. Determined that if an Indian war was inevitable the government should not be responsible for it, Grant urged Congress to make the necessary appropriations in order to carry out the treaties made by the Peace Commission.[111]

Tatum's "peace on the reservations, war off of them" became an accurate description of the situation by the end of the decade as Kiowa and Comanche men, frustrated at their confinement and dependence on government rations that were shoddy, inadequate, and irregular, left the reservations, stole horses and livestock, took captives and scalps, and then returned as winter approached and the raiding season ended.[112] In the spring of 1870 Satank's eldest son was killed during a raid into Texas. The grief-stricken old man carefully wrapped his son's bones in a blanket, placed the bundle on a separate pony, and carried it with him wherever he went. "Satank, who had pledged eternal friendship with the whites at Medicine Lodge, now burned with hatred for them."[113]

The public was outraged at a policy that seemed to feed and supply Indians who then went out and killed whites, and the army was determined to put a stop to the raids. Public indignation peaked after the infamous Warren Wagon Train Massacre in Texas in May 1871 when Kiowa, Comanche, and Apache warriors killed and mutilated seven teamsters, one of whom was tied to a wagon tongue and burned. Satanta, who boasted he had led the raid, Satank, and Big Tree were arrested when they returned to the reservation. Kicking Bird tried to prevent it: "You and I are going to die right here," he told General Sherman. But Sherman had no doubts about what should become of Satanta: "I think it is time to end his career," he wrote Sheridan. "He has been raiding in Texas to regain his influence as a great warrior." Sherman also announced that "Old Satank ought to have been shot long ago." Satanta's impudence in boasting of his murders showed that the Kiowas needed "pretty much the lesson you gave Black Kettle and Little Raven." As for Lone Wolf, he "ought to have been hung when you had him in hand." Sherman thought Kicking Bird was "about the only Kiowa that seems to understand their situation."[114] Kicking Bird understood more than Sherman knew. He remained committed to peace but he worried that his people could not take to the "new road for all the Indians in this country," and he feared the consequences. "The white man is strong," he said in a letter to the commissioner of Indian affairs, "but he cannot destroy us all in one year, it will take him two or three, maybe four years and then the world will turn to water or burn up. It cannot live when all the Indians are dead."[115]

The chiefs were to be sent back to Texas, for trial and hanging if found guilty. Satank was determined to die rather than go to Texas. When he was loaded into a wagon to transport him to Fort Richardson, he called to a Caddo scout who rode alongside the wagon, asking him to tell the Kiowas that Satank was dead. He then began to sing his death song:

"O sun, you remain forever, but we *Kâitse'ñko* must die.
O earth, you remain forever, but we *Kâitse'ñko* must die."

Slipping his handcuffs, he grabbed one of the guards' rifles and died in a hail of bullets, as he had intended.[116]

Satanta and Big Tree went on trial for the murder of the seven teamsters. The jury found them guilty and the judge sentenced them to hang. Agent Tatum persuaded Governor Edmund Davis of Texas to commute the sentence to life imprisonment (he thought it would be easier to control the Kiowas with Satanta in jail than with Satanta dead) and the two Kiowas were shipped to the state penitentiary in Huntsville.[117] Meanwhile, a delegation of Kiowa and Comanche chiefs was taken to Washington where they met with the commissioner of Indian affairs, received large silver medals, and saw the sights. The delegates included several Medicine Lodge signatories: Ten Bears, Lone Wolf, Stumbling Bear, and Woman's Heart. The trip took its toll on Ten Bears. By the time he returned to Fort Sill the old man was sick. The agent gave him a bed in his office and Ten Bears died there—in Colonel W. S. Nye's view "a pathetic figure, alone in the midst of an alien people, in an age he did not understand."[118] Shortly after Lone Wolf's trip to Washington, his son was killed by cavalry in December 1873.[119]

Kiowas continued to raid, however. Christopher C. Augur, now a brigadier general and commander of the Department of Texas orchestrating expeditions against the tribes, believed the Kiowas were "the meanest and cruelest Indians of the plains." He recommended to Sheridan that the whole tribe "be taken possession of and disarmed, and taken entirely out of the Indian Country, and distributed among Military posts at the North—not breaking up families, and that the Kiowas as a tribe be no longer recognized."[120]

Satanta and Big Tree worked on a chain gang laying railroad tracks (although they were taken out of prison to travel to St. Louis and meet the delegation of chiefs en route to Washington). The delegation carried on to Washington, and Satanta and Big Tree returned to Huntsville. In a controversial move that outraged the citizens of Texas as well as General Sherman, Governor Davis granted the chiefs a parole on condition that they made sure that Kiowa raids ceased. However, when the Red River War broke out in 1874, Comanches, Kiowas, and Apaches attacked the buffalo hunters invading their hunting grounds.

The Treaty of Medicine Lodge had established an informal boundary between white settlers (and railroad construction crews) north of the Arkansas River and Indian hunters south of the river, but it did not expressly forbid white *hunters* from the southern buffalo ranges, only from the Indian reservations. Bison hunters consequently paid little regard to the treaty. The treaty agreements, in Andrew Isenberg's words, "were ephemeral because the United States' recognition of autonomous Indian hunting territories was due to expire with the bison." Increasing human and environmental pressures had been pushing bison numbers downward for years and the Indians as well as the treaty commissioners understood that the herds were diminishing. Now, roads and railroads brought immigrants and hunters by the hundreds to the Indians' hunting grounds and in 1871 a Pennsylvania tannery found that buffalo hides could be used to manufacture machine belts. Thousands of hides were loaded onto trains and shipped east, feeding a growing tanning industry that produced the leather belts that drove the machinery of industrializing America. Buffalo hunters embarked on a systematic slaughter of the southern herds that in just a few short years brought the species to the brink of extinction. Colonel Richard Irving Dodge, who was stationed at Fort Dodge at the time, witnessed the slaughter firsthand. In 1871, he wrote, there was "apparently no limit to the numbers of buffalo." In 1872, he went out on many hunting expeditions, including one in the fall with three trigger-happy British gentlemen who "in their excitement bagged more buffalo than would have supplied a brigade." In the fall of 1873 he went with some of the same gentlemen over the same ground. "Where there were myriads of buffalo the year before, there were now myriads of carcasses. The air was foul with sickening stench, and the vast plain, which only a short twelvemonth before teemed with animal life, was a dead, solitary, putrid desert." The next fall, there seemed to be more buffalo hunters than buffalo. All this slaughter, Dodge acknowledged, was "in contravention of solemn treaties made with the Indians."[121]

The architects of US Indian policy always assumed that, faced with starvation, Indians would give up their hunting culture and settle down to become farmers. But one Yamparika Comanche chief named Tananaica (Hears the Sunrise, or Voice of the Sunrise) spoke for many of his people when, in a council held with American agents in 1872, he proclaimed in a booming voice that he would rather stay out on the prairie and eat dung than come in and be penned up in a reservation.[122] Rather than succumb to the government's starvation policies, the Indians struck back against the men who were slaughtering their food source.[123]

The Red River War, or Buffalo War as it was sometimes called, produced atrocities on both sides, but the attack by Cheyenne Dog Soldiers on the family of John and Lydia German in western Kansas in September 1874 and the lurid reports it generated of murder, mutilation, and gang rape fueled demands for rapid retribution.[124] The same year Colonel Ranald Mackenzie attacked a large village of Comanches, Kiowas, and Cheyennes encamped at Palo Duro Canyon. Few Indians died but Mackenzie destroyed their lodges and food supplies and slaughtered more than one thousand ponies. With winter approaching, other army columns pressing them hard, and the once-vast buffalo herds dwindling to near extinction, southern Plains warriors began to straggle in to Fort Sill. Grey Beard, one of the Dog Soldiers who had refused to sign the Treaty of Medicine Lodge, was one of the last Cheyenne chiefs to surrender.[125]

Leaders like Woman's Heart and White Horse were placed in cells. More than one hundred other warriors were confined under guard in an unfinished ice house; once a day soldiers tossed chunks of raw meat over the walls. "They fed us like we were lions," recalled one Kiowa.[126]

Satanta was inevitably assumed to be in the thick of the trouble, even though the evidence for his involvement was shaky at best. In late 1874 he was sent back to prison, this time for life. On October 10, 1878, in his sixties and growing feeble, Satanta asked if there was any chance of his being released. He was told there was none. "I cannot wither and die like a dog in chains," he said. The next day he slashed several arteries. Taken to the prison hospital, he jumped from the second-floor landing and died. He left two daughters and two sons. One of his sons enlisted in Troop L, the all-Indian troop of the Seventh Cavalry organized at Fort Sill in 1892; another attended boarding school in Carlisle, Pennsylvania. Big Tree, who was not sent back to prison with Satanta, converted to Christianity in his forties and became a deacon and Sunday school teacher in a Baptist church.[127]

Other warriors who fought in the Red River War were arrested for murder. Frontier feeling against the Indians was so intense that they had no chance of a fair trial. "It was therefore concluded," recounted Lieutenant Richard Henry Pratt, "best to punish the most notorious of the recent offenders by arbitrarily sending all of them to some remote eastern fort to be held indefinitely as prisoners of war." Pratt, who as an officer in the Tenth Cavalry had led African American "buffalo soldiers" and Indian scouts in the war, was now assigned to be the jailor. Seventy-two prisoners—thirty-two Cheyenne men and one Cheyenne woman, twenty-seven Kiowas, nine Comanches, two Arapahos, and one Caddo—were selected, shackled, and sent to Fort Sill, loaded on trains bound for Fort Leavenworth, and finally shipped to Fort Marion in Saint Augustine, Florida.[128] Kicking Bird assisted the government in selecting those Kiowas to be exiled. Soon after he was assassinated by poison, although some Kiowas attributed his death to the prayers of Maman-ti, or Touching the Sky, also known as Dohate, the Owl Prophet, who was reputed to have led the wagon raid in 1871 and had great power.[129] Kicking Bird was given a Christian burial.

Among the prisoners, Heap of Birds had signed the Treaty of Medicine Lodge for the Cheyennes; Mayetin, or Woman's Heart, now an old chief, had signed for the Kiowas. Grey Beard, who refused to sign, attempted suicide while he was in prison in Fort Leavenworth and never made it to Florida. Pratt, who accompanied the Indians on their cross-country journey, encountered him on the train:

> Going through the cars with my oldest daughter, then six years of age, I
> stopped to talk with Grey Beard. He said he had only one child and that

was a little girl just about my daughter's age. He asked me how I would like to have chains on my legs as he had and to be taken a long distance from my home, my wife, and little girl, as he was, and his voice trembled with deepest emotion. It was a hard question.

As the train neared the Georgia-Florida state line, Grey Beard jumped from a window at night and was shot trying to escape. Before he died, he said "he had wanted to die ever since being chained and taken from home." Another Cheyenne, Lean Bear, stabbed himself several times in the neck and chest on the journey and starved himself to death at Fort Marion.[130] Woman's Heart was reputed to be one of the most notorious Kiowa raiders but Pratt said he was "especially noted for the strength of his family affection." In prison in Florida he suffered from homesickness and wore the little moccasin of one of his children around his neck.[131] Maman-ti, who was said to have predicted his own death for using his power to kill Kicking Bird, died of tuberculosis at Fort Marion in July 1875.[132]

At Fort Marion, Pratt subjected his Indian prisoners to an immersion program that he later incorporated into the Indian Industrial School he opened in Carlisle, Pennsylvania, and that became the core of federal assimilation policy for thousands of Indian children for more than half a century. Freed of their shackles, the prisoners were stripped of their clothing and had their hair cut short. Pratt gave them military uniforms, organized their daily lives according to a strict military regimen, and taught them reading, writing, Christianity, and American values. Some of the Kiowa and Southern Cheyenne men, bored and restless in confinement and with access to paper and drawing materials, depicted new sights and experiences in Florida as well as old scenes of fighting and hunting on the Plains. Some of the artists sold their drawings to tourists; some continued to draw after their release. Howling Wolf, one of the most prominent of the Fort Marion artists, made a drawing of the Medicine Lodge treaty council (figure 6.6); as a young unmarried man he would have been living in Black Kettle's village at the time.[133]

Woman's Heart was one of the first prisoners to return home. In the spring of 1877 he was allowed to accompany an old and ailing Kiowa named Coming to the Grove on his trip out of exile. Back on the reservation, Woman's Heart lobbied for the release of the other prisoners. He also urged his people to follow the new road, settle down, and attend church, although when Pratt's son visited him in 1882 just before he died, the old man looked like "a regular Indian" and had "turned against the agency."[134] The Fort Marion prisoners who returned home faced dark days and hard times. Kiowa calendars recorded the summer of 1879 as the "horse-eating sun dance": with the buffalo gone and government rations woefully inadequate, the people had to kill and eat their own horses.[135] Lone Wolf died of malaria in 1879 shortly after being allowed to return home.

Before he died, he passed his name, together with his shield and his medicine, to his adopted son, Mamaydayte.[136] Lone Wolf "junior" carried the story of Medicine Lodge into the twentieth century.

In 1917 the citizens of the town of Medicine Lodge initiated efforts to commemorate the treaty that occurred fifty years before. World War I delayed things and it was another ten years before the town first marked the event with a historical pageant. I-See-O, a Kiowa who had attended the treaty as a young boy and later served as a sergeant in the US army, identified the site and the pageant was staged in a natural amphitheater designated as the Memorial Peace Park. Every five years until the 1960s, and since then every three years, citizens of Medicine Lodge and its vicinity and members of the tribes who attended the treaty council participate in a pageant billed as a commemoration of "the great Peace Council of 1867 between the US government and the proud civilization of the Plains Indians." In fact, the Medicine Lodge treaty reenactment "compresses 300 years of history into two hours of entertainment and education." Visitors watch history unfold as Coronado, Lewis and Clark, and other historical actors "come alive on the prairie" and Medicine Lodge "transforms into a frontier town," complete with parades and a reenactment of a bank robbery.[137] As the French historian Ernest Renan said, "forgetting…is a crucial factor in the creation of a nation."[138]

{ Conclusion }

THE DEATH AND REBIRTH OF INDIAN TREATIES

After the Treaty of Medicine Lodge, the Peace Commissioners returned to St. Louis, and they then headed north again to resume talks with the Sioux. They made a treaty with the Crows in November and had talks with the Brulé chief, Spotted Tail, but full peace with the Sioux had to be delayed until the following spring. In December 1867 the commission convened in Washington, and in January the commissioners submitted a report to the president. In the spring they (minus Senator Henderson who remained in Washington for President Johnson's impeachment trial) returned to Fort Laramie for another round of treaty negotiations. There, Harney, Sanborn, Tappan, Terry, and Augur negotiated a treaty with the several bands of Sioux, Northern Cheyennes, and Arapahos, bringing an end to the war that the Oglala chief Red Cloud and his allies had waged to close the Bozeman Trail. The Treaty at Fort Laramie contained many of the same provisions as the treaty made at Medicine Lodge. The Indians agreed to permit the building of railroads, move on to a reservation, settle down, farm, and send their children to school. The government allowed them to continue hunting buffalo in certain territory so long as there were sufficient buffalo "to justify the chase"; promised to feed, clothe, and educate them; and guaranteed that no additional lands would be taken without consent of three-quarters of the adult male population. The Laramie treaty set aside most of what is now South Dakota as "the Great Sioux Reservation" and guaranteed the Sioux possession of the Black Hills, the sacred center of their world.[1]

Over a six-month period, 159 chiefs from ten Sioux bands "touched the pen" to the treaty. The commissioners left in May without meeting Red Cloud. Only after the forts on the Bozeman Trail were abandoned and burned did Red Cloud ride into Fort Laramie and sign the treaty with the post commander in November. Red Cloud later denied agreeing to the terms the commissioners recorded in the official document and said he had signed his name merely to make peace. In a speech to the Cooper Union in New York two years later, he said, "In 1868, men came out and brought papers. We could not read them and they did not tell us truly what was in them. We thought the treaty was to remove the forts and for us to cease from fighting." As the historian Jeffrey Ostler notes, the terms of the treaty "were complicated and ambiguous to begin with and the commissioners did a poor job of explaining them. In fact, the record strongly indicates that the commissioners generally avoided saying things that might raise Lakota suspicions and deter them from signing."[2] The Bozeman Trail had been the sticking point in the negotiations but in 1868 the railroad moved beyond the contested area, opening up a better access route to Montana. The Bozeman Trail was no longer worth fighting for. "It was the single episode in United States history where an Indian treaty was signed on Indian terms, but in truth it was not much of a victory. It was simply that the railroad made the battle obsolete."[3] Nevertheless, having signed the treaty, Red Cloud kept the peace. The United States did not.

While Harney, Sanborn, and Terry remained, collecting signatures from various Sioux bands, Sherman and Tappan headed south to make a treaty in June with the Navajos. After four years' incarceration at Bosque Redondo in New Mexico, an expensive failure the government was ready to terminate, the Navajos were allowed to return to their homeland in Arizona and were provided with livestock to rebuild their pastoral economy. The Navajos agreed to send their children to American schools and to permit railroad construction through their territory.[4] Sherman and Tappan rejoined the other members of the commission in time to make a treaty with the Bannocks and Shoshonis at Fort Bridger in western Wyoming a month later.[5]

In August, Commissioner Taylor signed the last formal Indian treaty ratified by the US Senate. In 1863 the Nez Perce chief Lawyer, who had been so quick to approve the Treaty of Walla Walla with Isaac Stevens in 1855, and fifty-one other chiefs signed another treaty in the Lapwai Valley. Lawyer began the negotiations by reading aloud some of Stevens's statements, which the chief had written down word for word in a small pocket notebook, but he then ceded almost 90 percent of the reservation lands established by the Walla Walla treaty, almost seven million acres for about 8 cents an acre. Most of the ceded land belonged to other Nez Perce bands. Dealing with compliant chiefs had long been standard practice in American Indian diplomacy. Lawyer viewed himself as head chief and the government chose to deal with him as such and to regard the treaty as binding on all Nez Perces. Now, in 1868, Lawyer and three chiefs (one of whom died) traveled to Washington, D.C., and signed another treaty making "certain amendments" to the 1863 treaty. Other Nez Perces who were not present at what Yellow Wolf called the "lie-talk council" in 1863 refused to be bound by the "land-stealing treaty." "It was these Christian Nez Perces who made with the Government a *thief* treaty," said Yellow Wolf, and "sold what did not belong to them." Confronted with American assertions that his people had sold their coveted Wallowa Valley homeland and that they must move to the new reservation, Chief Joseph, leader of one of the "nontreaty bands," later responded:

> Suppose a white man should come to me and say, "Joseph, I like your horses, and I want to buy them." I say to him, "No, my horses suit me, I will not sell them." Then he goes to my neighbor, and says to him: "Joseph has some good horses. I want to buy them, but he refuses to sell." My neighbor answers, "Pay me the money, and I will sell you Joseph's horses." The white man returns to me and says, "Joseph, I have bought your horses, and you must let me have them." If we sold our lands to the Government, this is the way they were bought."[6]

Joseph would have understood the kind of horse-trading that had gone on at Fort Stanwix in 1768, New Echota in 1835, and scores of other locations. It was, in many ways, a fitting final comment on the treaty making that had transferred so many Indian homelands into American hands. The Nez Perces, who had befriended Lewis and Clark in 1805, had asked for Christianity in 1831, and had held steadfastly to peace, were soon at war with the United States. In the last great Indian war, eight hundred Nez Perce people and their livestock tried to escape to Canada in an epic and ultimately tragic 1,500-mile odyssey.[7] For ninety years US Indian policy had seen the treaty system as a "fair and honorable" way to acquire the continent from its original inhabitants but it had been reduced, finally, to American armies harrying hungry women, children, and old people through the snow and rounding them up for exile to Indian Territory.

By then the treaty system was dead. The Medicine Lodge and Fort Laramie treaties helped to kill it. The signs were there even before the Peace Commission disbanded, even before the first signatures on the Medicine Lodge treaty were dry. Senator E. G. Ross of Kansas fired off a letter to the *Lawrence Tribune* as soon as he returned from the Medicine Lodge treaty grounds. Briefly reviewing the terms of the treaty, he urged congressional delegates throughout the West to get behind the movement "for the speedy abandonment of the present absurd Indian treaty policy" and to incorporate the Indians into American society, subject to US laws. "Our own self-respect forbids that we should continue to recognize a few squalid nomads as independent nations, and the sooner the Government places them in their proper relation to itself and the community, the better it will be for all concerned." Doing so would require patience and careful consideration, Ross allowed: "The treaty system was adopted when the Indians were the stronger party, and having grown into a settled feature of our Indian jurisprudence, it cannot be hastily abandoned without encountering grave legal obstacles." Nevertheless, "the idea of a nation of thirty millions of people constantly warring with, or suffering itself to be constantly harassed by a handful of miserable savages, is even more discreditable than that of continuing the petty, mock sovereignties into which they are divided. We can never have permanent peace so long as their present absurd status is continued."[8]

In October 1868 the members of the Peace Commission assembled for a two-day meeting at Tremont House in Chicago. The Republican nominee for president, Ulysses S. Grant, attended as an observer. Senator Henderson was still absent on impeachment business. After their long travels, hard work, and frequent frustrations, the commissioners were tired and testy. It was clear they had not brought peace to the Plains—the Treaty of Medicine Lodge was already a shambles and Red Cloud had yet to sign the Treaty of Fort Laramie. It was a time for review and rethinking. The commission generals—Sherman, Terry, Harney, and Augur—pushed their agenda over the opposition of Taylor and Tappan. General Terry proposed recommending to Congress that the Bureau of Indian Affairs be transferred back to the War Department. The army blamed civilian control for the inefficiency and corruption that plagued the system, produced hunger and suffering on the reservations, and drove Indians to war. Military control would instill more professionalism and humanity in the conduct of Indian affairs. Terry's resolution prompted lengthy debate. Commissioner Taylor objected that such a move and placing troops in Indian country would promote war, not peace, and that the record of wars against the Indians showed that the costs and losses incurred by military action were huge, relative to the few Indians killed—unless, of course, Indians were surprised, surrounded, and butchered in large numbers as at Sand Creek. "As a rule, with rare exceptions, if any, Indian tribes never break the peace without powerful provocation or actual wrong perpetrated against them first," he said. "Respect their wishes, fulfill our treaty stipulations promptly and faithfully, keep them well fed, and there will be no need of armies among them. But violate our pledges; postpone, neglect, or refuse the fulfillment of our treaty engagements with them; permit them to get hungry and half starved, and the presence of armies will not restrain them from war."[9]

The BIA remained in the Department of Interior. But another resolution offered by General Terry was unanimously adopted:

That in the opinion of this Commission, the time has come when the Government should cease to recognize the Indian tribes as "domestic dependent nations" except so far as it may be required to recognize them as such by existing treaties and by treaties made but not yet ratified; that hereafter all Indians should be considered and held to be individually subject to the laws of the United States, except where and while it is otherwise provided in said treaties: and that they should be entitled to the same protection from said laws as other persons owing allegiance to the Government enjoy.[10]

The treaty system came under increasing attack. Henry B. Whipple, the Episcopal Bishop of Minnesota and known as a champion of Indian rights and a critic of federal Indian policy, was scathing in his indictment of the treaty-making process. It was, he wrote in the *North American Review* in 1864, "one of those blunders which is worse than a crime" to "treat as an independent nation a people whom we will not permit to exercise one single element of that sovereign power which is necessary to a nation's existence." Ostensibly negotiated between a Christian nation and the Indians for the avowed purpose of acquiring certain lands at a fair price and advancing civilization, treaties were "usually conceived and executed in fraud" and the beneficiaries were the Indian agents, politicians, and traders whose debts were settled. Whipple continued his condemnation in the *New York Times* in October 1868: "We recognize them as nations; we pledge them our faith; we enter on solemn treaties, and these treaties are ratified as with all foreign Powers, by the highest authority in the nation. You know—every man who ever looked into our Indian affairs knows—it is a shameless lie."[11] Colonel Richard Dodge agreed, calling the treaty system "absurd." "We 'covenant and agree' to keep white men out of the limits of the new reservation, though we well know that a government constituted as ours, resting on a popular basis, and with a tide of immigration unparalleled in modern times, can by no possibility keep the faith of any such treaty." Dodge denounced the negligence and corruption that skimmed off the annuities pledged to Indians on the reservations.[12] Others, in Congress, in the press, on the frontiers, and in the army, were outraged that the treaties seemed to protect and feed Indians during the winter months, only for them to resume their raids come spring. Less than a month before he died at the Washita, Major Joel Elliott complained that the peace commissioners were "making heroes and saints" of Indians with blood on their hands. "Our whole system of treaties with Indians is a downright farce," wrote another soldier.[13]

The Peace Commission failed to establish lasting peace, incurred excessive costs, and appeared to ignore or undermine the responsibilities of the House of Representatives in Indian affairs. (The reservation lands selected were supposed to be submitted for congressional approval but never were.) The contents and costs of the treaties attracted criticism. The House resented appropriating funds to fulfill treaty obligations that the Senate had ratified. It balked at the vast increase in expenditures required by the treaties of 1867–68, and it renewed its attack on Senate control of the Indian treaty system. Debate continued during the commission's lifetime about whether the president and Senate or the House of Representatives had the constitutional authority to conduct Indian treaties and whether Indian affairs should be under the jurisdiction of the

Interior Department or the War Department. Military and civilian authorities wrangled over who should do what and how and about who was responsible for the sorry state of Indian affairs. But what killed the treaty system was a consensus in Congress that "the documents perpetuated an outdated, unrealistic, and to some unfair relationship between the United States and the Indian peoples." Even Grant's commissioner of Indian affairs, Ely S. Parker, a Seneca, advocated abandoning the treaty system. "A treaty," wrote Parker, "involves the idea of a compact between two or more sovereign powers, each possessing sufficient authority and force to compel a compliance with the obligations incurred." The tribes lacked organized governments capable of enforcing compliance with their treaty commitments and could not be considered sovereign nations on an equal basis with the United States, he said. Treaty making was a "cruel farce" that had given Indians a false impression of national independence.[14] The issue came to a head with the Indian appropriations bill in March 1871 to which was attached a rider "that hereafter no Indian nation or tribe within the territory of the United States shall be acknowledged or recognized as an independent nation, tribe, or power with whom the United States may contract by treaty." Though some members of Congress expressed doubts about the constitutionality of the rider, the treaty system was effectively ended.[15]

That May a delegation of chiefs that included Little Raven and Powder Face of the Arapahos and Stone Calf and Little Robe of the Cheyennes, with John Simpson Smith and Philip McCusker as interpreters, arrived in Washington, D.C. They met President Grant. They traveled home via New York City, Boston, Philadelphia, and Chicago. In Boston, they toured Harvard College. At a large assembly in the city, Stone Calf and Little Raven gave long speeches. Stone Calf declared the government had not kept the promises made at Medicine Lodge, and he appealed in vain for an end to railroad construction across Cheyenne country. In New York they visited the Central Park Zoo (where said Little Raven, "My eyes saw more than they could carry") and sat for a photograph (figure C.1). It was the last known photograph of Smith. He died a month later, back in Indian Territory with his Cheyenne family.[16] It was just three months after the appropriations bill ended the treaty-making era. Perhaps it was a fitting time for the sixty-one-year-old veteran of numerous treaty councils and several delegations to Washington (and a massacre) to depart the scene.

The end of treaty making did not, of course, end the transfer of Indian lands into American hands. The United States continued to acquire land through agreements, executive orders, "conventions," and other treaty substitutes.[17] Unlike treaties that were ratified by the Senate alone, agreements required approval by both houses of Congress. Congress continued to authorize commissioners to go to reservations and obtain land cessions, and it then ratified the agreements by incorporating the texts into federal statutes. Statutes, rather than treaties, came

"LITTLE RAVEN,"
Head Chief of the Arrapahoes.

"BIRD CHIEF,"
Second War Chief of the Arrapahoes.

"LITTLE ROBE,"
Head Chief of the Cheyennes.

"BUFFALO GOAD,"
Chief of the Wichita.

EDWARD GEARY,
Indian Interpreter.

MAHLON STUBBS, Esq.,
Superintendent of Indian Affairs.

JOHN S. SMITH,
U. S. Indian Interpreter.

PHILIP McCUSKER,
U. S. Indian Interpreter.

FIGURE C.1 **Indian delegation, New York, 1871.** *The members of the delegation pictured here are (seated) Little Raven (front left, with cane), Bird Chief, Little Robe, and a Wichita chief named Buffalo Goad. Standing left to right are the interpreter Edmund Guerrier (with the long hair), the Indian agent Mahlon Stubbs, and John Simpson Smith, leaning with his arm on the shoulder of the Comanche interpreter Philip McCusker. Smith died shortly after he returned home. (Smithsonian Institution, National Anthropological Archives and Human Studies Film Archives)*

to define Indian rights.[18] It marked a critical shift in US-Indian relations: after more than a century of nation-to-nation dealings with the tribes, the United States now treated them more like domestic entities, bringing them more firmly into the American political system and more directly under colonial adminis-tration. Lewis Downing, principal chief of the Cherokees, thought the change ominous: "it appears to us that when once cut loose from our treaty moorings," he wrote the Board of Indian Commissioners in 1870, "we will roll and tumble upon the tempestuous ocean of American politics and congressional legislation, and shipwreck will be our inevitable destination."[19]

The 1871 resolution did not put an end to *existing* treaty relations between the United States and the tribes, but they, too, came under assault. Stand Watie and his nephew Elias C. Boudinot established a tobacco company on Cherokee land in the 1860s and refused to pay federal taxes on the business, arguing that the Treaty of 1866 exempted them from the Internal Revenue Act of 1868. Article 10 of the treaty stated that any resident of the Cherokee nation "shall have the right to sell any products of his farm...without restraint, paying any tax thereon which is now or may be levied by the United States." In its decision on the *Cherokee Tobacco* case of 1870, issued just a couple of months after Congress voted to end treaty making, the US Supreme Court held that an act of Congress could supersede a prior treaty.[20]

Boudinot lost his property in order to pay back taxes. Having rested his hopes on a treaty and lost, he now denounced treaties as a charade and argued for ending the special legal status of the tribes and for abolishing Indian Territory. He maintained that the Indians' only hope lay in doing away with tribal governments, acquiring citizenship, and ending common landholdings. His position also had something to do with the fact that he tried to restore his fortunes by cultivating relations with railroad companies whose land grants depended on Indian land cessions or the dissolution of Indian Territory. Boudinot lobbied for territorial government, grants to railroads, and opening up Indian lands. He claimed he was acting in the best interests of the Cherokee people, but most Cherokees regarded him as a self-serving traitor: like father, like son. Unlike his father, he was not murdered, although his life was threatened. He pursued various business schemes and continued to argue for the abolition of Indian Territory, reopening old divisions between the Boudinot-Watie faction and the majority of Cherokees.[21]

The United States broke the Treaty of Fort Laramie six years after it was signed. In 1874 George Custer led an expedition into the Black Hills of South Dakota and verified reports of gold in the region. A government commission offered to purchase the Black Hills, but the Sioux dismissed its offers; Sitting Bull said that the hills were simply not for sale. The United States took them anyway. The army sent an ultimatum ordering all Sioux and Northern Cheyenne bands onto the reservations by January 31, 1876, and then launched a three-pronged "pacification campaign" against the "hostiles" who refused to come in. In June, Crazy Horse, the renowned Oglala war chief, turned back General George Crook at the Battle of the Rosebud and the Sioux and Cheyennes annihilated Custer's command at the Battle of the Little Bighorn a week later. But the army hunted down the various bands in the next year or two. Sitting Bull fled to Canada; Crazy Horse surrendered in 1877 and was bayoneted to death in a guardroom scuffle.[22] Another commission, led by George Manypenny, arrived on the reservations to obtain consent to the transfer to the United States of the "unceded territory" that included the Black Hills. Congress cut funding for rations to the agencies until the Lakotas agreed to cede the land. People recalled having to negotiate while under the guns of American soldiers. The Lakotas protested but the reservation chiefs signed. The commissioners managed to secure the agreement of only about 10 percent of the adult males—about 65 percent short of what the Treaty of Fort Laramie required—but in the wake of the "Custer Massacre" the government was in no mood to worry about such niceties. In February 1877 Congress passed a law taking the Black Hills and extinguishing all Sioux rights outside the Great Sioux Reservation. The "Great Sioux Nation" had shrunk from about 134 million acres as recognized in the 1851 Treaty of Fort Laramie to less than 15 million acres.

Ten years later, Congress passed the Dawes, or General Allotment, Act. The United States had included a provision for allotting lands to individuals who met certain requirements in about seventy of its Indian treaties, and most treaties negotiated after the mid-nineteenth century contained clauses providing for the division of tribal lands in severalty.[23] But the new legislation, named after Senator Henry Dawes of Massachusetts who introduced it, triggered a renewed and massive assault on Native American landholdings. The reservations established by treaties like Medicine Lodge were supposed to be places where, under the tutelage of agents, farmers, and teachers, Indians would learn new ways and new values and gradually cease to be Indians. Instead, as Indian people resisted the imposition of alien ways and clung to traditional values in what remained of their homelands, reformers saw reservations functioning as obstacles to progress. Communal landholding and the Natives' moral economy of sharing seemed to be holding them back. Reformers and the government lost patience with the reservation system; progress surely required breaking up the reservations into plots of private property and instilling in Indian people the values of hard work, thrift, and individual competition that they would need to survive in the capitalist world that was about to engulf them. Under the Dawes Act, reservation lands were surveyed, divided up, and allotted in 160-acre parcels to the heads of families. "Surplus lands" were opened for sale to non-Indians. The government dispatched commissions into Indian country to put allotment into effect and reservation lands established by treaties were opened for settlement.

The Sioux Act of 1888 applied the allotment act to the Great Sioux Reservation, dividing the Lakotas into six separate reservations and making "surplus lands" available for settlement. Congress passed another Sioux Act in 1889 and dispatched another commission, this one led by General George Crook, who told the Indians that a flood was coming and they must save what they could or see it all swept away. The Lakotas in their own councils had decided against agreement with the US government and already presented a united front. Finding that "it was impossible to deal with the Indians as a body in general councils," the commissioners went to work "to convince individuals that substantial advantages to the Indians as a whole would result from an acceptance of the bill." For a time, Crook said in his report, "the task seemed almost hopeless, but persistence prevailed and interest was awakened. As soon as the question became debatable the situation changed and success was assured." Congress cut the amount of rations the commission promised, and another nine million acres were stripped away from the reservation. Angry and divided, Lakota people watched as American settlers moved onto lands that less than twenty-five years earlier had been set apart for the Indians' "absolute and undisturbed use and occupation."[24]

Between 1889 and 1893, the Cherokee Commission (frequently known as the Jerome Commission after its chair, David H. Jerome) purchased fifteen million acres of land in what was to become the State of Oklahoma. In addition to the Cherokees, it made agreements with the Iowas, Sac and Fox, Kickapoos, Potawatomis, Shawnees, Wichitas, Tonkawas, Poncas, Pawnees, Choctaws, and Chickasaws, and with the five tribes whose reservations were established by the treaties they made at Medicine Lodge. Restricted by Congress to pay no more than $1.25 per acre, the commissioners frequently resorted to deception, coercion, and intimidation.[25]

The tribes who had been at Medicine Lodge knew that the treaty was supposed to run until 1897 and saw no reason to negotiate for a reduction in their land before then. When the commissioners arrived on the Cheyenne and Arapaho reservation in 1890, the Arapahos were willing to consider their offers but most Cheyennes refused to sell or even to discuss selling. "The Great Spirit knows what you are saying and we don't propose to give up this land and chop it up and take farms for the Indians in this reservation till the seven years are up," declared a Cheyenne named Little Medicine. But the commissioners stuck to their task. With the help of George Bent and a team of attorneys (who were handsomely compensated for their services from the money paid to the Indians) they eventually managed to obtain the signatures they needed, and they acquired the Cheyenne and Arapaho land for about fifty cents per acre. In the 1960s the tribes brought their case before the Indian Claims Commission, arguing that the $1.5 million they received for the lands they ceded in 1890 was "unconscionable." The Justice Department agreed and the government settled all the claims of the Southern Cheyennes and Southern Arapahos for $15 million.[26]

The commission had secured nine cession agreements from other tribes by the time it arrived on the Kiowa, Comanche, and Apache reservation. There, its primary purpose was to collect the signatures of three-fourths of the adult male Indians as a prerequisite for any further land cessions. The commission met opposition from the start. The old Yamparika Comanche Howea, or Gap in the Woods, one of only two living signers of the Medicine Lodge treaty, presented the commissioners with a copy of the treaty. Stumbling Bear, the surviving signer among the Kiowas, and other old Indians recalled the pledges the United States had made to them and refused to negotiate before the treaty terms expired. Big Tree cited the condition of the Cheyennes and Arapahos who had accepted allotments as reason enough for the Kiowas to resist. But the commissioners pointed to the clause in the treaty that the president could "at any time, order a survey of the reservation" and that Congress could "fix the character of the title held by each [Indian]." The proceedings, writes Native scholar Blue Clark, "rapidly grew confused, turned to turmoil, and finally degenerated into outright fraud."[27]

Indians accused the commissioners and their interpreters of employing deception and coercion. "When the President of the United States sent you here," asked a Kiowa named Apiatan, "did he tell you also, outside the general council, to get signers in a dishonest way?" Jerome was furious—"I will not be talked to that way"—and declared the council at an end. The Indians "left in an uproar," and Jerome left with 456 signatures—more than the three-fourths he needed according to the Indian agent's low count of 562 eligible signers. (Interior Department evidence indicated that the actual number of adult Indian men was between 631 and 725.) Suspecting they had been deceived by incorrect translation of the terms of the agreement they had signed, Lone Wolf and a group of Indians asked to see the document and to have their names erased. Both requests were denied.[28]

Satank's son played a key role as an interpreter. A graduate of Pratt's Indian Industrial School in Carlisle, he was a Presbyterian missionary and principal of an Indian school near Anadarko. He had taken a new name, Joshua Given or Givens, after the agency physician. Kiowas accused him of selling them out to the government. As the commissioners went about their work and compiled signatures, the son of the great war chief had to be guarded against irate Kiowas. Warned that he would pay for his misdeeds with his life, Joshua died shortly after; some said it was the result of a curse. The commission's deception continued even back in Washington, where a new document was substituted containing counterfeit signatures. By various means, they came up with enough signatures to satisfy the three-quarter consent clause of the Medicine Lodge treaty.[29] The reservation would be divided up into 160-acre allotments and the remainder of the lands opened for settlement.

There were protests immediately. Many of those who signed claimed the commissioners had deceived them as to what exactly they were signing. Lone Wolf, who had already been to Washington, D.C., in 1887 in a vain attempt to fight against passage of the Dawes Act, returned to the capital with a tribal delegation to lobby against congressional approval of the Jerome agreement. Tribal members from the Kiowa, Comanche, and Apache reservation submitted petitions repudiating the agreement, complaining about "mendacity, fraud, and coercion" in the commission's dealings, pointing out that the Treaty of Medicine Lodge stipulated that each allotment would be 320 acres, not 160 acres. "The Kiowas, Comanches and Apaches are almost without exception, now that they understand it, uniformly opposed to the agreement," reported Captain Hugh Brown, the acting agent on the reservation in August 1893. A petition submitted to Congress in January 1900 and signed by 571 Indian men said that they were following the path laid out at Medicine Lodge and preparing for the new days they realized were coming but that opening the reservation prematurely to white settlers would be a disaster: "We now realize that if this treaty is ratified we are doomed to destruction as a people."[30]

The Indian Rights Association, a non-Indian reform group founded in 1882 to "bring about the complete civilization of the Indians and their admission to citizenship," took up the Indians' cause. For seven years the Indians and those who lobbied on their behalf managed to delay congressional ratification of the Jerome agreement. But this reservation was one of the last to be opened in Indian Territory and Congress was under enormous pressure to do so from railroad companies, land boomers, and whites around the reservation. In June 1900, the United States took possession and title to the almost three million acres of the reservation. It set aside 480,000 acres as common grazing land, allotted 445,000 acres in severalty, and earmarked 10,310 acres for agency, school, religious, and other purposes. That left two million acres of "surplus land" to be opened to settlement. The government paid the Kiowas just over 93 cents per acre.[31] Americans by the thousands gathered on the borders of the reservation, registering claims and waiting eagerly for the reservation to be opened; others trespassed in search of quick profits.

The Comanche chief Quanah Parker acquiesced in the allotment but Lone Wolf kept up the fight. He returned to Washington with a delegation of nine Kiowas and Comanches in June 1901 and retained a former congressman and federal judge, William Springer, as an attorney. Secretary of the Interior Ethan Allen Hitchcock refused to recognize the delegation. With the support of the Indian Rights Association, Lone Wolf and Springer brought suit to try and prevent the allotment of the reservation. They based their case on the Treaty of Medicine Lodge and took it all the way to the Supreme Court. In *US v. Kagama* in 1886, the Supreme Court, citing the 1871 resolution, had affirmed congressional power over Indian country in jurisdiction over major crimes; in January 1903 the Court went a step further in its decision on Lone Wolf. To uphold Lone Wolf's claim would mean "that the indirect operation of the treaty was to materially limit and qualify the controlling authority of Congress in respect to the care and protection of Indians, and to deprive Congress, in a possible emergency, when the necessity might be urgent for a partition and disposal of the tribal lands, of all power to act if the assent of the Indians could not be obtained." According to the Court, Congress had always exercised plenary power over Indians and could, if it saw fit, abrogate its own treaties with Indians. In other words, Indians had no rights that Congress was bound to protect. Whites streamed into the reservation. Kiowa reservation landholdings fell by 90 percent, from almost three million acres to just above three thousand acres by 1934.[32]

Like the Cheyennes and Arapahos, the Kiowas, Comanches, and Apaches subsequently received additional compensation: in 1955 the Indian Claims Commission awarded the three tribes more than $2 million for the lands they sold to the United States under the 1892 agreement. Then, in the 1970s the commission ordered the government to pay them more than $35 million for its "unconscionable" purchases of huge areas of land acquired under the treaties negotiated in 1865 and at Medicine Lodge in 1867.[33] But *Lone Wolf v. Hitchcock* had ramifications well beyond the Kiowa reservation. The decision deprived all Indians of their land base and their treaty rights; "all aspects of tribal political and property rights were now subject to radical changes at the whim of the legislative branch." In Blue Clark's words, "The opinion cast a whole people into despair when not only their guardian but their friends abandoned them." The decision "enshrined one of the fundamental rules in federal-Indian law, plenary power" and gave "the American frontier juggernaut . . . legal justification." The "plenary power doctrine" still stands and with it Congress's authority to abrogate Indian treaties.[34]

The Supreme Court, however, also developed canons of construction guiding the interpretation of Indian treaties. Acknowledging that the United States typically had the advantage in power, literacy, and language when treaties were negotiated, the Supreme Court in *US v. Winans* in 1905 ruled that treaties should be interpreted as Indians would have understood them at the time and that treaties were "not a grant of rights to the Indians, but a grant of rights from them." In other words, rights, resources, and powers that were not expressly given up in a treaty or taken by federal statute were reserved to the Indians. In *Winters v. US* in 1908, the same Court ruled that if ambiguities occurred in the interpretation of treaties they should be construed in favor of the tribes.[35] The courts have not always followed these canons of construction but treaties, ratified by the Senate, remain the law of the land and are preserved in Native American communal memories as still-binding commitments. In a sense, those treaties—those laws—were all that Indian people had to show for the loss of 97 percent of the land base of the United States. Typically quickly broken and long forgotten by Americans, treaties have been dusted off and scrutinized by Indian tribes and their attorneys and have often to come back to bite the power that dictated them. In documented commitments made to the tribes, sometimes in perpetuity, they inscribe Indian rights and provide the moral and legal leverage to assert those rights in modern America. Many tribes have upheld their treaties as sacred texts, even if the United States has not. In *Federal Power Commission v. Tuscarora Indian Nation* in 1960 (a case involving the taking of Indian land protected by treaty for a reservoir, in which the Supreme Court found in favor of the power commission), Justice Hugo Black wrote the dissenting opinion: "The solemn pledge of the United States to its wards is not to be construed like a money-lender's mortgage....Great nations, like great men, should keep their word."[36]

Indian people in modern America have insisted that the United States keep its word. Damaging as treaties were, Indian people focused their anger on the breach and disregard of treaties more often than on the treaties themselves. After all, treaties recognized tribal sovereignty and established important rights; it was military action, legislation, and judicial decisions that negated that status and those rights. "The betrayal of treaty promises has in this generation created a greater feeling of unity among Indian people than any other subject," Vine Deloria, Jr., wrote in *Custer Died for Your Sins* in 1969.[37] The American Indian Movement (AIM) regularly invoked treaties in its campaigns. The Trail of Broken Treaties, a march on Washington, D.C., organized by AIM in 1972, demanded observance of past treaty commitments and restoration of constitutional treaty making as essential components of a "manifesto for construction of an Indian future in America."[38] AIM holdouts at the siege of Wounded Knee in 1973 demanded the boundaries of the Oglala Nation be restored according to those guaranteed by the 1868 Treaty of Fort Laramie. Indians and their attorneys, often with the support of the Native American Rights Fund founded in 1970, reached back into history and invoked treaties that were supposed to guarantee and protect their rights but that were often ignored in days when Indians had no voice in the courts.

In the new social and political climate of reform created by the upheavals of the 1960s and 1970s, judicial opinion was more sympathetic to Justice Black's notion that the nation should live up to its treaty commitments. Treaties that dispossessed Indian people in the eighteenth and nineteenth centuries often became keys to Indian hope and sovereignty in the twentieth and twenty-first centuries. As early as 1959, in *Williams v. Lee*, a case that the legal scholar Charles Wilkinson regards as opening the modern era of federal Indian law, the Supreme Court held that the Navajos' treaty in 1868 protected the tribe's authority over internal issues and ruled that a non-Indian's suit to collect a debt incurred by an Indian on the reservation fell under the exclusive jurisdiction of the tribal courts.[39] In subsequent cases (*Warren Trading Post Co. v. Arizona Tax*

Commission in 1965 and *McClanahan v. Arizona Tax Commission* in 1973) the Supreme Court turned again to the 1868 treaty and ruled that the state could not collect taxes from non-Indian businesses on the reservation or from Indians whose incomes were derived from reservation sources.

In the 1960s and 1970s, Northwest Coast Indians began to reassert their fishing rights that had been guaranteed in the treaties with Isaac Stevens in the mid-1850s by staging a series of "fish-ins." Overfishing, pollution, dam building, and the destruction of habitat had steadily depleted salmon runs and many non-Indian fishermen reacted angrily, and sometimes violently, to what they saw as an Indian threat to a declining resource. The issue went to US District Court. Reviewing the treaties after almost 120 years, Judge George Boldt noted in his opinion that "the treaties were written in English, a language unknown to most of the tribal representatives, and translated for the Indians by an interpreter in the service of the United States using Chinook Jargon, which was also unknown to some tribal representatives. Having only about three hundred words in its vocabulary, the Jargon was capable of conveying only rudimentary concepts, but not the sophisticated or implied meaning of treaty provisions about which highly learned jurists and scholars differ." Boldt found in favor of the Indians, interpreting "fish in common" to mean "take an equal share" of the salmon and steelhead harvest. "Because the right of each Treaty Tribe to take anadromous fish arises from a treaty with the United States," wrote Boldt, "that right is preserved and protected under the supreme law of the land, does not depend on State law, is distinct from rights or privileges held by others, and may not be qualified by any action of the State." The decision sparked a virulent racist response from commercial and sports fishermen and met stiff resistance in Washington State but was upheld on review by the US Supreme Court in 1979.[40] Great Lakes tribes have likewise invoked nineteenth-century treaties to secure their rights to hunt, fish, and gather wild rice. In 1983 the US Court of Appeals for the Seventh Circuit upheld the claims of Wisconsin Ojibwes that the treaties that had been signed guaranteed their rights to continue hunting, fishing, and gathering in the areas ceded by those treaties. The decision generated a backlash among local fishermen, and there was racial violence every spring during spearfishing season during the 1980s as Indians attempted to exercise their rights. In 1999 the Supreme Court ruled in a 5–4 majority that the Mille Lacs band of Ojibwe in Minnesota retained hunting, fishing, and gathering rights on lands it had ceded to the federal government in the treaty of 1837. No subsequent action by the federal government had expressly extinguished those rights. Anger and tensions over treaty rights remained high in that state, too.[41]

The Sioux never accepted the loss of the Black Hills.[42] In 1923 they filed suit with the US Court of Claims, demanding compensation. The Court of Claims dragged its feet before dismissing the claim in 1942, and the US Supreme Court refused to review the decision. The Sioux tried again with the Indian Claims Commission but the commission dismissed the case in 1954 on the grounds that the claim had already been denied. The Sioux then fired their lawyer and had their claim reinstated on the basis that they had been represented by "inadequate counsel." In 1974 the Indian Claims Commission decided that the government had taken the land in violation of the Fifth Amendment and had not paid just compensation; the commission awarded the Sioux $17.5 million plus interest. The government appealed, and the Court of Claims reversed the decision on the basis of *res judicata,* stating that the claim had already been litigated and decided back in 1942. But the court acknowledged "a more ripe and rank case of dishonorable dealings will never, in all probability, be found in our history," and this opened the door for the Sioux to seek compensation on the grounds of dishonorable dealings.[43] In 1978 Congress passed an act enabling the Court of Claims to rehear the case. The Court of Claims found that the United States had taken the Black Hills unconstitutionally and reinstated the $17.5 million award, plus 5 percent interest, for a total of $122.5 million. The Justice Department appealed the decision, and finally, in 1980—fifty-seven years after the Sioux first brought suit—the Supreme Court heard the Black Hills case. It found that the annexation act of 1877 constituted "a taking of tribal property which had been set aside by the treaty of Fort Laramie for the Sioux's exclusive occupation" and upheld the award. Having won their long-sought victory, the Sioux turned down the money. They remained adamant that the Black Hills must be returned. The award remains uncollected and with accumulated interest now stands at more than $1 billion.

In Maine, Penobscot and Passamaquoddy Indians brought suit for the return of about two-thirds of the state's land to the tribes. The Indian Trade and Intercourse Act of 1790 had declared that transfers of Indian land were invalid unless they had the approval of Congress. Massachusetts and, after it became a state in 1820, Maine continued to make treaties with the Indians but none of the land sales that occurred after 1790 were submitted for approval. If the United States were to respect its own laws, the Indians believed they had a watertight case. In 1980 President Jimmy Carter signed the Maine Indian Claims Settlement Act, paying the Indians $81.5 million in compensation for lands taken in contravention of the 1790 law.

After the legal victories of the 1970s and early 1980s, a more conservative Supreme Court began to reverse the trend of rulings on Indian rights and by the turn of the millennium seemed to be making a sustained assault on tribal sovereignty.[44] Nevertheless, Indian treaties remain the law of the land, and long-time scholar of Indian law Charles Wilkinson believes these old laws "emanate a kind of morality profoundly rare in our jurisprudence." It goes beyond guilt or obligation. "Real promises were made... and the Senate of the United States approved them, making them real laws. My sense is that most judges cannot shake that. Their training, their experience, and finally, their humanity—all of the things that blend into the rule of law—brought them up short when it came to signing opinions that would have obliterated those promises."[45]

Long after they were negotiated and signed, despite a sordid record of broken promises and despite being interpreted as strictly legal documents rather than as sacred pledges made by one people to another, treaties, resurrected and reaffirmed, could be a means for Indians to preserve themselves as a people.[46] In the Indian way, treaties were not made to be broken; they had to be maintained and renewed, by repeatedly revisiting and honoring the agreement, exchanging gifts, and rebuilding trust and friendship. Treaties that functioned as instruments of colonialism can also be the means of restoring respectful relations between the United States and the Indian nations within its borders. More than thirty years ago, legal scholars Russell Barsh and James Youngblood Henderson called for "treaty federalism"—incorporating tribes into the federal system on the basis of treaty compacts. "The significance of treaties," they wrote, "lies not in their specific promises of so many blacksmiths, or so many schoolhouses, which have little contemporary relevance, nor in the proprietary arrangements for boundaries, fishing rights, and the like, which retain great economic value and are responsible for most recent treaty-rights litigation. Treaties are a form of political recognition and a measurement of the consensual distribution of powers between tribes and the United States."[47] When Congress ended treaty making and then acted as if it had plenary power in its relations with Indian tribes (rather than simply the power to conduct those relations, which is what the commerce clause of the Constitution actually bestows), the United States rejected bilateral relations with Indian tribes and abandoned "the fundamental principle that our national government is one of limited powers." Restoring respectful bilateral relations, argues Houma legal scholar N. Bruce Duthu, "would require a return to treaty-making, the only constitutionally sanctioned mechanism by which the federal government is empowered to engage in relations with Indian tribes." That would not entail returning to nineteenth-century-style treaty making with individual tribes but could take the form of a convention, a kind of "master treaty" that would help establish "a firmer foundation for respectful coexistence" among the nation's three sovereigns—the United States, the states, and the tribes.[48]

Treaty rights, law professor Rebecca Tsosie points out, carry moral as well as legal obligations. The federal government may have or claim the legal right to abrogate a treaty, but it has a moral obligation to act in good faith to racially and culturally distinct groups that have been unjustly treated. For Native peoples, the discourse of treaty rights is essentially about "the need to assert, maintain, and even demand recognition for tribal sovereignty." The discourse of treaty rights involves calls for a recognition of the history of conquest and colonialism and a recognition of tribal sovereignty. "The treaties between the United States and Indian nations exemplify the commitment to tribalism and group-based separatism that Indian nations look to today in their efforts to gain recognition for their rights to self-determination."[49]

The United States also has an obligation under international human rights to ensure the survival of distinctive ethnic groups. Article 37 of the United Nations Declaration on the Rights of Indigenous Peoples states: "Indigenous peoples have the right to the recognition, observance and enforcement of treaties, agreements and other constructive arrangements concluded with States or their successors and to have States honour and respect such treaties, agreements and other constructive arrangements."[50] One hundred forty-three nations adopted the declaration in 2007; eleven abstained, and only Australia, Canada, New Zealand, and the United States voted against it. Those four nations subsequently reversed their position. The United States signed on to the declaration in December 2010—the last nation to do so.

Treaties that functioned so often to separate Native peoples from their lands and cultures also established Native rights and recognized tribal sovereignty; when observed and honored in good faith, they have the potential to be instruments of restorative justice and healing. As tribal leaders, lawyers, judges, and academics wrestle with the meanings and implications of the specific terms of treaties, the relationships those treaties were supposed to establish between Indian tribes and the United States await renewal. Restoring treaty relations between the United States and Native nations offers a path toward reconciliation and cooperation based on good relations between the groups—the very thing that Indian people understood treaties to accomplish in the first place. Looking back to treaty making in the colonial era, Native law professor Robert A. Williams, Jr., recalls "a time when the West had to listen seriously to these indigenous tribal visions of how different peoples might live together in relationships of trust, solidarity, and respect."[51] Perhaps it is time to do so again.

Of course, a treaty-based relationship between Indian nations and the United States would meet considerable opposition. Many non-Indians resist treaty rights in any shape or form—especially as they see them being mobilized by modern tribal governments—and they complain that they suffer injustices when Indians successfully assert those rights. Transforming "defenses of self-interest into defenses of core American values," conservative activists denounce the granting of "special rights" to historically disadvantaged Americans as un-American and a violation of the nation's commitment to equal rights. They lament "that 'ordinary,' forgotten Americans have become the new victims of a nation that panders to the interests of former victims, thereby sacrificing the equal rights of deserving citizens." No rights seem more special than Indian treaty rights, which elevate Indians to a class of "supercitizens." Treaty commitments made in very different times and circumstances should not apply in modern America, they say.[52] Whatever the merits and motivations of their arguments, some of the people who oppose Indian treaty rights would surely agree with the Ottawa chief Egushawa: treaties do indeed contain *"pen and ink witch-craft,* which they can make speak things we never intended, or had any idea of, even an hundred years hence."

{ Appendix }

THE TREATIES

The Treaty of Fort Stanwix

[Edmund B. O' Callaghan, ed. *Documents Relating to the Colonial History of the State of New York*. 15 vols. (Albany: Weed, Parsons, and Co., 1853–57), 8: 135–38.]

Deed Determining the Boundary Line between the Whites and the Indians

To all to whom, These presents shall come or may concern. We the Sachems & Cheifs of the Six confederate Nations, and of the Shawanese, Delawares, Mingoes of Ohio and other Dependant Tribes on behalf of our selves and of the rest of our Several Nations the Cheifs & Warriors of whom are now here convened by Sir William Johnson Baronet His Majestys Superintendant of our affairs send GREETING.

WHEREAS His Majesty was graciously pleased to propose to us in the year one thousand seven hundred and sixty five that a Boundary Line should be fixed between the English & us to ascertain & establish our Limitts and prevent those intrusions & encroachments of which we had so long and loudly complained and to put a stop to the many fraudulent advantages which had been so often taken of us in Land affairs which Boundary appearing to us a wise and good measure we did then agree to a part of a Line and promised to settle the whole finally when soever Sir William Johnson should be fully empowered to treat with us for that purpose[.]

AND WHEREAS His said Majesty has at length given Sir William Johnson orders to compleat the said Boundary Line between the Provinces and Indians in conformity to which orders Sir William Johnson has convened the Cheifs & Warriors of our respective Nations who are the true and absolute Proprietors of the Lands in question and who are here now to a very considerable Number.

AND WHEREAS many uneasinesses and doubts have arisen amongst us which have given rise to an apprehension that the Line may not be strictly observed on the part of the English in which case matters may be worse than before which apprehension together with the dependant state of some of our

Tribes and other circumstances which retarded the Settlement and became the subject of some Debate Sir William Johnson has at length so far satisfied us upon as to induce us to come to an agreement concerning the Line which is now brought to a conclusion the whole being fully explained to us in a large Assembly of our People before Sir William Johnson and in the presence of His Excellency the Governor of New Jersey the Commissioners from the Provinces of Virginia and Pensilvania and sundry other Gentlemen by which Line so agreed upon a considerable Tract of Country along several Provinces is by us ceded to His said Majesty which we are induced to and do hereby ratify & confirm to His said Majesty from the expectation and confidence we place in His royal Goodness that he will graciously comply with our humble requests as the same are expressed in the speech of the several Nations addressed to His Majesty through Sir William Johnson on Tuesday the first of the Present Month of November wherein we have declared our expectation of the continuance of His Majestys Favour and our desire that our ancient Engagements be observed and our affairs attended to by the officer who has the management thereof enabling him to discharge all these matters properly for our Interest. That the Lands occupied by the Mohocks around their villages as well as by any other Nation affected by this our Cession may effectually remain to them and to their Posterity and that any engagements regarding Property which they may now be under may be prosecuted and our present Grants deemed valid on our parts with the several other humble requests contained in our said Speech.

AND WHEREAS at the settling of the said Line it appeared that the Line described by His Majestys order was not extended to the Northward of Oswegy or to the Southward of Great Kanhawa river We have agreed to and continued the Line to the Northward on a supposition that it was omitted by reason of our not having come to any determination concerning its course at the Congress held in one thousand seven hundred and sixty five and in as much as the Line to the Northward became the most necessary of any for preventing encroachments at our very Towns & Residences We have given the Line more favorably to Pensylvania for the reasons & considerations mentioned in the Treaty, we have likewise continued it South to Cherokee River because the same is and we do declare it to be our true Bounds with the Southern Indians and that we have an undoubted right to the Country as far South as that River which makes our Cession to His Majesty much more advantageous than that proposed,

Now THEREFORE KNOW YE that we the Sachems and Cheifs aforementioned Native Indians and Proprietors of the Lands herein after described for and in behalf of ourselves and the whole of our Confederacy for the considerations herein before mentioned and also for and in consideration of a valuable

Present of the several articles in use amongst Indians which together with a large sums of money amounts in the whole to the sum of Ten thousand four Hundred and Sixty pounds seven shillings and three pence sterling to us now delivered and paid by Sir William Johnson Baronet His Majestys sole Agent and superintendant of Indian affairs for the Northern department of America in the Name and on behalf of our Soverreign Lord George the third by the Grace of God of Great Britain France and Ireland King Defender of the Faith the receipt whereof we do hereby acknowledge WE the said Indians HAVE for us and our Heirs and Successors granted bargained sold released and confirmed and by these presents DO Grant bargain sell release and confirm unto our said Sovereign Lord King George the third, ALL that Tract of Land situate in North America at the Back of the British Settlements bounded by a Line which we have now agreed upon and do hereby establish as the Boundary between us and the British Colonies in America beginning at the Mouth of Cherokee or Hogohege River where it emptys into the River Ohio and running from thence upwards along the South side of said River to Kittaning which is above Fort Pitt from thence by a direct Line to the nearest Fork of the west branch of Susquehanna thence through the Allegany Mountains along the South side of the said West Branch untill it comes opposite to the mouth of a Creek called Tiadaghton thence across the West Branch and along the South Side of that Creek and along the North Side of Burnetts Hills to a Creek called Awandae thence down the same to the East Branch of Susquehanna and across the same and up the East side of that River to Oswegy from thence East to Delawar River and up that River to opposite where Tianaderha falls into Susquehanna thence to Tianaderha and up the West side of its West Branch to the head thereof and thence by a direct Line to Canada Creek where it emptys into the wood Creek at the West of the Carrying Place beyond Fort Stanwix and extending Eastward from every part of the said Line as far as the Lands formerly purchased so as to comprehend the whole of the Lands between the said Line and the purchased Lands or settlements, except what is within the Province of Pensilvania, together with all the Hereditaments and Appurtenances to the same belonging or appertaining in the fullest & most ample manner and all the Estate Right Title Interest Property Possession Benefit claim and Demand either in Law or Equity of each & every of us of in or to the same or any part thereof TO HAVE AND TO HOLD the whole Lands and Premises hereby granted bargained sold released and confirmed as aforesaid with the Hereditaments and appurtenances thereunto belonging under the reservations made in the Treaty unto our said Sovereign Lord King George the third his Heirs & Successors to and for his and their own proper use and behoof for ever.

   In WITNESS whereof We the Cheifs of the Confederacy have hereunto set our marks and Seals at FORT STANWIX the fifth day of November one

Thousand seven hundred and sixty eight in the ninth year of His Majestys Reign

for the Mohocks
TYORHANSERE als ABRAHAM
for the Oneidas
CANAGHQUIESON
for the Tuscaroras
SEQUARUSERA
for the Onondagas
OTSINOGHIYATA als BUNT
for the Cayugas
TEGAAIA
for the Senecas
GUASTRAX
Sealed and delivered and the consideration paid in the presence of
Wm Franklin Governor of New Jersey
Fre. Smyth Cheif Justice of New Jersey
Thomas Walker Commissioner for Virginia
Of the Council of Pensylvania
Richard Peters
James Tilghman

The above Deed was executed in my presence at Fort Stanwix the day and year above Written
W JOHNSON

The Treaty of New Echota

[Charles J. Kappler, comp. *Indian Affairs: Laws and Treaties. Vol. 2: Treaties.* (Washington, D.C.: Government Printing Office, 1904), 439–49.]

Articles of a treaty, concluded at New Echota in the State of Georgia on the 29th day of Decr. 1835 by General William Carroll and John F. Schermerhorn commissioners on the part of the United States and the Chiefs Head Men and People of the Cherokee tribe of Indians.

WHEREAS the Cherokees are anxious to make some arrangements with the Government of the United States whereby the difficulties they have experienced by a residence within the settled parts of the United States under the jurisdiction and laws of the State Governments may be terminated and adjusted; and with a view to reuniting their people in one body and securing a permanent home for themselves and their posterity in the country selected by their forefathers without the territorial limits of the State sovereignties, and where they can establish and enjoy a government of their choice and perpetuate such a state of society as may be most consonant with their views, habits and condition; and as may tend to their individual comfort and their advancement in civilization.

And whereas a delegation of the Cherokee nation composed of Messrs. John Ross Richard Taylor Danl. McCoy Samuel Gunter and William Rogers with full power and authority to conclude a treaty with the United States did on the 28th day of February 1835 stipulate and agree with the Government of the United States to submit to the Senate to fix the amount which should be allowed the Cherokees for their claims and for a cession of their lands east of the Mississippi river, and did agree to abide by the award of the Senate of the United States themselves and to recommend the same to their people for their final determination.

And whereas on such submission the Senate advised "that a sum not exceeding five millions of dollars be paid to the Cherokee Indians for all their lands and possessions east of the Mississippi river."

And whereas this delegation after said award of the Senate had been made, were called upon to submit propositions as to its disposition to be arranged in a treaty which they refused to do, but insisted that the same "should be referred to their nation and there in general council to deliberate and determine on the subject in order to ensure harmony and good feeling among themselves."

And whereas a certain other delegation composed of John Ridge Elias Boudinot Archilla Smith S. W. Bell John West Wm. A. Davis and Ezekiel West, who represented that portion of the nation in favor of emigration to the Cherokee country west of the Mississippi entered into propositions for a treaty with John F. Schermerhorn commissioner on the part of the United States which were to be submitted to their nation for their final action and determination:

And whereas the Cherokee people at their last October council at Red Clay, fully authorized and empowered a delegation or committee of twenty persons of their nation to enter into and conclude a treaty with the United States commissioner then present, at that place or elsewhere and as the people had good reason to believe that a treaty would then and there be made or at a subsequent council at New Echota which the commissioners it was well known and understood, were authorized and instructed to convene for said purpose; and since the said delegation have gone on to Washington city, with a view to close negotiations there, as stated by them notwithstanding they were officially informed by the United States commissioner that they would not be received by the President of the United States; and that the Government would transact no business of this nature with them, and that if a treaty was made it must be done here in the nation, where the delegation at Washington last winter urged that it should be done for the purpose of promoting peace and harmony among the people; and since these facts have also been corroborated to us by a communication recently received by the commissioner from the Government of the United States and read and explained to the people in open council and therefore believing said delegation can effect nothing and since our difficulties are daily increasing and our situation is rendered more and more precarious uncertain and insecure in consequence of the legislation of the States; and seeing no effectual way of relief, but in accepting the liberal overtures of the United States.

And whereas Genl William Carroll and John F. Schermerhorn were appointed commissioners on the part of the United States, with full power and authority to conclude a treaty with the Cherokees east and were directed by the President to convene the people of the nation in general council at New Echota and to submit said propositions to them with power and authority to vary the same so as to meet the views of the Cherokees in reference to its details.

And whereas the said commissioners did appoint and notify a general council of the nation to convene at New Echota on the 21st day of December 1835; and informed them that the commissioners would be prepared to make a treaty with the Cherokee people who should assemble there and those who did not come they should conclude gave their assent and sanction to whatever should be transacted at this council and the people having met in council according to said notice.

Therefore the following articles of a treaty are agreed upon and concluded between William Carroll and John F. Schermerhorn commissioners on the part of the United States and the chiefs and head men and people of the Cherokee nation in general council assembled this 29th day of Decr 1835.

ARTICLE 1

The Cherokee nation hereby cede relinquish and convey to the United States all the lands owned claimed or possessed by them east of the Mississippi river, and hereby release all their claims upon the United States for spoliations of every kind for and in consideration of the sum of five millions of dollars to be expended paid and invested in the manner stipulated and agreed upon in the following articles But as a question has arisen between the commissioners and the Cherokees whether the Senate in their resolution by which they advised "that a sum not exceeding five millions of dollars be paid to the Cherokee Indians for all their lands and possessions east of the Mississippi river" have included and made any allowance or consideration for claims for spoliations it is therefore agreed on the part of the United States that this question shall be again submitted to the Senate for their consideration and decision and if no allowance was made for spoliations that then an additional sum of three hundred thousand dollars be allowed for the same.

ARTICLE 2

Whereas by the treaty of May 6th 1828 and the supplementary treaty thereto of Feb. 14th 1833 with the Cherokees west of the Mississippi the United States guarantied and secured to be conveyed by patent, to the Cherokee nation of Indians the following tract of country "Beginning at a point on the old western territorial line of Arkansas Territory being twenty-five miles north from the point where the territorial line crosses Arkansas river, thence running from said north point south on the said territorial line where the said territorial line crosses Verdigris river; thence down said Verdigris river to the Arkansas river; thence down said Arkansas to a point where a stone is placed opposite the east or lower bank of Grand river at its junction with the Arkansas; thence running south forty-four degrees west one mile; thence in a straight line to a point four miles northerly, from the mouth of the north fork of the Canadian; thence along the said four mile line to the Canadian; thence down the Canadian to the Arkansas; thence down the Arkansas to that point on the Arkansas where the eastern Choctaw boundary strikes said river and running thence with the western line of Arkansas Territory as now defined, to the southwest corner of Missouri; thence along the western Missouri line to the land assigned the Senecas; thence on the south line of the Senecas to Grand river; thence up said Grand river as far as the south line of the Osage reservation, extended if necessary; thence up and between said south Osage line extended west if necessary, and a line drawn due west from the point of beginning to a certain distance west, at which a line running north and south from said Osage line to said due west line will make seven millions of acres within the whole described boundaries. In addition to the seven millions of acres of land thus provided for and bounded, the United States further guaranty to the Cherokee nation a perpetual outlet west, and a free and unmolested use of all the country west of the western boundary of said seven millions of acres, as far west as the sovereignty of the United States and their right of soil extend:
Provided however That if the saline or salt plain on the western prairie shall fall within said limits prescribed for said outlet, the right is reserved to the United States to permit other tribes of red men to get salt on said plain in common with the Cherokees; And letters patent shall be issued by the United States as soon as practicable for the land hereby guarantied."
And whereas it is apprehended by the Cherokees that in the above cession there is not contained a sufficient quantity of land for the accommodation of the whole nation on their removal west of the Mississippi the United States in consideration of the sum of five hundred thousand dollars therefore hereby covenant and agree to convey to the said Indians, and their descendants by patent, in fee simple the following additional tract of land situated between the west line of the State of Missouri and the Osage reservation beginning at the

southeast corner of the same and runs north along the east line of the Osage lands fifty miles to the northeast corner thereof; and thence east to the west line of the State of Missouri; thence with said line south fifty miles; thence west to the place of beginning; estimated to contain eight hundred thousand acres of land; but it is expressly understood that if any of the lands assigned the Quapaws shall fall within the aforesaid bounds the same shall be reserved and excepted out of the lands above granted and a pro rata reduction shall be made in the price to be allowed to the United States for the same by the Cherokees.

ARTICLE 3

The United States also agree that the lands above ceded by the treaty of Feb. 14, 1833, including the outlet, and those ceded by this treaty shall all be included in one patent executed to the Cherokee nation of Indians by the President of the United States according to the provisions of the act of May 28, 1830. It is, however, agreed that the military reservation at Fort Gibson shall be held by the United States. But should the United States abandon said post and have no further use for the same it shall revert to the Cherokee nation. The United States shall always have the right to make and establish such post and military roads and forts in any part of the Cherokee country, as they may deem proper for the interest and protection of the same and the free use of as much land, timber, fuel and materials of all kinds for the construction and support of the same as may be necessary; provided that if the private rights of individuals are interfered with, a just compensation therefor shall be made.

ARTICLE 4

The United States also stipulate and agree to extinguish for the benefit of the Cherokees the titles to the reservations within their country made in the Osage treaty of 1825 to certain half-breeds and for this purpose they hereby agree to pay to the persons to whom the same belong or have been assigned or to their agents or guardians whenever they shall execute after the ratification of this treaty a satisfactory conveyance for the same, to the United States, the sum of fifteen thousand dollars according to a schedule accompanying this treaty of the relative value of the several reservations.

And whereas by the several treaties between the United States and the Osage Indians the Union and Harmony Missionary reservations which were established for their benefit are now situated within the country ceded by them to the United States; the former being situated in the Cherokee country and the latter in the State of Missouri. It is therefore agreed that the United States shall pay the American Board of Commissioners for Foreign Missions for the improvements on the same what they shall be appraised at by Capt. Geo. Vashon Cherokee sub-agent Abraham Redfield and A. P. Chouteau or such persons as the President of the United States shall appoint and the money allowed for the same shall be expended in schools among the Osages and improving their condition. It is understood that the United States are to pay the amount allowed for the reservations in this article and not the Cherokees.

ARTICLE 5

The United States hereby covenant and agree that the lands ceded to the Cherokee nation in the forgoing article shall, in no future time without their consent, be included within the territorial limits or jurisdiction of any State or Territory. But they shall secure to the Cherokee nation the right by their national councils to make and carry into effect all such laws as they may deem necessary for the government and protection of the persons and property within their own country belonging to their people or such persons as have connected themselves with them: provided always that they shall not be inconsistent with the constitution of the United States and such acts of Congress as have been or may be passed regulating trade and intercourse with the Indians; and also, that they stall not be considered as extending to such citizens and army of the United States as may travel or reside in the Indian country by permission according to the laws and regulations established by the Government of the same.

ARTICLE 6

Perpetual peace and friendship shall exist between the citizens of the United States and the Cherokee Indians. The United States agree to protect the Cherokee nation from domestic strife and foreign enemies and against intestine wars between the several tribes. The Cherokees shall endeavor to preserve and maintain the peace of the country and not make war upon their neighbors they shall also be protected against interruption and intrusion from citizens of the United States, who may attempt to settle in the country without their consent; and all such persons shall be removed from the same by order of the President of the United States. But this is not intended to prevent the residence among them of useful farmers mechanics and teachers for the instruction of Indians according to treaty stipulations.

ARTICLE 7

The Cherokee nation having already made great progress in civilization and deeming it important that every proper and laudable inducement should be offered to their people to improve their condition as well as to guard and secure in the most effectual manner the rights guarantied to them in this treaty, and with a view to illustrate the liberal and enlarged policy of the Government of the United States towards the Indians in their removal beyond the territorial limits of the States, it is stipulated that they shall be entitled to a delegate in the House of Representatives of the United States whenever Congress shall make provision for the same.

ARTICLE 8

The United States also agree and stipulate to remove the Cherokees to their new homes and to subsist them one year after their arrival there and that a sufficient number of steamboats and baggage-wagons shall be furnished to remove them comfortably, and so as not to endanger their health, and that a physician well supplied with medicines shall accompany each detachment of emigrants removed by the Government. Such persons and families as in the opinion of the emigrating agent are capable of subsisting and removing themselves shall be permitted to do so; and they shall be allowed in full for all claims for the same twenty dollars for each member of their family; and in lieu of their one year's rations they shall be paid the sum of thirty-three dollars and thirty-three cents if they prefer it.

Such Cherokees also as reside at present out of the nation and shall remove with them in two years west of the Mississippi shall be entitled to allowance for removal and subsistence as above provided.

ARTICLE 9

The United States agree to appoint suitable agents who shall make a just and fair valuation of all such improvements now in the possession of the Cherokees as add any value to the lands; and also of the ferries owned by them, according to their net income; and such improvements and ferries from which they have been dispossessed in a lawless manner or under any existing laws of the State where the same may be situated.

The just debts of the Indians shall be paid out of any monies due them for their improvements and claims; and they shall also be furnished at the discretion of the President of the United States with a sufficient sum to enable them to obtain the necessary means to remove themselves to their new homes, and the balance of their dues shall be paid them at the Cherokee agency west of the Mississippi. The missionary establishments shall also be valued and appraised in a like manner and the amount of them paid over by the United States to the treasurers of the respective missionary societies by whom they have been established and improved in order to enable them to erect such buildings and make such improvements among the Cherokees west of the Mississippi as they may deem necessary for their benefit. Such teachers at present among the Cherokees as this council shall select and designate shall be removed west of the Mississippi with the Cherokee nation and on the same terms allowed to them.

ARTICLE 10

The President of the United States shall invest in some safe and most productive public stocks of the country for the benefit of the whole Cherokee nation who have removed or shall remove to the lands assigned by this treaty to the Cherokee nation west of the Mississippi the following sums as a permanent fund for the purposes hereinafter specified and pay over the net income of the same annually to such person or persons as shall be authorized or appointed by the Cherokee nation to receive the same and their receipt shall be a full discharge for the amount paid to them viz: the sum of two hundred thousand dollars in addition to the present annuities of the nation to constitute a general fund the interest of which shall be applied annually by the council of the nation to such purposes as they may deem best for the general interest of their people. The sum of fifty thousand dollars to constitute an orphans' fund the annual income of which shall be expended towards the support and education of such orphan children as are destitute of the means of subsistence. The sum of one hundred and fifty thousand dollars in addition to the present school fund of the nation shall constitute a permanent school fund, the interest of which shall be applied annually by the council of the nation for the support of common schools and such a literary institution of a higher order as may be established in the Indian country. And in order to secure as far as possible the true and beneficial application of the orphans' and school fund the council of the Cherokee nation when required by the President of the United States shall make a report of the application of those funds and he shall at all times have the right if the funds have been misapplied to correct any abuses of them and direct the manner of their application for the purposes for which they were intended. The council of the nation may by giving two years' notice of their intention withdraw their funds by and with the consent of the President and Senate of the United States, and invest them in such manner as they may deem most proper for their interest. The United States also agree and stipulate to pay the just debts and claims against the Cherokee nation held by the citizens of the same and also the just claims of citizens of the United States for services rendered to the nation and the sum of sixty thousand dollars is appropriated for this purpose but no claims against individual persons of the nation shall be allowed and paid by the nation. The sum of three hundred thousand dollars is hereby set apart to pay and liquidate the just claims of the Cherokees upon the United States for spoliations of every kind, that have not been already satisfied under former treaties.

ARTICLE 11

The Cherokee nation of Indians believing it will be for the interest of their people to have all their funds and annuities under their own direction and future disposition hereby agree to commute their permanent annuity of ten thousand dollars for the sum of two hundred and fourteen thousand dollars, the same to be invested by the President of the United States as a part of the general fund of the nation; and their present school fund amounting to about fifty thousand dollars shall constitute a part of the permanent school fund of the nation.

ARTICLE 12

Those individuals and families of the Cherokee nation that are averse to a removal to the Cherokee country west of the Mississippi and are desirous to become citizens of the States where they reside and such as are qualified to take care of themselves and their property shall be entitled to receive their due portion of all the personal benefits accruing under this treaty for their claims, improvements and per capita; as soon as an appropriation is made for this treaty.

Such heads of Cherokee families as are desirous to reside within the States of No. Carolina, Tennessee, and Alabama subject to the laws of the same; and who are qualified or calculated to become useful citizens shall be entitled, on the certificate of the commissioners to a preemption right to one hundred and sixty acres of land or one quarter section at the minimum Congress price; so as to include the present buildings or improvements of those who now reside there and such as do not live there at present shall be permitted to locate within two years any lands not already occupied by persons entitled to pre-emption privilege under this treaty and if two or more families live on the same quarter section and they desire to continue their residence in these States and are qualified as above specified they shall, on receiving their pre-emption certificate be entitled to the right of pre-emption to such lands as they may select not already taken by any person entitled to them under this treaty.

It is stipulated and agreed between the United States and the Cherokee people that John Ross, James Starr, George Hicks, John Gunter, George Chambers, John Ridge, Elias Boudinot, George Sanders, John Martin, William Rogers, Roman Nose Situwake, and John Timpson shall be a committee on the part of the Cherokees to recommend such persons for the privilege of pre-emption rights as may be deemed entitled to the same under the above articles and to select the missionaries who shall be removed with the nation; and that they be hereby fully empowered and authorized to transact all business on the part of the Indians which may arise in carrying into effect the provisions of this treaty and settling the same with the United States. If any of the persons above mentioned should decline acting or be removed by death; the vacancies shall be filled by the committee themselves.

It is also understood and agreed that the sum of one hundred thousand dollars shall be expended by the commissioners in such manner as the committee deem best for the benefit of the poorer class of Cherokees as shall remove west or have removed west and are entitled to the benefits of this treaty. The same to be delivered at the Cherokee agency west as soon after the removal of the nation as possible.

ARTICLE 13

In order to make a final settlement of all the claims of the Cherokees for reservations granted under former treaties to any individuals belonging to the nation by the United States it is therefore hereby stipulated and agreed and expressly understood by the parties to this treaty—that all the Cherokees and their heirs and descendants to whom any reservations have been made under any former treaties with the United States, and who have not sold or conveyed the same by deed or otherwise and who in the opinion of the commissioners have complied with the terms on which the reservations were granted as far as practicable in the several cases; and which reservations have since been sold by the United States shall constitute a just claim against the United States and the original reservee or their heirs or descendants shall be entitled to receive the present value thereof from the United States as unimproved lands. And all such reservations as have not been sold by the United States and where the terms on which the reservations were made in the opinion of the commissioners have been complied with as far as practicable, they or their heirs or descendants shall be entitled to the same. They are hereby granted and confirmed to them—and also all persons who were entitled to reservations under the treaty of 1817 and who as far as practicable in the opinion of the commissioners, have complied with the stipulations of said treaty, although by the treaty of 1819 such reservations were included in the unceded lands belonging to the Cherokee nation are hereby confirmed to them and they shall be entitled to receive a grant for the same. And all such reservees as were obliged by the laws of the States in which their reservations were situated, to abandon the same or purchase them from the States shall be deemed to have a just claim against the United States for the amount by them paid to the States with interest thereon for such reservations and if obliged to abandon the same, to the present value of such reservations as unimproved lands but in all cases where the reservees have sold their reservations or any part thereof and conveyed the same by deed or otherwise and have been paid for the same, they their heirs or descendants or their assigns shall not be considered as having any claims upon the United States under this article of the treaty nor be entitled to receive any compensation for the lands thus disposed of. It is expressly understood by the parties to this treaty that the amount to be allowed for reservations under this article shall not be deducted out of the consideration money allowed to the Cherokees for their claims for spoilations and the cession of their lands; but the same is to be paid for independently by the United States as it is only a just fulfillment of former treaty stipulations.

ARTICLE 14

It is also agreed on the part of the United States that such warriors of the Cherokee nation as were engaged on the side of the United States in the late war with Great Britain and the southern tribes of Indians, and who were wounded in such service shall be entitled to such pensions as shall be allowed them by the Congress of the United States to commence from the period of their disability.

ARTICLE 15

It is expressly understood and agreed between the parties to this treaty that after deducting the amount which shall be actually expended for the payment for improvements, ferries, claims, for spoilations, removal subsistence and debts and claims upon the Cherokee nation and for the additional quantity of lands and goods for the poorer class of Cherokees and the several sums to be invested for the general national funds; provided for in the several articles of this treaty the balance whatever the same may be shall be equally divided between all the people belonging to the Cherokee nation east according to the census just completed; and such Cherokees as have removed west since June 1833 who are entitled by the terms of their enrollment and removal to all the benefits resulting from the final treaty between the United States and the Cherokees east they shall also be paid for their improvements according to their approved value before their removal where fraud has not already been shown in their valuation.

ARTICLE 16

It is hereby stipulated and agreed by the Cherokees that they shall remove to their new homes within two years from the ratification of this treaty and that during such time the United States shall protect and defend them in their possessions and property and free use and occupation of the same and such persons as have been dispossessed of their improvements and houses; and for which no grant has actually issued previously to the enactment of the law of the State of Georgia, of December 1835 to regulate Indian occupancy shall be again put in possession and placed in the same situation and condition, in reference to the laws of the State of Georgia, as the Indians that have not been dispossessed; and if this is not done, and the people are left unprotected, then the United States shall pay the several Cherokees for their losses and damages sustained by them in consequence thereof. And it is also stipulated and agreed that the public buildings and improvements on which they are situated at New Echota for which no grant has been actually made previous to the passage of the above recited act if not occupied by the Cherokee people shall be reserved for the public and free use of the United States and the Cherokee Indians for the purpose of settling and closing all the Indian business arising under this treaty between the commissioners of claims and the Indians.

The United States, and the several States interested in the Cherokee lands, shall immediately proceed to survey the lands ceded by this treaty; but it is expressly agreed and understood between the parties that the agency buildings and that tract of land surveyed and laid off for the use of Colonel R. J. Meigs Indian agent or heretofore enjoyed and occupied by his successors in office shall continue subject to the use and occupancy of the United States, or such agent as may be engaged specially superintending the removal of the tribe.

ARTICLE 17

All the claims arising under or provided for in the several articles of this treaty, shall be examined and adjudicated by such commissioners as shall be appointed by the President of the United States by and with the advice and consent of the Senate of the United States for that purpose and their decision shall be final and on their certificate of the amount due the several claimants they shall be paid by the United States. All stipulations in former treaties which have not been superseded or annulled by this shall continue in full force and virtue.

ARTICLE 18

Whereas in consequence of the unsettled affairs of the Cherokee people and the early frosts, their crops are insufficient to support their families and great distress is likely to ensue and whereas the nation will not, until after their removal be able advantageously to expend the income of the permanent funds of the nation it is therefore agreed that the annuities of the nation which may accrue under this treaty for two years, the time fixed for their removal shall be expended in provision and clothing for the benefit of the poorer class of the nation and the United States hereby agree to advance the same for that purpose as soon after the ratification of this treaty as an appropriation for the same shall be made. It is however not intended in this article to interfere with that part of the annuities due the Cherokees west by the treaty of 1819.

ARTICLE 19

This treaty after the same shall be ratified by the President and Senate of the United States shall be obligatory on the contracting parties.

ARTICLE 20

[Supplemental article. Stricken out by Senate.]

In testimony whereof, the commissioners and the chiefs, head men, and people whose names are hereunto annexed, being duly authorized by the people in general council assembled, have affixed their hands and seals for themselves, and in behalf of the Cherokee nation. I have examined the foregoing treaty, and although not present when it was made, I approve its provisions generally, and therefore sign it.

Wm. Carroll,
J. F. Schermerhorn.
Major Ridge, his x mark, [L. S.]
James Foster, his x mark, [L. S.]
Tesa-ta-esky, his x mark, [L. S.]
Charles Moore, his x mark, [L. S.]
George Chambers, his x mark, [L. S.]
Tah-yeske, his x mark, [L. S.]
Archilla Smith, his x mark, [L. S.]
Andrew Ross, [L. S.]
William Lassley, [L. S.]
Cae-te-hee, his x mark, [L. S.]
Te-gah-e-ske, his x mark, [L. S.]
Robert Rogers, [L. S.]
John Gunter, [L. S.]
John A. Bell, [L. S.]
Charles F. Foreman, [L. S.]
William Rogers, [L. S.]

George W. Adair, [L. S.]

Elias Boudinot, [L. S.]

James Starr, his x mark, [L. S.]

Jesse Half-breed, his x mark, [L. S.]

Signed and sealed in presence of—

Western B. Thomas, secretary.

Ben. F. Currey, special agent.

M. Wolfe Batman, first lieutenant, sixth U.S. infantry, disbursing agent.

Jon. L. Hooper, lieutenant, fourth Infantry.

C. M. Hitchcock, M. D., assistant surgeon, U.S.A.

G. W. Currey,

Wm. H. Underwood,

Cornelius D. Terhune,

John W. H. Underwood.

In compliance with instructions of the council at New Echota, we sign this treaty.

Stand Watie,

John Ridge.

March 1, 1836.

Witnesses:

Elbert Herring,

Alexander H. Everett,

John Robb,

D. Kurtz,

Wm. Y. Hansell,

Samuel J. Potts,

Jno. Litle,

S. Rockwell.

Dec. 31, 1835|7 Stat., 487. Whereas the western Cherokees have appointed a delegation to visit the eastern Cherokees to assure them of the friendly disposition of their people and their desire that the nation should again be united as one people and to urge upon them the expediency of accepting the overtures of the Government; and that, on their removal they may be assured of a hearty welcome and an equal participation with them in all the benefits and privileges of the Cherokee country west and the undersigned two of said delegation being the only delegates in the eastern nation from the west at the signing and sealing of the treaty lately concluded at New Echota between their eastern brethren and the United States; and having fully understood the provisions of the same they agree to it in behalf of the western Cherokees. But it is expressly understood that nothing in this treaty shall affect any claims of the western Cherokees on the United States.

In testimony whereof, we have, this 31st day of December, 1835, hereunto set our hands and seals.

James Rogers,

John Smith. Delegates from the western Cherokees.

Test:

Ben. F. Currey, special agent.

M. W. Batman, first lieutenant, Sixth Infantry,

Jno. L. Hooper, lieutenant, Fourth Infantry,

Elias Boudinot.

Supplementary articles to a treaty concluded at New Echota, Georgia, December 29, 1835, between the United States and Cherokee people. March 1, 1836. | 7 Stat., 488. | Proclamation, May 23, 1836.

WHEREAS the undersigned were authorized at the general meeting of the Cherokee people held at New Echota as above stated, to make and assent to such alterations in the preceding treaty as might be thought necessary, and whereas the President of the United States has expressed his determination not to allow any pre-emptions or reservations his desire being that the whole Cherokee people should remove together and establish themselves in the country provided for them west of the Mississippi river.

ARTICLE 1

It is therefore agreed that all the pre-emption rights and reservations provided for in articles 12 and 13 shall be and are hereby relinquished and declared void.

ARTICLE 2

Whereas the Cherokee people have supposed that the sum of five millions of dollars fixed by the Senate in their resolution of —— day of March, 1835, as the value of the Cherokee lands and possessions east of the Mississippi river was not intended to include the amount which may be required to remove them, nor the value of certain claims which many of their people had against citizens of the United States, which suggestion has been confirmed by the opinion expressed to the War Department by some of the Senators who voted upon the question and whereas the President is willing that this subject should be referred to the Senate for their consideration and if it was not intended by the Senate that the above-mentioned sum of five millions of dollars should include the objects herein specified that in that case such further provision should be made therefor as might appear to the Senate to be just.

ARTICLE 3

It is therefore agreed that the sum of six hundred thousand dollars shall be and the same is hereby allowed to the Cherokee people to include the expense of their removal, and all claims of every nature and description against the Government of the United States not herein otherwise expressly provided for, and to be in lieu of the said reservations and pre-emptions and of the sum of three hundred thousand dollars for spoliations described in the 1st article of the above-mentioned treaty. This sum of six hundred thousand dollars shall be applied and distributed agreeably to the provisions of the said treaty, and any surplus which may remain after removal and payment of the claims so ascertained shall be turned over and belong to the education fund. But it is expressly understood that the subject of this article is merely referred hereby to the consideration of the Senate and if they shall approve the same then this supplement shall remain part of the treaty.

ARTICLE 4

It is also understood that the provisions in article 16, for the agency reservation is not intended to interfere with the occupant right of any Cherokees should their improvement fall within the same. It is also understood and agreed, that the one hundred thousand dollars appropriated in article 12 for the poorer class of Cherokees and intended as a set-off to the pre-emption rights shall now be transferred from the funds of the nation and added to the general national fund of four hundred thousand dollars so as to make said fund equal to five hundred thousand dollars.

ARTICLE 5

The necessary expenses attending the negotiations of the aforesaid treaty and supplement and also of such persons of the delegation as may sign the same shall be defrayed by the United States.

In testimony whereof, John F. Schermerhorn, commissioner on the part of the United States, and the undersigned delegation have hereunto set their hands and seals, this first day of March, in the year one thousand eight hundred and thirty-six.

J. F. Schermerhorn.
Major Ridge, his x mark, [L. S.]
James Foster, his x mark, [L. S.]
Tah-ye-ske, his x mark, [L. S.]
Long Shell Turtle, his x mark, [L. S.]

John Fields, his x mark, [L. S.]
James Fields, his x mark, [L. S.]
George Welch, his x mark, [L. S.]
Andrew Ross, [L. S.]
William Rogers, [L. S.]
John Gunter, [L. S.]
John A. Bell, [L. S.]
Jos. A. Foreman,
Robert Sanders, [L. S.]
Elias Boudinot, [L. S.]
Johnson Rogers, [L. S.]
James Starr, his x mark, [L. S.]
Stand Watie, [L. S.]
John Ridge, [L. S.]
James Rogers, [L. S.]
John Smith, his x mark, [L. S.]
Witnesses:
Elbert Herring,
Thos. Glascock,
Alexander H. Everett,
Jno. Garland, Major, U.S. Army,
C. A. Harris,
John Robb,
Wm. Y. Hansell,
Saml. J. Potts,
Jno. Litle,
S. Rockwell.

The Treaties at Medicine Lodge

[Charles J. Kappler, comp. *Indian Affairs: Laws and Treaties. Vol. 2: Treaties* (Washington, D.C.: Government Printing Office, 1904), 977–89.]

Articles of a treaty and agreement made and entered into at the Council Camp, on Medicine Lodge Creek, seventy miles south of Fort Larned, in the State of Kansas, on the twenty-first day of October, one thousand eight hundred and sixty-seven, by and between the United States of America, represented by its commissioners duly appointed thereto, to wit, Nathaniel G. Taylor, William S. Harney, C. C. Augur, Alfred S.[H.] Terry, John B. Sanborn, Samuel F. Tappan, and J. B. Henderson, of the one part, and the confederated tribes of Kiowa and Comanche Indians, represented by their chiefs and headmen, duly authorized and empowered to act for the body of the people of said tribes, (the names of said chiefs and head-men being hereto subscribed,) of the other part, witness:

ARTICLE 1

From this day forward all war between the parties to this agreement shall forever cease. The Government of the United States desires peace, and its honor is here pledged to keep it. The Indians desire peace, and they now pledge their honor to maintain it. If bad men among the whites, or among other people subject to the authority of the United States, shall commit any wrong upon the person or property of the Indians, the United States will, upon proof made to the agent and forwarded to the Commissioner of Indian Affairs at Washington City, proceed at once to cause the offender to be arrested and punished according to the laws of the United States, and also re-imburse the injured person for the loss sustained. If bad men among the Indians shall commit a wrong or depredation upon the person or property of any one, white, black, or Indians, subject to the authority of the United States and at peace therewith, the tribes herein named solemnly agree that they will, on proof made to their agent and notice by him, deliver up the wrong-doer to the United States, to be tried and punished according to its laws, and in case they wilfully refuse so to do, the person injured shall be re-imbursed for his loss from the annuities or other moneys due or to become due to them under this or other treaties made with the United States. And the President, on advising with the Commissioner of Indian Affairs shall prescribe such rules and regulations for ascertaining damages under the provisions of this article as, in his judgment, may be proper; but no such damages shall be adjusted and paid until thoroughly examined and passed upon by the Commissioner of Indian Affairs and the Secretary of the Interior; and no one sustaining loss, while violating or because of his violating, the provisions of this treaty or the laws of the United States, shall be re-imbursed therefor.

ARTICLE 2

The United States agrees that [the*] following district of country, to wit: commencing at a point where the Washita River crosses the 98th meridian, west from Greenwich; thence up the Washita River, in the middle of the main channel thereof, to a point thirty miles, by river, west of Fort Cobb, as now established; thence, due west to the north fork of Red River, provided said line strikes said river east of the one hundredth meridian of west longitude; if not, then only to said meridian-line, and thence south, on said meridian-line, to the said north fork of Red River; thence down said north fork, in the middle of the main channel thereof, from the point where it may be first intersected by the lines above described, to the main Red River; thence down said river, in the middle of the main channel thereof to its intersection with the ninety-eighth meridian of longitude west from Greenwich; thence north, on said meridian-line, to the place of beginning, shall be and the same is hereby set apart for the absolute and undisturbed use and occupation of the tribes herein named, and for such other friendly tribes or individual Indians as, from time to time, they may be willing [with the consent of the United States*] to admit among them; and the United States now solemnly agrees that no persons except those herein authorized so to do and except such officers, agents, and employés of the Government as may be authorized to enter upon Indian reservation in discharge of duties enjoined by law, shall ever be permitted to pass over, settle upon, or reside in the territory described in this article, or in such territory as may be added to this reservation, for the use of said Indians.

ARTICLE 3

If it should appear from actual survey or other satisfactory examination of said tract of land, that it contains less than one hundred and sixty acres of tillable land, for each person, who at the time may be authorized to reside on it under the provisions of this treaty, and a very considerable number of such persons shall be disposed to commence cultivating the soil as farmers, the United States agrees to set apart for the use of said Indians, as herein provided, such additional quantity of arable land adjoining to said reservation, or as near the same as it can be obtained, as may be required to provide the necessary amount.

ARTICLE 4

The United States agrees at its own proper expense to construct at some place, near the centre of said reservation, where timber and water may be convenient, the following buildings, to wit: A warehouse or store-room for the use of the agent, in storing goods belonging to the Indians, to cost not exceeding fifteen hundred dollars: an agency-building for the residence of the agent, to cost not exceeding three thousand dollars; a residence for the physician, to cost not more than three thousand dollars; and five other buildings, for a carpenter, farmer, blacksmith, miller, and engineer, each to cost not exceeding two thousand dollars; also a school-house or mission-building, so soon as a sufficient number of children can be induced by the agent to attend school, which shall not cost exceeding five thousand dollars. The United States agrees further to cause to be erected on said reservation, near the other buildings herein authorized, a good steam circular saw mill, with a grist-mill and shingle-machine attached: the same to cost not exceeding eight thousand dollars.

ARTICLE 5

The United States agrees that the agent for the said Indians in the future shall make his home at the agency-building: that he shall reside among them, and keep an office open at all times, for the purpose of prompt and diligent inquiry into such matters of complaint by and against the Indians as may be presented for investigation under the provisions of their treaty stipulations, as also for the faithful discharge of other duties enjoined on him by law. In all cases of depredation on person or property, he shall cause the evidence to be taken in writing and forwarded, together with his findings to the Commissioner of Indian Affairs, whose decision, subject to the revision of the Secretary of the Interior, shall be binding on the parties to this treaty.

ARTICLE 6

If any individual belonging to said tribes of Indians, or legally incorporated with them, being the head of a family, shall desire to commence farming, he shall have the privilege to select, in the presence and with the assistance of the agent then in charge, a tract of land within said reservation, not exceeding three hundred and twenty acres in extent, which tract, when so selected, certified, and recorded in the "land book" as herein directed, shall cease to be held in common, but the same may be occupied and held in the exclusive possession of the person selecting it, and of his family so long as he or they may continue to cultivate it. Any person over eighteen years of age, not being the head of a family, may in like manner select and cause to be certified to him or her, for purposes of cultivation, a quantity of land not exceeding eighty acres in extent, and thereupon, be entitled to the exclusive possession of the same as above directed. For each tract of land so selected, a certificate, containing a description thereof and the name of the person selecting it, with a certificate indorsed thereon that the same has been recorded, shall be delivered to the party entitled to it, by the agent, after the same shall have been recorded by him in a book to be kept in his office, subject to inspection, which said book shall be known as the "Kiowa and Comanche land book." The President may, at any time, order a survey of the reservation, and, when so surveyed, Congress shall provide for protecting the rights of settlers, in their improvements, and may fix the character of the title held by each. The United States may pass such laws, on the subject of alienation and descent of property and on all subjects connected with the government of the said Indians on said reservations, and the internal police thereof, as may be thought proper.

ARTICLE 7

In order to insure the civilization of the tribes, entering into this treaty, the necessity of education is admitted, especially by such of them as are or may be settled on said agricultural reservations: and they therefore pledge themselves to compel their children, male and female, between the ages of six and sixteen years, to attend school; and it is hereby made the duty of the agent for said Indians to see that this stipulation is strictly complied with; and the United States agrees that for every thirty children between said ages, who can be induced or compelled to attend school, a house shall be provided, and a teacher competent to teach the elementary branches of an English education, shall be furnished, who will reside among said Indians, and faithfully discharge his or her duties as a teacher. The provisions of this article to continue for not less than twenty years.

ARTICLE 8

When the head of a family or lodge shall have selected lands and received his certificate as above directed, and the agent shall be satisfied that he intends in good faith to commence cultivating the soil for a living, he shall be entitled to receive seeds and agricultural implements for the first year not exceeding in value one hundred dollars, and for each succeeding year he shall continue to farm for a period of three years more, he shall be entitled to receive seeds and implements as aforesaid not exceeding in value twenty-five dollars. And it is further stipulated that such persons as commence farming shall receive instruction from the farmer herein provided for, and whenever more than one hundred persons shall enter upon the cultivation of the soil a second blacksmith shall be provided, together with such iron, steel, and other material as may be needed.

ARTICLE 9

At any time after ten years from the making of this treaty the United States shall have the privilege of withdrawing the physician, farmer, blacksmiths, carpenter, engineer, and miller herein provided for; but, in case of such withdrawal, an additional sum thereafter of ten thousand dollars per annum shall be devoted to the education of said Indians, and the Commissioner of Indian Affairs shall, upon careful inquiry into the condition of said Indians, make such rules and regulations for the expenditure of said sum as will best promote the educational and moral improvement of said tribes.

ARTICLE 10

In lieu of all sums of money or other annuities provided to be paid to the Indians, herein named, under the treaty of October eighteenth, one thousand eight hundred and sixty-five, made at the mouth of the "Little Arkansas," and under all treaties made previous thereto, the United States agrees to deliver at the agency-house on the reservation herein named, on the fifteenth day of October of each year, for thirty years, the following articles, to wit: For each male person over fourteen years of age, a suit of good substantial woollen clothing, consisting of coat, pantaloons, flannel shirt, hat, and a pair of home-made socks. For each female over twelve years of age, a flannel skirt, or the goods necessary to make it, a pair of woolen hose, and twelve yards of calico, and twelve yards of "domestic." For the boys and girls under the ages named, such flannel and cotton goods as may be needed, to make each a suit as aforesaid, together with a pair of woollen hose for each; and in order that the Commissioner of Indian Affairs may be able to estimate properly for the articles herein named, it shall be the duty of the agent, each year, to forward him a full and exact census of the Indians on which the estimates from year to year can be based; and, in addition to the clothing herein named, the sum of twenty-five thousand dollars shall be annually appropriated for a period of thirty years, to be used by the Secretary of the Interior in the purchase of such articles, upon the recommendation of the Commissioner of Indian Affairs, as from time to time the condition and necessities of the Indians may indicate to be proper; and if at any time within the thirty years it shall appear that the amount of money needed for clothing under this article can be appropriated to better uses for the tribes herein named, Congress may by law change the appropriation to other purposes, but in no event shall the amount of this appropriation be withdrawn or discontinued for the period named; and the President shall, annually, detail an officer of the Army to be present and attest the delivery of all the goods herein named to the Indians, and he shall inspect and report on the quantity and quality of the goods and the manner of their delivery.

ARTICLE 11

In consideration of the advantages and benefits conferred by this treaty and the many pledges of friendship by the United States, the tribes who are parties to this agreement hereby stipulate that they will relinquish all right to occupy permanently the territory outside of their reservation, as herein defined, but they yet reserve the right to hunt on any lands south of the Arkansas [River,*] so long as the buffalo may range thereon in such numbers as to justify the chase, [and no white settlements shall be permitted on any part of the lands contained in the old reservation as defined by the treaty made between the United

States and the Cheyenne, Arapahoe, and Apache tribes of Indians at the mouth of the Little Arkansas, under date of October fourteenth, one thousand eight hundred and sixty-five, within three years from this date;*] and they, [the said tribes,*] further expressly agree—

1st. That they will withdraw all opposition to the construction of the railroad now being built on the Smoky Hill River, whether it be built to Colorado or New Mexico. 2d. That they will permit the peaceable construction of any railroad not passing over their reservation as herein defined. 3d. That they will not attack any persons at home, nor travelling, nor molest or disturb any wagon-trains, coaches, mules, or cattle belonging to the people of the United States, or to persons friendly therewith. 4th. They will never capture or carry off from the settlements white women or children. 5th. They will never kill nor scalp white men nor attempt to do them harm. 6th. They withdraw all pretence of opposition to the construction of the railroad now being built along the Platte River and westward to the Pacific Ocean; and they will not, in future, object to the construction of railroads, wagon-roads, mail-stations, or other works of utility or necessity which may be ordered or permitted by the laws of the United States. But should such roads or other works be constructed on the lands of their reservation, the Government will pay the tribes whatever amount of damage may be assessed by three disinterested commissioners, to be appointed by the President for that purpose; one of said commissioners to be a chief or head-man of the tribes. 7th. They agree to withdraw all opposition to the military posts now established in the western Territories.

ARTICLE 12

No treaty for the cession of any portion or part of the reservation herein described, which may be held in common, shall be of any validity or force as against the said Indians, unless executed and signed by at least three-fourths of all the adult male Indians occupying the same, and no cession by the tribe shall be understood or construed in such manner as to deprive, without his consent, any individual member of the tribe of his rights to any tract of land selected by him as provided in Article III [VI] of this treaty.

ARTICLE 13

The Indian agent, in employing a farmer, blacksmith, miller, and other employés herein provided for, qualifications being equal, shall give the preference to Indians.

ARTICLE 14

The United States hereby agrees to furnish annually to the Indians the physician, teachers, carpenter, miller, engineer, farmer, and blacksmiths, as herein contemplated, and that such appropriations shall be made from time to time, on the estimates of the Secretary of the Interior, as will be sufficient to employ such persons.

ARTICLE 15

It is agreed that the sum of seven hundred and fifty dollars be appropriated for the purpose of building a dwelling-house on the reservation for "Tosh-e-wa," (or the Silver Brooch,) the Comanche chief who has already commenced farming on the said reservation. And the sum of five hundred dollars annually, for three years from date, shall be expended in presents to the ten persons of said tribes who in the judgment of the agent may grow the most valuable crops for the period named.

ARTICLE 16

The tribes herein named agree, when the agency-house and other buildings shall be constructed on the reservation named, they will make said reservation their permanent home and they will make no permanent settlement elsewhere, but they shall have the right to hunt on the lands south of the Arkansas River, formerly called theirs, in the same manner, subject to the modifications named in this treaty, as agreed on by the treaty of the Little Arkansas, concluded the eighteenth day of October, one thousand eight hundred and sixty-five.

In testimony of which, we have hereunto set our hands and seals on the day and year aforesaid.

N. G. Taylor, [SEAL.] President of Indian Commission.

Wm. S. Harney, [SEAL.] Brevet Major-General.

C. C. Augur, [SEAL.] Brevet Major-General.

Alfred H. Terry, [SEAL.] Brigadier and Brevet Major-General.

John B. Sanborn, [SEAL.]

Samuel F. Tappan, [SEAL.]

J. B. Henderson. [SEAL.]

Attest:

Ashton S. H. White, secretary.

Kioways:

Satank, or Sitting Bear, his x mark. [SEAL.]

Sa-tan-ta, or White Bear, his x mark. [SEAL.]
Wa-toh-konk, or Black Eagle, his x mark. [SEAL.]
Ton-a-en-ko, or Kicking Eagle, his x mark. [SEAL.]
Fish-e-more, or Stinking Saddle, his x mark. [SEAL.]
Ma-ye-tin, or Woman's Heart, his x mark. [SEAL.]
Sa-tim-gear, or Stumbling Bear, his x mark. [SEAL.]
Sit-par-ga, or One Bear, his x mark. [SEAL.]
Corbeau, or The Crow, his x mark. [SEAL.]
Sa-ta-more, or Bear Lying Down. [SEAL.]

Comanches:
Parry-wah-say-men, or Ten Bears, his x mark. [SEAL.]
Tep-pe-navon, or Painted Lips, his x mark. [SEAL.]
To-sa-in, or Silver Brooch, his x mark. [SEAL.]
Cear-chi-neka, or Standing Feather, his x mark. [SEAL.]
Ho-we-ar, or Gap in the Woods, his x mark. [SEAL.]
Tir-ha-yah-guahip, or Horse's Back, his x mark. [SEAL.]
Es-a-nanaca, or Wolf's Name, his x mark. [SEAL.]
Ah-te-es-ta, or Little Horn, his x mark. [SEAL.]
Pooh-yah-to-yeh-be, or Iron Mountain, his x mark. [SEAL.]
Sad-dy-yo, or Dog Fat, his x mark. [SEAL.]

Attest:
Jas. A. Hardie, Inspector-General, U.S. Army.
Sam'l S. Smoot, U.S. surveyor.
Philip McCusker, interpreter.
J. H. Leavenworth, United States Indian agent.
Thos. Murphy, superintendent Indian affairs.
Henry Stanley, correspondent.
A. A. Taylor, assistant secretary.
Wm. Fayel, correspondent.
James O. Taylor, artist.
Geo. B. Willis, phonographer.
C. W. Whitraker, trader.

Articles of a treaty concluded at the Council Camp on Medicine Lodge Creek, seventy miles south of Fort Larned, in the State of Kansas, on the twenty-first day of October, eighteen hundred and sixty-seven, by and between the United States of America, represented by its commissioners duly appointed thereto to-wit: Nathaniel G. Taylor, William S. Harney, C. C. Augur, Alfred S. [H.] Terry, John B. Sanborn, Samuel F. Tappan, and J. B. Henderson, of the one part, and the Kiowa, Comanche, and Apache Indians, represented by their chiefs and headmen duly authorized and empowered to act for the body of the people of said tribes (the names of said chiefs and headmen being hereto subscribed) of the other part, witness:

Whereas, on the twenty-first day of October, eighteen hundred and sixty-seven, a treaty of peace was made and entered into at the Council Camp, on Medicine Lodge Creek, seventy miles south of Fort Larned, in the State of Kansas, by and between the United States of America, by its commissioners Nathaniel G. Taylor, William S. Harney, C. C. Augur, Alfred H. Terry, John B. Sanborn, Samuel F. Tappan, and J. B. Henderson, of the one part, and the Kiowa and Comanche tribes of Indians, of the Upper Arkansas, by and through their chiefs and headmen whose names are subscribed thereto, of the other part, reference being had to said treaty; and whereas, since the making and signing of said treaty, at a council held at said camp on this day, the chiefs and headmen of the Apache nation or tribe of Indians express to the commissioners on the part of the United States, as aforesaid, a wish to be confederated with the said Kiowa and Comanche tribes, and to be placed, in every respect, upon an equal footing with said tribes; and whereas, at a council held at the same place and on the same day, with the chiefs and headmen of the said Kiowa and Comanche Tribes, they consent to the confederation of the said Apache tribe, as desired by it, upon the terms and conditions hereinafter set forth in this supplementary treaty: Now, therefore, it is hereby stipulated and agreed by and between the aforesaid commissioners, on the part of the United States, and the chiefs and headmen of the Kiowa and Comanche tribes, and, also, the chiefs and headmen of the said Apache tribe, as follows, to-wit:

ARTICLE 1

The said Apache tribe of Indians agree to confederate and become incorporated with the said Kiowa and Comanche Indians, and to accept as their permanent home the reservation described in the aforesaid treaty with said Kiowa and Comanche tribes, concluded as aforesaid at this place, and they pledge themselves to make no permanent settlement at any place, nor on any lands, outside of said reservation.

ARTICLE 2

The Kiowa and Comanche tribes, on their part, agree that all the benefits and advantages arising from the employment of physicians, teachers, carpenters, millers, engineers, farmers, and blacksmiths, agreed to be furnished under the provisions of their said treaty, together with all the advantages to be derived from the construction of agency buildings, warehouses, mills, and other structures, and also from the establishment of schools upon their said reservation, shall be jointly and equally shared and enjoyed by the said Apache Indians, as though they had been originally a part of said tribes; and they further agree that all other benefits arising from said treaty shall be jointly and equally shared as aforesaid.

ARTICLE 3

The United States, on its part, agrees that clothing and other articles named in Article X. of said original treaty, together with all money or other annuities agreed to be furnished under any of the provisions of said treaty, to the Kiowa and Comanches, shall be shared equally by the Apaches. In all cases where specific articles of clothing are agreed to be furnished to the Kiowas and Comanches, similar articles shall be furnished to the Apaches, and a separate census of the Apaches shall be annually taken and returned by the agent, as provided for the other tribes. And the United States further agrees, in consideration of the incorporation of said Apaches, to increase the annual appropriation of money, as provided for in Article X. of said treaty, from twenty-five thousand to thirty thousand dollars; and the latter amount shall be annually appropriated, for the period therein named, for the use and benefit of said three tribes, confederated as herein declared; and the clothing and other annuities, which may from time to time be furnished to the Apaches, shall be based upon the census of the three tribes, annually to be taken by the agent, and shall be separately marked, forwarded, and delivered to them at the agency house, to be built under the provisions of said original treaty.

ARTICLE 4

In consideration of the advantages conferred by this supplementary treaty upon the Apache tribe of Indians, they agree to observe and faithfully comply with all the stipulations and agreements entered into by the Kiowas and Comanches in said original treaty. They agree, in the same manner, to keep the peace toward the whites and all other persons under the jurisdiction of the United States, and to do and perform all other things enjoined upon said tribes by the provisions of said treaty; and they hereby give up and forever relinquish to the United States all rights, privileges, and grants now vested in them, or intended to be transferred to them, by the treaty between the United States and the Cheyenne and Arapahoe tribes of Indians, concluded at the camp on the Little Arkansas River, in the State of Kansas, on the fourteenth day of October, one thousand eight hundred and sixty-five, and also by the supplementary treaty, concluded at the same place on the seventeenth day of the same month, between the United States, of the one part, and the Cheyenne, Arapahoe, and Apache tribes, of the other part.

In testimony of all which, the said parties have hereunto set their hands and seals at the place and on the day hereinbefore stated.

N. G. Taylor, [SEAL.] President of Indian Commission.

Wm. S. Harney, [SEAL.] Brevet Major-General, Commissioner, &c.

C. C. Augur, [SEAL.] Brevet Major-General.

Alfred H. Terry, [SEAL.] Brevet Major-General and Brigadier-General.

John B. Sanborn, [SEAL.]

Samuel F. Tappan, [SEAL.]

J. B. Henderson, [SEAL.]

On the part of the Kiowas:

Satanka, or Sitting bear, his x mark, [SEAL.]

Sa-tan-ta, or White Bear, his x mark, [SEAL.]

Wah-toh-konk, or Black Eagle, his x mark, [SEAL.]

Ton-a-en-ko, or Kicking Eagle, his x mark, [SEAL.]

Fish-e-more, or Stinking Saddle, his x mark, [SEAL.]

Ma-ye-tin, or Woman's Heart, his x mark, [SEAL.]

Sa-tim-gear, or Stumbling Bear, his x mark, [SEAL.]

Sa-pa-ga, or One Bear, his x mark, [SEAL.]

Cor-beau, or The Crow, his x mark, [SEAL.]

Sa-ta-more, or Bear Lying Down, his x mark, [SEAL.]

On the part of the Comanches:

Parry-wah-say-men, or Ten Bears, his x mark, [SEAL.]

Tep-pe-navon, or Painted Lips, his x mark, [SEAL.]

To-she-wi, or Silver Brooch, his x mark, [SEAL.]

Cear-chi-neka, or Standing Feather, his x mark, [SEAL.]

Ho-we-ar, or Gap in the Woods, his x mark, [SEAL.]

Tir-ha-yah-gua-hip, or Horse's Back, his x mark, [SEAL.]

Es-a-man-a-ca, or Wolf's Name, his x mark, [SEAL.]

Ah-te-es-ta, or Little Horn, his x mark, [SEAL.]

Pooh-yah-to-yeh-be, or Iron Mountain, his x mark, [SEAL.]

Sad-dy-yo, or Dog Fat, his x mark, [SEAL.]

On the part of the Apaches:

Mah-vip-pah, or Wolf's Sleeve, his x mark, [SEAL.]

Kon-zhon-ta-co, or Poor Bear, his x mark, [SEAL.]

Cho-se-ta, or Bad Back, his x mark, [SEAL.]

Nah-tan, or Brave Man, his x mark, [SEAL.]

Ba-zhe-ech, or Iron Shirt, his x mark, [SEAL.]

Til-la-ka, or White Horn, his x mark, [SEAL.]

Attest:Ashton S. H. White, secretary.

Geo. B. Willis, reporter.

Philip McCusker, interpreter.

John D. Howland, clerk Indian Commission.

Sam'l S. Smoot, United States surveyor.

A. A. Taylor.

J. H. Leavenworth, United States Indian agent.

Thos. Murphy, superintendent Indian affairs.

Joel H. Elliott, major, Seventh U.S. Cavalry.

Articles of a treaty and agreement made and entered into at the Council Camp on Medicine Lodge Creek, seventy miles south of Fort Larned, in the State of Kansas, on the twenty-eighth day of October, eighteen hundred and sixty-seven, by and between the United States of America, represented by its commissioners duly appointed thereto, to wit: Nathaniel G. Taylor, William S. Harney, C. C. Augur, Alfred H. Terry, John B. Sanborn, Samuel F. Tappan and John B. Henderson, of the one part, and the Cheyenne and Arapahoe tribes of Indians, represented by their chiefs and head-men duly authorized and empowered to act for the body of the people of said tribes—the names of said chiefs and head-men being hereto subscribed—of the other part, witness:

ARTICLE 1

From this day forward all war between the parties to this agreement shall forever cease. The Government of the United States desires peace, and its honor is here pledged to keep it. The Indians desire peace, and they now pledge their honor to maintain it.

If bad men among the whites, or among other people subject to the authority of the United States, shall commit any wrong upon the person or property of the Indians, the United States will, upon proof made to the agent and forwarded to the Commissioner of Indian Affairs at Washington City, proceed at once to cause the offender to be arrested and punished according to the laws of the United States, and also reimburse the injured person for the loss sustained.

If bad men among the Indians shall commit a wrong or depredation upon the person or property of any one, white, black, or Indian, subject to the authority of the United States and at peace therewith, the tribes herein named solemnly agree that they will, on proof made to their agent, and notice by him, deliver up the wrongdoer to the United States, to be tried and punished according to its laws; and in case they wilfully refuse so to do, the person injured shall be re-imbursed for his loss from the annuities or other moneys due or to become due to them under this or other treaties made with the United States. And the President, on advising with the Commissioner of Indian Affairs, shall prescribe such rules and regulations for ascertaining damages, under the provisions of this article, as in his judgment may be proper. But no such damages shall be adjusted and paid until thoroughly examined and passed upon by the

Commissioner of Indian Affairs and the Secretary of the Interior, and no one sustaining loss, while violating, or because of his violating, the provisions of this treaty or the laws of the United States, shall be re-imbursed therefor.

ARTICLE 2

The United States agrees that the following district of country, to wit: commencing at the point where the Arkansas River crosses the 37th parallel of north latitude, thence west on said parallel—the said line being the southern boundary of the State of Kansas—to the Cimarone River, (sometimes called the Red Fork of the Arkansas River), thence down said Cimarone River, in the middle of the main channel thereof, to the Arkansas River; thence up the Arkansas River, in the middle of the main channel thereof, to the place of beginning, shall be and the same is hereby set apart for the absolute and undisturbed use and occupation of the Indians herein named, and for such other friendly tribes or individual Indians, as from time to time they may be willing, with the consent of the United States, to admit among them; and the United States now solemnly agrees that no persons except those herein authorized so to do, and except such officers, agents, and employés of the Government as may be authorized to enter upon Indian reservations in discharge of duties enjoined by law, shall ever be permitted to pass over, settle upon, or reside in the territory described in this article, or in such territory as may be added to this reservation for the use of said Indians.

ARTICLE 3

If it should appear from actual survey or other examination of said tract of land, that it contains less than one hundred and sixty acres of tillable land for each person who at the time may be authorized to reside on it, under the provisions of this treaty, and a very considerable number of such persons shall be disposed to commence cultivating the soil as farmers, the United States agrees to set apart for the use of said Indians as herein provided, such additional quantity of arable land adjoining to said reservation, or as near the same as it can be obtained, as may be required to provide the necessary amount.

ARTICLE 4

The United States agrees at its own proper expense to construct at some place near the center of said reservation, where timber and water may be convenient, the following buildings, to wit: a warehouse or store-room for the use of the agent in storing goods belonging to the Indians, to cost not exceeding fifteen hundred dollars; an agency-building for the residence of the agent, to cost not exceeding three thousand dollars; a residence for the physician, to cost not more than three thousand dollars; and five other buildings, for a carpenter, farmer, blacksmith, miller, and engineer, each to cost not exceeding two thousand dollars; also a school-house or mission-building, so soon as a sufficient number of children can be induced by the agent to attend school, which shall not cost exceeding five thousand dollars. The United States agrees, further, to cause to be erected on said reservation, near the other buildings herein authorized, a good steam circular saw-mill, with a grist-mill and shingle machine attached; the same to cost not exceeding eight thousand dollars.

ARTICLE 5

The United States agrees that the agent for said Indians in the future shall make his home at the agency building; that he shall reside among them, and keep an office open at all times for the purpose of prompt and diligent inquiry into such matters of complaint by and against the Indians as may be presented for investigation, under the provisions of their treaty stipulations, as also for the faithful discharge of other duties enjoined on him by law. In all cases of depredation on person or property, he shall cause the evidence to be taken in writing and forwarded, together with his finding, to the Commissioner of Indian Affairs, whose decision, subject to the revision of the Secretary of the Interior, shall be binding on the parties to this treaty.

ARTICLE 6

If any individual, belonging to said tribes of Indians, or legally incorporated with them, being the head of a family, shall desire to commence farming, he shall have the privilege to select, in the presence and with the assistance of the agent then in charge, a tract of land within said reservation not exceeding three hundred and twenty acres in extent, which tract when so selected, certified, and recorded in the land-book as herein directed, shall cease to be held in common, but the same may be occupied and held in the exclusive possession of the person selecting it, and of his family, so long as he or they may continue to cultivate it. Any person over eighteen years of age, not being the head of a family, may in like manner select and cause to be certified to him, or her, for purposes of cultivation, a quantity of land not exceeding eighty acres in extent, and thereupon be entitled to the exclusive possession of the same as above directed.

For each tract of land so selected, a certificate containing a description thereof, and the name of the person selecting it, with a certificate indorsed thereon, that the same has been recorded, shall be delivered to the party entitled to it by the agent, after the same shall have been recorded by him in a book to be kept in his office, subject to inspection, which said book shall be known as the "Cheyenne and Arapahoe Land Book." The President may at any time order a survey of the reservation, and, when so surveyed, Congress shall provide for protecting the rights of settlers in their improvements, and may fix the character of the title held by each.

The United States may pass such laws on the subject of alienation and descent of property, and on all subjects connected with the government of the Indians on said reservations, and the internal police thereof as may be thought proper.

ARTICLE 7

In order to insure the civilization of the tribes entering into this treaty, the necessity of education is admitted, especially by such of them as are or may be settled on said agricultural reservation, and they therefore pledge themselves to compel their children, male and female, between the ages of six and sixteen years, to attend school; and it is hereby made the duty of the agent for said Indians to see that this stipulation is strictly complied with; and the United States agrees that for every thirty children between said ages, who can be induced or compelled to attend school, a house shall be provided, and a teacher competent to teach the elementary branches of an English education shall be furnished, who will reside among said Indians, and faithfully discharge his or her duties as a teacher. The provisions of this article to continue for not less than twenty years.

ARTICLE 8

When the head of a family or lodge shall have selected lands and received his certificate as above directed, and the agent shall be satisfied that he intends in good faith to commence cultivating the soil for a living, he shall be entitled to receive seeds and agricultural implements for the first year, not exceeding in value one hundred dollars; and for each succeeding year he shall continue to farm for a period of three years more, he shall be entitled to receive seeds and implements as aforesaid, not exceeding in value twenty-five dollars.

And it is further stipulated that such persons as commence farming shall receive instruction from the farmer herein provided for; and whenever more than one hundred persons shall enter upon the cultivation of the soil, a second blacksmith shall be provided, with such iron, steel, and other material as may be needed.

ARTICLE 9

At any time after ten years from the making of this treaty the United States shall have the privilege of withdrawing the physician, farmer, blacksmith, carpenter, engineer, and miller, herein provided for, but in case of such withdrawal, an additional sum, thereafter, of ten thousand dollars per annum shall be devoted to the education of said Indians, and the Commissioner of Indian Affairs shall upon careful inquiry into their condition make such rules and regulations for the expenditure of said sum as will best promote the educational and moral improvement of said tribes.

ARTICLE 10

In lieu of all sums of money or other annuities provided to be paid to the Indians herein named, under the treaty of October fourteenth, eighteen hundred and sixty-five, made at the mouth of Little Arkansas, and under all treaties made previous thereto, the United States agrees to deliver at the agency house on the reservation herein named, on the fifteenth day of October, of each year, for thirty years, the following articles, to wit:
For each male person over fourteen years of age, a suit of good, substantial woolen clothing, consisting of coat, pantaloons, flannel shirt, hat, and a pair of home-made socks. For each female over twelve years of age, a flannel skirt, or the goods necessary to make it, a pair of woolen hose, twelve yards of calico and twelve yards of cotton domestics. For the boys and girls under the ages named, such flannel and cotton goods as may be needed to make each a suit as aforesaid, together with a pair of woolen hose for each. And in order that the Commissioner of Indian Affairs may be able to estimate properly for the articles herein named, it shall be the duty of the agent each year to forward to him a full and exact census of the Indians on which the estimate from year to year can be based.

And, in addition to the clothing herein named, the sum of twenty thousand dollars shall be annually appropriated for a period of thirty years, to be used by the Secretary of the Interior in the purchase of such articles as, from time to time, the condition and necessities of the Indians may indicate to be proper. And if at any time, within the thirty years, it shall appear that the amount of money needed for clothing, under this article, can be appropriated to better uses for the tribe herein named, Congress may, by law, change the appropriation to other purposes; but, in no event, shall the amount of this appropriation be withdrawn or discontinued for the period named. And the President shall, annually, detail an officer of the Army to be present, and attest the delivery of all the goods herein named to the Indians, and he shall inspect and report on the quantity and quality of the goods and the manner of their delivery.

ARTICLE 11

In consideration of the advantages and benefits conferred by this treaty, and the many pledges of friendship by the United States, the tribes who are parties to this agreement hereby stipulate that they will relinquish all right to occupy permanently the territory outside of their reservation as herein defined, but they yet reserve the right to hunt on any lands south of the Arkansas so long as the buffalo may range thereon in such numbers as to justify the chase; and no white settlements shall be permitted on any part of the lands contained in the old reservation as defined by the treaty made between the United States and the Cheyenne, Arapahoe, and Apache tribes of Indians, at the mouth of the Little Arkansas, under date of October fourteenth, eighteen hundred and sixty-five, within three years from this date, and they, the said tribes, further expressly agree:

1st. That they will withdraw all opposition to the construction of the railroad now being built on the Smoky Hill River, whether it be built to Colorado or New Mexico. 2d. That they will permit the peaceable construction of any railroad not passing over their reservation, as herein defined. 3d. That they will not attack any persons at home or travelling, nor molest or disturb any wagon-trains, coaches, mules, or cattle belonging to the people of the United States or to persons friendly therewith. 4th. They will never capture or carry off from the settlements white women or children. 5th. They will never kill or scalp white men, nor attempt to do them harm. 6th. They withdraw all pretense of opposition to the construction of the railroad now being built along the Platte River, and westward to the Pacific Ocean; and they will not in future object to the construction of railroads, wagon-roads, mail-stations, or other works of utility or necessity, which may be ordered or permitted by the laws of the United States. But should such roads or other works be constructed on the lands of their reservation, the Government will pay the tribe whatever amount of damage may be assessed by three disinterested commissioners to be appointed by the President for that purpose, one of said commissioners to be a chief or head-man of the tribe. 7th. They agree to withdraw all opposition to the military posts or roads now established, or that may be established, not in violation of treaties heretofore made or hereafter to be made with any of the Indian tribes.

ARTICLE 12

No treaty for the cession of any portion or part of the reservation herein described, which may be held in common, shall be of any validity or force as against the said Indians unless executed and signed by at least three-fourths of all the adult male Indians occupying or interested in the same; and no cession by the tribe shall be understood or construed in such manner as to deprive without his consent any individual member of the tribe of his rights to any tract of land selected by him as provided in Article 6 of this treaty.

ARTICLE 13

The United States hereby agree to furnish annually to the Indians the physician, teachers, carpenter, miller, engineer, farmer, and blacksmiths, as herein contemplated, and that such appropriations shall be made from time to time, on the estimates of the Secretary of the Interior, as will be sufficient to employ such persons.

ARTICLE 14

It is agreed that the sum of five hundred dollars, annually, for three years from date, shall be expended in presents to the ten persons of said tribe who, in the judgment of the agent, may grow the most valuable crops for the respective year.

ARTICLE 15

The tribes herein named agree that when the agency-house and other buildings shall be constructed on the reservation named, they will regard and make said reservation their permanent home, and they will make no permanent settlement elsewhere, but they shall have the right, subject to the conditions and modifications of this treaty, to hunt on the lands south of the Arkansas River, formerly called theirs, in the same manner as agreed on by the treaty of the "Little Arkansas," concluded the fourteenth day of October, eighteen hundred and sixty-five.

In testimony of which, we have hereunto set our hands and seals, on the day and year aforesaid.

N. G. Taylor, [SEAL.] President of Indn. Commission.
Wm. S. Harney, [SEAL.] Major-General, Brevet, &c.
C. C. Augur, [SEAL.] Brevet Major-General.
Alfred H. Terry, [SEAL.] Brevet Major-General.
John B. Sanborn, [SEAL.] Commissioner.
Samuel F. Tappan. [SEAL.]
J. B. Henderson. [SEAL.]
Attest:Ashton S. H. White, secretary.

Geo. B. Willis, phonographer.
On the part of the Cheyennes:
O-to-ah-nac-co, Bull Bear, his x mark, [SEAL.]
Moke-tav-a-to, Black Kettle, his x mark, [SEAL.]
Nac-co-hah-ket, Little Bear, his x mark, [SEAL.]
Mo-a-vo-va-ast, Spotted Elk, his x mark, [SEAL.]
Is-se-von-ne-ve, Buffalo Chief, his x mark, [SEAL.]
Vip-po-nah, Slim Face, his x mark, [SEAL.]
Wo-pah-ah, Gray Head, his x mark, [SEAL.]
O-ni-hah-ket, Little Rock, his x mark, [SEAL.]
Ma-mo-ki, or Curly Hair, his x mark, [SEAL.]
O-to-ah-has-tis, Tall Bull, his x mark, [SEAL.]
Wo-po-ham, or White Horse, his x mark, [SEAL.]
Hah-ket-home-mah, Little Robe, his x mark, [SEAL.]
Min-nin-ne-wah, Whirlwind, his x mark, [SEAL.]
Mo-yan-histe-histow, Heap of Birds, his x mark, [SEAL.]
On the part of the Arapahoes:
Little Raven, his x mark, [SEAL.]
Yellow Bear, his x mark, [SEAL.]
Storm, his x mark, [SEAL.]
White Rabbit, his x mark, [SEAL.]
Spotted Wolf, his x mark, [SEAL.]
Little Big Mouth, his x mark, [SEAL.]
Young Colt, his x mark, [SEAL.]
Tall Bear, his x mark, [SEAL.]

Attest:
C. W. Whitaker, interpreter.
H. Douglas, major, Third Infantry.
Jno. D. Howland, clerk Indian Commission.
Sam'l. S. Smoot, United States surveyor.
A. A. Taylor.
Henry Stanley, correspondent.
John S. Smith, United States interpreter.
George Bent, interpreter.
Thos. Murphy, superintendent Indian affairs.

{ NOTES }

Abbreviations

ARCIA   *Annual Reports of the Commissioner of Indian Affairs for the years 1824–1920.* Washington, D.C.: Government Printing Office

ASPIA   *American State Papers: Documents, Legislative and Executive, of the Congress of the United States. Class II: Indian Affairs.* Selected and edited by Walter Lowrie and Matthew St. Clair Clarke. 2 vols. Washington: Gales and Seaton, 1832.

DRCHNY   Edmund B. O' Callaghan, ed. *Documents Relating to the Colonial History of the State of New York.* 15 vols. Albany, N.Y.: Weed, Parsons, and Co., 1853–57.

EAID   Alden T. Vaughan, gen. ed. *Early American Indian Documents: Treaties and Laws, 1607–1789.* 20 vols. Bethesda, Md.: University Publications of America, 1979–2004.* See below for individual volumes.

IALT   Charles J. Kappler, comp. *Indian Affairs: Laws and Treaties. Vol. 2: Treaties.* Washington, D.C.: Government Printing Office, 1904.

LROAG   National Archives, Letters Received by the Office of the Adjutant General (Main Series), 1861–70. Microfilm M619.

LROIA   National Archives, RG 75, Letters Received by the Office of Indian Affairs, 1824–81, Microfilm M234.

NASPIA   *The New American State Papers: Indian Affairs, 1789–1860.* 13 vols. Wilmington, Del.: Scholarly Resources, 1972.

RG 48, 665   National Archives, RG 48: Records of the Secretary of the Interior, Entry 665, 2 vols.

Ross Papers   Gary E. Moulton, ed. *The Papers of Chief John Ross.* 2 vols. Norman: University of Oklahoma Press, 1985.

WJP   James Sullivan et al., eds. *The Papers of Sir William Johnson.* 14 vols. Albany: University of the State of New York, 1921–65.

EAID volumes cited:
1. Donald H. Kent, ed. *Pennsylvania and Delaware Treaties, 1629–1737.*
2. Donald H. Kent, ed. *Pennsylvania Treaties, 1737–1756.*
3. Alison Duncan Hirsch, ed. *Pennsylvania Treaties, 1756–1775.*
4. W. Stitt Robinson, ed. *Virginia Treaties, 1607–1722.*
5. W. Stitt Robinson, ed. *Virginia Treaties, 1723–1775.*
6. W. Stitt Robinson, ed. *Maryland Treaties, 1632–1775.*
9. Barbara Graymont, ed. *New York and New Jersey Treaties, 1714–1753.*
10. Barbara Graymont, ed. *New York and New Jersey Treaties, 1754–1775.*
12. John T. Juricek, ed. *Georgia and Florida Treaties, 1763–1776.*

13. W. Stitt Robinson, ed. *North and South Carolina Treaties, 1654–1756.*
14. W. Stitt Robinson, ed. *North and South Carolina Treaties, 1756–1775.*
17. Alden T. Vaughan and Deborah A. Rosen, eds. *New England and Middle Atlantic Laws.*
18. Colin G. Calloway, ed. *Revolution and Confederation.*
19. Daniel R. Mandell, ed. *New England Treaties, Southeast, 1524–1761.*
20. Daniel R. Mandell, ed. *New England Treaties, North and West, 1650–1776.*

Acknowledgments and a Note on Terminology

1. Taiaiake Alfred, *Peace, Power, Righteousness: An Indigenous Manifesto* (New York: Oxford University Press, 1999), xxv–vi, 67–69.

Introduction

1. *DRCHNY*, 4: 337.
2. A. M. Drummond and Richard Moody, "Indian Treaties: The First American Dramas," *Quarterly Journal of Speech* 39 (February 1953), 15–24.
3. Gilles Havard, *The Great Peace of Montreal in 1701: French-Native Diplomacy in the Seventeenth Century* (Montreal: McGill-Queens University Press, 2001); Alain Beaulieu and Roland Viau, *The Great Peace: Chronicle of a Diplomatic Saga* (Ottawa: Canadian Museum of Civilization, 2001); Timothy J. Shannon, *Iroquois Diplomacy on the Early American Frontier* (New York: Penguin, 2008), 50–62; J. A. Brandão and William A. Starna, "The Treaties of 1701: A Triumph of Iroquois Diplomacy," *Ethnohistory* 43 (Spring 1996), 209–44. Jon Parmenter, *The Edge of the Woods: Iroquoia, 1534–1701* (East Lansing: Michigan State University Press, 2010), ch. 6, downplays the crisis confronting the Iroquois and emphasizes their achievement at the peace settlement in making Iroquoia a crucial central space between neighboring Native nations and settler colonies.
4. Georgiana C. Nammack, *Fraud, Politics, and the Dispossession of the Indians: The Iroquois Land Frontier in the Colonial Period* (Norman: University of Oklahoma Press, 1969); Paul VanDevelder, *Savages and Scoundrels: The Untold Story of America's Road to Empire through Indian Territory* (New Haven: Yale University Press, 2009); *Minutes of Debates in Council on the banks of the Ottawa River, November 1791 Said to be held there by the Chiefs of the several Indian Nations, who defeated the Army of the United States, on the 4th of that Month* (Philadelphia: William Young, 1792), 11.
5. Scott Richard Lyons, *X-Marks: Native Signatures of Assent* (Minneapolis: University of Minnesota Press, 2010), 1.
6. Walter R. Echo-Hawk, *In the Courts of the Conqueror: The 10 Worst Indian Law Cases Ever Decided* (Golden, Colo.: Fulcrum, 2010).
7. Robert A. Williams, Jr., *The American Indian in Western Legal Thought: The Discourses of Conquest* (New York: Oxford University Press, 1990), 326–27; Taiaiake Alfred, *Peace, Power, Righteousness: An Indigenous Manifesto* (New York: Oxford University Press, 1999), 49.
8. Patricia Seed, *Ceremonies of Possession in Europe's Conquest of the New World, 1492–1640* (Cambridge: Cambridge University Press, 1995).
9. Colin G. Calloway, *One Vast Winter Count: The Native American West before Lewis and Clark* (Lincoln: University of Nebraska Press, 2003), 244–45. On the limitations of this and

other such French rituals for understanding, let alone controlling, a mobile web of kinship ties and shifting identities, see Michael Witgen, "The Rituals of Possession: Native Identity and the Invention of Empire in Seventeenth-Century Western North America," *Ethnohistory* 45 (Fall 2007), 639–68.

10. Williams, *The American Indian in Western Legal Thought*; Robert J. Miller, Jacinta Ruru, Larissa Behrendt, and Tracey Lindberg, eds., *Discovering Indigenous Lands: The Doctrine of Discovery in the English Colonies* (New York: Oxford University Press, 2010) examine the application of the doctrine in the United States, Canada, Australia, and New Zealand.

11. Blake A. Watson, *Buying America from the Indians: Johnson v. McIntosh and the History of Native Land Rights* (Norman: University of Oklahoma Press, 2012), Williams quote at 11; Stuart Banner, *How the Indians Lost Their Land: Law and Power on the Frontier* (Cambridge, Mass.: Harvard University Press, 2005), ch. 3.

12. Watson, *Buying America from the Indians*; Robert J. Miller, *Native America, Discovered and Conquered: Thomas Jefferson, Lewis and Clark, and Manifest Destiny* (Westport, Conn.: Praeger, 2006); Lindsay J. Robertson, *Conquest by Law: How the Discovery of America Dispossessed Indigenous Peoples of Their Lands* (New York: Oxford University Press, 2005); Banner, *How the Indians Lost Their Land*, ch. 5; Williams, *American Indian in Western Legal Thought*, 325 ("perfect instrument"); Patrick Wolfe, "Against the Intentional Fallacy: Logocentrism and Continuity in the Rhetoric of Indian Dispossession," *American Indian Culture and Research Journal* 36 (2012), 9–12.

13. Colin G. Calloway, Gerd Gemünden, and Suzanne Zantop, eds., *Germans and Indians: Fantasies, Encounters, Projections* (Lincoln: University of Nebraska Press, 2002), 57–58; Vine Deloria, Jr., and Raymond J. DeMallie, eds., *Documents of American Indian Diplomacy: Treaties, Agreements, and Conventions, 1775–1979*, 2 vols. (Norman: University of Oklahoma Press, 1999), 2: 1493–94.

14. John R. Wunder, "'That No Thorn Will Pierce Our Friendship': The Ute-Comanche Treaty of 1786," *Western Historical Quarterly* 42 (Spring 2011), 5–27.

15. Susan Kalter, ed., *Benjamin Franklin, Pennsylvania, and the First Nations: The Treaties of 1736–62* (Urbana: University of Illinois Press, 2006).

16. For colonial treaties: *EAID*; Robert Clinton, Kevin Gover, and Rebecca Tsosie, eds., introduction, *Colonial and American Indian Treaties: A Collection* (Arizona State University College of Law, 2004); for US treaties, *IALT*, also online at http://digital.library.ok.state.edu/kappler/vol2/toc.htm; and the more complete Deloria and DeMallie, eds., *Documents of American Indian Diplomacy*; http://early treaties.unl.edu/index.html.

17. Among these are Donald E. Worcester, ed., *Forked Tongues and Broken Treaties* (Caldwell, Idaho: Caxton Printers, 1975); Rupert Costo and Jeanette Henry, *Indian Treaties: Two Centuries of Dishonor* (San Francisco: Indian Historian Press, 1977); Dorothy V. Jones, *License for Empire: Colonialism by Treaty in Early America* (Chicago: University of Chicago Press, 1982); Francis Paul Prucha, *American Indian Treaties: The History of a Political Anomaly* (Berkeley: University of California Press, 1994); Robert A. Williams, *Linking Arms Together: American Indian Treaty Visions of Law and Peace, 1600–1800* (New York: Oxford University Press, 1997); Jill St. Germain, *Indian Treaty-Making Policy in the United States and Canada, 1867–1877* (Lincoln: University of Nebraska Press, 2001); Stan Hoig, *White Man's Paper Trail: Grand Councils and Treaty Making on the Central Plains* (Boulder: University Press of Colorado, 2006).

18. Raymond J. DeMallie, "Touching the Pen: Plains Indian Treaty Councils in Ethnohistorical Perspective," in *Ethnicity on the Great Plains*, ed. Frederick C. Luebke (Lincoln: University of Nebraska Press, 1980), 38–53; Williams, *Linking Arms Together*.

19. *A Journey from Pennsylvania to Onondaga in 1743 by John Bartram, Lewis Evans, and Conrad Weiser* (Barre, Mass.: Imprint Society, 1973), 90.

20. For example, see Benjamin Ramirez-Shkwegnaabi, "The Dynamics of American Indian Diplomacy in the Great Lakes Region," *American Indian Culture and Research Journal* 27, no. 4 (2003), 53–77.

21. Lawrence C. Wroth, "The Indian Treaty as Literature," *Yale Review* 17 (1928), 749–50, 766.

22. James H. Merrell, *Into the American Woods: Negotiators on the Pennsylvania Frontier* (New York: W. W. Norton, 1999), 254.

23. *Anishnabek News* 24, no. 6 (July–August 2012), 2; Chief Irving Powless, Jr., "Treaty Making," in *Treaty of Canandaigua 1794: 200 Years of Treaty Relations between the Iroquois Confederacy and the United States*, ed. G. Peter Jemison and Anna M. Schein (Santa Fe: Clear Light Publishers, 2000), 31.

24. Cf. J. R. Miller, *Compact, Contract, Covenant: Aboriginal Treaty-Making in Canada* (Toronto: University of Toronto Press, 2009), 5.

Chapter 1

1. *WJP*, 6: 400.

2. On the marking and meanings of indigenous boundaries, see Kathleen DuVal, *The Native Ground: Indians and Colonists in the Heart of the Continent* (Philadelphia: University of Pennsylvania Press, 2006), 28; Julianna Barr, "Geographies of Power: Mapping Indian Borders in the 'Borderlands' of the Early Southwest," *William and Mary Quarterly*, 3rd ser., 68 (January 2011), 5–46; Patricia Albers and Jeanne Kay, "Sharing the Land: A Study in American Indian Territoriality," in *A Cultural Geography of North American Indians*, ed. Tyrel G. Moore and Thomas E. Ross, (Boulder, Colo: Westview Press, 1987), 47–91.

3. Peter Wraxall, *An Abridgment of the Indian Affairs Contained in Four Folio Volumes, Transacted in the Colony of New York, from the year 1678 to the year 1751* (Cambridge, Mass.: Harvard University Press, 1915), 195.

4. Cynthia J. Van Zandt, *Brothers among Nations: The Pursuit of Intercultural Alliances in Early America, 1580–1660* (New York: Oxford University Press, 2008), quote at 12; Tom Arne Midtrød, *The Memory of All Ancient Customs: Native American Diplomacy in the Colonial Hudson Valley* (Ithaca, N.Y.: Cornell University Press, 2012); Jenny Hale Pulsipher, "Gaining the Diplomatic Edge: Kinship, Trade, Ritual, and Religion in Amerindian Alliances in Early North America," in *Empires and Indigenes: Intercultural Alliance, Imperial Expansion, and Warfare in the Early Modern World*, ed. Wayne E. Lee, (New York: New York: University Press, 2011), 19–47; Leanne Simpson, "Looking after Gdoo-naaganinaa: Precolonial Nishnaabeg Diplomatic and Treaty Relationships," *Wicazo Sa Review: A Journal of Native American Studies* 23 (Fall 2008), 29–42.

5. Smith's account of his rescue, embellished in a letter to the Queen of England at the time Pocahontas visited London, is reprinted in Karen Ordahl Kupperman, ed., *Captain John Smith: A Select Edition of His Writings* (Chapel Hill: University of North Carolina Press, 1988),

69; Helen C. Rountree, *Pocahontas's People: The Powhatan Indians of Virginia through Four Centuries* (Norman: University of Oklahoma Press, 1990), 38 (Smith's life saved three times); Frederic W. Gleach, *Powhatan's World and Colonial Virginia: A Conflict of Cultures* (Lincoln: University of Nebraska Press, 1997); ch. 4; Van Zandt, *Brothers among Nations*, ch. 3.

6. *EAID*, 19: 26.

7. Colin G. Calloway, ed., *The World Turned Upside Down: Indian Voices from Early America* (Boston: Bedford Books, 1994), 79–83, 91–94; Jenny Hale Pulsipher, *Subjects unto the Same King: Indians, English, and the Contest for Authority in Colonial New England* (Philadelphia: University of Pennsylvania Press, 2005).

8. Richard White, *The Middle Ground: Indians, Empires, and Republics in the Great Lakes Region, 1650–1815* (Cambridge: Cambridge University Press, 1991).

9. Dorothy V. Jones, "British Colonial Treaties," in *Handbook of North American Indians*, ed. William C. Sturtevant, Vol. 4: *History of Indian-White Relations*, ed. Wilcomb E. Washburn (Washington, D.C.: Smithsonian Institution, 1988), 185–86; Timothy J. Shannon, *Iroquois Diplomacy on the Early American Frontier* (New York: Penguin, 2008), ch. 3; DuVal, *Native Ground*; Michael M. Pomedi, "Eighteenth-Century Treaties: Amended Iroquois Condolence Rituals," *American Indian Quarterly* 19 (Summer 1995), 3129–39; Colin G. Calloway, *New Worlds for All: Indians, Europeans, and the Remaking of Early America* (Baltimore: Johns Hopkins University Press, 1997), 115–33.

10. Wilbur R. Jacobs, ed., *The Appalachian Indian Frontier: The Edmond Atkin Report and Plan of 1755* (Lincoln: University of Nebraska Press, 1967), 38; *WJP*, 5: 39 (Croghan quote).

11. Lawrence C. Wroth, "The Indian Treaty as Literature," *Yale Review* 17 (1928), 752.

12. Francis Jennings, William N. Fenton et al., eds., *The History and Culture of Iroquois Diplomacy: An Interdisciplinary Guide to the Treaties of the Six Nations and Their League* (Syracuse, N.Y.: Syracuse University Press, 1985), xv.

13. *EAID*, 2: 244; 3: 204.

14. Donald L. Fixico, ed., *Treaties with American Indians: An Encyclopedia of Rights, Conflicts, and Sovereignty*. 3 vols. (Santa Barbara, Calif.: ABC-CLIO, 2008) 1: xxi; Vine Deloria, Jr., and Raymond J. DeMallie, eds., *Documents of American Indian Diplomacy: Treaties, Agreements, and Conventions, 1775–1979*, 2 vols. (Norman: University of Oklahoma Press, 1999), 1: 103, 106–8; Peter Silver, "Indians Abroad," *William and Mary Quarterly* 67 (January 2010), 153 ("crude theater").

15. *EAID*, 13: 163.

16. *EAID*, 18: 58–59.

17. Jennings, *History and Culture of Iroquois Diplomacy*, 18–21; Williams, *Linking Arms Together*, 54–61.

18. Jones, *License for Empire*, 30; Pomedi, "Eighteenth-Century Treaties."

19. *EAID*, 14: 81.

20. *WJP*, 2: 442–43.

21. Williams, *Linking Arms Together*, 32–37, 62, 71, 81–82, 100–102 (quote).

22. Deloria and DeMallie, *Documents of American Indian Diplomacy*, 1: 7.

23. Raymond J. DeMallie, "Touching the Pen: Plains Indian Treaty Councils in Ethnohistorical Perspective," in *Ethnicity on the Great Plains* ed. Frederick C. Luebke (Lincoln: University of Nebraska Press, 1980), 39–40, 42; Williams, *Linking Arms Together*.

24. Cadwallader Colden, *The History of the Five Indian Nations Depending on the Province of New-York in America* (Part 1 and 2, 1727 and 1747; Ithaca, N.Y.: Cornell University Press, 1964), xx.

25. Milo Milton Quaife, ed., *John Long's Voyages and Travels in the Years 1768–1788* (Chicago: R. R. Donnelley and Sons, 1922), 40.

26. Samuel Cole Williams, ed., *Adair's History of the American Indians* (Johnston City, Tenn., 1930), 460.

27. William N. Fenton, *The Great Law and the Longhouse: A Political History of the Iroquois Confederacy* (Norman: University of Oklahoma Press, 1998), 7; Nancy Shoemaker, *A Strange Likeness: Becoming Red and White in Eighteenth-Century North America* (New York: Oxford University Press, 2004), 65; Cary Miller, *Ogimaag: Anishinaabeg Leadership, 1760–1845* (Lincoln: University of Nebraska Press, 2010), quote at 74.

28. Quaker quoted in Henry Harvey, *History of the Shawnee Indians, from the Year 1681 to 1854* (Cincinnati: Ephraim Morgan and Sons, 1855), 51–52; and Gunlög Fur, *A Nation of Women: Gender and Colonial Encounters among the Delaware Indians* (Philadelphia: University of Pennsylvania Press, 2009), 40.

29. For example, *EAID*, 6: 221, 228–230; 19: 342, 344–47, 373; Calloway, *World Turned Upside Down*, 85–86.

30. Julianna Barr, *Peace Came in the Form of a Woman: Indians and Spaniards in the Texas Borderlands* (Chapel Hill: University of North Carolina Press, 2007).

31. Greg O'Brien, "The Conqueror Meets the Unconquered: Negotiating Cultural Boundaries, on the Post-Revolutionary Southern Frontier," *Journal of Southern History* 67 (February 2001), 59.

32. Michelle LeMaster, *Brothers Born of One Mother: Gender and Family in British-Native American Relations in the Colonial Southeast* (Charlottesville: University of Virginia Press, 2012), ch. 5.

33. Loretta Fowler, *Wives and Husbands: Gender and Age in Southern Arapaho History* (Norman: University of Oklahoma Press, 2010), 68.

34. Fur, *A Nation of Women;* Nancy Shoemaker, "An Alliance between Men: Gender Metaphors in Eighteenth-Century American Indian Diplomacy East of the Mississippi," *Ethnohistory* 46 (Spring 1999), 239–63.

35. James Axtell, ed., *The Indian Peoples of Eastern America: A Documentary History of the Sexes* (New York: Oxford University Press, 1981), 154–57; *EAID*, 10: 236 (Mohawk women's request).

36. *WJP*, 3: 707–8; *EAID*, 10: 387.

37. Reuben G. Thwaites, ed., *The Jesuit Relations and Allied Documents*, 71 vols. (Cleveland: Burrows Brothers, 1896–1901), 21: 46–47.

38. Wilbur R. Jacobs, *Wilderness Politics and Indian Gifts: The Northern Colonial Frontier, 1748–1763* (1950; reprint: Lincoln: University of Nebraska Press, 1966); Joseph M. Hall, Jr., *Zamuno's Gifts: Indian-European Exchange in the Colonial Southeast* (Philadelphia: University of Pennsylvania Press, 2009); Cary Miller, "Gifts as Treaties: The Political Use of Received Gifts in Anishinaabeg Communities, 1820–1832," *American Indian Quarterly* 26 (Spring 2002), 221–45.

39. *EAID*, 19: 36–37; Pulsipher, *Subjects unto the Same King*, 20. Canonicus's gift may have had subtler spiritual meanings that were lost on the colonists; R. Todd Romero, *Making War and Minting Christians: Masculinity, Religion, and Colonialism in Early New England* (Amherst: University of Massachusetts Press, 2011), 141–49.

40. "The Treaty of Logg's Town, 1752," *Virginia Magazine of History and Biography* 13 (October 1905), 153.

41. Alfred Barnaby Thomas, *The Plains Indians and New Mexico, 1751–1778* (Albuquerque: University of New Mexico Press, 1940), 134–35, 151.

42. *DRCHNY*, 7: 186.

43. Timothy J. Shannon, "War, Diplomacy, and Culture: The Iroquois Experience in the Seven Years' War," in *Cultures in Conflict: The Seven Years' War in North America*, ed. Warren R. Hofstra (Lanham, Md.: Rowman and Littlefield, 2007), 93–95.

44. *EAID*, 2: 164, 399–400.

45. *DRCHNY*, 10: 563.

46. *EAID*, 3: 458–60; 10: 345–46.

47. F. Kent Reilly III, "Displaying the Source of the Sacred: Shell Gorgets, Peace Medals, and the Accessing of Supernatural Power," in *Peace Medals: Negotiating Power in Early America*, ed. Robert B. Pickering et al. (Tulsa, Okla.: Gilcrease Museum, 2011), 9–17; Richard White, *The Roots of Dependency: Subsistence, Environment, and Social Change among the Choctaws, Pawnees, and Navajos* (Lincoln: University of Nebraska Press, 1983), chs. 3–4; John C. Ewers, "Symbols of Chiefly Authority in Spanish Louisiana," in *The Spanish in the Mississippi Valley, 1762–1804*, ed. John Francis McDermott (Urbana: University of Illinois Press, 1974), 272–84; Greg O'Brien, *Choctaws in a Revolutionary Age, 1750–1830* (Lincoln: University of Nebraska Press, 2002), 72, 79; Charles A. Weeks, *Paths to a Middle Ground: The Diplomacy of Natchez, Boukfouka, Nogales, and San Fernando de las Barrancas, 1791–1795* (Tuscaloosa: University of Alabama Press, 2005), 27–28, 35–36; "Superintendent Stuart's 1765 Roster of Leading Choctaw Chiefs," *EAID*, 12: 278–79.

48. Alfred Barnaby Thomas, ed., *Forgotten Frontiers: A Study of the Spanish Indian Policy of Don Juan Bautista de Anza, Governor of New Mexico* (Norman: University of Oklahoma Press, 1932), 320.

49. Jacobs, *Wilderness Politics and Indian Gifts*, 180–85; White, *Middle Ground*, 256–68; Eric Hinderaker, *Elusive Empires: Constructing Colonialism in the Ohio Valley, 1673–1800* (Cambridge: Cambridge University Press, 1997), 147–49; *WJP*, 3: 185–86, 345, 530–31, 733; 10: 649 (Amherst quote), 652, 657.

50. Thwaites, *Jesuit Relations*, 3: 225; 6: 243.

51. William M. Clements, *Oratory in North America* (Tucson: University of Arizona Press, 2002), 84.

52. Thwaites, *Jesuit Relations*, 10: 219.

53. "Glossary of Figures of Speech in Iroquois Political Rhetoric," in Jennings, *History and Culture of Iroquois Diplomacy*, 115–24; "Extract from my Journal of the 1st May 1774 Containing Indian Transactions &c" (August 4, 1774, p. 52), New York Public Library, Chalmers Collection: Papers Relating to Indians 1750–75 ("bad Birds"); *EAID*, 3: 114 ("Teeth outwards"); James H. Merrell, ed., *The Lancaster Treaty of 1744 with Related Documents* (Boston: Bedford/St. Martin's, 2008), 70; and Susan Kalter, ed., *Benjamin Franklin, Pennsylvania, and the First Nations: The Treaties of 1736–62* (Urbana: University of Illinois Press, 2006), 106 (two penises).

54. Heidi Kiiwetinepinesiik Stark, "Marked by Fire: Anishinaabe Articulations of Nationhood in Treaty Making with the United States and Canada," *American Indian Quarterly* 36 (Spring 2012), 122; Williams, *Linking Arms Together*, ch. 4, quote at 92.

55. Clements, *Oratory in North America*, 107–8; Thwaites, *Jesuit Relations,* 27: 259.

56. William A. Starna, "The Diplomatic Career of Canasatego," in *Friends and Enemies in Penn's Woods: Indians, Colonists, and the Racial Construction of Pennsylvania*, ed. William A. Pencak and Daniel K. Richter (University Park: Pennsylvania State University Press, 2004), 344–63; Merrell, *The Lancaster Treaty of 1744*, 1, 4, 84–86; Kalter, *Benjamin Franklin, Pennsylvania, and the Six Nations*, 117–19. The longer version of Canasatego's speech to the Virginians is in Leonard W. Labaree, ed., *The Papers of Benjamin Franklin*, 39 vols. (New Haven: Yale University Press, 1959–), 4: 483.

57. Wroth, "The Indian Treaty as Literature," 753.

58. Shannon, *Iroquois Diplomacy on the Early American Frontier*, 93; DeMallie, "Touching the Pen."

59. Samuel Alexander Harrison, *Memoir of Lieutenant Colonel Tench Tilghman: Secretary and Aid to Washington* (1876; reprint, New York: Arno Press, 1971), 94.

60. Jones, *License for Empire*, 35.

61. Jennings, *History and Culture of Iroquois Diplomacy*, 38 ("no member").

62. *DRCHNY*, 6: 781–88, 853–92; *EAID*, 10: 14–57. "Journal of the Proceedings of the Congress held at Albany, in 1754," *Collections of the Massachusetts Historical Society*, 3rd ser., 5 (1836), 5–100, esp. 20; Timothy J. Shannon, *Indians and Colonists at the Crossroads of Empire: The Albany Congress of 1754* (Ithaca, N.Y.: Cornell University Press, 2000).

63. Shannon, *Iroquois Diplomacy on the Early American Frontier*, 23.

64. White, *Middle Ground*, ch. 2; Patricia Galloway, "'The Chief Who Is Your Father': Choctaw and French Views of the Diplomatic Relation," in *Powhatan's Mantle: Indians in the Colonial Southeast*, ed. Peter H. Wood, Gregory A. Waselkov, and M. Thomas Hatley (Lincoln: University of Nebraska Press, 1989), 254–78; Williams, *Linking Arms Together*, 71–74.

65. Hendrick Aupaumut, "A Narrative of an Embassy to the Western Indians," *Memoirs of the Historical Society of Pennsylvania* 2, part 1 (1827), 76–77; Carl F. Klinck and James J. Talman, eds., *The Journal of John Norton, 1816* (Toronto: Champlain Society, 1970), 84–85.

66. Jennings, *History and Culture of Iroquois Diplomacy*, 235, 246–47.

67. William Fenton, ed., "Answers to Governor Cass's Questions by Jacob Jemison, a Seneca [ca. 1821–1825]," *Ethnohistory* 16 (Spring 1969), 122; *EAID*, 3: 553 (Teedyuscung); John Heckewelder, *History, Manners, and Customs of the Indian Nations Who Once Inhabited Pennsylvania and the Neighboring States* (1876; reprint, New York: Arno Press and the New York Times, 1971), 180–84.

68. Andrew Burnaby, *Travels through the Middle Settlements in North America in the Years 1759 and 1760 with Observations upon the State of the Colonies* (New York: Augustus M. Kelley, 1970), 112.

69. *EAID*, 17: 499–500.

70. More than 150 wampum belts are reproduced in *Iroquois Indians: A Documentary History of the Diplomacy of the Six Nations and Their League*, 50 reels (Woodbridge, Conn.: Research Publications, 1984).

71. James H. Merrell, *Into the American Woods: Negotiators on the Pennsylvania Frontier* (New York: W. W. Norton, 1999), 187.

72. Lawrence H. Leder, ed., *The Livingston Indian Records, 1666–1723* (Gettysburg: Pennsylvania Historical Association, 1956), 201.

73. *EAID*, 20: 745 (Shirley); *WJP*, 9: 604 (Mohawk).

74. Jennings, *History and Culture of Iroquois Diplomacy*, xv; Jennings, *The Invasion of America: Indians, Colonialism, and the Cant of Conquest* (New York: W. W. Norton, 1975), 121.

75. *EAID*, 9: 51.

76. "The Treaty of Logg's Town, 1752," 156, 162.

77. Jane T. Merritt, "Metaphor, Meaning, and Misunderstanding: Language and Power on the Pennsylvania Frontier," in *Contact Points: American Frontiers from the Mohawk Valley to the Mississippi, 1750–1830*, ed. Andrew R. L. Cayton and Frederika J. Teute (Chapel Hill: University of North Carolina Press, 1998), incident quoted at 72; David Murray, *Forked Tongues: Speech, Writing and Representation in North American Indian Texts* (Bloomington: Indiana University Press, 1991), 25.

78. Heckewelder, *History, Manners, and Customs*, 108.

79. Fenton, "Iroquois Treaty Making," 17; Jennings, *History and Culture of Iroquois Diplomacy*, 88–90, 99–114.

80. Alain Beaulieu and Roland Viau, *The Great Peace: Chronicle of a Diplomatic Saga* (Ottawa: Canadian Museum of Civilization, 2001), 37.

81. Jasper Danckaerts, "Journal of a Voyage to New York and a Tour in Several of the American Colonies in 1679–1680," in *In Mohawk Country: Early Narratives about a Native People*, ed. Dean R. Snow, Charles T. Gehring, and William A. Starna (Syracuse, N.Y.: Syracuse University Press, 1996), 210–11.

82. *A Journey from Pennsylvania to Onondaga in 1743 by John Bartram, Lewis Evans, and Conrad Weiser* (Barre, Mass.: Imprint Society, 1973), 75–77, 116–31; *EAID*, 2: 65–72; cf. Jennings, *History and Culture of Iroquois Diplomacy*, 28–30.

83. *DRCHNY*, 10: 556.

84. Heckewelder, *History, Manners, and Customs*, 107–8.

85. Heckewelder, *History, Manners, and Customs*, 109.

86. *NASPIA*, 6: 49, 62.

87. John T. Juricek, *Colonial Georgia and the Creeks: Anglo-Indian Diplomacy on the Southern Frontier, 1733–1763* (Gainesville: University Press of Florida, 2010), 6; Williams, *Adair's History of the American Indians*, 63.

88. *EAID*, 13: 139.

89. *EAID*, 14: 92.

90. *EAID*, 18: 213–14. Some belts were more than two yards long, wrote US Indian agent Thomas Forsyth: "if for peace or friendship the Belts are composed solely of white grained wampum, if for war, they are made of the blue grained wampum painted red with vermillion, the greater the size of the Belt, the more force of expression is meant by it to convey." Emma Helen Blair, ed., *The Indian Tribes of the Upper Mississippi Valley and Region of the Great Lakes*, 2 vols. (1911–12; reprint, Lincoln: University of Nebraska Press, 1996), 2: 185, 188, 238–39.

91. *WJP*, 10: 845–46; *EAID*, 10: 412; Shannon, *Indians and Colonists at the Crossroads of Empire*, 4–6.

92. Fenton, "Answers to Governor Cass's Questions," 122.

93. Leder, *Livingston Indian Records*, 46, 91.

94. *DRCHNY*, 3: 780 ("venomous and detestable"); 4: 561 (five belts kicked); 9: 578 (Frontenac); *EAID*, 3: 374–75.

95. *An Account of Conferences and Treaties made Between Major-general Sir William Johnson, Bart. And The Chief Sachems and Warriours of the... Indian Nations in North America... in the Years 1755 and 1756* (London, 1756), 27.

96. Quaife, *John Long's Voyages and Travels*, 62–63.

97. Thwaites, *Jesuit Relations*, 58: 97–99; 59: 129–31.

98. Colin G. Calloway, *One Vast Winter Count: The Native American West before Lewis and Clark* (Lincoln: University of Nebraska Press, 2003), 237–38; White, *Middle Ground*, 20–23; Tanis C. Thorne, *The Many Hands of My Relations: French and Indians on the Lower Missouri* (Columbia: University of Missouri Press, 1996), ch. 1; Castle McLaughlin, "The Language of Pipes," in *Arts of Diplomacy: Lewis and Clark's Indian Collection*, ed. Castle McLaughlin (Cambridge, Mass.: Peabody Museum, Harvard; Seattle: University of Washington Press, 2003), 201–49.

99. Norman Gelb, ed., *Jonathan Carver's Travels through America, 1766–1768* (New York: John Wiley and Sons, 1993), 175.

100. *EAID*, 9: 137.

101. *EAID*, 3: 351.

102. Williams, *Linking Arms Together*, 75–76; Miller, *Compact, Contract, Covenant*, 20, 286, 295.

103. Quaife, *John Long's Voyages and Travels*, 61–62.

104. George Sabo III, "Rituals of Encounter: Interpreting Native American Views of European Explorers," in *Cultural Encounters in the Early South*, ed. Jeanne Whayne (Fayetteville: University of Arkansas Press, 1995), 76–87.

105. Jacques Le Sueur, "History of the Calumet and of the Dance," *Contributions from the Museum of the American Indian, Heye Foundation* 12, no. 5 (1952), 1–22; Donald J. Blakeslee, "Origin and Spread of the Calumet Ceremony," *American Antiquity* 46 (1981), 759–68; William N. Fenton, *The Iroquois Eagle Dance: An Offshoot of the Calumet Dance* (Syracuse, N.Y.: Syracuse University Press, 1953).

106. Fenton, "Answers to Governor Cass's Questions," 122.

107. Wraxall, *Abridgment of the Indian Affairs*, 70 (Ottawa pipe); 193 (1735 meeting); *WJP*, 9: 376–77 (Onondaga pipe); Fenton, *Great Law and the Longhouse*, 404, 486.

108. Blair, *Indian Tribes of the Upper Mississippi Valley*, 1: 184–86.

109. *EAID*, 4: 266.

110. "The Treaty of Logg's Town, 1752," 154.

111. Weeks, *Paths to a Middle Ground*, 27.

112. *The Sacred Pipe: Black Elk's Account of the Seven Rites of the Oglala Sioux*, recorded and edited by Joseph Epes Brown (1953; reprint, Norman: University of Oklahoma Press, 1989), 115.

113. *EAID*, 2: 180.

114. William L. McDowell, Jr., ed., *Colonial Records of South Carolina: Documents Relating to Indian Affairs, 1750–1754* (Columbia: South Carolina Archives Dept., 1958), 164.

115. Merrell, *The Lancaster Treaty of 1744*, 66.

116. Quoted in Merrell, *Into the American Woods*, 216–17.

117. *EAID*, 1: 206.

118. Harrison, *Memoir of Lieutenant Colonel Tench Tilghman*, 99.

119. Shoemaker, *Strange Likeness*, 76–81.

120. Matt Cohen, *The Networked Wilderness: Communicating in Early New England* (Minneapolis: University of Minnesota Press, 2010).

121. *DRCHNY*, 5: 563, 566.

122. James Axtell, "The Power of Print in the Eastern Woodlands," in his *After Columbus: Essays in the Ethnohistory of Colonial North America* (New York: Oxford University Press,

1988), 86–99; Hilary E. Wyss, *Writing Indians: Literacy, Christianity, and Native Community in Early America* (Amherst: University of Massachusetts Press, 2000); Lisa Brooks, *The Common Pot: The Recovery of Native Space in the Northeast* (Minneapolis: University of Minnesota Press, 2008).

123. Merrell, *Lancaster Treaty of 1744*, 55.

124. Jennings, *History and Culture of Iroquois Diplomacy*, 87.

125. *WJP*, 6: 761–62. The treaty the Esopus Indians made with Governor Richard Nicolls in 1665 is in the Ulster County Archives in Kingston, New York, and is available as a publication of the Ulster County Clerk's Records Management Program.

126. For a close and insightful textual analysis, see James H. Merrell, "'I desire all that I have said… may be taken down aright': Revisiting Teedyuscung's 1756 Treaty Council Speeches," *William and Mary Quarterly* 58 (October 2006), 777–826.

127. Merrell, "'I desire all that I have said.'"

128. Charles Thomson, *An Enquiry into the Causes of the Alienation of the Delaware and Shawanese Indians from the British Interest, And into the Measures taken for recovering their Friendship* (London: Printed for J. Wilkie, 1759), 67.

129. Calloway, *World Turned Upside Down*, 92–94; *EAID*, 20: 316–18. Such misconstructions were not rare: David L. Ghere, "Mistranslations and Misinformation: Diplomacy on the Maine Frontier, 1725 to 1755," *American Indian Culture and Research Journal* 8, no. 4 (1984), 3–26.

130. Anthony F. C. Wallace, *King of the Delawares: Teedyuscung, 1700–1763* (1949; Syracuse, N.Y.: Syracuse University Press, 1990).

131. *EAID*, 1: 455–59.

132. *EAID*, 2: 24–25, 45–49; 3: 126 (rawboned), 149, 313; Kalter, *Benjamin Franklin, Pennsylvania, and the First Nations*, 206, 208–10, 213–14.

133. *WJP*, 3: 767.

134. Kalter, *Benjamin Franklin, Pennsylvania, and the First Nations*, 196; Merrell, "'I desire all that I have said,'" 803–4; Merrell, *Into the American Woods*, 219–20; *EAID*, 3: 255–56; Thomson, *An Enquiry into the Causes of the Alienation of the Delaware and Shawanese Indians*, 110–12.

135. "Extracts of the Treaty held at Easton July 1757," New York Public Library, Chalmers Collection: Papers Relating to Indians, 1750–75.

136. *WJP*, 7: 324.

137. *WJP*, 7: 852.

138. Juricek, *Colonial Georgia and the Creeks*, 5–6.

139. Eric Cheyfitz, *The Poetics of Imperialism: Translation and Colonization from the Tempest to Tarzan* (New York: Oxford University Press, 1991), 104.

140. Quoted in Calloway, *New Worlds for All*, 124.

141. Merrell, *Into the American Woods*, 211.

142. Patricia Galloway, "Talking with Indians: Interpreters and Diplomacy in French Louisiana," in *Race and Family in the Colonial South*, ed. Winthrop D. Jordan and Sheila L. Skemp (Jackson: University of Mississippi Press, 1987), 109–29.

143. Yasuhide Kawashima, "Forest Diplomats: The Role of Interpreters in Indian-White Relations on the Early American Frontier," *American Indian Quarterly* 13 (Winter 1990), 1–14; Nancy Lee Hagedorn, "'A Friend to Go Between Them': Interpreters among the Iroquois, 1664–1775," Ph.D. dissertation, College of William and Mary, 1995.

144. Wraxall, *Abridgment of the Indian Affairs*, 212.

145. Merrell, *Into the American Woods*, 33, 59, 66; Paul A. Wallace, *Conrad Weiser, 1696–1760: Friend of Colonist and Mohawk* (Philadelphia: University of Pennsylvania Press, 1945).

146. Merrell, *Lancaster Treaty of 1744*, 111.

147. *EAID*, 3: 565–66. Weiser, of course, was German, not English.

148. Daniel K. Richter, "Cultural Brokers and Intercultural Politics: New York-Iroquois Relations, 1664–1701," *Journal of American History* 75 (June 1988), 40–67, quote at 42.

149. "The Treaty of Logg's Town, 1752," 171–72.

150. W. W. Abbott and Dorothy Twohig, eds., *The Papers of George Washington, Colonial Series*, 10 vols. (Charlottesville: University Press of Virginia, 1983–), 1: 121, 124–25, 131, 146.

151. Jane T. Merritt, *At the Crossroads: Indians and Empires on a Mid-Atlantic Frontier, 1700–1763* (Chapel Hill: University of North Carolina Press, 2003), ch. 6.

152. James H. Merrell, "Shickellamy, 'A Person of Consequence,'" in *Northeastern Indian Lives, 1632–1816*, ed. Robert S. Grumet (Amherst: University of Massachusetts Press, 1996), 241.

153. Colden, *The History of the Five Indian Nations*, xi.

154. DeMallie, "Touching the Pen," 39.

155. Merrell, *Into the American Woods*, 296.

156. Colin G. Calloway, *The Indian History of an American Institution: Native Americans and Dartmouth* (Hanover, N.H.: University Press of New England, 2010), 58–61; Karim M. Tiro, "James Dean in Iroquoia," *New York History* 80 (1999), 397–422.

157. Kalter, *Benjamin Franklin, Pennsylvania, and the Six Nations*, 72; *EAID*, 2: 38.

158. Merrell, *Lancaster Treaty of 1744*, 53–54; Kalter, *Benjamin Franklin, Pennsylvania, and the Six Nations,* 94–96; Shannon, *Iroquois Diplomacy on the Early American Frontier*, 112–13.

159. Merrell, *Lancaster Treaty of 1744*, 30.

160. Andro Linklater, *Measuring America* (New York: Walker and Co., 2002), 42–43.

161. *Pennsylvania Archives*, ser. 4, 2: 704; Shannon, *Indians and Colonists at the Crossroads of Empire*, 166–68. On the life and identity of this Hendrick, see Eric Hinderaker, *The Two Hendricks: Unraveling a Mohawk Mystery* (Cambridge, Mass.: Harvard University Press, 2010).

162. Francis Jennings, *The Ambiguous Iroquois Empire: The Covenant Chain Confederation of Indian Tribes with English Colonies from Its Beginnings to the Lancaster Treaty of 1744* (New York: W. W. Norton, 1984).

163. Peter C. Mancall, *Deadly Medicine: Indians and Alcohol in Early America* (Ithaca, N.Y.: Cornell University Press, 1995).

164. *EAID*, 5: 182; 2: 32–33, 66–67.

165. *EAID*, 5: 187.

166. *EAID*, 2: 188; 5: 191–93.

167. Wraxall, *Abridgment of the Indian Affairs*, 161–62.

168. Merrell, *Lancaster Treaty of 1744*, 44, 114–16.

169. *EAID*, 3: 541–42.

170. *DRCHNY,* 6: 984; *EAID*, 10: 107.

171. Heidi Bohaker, "Reading Identities: Meaning and Metaphor in *Nindoodem* Pictographs," *Ethnohistory* 57 (Winter 2010), 11–33. On the distortion and omission of totems,

see Patricia Kennedy, "Treaty Texts: When Can We Trust the Written Word?" *Social Sciences and Humanities Aboriginal Research Exchange* 3, No. 1 (Spring/Summer 1995), 1–24.

172. Albers and Kay, "Sharing the Land: A Study in American Indian Territoriality."

173. *NASPIA*, 6: 48, 51; Angela Pulley Hudson, *Creek Paths and Federal Roads: Indians, Settlers, and Slaves and the Making of the American South* (Chapel Hill: University of North Carolina Press, 2010), ch. 2.

174. *WJP*, 10: 411. (Panis was a generic term for Indian slaves captured on the Plains and did not necessarily mean that this captive was a Pawnee.) Brett Rushforth, *Bonds of Alliance: Indigenous and Atlantic Slaveries in New France* (Chapel Hill: University of North Carolina Press, 2012), quote at 64.

175. Kalter, *Benjamin Franklin, Pennsylvania, and the First Nations*, 191–92 ("from the Teeth outwards"; Reuben G.Thwaites , ed., *Early Western Travels 1748–1765* (1904; reprinted Lewisburg, Pa: Wennawoods Publishing, 1998), 199 ("wanted brains"); William Smith, *An Historical Account of the Expedition against the Ohio Indians in the year 1764* (Philadelphia, 1766), 25–37.

176. *EAID*, 9: 10.

177. Juricek, *Colonial Georgia and the Creeks*, 7; *EAID*, 14: 7, 11–12 ("has not the consent").

Chapter 2

1. William J. Campbell, "Converging Interests: Johnson, Croghan, the Six Nations, and the 1768 Treaty of Fort Stanwix," *New York History* 89 (Spring 2008), 138; Campbell, *Speculators in Empire: Iroquoia and the 1768 Treaty of Fort Stanwix* (Norman: University of Oklahoma Press, 2012).

2. Timothy J. Shannon, *Iroquois Diplomacy on the Early American Frontier* (New York: Penguin, 2008).

3. Timothy J. Shannon, "Dressing for Success on the Mohawk Frontier: Hendrick, William Johnson, and the Indian Fashion," *William and Mary Quarterly* 53 (January 1996), 13–42.

4. *EAID*, 9: 595, 612; *DRCHNY*, 6: 739 (Clinton).

5. Gail D. Danvers, "Gendered Encounters: Warriors, Women, and William Johnson," *Journal of American Studies* 35, no. 2 (2001), 187–202; and Gail D. MacLeitch, *Imperial Entanglements: Iroquois Change and Persistence on the Frontiers of Empire* (Philadelphia: University of Pennsylvania Press, 2011), ch. 4; Lois M. Feister and Bonnie Pulis, "Molly Brant: Her Domestic and Political Roles in Eighteenth-Century New York," in *Northeastern Indian Lives, 1632–1816*, ed. Robert S. Grumet (Amherst: University of Massachusetts Press, 1996), 295–320, persuaded chiefs quote at 302; Samuel Alexander Harrison, *Memoir of Lieutenant Colonel Tench Tilghman: Secretary and Aid to Washington* (1876; reprint, New York: Arno Press, 1971), 83.

6. Feister and Pulis, "Molly Brant," 303.

7. *EAID*, 3: 573.

8. Milo Milton Quaife, ed., *John Long's Voyages and Travels in the Years 1768–1788* (Chicago: R. R. Donnelley and Sons, 1922), 112–13; other versions are in Thomas Perkins Abernethy, *Western Lands and the American Revolution* (New York: Russell and Russell, 1959), 16.

9. *WJP*, 1: 430.

10. *WJP*, 3: 269–75, quote at 271.

11. Alan Taylor, "The Collaborator," *New Republic* (September 11, 2006), 33–37.

12. Dorothy V. Jones, *License for Empire: Colonialism by Treaty in Early America* (Chicago: University of Chicago Press, 1982), 59.

13. *WJP*, 10: 360.

14. William N. Fenton, *The Great Law and the Longhouse: A Political History of the Iroquois Confederacy* (Norman: University of Oklahoma Press, 1998), 501, 510; *EAID*, 10: 90 ("raised up"), 703.

15. *WJP*, 10: 69.

16. McConnell, Michael N., *A Country Between: The Upper Ohio Valley and Its Peoples, 1724–1774* (Lincoln: University of Nebraska Press, 1992); Jon W. Parmenter, "The Iroquois and the Native American Struggle for the Ohio Valley," in *The Sixty Years' War for the Great Lakes, 1754–1814*, ed. David Curtis Skaggs and Larry L. Nelson (East Lansing: Michigan State University Press, 2001), 105–24.

17. *WJP*, 3: 457.

18. "The Fitch Papers: Correspondence and Documents during Thomas Fitch's Governorship of the Colony of Connecticut, 1754–1766," *Collections of the Connecticut Historical Society* 18 (1920): 224; *DRCHNY*, 7: 520–21.

19. Gregory Evans Dowd, *War under Heaven: Pontiac, the Indian Nations, and the British Empire* (Baltimore: Johns Hopkins University Press, 2002); David Dixon, *Never Come to Peace Again: Pontiac's Uprising and the Fate of the British Empire in North America* (Norman: University of Oklahoma Press, 2005); Richard Middleton, *Pontiac's War: Its Causes and Consequences* (New York: Routledge, 2007); William R. Nester, *Haughty Conquerors: Amherst and the Great Indian Uprising of 1763* (Westport, Conn.: Praeger, 2000), 50–52; Jon William Parmenter, "Pontiac's War: Forging New Links in the Anglo-Iroquois Covenant Chain, 1758–1766," *Ethnohistory* 44 (Autumn 1997), 617–54. On the Seneca role, see Anthony F. C. Wallace, *The Death and Rebirth of the Seneca* (New York: Vintage, 1969), 115–16.

20. "Journal of William Trent," in *Pen Pictures of Early Western Pennsylvania*, ed. John W. Harpster (Pittsburgh: University of Pittsburgh Press, 1938), 103–4; Elizabeth A. Fenn, "Biological Warfare in Eighteenth-Century North America: Beyond Jeffery Amherst," *Journal of American History* 86 (March 2000), 1552–80; Philip Ranlet, "The British, the Indians, and Smallpox: What Actually Happened at Fort Pitt in 1763?" *Pennsylvania History* 67 (Summer 2000), 427–41.

21. Peter Silver, *Our Savage Neighbors: How Indian War Transformed Early America* (New York: W. W. Norton, 2008); Kevin Kenny, *Peaceable Kingdom Lost: The Paxton Boys and the Destruction of William Penn's Holy Experiment* (New York: Oxford University Press, 2009).

22. Colin G. Calloway, *The Scratch of a Pen: 1763 and the Transformation of North America* (New York: Oxford University Press, 2006).

23. The proclamation was issued as a broadside and was also published in *The Gentleman's Magazine* in October 1763. It is reprinted in Adam Shortt and Arthur G. Doughty, eds., *Documents Relating to the Constitutional History of Canada, 1759–1791*, 2 vols. (Ottawa: Historical Documents Publication Board, 1918), 163–68, as well as in *WJP*, 10: 977–85.

24. *WJP*, 4: 330–31 ("At this Treaty"); John Borrows, "Wampum at Niagara: The Royal Proclamation, Canadian Legal History, and Self-Government," in *Aboriginal and Treaty Rights in Canada*, ed. Michael Asch (Vancouver: University of British Columbia Press, 1997), 155–72. The Niagara treaty is in *WJP*, 11: 278–324, and *EAID*, 10: 440–68.

25. J. R. Miller, *Compact, Contract, Covenant: Aboriginal Treaty-Making in Canada* (Toronto: University of Toronto Press, 2009), 66–70.

26. Daniel K. Richter, "Native Americans, the Plan of 1764, and a British Empire That Never Was," in *Cultures and Identities in Colonial British America*, ed. Robert Olwell and Alan Tully (Baltimore: Johns Hopkins University Press, 2006), 269–92. Indian complaints in Croghan to Franklin, October 2, 1767, in Howard H. Peckham, ed., *George Croghan's Journal of his Trip to Detroit in 1767 with his Correspondence Relating Thereto* (Ann Arbor: University of Michigan Press, 1939), 23.

27. Woody Holton, *Forced Founders: Indians, Debtors, Slaves, and the Making of the American Revolution in Virginia* (Chapel Hill: University of North Carolina Press, 1999), ch. 1, esp. 7–8, 29–31; Stuart Banner, *How the Indians Lost Their Land: Law and Power on the Frontier* (Cambridge, Mass.: Harvard University Press, 2005), 100–109; Abernethy, *Western Lands and the American Revolution*, ch. 2.

28. Jones, *License for Empire*, 3–4.

29. *DRCHNY*, 7: 572–81, quote at 578.

30. Jones, *License for Empire*, 76–78.

31. Peter Marshall, "Colonial Policy and Imperial Retrenchment: Indian Policy 1764–1768," *Journal of American Studies* 5 (1971), 1–17; Richter, "Native Americans."

32. James H. Merrell, *Into the American Woods: Negotiators on the Pennsylvania Frontier* (New York: W. W. Norton, 1999), 81, 295; Alan Taylor, *William Cooper's Town: Power and Persuasion on the Frontier of the Early American Republic* (New York: Knopf, 1995), 45; William J. Campbell, "An Adverse Patron: Land, Trade, and George Croghan," *Pennsylvania History* 76 (Spring 2009), 117–40.

33. Nicholas B. Wainwright, *George Croghan: Wilderness Diplomat* (Chapel Hill: University of North Carolina Press, 1959), 28 (1749 grant); Albert T. Volwiler, *George Croghan and the Westward Movement, 1741–1782* (Cleveland: Arthur H. Clark, 1926); Nancy Lee Hagedorn, "'A Friend to Go Between Them': Interpreters among the Iroquois, 1664–1775," Ph.D. dissertation, College of William and Mary, 1995, 226–27.

34. Wainwright, *George Croghan*, 189; *WJP*, 3: 987; 4: 63.

35. Wainwright, *George Croghan*, 4, 212.

36. For example, see *WJP*, 5: 386; 6: 312; 12: 68, 74, 423.

37. Volwiler, *George Croghan and the Westward Movement*, 246–47.

38. Campbell, "Converging Interests," 127–41, quote at 130.

39. Peter Marshall, "Lord Hillsborough, Samuel Wharton and the Ohio Grant, 1769–1775," *English Historical Review* 80 (1965), 717.

40. *WJP*, 4: 264–66 (tavern meeting), 270–71 (memorial), 399 (quote from Croghan letter); Abernethy, *Western Lands and the American Revolution*, 22–32; Jack M. Sosin, *Whitehall and the Wilderness: The Middle West in British Colonial Policy, 1760–1775* (Lincoln: University of Nebraska Press, 1961), 145–46.

41. James Thomas Flexner, *Mohawk Baronet: A Biography of Sir William Johnson* (1959; reprint, Syracuse, N.Y.: Syracuse University Press, 1989), 277.

42. Jones, *License for Empire*, 78–79.

43. Campbell, "Converging Interests," 132–33.

44. Jones, *License for Empire*, 79–83; *DRCHNY*, 7: 718–41 (Onondaga quote at 726), 750–58; "Journal of George Croghan at Pittsburgh," *EAID*, 3: 702–11. Samuel Wharton included the Onondaga's response in his *View of the title to Indiana, a tract of country on the*

river Ohio: containing Indian conferences at Johnson-Hall, in May, 1765; the deed of the Six Nations to the proprietors of Indiana; the minutes of the congress at Fort Stanwix, in October and November, 1768; the deed of the Indians, settling the boundary line between the English and Indians lands; and the opinion of counsel on the title of the proprietors of Indiana (Philadelphia? 1775), 4.

45. "Croghan's Journal, 1765," in *Early Western Journals, 1748–1765*, ed. Reuben G. Thwaites (Lewisburg, Pa.: Wennawoods, 1998), 139; *WJP*, 11: 836–38, 841, 853–55.

46. James H. Hutson, "Benjamin Franklin and the West," *Western Historical Quarterly* 4 (1973), 425–34; Sosin, *Whitehall and the Wilderness*, 146; Leonard W. Labaree, *The Papers of Benjamin Franklin*, 39 vols. (New Haven: Yale University Press, 1959–), 12: 398, 403–06; 13: 395–402.

47. Quoted in Sosin, *Whitehall and the Wilderness*, 147.

48. *WJP*, 12: 234–38.

49. Sosin, *Whitehall and the Wilderness*, 162; Labaree, *Papers of Benjamin Franklin*, 14: 257–60 (Wharton quote at 259), 266–71.

50. Labaree, *Papers of Benjamin Franklin*, 14: 324–26.

51. Peckham, *George Croghan's Journal of His Trip to Detroit in 1767*.

52. Julian P. Boyd, ed., *The Susquehannah Company Papers*, 11 vols. (Cornell University Press for the Wyoming Historical and Genealogical Society, 1962), 2: 175–300 ("did not understand" at 299); "The Fitch Papers," 224–27 (horrors of Indian war at 225), 229–334, "Thousand Families" at 230, 237–40; Anthony F. C. Wallace, *King of the Delawares: Teedyuscung, 1700–1763* (1949; reprint, Syracuse, N.Y.: Syracuse University Press, 1990), 258–61.

53. *WJP*, 12: 392.

54. *DRCHNY*, 7: 1004–5.

55. *WJP*, 6: 22–23.

56. *WJP*, 12: 385.

57. *DRCHNY*, 8: 2; *WJP*, 12: 405–6.

58. Marshall, "Colonial Protest and Imperial Retrenchment," quote at 17.

59. *DRCHNY*, 8: 2, 35–36.

60. *DRCHNY*, 8: 23; Jones, *License for Empire*, 88.

61. Alden T. Vaughan, *Transatlantic Encounters: American Indians in Britain, 1500–1776* (Cambridge: Cambridge University Press, 2006), 143.

62. *WJP*, 12: 21, 337–40, 360, 456–58; *DRCHNY*, 8: 38–53, quotes at 42–43; Theda Perdue, "Cherokee Relations with the Iroquois in the Eighteenth Century," in *The Iroquois and Their Neighbors in Indian North America, 1600–1800*, ed. Daniel K. Richter and James H. Merrell (Syracuse, N.Y.: Syracuse University Press, 1987), 135–49.

63. David L. Preston, *The Texture of Contact: European and Indian Settler Communities on the Frontiers of Iroquoia, 1667–1783* (Lincoln: University of Nebraska Press, 2009).

64. *DRCHNY*, 8: 40, 47.

65. *DRCHNY*, 7: 946–47.

66. *DRCHNY*, 8: 76 (for later trips, *WJP*, 8: 837–38).

67. "Letters of Colonel George Croghan," *Pennsylvania Magazine of History and Biography* 15 (1891), 429–30; *Minutes of Conferences held at Fort-Pitt in April and May 1768, under the direction of George Croghan* (Philadelphia: William Goddard, 1769), quotes at 12, 16; *EAID*, 3: 720–45, quotes at 732, 737.

68. "Journal of the Proceedings of the Congress held at Albany, in 1754," *Collections of the Massachusetts Historical Society*, 3rd ser. 5 (1836), 36.

69. *WJP*, 12: 529–42, 566–67, 572–78, quotes at 577–78. Georgianna C. Nammack, *Fraud, Politics, and the Dispossession of the Indians: The Iroquois Land Frontier in the Colonial Period* (Norman: University of Oklahoma Press, 1969), 53–69.

70. *WJP*, 12: 476–77, 564.

71. *WJP*, 12: 605–6, 608, 621, 627, 636.

72. Labaree, *Papers of Benjamin Franklin*, 15: 275.

73. *WJP*, 12: 617–19.

74. "Proceedings of Sir William Johnson with the Indians at Fort Stanwix to Settle a Boundary Line," in *DRCHNY*, 8:111–12; *WJP*, 12: 617–20.

75. Wainwright, *George Croghan*, 256; Volwiler, *George Croghan and the Westward Movement*, 222.

76. Volwiler, *George Croghan and the Westward Movement*, 268 (bounds of 2.5 million acres).

77. Daniel M. Friedenberg, *Life, Liberty, and the Pursuit of Land: The Plunder of Early America* (Buffalo, N.Y.: Prometheus Books, 1992), 114 (finger quote); *EAID*, 5: 321–22, 335–36; Fenton, *Great Law and the Longhouse*, 536, 539.

78. Shannon, *Indians and Colonists at the Crossroads of Empire*, 165–69.

79. Merrell, *Into the American Woods*, 82.

80. Hubertis Cummings, *Richard Peters: Provincial Secretary and Cleric, 1704–1776* (Philadelphia: University of Pennsylvania Press, 1944), 8–11.

81. Wainwright, *George Croghan*, 22–23.

82. James. H. Merrell, "'I desire all that I have said… may be taken down aright': Revisiting Teedyuscung's 1756 Treaty Council Speeches," *William and Mary Quarterly* 58 (October 2006), 806–12.

83. "Proceedings of Sir William Johnson with the Indians at Fort Stanwix," 112; *WJP*, 12: 628–29; Johnson to Henry Moore, November 24, 1768, New York Public Library, Philip Schuyler Mss., Indian Affairs Papers, reel 7, box 13. Johnson said 3,008 at the opening "and more came in afterwards." Wharton estimated 3,400 Indians attended; Labaree, *Papers of Benjamin Franklin*, 15: 275.

84. Quoted in MacLeitch, *Imperial Entanglements*, 227.

85. Francis Jennings, William N. Fenton et al., eds., *The History and Culture of Iroquois Diplomacy: An Interdisciplinary Guide to the Treaties of the Six Nations and Their League* (Syracuse, N.Y.: Syracuse University Press, 1985), 239, 241, 252–53; Fenton, *Great Law and the Longhouse*, 510, 524, 529, 542; *WJP*, 12: 18; Thomas S. Abler, "Kaieñãkwaahtoñ," *Dictionary of Canadian Biography* Online, vol. 4.

86. Randolph C. Downes, *Council Fires on the Upper Ohio* (1940; Pittsburgh: University of Pittsburgh Press, 1968), 143.

87. Tanaghirison's speech is in "The Treaty of Logg's Town, 1752," *Virginia Magazine of History and Biography* 13 (1905), 165; Peters's comment in *EAID*, 2: 303. Nancy Lee Hagedorn, "'A Friend to Go Between Them': Interpreters among the Iroquois, 1664–1775," Ph.D. dissertation, College of William and Mary, 1995, 16, 169–80; Hagedorn, "'Faithful, Knowing, and Prudent': Andrew Montour as Interpreter and Cultural Broker," in *Between Indian and White Worlds: The Cultural Broker*, ed. Margaret Connell Szasz (Norman: University of Oklahoma Press, 1994), 53–60; James H. Merrell, "'The Cast of His Countenance:' Reading Andrew

Montour," in *Through a Glass Darkly: Reflections on Personal Identity in Early America*, ed. Ronald Hoffman, Mechal Sobel, and Frederika J. Teute (Chapel Hill: University of North Carolina Press, 1997), 9–39.

88. Hagedorn, "A Friend to Go Between Them," 223; R. Arthur Bowler and Bruce G. Wilson, "John Butler," *Dictionary of Canadian Biography Online*, vol. 4.

89. Hagedorn, "A Friend to Go Between Them," 236.

90. *DRCHNY*, 8: 180; *WJP*, 6: 472–73.

91. William N. Fenton, "Structure, Continuity, and Change in the Process of Iroquois Treaty Making," in Jennings, *History and Culture of Iroquois Diplomacy*, 23, 27.

92. "Proceedings of Sir William Johnson with the Indians at Fort Stanwix," 114–15.

93. "Proceedings of Sir William Johnson with the Indians at Fort Stanwix," 115–17; Labaree, *Papers of Benjamin Franklin*, 15: 264.

94. Fenton, *Great Law and the Longhouse*, 543.

95. Fenton, *Great Law and the Longhouse*, 537.

96. "Proceedings of Sir William Johnson with the Indians at Fort Stanwix," 117–19; Labaree, *Papers of Benjamin Franklin*, 15: 276 (Wharton estimate).

97. "Proceedings of Sir William Johnson with the Indians at Fort Stanwix," 119.

98. "Proceedings of Sir William Johnson with the Indians at Fort Stanwix," 120.

99. "Proceedings of Sir William Johnson with the Indians at Fort Stanwix," 121.

100. "Proceedings of Sir William Johnson with the Indians at Fort Stanwix," 121–22.

101. "Proceedings of Sir William Johnson with the Indians at Fort Stanwix," 123–24.

102. Karim M. Tiro, *The People of the Standing Stone: The Oneida Nation from the Revolution through the Era of Removal* (Amherst: University of Massachusetts Press, 2011), 30; "Proceedings of Sir William Johnson with the Indians at Fort Stanwix," 124.

103. *WJP*, 12: 656–57.

104. "Proceedings of Sir William Johnson with the Indians at Fort Stanwix," 124–25; *WJP*, 12: 656–59.

105. "Proceedings of Sir William Johnson with the Indians at Fort Stanwix," 125–26.

106. "Proceedings of Sir William Johnson with the Indians at Fort Stanwix," 122; *WJP*, 6: 472, 492, 529–30; Johnson to Henry Moore, November 24, 1768, New York Public Library, Philip Schuyler Mss., Indian Affairs Papers, reel 7, box 13.

107. "Proceedings of Sir William Johnson with the Indians at Fort Stanwix," 127.

108. "Proceedings of Sir William Johnson with the Indians at Fort Stanwix," 128, 135.

109. "Proceedings of Sir William Johnson with the Indians at Fort Stanwix," 128; Campbell, "An Adverse Patron," 132 ("convenient" falling); Campbell, *Speculators in Empire*, 154–60 (excluding Lydius, 156).

110. "Proceedings of Sir William Johnson with the Indians at Fort Stanwix," 123.

111. "Proceedings of Sir William Johnson with the Indians at Fort Stanwix," 130–32.

112. Labaree, *Papers of Benjamin Franklin*, 15: 277; "Proceedings of Sir William Johnson with the Indians at Fort Stanwix," 134–35. A copy of the deed and the chiefs' marks is in Philip Schuyler Mss., Indian Papers, reel 7, box 13.

113. Jones, *License for Empire*, 107.

114. Shannon, *Iroquois Diplomacy on the Early American Frontier*, 168.

115. *WJP*, 6: 569; 12: 665–68.

116. Flexner, *Mohawk Baronet*, 330.

117. *WJP*, 6: 472.

118. *WJP*, 6: 517.

119. Labaree, *Papers of Benjamin Franklin*, 15: 278–79.

120. Fenton, *Great Law and the Longhouse*, 540.

121. Campbell, *Speculators in Empire*, 165.

122. *WJP*, 6: 513.

123. *WJP*, 12: 674; 6: 652.

124. *WJP*, 12: 709–10.

125. *WJP*, 12: 715.

126. Stuart's journal of the proceedings at Hard Labor is in *EAID*, 14: 272–81; the treaty is in *EAID*, 5: 326–30 and 14: 282–85.

127. *EAID*, 12: 66–71.

128. "Virginia and the Cherokees, &c: The Treaties of 1768 and 1770," *Virginia Magazine of History and Biography* 13 (1905), 20–36; K. G. Davies, ed., *Documents of the American Revolution 1770–1783* (Colonial Office Series), 20 vols. (Shannon: Irish University Press, 1972), 2: 261–62.

129. *EAID*, 5: 360–71 (Attakullakulla quote at 365); 14: 298–99, 304–5, 320–21; Louis De Vorsey, Jr., *The Indian Boundary in the Southern Colonies, 1763–1775* (Chapel Hill: University of North Carolina Press, 1961), 64–92. The Kentucky River was also called the Catawba River at the time and, according to some sources, the Louisa, although the Louisa and Kentucky rivers may have been deliberately conflated with the Kentucky during the running of the boundary; Clarence Walworth Alvord, *The Mississippi Valley in British Politics*, 2 vols. (Cleveland: Arthur H. Clark Co., 1917), 2: 84–89.

130. Labaree, *Papers of Benjamin Franklin*, 19: 3–4.

131. Matthew L. Rhoades, *Long Knives and the Longhouse: Anglo-Iroquois Politics and the Expansion of Colonial Virginia* (Madison, N.J.: Fairleigh Dickinson University Press, 2011), 15.

132. *DRCHNY*, 8: 145.

133. *DRCHNY*, 8: 158–63, quote at 160.

134. *WJP*, 7: 215–16.

135. Abernethy, *Western Lands and the American Revolution*, ch. 3; Sosin, *Whitehall and the Wilderness*, ch. 8; Alvord, *Mississippi Valley in British Politics*, 2: chs. 4–6 ("better connections" quote at 96); Marshall, "Lord Hillsborough, Samuel Wharton and the Ohio Grant, 1769–75," 717–39 ("unscrupulous" at 738, "casualties of war" at 737); James Donald Anderson, "Vandalia: The First West Virginia?" *West Virginia History* 40 (1979), 375–92; Hutson, "Benjamin Franklin and the West," 434 ("absolutely nothing"); Labaree, *Papers of Benjamin Franklin*, 16: 163–69; 17: 8–11.

136. *WJP*, 7: 78, 92, 221. For a full treatment of Croghan's wheeling and dealing, see Campbell, *Speculators in Empire*.

137. *WJP*, 7: 388.

138. *WJP*, 7: 653; Holton, *Forgotten Founders*, 23; Wainwright, *George Croghan*, 275–77.

139. Abernethy, *Western Lands and the American Revolution*, 69.

140. Jones, *License for Empire*, 4 and ch. 5.

141. Timothy J. Shannon, "War, Diplomacy, and Culture: The Iroquois Experience in the Seven Years' War," in *Cultures in Conflict: The Seven Years' War in North America*, ed. Warren R. Hofstra (Lanham, Md.: Rowman and Littlefield, 2007), 96.

142. Jones, *License for Empire*, 117–19.

143. Eric Hinderaker, *Elusive Empires: Constructing Colonialism in the Ohio Valley, 1673–1800* (Cambridge: Cambridge University Press, 1997), 170.

144. Holton, *Forced Founders*, 11–12; Samuel Wharton, *Plain facts: being an examination into the rights of the Indian nations of America, to their respective countries; and a vindication of the grant, from the Six United Nations of Indians, to the proprietors of Indiana, against the decision of the legislature of Virginia; together with authentic documents, proving that the territory, westward of the Allegany mountain, never belonged to Virginia, &c.* (Philadelphia: R. Aitken, 1781); Blake Watson, *Buying America from the Indians: Johnson v. McIntosh and the History of Native Land Rights* (Norman: University of Oklahoma Press, 2012), 28, 140–43.

145. Alvord, *The Mississippi Valley in British Politics*, 2: 113 (Croghan quote); *WJP*, 7: 185 (McKee quote).

146. *EAID*, 3: 754–55.

147. MacLeitch, *Imperial Entanglements*, 201; Francis W. Halsey, ed., *A Tour of the Hudson, the Mohawk, the Susquehanna, and the Delaware in 1769: Being the Journal of Richard Smith* (Port Washington, N.Y.: Ira J. Friedman, 1964; New York: Purple Mountain Press, 1989), 84.

148. *DRCHNY*, 8: 239.

149. *DRCHNY*, 8: 304–6; Davies, *Documents of the American Revolution*, 3: 155–56.

150. *WJP*, 7: 184, 316; Davies, *Documents of the American Revolution*, 2: 22.

151. *WJP*, 7: 406–8; Davies, *Documents of the American Revolution*, 1: 159, 315; 2: 22, 24, 28, 87, 105, 204, 253–54, 261–62; 3: 85, 174.

152. Jones, *License for Empire*, 100–103; Davies, *Documents of the American Revolution*, 2: 204.

153. Davies, *Documents of the American Revolution*, 3: 43.

154. Davies, *Documents of the American Revolution*, 3: 135; *DRCHNY*, 8: 302.

155. Wilbur R. Jacobs, *Dispossessing the American Indian* (New York: Scribners, 1972), 100.

156. Stephen Aron, *How the West Was Lost: The Transformation of Kentucky from Daniel Boone to Henry Clay* (Baltimore: Johns Hopkins University Press, 1996), 18–19; John Mack Faragher, *Daniel Boone: The Life and Legend of an American Pioneer* (New York: Henry Holt, 1992), 76–81, 89–97.

157. Aron, *How the West Was Lost*, ch. 1; Stephen Aron, "Pigs and Hunters: 'Rights in the woods' on the Trans-Appalachian Frontier," in *Contact Points: American Frontiers from the Mohawk Valley to the Mississippi, 1750–1830*, ed. Andrew R. L. Clayton and Frederika J. Teute (Chapel Hill: University of North Carolina Press, 1998), 175–204; Colin G. Calloway, *The Shawnees and the War for America* (New York: Penguin, 2007), 49–51; "crazy people" quote in John Sugden, *Blue Jacket: Warrior of the Shawnees* (Lincoln: University of Nebraska Press, 2000), 46.

158. Letter from Oconostota, April 26, 1772, New York Public Library, Chalmers Collection: Papers Relating to Indians, 1750–75.

159. "Letters of Colonel George Croghan," 434–37.

160. *DRCHNY*, 8: 396.

161. *WJP*, 12: 1038–39; *DRCHNY*, 8: 462.

162. *WJP*, 12: 1045.

163. Davies, *Documents of the American Revolution*, 2: 38 (cut throats); Jack M. Sosin, "The British Indian Department and Dunmore's War," *Virginia Magazine of History and*

Biography 74 (1966), 34–50. The bulk of the papers in Chalmers Collection: Papers Relating to Indian Affairs, 1750–75, New York Public Library, deal with the diplomatic maneuverings leading up to Dunmore's War.

164. Patrick Griffin, *American Leviathan: Empire, Nation, and Revolutionary Frontier* (New York: Hill and Wang, 2007), 91.

165. Fintan O'Toole, *White Savage: William Johnson and the Invention of America* (New York: Farrar, Straus, and Giroux, 2005), 325.

166. *DRCHNY*, 8: 460–61.

167. *DRCHNY*, 8: 474–79 (Serihowane quote at 476).

168. *DRCHNY*, 8: 480–82.

169. Fenton, *Great Law and the Longhouse*, 573–77.

170. *DRCHNY*, 8: 521.

171. Holton, *Forced Founders*, 28–31.

172. Reuben Gold Thwaites and Louise Phelps Kellogg, eds., *Documentary History of Dunmore's War, 1774* (Madison: Wisconsin Historical Society, 1905).

173. "Letters of George Croghan," 437–38.

174. Charles A. Stuart, ed., *Memoir of Indian Wars, and Other Occurrences, by the Late Colonel Stuart, of Greenbrier* (New York: New York Times and Arno Press, 1971), 46–48; Thwaites and Kellogg, *Documentary History of Dunmore's War*, 256, 259, 261–66, 275, 343, 346.

175. Jones, *License for Empire*, 107.

176. Robert L. Scribner et al., eds., *Revolutionary Virginia, The Road to Independence: A Documentary Record*, 7 vols. (Charlottesville: University Press of Virginia, 1973–83), 7: 770.

177. *EAID*, 18: 125–47, quotes at 145–47; Cornstalk's speech to Congress, November 7, 1776, in "Letter Book of George Morgan 1776," Pennsylvania Historical Commission, Harrisburg, Pa.; reproduced in *Iroquois Indians: A Documentary History*, reel 32.

178. On Cornstalk's murder, see Stuart, *Memoir of Indian Wars*, 58–62; Draper Mss., State Historical Society of Wisconsin, microfilm, 3D164–73, 2YY91–94; Reuben G. Thwaites and Louise P. Kellogg, eds., *Frontier Defense on the Upper Ohio, 1777–1778* (Madison: Wisconsin State Historical Society, 1912), 126–27, 149, 157–63, 175–77, 188–89, 205–9, 258–61.

179. *EAID*, 18: 161–69.

180. Davies, *Documents of the American Revolution*, 3: 72; William L. Saunders and Walter Clark, eds., *The Colonial and State Records of North Carolina*, 30 vols. (Raleigh: Department of State, 1886–90), 10: 764.

181. Colin G. Calloway, "Declaring Independence and Rebuilding a Nation: Dragging Canoe and the Chickamauga Revolution," in *Revolutionary Founders: Rebels, Radicals, and Reformers in the Making of the Nation*, ed. Alfred F. Young, Gary B. Nash, and Ray Raphael (New York: Knopf, 2011), 185–98; Saunders and Clark, *Colonial and State Records of North Carolina*, 10: 660–61, 763–85; Davies, *Documents of the American Revolution*, 12: 191–208, esp. 202–3.

182. Fenton, *Great Law and the Longhouse*, 589–94.

183. Tiro, *People of the Standing Stone*, ch. 3; Joseph T. Glatthaar and James Kirby Martin, *Forgotten Allies: The Oneida Indians in the American Revolution* (New York: Hill and Wang, 2006); Walter Pilkington, ed., *The Journals of Samuel Kirkland* (Clinton, N.Y.: Hamilton College, 1980), 106–7.

184. Bowler and Wilson, "John Butler," *Dictionary of Canadian Biography Online*, vol. 4; Alan Taylor, *The Divided Ground: Indians, Settlers, and the Northern Borderland of the American Revolution* (New York: Knopf, 2006), 177–79; "Proceedings of a Ceremony of Condolence on the death of Lieut. Col. Butler," in *The Correspondence of Lieut. Governor John Graves Simcoe, with allied Documents Relating to His Administration of the Government of Upper Canada*, ed. E. A. Cruikshank, 5 vols. (Toronto: Ontario Historical Society, 1923–31), 4: 265–66.

185. Colin G. Calloway, *The American Revolution in Indian Country* (Cambridge: Cambridge University Press, 1995), ch. 5, quote at 132–33; Thomas S. Abler, ed., *Chainbreaker: The Revolutionary War Memoirs of Governor Blacksnake* (Lincoln: University of Nebraska Press, 1989), 69, 85, 90.

186. Caitlin A. Fritz, "'Suspected on both sides': Little Abraham, Iroquois Neutrality, and the American Revolution," *Journal of the Early Republic* 28 (2008), 299–335.

187. Cummings, *Richard Peters*, 328.

188. Volwiler, *George Croghan and the Westward Movement*, 323–36; Wainwright, *George Croghan*, 294–307.

189. Wainwright, *George Croghan*, 296.

190. Will and Codicil of Benjamin Franklin, July 17, 1788 (signed June 23, 1789), http://franklinpapers.org/franklin.

191. Colin G. Calloway, "Suspicion and Self-Interest: The British-Indian Alliance and the Peace of Paris," *The Historian* 49 (November 1985), 41–60; Colin G. Calloway, *Crown and Calumet: British-Indian Relations, 1783–1815* (Norman: University of Oklahoma Press, 1987), 5–13; National Archives, U.K., Colonial Office Records 5/82: 446–47 (Little Turkey); *EAID*, 18: 278–79.

Chapter 3

1. "Minutes of the Proceedings of the Commissioners for the Northern Department Commencing 29 April 1776," New York Public Library, Philip Schuyler Mss., Indian Affairs Papers, reel 7, box 13; *EAID*, 18: 5–38, 43–57, 66–76.

2. "Letter Book of George Morgan 1776," Pennsylvania Historical Commission, Harrisburg, Pa.; reproduced in *Iroquois Indians: A Documentary History of the Diplomacy of the Six Nations and Their League*, 50 reels (Woodbridge, Conn.: Research Publications, 1984), reel 32; Col. George Morgan Letter Books, I-II, Carnegie Library of Pittsburgh; Gregory Schaaf, *Wampum Belts and Peace Trees: George Morgan, Native Americans, and Revolutionary Diplomacy* (Golden, Colo.: Fulcrum, 1990).

3. Eliga H. Gould, *Among the Powers of the Earth: The American Revolution and the Making of a New World Empire* (Cambridge, Mass.: Harvard University Press, 2012); Leonard J. Sadosky, *Revolutionary Negotiations: Indians, Empires, and Diplomats in the Founding of America* (Charlottesville: University of Virginia Press, 2009).

4. Col. George Morgan Letter Books, III: 92–102, 106, 150–52, 164, 175; *EAID*, 18: 167–69, 173–74.

5. *EAID*, 18: xxv.

6. *NASPIA*, 6: 27.

7. Dorothy V. Jones, *License for Empire: Colonialism by Treaty in Early America* (Chicago: University of Chicago Press, 1982), 150–51, 155.

8. *EAID*, 18: 460; *NASPIA*, 6: 65.

9. Herman J. Viola, *Diplomats in Buckskins: A History of Indian Delegations in Washington City* (Washington, D.C.: Smithsonian Institution Press, 1981).

10. Robert B. Pickering et al., *Peace Medals: Negotiating Power in Early America* (Tulsa, Okla.: Gilcrease Museum, 2011); Francis Paul Prucha, *Indian Peace Medals in American History* (Madison: State Historical Society of Wisconsin, 1971); McKenney quoted in Viola, *Diplomats in Buckskins,* 104.

11. Carolyn Eastman, "The Indian Censures the White Man: 'Indian Eloquence' and Early American Reading Audiences in the Early Republic," *William and Mary Quarterly* 65 (July 2008), 535–64.

12. *NASPIA*, 6: 65.

13. *EAID*, 18: 299–301.

14. Items dated July 2, 1783, and January 11, 1784, "Second Report on Indian Affairs and Western Country," all in New York Public Library, Philip Schulyer Mss., Indian Affairs Papers, reel 7, box 14; *EAID*, 18: 290–91.

15. *EAID*, 18: 278–79.

16. "Proceedings of the United States and the Six Nations at Fort Stanwix" and "Treaty of Fort Stanwix," in *EAID*, 18: 313–27; Henry S. Manly, *The Treaty of Fort Stanwix, 1784* (Rome, N.Y.: Rome Sentinel Co., 1932); Sadosky, *Revolutionary Negotiations*, 127–40.

17. *ASPIA*, 1: 140, 143; *NASPIA*, 4: 25, 27.

18. *EAID*, 18: 332–38, quote at 335.

19. Franklin B. Hough, ed., *Proceedings of the Commissioners of Indian Affairs, Appointed by Law for the Extinguishment of Indian Titles in the State of New York*, 2 vols. (Albany, N.Y.: Munsell, 1861), 1: 214 (Beech Tree quote); Anthony Wonderley, "Good Peter's Narrative of Several Transactions Respecting Indian Lands: An Oneida View of Dispossession, 1785–1788," *New York History* 84 (2003), 237–73, quote on 261.

20. Hough, *Proceedings of the Commissioners of Indian Affairs*, 2: 274, 279, 299–300.

21. Quoted in Karim M. Tiro, *The People of the Standing Stone: The Oneida Nation from the Revolution through the Era of Removal* (Amherst: University of Massachusetts Press, 2011), 85; and David J. Silverman, *Red Brethren: The Brothertown and Stockbridge Indians and the Problem of Race in Early America* (Ithaca, N.Y.: Cornell University Press, 2010), 140.

22. *EAID*, 18: 328–31 ("high tone" at 329); "Treaty with the Western Indians, Dec. 3, 1784," Massachusetts Historical Society, Timothy Pickering Papers, 59: 119–26 ("give not to receive" at 122–23).

23. *EAID*, 18: 340–41; *Military Journal of Ebenezer Denny: An Officer in the Revolutionary and Indian Wars* (Philadelphia: J. B. Lippincott, 1850), 69–70.

24. *EAID*, 18: 158–59.

25. *EAID*, 18: 346–47, 593n.75; *Military Journal of Ebenezer Denny*, 73, 75; *Minutes of Debates in Council on the banks of the Ottawa River, November 1791 Said to be held there by the Chiefs of the several Indian Nations, who defeated the Army of the United States, on the 4th of that Month* (Philadelphia: William Young, 1792), 10.

26. *NASPIA*, 6: 48–49, 51–53.

27. *EAID*, 18: 444.

28. *NASPIA*, 6: 60; Greg O'Brien, "The Conqueror Meets the Unconquered: Negotiating Cultural Boundaries on the Post-Revolutionary Southern Frontier," *Journal of Southern History* 67 (February 2001), 39–72.

29. *NASPIA*, 4: 17–18.

30. Reginald Horsman, *Expansion and American Indian Policy, 1783–1812* (1967; Norman: University of Oklahoma Press, 1992), 30–49; *ASPIA*, 1: 9–10 (quotations); *EAID*, 18: 438–39, 481–97; *Military Journal of Major Ebenezer Denny*, 127–30.

31. *Minutes of Debates in Council on the banks of the Ottawa River,* 8–11, 14.

32. Robert M. Kvasnicka, "United States Indian Treaties and Agreements," in *Handbook of North American Indians*, ed. William C. Sturtevant, Vol. 4: *History of Indian-White Relations*, ed. Wilcomb E. Washburn (Washington, D.C.: Smithsonian Institution, 1988), 195–201.

33. Hough, *Proceedings of the Commissioners of Indian Affairs*, Washington quote at 1: 166.

34. David Andrew Nichols, *Red Gentlemen and White Savages: Indians, Federalists, and the Search for Order on the American Frontier* (Charlottesville: University of Virginia Press, 2008).

35. *IALT*, 25–29.

36. *NASPIA*, 6: 139; 7, passim.

37. *ASPIA* 1: 203–6; Carole Goldberg, "Federal Policy and Treaty Making: A Federal View," in *Treaties with American Indians: An Encyclopedia of Rights, Conflicts, and Sovereignty*, ed. Donald L. Fixico, 3 vols. (Santa Barbara, Calif.: ABC-CLIO, 2008), 1: 13.

38. *ASPIA* 1: 205; 6: 105.

39. *NASPIA*, 6: 140.

40. "Indian Council at the Glaize, 1792," in *The Correspondence of Lieut. Governor John Graves Simcoe, with Allied Documents Relating to His Administration of the Government of Upper Canada*, ed. E. A. Cruikshank, 5 vols. (Toronto: Ontario Historical Society, 1923–31), 1: 218–29; Hendrick Aupaumut, "A Narrative of an Embassy to the Western Indians," *Memoirs of the Historical Society of Pennsylvania* 2, pt. 1 (1827), 118.

41. Colin G. Calloway, "Simon Girty: Interpreter and Intermediary," in *Being and Becoming Indian: Biographical Studies of North American Frontiers*, ed. James A. Clifton (Chicago: Dorsey Press, 1989), 38–58, quotes at 52; *NASPIA*, 4: 137; Benjamin Lincoln, "Journal of a Treaty Held in 1793, with the Indian Tribes North-West of the Ohio," *Collections of the Massachusetts Historical Society*, 3rd series, 5 (1836), 150.

42. Cruikshank, *Correspondence of Lieut. Governor John Graves Simcoe*, 2: 17–19 (Indian speech); *ASPIA*, 1: 352–54, 356–57 (Indian speech); *NASPIA* 4: 136 ("impossible"), 139–40; Lincoln, "Journal of a Treaty Held in 1793," 109–76 (Indian speech at 165–66).

43. Granville Ganter, ed., *The Collected Speeches of Sagoyewatha, or Red Jacket* (Syracuse, N.Y.: Syracuse University Press, 2006), 1–15, 22–32. The proceedings of the councils at Tioga in 1790 and Newtown Point in 1791 are in Timothy Pickering Papers, reel 60, 69–112 (Red Jacket's speeches at 92, 96, 105–6, 110), and reel 61, 55–100 (Red Jacket's speeches at 62, 71, 82–83, 93).

44. Jack Campisi and William A. Starna, "On the Road to Canandaigua: The Treaty of 1794," *American Indian Quarterly* 19 (Autumn 1995), 467–90; Ganter, *The Collected Speeches of Sagoyewatha, or Red Jacket*, 67 ("would not proceed"); "The Savery Journal: The Canandaigua Treaty Excerpt," in *Treaty of Canandaigua 1794: 200 Years of Treaty Relations between the Iroquois Confederacy and the United States*, ed. G. Peter Jemison and Anna M. Schein (Santa Fe, N.M.: Clear Light, 2000), 260–93 ("to no purpose" quote at 287); William N. Fenton, ed., "The Journal of James Emlen Kept on a Trip to Canandaigua, New York, September 15 to October 30, 1794, to Attend the Treaty between the United Sates and the Six

Nations," *Ethnohistory* 12 (Fall 1965), 279–342 ("made the Men" quote at 306; "masters of their time" quote at 333).

45. Timothy Pickering Papers, reel 60, 221–22, 225; Laurence M. Hauptman, *Conspiracy of Interests: Iroquois Dispossession and the Rise of New York State* (Syracuse, N.Y.: Syracuse University Press, 1999), 74 (Oneida land loss).

46. "The Savery Journal," 271, 287.

47. Timothy Pickering Papers, reel 60, 224–225.

48. Timothy Pickering Papers, reel 60, 207–8. The treaty is in *IALT*, 34–37.

49. *IALT*, 37–39; Hauptman, *Conspiracy of Interests*, 74, 80.

50. The minutes and terms of the treaty are in *NASPIA*, 4: 150–77 (quotes at 152–53).

51. Andrew R. L. Cayton, "'Noble Actors' upon 'the Theatre of Honour': Power and Civility in the Treaty of Greenville," in *Contact Points: American Frontiers from the Mohawk Valley to the Mississippi, 1750–1830*, ed. Andrew R. L. Cayton and Frederika J. Teute (Chapel Hill: University of North Carolina Press, 1998), 235–69. Barbara Mann takes a very different view of American behavior at Greenville. Wayne was rude, insulting, and inept in council protocol and the treaty itself was the culmination of almost half a century of fraudulent dealings in the Ohio county: see Barbara Alice Mann, "The Greenville Treaty of 1795: Pen-and-Ink Witchcraft in the Struggle for the Old Northwest," in *Enduring Legacies: Native American Treaties and Contemporary Controversies*, ed. Bruce E. Johansen (Westport, Conn.: Praeger, 2004), 135–201.

52. *NASPIA*, 4: 153, 174.

53. *IALT*, 39–45, signatories at 44.

54. Paul A. Hutton, "William Wells: Frontier Scout and Indian Agent," *Indiana Magazine of History* 74 (September 1978), 183–222.

55. Timothy Pickering Papers, reel 20, 254; John C. Fitzpatrick, ed., *The Writings of George Washington from the Original Manuscript Sources, 1745–1799*, 39 vols. (Washington, D.C.: Government Printing Office, 1931–44), 25: 112.

56. Laurence M. Hauptman, *The Tonawanda Senecas' Heroic Battle against Removal* (Albany: State University of New York Press, 2011), 5–6, 13 (quotation).

57. Jay Gitlin, "Private Diplomacy to Private Property: States, Tribes, and Nations in the Early National Period," *Diplomatic History* 22 (Winter 1998), 91–94.

58. Jefferson's letter to the Delawares was reprinted in Henry Harvey, *History of the Shawnee Indians* (Cincinnati: Ephraim Morgan and Sons, 1855), 129–31; Jefferson to Harrison in Francis Paul Prucha, ed., *Documents of United States Indian Policy* (Lincoln: University of Nebraska Press, 1975), 22–23; Anthony F. C. Wallace, *Jefferson and the Indians: The Tragic Fate of the First Americans* (Cambridge, Mass.: Harvard University Press, 1999).

59. William S. Coker and Thomas D. Watson, *Indian Traders of the Southeastern Spanish Borderlands: Panton, Leslie and Company and John Forbes and Company, 1783–1847* (Pensacola: University of West Florida Press, 1986), 228–29, 366, 370, and ch. 12 (quote at 229, map of 1805 cessions at 264, figures on 265, 271–72); Joel W. Martin, "Cultural Contact and Crises in the Early Republic: Native American Religious Renewal, Resistance, and Accommodation," in *Native Americans and the Early Republic*, ed. Frederick E. Hoxie, Ronald Hoffman, and Peter J. Albert (Charlottesville: University Press of Virginia, 1999), 244–46 (quote).

60. *IALT*, 87–88; Clarence Edwin Carter, comp. and ed., *The Territorial Papers of the United States*, 28 vols. (Washington, D.C.: Government Printing Office, 1934–75), 4: 173 ("friend to the United States").

61. Donald Jackson, ed., *Black Hawk, An Autobiography* (Urbana: University of Illinois Press, 1955), 54, 87, 101.

62. Robert M. Owens, *Mr. Jefferson's Hammer: William Henry Harrison and the Origins of American Indian Policy* (Norman: University of Oklahoma Press, 2007).

63. Owens, *Mr. Jefferson's Hammer*, 200–206 ("just to all" at 206); Harrison to Indians quoted in Goldberg, "Federal Policy and Treaty Making," 20.

64. *NASPIA*, 4: 194.

65. *NASPIA*, 6: 339; *IALT*, 107–10.

66. Sadosky, *Revolutionary Negotiations*, 204.

67. Documents relating to the Treaty of Indian Springs are in *NASPIA*, 7 and 8: passim; 7: 28 ("horrid state"), 155 ("base treachery"), 157–58, 276–78 (lists of chiefs); Michael D. Green, *The Politics of Indian Removal: Creek Government and Society in Crisis* (Lincoln: University of Nebraska Press, 1982), 54–57, 69–97; Grace M. Schwartzman and Susan K. Barnard, "A Trail of Broken Promises: Georgians and Muskogee/Creek Treaties," *Georgia Historical Quarterly* 75 (1991), 697–718; *IALT*, 86, 109, 156, 196–97, 215. Documents relating to McIntosh's killing are in *ASPIA*, 2: 760–74.

68. Charles J. Latrobe, *The Rambler in North America, 1832–1833*, 2 vols. (New York: Harper and Brothers, 1835), 2: 149–54, 156–59; Anselm J. Gerwing, "The Chicago Indian Treaty of 1833," *Journal of the Illinois State Historical Society* 57 (Summer 1964), 117–42; Milo M. Quaife, ed., "The Chicago Treaty of 1833," *Wisconsin Magazine of History* 1 (March 1918), 287–303; James A. Clifton, "Chicago, September 14, 1833: The Last Great Indian Treaty in the Old Northwest," *Chicago History* 9 (Summer 1980), 86–97. The treaty is in *IALT*, 2: 402–15 (schedule B lists the debts paid); the proceedings and other related documents are in "Documents relating to the negotiation of ratified and unratified treaties with various tribes of Indians," T494, reels 2–3. "The United Nation of Chippewa, Ottawa and Potawatomi" in the treaty document included members of other Anishinaabe tribes who were affiliated with Potawatomi communities.

69. *IALT*, 273–77, 283–84, 292–300, 428–31, 450, 457–60, 462–63, 470–72, 486–87, 488.

70. Hauptman, *Conspiracy of Interests*, quote at 176; *IALT*, 502–16.

71. For example, see *NASPIA*, 6: 49.

72. Cary Miller, "Gifts as Treaties: The Political Use of Received Gifts in Anishinaabeg Communities, 1820–1832," *American Indian Quarterly* 26 (Spring 2002), 230.

73. Benjamin Ramirez-Shkwegnaabi, "The Dynamics of American Indian Diplomacy in the Great Lakes Region," *American Indian Culture and Research Journal* 27, no. 4 (2003), 67–71; Heidi Kiiwetinepinesiik Stark, "Marked by Fire: Anishinaabe Articulations of Nationhood in Treaty Making with the United States and Canada," *American Indian Quarterly* 36 (Spring 2012), 122–23.

74. H. S. Halbert, "Story of the Treaty of Dancing Rabbit Creek," *Publications of the Mississippi Historical Society* 6 (1902), 382–85; Michelene E. Pesantubee, "Beyond Domesticity: Choctaw Women Negotiating the Tension between Choctaw Culture and Protestantism," in *Native Women's History in Eastern North America before 1900: A Guide to Research and Writing*, ed. Rebecca Kugel and Lucy Eldersveld Murphy (Lincoln: University of Nebraska Press, 2007), 442–43.

75. Hauptman, *The Tonawanda Senecas' Heroic Battle against Removal*; Colin G. Calloway, *The Indian History of an American Institution: Native Americans and Dartmouth* (Hanover, N.H.: University Press of New England, 2010), 90–91; *Address on the Present Condition and*

Prospects of the Aboriginal Inhabitants of North America, with particular reference to the Seneca Nation. Delivered at Buffalo, New York, by M. B. Pierce, a Chief of the Seneca Nation, and a Member of Dartmouth College (Philadelphia: J. Richards, 1839); *IALT*, 537–42.

Chapter 4

1. Donald E. Worcester, ed., *Forked Tongues and Broken Treaties* (Caldwell, Idaho: Caxton, 1975), 38.

2. William G. McLoughlin, *Cherokee Renascence in the New Republic* (Princeton: Princeton University Press, 1986).

3. McLoughlin, *Cherokee Renascence in the New Republic,* ch. 16; Tiya Miles, *The House on Diamond Hill: A Cherokee Plantation Story* (Chapel Hill: University of North Carolina Press, 2010).

4. Thurman Wilkins, *Cherokee Tragedy: The Ridge Family and the Decimation of a People* (1970; reprint, Norman: University of Oklahoma Press, 1986), 38–41; William Anderson, Jane L. Brown, and Anne F. Rogers, eds., *The Payne-Butrick Papers, Volumes 1, 2, 3* (Lincoln: University of Nebraska Press, 2010), 102–5. The Treaty of 1805 is in *IALT*, 84.

5. McLoughlin, *Cherokee Renascence in the New Republic*, 104–5, 120–21; Wilkins, *Cherokee Tragedy*, 41.

6. Wilkins, *Cherokee Tragedy*, ch. 3.

7. Wilkins, *Cherokee Tragedy*, 94–96; Theda Perdue and Michael D. Green, eds., *The Cherokee Removal: A Brief History with Documents*. 2nd ed. (Boston: Bedford/St. Martin's, 2005), 131–33; Theda Perdue and Michael D. Green, *The Cherokee Nation and the Trail of Tears* (New York: Penguin, 2007), 38–40, 45; Theda Perdue, "Cherokee Women and the Trail of Tears," *Journal of Women's History* 1 (Spring 1989), 14–30; Tiya Miles, "Circular Reasoning: Recentering Cherokee Women in the Antiremoval Campaigns," *American Quarterly* 61 (June 2009), 221–43; Cherokee delegation to John C. Calhoun, February 11, 1824, LROIA, reel 71.

8. Wilkins, *Cherokee Tragedy*, 114–15.

9. Wilkins, *Cherokee Tragedy*, 144–45, 165–67; Anderson, Brown, and Rogers, *The Payne-Butrick Papers*, 194–99; *NASPIA*, 8: 32–33 (McIntosh expelled from Cherokee General Council).

10. 29th Congress, 1st session, House Document 185: 50.

11. Wilkins, *Cherokee Tragedy*, ch. 6.

12. Wilkins, *Cherokee Tragedy*, 130–31.

13. Wilkins, *Cherokee Tragedy*, 131–34, 146–53.

14. Theda Perdue, ed., *Cherokee Editor: The Writings of Elias Boudinot* (Knoxville: University of Tennessee Press, 1983), 68–79.

15. Perdue, *Cherokee Editor*, 10–11.

16. Wilkins, *Cherokee Tragedy*, 186–89.

17. Wilkins, *Cherokee Tragedy*, 189–90.

18. Margaret Bender, *Signs of Cherokee Culture: Sequoyah's Syllabary in Eastern Cherokee Life* (Chapel Hill: University of North Carolina Press, 2002), 25–26; Ellen Cushman, *The Cherokee Syllabary: Writing the People's Perseverance* (Norman: University of Oklahoma Press, 2011).

19. The Cherokee Constitution of 1827 is in 20th Congress, 1st session, House Document 106: 31–40, and *NASPIA*, 9: 41–50.

20. Wilkins, *Cherokee Tragedy*, 198–99.

21. Phillip H. Round, *Removable Type: Histories of the Book in Indian Country, 1663–1880* (Chapel Hill: University of North Carolina Press, 2010), 123, 139.

22. Andrew Denson, *Demanding the Cherokee Nation: Indian Autonomy and American Culture, 1830–1900* (Lincoln: University of Nebraska Press, 2004), ch. 1; Maureen Konkle, *Writing Indian Nations: Native Intellectuals and the Politics of Historiography, 1827–1863* (Chapel Hill: University of North Carolina Press, 2004), ch. 1.

23. On Ross's ancestry, and the broader phenomenon of Scots-Cherokee intermarriage, see Colin G. Calloway, *White People, Indians, and Highlanders: Tribal Peoples and Colonial Encounters in Scotland and America* (New York: Oxford University Press, 2008), esp. 150–54.

24. Wilkins, *Cherokee Tragedy*, 208–9.

25. Perdue and Green, *The Cherokee Removal*, 114–21; Konkle, *Writing Indian Nations*, 61–78.

26. Lisa Ford, *Settler Sovereignty: Jurisdiction and Indigenous People in America and Australia, 1788–1836* (Cambridge, Mass.: Harvard University Press, 2010), quote at 189.

27. *Acts of the Georgia General Assembly*, 1827, 1: 249; Report of the Georgia Legislature, December 19, 1827, LROIA, reel 72; "Resolutions of the Legislature of Georgia," February 4, 1828, 20th Congress, 1st session, House Document 80: 12; *NASPIA*, 9: 61.

28. Perdue, *Cherokee Editor*, 105–6.

29. "Memorial of John Ross and Others," March 3, 1829, 20th Congress, 2nd session, House Document 145: 1–3; *NASPIA*, 9: 139–41.

30. *Ross Papers*, 1: 167; "Correspondence on the Subject of the Emigration of Indians," 1831–1833, 23rd Congress, 1st session, Senate Document 512, 2: 180–81.

31. Wilkins, *Cherokee Tragedy*, 212.

32. Francis Paul Prucha, ed. *Cherokee Removal: The "William Penn" Essays and Other Writings by Jeremiah Evarts* (Knoxville: University of Tennessee Press, 1981), 120, 194, 244, 251.

33. Ronald F. Reid, *Edward Everett, Union Orator* (Westport, Conn.: Greenwood, 1990), 118–20.

34. *Register of Debates in Congress, 1824–1837*, 14 vols. (Washington, D.C.: Gales and Seaton), vol. 6, pt. 1 (Senate), 456; vol. 6, pt. 2 (House): 383, 1133; 21st Congress, 1st session: *Senate Journal*, 266–68; *Journal of the House of Representatives*, 729–30; Ronald N. Satz, *American Indian Policy in the Jacksonian Era* (Lincoln: University of Nebraska Press, 1975), 40–41, 53 (Webster's stance).

35. "Correspondence on the Subject of the Emigration of Indians," 1831–1833, 23rd Congress, 1st session, Senate Document 512, 2: 14–15, 365–66.

36. "Correspondence on the Subject of the Emigration of Indians," 1831–1833, 23rd Congress, 1st session, Senate Document 512, 2: 229–36; Wilkins, *Cherokee Tragedy*, 210; McLoughlin, *Cherokee Renascence in the New Republic*, 437.

37. "Memorial of a Delegation from the Cherokee Indians," January 18, 1831, 21st Congress, 2nd session, House Document 57: 19, quote at 2; "Correspondence on the Subject of the Emigration of Indians," 1831–33, 23rd Congress, 1st session, Senate Document 512, 2: 203; 3: 241.

38. Clay to John Gunter, June 6, 1831, enclosed in Benjamin Currey to Harris, September 30, 1836, LROIA, reel 113.

39. Perdue, *Cherokee Editor*, 121.

40. *Worcester v. Georgia*, 31 U.S. 515, 559–60 (1832); Jill Norgren, *The Cherokee Cases: Two Landmark Federal Decisions in the Fight for Sovereignty* (Norman: University of Oklahoma Press, 2004).

41. *Ross Papers*, 2: 242–43.

42. 29th Congress, 1st session, House Document 185, 50.

43. David Greene to John Ridge, May 3, 1832, Houghton Library, Harvard University, American Board of Commissioners for Foreign Missions [ABCFM] 1.3.1I: 1; quoted in Wilkins, *Cherokee Tragedy*, 240.

44. Wilkins, *Cherokee Tragedy*, 246.

45. Perdue, *Cherokee Editor*, 27–29, 31–33; Bethany Schneider, "Boudinot's Change: Boudinot, Emerson, and Ross on Cherokee Removal," *English Literary History* 75 (Spring 2008), 151–77; Daniel Blake Smith, *An American Betrayal: Cherokee Patriots and the Trail of Tears* (New York: Henry Holt, 2011), 136–46.

46. Theda Perdue, "The Conflict Within: The Cherokee Power Structure and Removal," *Georgia Historical Quarterly* 73 (Fall 1989), 482–88.

47. Perdue, *Cherokee Editor*, 163; *Ross Papers*, 1: 247–50.

48. Perdue, *Cherokee Editor*, 26.

49. Quoted in Wilkins, *Cherokee Tragedy*, 246.

50. Dunlap to Jackson, August 25, 1833, LROIA, reel 75, quoted in Wilkins, *Cherokee Tragedy*, 257.

51. Wilson Lumpkin, *The Removal of the Cherokee Indians from Georgia, 1827–1841*, 2 vols. (New York: Dodd, Mead, and Co., 1907), 1: 128, 186–87, 345.

52. Lumpkin, *The Removal of the Cherokee Indians*, 1: 221–22.

53. Ross et al. to Jackson, March 12, March 28, 1834, LROIA, reel 76.

54. [Cherokees] to Cass, May 3, 1834, LROIA, reel 76.

55. "Memorial and Protest of the Cherokee Nation," 24th Congress, 1st session, House Document 286: 133–37.

56. Gary E. Moulton, *John Ross, Cherokee Chief* (Athens: University of Georgia Press, 1978), 57, 60.

57. Currey to Herring, August 25, 1834: John Ridge's account of the August 1834 council in Currey to Cass, September 15, 1834, LROIA, reel 76.

58. John Ridge et al. to Currey, November 1834, LROIA, reel 76.

59. "Report of the Secretary of War... in relation to the Cherokee Treaty of 1835," 25th Congress, 2nd session, Senate Document 120: 348–50; *Ross Papers*, 1: 314–18.

60. "Memorial and Protest of the Cherokee Nation," 24th Congress, 1st session, House Document 286: 126–29.

61. "Memorial of a Council Held at Running Waters," 23rd Congress, 2nd session, House Document 91: 1–7.

62. "Correspondence on the Subject of the Emigration of Indians," 1831–33, 23rd Congress, 1st session, Senate Document 512, 3: 506–07.

63. Schermerhorn's life and career are traced in James W. Van Hoeven, "Salvation and Indian Removal," *The Reformed Review* 39 (1986?), 255–70.

64. The treaties are in *IALT*, 383–91, 394–97; proceedings and related correspondence are in "Documents relating to the negotiation of ratified and unratified treaties with various tribes of Indians," National Archives microfilm T494, reels 2–3.

65. "Documents relative to a council held with the Potawatomie Indians at Logan's Post, Indiana, June 17, 1833," and "Documents relative to a Council of the Six Nations, Sept. 18, 1833," both in "Documents relating to the negotiation of ratified and unratified treaties with various tribes of Indians," T494, reel 2.

66. "Correspondence on the Subject of the Emigration of Indians," 1831–33, 23rd Congress, 1st session, Senate Document 512, 4: 577 (Schermerhorn's account); Anselm J. Gerwing, "The Chicago Indian Treaty of 1833," *Journal of the Illinois State Historical Society* 57 (Summer 1964), 117–42 (Senate amendment and quote at 138). The treaty is in *IALT*, 402–15; the proceedings and other related documents are in "Documents relating to the negotiation of ratified and unratified treaties with various tribes of Indians," T494, reels 2–3. The charges brought against Governor Porter and his refutation are in Milo M. Quaife, ed., "The Chicago Treaty of 1833," *Wisconsin Magazine of History* 1 (March 1918), 287–303 ($10,000 bribe at 290, 298).

67. "Correspondence on the Subject of the Emigration of Indians," 1831–33, 23rd Congress, 1st session, Senate Document 512, 4: 724; Jay Gitlin, "Private Diplomacy to Private Property: States, Tribes, and Nations in the Early National Period," *Diplomatic History* 22 (Winter 1998), 96. On Richardville's changing stance on removal treaties, see Melissa Rinehart, "Miami Resistance and Resilience during the Removal Era," in *Contested Territories: Native Americans and Non-Natives in the Lower Great Lakes, 1700–1850*, ed. Charles Beatty-Medina and Melissa Rinehart (East Lansing: Michigan State University Press, 2012), ch. 6.

68. LROIA, reel 79, Cherokee Agency, 1834–36. The 1828 treaty with the western Cherokees is in *IALT*, 286–92.

69. Wilkins, *Cherokee Tragedy*, 267–68; "Report of the Secretary of War... in relation to the Cherokee Treaty of 1835," 25th Congress, 2nd session, Senate Document 120: 94–104. The unratified treaty of March 1835 and Jackson's proclamation of March 16, 1835, are in "Documents relating to the negotiation of ratified and unratified treaties with various tribes of Indians," T494, reel 3.

70. "Report of the Secretary of War... in relation to the Cherokee Treaty of 1835," 25th Congress, 2nd session, Senate Document 120: 359–60; "Memorial and Protest of the Cherokee Nation," 24th Congress, 1st session, House Document 286: 355–63; Ridge to Cass, March 13, 1835, LROIA, reel 76.

71. Edward Everett Dale and Gaston Litton, eds., *Cherokee Cavaliers: Forty Years of Cherokee History as Told in the Correspondence of the Ridge-Watie-Boudinot Family* (Norman: University of Oklahoma Press, 1939), 8 ("the Chicken Snake General Jackson"); Wilkins, *Cherokee Tragedy*, 269.

72. Currey to Ross, April 19, 1835, LROIA, reel 76; Currey to Herring, August 30, 1835, LROIA, reel 76.

73. *Ross Papers*, 1: 7.

74. Anderson, Brown, and Rogers, *Payne-Butrick Papers*, xiv–xvii, quote at 84.

75. "Report of the Secretary of War... in relation to the Cherokee Treaty of 1835," 25th Congress, 2nd session, Senate Document 120: 380–462; Schermerhorn's report on the council, 450–62; quotes at 454, 459–60; Payne's account in Anderson, Brown, and Rogers, *Payne-Butrick Papers*, 178–83; Meigs to Cass, August 20, 1835, LROIA, reel 76.

76. "Report of the Secretary of War... in relation to the Cherokee Treaty of 1835," 25th Congress, 2nd session, Senate Document 120: 463.

77. Kenny A. Franks, *Stand Watie and the Agony of the Cherokee Nation* (Memphis: Memphis State University Press, 1979), 21–22; "Report of the Secretary of War… in relation to the Cherokee Treaty of 1835," 25th Congress, 2nd session, Senate Document 120: 492–94, 538, 591–92.

78. Lumpkin, *Removal of the Cherokee Indians*, 1: 340 (farce), 347–48 (move or starve), 361, 364 (treaty unnecessary).

79. Duane H. King and E. Raymond Evans, eds., "The Trail of Tears: Primary Documents of the Cherokee Removal," *Journal of Cherokee Studies* 3, no. 3 (Summer 1978), 133; "Report of the Secretary of War… in relation to the Cherokee Treaty of 1835," 25th Congress, 2nd session, Senate Document 120; 485, 518, 532–34; copies of talk delivered at the Red Clay council, October 30, 1835, LROIA, reel 76.

80. John Hooper to Gen. R. Jones, November 10, 1835, LROIA, reel 76; Currey to Cass, November 1835, LROIA, reel 76; Anderson, Brown, and Rogers, *Payne-Butrick Papers*, xvii–xviii.

81. *NASPIA*, 1: 262.

82. "Report of the Secretary of War… in relation to the Cherokee Treaty of 1835," 25th Congress, 2nd session, Senate Document 120: 490–91.

83. John F. Schermerhorn, "A Journal of the proceedings of the council held at New Echota," December 21–30th, LROIA, reel 76, and in 25th Congress, 2nd session, Senate Document 120: 514.

84. Perdue, "Cherokee Women and the Trail of Tears," 14.

85. "Memorial and Protest of the Cherokee Nation," 24th Congress, 1st session, House Document 286: 120; *Ross Papers*, 1: 379.

86. Quoted in Wilkins, *Cherokee Tragedy*, 286–87 (Ridge), and Perdue, *Cherokee Editor*, 27 (Boudinot).

87. Copy of the minutes of the council at New Echota (accompanying Schermerhorn's journal of proceedings), LROIA, reel 76.

88. *IALT*, 439–48.

89. *IALT*, 448–49.

90. "Memorial and Protest of the Cherokee Nation," 24th Congress, 1st session, House Document 286: 120; *Ross Papers*, 1: 379.

91. Daniel Heath Justice, *Our Fire Survives the Storm: A Cherokee Literary History* (Minneapolis: University of Minnesota Press, 2006), 58 (quote), 81–86.

92. Report of Secretary of War to the Senate, February 9, 1829, Senate Document 72, 20–22, serial 181: 17–19, quoted in Francis Paul Prucha, *American Indian Treaties: The History of a Political Anomaly* (Berkeley: University of California Press, 1994), 211.

93. Wilkins, *Cherokee Tragedy*, 289.

94. A. D. Shackleford to William Wilkins, March 25, 1844, LROIA, reel 116.

95. Schermerhorn, "A Journal of the proceedings of the council held at New Echota," 517.

96. "Report of the Secretary of War… in relation to the Cherokee Treaty of 1835," 25th Congress, 2nd session, Senate Document 120: 495–96.

97. "Report of the Secretary of War… in relation to the Cherokee Treaty of 1835," 25th Congress, 2nd session, Senate Document 120: 519, 528.

98. "Memorial of a Delegation of the Cherokee Nation, Remonstrating against the instrument of writing (treaty) of December, 1835," 25th Congress, 2nd session, House Document 99: 10–11.

99. "Memorial and Protest of the Cherokee Nation," 24th Congress, 1st session, House Document 286, quotes at 2, 13, 15; "Report of the Secretary of War… in relation to the Cherokee Treaty of 1835," 25th Congress, 2nd session, Senate Document 120: 799–814; *Ross Papers*, 1: 394–413; Ross et al. to Cass, January 14, February 9, and February 29, 1836, LROIA, reel 76.

100. It is this petition, not the treaty, that modern Cherokees chose to exhibit at the National Museum of the American Indian. Thanks to Theda Perdue for bringing this to my attention.

101. 25th Congress, 2nd session, Senate Document 120: 530, 535; Schermerhorn to Cass, March 3, 1836, LROIA, reel 80.

102. Quoted in Wilkins, *Cherokee Tragedy*, 292.

103. Hugh Park, *Reminiscences of the Indians by Cephas Washburn* (Van Buren, Ark.: Press-Argus, 1955), 49.

104. Anderson, Brown, and Rogers, *Payne-Butrick Papers,* xxi.

105. Benton quoted in Moulton, *John Ross*, 77.

106. Lumpkin, *Removal of the Cherokee Indians*, 2: 87.

107. Kenny, *Stand Watie*, 37; 25th Congress, 2nd session, Senate Document 120: 593.

108. "The Death of Harriet Gold Boudinot," *Journal of Cherokee Studies* 4, no. 2 (Spring 1979), 102–7; Perdue, *Cherokee Editor,* 30.

109. The Ridges to President Jackson, June 30, 1836, LROIA, reel 80; 25th Congress, 2nd session, Senate Document 120: 600–601, 607–8.

110. Worcester, *Forked Tongues and Broken Treaties*, 63.

111. "Report of the Secretary of War… in relation to the Cherokee Treaty of 1835," 25th Congress, 2nd session, Senate Document 120: 67; Wool to the Cherokee People, September 19, 1836, LROIA, reel 80; "Proclamation to the Chiefs, Headmen, and People of the Cherokee Nation," December 28, 1837, LROIA, reel 82.

112. Lumpkin, *Removal of the Cherokee Indians*, 2: 8 (no one contributed more; liberal provisions), 45 (ignorant and depraved), 51 (execute, not negotiate); Wilson Lumpkin and John Kennedy to Harris, June 5, 1837, LROIA, reel 114 ("intelligent and wealthy").

113. Lumpkin, *Removal of the Cherokee Indians*, 12 (fraud and corruption), 193 (legislate directly), 225 ("never cease").

114. Lumpkin and Kennedy to Harris, June 5, 1837, and Lindsay to Poinsett, July 20, 1837, LROIA, reel 114.

115. Elias Boudinot, *Letters and Other Papers Relating to Cherokee Affairs; Being in Reply to Sundry Publications Authorized by John Ross* (Athens, 1837); reprinted in Perdue, *Cherokee Editor,* 155–225 (quotations at 162, 177), and in "Documents in relation to the Validity of the Cherokee Treaty of 1835," 25th Congress, 2nd session, Senate Document 121.

116. *Ross Papers*, 1: 471–74 (quote at 473), 480–87 ("Our fate is in your hands" at 486).

117. Petition to Congress, February 22, 1838, LROIA, M234, reel 82; "Memorial of the Cherokee Delegation, Submitting the memorial and protest of the Cherokee people to Congress," April 9, 1838, 25th Congress, 2nd session, House Document 316: 1–4.

118. Nathan Smith to congressional delegates, February 2, 1838, and George Gilmer to Joel Poinsett, March 5, 1838, LROIA, reel 115.

119. Perdue and Green, *Cherokee Nation and the Trail of Tears*, 120–23.

120. Lumpkin to C. A. Harris, March 23, 1837, LROIA, reel 81.

121. Wilkins, *Cherokee Tragedy*, 311, 315.

122. Scott's address in King and Evans, "The Trail of Tears: Primary Documents of the Cherokee Removal," 145; Scott to Poinsett, June 7, 1838, LROIA, reel 115. Both documents also in "Removal of the Cherokees," 25th Congress, 2nd session, House Document 453: 11–12, 18–21.

123. Scott to Poinsett, July 20, 1838, LROIA, reel 115.

124. Ross et al. to Scott, July 23, 1838, and Scott to Ross et al., July 25, 1838, and Resolution of July 26, 1838, LROIA, reel 115; "Memorial of the Delegation of the Cherokee Nation," March 9, 1840, 26th Congress, 1st session, House Document 129: 34–38, 48–49; William G. McLoughlin, *After the Trail of Tears: The Cherokees' Struggle for Sovereignty, 1839–1880* (Chapel Hill: University of North Carolina Press, 1993), 2–5.

125. Carl J. Vipperman, "The Bungled Treaty of New Echota: The Failure of Cherokee Removal, 1836–1838," *Georgia Historical Quarterly* 78 (Fall 1989), 540–58.

126. *IALT*, 443.

127. Williams to Poinsett, April 11, 1838, LROIA, reel 81 (quote at page 5); Scott to Collins, August 10, 1837, reel 115. Settling payments due under article 8 went on for many years after removal: see LROIA, reel 116.

128. Wilkins, *Cherokee Tragedy*, 323; *Ross Papers*, 1: 9; Moulton, *John Ross*, ch. 6.

129. King and Evans, "The Trail of Tears," 180–85.

130. Quoted in Wilkins, *Cherokee Tragedy*, 322.

131. Butler to Greene, January 25, 1839, Houghton Library, ABCFM, 18.3.1X: 73; quoted in Wilkins, *Cherokee Tragedy*, 328.

132. "Statement showing the number of Indians annually removed from the eastern to the western side of the Mississippi, from 1789 to 1838, inclusive," *NASPIA*, 1: 575.

133. David J. Silverman, *Red Brethren: The Brothertown and Stockbridge Indians and the Problem of Race in Early America* (Ithaca, N.Y.: Cornell University Press, 2010), 188–91.

134. Van Hoeven, "Salvation and Indian Removal," 267.

135. Perdue and Green, *Cherokee Nation and the Trail of Tears*, 143–45.

136. McLoughlin, *After the Trail of Tears*, 4–17; "Memorial of the Delegation of the Cherokee Nation," March 9, 1840, 26th Congress, 1st session, House Document 129: 50–51.

137. Wilkins, *Cherokee Tragedy*, 334–39; James W. Parins, *John Rollin Ridge: His Life and Works* (Lincoln: University of Nebraska Press, 1991), 30–31; Kenny, *Stand Watie*, 56; "The Murder of Elias Boudinot," *Chronicles of Oklahoma* 12 (March 1934), 9–24 (Allen Ross's account); "Message of the President of the United States, relative to the internal feuds among the Cherokees," April 13, 1846, 29th Congress, 1st session, Senate Document 289, House Document 185: 54–55; Ross to Arbuckle, June 22, 1839, and Arbuckle to Brig. Gen. Jones, November 24, 1839, LROIA, reel 84 (Mrs. Boudinot's warnings).

138. "A Tribute to John Ridge," *Journal of Cherokee Studies* 4. no. 2 (Spring 1979), 111–17.

139. Lumpkin, *Removal of the Cherokee Indians from Georgia*, 1: 192.

140. Arbuckle to J. B. Grayson, June 26, 1839; Capt. Nathan Boone to Major C. Wharton, July 9, 1839; and Edmund Gaines to Commanding Officers, July 13, 1839, LROIA, reel 83.

141. "Names of Cherokees charged with the murder of the Ridges and Boudinot," November 27, 1839, and Arbuckle to Poinsett, December 26, 1839, LROIA, reel 84. Documents relating to the issue of Arbuckle's intervention are in "Letter from the Secretary of War … respecting the interference of any officer or agent of the Government with the Cherokee Indians in the formation of a government for the regulation of their own

internal affairs," 26th Congress, 1st session, House Document 188 (names of Cherokees charged at 17).

142. *Ross Papers*, 1: 764–70; "Memorial of John Ross and Others," March 3, 1829, 20th Congress, 2nd session, House Document 145: 7–9; Ross to Arbuckle, November 4, 1839, LROIA, reel 84, reprinted in 26th Congress, 1st session, House Document 188, 15–17.

143. Dianne Everett, *The Texas Cherokees: A People between Two Fires, 1819–1840* (Norman: University of Oklahoma Press, 1990), ch. 5; Gary Clayton Anderson, *The Conquest of Texas: Ethnic Cleansing in the Promised Land, 1820–1875* (Norman: University of Oklahoma Press, 2005), 177–80.

144. *Ross Papers*, 2: 11, 23; Moulton, *John Ross*, 115–16. The Cherokee Constitution and other documents relating to these events are in LROIA, reels 83–84.

145. David LaVere, *Contrary Neighbors: Southern Plains and Removed Indians in Indian Territory* (Norman: University of Oklahoma Press, 2000), ch. 4; John P. Bowes, *Exiles and Pioneers: Eastern Indians in the Trans-Mississippi West* (Cambridge: Cambridge University Press, 2007), 122–23 (quote at 123), 141–47.

146. *Ross Papers*, 2: 65, 74–75; Address of General Arbuckle to Deputations from the Old Settlers and late Emigrant Cherokees, April 21, 1840, and Cherokee Council to Arbuckle, April 22, 1840, LROIA, reel 84.

147. *Ross Papers*, 2: 87.

148. *Ross Papers*, 2: 150–51.

149. John Howard Payne, *Indian Justice: A Cherokee Murder Trial at Tahlequah in 1840* (Norman: University of Oklahoma Press, 2002).

150. "Report of the Secretary of War [on] difficulties among the Cherokee Indians," February 24, 1845, 28th Congress, 2nd session, Senate Document 140: 95.

151. *Ross Papers*, 2: 124–26, 143; Kenny, *Stand Watie*, 80–81, 83–88; George Paschal, "The Trial of Stand Watie," ed. Grant Foreman *Chronicles of Oklahoma* 12 (September 1934), 305–39. Paschal was married to the daughter of John Ridge and was therefore a strong supporter of Watie.

152. Kenny, *Stand Watie*, 83.

153. *Ross Papers*, 2: 170–77; Moulton, *John Ross*, 149.

154. Parins, *John Rollin Ridge*, 37.

155. "Memorial of John Ross and Others," May 4, 1846, 29th Congress, 1st session, Senate Document 331: 12–13; *Ross Papers*, 2: 272–73, 279–80, 298–300; Kenny, *Stand Watie*, 96.

156. McLoughlin, *After the Trail of Tears*, 34, 40–41; "Memorial of John Ross and Others," 29th Congress, 1st session, Senate Document 331: 20, 30.

157. "Memorial of John Rogers, Principal Chief, et al.," April 13, 1844, 29th Congress, 1st session, House Document 235, quotes at 13, 14, 34.

158. "Message of the President of the United States, relative to the internal feuds among the Cherokees," April 13, 1846, 29th Congress, 1st session, Senate Document 289, House Document 185: 55–58.

159. *Ross Papers*, 2: 228–42.

160. Dale and Litton, *Cherokee Cavaliers*, 35; Parins, *John Rollin Ridge*, 45.

161. *Ross Papers*, 2: 283–85.

162. "Message of the President of the United States, relative to the Cherokees Difficulties," April 13, 1846, 29th Congress, 1st session, House Document 185, Senate Document 289, quote at 2.

163. *Ross Papers*, 2: 285.

164. McLoughlin, *After the Trail of Tears*, 56–58; *Ross Papers*, 2: 312, 316–19.

165. McLoughlin, *After the Trail of Tears*, 60–62; Moulton, *John Ross*, 153–54; Perdue and Green, *Cherokee Nation and the Trail of Tears*, 160.

166. Wilkins, *Cherokee Tragedy*, 344.

167. Parins, *John Rollin Ridge*, 55–60; Dale and Litton, *Cherokee Cavaliers*, 64 (principle of revenge).

168. Clarissa W. Confer, *The Cherokee Nation in the Civil War* (Norman: University of Oklahoma Press, 2007); Denson, *Demanding the Cherokee Nation*, ch. 2.

169. *Ross Papers*, 2: 469–70, 476, 480.

170. *Ross Papers*, 2: 492–95; *The War of the Rebellion: A Compilation of the Official Records of the Union and Confederate Armies*, 70 vols. (Washington, D.C.: Government Printing Office, 1880–1901), Series 1, 4: 669–87.

171. Laurence M. Hauptman, *Between Two Fires: American Indians in the Civil War* (New York: Free Press, 1995), ch. 3, quote at 48.

172. *Ross Papers*, 2: 590–92, 624–27.

173. Moulton, *John Ross*, 177, 182.

174. Dale and Litton, *Cherokee Cavaliers*, chs. 3–4, Saladin quote at 128, "peace once more" at 170; Kenny, *Stand Watie*, chs. 7–9, "short time in peace" at 160.

175. Hauptman, *Between Two Fires*, 42.

176. Kenny, *Stand Watie*, 196, 200; Dale and Litton, *Cherokee Cavaliers*, 234, 256, 265.

177. Kenny, *Stand Watie*, 208.

Chapter 5

1. James P. Ronda, *Lewis and Clark among the Indians* (Lincoln: University of Nebraska Press, 1984), quote at 1.

2. Quoted in Paul VanDevelder, *Savages and Scoundrels: The Untold Story of America's Road to Empire through Indian Territory* (New Haven: Yale University Press, 2009), 89.

3. Colin G. Calloway, *One Vast Winter Count: The Native American West before Lewis and Clark* (Lincoln: University of Nebraska Press, 2003).

4. Calloway, *One Vast Winter Count*, 250–60; Juliana Barr, *Peace Came in the Form of a Woman: Indians and Spaniards in the Texas Borderlands* (Chapel Hill: University of North Carolina Press, 2007), ch. 1; Juliana Barr, "Beyond Their Control: Spaniards in Native Texas," in *Choice, Persuasion, and Coercion: Social Control on Spain's North American Frontier*, ed. Jesús F. de la Teja and Ross Frank (Albuquerque: University of New Mexico Press, 2005), 154–58.

5. Gilbert C. Din and Abraham P. Nasatir, *The Imperial Osages: Spanish-Indian Diplomacy in the Mississippi Valley* (Norman: University of Oklahoma Press, 1983); Willard H. Rollings, *The Osage: An Ethnohistorical Study of Hegemony on the Prairie-Plains* (Columbia: University of Missouri Press, 1992).

6. Pekka Hämäläinen, *The Comanche Empire* (New Haven: Yale University Press, 2008); Ned Blackhawk, *Violence over the Land: Indians and Empires in the Early American West* (Cambridge, Mass.: Harvard University Press, 2006), 35–54.

7. Alfred Barnaby Thomas, ed., *The Plains Indians and New Mexico: A Collection of Documents Illustrative of the History of the Eastern Frontier of New Mexico* (Albuquerque: University of New Mexico Press, 1940), 137.

8. Thomas, *Plains Indians and New Mexico*, 63–156, quote at 132.

9. Thomas, *Plains Indians and New Mexico*, 148–54, quote at 151.

10. Alfred Barnaby Thomas, trans. and ed., *Forgotten Frontiers: A Study of the Spanish Indian Policy of Don Juan Bautista de Anza, Governor of New Mexico, 1777–1787* (Norman: University of Oklahoma Press, 1932), 317.

11. Barr, *Peace Came in the Form of a Woman*, 276–86.

12. John R. Wunder, "'That No Thorn Will Pierce Our Friendship': The Ute-Comanche Treaty of 1786," *Western Historical Quarterly* 42 (Spring 2011), 5–27; Thomas, *Forgotten Frontiers*, 294–321.

13. Gary E. Moulton, ed., *The Lewis and Clark Journals: An American Epic of Discovery* (Lincoln: University of Nebraska Press, 2003), 28.

14. Castle McLaughlin, *Arts of Diplomacy: Lewis and Clark's Indian Collection* (Cambridge, Mass.: Peabody Museum, Harvard University; Seattle: University of Washington Press, 2003), 206; Moulton, *Lewis and Clark Journals*, 52.

15. Moulton, *Lewis and Clark Journals*, 47–52, 57.

16. Moulton, *Lewis and Clark Journals*, 24, 28, 41, 50 (Brulé and Spanish flags), 65–66, 71 (quote), 72, 87, 176, 213, 241, 342, 368.

17. A. P. Nasatir, ed., *Before Lewis and Clark: Documents Illustrating the History of the Missouri, 1785–1804*, 2 vols. (1952; reprint, Lincoln: University of Nebraska Press, 1990), 1: 305; John C. Ewers, "Symbols of Chiefly Authority in Spanish Louisiana," in *The Spanish in the Mississippi Valley, 1762–1804*, ed. John Francis McDermott (Urbana: University of Illinois Press, 1974), 279.

18. McLaughlin, "The Language of Pipes," in *Arts of Diplomacy*, 201–49; Moulton, *Lewis and Clark Journals*, 176.

19. Moulton, *Lewis and Clark Journals*, 202.

20. Tracy Potter, *Sheheke, Mandan Indian Diplomat: The Story of White Coyote, Thomas Jefferson, and Lewis and Clark* (Helena, Mont.: Farcountry Press; Washburn, N.D.: Fort Mandan Press, 2003).

21. Herman J. Viola, *Diplomats in Buckskins: A History of Indian Delegations in Washington City* (Washington, D.C.: Smithsonian Institution Press, 1981).

22. *IALT*, 95–99; Jay H. Buckley, *William Clark, Indian Diplomat* (Norman: University of Oklahoma Press, 2008), 75–78 ("hardest treaty" quote at 77).

23. *IALT*, 250–55; Heidi Kiiwetinepinesiik Stark, "Marked by Fire: Anishinaabe Articulations of Nationhood in Treaty Making with the United States and Canada," *American Indian Quarterly* 36 (Spring 2012), 130–33.

24. *IALT*, 225–46, 256–62.

25. Landon Y. Jones, *William Clark and the Shaping of the West* (New York: Hill and Wang, 2004), ch. 10; William E. Unrau, *The Rise and Fall of Indian Country, 1825–1855* (Lawrence: University Press of Kansas, 2007), ch. 5; Buckley, *William Clark, Indian Diplomat*, 112–13 (quote).

26. Report submitted to Senate by Secretary of War, February 9, 1829, Senate Document 72: 20–22, serial 181, pp. 17–19, quoted in Francis Paul Prucha, *American Indian Treaties: The History of a Political Anomaly* (Berkeley: University of California Press, 1994), 211.

27. Katherine M. Weist, "An Ethnohistorical Analysis of Crow Political Alliances," *Western Canadian Journal of Anthropology* 7-4 (1977), 34–54; Colin G. Calloway, "The Only

Way Open to Us: Intertribal Warfare and the Crow Struggle for Survival," *North Dakota History* 53 (Summer 1986), 24–34.

28. George Bird Grinnell, *The Fighting Cheyennes* (Norman: University of Oklahoma Press, 1956), 63–69; Joseph Jablow, *The Cheyenne in Plains Indian Trade Relations, 1795–1840* (1950; reprint, Lincoln: University of Nebraska Press, 1992), 72–77; Joyce M. Szabo, *Howling Wolf and the History of Ledger Art* (Albuquerque: University of New Mexico Press, 1994), 133.

29. Hämäläinen, *Comanche Empire*, 357–59; Brian DeLay, *War of a Thousand Deserts: Indian Raids and the U.S.-Mexican War* (New Haven: Yale University Press, 2008).

30. Gary Clayton Anderson, *The Conquest of Texas: Ethnic Cleansing in the Promised Land, 1820–1875* (Norman: University of Oklahoma Press, 2005), ch. 11.

31. Reginald Horsman, *Race and Manifest Destiny: The Origins of American Racial Anglo-Saxonism* (Cambridge, Mass.: Harvard University Press, 1981).

32. Prucha, *American Indian Treaties*, 236.

33. Unrau, *Rise and Fall of Indian Country*, ch. 9; Robert A. Trennert, Jr., *Alternative to Extinction: Federal Indian Policy and the Beginnings of the Reservation System, 1846–1851* (Philadelphia: Temple University Press, 1975).

34. Clifford E. Trafzer and Joel R. Hyer, eds., *Exterminate Them! Written Accounts of the Murder, Rape, and Enslavement of Native Americans during the California Gold Rush* (East Lansing: Michigan State University Press, 1999), 139.

35. George E. Anderson, W. H. Ellison, and Robert F. Heizer, *Treaty Making and Treaty Rejection by the Federal Government in California, 1850–1852* (Socorro, N.M.: Ballena Press, 1978), i (executive session), 27 (Fillmore quote); Robert F. Heizer, *The Eighteen Unratified Treaties of 1851–1852 between the California Indians and the United States Government* (Berkeley: Archaeological Research Facility, University of California, 1972), 5 ("farce"); Chad L. Hoopes, *Domesticate or Exterminate: California Indian Treaties Unratified and Made Secret in 1852* (n.p.: Redwood Coast, 1975).

36. John D. Unrau, Jr., *The Plains Across: The Overland Emigrants and the Trans-Mississippi West, 1840–60* (Urbana: University of Illinois Press, 1979), ch. 5.

37. James Mooney, *Calendar History of the Kiowa Indians* (Washington, D.C.: Government Printing Office, 1898; reprinted with an introduction by John C. Ewers, Washington D.C.: Smithsonian Institution Press, 1979), 290.

38. *IALT*, 588–93.

39. Patricia Albers and Jeanne Kay, "Sharing the Land: A Study in American Indian Territoriality," in *A Cultural Geography of North American Indians*, ed. Tyrel G. Moore and Thomas E. Ross (Boulder, Colo: Westview Press, 1987), 47–91; Raymond J. DeMallie, "Touching the Pen: Plains Indian Treaty Councils in Ethnohistorical Perspective," in *Ethnicity on the Great Plains*, ed. Frederick C. Luebke (Lincoln: University of Nebraska Press, 1980), 38–53; VanDevelder, *Savages and Scoundrels*, ch. 5 (Crow arrival at 186); *IALT*, 594–96.

40. Jeffrey Ostler, *The Plains Sioux and U.S. Colonialism* (Cambridge: Cambridge University Press, 2004), 38.

41. Stan Hoig, *The Western Odyssey of John Simpson Smith, Frontiersman and Indian Interpreter* (1974; Norman: University of Oklahoma Press, 2004), 85–87.

42. Kingsley M. Bray, "Lone Horn's Peace: A New View of Sioux-Crow Relations, 1851–1858," *Nebraska History* 66 (Spring 1985), 28–47, quote at 41.

43. VanDevelder, *Savages and Scoundrels*, 192, 217–18.

44. Unrau, *Rise and Fall of Indian Country*, 141.

45. Hoig, *Western Odyssey of John Simpson Smith*, 127–36; Viola, *Diplomats in Buckskins*, 99–102.

46. Stan Hoig, *The Sand Creek Massacre* (Norman: University of Oklahoma Press, 1961), ch. 9; Hoig, *Western Odyssey of John Simpson Smith*, ch. 9; George E. Hyde, *Life of George Bent, Written from his Letters*, ed. Savoie Lottinville (Norman: University of Oklahoma Press, 1968), 155, 248. The most complete compilations of materials relating to the massacre are in the official investigations: "Massacre of Cheyenne Indians," 38th Congress, 2nd session, Sen. Report 142, pt. 3; "Sand Creek Massacre," 39th Cong., 2d session, Senate Executive Document 26, and "Chivington Massacre," 39th Congress, 2nd session, Senate Report, 156.

47. *IALT*, 603–7, 655–60, 714–19, 740–42.

48. *IALT*, 661–77, 682–85, 719–25, 736–39; Prucha, *American Indian Treaties*, 250–55, Stevens quote at 251; Boxberger, "California, Hawaii, and the Pacific Northwest," 225–28; Richard Kluger, *The Bitter Waters of Medicine Creek: A Tragic Clash between White and Native America* (New York: Knopf, 2011). For the broader significance of the Stevens treaties, see Kent Richards, guest ed., "The Isaac I. Stevens and Joel Palmer Treaties, 1855–2005," *Oregon Historical Quarterly* 106 (Fall 2005), 342–491; and Alexandra Harmon, ed., *The Power of Promises: Rethinking Indian Treaties in the Pacific Northwest* (Seattle: University of Washington Press, 2008).

49. Alvin M. Josephy, Jr., *The Nez Perce Indians and the Opening of the Northwest* (New Haven: Yale University Press, 1965), ch. 8; Col. Lawrence Kip, *The Indian Council at Walla Walla, May and June, 1855: A Journal. Sources of the History of Oregon*, vol. 1, part 2 (*Contributions of the Department of Economics and History*, 1897), 10–11 (arrival), 13 (prayers).

50. Kip, *Indian Council at Walla Walla*, 15–16.

51. Kip, *Indian Council at Walla Walla*, 19–24 (quotes at 24).

52. Josephy, *Nez Perce Indians*, 332 ("most satisfactory"); McKay quoted in Robert H. Ruby and John A. Brown, *The Cayuse Indians* (Norman: University of Oklahoma Press, 1972), 203; David L. Nicandri, *Northwest Chiefs: Gustav Sohon's Views of the 1855 Stevens Treaty Councils* (Tacoma: Washington State Historical Society, 1986), 13–17. The Walla Walla treaties are in *IALT*, 694–706.

53. Robert Ignatius Burns, S.J., *The Jesuits and the Indian Wars of the Northwest* (New Haven: Yale University Press, 1966), 101.

54. William E. Farr, "'When We Were First Paid': The Blackfoot Treaty, the Western Tribes, and the Creation of the Common Hunting Ground, 1855," *Great Plains Quarterly* 21 (Spring 2001), 131–55; *IALT*, 736–40; Nicandri, *Northwest Chiefs*, 19–26.

55. U.S. Statutes at Large, 12: 489; Richard White, *Railroaded: The Transcontinentals and the Making of Modern America* (New York: W. W. Norton, 2011), 17–19, 23–25.

56. Elliott West, *The Last Indian War: The Nez Perce Story* (New York: Oxford University Press, 2009), xix–xxii; Elliott West, *The Essential West: Collected Essays* (Norman: University of Oklahoma Press, 2012), 6 (quote); *Congressional Globe*, 40th Congress, 1st session, 670.

57. Letter of the Secretary of the Interior, July 13, 1867, 40th Congress, 1st session, Senate Executive Document 13: 5–6.

Chapter 6

1. "Proceedings of the Indian Peace Commission," St. Louis, August 7, 1867, LROIA, Upper Platte Agency, 1867, roll 892.

2. *Congressional Globe*, 40th Congress, 1st session, 667–73, 678–79, 707–9; "Report to the President by the Indian Peace Commission," January 7, 1868, in *Message from the President of the United States, transmitting report of the Indian peace commissioners. January 14, 1868.—Referred to the Committee on Indian Affairs and ordered to be printed*, 40th Congress, 2nd session, House Executive Document 97: 1–2; Francis Paul Prucha, *American Indian Treaties: The History of a Political Anomaly* (Berkeley: University of California Press, 1997), 279–80; Douglas C. Jones, *The Treaty of Medicine Lodge: The Story of the Great Treaty Council as Told by Eyewitnesses* (Norman: University of Oklahoma Press, 1966), vii–viii, 1; Jill St. Germain, *Indian Treaty-Making Policy in the United States and Canada, 1867–1877* (Lincoln: University of Nebraska Press, 2001), 20, ch. 7.

3. George E. Hyde, *Life of George Bent, Written from His Letters*, ed. Savoie Lottinville (Norman: University of Oklahoma Press, 1968), 177, 244.

4. Stan Hoig, *White Man's Paper Trail: Grand Councils and Treaty Making on the Central Plains* (Boulder: University Press of Colorado, 2006), 125–29; *IALT*, 887–95. The proceedings of the treaty are in *Documents relating to the negotiation of ratified and unratified treaties with various tribes of Indians*, 10 reels, National Archives Microfilm T494; reel 7, ratified treaty no. 341.

5. William T. Hagan, *United States–Comanche Relations: The Reservation Years* (New Haven: Yale University Press 1976), 8.

6. *Congressional Globe*, 40th Congress, 1st session, 670; *IALT*, 889 (special request).

7. Charles Bogy and W. R. Irwin to Louis Bogy, December 1866, p. 6, in *Documents relating to the negotiation of ratified and unratified treaties with various tribes of Indians*, reel 7.

8. Hoig, *White Man's Paper Trail*, 130–32.

9. Bogy and Irwin to Bogy, December 1866, *Documents relating to the negotiation of ratified and unratified treaties*, p. 13.

10. William Y. Chalfant, *Hancock's War: Conflict on the Southern Plains* (Norman: University of Oklahoma Press, 2010); *ARCIA* for 1867: 18, 310–14; "Report to the President by the Indian Peace Commission," 12; *Proceedings of the Great Peace Commission of 1867–1868*, with an introduction by Vine Deloria, Jr., and Raymond DeMallie (Washington D.C.: Institute for the Development of Indian Law, 1975), 21–22. The original proceedings are in RG 48, 665.

11. St. Germain, *Indian Treaty-Making Policy*, 47.

12. "Report to the President by the Indian Peace Commission," 1–2, 7, 9; *Congressional Globe*, 40th Congress, 1st session, 667–70; *ARCIA*, 1868: 26, 32, 35.

13. *New York Times*, September 22, 1867, September 29, 1867.

14. *Congressional Globe*, 40th Congress, 1st session, 670, 679, 706; "Report to the President by the Indian Peace Commission," 18.

15. *Congressional Globe*, 40th Congress, 1st session, 668, 706, 712; St. Germain, *Indian Treaty-Making Policy*, 48–49 (quotations).

16. Jones, *Treaty of Medicine Lodge*, 18–19, 99; Henry M. Stanley, "A British Journalist Reports the Medicine Lodge Peace Councils of 1867," *Kansas Historical Quarterly* 33 (Autumn 1967), 253–54. (The above contains Stanley's complete letters from Kansas to the *Missouri Democrat*; those reprinted in Stanley's *My Early Travels and Adventures in America*

and Asia were incomplete and abridged.) *New York Times*, October 26, 1867, 8; Stanley, *My Early Travels and Adventures in America and Asia*, 2 vols. (New York: Charles Scribner's Sons, 1895), 1: 115–16 (on Augur); Joseph M. Marshall III, *The Day the World Ended at Little Bighorn: A Lakota History* (New York: Penguin, 2007), 117 (Harney's Lakota name); George Rollie Adams, *General William S. Harney, Prince of Dragoons* (Lincoln: University of Nebraska Press, 2001), xv–xvi.

17. John W. Bailey, *Pacifying the Plains: General Alfred Terry and the Decline of the Sioux, 1866–1890* (Westport, Conn.: Greenwood, 1979); Nathaniel Philbrick, *The Last Stand: Custer, Sitting Bull, and the Battle of the Little Bighorn* (New York: Viking, 2010), 101.

18. Peter Cozzens, ed., *Eyewitnesses to the Indian Wars, Vol. 2: Conquering the Southern Plains* (Mechanicsburg, Pa.: Stackpole Books, 2003), 664; Stanley, *Early Travels and Adventures*, 1: v–xiv; Tim Jeal, *Stanley: The Impossible Life of Africa's Greatest Explorer* (New Haven: Yale University Press, 2007), chs. 1–4. Jeal points out several discrepancies in Stanley's account of his early life. He also ignores his role at Medicine Lodge.

19. Jones, *Treaty of Medicine Lodge*, 25, ch. 3, and 210–19; Stanley, "A British Journalist Reports," 249, 255; Stanley, *Early Travels and Adventures*.

20. "Proceedings of the Indian Peace Commission," St. Louis, August 6–7, 1867, LROIA, Upper Platte Agency, 1867, roll 892, doc. 1–379 plus enclosure; RG 48, 665, 1: 1–4.

21. "Telegram to Superintendent Murphy," August 7, 1867, LROIA, Upper Platte Agency, 1867; Jones, *Treaty of Medicine Lodge*, 74–77; *Chicago Tribune*, September 26, 1867; *New York Times*, October 5, 1867, 5; *New York Times*, October 7, 1867, 1, 8; Hyde, *Life of George Bent*, 282.

22. William C. Meadows, *Kiowa, Apache, and Comanche Military Societies: Enduring Veterans, 1800 to the Present* (Austin: University of Texas Press, 1999), 40–41.

23. Charles M. Robinson, III, *Satanta: The Life and Death of a War Chief* (Austin: State House Press, 1997), 12; Theodore R. Davis, "A Summer on the Plains," *Harper's New Monthly Magazine* 36 (February 1868), 292–307, reprinted in Cozzens, *Eyewitnesses*, 2: 36, 39; Richard Taylor Jacob, Jr., "Military Reminiscences of Captain Richard T. Jacob," *Chronicles of Oklahoma* 2 (March 1924), 28 (quote).

24. Colonel W. S. Nye, *Carbine and Lance: The Story of Old Fort Sill* (1937; revised ed., Norman: University of Oklahoma Press, 1974), 35; James Mooney, *Calendar History of the Kiowa Indians* (Washington, D.C.: Government Printing Office, 1898; reprinted with an introduction by John C. Ewers, Washington, D.C.: Smithsonian Institution Press, 1979), 314; "Report to the President by the Indian Peace Commission," 11; Davis. "A Summer on the Plains," in Cozzens, *Eyewitnesses*, 2: 39.

25. Stanley, "A British Journalist Reports," 258; Stanley, *Early Travels and Adventures*, 1: 223.

26. Statement of F. F. Jones, February 9, 1867, LROIA, reel 375.

27. Robinson, *Satanta*, 62–63, 208n.12.

28. Robinson, *Satanta*, 63.

29. Arthur H. Mattingly, "The Great Peace Commission of 1867," *Journal of the West* 15 (1976), 29; *New York Times*, October 26, 1867, 8 ("special"); *New York Daily Tribune*, October 23, 1867; Stanley, "A British Journalist Reports," 260. Other reports said there were two Gatling guns but Edward Godfrey, who was detailed to command them, said there were four. Edward S. Godfrey, "The Medicine Lodge Treaty, Sixty Years Ago," in Cozzens, *Eyewitnesses*, 2: 69.

30. Jones, *Treaty of Medicine Lodge*, 67–68; Stanley, "A British Journalist Reports," 262; Stanley, *Early Travels and Adventures*, 1: 228–29; Godfrey, "The Medicine Lodge Treaty," 70–71; *New York Daily Tribune*, October 23, 1867 (quotes).

31. Jones, *Treaty of Medicine Lodge*, 72; Stanley, "A British Journalist Reports," 262–64; Stanley, *Early Travels and Adventures*, 1: 227, 229–30; *New York Times*, October 26, 1867, 8; *Chicago Tribune*, October 1, 1867, 1; *New York Daily Tribune*, October 23, 1867; Hyde, *Life of George Bent*, 283.

32. "Report to the President by the Indian Peace Commission," 4–5 (quote). On Black Kettle and his relations with the Dog Soldiers, see Stan Hoig, *Peace Chiefs of the Cheyennes* (Norman: University of Oklahoma Press, 1980), ch. 8 (Bull Bear as "the man" quote at 89).

33. Donald J. Berthrong, *The Southern Cheyennes* (Norman: University of Oklahoma Press, 1963), 56–57; Peter J. Powell, *People of the Sacred Mountain: A History of the Northern Cheyenne Chiefs and Warrior Societies, 1830–1879*, 2 vols. (San Francisco: Harper and Row, 1979), 1: 506–9, 521.

34. Godfrey, "The Medicine Lodge Treaty," 71.

35. Jones, *Treaty of Medicine Lodge*, 80–83; Stanley, "A British Journalist Reports," 264–68; Stanley, *Early Travels and Adventures*, 1: 231–33.

36. Leavenworth to Taylor, June 18, 1867, LROIA, reel 375.

37. Jones, *Treaty of Medicine Lodge*, 205; RG 48, 665, 1: 101.

38. Stanley, *Early Travels and Adventures*, 1: 235.

39. Jones, *Treaty of Medicine Lodge*, 84–86.

40. Jones, *Treaty of Medicine Lodge*, 94–95.

41. Stanley, "A British Journalist Reports," 269–70; Robinson, *Satanta*, 67–68.

42. Stanley, "A British Journalist Reports," 273–74; Robert M. Utley, ed., *Life in Custer's Cavalry: Diaries and Letters of Albert and Jennie Barnitz, 1867–1868* (New Haven: Yale University Press, 1977), 110–11; *Chicago Tribune*, October 24, 1867, 2.

43. Mooney, *Calendar History of the Kiowa Indians*, 321; John Galvin, ed., *Through the Country of the Comanche Indians in the Fall of the Year 1845: The Journal of a U. S. Army Expedition led by Lieutenant James W. Abert* (San Francisco: John Howell Books, 1970), 39 ("like falling water"); Richard H. Pratt, *Battlefield and Classroom: Four Decades with the American Indian, 1867–1904*, ed. Robert M. Utley (New Haven: Yale University Press, 1964; reprint, Norman: University of Oklahoma Press, 2003), 67, 96; Jones, *Treaty of Medicine Lodge*, 109 ($583.65); Sherman to J. C. Kelton, September 24, 1868, LROIA, reel 375 ($1,565).

44. Jones, *Treaty of Medicine Lodge*, 104–9; St. Germain, *Indian Treaty-Making Policy*, 61–62; *Chicago Tribune*, October 24, 1867, 2; David Fridtjof Halaas and Andrew E. Masich, *Halfbreed: The Remarkable Story of George Bent* (Cambridge, Mass.: Da Capo, 2004), 233–34, 237.

45. Loretta Fowler, *Wives and Husbands: Gender and Age in Southern Arapaho History* (Norman: University of Oklahoma Press, 2010), 22, 24–25, 27, 50–51; Stanley, "A British Journalist Reports," 265; Stanley, *Early Travels and Adventures*, 1: 231.

46. Jones, *Treaty of Medicine Lodge*, 110–17; Stanley, "A British Journalist Reports," 269; Stanley, *Early Travels and Adventures*, 1: 244; *New York Times*, October 30, 1867, 1; *Chicago Tribune*, October 25, 1867, 2.

47. Meadows, *Kiowa, Apache, and Comanche Military Societies*, 40; Robinson, *Satanta*, 7–9.

48. Jones, *Treaty of Medicine Lodge*, 111–12; Stanley, "A British Journalist Reports," 258, 279; Stanley, *Early Travels and Adventures*, 1: 223, 244.

49. Stanley, "A British Journalist Reports," 280–81; Stanley, *Early Travels and Adventures*, 1: 245–47; *Proceedings of the Great Peace Commission*, 68–69; RG 48, 665, 1: 98–100; *Papers Relating to Talks and Councils Held with the Indians in Dakota and Montana Territories in the Years 1866–1869* (Washington, D.C.: Government Printing Office, 1910), 57 ("our richest agricultural land"); *Chicago Tribune*, October 25, 1867, 2.

50. Stanley, "A British Journalist Reports," 282; Stanley, *Early Travels and Adventures*, 1: 247–49; *New York Times*, October 30, 1867; *Chicago Tribune*, October 25, 1867, 2; *Proceedings of the Great Peace Commission*, 69–70; RG 48, 665, 1: 100–101; *Papers Relating to Talks and Councils Held with the Indians in Dakota and Montana Territories*, 57–58.

51. Stanley, "A British Journalist Reports," 283–84; Stanley, *Early Travels and Adventures*, 1: 250–51; Jones, *Treaty of Medicine Lodge*, 110–16; *Proceedings of the Great Peace Commission*, 70; RG 48, 665, 1: 102–3; *Papers Relating to Talks and Councils Held with the Indians in Dakota and Montana Territories*, 58–59; *New York Times*, October 30, 1867, 1. Thomas W. Kavanagh, in *The Comanches: A History 1706–1875* (Lincoln: University of Nebraska Press, 1999), 410–18, identifies the various Comanches present at the treaty.

52. RG 48, 665, 1: 25–26, 110–12; *Papers Relating to Talks and Councils Held with the Indians in Dakota and Montana Territories*, 59; *New York Times*, October 30, 1867, 1.

53. Stanley, "A British Journalist Reports," 285–86; Stanley, *Early Travels and Adventures*, 1: 252–54; Robinson, *Satanta*, 71; Jones, *Treaty of Medicine Lodge*, 123–26; *Proceedings of the Great Peace Commission*, 71–72; RG 48, 665, 1: 104–6; *Papers Relating to Talks and Councils Held with the Indians in Dakota and Montana Territories*, 59–61; *New York Times*, October 30, 1867, 1.

54. Stanley, "A British Journalist Reports," 286–87; Stanley, *Travels and Adventures*, 253–56; *New York Times*, October 30, 1867; *New York Times*, October 30, 1867, 1; Jones, *Treaty of Medicine Lodge*, 127–28; *Papers Relating to Talks and Councils Held with the Indians in Dakota and Montana Territories*, 61; RG 48, 665, 1: 106–8; St. Germain, *Indian Treaty-Making Policy*, 132–33.

55. St. Germain, *Indian Treaty-Making Policy*, 83, 103.

56. *Papers Relating to Talks and Councils Held with the Indians in Dakota and Montana Territories*, 62: RG 48, 665, 1: 109.

57. Godfrey, "The Medicine Lodge Treaty," 71.

58. *IALT*, 977–82.

59. Blue Clark, *Lone Wolf v. Hitchcock: Treaty Rights and Indian Law at the End of the Nineteenth Century* (Lincoln: University of Nebraska Press, 1999), 23.

60. Jones, *Treaty of Medicine Lodge*, 131–32.

61. Jacqueline Fear-Segal, *White Man's Club: Schools, Race, and the Struggle of Indian Acculturation* (Lincoln: University of Nebraska Press, 2007), 5.

62. Jones, *Treaty of Medicine Lodge*, 134.

63. Stanley, "A British Journalist Reports," 288–89; *Proceedings of the Great Peace Commission*, 74; RG 48, 665: 109; *Papers Relating to Talks and Councils Held with the Indians in Dakota and Montana Territories*, 62.

64. Stanley, "A British Journalist Reports," 288; Jones, *Treaty of Medicine Lodge*, 136.

65. Jones, *Treaty of Medicine Lodge,* 137–42, 145–46, 151; Stanley, "A British Journalist Reports," 289–92; Stanley, *Early Travels and Adventures,* 1: 259–62; *Proceedings of the Great Peace Commission,* 77–78; RG 48, 665, 1: 113–15; *IALT,* 982–84.

66. Stanley, "A British Journalist Reports," 292–94. Claims then and since that the commissioners gave guns to murdering Indians who promptly turned them on innocent settlers seem to be ill-founded; few firearms appear to have been issued. Jones, *Treaty of Medicine Lodge,* 143–44; William E. Connelley, "The Treaty Held at Medicine Lodge, between the Peace Commissioners and the Comanche, Kiowa, Arapahoe, Cheyenne and Prairie Apache Tribes of Indians, in October 1867," *Collections of the Kansas State Historical Society* 17 (1926–28), 601–6.

67. Candace S. Greene, *One Hundred Summers: A Kiowa Calendar Record* (Lincoln: University of Nebraska Press, 2009), 94–95.

68. Jones, *Treaty of Medicine Lodge,* 146–49.

69. Stanley, "A British Journalist Reports," 294–96; also Jones, *Treaty of Medicine Lodge,* 155–57; *New York Times,* November 4, 1867; *Proceedings of the Great Peace Commission,* 83; RG 48, 665, 1: 123–26 (the proceedings here misidentify Satank as Satanta).

70. Stanley, "A British Journalist Reports," 298–307, 309–11; Jones, *Treaty of Medicine Lodge,* 159–69; Utley, *Life in Custer's Cavalry,* 114; *Chicago Tribune,* November 4, 1867, 1.

71. Stanley, "A British Journalist Reports," 312–13; Jones, *Treaty of Medicine Lodge,* 170–71; *Proceedings of the Great Peace Commission,* 79–80; RG 48, 665, 1: 116–19; *Papers Relating to Talks and Councils Held with the Indians in Dakota and Montana Territories,* 62–63; *Chicago Tribune,* November 4, 1867, 1.

72. Stanley, "A British Journalist Reports," 314–15; Jones, *Treaty of Medicine Lodge,* 172–73; *Papers Relating to Talks and Councils Held with the Indians in Dakota and Montana Territories,* 64–65; *Proceedings of the Great Peace Commission,* 80–81; RG 48, 665, 1: 119–21.

73. Stanley, "A British Journalist Reports," 315–16; Jones, *Treaty of Medicine Lodge,* 173–75; Mattingly, "Great Plains Peace Commission," 32–33; *New York Times,* November 1, 1867; *Chicago Tribune,* November 4, 1867, 1; *Proceedings of the Great Peace Commission,* 82; RG, 665, 1: 121–22; *Papers Relating to Talks and Councils Held with the Indians in Dakota and Montana Territories,* 65.

74. Jones, *Treaty of Medicine Lodge,* 175.

75. Raymond J. DeMallie, "Touching the Pen: Plains Indian Treaty Councils in Ethnohistorical Perspective," in *Ethnicity on the Great Plains,* ed. Frederick C. Luebke (Lincoln: University of Nebraska Press, 1980), 40.

76. Jones, *Treaty of Medicine Lodge,* 176–78; Stanley, "A British Journalist Reports," 315–16; *Chicago Tribune,* November 4, 1867, 1 ("obnoxious treaty clause"); St. Germain, *Indian Treaty-Making Policy,* 132; Powell, *People of the Sacred Mountain,* 1: 530–31; *IALT,* 984–89.

77. Stanley, "A British Journalist Reports," 315–16; *Chicago Tribune,* November 4, 1867, 1.

78. Utley, *Life in Custer's Cavalry,* 115.

79. Hyde, *Life of George Bent,* 285.

80. Jones, *Treaty of Medicine Lodge,* 181–82.

81. "By Western Union Telegraph Company," November 1, 1867, LROIA, Upper Platte Agency, 1867.

82. Stanley, *My Early Travels and Adventures,* 1: 289–90; Stanley, "A British Journalist Reports," 320.

83. Jeal, *Stanley*, 69–70.

84. LROIA, Upper Platte Agency, December 27, 1867.

85. Hagan, *United States-Comanche Relations*, 42 (quote).

86. *New York Times*, August 27, 1867, 2 ("humbug"); *New York Times*, November 8, 1867, 1; *Chicago Tribune*, November 8, 1867, 2 (order); Robert M. Utley, *Bluecoats and Redskins: The United States Army and the Indian, 1866–1891* (London: Cassell, 1975; American title: *Frontier Regulars*), 132 ("little difference"); Robert G. Athearn, *William Tecumseh Sherman and the Settlement of the West* (Norman: University of Oklahoma Press, 1956), 210–11 ("kill time").

87. Jones, *Treaty of Medicine Lodge*, 182.

88. "Report of the Indian Commission to the President." The *New York Times*, January 10, 1868, 5, provided an abstract of the report; the *Chicago Tribune,* January 11, 1868, 2, printed the report in full.

89. Major Joel H. Elliott, "Official Report, November 2, 1867," Letters Received, Department of the Missouri, Army-Navy Branch, National Archives, Washington, D.C., cited and discussed in Jones, *Treaty of Medicine Lodge*, 199–202.

90. *ARCIA* for 1869: 361.

91. St. Germain, *Indian Treaty-Making Policy*, 139–40.

92. *Proceedings of the Great Peace Commission*, 162–63; Sherman to Brevet Major General E. D. Townshend, September 5, 1868; Charles E. Mix, Acting Commissioner of Indian Affairs, to W. J. Otto, Acting Secretary of the Interior, September 12, 1868; Otto to Secretary of War, September 28, 1868, in "Correspondence relating to the implementation of the Medicine Lodge treaties with the Kiowa, Kiowa-Apache, Comanche, Cheyenne, and Arapaho Indians," July–September 1868, LROAG, M619, reel 629; *ARCIA* for 1870: 262; Jacki Thompson Rand, *Kiowa Humanity and the Invasion of the State* (Lincoln: University of Nebraska Press, 2008), chs. 3–4.

93. *ARCIA* for 1869: 385 (Kiowa complaints and corn); *ARCIA* for 1870: 260–65; Statement of Tosh-o-na [Silver Brooch], March 6, 1868, and McCusker to Commissioner of Indian Affairs, June 5, 1868, LROIA, reel 375.

94. *ARCIA* for 1867: 18; *ARCIA* for 1870: 254–55 (rights in Texas). Correspondence regarding captives from Texas is scattered through LROIA, reel 375.

95. Leavenworth to Taylor, May 21, 1868; Sheridan to Gen. Nichols, May 22, 1868 (Leavenworth unsuitable for his position); Commissioner of Indian Affairs to Secretary of Interior, July 1, 1868, LROIA, reel 375.

96. Rand, *Kiowa Humanity and the Invasion of the State*, 8, chs. 3–4.

97. Capt. Henry Alvord to Maj. Gen. Guerson, April 24, 1869, and Gen. Schofield to Sheridan, May 29, 1869, LROAG, M619, reel 722; Berthrong, *Southern Cheyennes*, 346.

98. "Correspondence relating to the implementation of the Medicine Lodge treaties with the Kiowa, Kiowa-Apache, Comanche, Cheyenne, and Arapaho Indians"; *ARCIA* for 1868: 2–3, 256–58, 260–61, 267.

99. Sherman to Maj. Gen. Schriver, September 17, 1868; and Sherman to Brig. Gen. J. C. Kelton, September 19, 1868, "Correspondence relating to the implementation of the Medicine Lodge treaties with the Kiowa, Kiowa-Apache, Comanche, Cheyenne, and Arapaho Indians"; Sherman to Gen. Schofield, September 26, 1868, LROIA, reel 375 ("to their hearts' content").

100. *ARCIA* for 1868: 258.

101. *Proceedings of the Great Peace Commission*, 170–71.

102. Robinson, S*atanta*, 88; General G. A. Custer, *My Life on the Plains, or Personal Experiences with Indians* (London: Folio Society, 1963), 172, 190; Hyde, *Life of George Bent*, 316–22; Stan Hoig, *The Battle of the Washita: The Sheridan-Custer Indian Campaign of 1867–69* (Norman: University of Oklahoma Press, 1976), 131–32, 154–62; 40th Congress, 3rd session, Senate Executive Documents 13, 18, 36: Letters and reports relating to the Battle of the Washita; George Bent, "She-Wolf's Account of the Death of Major Elliott," in Cozzens, *Eyewitnesses*, 2: 398–400.

103. Godfrey, "The Medicine Lodge Treaty," 73.

104. Greene, *One Hundred Summers*, 96–97.

105. Mooney, *Calendar History of the Kiowa Indians*, 322–24; Murphy to Charles E. Mix, September 21, 1868, LROIA, reel 375.

106. Sheridan quoted in Custer, *My Life on the Plains*, 199–200.

107. Interview of General Sheridan with Little Robe of the Cheyennes and Yellow Robe of the Arapahoes, January 1, 1869 ("do not care one cent"), LROAG, M 619, reel 718; Sheridan to Sherman, telegram, June 9, 1869, reel 722.

108. Hoig, *Peace Chiefs of the Cheyennes*, 94–103; Elliott West, *The Contested Plains: Indians, Goldseekers, and the Rush to Colorado* (Lawrence: University Press of Kansas, 1998), 313–16; Hyde, *Life of George Bent*, 331–34, 340.

109. General Orders, June 29, 1869, LROAG, reel 722.

110. Quoted in Robinson, *Satanta*, 104.

111. "Message of the President," March 8, 1870, 41st Congress, 2nd session, Senate Executive Document 57, 1–3.

112. Rand, *Kiowa Humanity and the Invasion of the State*, ch. 4.

113. Mooney, *Calendar History of the Kiowa Indians*, 327–28; Alice Marriott, *The Ten Grandmothers* (Norman: University of Oklahoma Press, 1945), 101–11; Robinson, *Satanta*, 116 (quotation).

114. Nye, *Carbine and Lance*, 132–43, 147.

115. Kicking Bird to CIA, n.d. (c. 1872), LROIA, Kiowa Agency, quoted in Fear-Segal, *White Man's Club*, 48.

116. Mooney, *Calendar History of the Kiowa Indians*, 329–33; Marriott, *The Ten Grandmothers*, 124–25; Nye, *Carbine and Lance*, 143–47.

117. Robinson, S*atanta*, ch. 10.

118. Nye, *Carbine and Lance*, 157–60.

119. Brad D. Lookingbill, *War Dance at Fort Marion: Plains Indian War Prisoners* (Norman: University of Oklahoma Press, 2006), 15.

120. Quoted in Robinson, S*atanta*, 156.

121. James L. Haley, *The Buffalo War: The History of the Red River Indian Uprising of 1874* (New York: Doubleday, 1976), ch. 2; Andrew C. Isenberg, *The Destruction of the Bison: An Environmental History, 1750–1920* (Cambridge: Cambridge University Press, 2000), ch. 5 (quote at 128); Richard Irving Dodge, *Our Wild Indians: Thirty-Three Years' Personal Experience among the Red Men of the Great West* (1882; reprint, Freeport, N.Y.: Books for Libraries Press, 1970), 293–96.

122. Nye, *Carbine and Lance*, 159.

123. Haley, *Buffalo War*, vii, 41–48.

124. Haley, *Buffalo War*, 143–46; Lookingbill, *War Dance at Fort Marion*, 22–23.

125. Powell, *People of the Sacred Mountain*, 1: 531; Berthrong, *Southern Cheyennes*, 396–99.

126. Nye, *Carbine and Lance*, 213–30.

127. Robinson, *Satanta*, 193–95; Nye, *Carbine and Lance*, 255–56, 261.

128. Pratt, *Battlefield and Classroom*, 105, 138–44 (list of prisoners).

129. Nye, *Carbine and Lance*, 127, 231–34; Lookingbill, *War Dance at Fort Marion*, 16–17, 44.

130. Pratt, *Battlefield and Classroom*, 109, 112–15; Richard H. Pratt, *American Indians, Chained and Unchained: Being an Address before the Pennsylvania Commandery of the Military Order of the Loyal Legion, Philadelphia...* (1912), 5–6.

131. Pratt, *Battlefield and Classroom*, 158.

132. Nye, *Carbine and Lance*, 234; Lookingbill, *War Dance at Fort Marion*, 66.

133. On the prisoners, see Lookingbill, *War Dance at Fort Marion*; on their art, see Rand, *Kiowa Humanity and the Invasion of the State*, 101–7; Joyce M. Szabo, *Art from Fort Marion: The Silberman Collection* (Norman: University of Oklahoma Press, 2007); Szabo, *Howling Wolf and the History of Ledger Art* (Albuquerque: University of New Mexico Press, 1994); Szabo, "Medicine Lodge Remembered," *American Indian Art Magazine* 14, no. 4 (1989), 52–59, 87 (Howling Wolf in Black Kettle's village, 58); Herman J. Viola, *Warrior Artists: Historic Cheyenne and Kiowa Indian Ledger Art Drawn by Making Medicine and Zotom* (Washington, D.C.: National Geographic Society, 1998); Karen Daniels Peterson, *Plains Indian Art from Fort Marion* (Norman: University of Oklahoma Press, 1971).

134. Lookingbill, *War Dance at Fort Marion*, 150–52, 186.

135. Mooney, *Calendar History of the Kiowa Indians*, 344.

136. Lookingbill, *War Dance at Fort Marion*, 175; Clark, *Lone Wolf v. Hitchcock*, 29–30.

137. Greene, *One Hundred Summers*, 187; "Medicine Lodge Treaties Celebrated by a Pageant," *New York Times*, October 23, 1927, 12; Douglas C. Jones, "Medicine Lodge Revisited," *Kansas Historical Quarterly* 35 (Summer 1969), 130–42; "Indian Peace Treaty Pageant," http://peacetreaty.org.

138. Ernest Renan, "What Is a Nation?" in *Nation and Narration*, ed. Homi K. Bhabha (London: Routledge, 1990), 11.

Conclusion

1. *IALT*, 998–1007.

2. Red Cloud quoted in Edward Lazarus, *Black Hills/White Justice: The Sioux Nation versus the United States, 1775 to the Present* (New York: HarperCollins, 1991), 62. A full version of Red Cloud's Cooper Union speech as reported in the *New York Times* is in Wayne Moquin and Charles Van Doren, eds., *Great Documents in American Indian History* (New York: Praeger, 1973), 211–13. Jeffrey Ostler, *The Lakotas and the Black Hills* (New York: Penguin, 2010), 66, 73.

3. Jill St. Germain, *Indian Treaty-Making Policy in the United States and Canada, 1867–1877* (Lincoln: University of Nebraska Press, 2001), 36. Challenging the "broken treaties refrain," Germain offers a more optimistic interpretation of the 1868 Treaty of Fort Laramie than is common in much of the literature; Jill St. Germain, *Broken Treaties: United States*

and Canadian Relations with the Lakotas and the Plains Cree, 1868–1885 (Lincoln: University of Nebraska Press, 2009).

4. *IALT*, 1015–20.

5. *IALT*, 1020–24.

6. The Nez Perce treaties are in *IALT*, 843–48, 1024–25. Lucullus Virgil McWhorter, *Yellow Wolf: His Own Story* (1940; Caldwell, Idaho: Caxton Printers, 1995), 35; Alvin M. Josephy, Jr., *The Nez Perce Indians and the Opening of the Northwest* (New Haven: Yale University Press, 1965), 421 (Lawyer's notebook); Elliott West, *The Last Indian War: The Nez Perce Story* (New York: Oxford University Press, 2009), 93–94 (90 percent at 8 cents an acre); Chief Joseph, "An Indian's View of Indian Affairs," *North American Review* (April 1879), 419, and quoted in Josephy, *Nez Perce Indians*, 488–89.

7. West, *The Last Indian War.*

8. Ross's letter reprinted in *New York Times*, November 5, 1867, 2.

9. *Proceedings of the Great Peace Commission of 1867–1868*, with an introduction by Vine Deloria, Jr., and Raymond DeMallie (Washington, D.C.: Institute for the Development of Indian Law, 1975), 157–71, quotations at 169; RG 48, 665, 2: 178–96; *Papers Relating to Talks and Councils Held with the Indians in Dakota and Montana Territories in the Years 1866–1869* (Washington, D.C.: Government Printing Office, 1910), 123, 128–31 (quotations at 131); *ARCIA*, 1868: 7–15; quote at 12.

10. *Proceedings of the Great Peace Commission*, 165; RG 48, 665, 2: 185; *Papers Relating to Talks and Councils Held with the Indians in Dakota and Montana Territories,* 123.

11. Henry B. Whipple, "The Indian System," *North American Review* 99 (1964), 449–64, quotes at 450–51; *New York Times* extract quoted as an epigram in Stan Hoig, *White Man's Paper Trail: Grand Councils and Treaty-Making on the Central Plains* (Boulder: University Press of Colorado, 2006).

12. Richard Irving Dodge, *Our Wild Indians: Thirty-Three Years' Personal Experience among the Red Men of the Great West.* (1882; reprint, Freeport, N.Y.: Books for Libraries Press, 1970), 89–90.

13. Peter Cozzens, ed., *Eyewitnesses to the Indian Wars, Vol. 2: Conquering the Southern Plains* (Mechanicsburg, Pa.: Stackpole, 2003), 250–51, 262.

14. *ARCIA* for 1869: 6.

15. St. Germain, *Indian Treaty-Making Policy*, ch. 9 (outdated and unfair quotation at 150); Deloria and DeMallie, *Documents of American Indian Diplomacy*, 1: ch. 6; Francis Paul Prucha, ed., *Documents of United States Indian Policy* (Lincoln: University of Nebraska Press, 1975), 136; John R. Wunder, "No More Treaties: The Resolution of 1871 and the Alteration of Indian Rights to Their Homelands," in *Working the Range: Essays on the History of Western Land Management and the Environment*, ed. John R. Wunder (Westport, Conn.: Greenwood, 1985), 39–56; Kevin Bruyneel, *The Third Space of Sovereignty: The Post-Colonial Politics of U.S.-Indigenous Relations* (Minneapolis: University of Minnesota Press, 2007), ch. 3.

16. Peter J. Powell, *People of the Sacred Mountain*, 2 vols. (San Francisco: Harper and Row, 1979), 2: 798–803; Stan Hoig, *The Western Odyssey of John Simpson Smith: Frontiersman and Indian Interpreter* (Norman: University of Oklahoma Press, 2004), 223–29.

17. Deloria and DeMallie, *Documents of American Indian Diplomacy*, 1: ch. 7.

18. Kevin Gover, "Statutes as Sources of Modern Indian Rights: Child Welfare, Gaming, and Repatriation," in *Treaties with American Indians: An Encyclopedia of Rights, Conflicts,*

and Sovereignty, ed. Donald L. Fixico, 3 vols. (Santa Barbara, Calif.: ABC-CLIO, 2008), 1: 109–29.

19. Bruyneel, *Third Space of Sovereignty,* ch. 3, Downing quotation at 70; Patrick Wolfe, "After the Frontier: Separation and Absorption in US Indian Policy," *Settler Colonial Studies* 1 (2011), 13, 33.

20. N. Bruce Duthu, *American Indians and the Law* (New York: Penguin, 2008), 120; James W. Parins, *Elias Cornelius Boudinot: A Life on the Cherokee Border* (Lincoln: University of Nebraska Press. 2006), ch. 5.

21. Richard White, *Railroaded: The Transcontinentals and the Making of Modern America* (New York: W. W. Norton, 2011), 134–39; H. Craig Miner, *The Corporation and the Indian: Tribal Sovereignty and Industrial Civilization in Indian Territory, 1865–1907* (1976; Norman: University of Oklahoma Press, 1989), 44–45, 81–82, 120–21; Parins, *Elias Cornelius Boudinot,* ch. 6.

22. Thomas Powers, *The Killing of Crazy Horse* (New York: Knopf, 2010).

23. Francis Paul Prucha, *American Indian Policy in Crisis: Christian Reformers and the Indian, 1865–1900* (Norman: University of Oklahoma Press, 1976), 231.

24. Robert M. Utley, *The Last Days of the Sioux Nation* (New Haven: Yale University Press, 1963), Crook quoted at 53. The 1889 agreement is in *IALT,* 1: 328–39, and Deloria and DeMallie, *Documents of American Indian Diplomacy,* 1: 307–15.

25. William T. Hagan, *Taking Indian Lands: The Cherokee (Jerome) Commission, 1889–1893* (Norman: University of Oklahoma Press, 2003).

26. Hagan *Taking Indian Lands,* ch. 4, Little Medicine quoted at 78. George Bent later became an informant and interpreter for the scholar George Bird Grinnell, gathering people for interviews and translating their answers to Grinnell's questions. He became acquainted with George Hyde, one of Grinnell's research assistants and around 1905 began a lengthy correspondence—hundreds of letters on the history and culture of the Southern Cheyennes—that continued almost until Bent's death in 1918. Hyde wrote a book from Bent's material, although it was not published until half a century later. The director of the University of Oklahoma Press rediscovered the manuscript and, with the support of the aged Hyde, edited and published the *Life of George Bent, Written from His Letters* (1968). Lincoln B. Faller, "Making Medicine against 'White Man's Side of Story': George Bent's Letters to George Hyde," *American Indian Quarterly* 24 (Winter 2000), 64–90; David Fridtjof Halaas and Andrew E. Masich, *Halfbreed: The Remarkable Story of George Bent* (Cambridge, Mass.: Da Capo, 2004), 313–26.

27. Hagan, *Taking Indian Lands,* ch. 9; Blue Clark, *Lone Wolf v. Hitchcock: Treaty Rights and Indian Law at the End of the Nineteenth Century* (Lincoln: University of Nebraska Press, 1999), ch. 5, quote at 46; Ann Laquer Estin, "*Lone Wolf v. Hitchcock*: The Long Shadow," in *The Aggressions of Civilization: Federal Indian Policy since the 1880s,* ed. Sandra L. Cadwalader and Vine Deloria, Jr. (Philadelphia: Temple University Press, 1984), 216–45.

28. Estin, "*Lone Wolf v. Hitchcock*: The Long Shadow," 222–26, 229.

29. Hagan, *Taking Indian Lands,* ch. 9; Clark, *Lone Wolf v. Hitchcock,* 45–48.

30. Estin, "*Lone Wolf v. Hitchcock*: The Long Shadow," 227–28, 229–30; 56th Congress, 1st session, 1900, Senate Document 76.

31. Clark, *Lone Wolf v. Hitchcock,* 54–55.

32. Estin, "*Lone Wolf v. Hitchcock*: The Long Shadow," 231–39; "Decision in the Case of Lone Wolf," 57th Congress, 2nd session, Senate Document 148; Clark, *Lone Wolf v. Hitchcock,* 95; Bruyneel, *Third Space of Sovereignty,* 80–89.

33. Hagan *Taking Indian Land*, 206–7.

34. Estin, "*Lone Wolf v. Hitchcock*: The Long Shadow," 239–40 ("at the whim"); Clark, *Lone Wolf v. Hitchcock*, ix–x. (David E. Wilkins, "The Reinvigoration of the Doctrine of 'Implied Repeals': A Requiem for Indigenous Treaty Rights," *The American Journal of Legal History* 43 [1999], 1–26, argues that the Supreme Court lacks constitutional authority to abrogate specific treaty rights by implication or to divest tribes of their rights; that power is vested in Congress.)

35. Fixico, *Treaties with American Indians*, 1: 41–43, 62, 151; Charles F. Wilkinson, *American Indians, Time, and the Law* (New Haven: Yale University Press, 1987), 46–52.

36. Quoted in Francis Paul Prucha, *American Indian Treaties: The History of a Political Anomaly* (Berkeley: University of California Press, 1994), 393.

37. Joanne Barker points out the "blatant contradictions.... between the recognition of the sovereignty of indigenous peoples through the entire apparatus of treaty making and the unmitigated negation of indigenous peoples' status and rights by national legislation, military action, and judicial decision." Joanne Barker, ed., *Sovereignty Matters: Locations of Contestation and Possibility in Indigenous Struggles for Self-Determination* (Lincoln: University of Nebraska Press, 2005), 6; Vine Deloria, Jr., *Custer Died for Your Sins: An Indian Manifesto* (1969; New York: Avon, 1970), 38, 56 (quote).

38. Bruyneel, *Third Space of Sovereignty*, 164–65.

39. Wilkinson, *American Indians, Time, and the Law*, 1–3.

40. Fay G. Cohen, *Treaties on Trial: The Continuing Controversy over Northwest Indian Fishing Rights* (Seattle: University of Washington Press, 1986); Kent Richards, guest ed., "The Isaac I. Stevens and Joel Palmer Treaties, 1855–2005," *Oregon Historical Quarterly* 106 (Fall 2005), 342–491, Boldt quotes in *U.S. v. Washington*, 1974, 384, Supp. 312.

41. Larry Nesper, *The Walleye War: The Struggle for Ojibwe Spearfishing and Treaty Rights* (Lincoln: University of Nebraska Press, 2002); James M. McClurken, comp., *Fish in the Lakes, Wild Rice, and Game in Abundance: Testimony on Behalf of Mille Lacs Ojibwe Hunting and Fishing Rights* (East Lansing: Michigan State University Press, 2000).

42. For a thorough account of the history of the Black Hills land claim, see Lazarus, *Black Hills*, and Ostler, *Lakotas and the Black Hills*.

43. Quoted in Lazarus, *Black Hills, White Justice*, 344.

44. Robert A. Williams, Jr., *Like a Loaded Weapon: The Rehnquist Court, Indian Rights, and the Legal History of Racism in America* (Minneapolis: University of Minnesota Press, 2005).

45. Wilkinson, *American Indians, Time, and the Law*, 121–22.

46. Vine Deloria, Jr., and Clifford M, Lytle, *The Nations Within: The Past and Future of American Indian Sovereignty* (New York: Pantheon, 1984), 8.

47. Russel Lawrence Barsh and James Youngblood Henderson, *The Road: Indian Tribes and Political Liberty* (Berkeley: University of California Press, 1980), 270.

48. Duthu, *American Indians and the Law*, 213–16.

49. Rebecca Tsosie, "Sacred Obligations: Intercultural Justice and the Discourse of Treaty Rights," *UCLA Law Review* 1615 (2000), 1615–1672, quotes at 1658, 1699.

50. http://social.un.org/index/IndigenousPeoples/DeclarationontheRightsofIndigenous Peoples.aspx

51. Robert A. Williams, Jr., *Linking Arms Together: American Indian Treaty Visions of Law and Peace, 1600–1800* (New York: Oxford University Press, 1997), 5.

52. Jeffrey R. Dudas, *The Cultivation of Resentment: Treaty Rights and the New Right* (Stanford: Stanford University Press, 2008), quotes at 4, 14.

BIBLIOGRAPHY

Manuscript Collections

Carnegie Library of Pittsburgh

Col. George Morgan Letter Books, 1775, 1776, 1778–79. Microfilm.

Massachusetts Historical Society, Boston

Timothy Pickering Papers. Microfilm. 69 reels. Reels 59–62: Pickering's Mission to the Indians, 1786–1809.

National Archives Washington, D. C.

"Correspondence relating to the implementation of the Medicine Lodge treaties with the Kiowa, Kiowa-Apache, Comanche, Cheyenne, and Arapaho Indians," July–Sept. 1868, Letters Received by the Office of the Adjutant General (Main Series), 1861–70. M619, reel 629.

Documents Relating to the Negotiation of Ratified and Unratified Treaties with Various Indian Tribes, 1801–69. MT494. 10 reels.

Letters Received by the Office of Indian Affairs, 1824–80, M234, reels 76, 79–84 (Cherokee Agency, 1834–40); 113–16 (Cherokee Emigration, 1828–54).

Letters Received by the Office of Indian Affairs, 1824–80, M234, reel 375 (Kiowa Agency, 1864–68).

Proceedings of the Indian Peace Commission, 1867–68. 2 vols. RG 48: Records of the Secretary of the Interior, Entry 665 (National Archives, College Park, Maryland).

"Proceedings of the Indian Peace Commission," St. Louis, August 7, 1867, Letters Received by the Office of Indian Affairs, Upper Platte Agency, 1867. M 234, roll 892.

Ratified Indian Treaties, 1722–1869. M668. 16 vols.

New York Public Library

Chalmers Collection: Papers Relating to Indians, 1750–75.

Philip Schuyler Manuscripts, 1710–97, Indian Affairs Papers, microfilm reels 7–7A.

Pennsylvania Historical Commission, Harrisburg, Pa.

"Letter Book of George Morgan 1776." Reproduced in *Iroquois Indians: A Documentary History of the Six Nations and Their League*. Microfilm. 50 reels. Woodbridge, Conn.: Research Publications, 1984, reel 32.

Government Documents

American State Papers: Documents, Legislative and Executive, of the Congress of the United States. Class II: Indian Affairs. Selected and edited by Walter Lowrie and Matthew St. Clair Clarke. 2 vols. Washington: Gales and Seaton, 1832.

Annual Reports of the Commissioner of Indian Affairs for the years 1824—1920. Washington, D. C.: Government Printing Office.

Congressional Globe, 40th Congress, 1st session.

"Correspondence on the Subject of the Emigration of Indians," 1831–33, 23rd Congress, 1st session, Senate Document 512. 5 vols. (Reprinted as *The Indian Removals.* New York: AMS Press, 1974.)

"Documents in relation to the Validity of the Cherokee treaty of 1835" [compiled by Elias Boudinot], 25th Congress, 2nd session, Senate Document 121.

Kappler, Charles J., comp. and ed. *Indian Affairs: Laws and Treaties.* Vol. 2 (Treaties). Washington, D.C.: Government Printing Office, 1904.

"Letter of the Secretary of the Interior [regarding] Indian hostilities on the frontier," 40th Congress, 1st session, Senate Doc. 13.

"Memorial and Protest of the Cherokee Nation...against the ratification, execution, and enforcement of the treaty negotiated at New Echota in December, 1835," 24th Congress, 1st session, House Document 286.

"Memorial of a Council Held at Running Waters," 23rd Congress, 2nd session, House Document 91.

"Memorial of a Delegation from the Cherokee Indians," January 18, 1831, 21st Congress, 2nd session, House Document 57.

"Memorial of a Delegation of the Cherokee Nation, Remonstrating against the instrument of writing (treaty) of December, 1835," 25th Congress, 2nd session, House Document 99.

"Memorial of John Rogers, Principal Chief, et al.," April 13, 1844, 29th Congress, 1st session, House Document 235.

"Memorial of John Ross and Others," March 3, 1829, 20th Congress, 2nd session, House Document 145.

"Memorial of John Ross and Others," May 4, 1846, 29th Congress, 1st session, Senate Document 331.

"Memorial of the Cherokee Delegation, Submitting the memorial and protest of the Cherokee people to Congress," April 9, 1838, 25th Congress, 2nd session, House Document 316.

"Memorial of the Delegation of the Cherokee Nation," March 9, 1840, 26th Congress, 1st session, House Document 129.

"Memorial of the 'Treaty Party' of the Cherokee Indians....," April 13, 1844, 28th Congress, 1st session, House Document 234.

"Message of the President of the United States, relative to the Cherokee Difficulties," April 13, 1846, 29th Congress, 1st session, House Document 185, Senate Document 298.

The New American State Papers: Indian Affairs, 1789–1860. 13 vols. Wilmington, Del.: Scholarly Resources, 1972.

Papers Relating to Talks and Councils Held with the Indians in Dakota and Montana Territories in the Years 1866–1869. Washington, D.C.: Government Printing Office, 1910 (includes Medicine Lodge).

"Peace with Indian Tribes." *Congressional Globe*, 40th Congress, 1st session, 667–73, 678–90, 702–15.

"Removal of the Cherokees" [correspondence between the War Dept. and General Winfield Scott], 25th Congress, 2nd session, House Document 453.

"Report of the Secretary of War...in relation to the Cherokee Treaty of 1835," 25th Congress, 2nd session, Senate Document 120.

"Report of the Secretary of War...[regarding] the discontents and difficulties among the Cherokee Indians," February 24, 1845, 28th Congress, 2nd session, Senate Document 140.

"Report to the President by the Indian Peace Commission," January 7, 1868, in Message from the President of the United States, transmitting report of the Indian peace commissioners. January 14, 1868.—Referred to the Committee on Indian Affairs and ordered to be printed. 40th Congress, 2nd session, House Executive Document 97. Also in *ARCIA*, 1868, Appendix A.

Schermerhorn, John F. "A Journal of the Proceedings of the Council held at New Echota." 25th Congress, 2nd session, Senate Document 120: 513–17.

Newspapers

The Cherokee Phoenix
Chicago Tribune, August 1867–January 1868
New York Times, August 1867–January 1868

Printed Primary Sources

Aupaumut, Hendrick. "A Narrative of an Embassy to the Western Indians." *Memoirs of the Historical Society of Pennsylvania* 2, part 1 (1827), 61–131.

Blair, Emma Helen, ed. *The Indian Tribes of the Upper Mississippi Valley and Region of the Great Lakes*. 2 vols., 1911–12; reprint, Lincoln: University of Nebraska Press, 1996.

Boudinot, Elias. *Letters and Other Papers Relating to Cherokee Affairs; Being in Reply to Sundry Publications Authorized by John Ross*. Athens, 1837.

Boyd, Julian P., ed. *Indian Treaties Printed by Benjamin Franklin, 1736–1762*. Philadelphia: The Historical Society of Pennsylvania, 1938.

Clinton, Robert, Kevin Gover, and Rebecca Tsosie, eds. *Colonial and American Indian Treaties: A Collection*. Arizona State University College of Law, 2004.

Colden, Cadwallader. *The History of the Five Indian Nations Depending on the Province of New-York in America*. 1727 and 1747; reprint, Ithaca, N.Y.: Cornell University Press, 1964.

Cozzens, Peter, ed. *Eyewitnesses to the Indian Wars, Vol. 2: Conquering the Southern Plains*. Mechanicsburg, Pa.: Stackpole Books, 2003.

Cruikshank, E. A., ed. *The Correspondence of Lieut. Governor John Graves Simcoe, with allied Documents Relating to His Administration of the Government of Upper Canada*. 5 vols. Toronto: Ontario Historical Society, 1923–31.

Dale, Edward Everett, and Gaston Litton, eds. *Cherokee Cavaliers: Forty Years of Cherokee History as Told in the Correspondence of the Ridge-Watie-Boudinot Family*. Norman: University of Oklahoma Press, 1939.

Davies, K. G., ed. *Documents of the American Revolution 1770–1783* (Colonial Office Series) 20 vols. Shannon: Irish University Press, 1972.

Deloria, Vine, Jr., and Raymond J. DeMallie, eds. *Documents of American Indian Diplomacy: Treaties, Agreements, and Conventions, 1775–1979.* 2 vols. Norman: University of Oklahoma Press, 1999.

Fenton, William N., ed. "Answers to Governor Cass's Questions by Jacob Jemison, a Seneca [ca. 1821–1825]." *Ethnohistory* 16 (Spring 1969), 113–39.

Fenton, William N., ed. "The Journal of James Emlen Kept on a Trip to Canandaigua, New York, September 15 to October 30, 1794, to Attend the Treaty between the United Sates and the Six Nations." *Ethnohistory* 12 (Fall 1965), 279–342.

Godfrey, Edward S. "The Medicine Lodge Treaty, Sixty Years Ago." In *Eyewitnesses to the Indian Wars*, ed. Cozzens, 69–73.

Harrison, Samuel Alexander. *Memoir of Lieutenant Colonel Tench Tilghman: Secretary and Aid to Washington.* 1876; reprint, New York: Arno Press, 1971.

Heckewelder, John. *History, Manners, and Customs of the Indian Nations Who Once Inhabited Pennsylvania and the Neighboring States.* 1876; reprint, New York: Arno Press and the *New York Times*, 1971.

Hough, Franklin B. ed. *Proceeedings of the Commissioners of Indian Affairs, Appointed by Law for the Extinguishment of Indian Titles in the State of New York.* Albany, N.Y.: Munsell, 1861.

Jackson, Donald, ed. *Black Hawk: An Autobiography.* Urbana: University of Illinois Press, 1955.

"Journal of the Proceedings of the Congress held at Albany, in 1754." *Collections of the Massachusetts Historical Society*, 3rd ser. 5 (1836), 5–100.

A Journey from Pennsylvania to Onondaga in 1743 by John Bartram, Lewis Evans, and Conrad Weiser. Barre, Mass.: Imprint Society, 1973.

Kalter, Susan, ed. *Benjamin Franklin, Pennsylvania, and the First Nations: The Treaties of 1736–62.* Urbana: University of Illinois Press, 2006.

King, Duane H., and E. Raymond Evans, eds. "The Trail of Tears: Primary Documents of the Cherokee Removal." *Journal of Cherokee Studies* 3, no. 3 (Summer 1978).

Kip, Col. Lawrence. *The Indian Council at Walla Walla, May and June, 1855: A Journal. Sources of the History of Oregon*, vol. 1, part 2, *Contributions of the Department of Economics and History*, 1897.

Labaree, Leonard W., ed. *The Papers of Benjamin Franklin.* 39 vols. New Haven: Yale University Press, 1959–.

Latrobe, Charles J. *The Rambler in North America, 1832–1833.* 2 vols. New York: Harper and Brothers, 1835.

Leder, Lawrence H., ed. *The Livingston Indian Records, 1666–1723.* Gettysburg: Pennsylvania Historical Association, 1956.

"Letters of Colonel George Croghan." *Pennsylvania Magazine of History and Biography* 15 (1891), 429–39.

Lumpkin, Wilson. *The Removal of the Cherokee Indians from Georgia, 1827–1841.* 2 vols. New York: Dodd, Mead, and Co., 1907.

Merrell, James H., ed. *The Lancaster Treaty of 1744 with Related Documents.* Boston: Bedford/St. Martin's, 2008.

Minutes of Conferences held at Fort-Pitt in April and May 1768, under the direction of George Croghan. Philadelphia: William Goddard, 1769.

Minutes of Debates in Council on the banks of the Ottawa River, November 1791 Said to be held there by the Chiefs of the several Indian Nations, who defeated the Army of the United States, on the 4th of that Month. Philadelphia: William Young, 1792.

Mooney, James. *Calendar History of the Kiowa Indians*. Washington, D.C.: Government Printing Office, 1898; reprinted with an introduction by John C. Ewers, Washington, D.C.: Smithsonian Institution Press, 1979.

Moulton, E. Gary, ed. *The Lewis and Clark Journals: An American Epic of Discovery*. Lincoln: University of Nebraska Press, 2003.

Moulton, E. Gary, ed. *The Papers of Chief John Ross*. 2 vols. Norman: University of Oklahoma Press, 1985.

"The Murder of Elias Boudinot." *Chronicles of Oklahoma* 12 (March 1934), 9–24.

O'Callaghan, Edmund B., ed. *Documents Relating to the Colonial History of the State of New York*. 15 vols. Albany: Weed, Parsons, and Co., 1853–57.

The Papers of Benjamin Franklin. Digital Edition by the Packard Humanities Institute. Sponsored by the American Philosophical Society and Yale University (http://franklin-papers.org/franklin).

Paschal, George. "The Trial of Stand Watie," ed. Grant Foreman, *Chronicles of Oklahoma* 12 (September 1934), 305–39.

Perdue, Theda, ed. *Cherokee Editor: The Writings of Elias Boudinot*. Knoxville: University of Tennessee Press, 1983.

"Proceedings of Sir William Johnson with the Indians at Fort Stanwix to Settle a Boundary Line," in E. B. O'Callaghan, ed., *Documents Relative to the Colonial History of the State of New York*. Vol. 8: 111–37. Albany: Weed, Parsons, and Co., 1857.

Proceedings of the Great Peace Commission of 1867–1868, with an introduction by Vine Deloria, Jr., and Raymond DeMallie. Washington, D.C.: Institute for the Development of Indian Law, 1975.

Prucha, Francis Paul, ed. *Cherokee Removal: The "William Penn" Essays and Other Writings by Jeremiah Evarts*. Knoxville: University of Tennessee Press, 1981.

Quaife, Milo M., ed. "The Chicago Treaty of 1833." *Wisconsin Magazine of History* 1 (March 1918), 287–303.

Quaife, Milo M., ed. *John Long's Voyages and Travels in the Years 1768–1788*. Chicago: R. R. Donnelley and Sons, 1922.

Savery, William. "The Savery Journal: The Canandaigua Treaty Excerpt." In *Treaty of Canandaigua 1794: 200 Years of Treaty Relations between the Iroquois Confederacy and the United States*, ed. G. Peter Jemison and Anna M. Schein, 260–93. Santa Fe, N.M.: Clear Light, 2000.

Stanley, Henry M. "A British Journalist Reports the Medicine Lodge Peace Councils of 1867." *Kansas Historical Quarterly* 33 (Autumn 1967), 249–320.

Stanley, Henry M. "The Medicine Lodge Peace Council." In *Eyewitnesses to the Indian Wars*, ed. Cozzens, 74–126. Mechanicsburg, Pa.: Stackpole Books, 2003.

Stanley, Henry M. *My Early Travels and Adventures in America and Asia*. 2 vols. New York: Charles Scribner's Sons, 1895.

Sullivan, James, et al., eds. *The Papers of Sir William Johnson*. 14 vols. Albany: University of the State of New York, 1921–65.

Thomson, Charles. *An Enquiry into the Causes of the Alienation of the Delaware and Shawanese Indians from the British Interest, And into the Measures taken for recovering their Friendship.* London: Printed for J. Wilkie, 1759.

Thwaites, Reuben G., ed. *Early Western Travels 1748–1765, by Conrad Wesier, 1748; George Croghan, 1750–1765; Frederick Post, 1758; and Thomas Morris, 1764.* 1904; reprinted Lewisburg, Pa: Wennawoods Publishing, 1998.

Thwaites, Reuben G., ed. *The Jesuit Relations and Allied Documents.* 71 vols. Cleveland: Burrows Brothers, 1896–1901.

"The Treaty of Logg's Town, 1752." *Virginia Magazine of History and Biography* 13 (October 1905), 143–74.

"A Tribute to John Ridge." *Journal of Cherokee Studies* 4, no. 2 (Spring 1979), 111–17.

Utley, Robert M., ed. *Life in Custer's Cavalry: Diaries and Letters of Albert and Jennie Barnitz, 1867–1868.* New Haven: Yale University Press, 1977.

Vaughan, Alden T., gen. ed. *Early American Indian Documents: Treaties and Laws, 1607–1789.* 20 vols. Bethesda, Md.: University Publications of America, 1979–2004.

"Virginia and the Cherokees, &c: The Treaties of 1768 and 1770." *Virginia Magazine of History and Biography* 13 (July 1905), 20–36.

Wharton, Samuel. *Facts and observations, respecting the country granted to His Majesty by the six united nations of Indians, on the South-East side of the river Ohio, in North America: The establishment of a new colony there; and the causes of the Indian war, which, last year, desolated the frontier settlements of the provinces of Pennsylvania, Maryland, and Virginia.* London, 1775.

Wharton, Samuel. *Plain facts: being an examination into the rights of the Indian nations of America, to their respective countries; and a vindication of the grant, from the Six United Nations of Indians, to the proprietors of Indiana, against the decision of the legislature of Virginia; together with authentic documents, proving that the territory, westward of the Allegany mountain, never belonged to Virginia, &c.* Philadelphia: R. Aitken, 1781.

Wharton, Samuel. *View of the title to Indiana, a tract of country on the river Ohio: containing Indian conferences at Johnson-Hall, in May, 1765; the deed of the Six Nations to the proprietors of Indiana; the minutes of the congress at Fort Stanwix, in October and November, 1768; the deed of the Indians, settling the boundary line between the English and Indians lands; and the opinion of counsel on the title of the proprietors of Indiana.* Philadelphia?, 1775.

Whipple, Henry B. "The Indian System." *North American Review* 99 (October 1864), 449–64.

Wraxall, Peter. *An Abridgment of the Indian Affairs Contained in Four Folio Volumes, Transacted in the Colony of New York, from the year 1678 to the year 1751.* Cambridge, Mass.: Harvard University Press, 1915.

Secondary Sources

Abernethy, Thomas Perkins. *Western Lands and the American Revolution.* New York: Russell and Russell, 1959.

Albers, Patricia, and Jeanne Kay, "Sharing the Land: A Study in American Indian Territoriality," in *A Cultural Geography of North American Indians*, ed. Tyrel G. Moore and Thomas E. Ross, 47–91 (Boulder, Colo: Westview Press, 1987).

Alvord, Clarence Walworth. *The Mississippi Valley in British Politics: A Study of the Trade, Land Speculation, and Experiments in Imperialism Culminating in the American Revolution.* 2 vols. Cleveland: Arthur H. Clark Co., 1917.

Anderson, George E., W. H. Ellison, and Robert F. Heizer. *Treaty Making and Treaty Rejection by the Federal Government in California, 1850–1852.* Socorro, N.M.: Ballena Press, 1978.

Barker, Joanne, ed. *Sovereignty Matters: Locations of Contestation and Possibility in Indigenous Struggles for Self-Determination.* Lincoln: University of Nebraska Press, 2005.

Barr, Julianna. "Geographies of Power: Mapping Indian Borders in the 'Borderlands' of the Early Southwest." *William and Mary Quarterly*, 68 (January 2011), 5–46.

Barr, Julianna. *Peace Came in the Form of a Woman: Indians and Spaniards in the Texas Borderlands.* Chapel Hill: University of North Carolina Press, 2007.

Barsh, Russel Lawrence, and James Youngblood Henderson. *The Road: Indian Tribes and Political Liberty.* Berkeley: University of California Press, 1980.

Beaulieu, Alain, and Viau, Roland. *The Great Peace: Chronicle of a Diplomatic Saga.* Ottawa: Canadian Museum of Civilization, 2001.

Borrows, John. "Wampum at Niagara: The Royal Proclamation, Canadian Legal History, and Self-Government." In *Aboriginal and Treaty Rights in Canada*, ed. Michael Asch, 155–72. Vancouver: University of British Columbia Press, 1997.

Brandão, J. A., and William A. Starna. "The Treaties of 1701: A Triumph of Iroquois Diplomacy." *Ethnohistory* 43 (Spring 1996), 209–44.

Bray, Kingsley M. "Lone Horn's Peace: A New View of Sioux-Crow Relations, 1851–1858." *Nebraska History* 66 (Spring 1985), 28–47.

Bruyneel, Kevin. *The Third Space of Sovereignty: The Post-Colonial Politics of U.S.-Indigenous Relations.* Minneapolis: University of Minnesota Press, 2007.

Buckley, Jay H. *William Clark, Indian Diplomat.* Norman: University of Oklahoma Press, 2008.

Calloway, Colin G. *The American Revolution in Indian Country.* Cambridge: Cambridge University Press, 1995.

Calloway, Colin G. *New Worlds for All: Indians, Europeans, and the Remaking of Early America.* Baltimore: Johns Hopkins University Press, 1997.

Calloway, Colin G. *One Vast Winter Count: The Native American West before Lewis and Clark.* Lincoln: University of Nebraska Press, 2003.

Calloway, Colin G. *The Scratch of a Pen: 1763 and the Transformation of North America.* New York: Oxford University Press, 2006.

Calloway, Colin G. *The Shawnees and the War for America.* New York: Penguin, 2007.

Calloway, Colin G. "Simon Girty: Interpreter and Intermediary." In *Being and Becoming Indian: Biographical Studies of North American Frontiers*, ed. James A. Clifton, 38–58. Chicago: Dorsey Press, 1989.

Campbell, William J. "An Adverse Patron: Land, Trade, and George Croghan." *Pennsylvania History* 76 (Spring 2009), 117–40.

Campbell, William J. "Converging Interests: Johnson, Croghan, the Six Nations, and the 1768 Treaty of Fort Stanwix." *New York History* 89 (Spring 2008), 127–41.

Campbell, William J. *Speculators in Empire: Iroquoia and the 1768 Treaty of Fort Stanwix*. Norman: University of Oklahoma Press, 2012.

Campisi, Jack, and William A. Starna. "On the Road to Canandaigua: The Treaty of 1794." *American Indian Quarterly* 19 (Autumn 1995), 467–90.

Cayton, Andrew R. L. "'Noble Actors' upon 'the Theatre of Honour': Power and Civility in the Treaty of Greenville." In *Contact Points: American Frontiers from the Mohawk Valley to the Mississippi, 1750–1830*, ed. Andrew R. L. Cayton and Fredrika J. Teute, 235–69. Chapel Hill: University of North Carolina Press, 1998.

Chalfant, William Y. *Hancock's War: Conflict on the Southern Plains*. Norman: University of Oklahoma Press, 2010.

Clark, Blue. *Lone Wolf v. Hitchcock: Treaty Rights and Indian Law at the End of the Nineteenth Century*. Lincoln: University of Nebraska Press, 1999.

Clements, William M. *Oratory in North America*. Tucson: University of Arizona Press, 2002.

Clifton, James A. "Chicago, September 14, 1833: The Last Great Indian Treaty in the Old Northwest." *Chicago History* 9 (Summer 1980), 86–97.

Cohen, Fay G. *Treaties on Trial: The Continuing Controversy over Northwest Indian Fishing Rights*. Seattle: University of Washington Press, 1986.

Costo, Rupert, and Jeanette Henry. *Indian Treaties: Two Centuries of Dishonor*. San Francisco: Indian Historian Press, 1977.

DeMallie, Raymond J. "Touching the Pen: Plains Indian Treaty Councils in Ethnohistorical Perspective." In *Ethnicity on the Great Plains*, ed. Frederick C. Luebke, 38–53. Lincoln: University of Nebraska Press, 1980.

Denson, Andrew. *Demanding the Cherokee Nation: Indian Autonomy and American Culture, 1830–1900*. Lincoln: University of Nebraska Press, 2004.

Drummond, A. M., and Richard Moody. "Indian Treaties: The First American Dramas." *Quarterly Journal of Speech* 39 (February 1953), 15–24.

Dudas, Jeffrey R. *The Cultivation of Resentment: Treaty Rights and the New Right*. Stanford: Stanford University Press, 2008.

Duthu, N. Bruce. *American Indians and the Law*. New York: Penguin, 2008.

DuVal, Kathleen. *The Native Ground: Indians and Colonists in the Heart of the Continent*. Philadelphia: University of Pennsylvania Press, 2006.

Estin, Ann Laquer. "*Lone Wolf v. Hitchcock*: The Long Shadow." In *The Aggressions of Civilization: Federal Indian Policy since the 1880s*, ed. Sandra L. Cadwalader and Vine Deloria, Jr., 216–45. Philadelphia: Temple University Press, 1984.

Ewers, John C. "Symbols of Chiefly Authority in Spanish Louisiana." In *The Spanish in the Mississippi Valley, 1762–1804*, ed. John Francis McDermott, 272–86. Urbana: University of Illinois Press, 1974.

Farr, William E. "'When We Were First Paid': The Blackfoot Treaty, the Western Tribes, and the Creation of the Common Hunting Ground, 1855," *Great Plains Quarterly*, 21 (Spring 2001), 131–55.

Fenton, William N. *The Great Law and the Longhouse: A Political History of the Iroquois Confederacy*. Norman: University of Oklahoma Press, 1998.

Fixico, Donald L., ed. *Treaties with American Indians: An Encyclopedia of Rights, Conflicts, and Sovereignty*. 3 vols. Santa Barbara, Calif.: ABC-CLIO, 2008.

Flexner, James Thomas. *Mohawk Baronet: A Biography of Sir William Johnson*. 1959; Syracuse, N.Y.: Syracuse University Press, 1989.

Ford, Lisa. *Settler Sovereignty: Jurisdiction and Indigenous People in America and Australia, 1788–1836*. Cambridge, Mass.: Harvard University Press, 2010.

Fowler, Loretta. *Wives and Husbands: Gender and Age in Southern Arapaho History.* Norman: University of Oklahoma Press, 2010.

Franks, Kenny A. *Stand Watie and the Agony of the Cherokee Nation*. Memphis: Memphis State University Press, 1979.

Friedenberg, Daniel M. *Life, Liberty, and the Pursuit of Land: The Plunder of Early America.* Buffalo, NY: Prometheus Books, 1992.

Fur, Gunlög. *A Nation of Women: Gender and Colonial Encounters among the Delaware Indians*. Philadelphia: University of Pennsylvania Press, 2009.

Galloway, Patricia. "'The Chief Who Is Your Father': Choctaw and French Views of the Diplomatic Relation." In *Powhatan's Mantle: Indians in the Colonial Southeast*, ed. Peter H. Wood, Gregory A. Waselkov, and M. Thomas Hatley, 254–78. Lincoln: University of Nebraska Press, 1989.

Galloway, Patricia. "Talking with Indians: Interpreters and Diplomacy in French Louisiana." In *Race and Family in the Colonial South*, ed. Winthrop D. Jordan and Sheila L. Skemp, 109–29. Jackson: University of Mississippi Press, 1987.

Gerwing, Anselm J. "The Chicago Indian Treaty of 1833." *Journal of the Illinois State Historical Society* 57 (Summer 1964), 117–42.

Ghere, David L. "Mistranslations and Misinformation: Diplomacy on the Maine Frontier, 1725 to 1755." *American Indian Culture and Research Journal* 8, no. 4 (1984), 3–26.

Gitlin, Jay. "Private Diplomacy to Private Property: States, Tribes, and Nations in the Early National Period." *Diplomatic History* 22 (Winter 1998), 85–99.

Greene, Candace S. *One Hundred Summers: A Kiowa Calendar Record*. Lincoln: University of Nebraska Press, 2009.

Hagan, William T. *Taking Indian Lands: The Cherokee (Jerome) Commission, 1889–1893.* Norman: University of Oklahoma Press, 2003.

Hagan, William T. *United States—Comanche Relations: The Reservation Years*. New Haven: Yale University Press, 1976.

Hagedorn, Nancy Lee. "'A Friend to Go Between Them': Interpreters among the Iroquois, 1664–1775." Ph.D. dissertation, College of William and Mary, 1995.

Halaas, David Fridtjof, and Andrew E. Masich. *Halfbreed: The Remarkable Story of George Bent*. Cambridge, Mass.: Da Capo, 2004.

Haley, James L. *The Buffalo War: The History of the Red River Indian Uprising of 1874.* New York: Doubleday, 1976.

Harmon, Alexandra. "Indian Treaty History: A Subject for Agile Minds." *Oregon Historical Quarterly* 106 (Fall 2005), 358–73.

Harmon, Alexandra, ed. *The Power of Promises: Rethinking Indian Treaties in the Pacific Northwest*. Seattle: University of Washington Press, 2008.

Hauptman, Laurence M. *Conspiracy of Interests: Iroquois Dispossession and the Rise of New York State*. Syracuse, N.Y.: Syracuse University Press, 1999.

Hauptman, Laurence M. *The Tonawanda Senecas' Heroic Battle against Removal*. Albany: State University of New York Press, 2011.

Havard, Gilles. *The Great Peace of Montreal in 1701: French-Native Diplomacy in the Seventeenth Century*. Montreal: McGill-Queens University Press, 2001.

Heizer, Robert F. *The Eighteen Unratified Treaties of 1851–1852 between the California Indians and the United States Government.* Berkeley: Archaeological Research Facility, University of California, 1972.

Hicks, Brian. *Toward the Setting Sun: John Ross, the Cherokees, and the Trail of Tears.* New York: Atlantic Monthly Press, 2011.

Hlebowicz, Bartosz, and Adam Piekarski, eds. *The Trail of Broken Treaties: Diplomacy in Indian Country from Colonial Times to Present.* Bydgoszcz, Poland: Wyższa Szkoła Gospodarki, 2011.

Hoig, Stan. *The Peace Chiefs of the Cheyennes.* Norman: University of Oklahoma Press, 1980.

Hoig, Stan. *The Western Odyssey of John Simpson Smith, Frontiersman and Indian Interpreter.* 1974; Norman: University of Oklahoma Press, 2004.

Hoig, Stan. *White Man's Paper Trail: Grand Councils and Treaty Making on the Central Plains.* Boulder: University Press of Colorado, 2006.

Holton, Woody. *Forced Founders: Indians, Debtors, Slaves, and the Making of the American Revolution in Virginia.* Chapel Hill: University of North Carolina Press, 1999.

Hoopes, Chad L. *Domesticate or Exterminate: California Indian Treaties Unratified and Made Secret in 1852.* N.p.: Redwood Coast, 1975.

Horsman, Reginald. *Expansion and American Indian Policy, 1783–1812.* 1967; Norman: University of Oklahoma Press, 1992.

Hudson, Angela Pulley. *Creek Paths and Federal Roads: Indians, Settlers, and Slaves and the Making of the American South.* Chapel Hill: University of North Carolina Press, 2010.

Hutson, James H. "Benjamin Franklin and the West." *Western Historical Quarterly* 4 (October 1973), 425–34.

Hyde, George. *Life of George Bent, Written from his Letters,* ed. Savoie Lottinville. Norman: University of Oklahoma Press, 1968.

Jacobs, Wilbur R. *Wilderness Politics and Indian Gifts: The Northern Colonial Frontier, 1748–1763.* 1950; Lincoln: University of Nebraska Press, 1966.

Jemison, G. Peter, and Anna M. Schein, eds. *Treaty of Canandaigua 1794: 200 Years of Treaty Relations between the Iroquois Confederacy and the United States.* Santa Fe, N.M.: Clear Light, 2000.

Jennings, Francis. *The Ambiguous Iroquois Empire: The Covenant Chain Confederation of Indian Tribes with English Colonies from Its Beginnings to the Lancaster Treaty of 1744.* New York: W. W. Norton, 1984.

Jennings, Francis. *The Invasion of America: Indians, Colonialism, and the Cant of Conquest.* New York: W. W. Norton, 1975.

Jennings, Francis, William N. Fenton, et al., eds. *The History and Culture of Iroquois Diplomacy: An Interdisciplinary Guide to the Treaties of the Six Nations and Their League.* Syracuse, N.Y.: Syracuse University Press, 1985.

Johansen, Bruce E., ed. *Enduring Legacies: Native American Treaties and Contemporary Controversies.* Westport, Conn.: Praeger, 2004.

Jones, Dorothy V. "British Colonial Treaties." In *Handbook of North American Indians,* ed. William C. Sturtevant, Vol. 4: *History of Indian-White Relations,* ed. Wilcomb E. Washburn, 185–94. Washington, D.C.: Smithsonian Institution, 1988.

Jones, Dorothy V. *License for Empire: Colonialism by Treaty in Early America.* Chicago: University of Chicago Press, 1982.

Jones, Douglas C. "Medicine Lodge Revisited." *Kansas Historical Quarterly* 35 (Summer 1969), 130–42.

Jones, Douglas C. *The Treaty of Medicine Lodge: The Story of the Great Treaty Council as Told by Eyewitnesses.* Norman: University of Oklahoma Press, 1966.

Juricek, John T. *Colonial Georgia and the Creeks: Anglo-Indian Diplomacy on the Southern Frontier, 1733–1763.* Gainesville: University Press of Florida, 2010.

Kawashima, Yasuhide. "Forest Diplomats: The Role of Interpreters in Indian-White Relations on the Early American Frontier." *American Indian Quarterly* 13 (Winter 1989), 1–14.

Kennedy, Patricia. "Treaty Texts: When Can We Trust the Written Word?" *Social Sciences and Humanities Aboriginal Research Exchange* 3, no. 1 (Spring/Summer 1995), 1–24.

Kluger, Richard. *The Bitter Waters of Medicine Creek: A Tragic Clash between White and Native America.* New York: Knopf, 2011.

Kvasnicka, Robert M. "United States Indian Treaties and Agreements." In *Handbook of North American Indians,* ed. William C. Sturtevant, Vol. 4: *History of Indian-White Relations,* ed. Wilcomb E. Washburn, 195–201. Washington, D.C.: Smithsonian Institution, 1988.

LeMaster, Michelle. *Brothers Born of One Mother: British-Native American Relations in the Colonial Southeast.* Charlottesville: University of Virginia Press, 2012.

Long, John S. *Treaty No. 9: Making the Agreement to Share the Land in Far Northern Ontario in 1905.* Montreal: McGill-Queen's University Press, 2010.

Lookingbill, Brad D. *War Dance at Fort Marion: Plains Indian War Prisoners.* Norman: University of Oklahoma Press, 2006.

Lyons, Scott Richard. *X-Marks: Native Signatures of Assent.* Minneapolis: University of Minnesota Press, 2010.

MacLeitch, Gail D. *Imperial Entanglements: Iroquois Change and Persistence on the Frontiers of Empire.* Philadelphia: University of Pennsylvania Press, 2011.

McConnell, Michael N. *A Country Between: The Upper Ohio Valley and Its Peoples, 1724–1774.* Lincoln: University of Nebraska Press, 1992.

McLaughlin, Castle. *Arts of Diplomacy: Lewis and Clark's Indian Collection.* Cambridge, Mass.: Peabody Museum of Archaeology and Ethnology, Harvard University, and Seattle: University of Washington Press, 2003.

McLoughlin, William G. *After the Trail of Tears: The Cherokees' Struggle for Sovereignty, 1839–1880.* Chapel Hill: University of North Carolina Press, 1993.

McLoughlin, William G. *Cherokee Renascence in the New Republic.* Princeton: Princeton University Press, 1986.

Manly, Henry S. *The Treaty of Fort Stanwix, 1784.* Rome, N.Y.: Rome Sentinel Co., 1932.

Marshall, Peter. "Colonial Policy and Imperial Retrenchment: Indian Policy 1764–1768." *Journal of American Studies* 5 (April 1971), 1–17.

Marshall, Peter. "Lord Hillsborough, Samuel Wharton and the Ohio Grant, 1769–1775." *English Historical Review* 80 (1965), 717–39.

Marshall, Peter. "Sir William Johnson and the Treaty of Fort Stanwix, 1768." *Journal of American Studies* 1 (August 1968), 149–79.

Mattingly, Arthur H. "The Great Peace Commission of 1867." *Journal of the West* 15 (1976), 23–37.

Merrell, James H. "'The Cast of His Countenance:' Reading Andrew Montour." In *Through a Glass Darkly: Reflections on Personal Identity in Early America,* ed. Ronald Hoffman,

Mechal Sobel, and Fredericka J. Teute, 9–39. Chapel Hill: University of North Carolina Press, 1997.

Merrell, James H. "'I desire all that I have said…may be taken down aright': Revisiting Teedyscung's 1756 Treaty Council Speeches." *William and Mary Quarterly* 58 (2006), 777–826.

Merrell, James H. *Into the American Woods: Negotiators on the Pennsylvania Frontier.* New York: W. W. Norton, 1999.

Merritt, Jane T. *At the Crossroads: Indians and Empires on a Mid-Atlantic Frontier, 1700–1763.* Chapel Hill: University of North Carolina Press, 2003.

Merritt, Jane T. "Metaphor, Meaning, and Misunderstanding: Language and Power on the Pennsylvania Frontier." In *Contact Points: American Frontiers from the Mohawk Valley to the Mississippi, 1750–1830,* ed. Andrew R. L. Cayton and Frederika J. Teute, 60–87. Chapel Hill: University of North Carolina Press, 1998.

Midtrød, Tom Arne. *The Memory of All Ancient Customs: Native American Diplomacy in the Colonial Hudson Valley.* Ithaca, N.Y.: Cornell University Press, 2012.

Miller, Cary. "Gifts as Treaties: The Political Use of Received Gifts in Anishinaabeg Communities, 1820–1832." *American Indian Quarterly* 26 (Spring 2002), 221–45.

Miller, Cary. *Ogimaag: Anishinaabbeg Leadership, 1760–1845.* Lincoln: University of Nebraska Press, 2010.

Miller, J. R. *Compact, Contract, Covenant: Aboriginal Treaty-Making in Canada.* Toronto: University of Toronto Press, 2009.

Miller, Robert J. *Native America, Discovered and Conquered: Thomas Jefferson, Lewis and Clark, and Manifest Destiny.* Westport, Conn.: Praeger, 2006.

Miller, Robert J., Jacinta Ruru, Larissa Behrendt, and Tracey Lindberg, eds. *Discovering Indigenous Lands: The Doctrine of Discovery in the English Colonies.* New York: Oxford University Press, 2010.

Moulton, Gary E. *John Ross, Cherokee Chief.* Athens: University of Georgia Press, 1978.

Murray, David. *Forked Tongues: Speech, Writing and Representation in North American Indian Texts.* Bloomington: University of Indiana Press, 1991.

Nammack, Georgiana C. *Fraud, Politics, and the Dispossession of the Indians: The Iroquois Land Frontier in the Colonial Period.* Norman: University of Oklahoma Press, 1969.

Nicandri, David L. *Northwest Chiefs: Gustav Sohon's Views of the 1855 Stevens Treaty Councils.* Tacoma: Washington State Historical Society, 1986.

O'Brien, Greg. "The Conqueror Meets the Unconquered: Negotiating Cultural Boundaries on the Post-Revolutionary Southern Frontier." *Journal of Southern History* 67 (February 2001), 39–72.

Oman, Kerry. "The Beginning of the End: The Indian Peace Commission of 1867–1868." *Great Plains Quarterly* 22 (Winter 2002), 35–51.

Ostler, Jeffrey. *The Lakotas and the Black Hills: The Struggle for Sacred Ground.* New York: Penguin, 2010.

O'Toole, Fintan. *White Savage: William Johnson and the Invention of America.* New York: Farrar, Straus, and Giroux, 2005.

Parmenter, Jon. *The Edge of the Woods: Iroquoia, 1534–1701.* East Lansing: Michigan State University Press, 2010.

Parmenter, Jon. "The Iroquois and the Native American Struggle for the Ohio Valley." In *The Sixty Years' War for the Great Lakes, 1754–1814,* ed. David Curtis Skaggs and Larry L. Nelson, 105–24. East Lansing: Michigan State University Press, 2001.

Parmenter, Jon. "Rethinking Willian Penn's Treaty with the Indians: Benjamin West, Thomas Penn, and the Legacy of Native-Newcomer Relations in Colonial Pennsylvania." *Proteus: A Journal of Ideas* 19 (2002), 38–44.

Parins, James W. *Elias Cornelius Boudinot: A Life on the Cherokee Border*. Lincoln: University of Nebraska Press. 2006.

Parins, James W. *John Rollin Ridge: His Life and Works*. Lincoln: University of Nebraska Press, 1991.

Perdue, Theda. "The Conflict Within: The Cherokee Power Structure and Removal." *Georgia Historical Quarterly* 73 (Fall 1989), 467–91.

Perdue, Theda, and Michael D. Green. *The Cherokee Nation and the Trail of Tears*. New York: Penguin, 2007.

Pickering, Robert B. et al. *Peace Medals: Negotiating Power in Early America*. Tulsa, Okla.: Gilcrease Museum, 2011.

Pomedi, Michael M. "Eighteenth-Century Treaties: Amended Iroquois Condolence Rituals." *American Indian Quarterly* 19 (Summer 1995), 319–39.

Powell, Peter J. *People of the Sacred Mountain: A History of the Northern Cheyenne Chiefs and Warrior Societies, 1830–1879*. 2 vols. San Francisco: Harper and Row, 1979.

Prucha, Francis Paul. *American Indian Treaties: The History of a Political Anomaly*. Berkeley: University of California Press, 1994.

Prucha, Francis Paul. *Indian Peace Medals in American History*. Madison: State Historical Society of Wisconsin, 1971.

Pulsipher, Jenny Hale. "Gaining the Diplomatic Edge: Kinship, Trade, Ritual, and Religion in Amerindian Alliances in Early North America," in *Empires and Indigenes: Intercultural Alliance, Imperial Expansion, and Warfare in the Early Modern World*, ed. Wayne E. Lee, 19–47. New York: New York University Press, 2011.

Pulsipher, Jenny Hale. *Subjects unto the Same King: Indians, English, and the Contest for Authority in Colonial New England*. Philadelphia: University of Pennsylvania Press, 2005.

Ramirez-Shkwegnaabi, Benjamin. "The Dynamics of American Indian Diplomacy in the Great Lakes Region." *American Indian Culture and Research Journal* 27, no. 4 (2003), 53–77.

Rand, Jacki Thompson. *Kiowa Humanity and the Invasion of the State*. Lincoln: University of Nebraska Press, 2008.

Rhoades, Matthew L. *Long Knives and the Longhouse: Anglo-Iroquois Politics and the Expansion of Colonial Virginia*. Madison, N.J.: Fairleigh Dickinson University Press, 2011.

Richards, Kent, guest ed. "The Isaac I. Stevens and Joel Palmer Treaties, 1855–2005." *Oregon Historical Quarterly* 106 (Fall 2005), 342–491.

Richter, Daniel K. "Cultural Brokers and Intercultural Politics: New York-Iroquois Relations, 1664–1701." *Journal of American History* 75 (June 1988), 40–67.

Richter, Daniel K. "Native Americans, the Plan of 1764, and a British Empire That Never Was." In *Cultures and Identities in Colonial British America*, ed. Robert Olwell and Alan Tully, 269–92. Baltimore: Johns Hopkins University Press, 2006.

Robertson, Lindsay J. *Conquest by Law: How the Discovery of America Dispossessed Indigenous Peoples of Their Lands*. New York: Oxford University Press, 2005.

Robinson, Charles M. *Satanta: The Life and Death of a War Chief*. Austin: State House Press, 1997.

Royce, Charles C. *Indian Land Cessions in the United States*. Bureau of American Ethnology, *Eighteenth Annual Report*, 1896–97. Washington, D.C.: Government Printing Office, 1899.

Rushforth, Brett. *Bonds of Alliance: Indigenous and Atlantic Slaveries in New France*. Chapel Hill: University of North Carolina Press, 2012.

Sabo, George III. "Rituals of Encounter: Interpreting Native American Views of European Explorers." In *Cultural Encounters in the Early South*, ed. Jeanne Whayne, 76–87. Fayetteville: University of Arkansas Press, 1995.

Sadosky, Leonard J. *Revolutionary Negotiations: Indians, Empires, and Diplomats in the Founding of America*. Charlottesville: University of Virginia Press, 2009.

St. Germain, Jill. *Broken Treaties: United States and Canadian Relations with the Lakotas and the Plains Cree, 1868–1885*. Lincoln: University of Nebraska Press, 2009.

St. Germain, Jill. *Indian Treaty-Making Policy in the United States and Canada, 1867–1877*. Lincoln: University of Nebraska Press, 2001.

Schaaf, Gregory. *Wampum Belts and Peace Trees: George Morgan, Native Americans, and Revolutionary Diplomacy*. Golden, Colo.: Fulcrum, 1990.

Schneider, Bethany. "Boudinot's Change: Boudinot, Emerson, and Ross on Cherokee Removal." *English Literary History* 75 (2008), 151–77.

Seed, Patricia. *Ceremonies of Possession in Europe's Conquest of the New World, 1492–1640*. Cambridge: Cambridge University Press, 1995.

Shannon, Timothy J. *Indians and Colonists at the Crossroads of Empire: The Albany Congress of 1754*. Ithaca, N.Y.: Cornell University Press, 2000.

Shannon, Timothy J. *Iroquois Diplomacy on the Early American Frontier*. New York: Penguin, 2008.

Shoemaker, Nancy. "An Alliance between Men: Gender Metaphors in Eighteenth-Century American Indian Diplomacy East of the Mississippi." *Ethnohistory* 46 (Spring 1999), 239–63.

Shoemaker, Nancy. *A Strange Likeness: Becoming Red and White in Eighteenth-Century North America*. New York: Oxford University Press, 2004.

Simpson, Leanne. "Looking after Gdoo-naaganinaa: Precolonial Nishnaabeg Diplomatic and Treaty Relationships," *Wicazo Sa Review: A Journal of Native American Studies*, 23 (Autumn, 2008), 29–42.

Smith, Daniel Blake. *An American Betrayal: Cherokee Patriots and the Trail of Tears*. New York: Henry Holt, 2011.

Smith, Ralph. "The Fantasy of a Treaty to End Treaties." *Great Plains Journal* 12 (Fall 1972), 26–51.

Stark, Heidi Kiiwetinepinesiik. "Marked by Fire: Anishinaabe Articulations of Nationhood in Treaty Making with the United States and Canada," *American Indian Quarterly*, 36 (Spring 2012), 119–49.

Starna, William A. "The Diplomatic Career of Canasatego." In *Friends and Enemies in Penn's Woods: Indians, Colonists, and the Racial Construction of Pennsylvania*, ed. William A. Pencak and Daniel K. Richter, 344–63. University Park: Pennsylvania State University Press, 2004.

Szabo, Joyce M. "Medicine Lodge Treaty Remembered." *American Indian Art Magazine* 14 (Autumn 1989), 52–59.

Tiro, Karim M. *The People of the Standing Stone: The Oneida Nation from the Revolution through the Era of Removal*. Amherst: University of Massachusetts Press, 2011.

Trennert, Robert A., Jr. *Alternative to Extinction: Federal Indian Policy and the Beginnings of the Reservation System, 1846–1851*. Philadelphia: Temple University Press, 1975.

Unrau, William E. *The Rise and Fall of Indian Country, 1825–1855*. Lawrence: University Press of Kansas, 2007.

VanDevelder, Paul. *Savages and Scoundrels: The Untold Story of America's Road to Empire Through Indian Territory*. New Haven: Yale University Press, 2009.

Van Hoeven, James W. "Salvation and Indian Removal." *The Reformed Review* 39 (1986?), 255–70.

Van Zandt, Cynthia J. *Brothers among Nations: The Pursuit of Intercultural Alliances in Early America, 1580–1660*. New York: Oxford University Press, 2008.

Viola, Herman J. *Diplomats in Buckskins: A History of Indian Delegations in Washington City*. Washington, D.C.: Smithsonian Institution Press, 1981.

Vipperman, Carl J. "The Bungled Treaty of New Echota: The Failure of Cherokee Removal, 1836–1838." *Georgia Historical Quarterly* 78 (Fall 1989), 540–58.

Volwiler, Albert T. *George Croghan and the Westward Movement, 1741–1782*. Cleveland: Arthur H. Clark Co., 1926.

Wainwright, Nicholas B. *George Croghan: Wilderness Diplomat*. Chapel Hill: University of North Carolina Press, 1959.

Watson, Blake A. *Buying America from the Indians: Johnson v. McIntosh and the History of Native Land Rights*. Norman: University of Oklahoma Press, 2012.

Weeks, Charles A. *Paths to a Middle Ground: The Diplomacy of Natchez, Boukfouka, Nogales, and San Fernando de las Barrancas, 1791–1795*. Tuscaloosa: University of Alabama Press, 2005.

White, Jerry P., Erik Anderson, Jean-Pierre Morin, and Dan Beavon, eds. *Aboriginal Policy Research. Vol. 7: A History of Treaties and Policies*. Toronto: Thompson Educational Publishing, 2010.

White, Richard. *The Middle Ground: Indians, Empires and Republics in the Great Lakes Region, 1650–1815*. Cambridge: Cambridge University Press, 1991.

Wilkins, Thurman. *Cherokee Tragedy: The Ridge Family and the Decimation of a People*. 1970; reprint, Norman: University of Oklahoma Press, 1986.

Wilkinson, Charles F. *American Indians, Time, and the Law*. New Haven: Yale University Press, 1987.

Williams, Robert A., Jr. *The American Indian in Western Legal Thought: The Discourses of Conquest*. New York: Oxford University Press, 1990.

Williams, Robert A., Jr. *Linking Arms Together: American Indian Treaty Visions of Law and Peace, 1600–1800*. New York: Oxford University Press, 1997.

Witgen, Michael. "The Rituals of Possession: Native Identity and the Invention of Empire in Seventeenth-Century Western North America." *Ethnohistory* 45 (Fall 2007), 639–68.

Wolfe, Patrick. "After the Frontier: Separation and Absorption in US Indian Policy," *Settler Colonial Studies*, 1 (2011), 13–51.

Wolfe, Patrick. "Against the Intentional Fallacy: Logocentrism and Continuity in the Rhetoric of Indian Dispossession," *American Indian Culture and Research Journal*, 36, no. 1 (2012), 9–12.

Wonderley, Anthony. "Good Peter's Narrative of Several Transactions Respecting Indian Lands: An Oneida View of Dispossession, 1785–1788." *New York History* 84 (2003), 237–73.

Worcester, Donald E., ed. *Forked Tongues and Broken Treaties*. Caldwell, Idaho: Caxton Printers, 1975.

Worcester , Donald E., ed. "Satanta." In *American Indian Leaders: Studies in Diversity*, ed. R. David Edmunds, 107–30. Lincoln: University of Nebraska Press, 1980.

Wright, J. Leitch, Jr. "The Creek-American Treaty of 1790: Alexander McGillivray and The Diplomacy of The Old Southwest." *Georgia Historical Quarterly* 51 (December 1967), 379–400.

Wroth, Lawrence C. "The Indian Treaty as Literature." *Yale Review* 17 (1928), 749–66.

Wunder, John R. "Indigenous Colonial Treaties of North America in Comparative Perspective." In *Reconfigurations of Native North America: An Anthology of New Perspectives*, ed. John R. Wunder and Kurt E. Kinbacher, 13–31. Lubbock: Texas Tech University Press, 2009.

Wunder, John R. "No More Treaties: The Resolution of 1871 and the Alteration of Indian Rights to Their Homelands." In *Working the Range: Essays on the History of Western Land Management and the Environment*, ed. John R. Wunder, 39–56. Westport, Conn.: Greenwood, 1985.

Wunder, John R. "'That No Thorn Will Pierce Our Friendship': The Ute-Comanche Treaty of 1786." *Western Historical Quarterly* 42 (Spring 2011), 5–27.

{ INDEX }

ABCFM (American Board
of Commissioners for
Foreign Missions), 125,
127, 131, 135, 139
Abenakis, 34, 47
Abraham (Little Abraham)
(Tayorheasere,
Teyarhasere, Tyorhansera,
Tigoransera,
Teirhenshsere) (Mohawk)
Albany conference (1775)
and, 92
death of, 93
Fort Stanwix Treaty and, 68,
70, 71, 72, 77, 248
W. Johnson and, 65, 73, 85
on settlers, 89
Adair, James, 17
Adams, John, 99
Adams, John Quincy, 147
Adams, Margaret (Fitzpatrick)
(Wilmarth) (Wilmott)
(Walking Woman)
(Arapaho), 184, 197, 198,
210
adoptions, 13, 18, 47–48. *see
also* kinship
agriculture
Blackfeet and, 180
Cherokees and, 122–23,
146, 233
Cheyennes and, 212, 235
"civilization" and, 114
Fort Laramie Treaty and,
175, 226
Little Raven on, 210
Medicine Lodge Treaty and,
10, 199, 201, 202, 203,
204, 209, 214, 234
in text of Medicine Lodge
Treaty, 266, 267, 268,
270–71, 273, 277, 278,
279, 280, 282

New Echota Treaty and, 253
reservations and, 181
Ridges and, 128
Tananaica on, 222
Texas and, 165
the West and, 117, 173
women and, 18
AIM (American Indian
Movement), 239
Alabama, 98, 115, 117, *122,*
131, 268
Albany Congress (1754), 24,
44–45, 65, 67
alcohol. *see* liquor
Algonquian languages, 42,
175, 196
Algonquins, 40
allegiances, 21, 49
alliances
captive and, 47
Chain of Friendship and, 24
Cherokees and, 156, 162
Delawares and, 97
French and Indian, 1, 4,
57, 165
gifts and, 19–20
interpreters and, 31–32
Iroquois and, 2, 81, 85, 91
W. Johnson and, 51, 71
kinship and, 12–13
Lewis and Clark and,
164–65, 168
Plains Indians and, 165,
171–72
Revolutionary War and,
92, 96
Spaniards and, 98
trade and, 165, 167
treaties and, 48, 84, 98, 173,
174
US Civil War and, 161, 162
wampum and, 30, 71
writing and, 35

allotments, 79, 202, 234–37
"amalgamation," 138
American Board of
Commissioners for
Foreign Missions
(ABCFM), 125, 127, 131,
135, 139
American Indian Movement
(AIM), 239
Americans. *see* settlers,
American; *entries
beginning US…*
Amherst, Jeffery, 21–22, 54
annexation act of 1877, 241
annuities. *see also*
appropriations
Blackfoot peace conference
and, 180
Cherokees and, 138
corruption and, 230
Fort Laramie Treaty, 175,
176
Fort Stanwix Treaty and, 84
Harrison and, 116
Little Arkansas Treaty and,
183, 184
Medicine Lodge Treaty and,
201, 202, 205, 208, 210,
214, 216
in text of Medicine Lodge
Treaty, 265, 269, 274,
276, 280
New Echota Treaty and,
255, 256, 260
Potawatomis and, 139
US Congress and, 106
Anza, Juan Bautista de,
21, 166
Apaches. *see also* Plains
Indians; *individual
Apaches*
additional compensation,
238

Apaches (*Cont.*)
    attacks south of Rio
        Grande, 172
    Cheyennes and, 171
    Fort Atkinson Treaty and,
        176
    Jerome Commission and,
        235–36, 237
    Little Arkansas Treaty and,
        183
    Medicine Lodge Treaty and,
        182, 193, 198
    New Mexico and, 166
    reservations, 163, 205, 214,
        215
    Spain and, 166
    Texas and, 216
    US Indian Peace
        Commission and, 186
    violence of, 220
Apiatan (Kiowa), 236
Appalachian Mountains, 54,
    55, 81
appropriations, 214, 230–31,
    269, 271, 280, 282. *see
    also* annuities
Arapahos. *see also* Plains
    Indians; *individual
    Arapahos*
    alliances, 171
    Black Kettle and, 183
    Cheyennes and, 209–10
    Fort Laramie Treaty and,
        175, 226
    Fort Wise Treaty and, 176
    gifts from, 206
    Jerome Commission and,
        235
    Little Arkansas Treaty and,
        183, 184
    Medicine Lodge Treaty
        and, 182, 189, 193, 194,
        196, 209
    as prisoners, 223
    Red Cloud War and,
        184–85
    reservations, 163, *215,* 217,
        219
    Sheridan and, 219
    US Indian Peace
        Commission and, 186
    violence of, 217, 218
Arbuckle, Matthew, 155, 157
Arikaras, 167, 170, 172, 175.
    see also Plains Indians

Arizona, 227
*Arizona Tax Commission,
    Warren Trading Post Co.
    v.* (1965), 239–40
Arkansas, 33–34, 118, 158,
    159, 169
Arkansas River Valley, 171, 201
"Articles of Government"
    (Cherokees), *124*
artists, 224
Ash Hollow (Nebraska), 176
Assaryquoa (Assaraquoa)
    (long knife) (sword),
    25, 29
assimilation, 123, 224, 234
Assiniboines, 175. *see also*
    Plains Indians
Athapaskan language, 197
Athens Courier (newspaper),
    148
Atkin, Edmond, 14
Atkinson, Henry, 170, 171
Attakullakulla (Little
    Carpenter) (Cherokee),
    63, 81, 91
Augooshaway (Egushawa)
    (Gushgushagwa)
    (Ottawa), 106, 113, 244
Augur, Christopher, 187, *187,*
    194, 221, 226, 229
Aupaumut, Hendrick
    (Mahican), 25, 108
Australia, 243
authority. *see also* legality;
    sovereignty
    Botetort and, 81
    British, 85
    Cherokee land and, 143
    Cherokee Nation and, 145,
        155, 158, 249, 250
    Indian, 17, 22, 34, 48, 60,
        108, 239
    Iroquois, 56, 62, 77, 80,
        85, 98
    W. Johnson and, 63, 79, 80
    Navajos and, 239
    Peace Commission and, 185
    traders and, 9, 88
    treaties and, 231
    Treaty Party and, 136, 138
    US government, 4, 24,
        98, 107, 132, 164, 230,
        237–38
autonomy of bands, 120
Bannocks, 227

Bao (Cat) (Having Horns)
    (Kiowa), 196
Barker, Joanne, 333n37
Barnitz, Alfred, 212
Barsh, Russell, 242
Bartram, John, 7, 29
Battle of Beecher's Island
    (1868), 218
Battle of Devil's Hole (1763),
    54
Battle of Fallen Timbers
    (1794), 110
Battle of Fort Niagara (1759),
    54, 68
Battle of Horseshoe Bend
    (Tohopeka) (1814), 117,
    118, 123
Battle of Lake George (1755),
    51
Battle of Monongahela (1755),
    57
Battle of Neches River (1839),
    156
Battle of Oriskany (1777), 93
Battle of Point Pleasant, 90
Battle of Summit Springs
    (1869), 219
Battle of the Little Bighorn
    (1876), 233
Battle of the Rosebud (1876),
    233
Battle of the Washita (1868),
    215
Battle of Tohopeka (Horseshoe
    Bend) (1814), 117, 118,
    123
Baynton, John, 58, 60,
    61, 66
Baynton, Wharton, and
    Morgan, 96
Beech Tree (Oneyanha)
    (Oneida), 101
Bell, John, 157
Bell, Sarah Caroline (Watie),
    157, 162, 163
Bent, Charles, 184
Bent, Charley, 189, 190, 196,
    198
Bent, George
    Cheyennes and, 189, 212,
        219
    Custer's raid and, 218
    as interpreter, 219
    Jerome Commission and,
        235

life history, 190, 332n26
Medicine Lodge Treaty and, 196, 198, 211
photo, *190*
Bent, Julia (Guerrier), 196, 197, 198
Bent, Robert, 190
Bent, William, 184, 189, 190, 196
Bent, Yellow Woman (Cheyenne), 184
Benton, Hart, 147
Biard, Pierre, 22
Big Tree (Seneca), 100–101, 220, 221, 223, 236
Bird Chief (Arapaho), *232*
Black, Hugo, 239
Black Beaver (Delaware), 196
Black Buffalo (Brulé), 167
Black Eagle (Kiowa), 194, 212
Black Elk (Oglala Lakota), 35
Blackfeet, 176, 179–80, 197. *see also* Plains Indians
Black Hawk (Oglala), 175
Black Hawk (Sauk), 115
Black Hills (SD), 226, 233–34, 240–41
Black Hoof (Shawnee), 113
Black Kettle (Cheyenne)
Custer and, 218
death of, 218
Dog Soldiers and, 195
kin, 190
Medicine Lodge Treaty and, 193, 198, 205, 216
raids of, 183
Sand Creek massacre and, 177
Sheridan and, 218
Blacksnake (Seneca), 68
Bloody Fellow (Cherokee), 108
Blount, William, 104, 108
Blue Jacket (Shawnee), 113
Board of Trade (Britain), 56, 58, 60, 61, 62, 63, 81, 82
Bogy, Charles, 184
Boldt, George, 240
Boone, Daniel, 86–87
Boone, James, 87
Bosque Redondo (NM), 227
Botetort, Lord, 81
Boudinot, Delight, 154
Boudinot, Elias (Galagina) (Buck Watie) (Cherokee).

see also Cherokee Phoenix (newspaper); Treaty Party
E. Butler on, 153
on Corn Tassel, 134
death penalty and, 9, 154
image, *207*
Jackson and, 143
on leadership, 149
namesake of, 125
on New Echota Treaty, 147
New Echota Treaty and, 9, 144, 154
on removal, 136, 137–38
Ross on, 159
US Civil War and, 161–62
US government and, 159
wives and children, 126–27, 147, 162, 163
Boudinot, Elias Cornelius, 162–63, 233
boundaries. *see also* fences; reservations; *specific treaties*
AIM and, 239
Croghan and, 66
Fort Laramie Treaty and, 175
Fort Stanwix Treaty and, 8, 9, 49–65, 71–77, *78,* 80–82, 83, 84, 86, 87, 88, 90, 95, 245, 247, 251
Gage on, 80–81
Greenville Treaty and, 113
Hard Labor Treaty and, 81
Indian wars and, 99
indigenous, 12
W. Johnson and, 62–63, 71–73, 76
kinship and, 46–47
Medicine Lodge Treaty and, 221, 277
Peace of Paris (1763) and, 54
Prairie du Chien Treaty and, 170
resistance to, 120
Revolutionary War and, *122*
Shawnees and, 103, 108
Tecumseh and, 116
US expansion and, 165, 172, 173, 174
US government and, 98, 99, 100, 104, 105, 107, 109, 174
wars and, 170

Bouquet, Henry, 47
Bowles (Duwali) (Cherokee), 156
Bozeman Trail, 184–85, 226, 227
Braddock, Edward, 57
Bradford, William, 13–14, 19–20
Brainerd mission, 125
Brant, Joseph (Mohawk), 51–52, 57, 72, 92, 93, 108
Brant, Molly (Mary), 19, 51, 52, 57
Bray, Kingsley, 175
bribery, 107, 108, 115, 119, 123, 125, 139–40
Bridger, Jim, 174–75
Britain and the British. *see also* Irish traders; Paris, Peace of (1763, 1783); Privy Council (Britain); Treaty of Fort Stanwix (1768)
Cherokees and, 122
colonial era and, 4
Covenant Chain and, 24
Fort Stanwix Treaty and, 49, 77–78, 80
France and, 20, 53, 76
Indian culture and, 14
Iroquois and, 49–50, 53, 54, 85–86
Ohio River and Valley and, 45, 54, 65, 84
Revolutionary War and, 90
settlers, American, and, 92
Shawnees and, 65–66, 88, 91
southeast US and, 117
treaties and, 4, 98
western frontier and, 55–57
Wharton and, 58–59, 82
Broken Hand (Thomas Fitzpatrick), 174, 175, 184, 197
"brother," 24–25
Brothertown Indians, 153
Brown, George, 189
Brown, Hugh, 237
Brown, John (Cherokee), 154
Brulé Sioux, 167, 171, 176, 226
Buchanan, James, 198
Budd, H. J., 189, 209
Buffalo Chief (Cheyenne), 210–11
Buffalo Goad (Wichita), *232*

buffalos
  Blackfoot peace conference
    and, 179–80
  cattle and, 180
  Cheyennes and, 209
  demise of, 200, 221–22, 224
  Fort Laramie Treaty and,
    226
  Indians' opinion and, 202
  Little Arkansas Treaty and,
    184
  Medicine Lodge Treaty
    and, 200, 201, 204, 211,
    215, 216
  railroads and, 186
  Red Cloud War and, 185
  Red River War and, 221
  settlers and, 221–22
  Sherman on, 217
  white hunters and, 193, 200
Buffalo War (Red River War),
  221, 222–23
Bulkley, Solomon T., 189, 197
Bull Bear (Cheyenne Dog
  Soldier), 184, 193, 211,
  212, 219
Bunt (Otsinoghiyata)
  (Onondaga), 68, 77, 89,
  248
Bureau of Indian Affairs
  (Indian Office), 173, 229
Burnett, John G., 152–53
Burns, Robert Ignatius, 179
Bushyhead, Isaac, 157
Bushyhead, Jesse, 142
Butler, Elijah, 134, 153
Butler, John, 68, 69, 92–93, 94
Butler, Richard, 94, 100, 102,
  103
Butler, Thomas, 92
Butler, Walter, 92
Butrick, Daniel, 147

Cachupín, Tomás Vélez, 166
Caddos, 165, 219, 223
Caldwell, Billy (Sauganash)
  (Potawatomi), 139–40
California, 5, 172, 173–74,
  180, 186
calumets. *see* pipes and
  smoking
Campbell, C., 175
Canada, 5, 31–32, 34, 54, 76,
  83, 92, 95, 98, 168, 228,
  233, 243

Canada Creek, 74, 75, 247
Canadian Charter of Rights
  and Freedoms, 55
Canaghquieson (Oneida). *see*
  Conoghquieson
Canajoharie, 50
Canasatego (Onondaga), 23,
  29, 36, 39, 43–44
Canonicus (Narragansett),
  19–20, 290n39
Captain Bull (Delaware), 62
Captain John (Onondiyo)
  (Oneida), 110–11
captives, 47–48, 69, 167, 183,
  206, 223
Carolina people (Americans),
  108
Carroll, William, 145, 148, 248
Carrying Place, 73–74, 92
Carter, Jimmy, 241
Cartier, Jacques, 40
Carver, Robert, 32–33
Cass, Lewis, 131, 135, 136, 138,
  140, 145, 170, 171
Catawba (Kentucky) River, 81,
  303n129
Cat (Bao) (Having Horns)
  (Kiowa), 196
Catherine (Mohawk), 57
Cattaraugus reservation, 120
cattle, 87, 122, 162, 180, 199,
  270, 281
Cavalier, Robert, Sieur de La
  Salle, 33–34
Cayugas, 1, 24, 77, 101, 111,
  248. *see also* Iroquois
Cayuses, 177
Central Pacific Railroad, 180
ceremonies, 16, 29. *see also*
  pipes and smoking;
  wampum
cession treaties (1817,1819),
  125
Chain of Friendship, 24
Champlain, Samuel de, 40
Charbonneau, Sakakawea
  (Shoshoni), 169
Charbonneau, Toussaint, 169
Charles (Prince), 10
Charles I, 14
Charlestown, 14, 15
"cheat like a white man," 102
Chechebinquey (Alexander
  Robinson) (Potawatomi),
  139–40

Cherokee Commission (Jerome
  Commission), 235–37
Cherokee constitution, 124,
  128, 131, 133
Cherokee National Committee,
  124, 151
Cherokee National Council
  Arbuckle and, 157
  Georgia and, 133
  on land sales, 129
  New Echota Treaty and, 145
  Payne and, 141
  removal and, 124–25, 136,
    151, 154
  Ridges and, 136, 138
  slaves and, 123
  Watie and, 161
Cherokee Nation v. Georgia,
  134
Cherokee Phoenix (newspaper),
  9, 129, 131, 136, 142
Cherokees. *see also* National
  Party; removal; Treaty
  of Hard Labor; Treaty
  of Lochaber (1770);
  Treaty of New Echota
  (Ridge's Treaty) (1835);
  Treaty Party; *individual
  Cherokees; entries
  beginning* Cherokee...;
  subtribes
  1731–1835, 121–34 (*see also*
    removal)
  Arbuckle and, 157
  Boone and, 87
  boundaries and, 62, 72
  Choctaws and, 25
  "civilized," 127
  civil wars of, 153–63
  Creeks and, 25, 123
  Delawares and, 25, 76
  Detroit conference and, 105
  feathers and, 30
  Fort Stanwix cessions and,
    91
  Georgia and, 108, 131, 135
  Holston Treaty and, 108
  homelands, *122*
  Hopewell Treaty and, 103–4
  Iroquois and, 25, 63–65
  Jackson and, 117, 129–30,
    148
  Johnson on, 80–81
  Medicine Lodge Treaty
    and, 182

North Carolina and, 118, 121

number of treaties made, 5

renaissance of, 121–23

reservations and, 183

rights of, 121

Shawnees and, 76, 86, 92

Stuart and, 88

US Civil War and, 161–63

US Constitution and, 134–35

US government and, 146–47

Virginia and, 67

wampum and, 31

western, 139, 140, 158

written treaties and, 128

Cherokee Strip, 163

Cherokee Tobacco case (1870), 233

Cheyennes. *see also* Plains Indians; *individual Cheyennes*

alliances, 171

Arapahos and, 209–10

artists, 224

G. Bent and, 332n26

Cimarron, 205, 209, 211, 222, 223–24

Crows and, 171

Fort Laramie Treaty and, 175, 226

Fort Wise Treaty and, 176

gifts and, 171–72

Indian wars and, 199

Jerome Commission and, 235

Kiowas and, 5, 171, 197, 210

Little Arkansas Treaty and, 183, 184

Lone Horn and, 175

medals and, 167

Medicine Lodge Treaty and, 182, 189, 193, 194–95, 198, 200, 205, 209–10, 211–12

as prisoners, 223

Red Cloud War and, 184–85

reservations, 163, *215*, 217, 219

Sheridan and, 219

US Indian Peace Commission and, 186

US military and, 233

US sovereignty and, 170

violence of, 217, 218, 219

Chicago newspapers, 188, 189, 209

Chickamauga Cherokees, 92

Chickasaws, 25, 34, 104, 114, 203, 235, 247

"chief," 17

chief salaries, 107–8

Chinook Jargon, 240

Chisholm, Jesse, 196

Chivington, John, 177

Choctaws

Cherokees and, 25

Hopewell Treaty and, 103–5

Jackson and, 118

medals and, 21

Mount Dexter Treaty and, 115

Oklahoma and, 235

reservations and, 203

US government and, 117, 118

women, 120

Chota, 30, 91, 104, 134

Chouteau, Pierre, 169

Christianity

Cherokee Phoenix and, 129

Indian converts, 51, 136, 178, 223, 227, 228

prisoners and, 224

removal of Christian Indians, 153

treaties and, 95, 147, 227, 230

Cimarron Cheyennes, 205, 209, 211, 222, 223–24

Cincinnati newspapers, 189

"civilization"

agriculture and, 114, 122, 199

Boudinot on, 127

Indians' opinion of, 202

Medicine Lodge Treaty and, 182, 185–86, 199, 204

New Echota Treaty and, 9

N. Taylor on, 181

treaties and, 230

US Department of Interior and, 173

US Indian Peace Commission and, 185

Clare, Lord, 61

Clark, Blue, 236, 238

Clark, George Rogers, 58, 102, 103, 169, 170

Clark, William, 5, 145, 164, 167–71

Claus, Daniel, 57, 66

Clay, Henry, 132, 133, 135

clerks, 37, 39

Clinton, George, 51, 101

clothing, 14, 20

Chicago treaty and, 118–19

Fort Finney conference and, 102

Fort Stanwix Treaty and, 71

as gifts, 20, 21

Hendrick and, 51

W. Johnson and, 52

Medicine Lodge Treaty and, 194, 196, 197–98, 202

Montour and, 69

19th century, *28*

treaty and, 167

Wells and, 113

coercion

Cherokee commission and, 236

W. Clark and, 169

colonial era and, 4

Fort Pitt Treaty and, 97

Harrison and, 115

Indian government and, 17

Jackson and, 117

Jerome Commission and, 235

New Echota Treaty and, 143–44, 151

Shawnees and, 103

sign of consent and, 3

starvation and, 214

US commissioners and, 115

Yakama treaty and, 179

Coeur d'Alenes, 180

Cohen, Felix, 164

Colden, Cadwallader, 17, 42, 51

Colley, Samuel, 176

colonial era

British and, 56

Cherokees and, 122

diplomacy, 12–19

education of Indians and, 204

European treaties and, 4

gifts, 19–22

interpreters and go-betweens, 40–43

Iroquois and, 49

land, liquor, and captives, 43–48

motives, 7

colonial era (*Cont.*)
  power of words, 22–25
  respect and, 243
  wampum and pipes, 25–35
  writing and memory, 35–40
Colorado
  Arapahos and, 210, *215,*
    217, 270, 281 (*see also*
    Sand Creek massacre
    (1864))
  Cheyenne attacks, 183
  Fort Wise Treaty and, 176
  Guadalupe Hidalgo Treaty
    and, 172
  map, *215*
  Medicine Lodge Treaty and,
    210–11
  trade and, 184
  violence and, 217
Colvilles, 180
Comanche-Kiowa treaty, 189
Comanches. *see also* Plains
    Indians; *individual*
    Comanches; specific
    bands; specific subtribes
  additional compensation,
    238
  alliances, 171
  attacks south of Rio
    Grande, 172
  Black Kettle and, 183
  Cheyennes and, 171
  cholera and, 174
  delegation to Washington,
    221
  as dominant power, 166
  Fort Atkinson Treaty and,
    176
  Germans and, 5
  horses and, 166
  Jerome Commission and,
    235–36, 237
  Kiowas and, 201, 210
  Medicine Lodge Treaty and,
    163, 193, 194, 198, 199,
    200, 201, 204, 205, 206,
    210, 216
  New Mexico and, 20, 21,
    166–67
  as prisoners, 223
  reservations, 163, 183, 203,
    205, 214, *215,* 219
  Texas and, 184, 206
  US Indian Peace
    Commission and, 182, 186

Utes and, 5, 167
Coming to the Grove (Kiowa),
    224
commissioners, 7, 16, 186.
    see also individual
    commissioners; specific
    treaties
  image, 187
Compromises of 1820 and
    1850, 176
condolence ceremony, 16
Conestogas, 55
confederacy, north of the
    Ohio, 108
confederacy, Shawnee, 86
confederacy, US, 5
confederated nations, 108
Confederate Indian Cavalry
    Brigade, 162
Confederation Congress, 98
conferences. *see also entries*
    beginning Treaty of . . . ;
    specific conferences
conferences, Albany, 42
conference, Albany (1701), 2
conference, Albany (1714), 48
conference, Albany (1723), 33
conference, Albany (1725–26),
    45
conference, Albany
    (1735), 34
conference, Albany (1746), 50
conference, Albany Congress
    (1754), 24, 31, 44–45,
    65, 67
conference, Albany (1775),
    91, 92
conference, Albany
    (Denniston's Tavern)
    (1789), 101
conference, Aquokee Camp,
    151
conference, Auglaize River
    (1792), 108
conference, Blackfoot peace
    (1855), 179–80
conference, Carlisle,
    Pennsylvania, (1753), 27
conference, Chota, Tennessee,
    (1776), 30–31, 91–92
conference, Detroit (1786), 105;
    (1812), 116
conference, Easton,
    Pennsylvania (1756), 39,
    47; (1758), 20, 21

conference, Fort Benton
    (1855), 179
conference, Fort Duquesne
    (1758), 32
conference, Fort Finney (1786),
    102–3, 106
conference, Fort Johnson
    (1755), 51; (1756), 20, 32
conference, Fort Laramie
    (1867), 189
conference, Fort Laramie
    (1868), 226
conference, Fort Larned
    (1867), 189
conference, Fort McIntosh
    (1785), 102
conference, Fort Pitt (1763), 68
conference, Fort Pitt (1765), 60
conference, Fort Pitt (1767),
    61, 86
conference, Fort Pitt
    (1776), 90
conference, Fort Pitt (1778), 91
conference, German Flatts,
    New York, (1775), 24
conference, Illinois
    Campground (Tahlequah)
    (1839), 156
conference, Johnson Hall
    (1762), 19, 31, 52
conference, Johnson Hall
    (1765), 59–60
conference, Johnson Hall
    (1768), 63–65
conference, Johnson Hall
    (1774), 88–89
conference, Lancaster,
    Pennsylvania (1744), 8,
    23, 35, 41, 43–44, 45–46,
    50, 81; (1748), 35
conference, Montreal (1701),
    1–2, 8, 15; (1756) 20,
    29–30, 49
conference, New Orleans
    (1769), 34–35
conference, Okmulgee (1870),
    163
conference, Onondaga (1758),
    19
conference, Philadelphia
    (1743), 45; (1758), 33
conference, Red Clay (1834),
    138, (1835), 142, 143
conference, representation at,
    17, 48

conference, Running Water
(1834), 138; (1835), 141
conference, Sandusky (1793),
93, 108–9
conference, speeches, 23–24
conference, Susquehanna River
(1706), 18
conference, Tahlequah (Illinois
Campground) (1839), 156
conference, Tahlequah (1843),
156
conference, Takatoka (1839),
154
conference, Tremont House
(Chicago), 229
conference, Walla Walla Valley
(1855), 177–79
conference, Williamsburg
(1721), 34
conference, Winchester (1753),
45
Connecticut, 61–62, 75, 125,
127
Connolly, John, 84
Conoghquieson
(Canaghquieson)
(Kanaghqweasea)
(Kanaghwaes)
(Kanongyweniyah)
("standing ears of corn")
(Oneida)
Albany conference and, 92
on boundaries, 72, 74
Fort Stanwix Treaty and,
54, 68, 70–71, 73, 77, 85,
88–89, 248
W. Johnson and, 64, 89
on land sales, 53–54
on liquor, 46, 53–54
on women, 19
Conquering Bear (Frightening
Bear) (Sioux), 176
consensus, 17, 136–37
consent of the people, 17–18,
48
consequences of treaties, 8
Constitution Act of 1982
(Canada), 55
Constitution of the United
Cherokee Nation, 156
constitutions, 128
Continental Congress, 92
contracts, 29, 206
Coodey, William (Cherokee),
157

Coosawatie district, 137
Corlaer, 25
Cornelius, Elias, 125
Cornplanter (Seneca), 100,
110, 113
Cornstalk (Shawnee), 90–91
Corn Tassel (Cherokee), 104
Corn Tassel, George
(Cherokee), 133–34
Corps of Discovery, 164
corruption, 148. *see also*
bribery
cotton industry, 117
Cotton Kingdom, 117, 147
Covenant Chain, 24, 74
Crawford, Samuel, 188, 189
Crawford, William, 83
Crazy Horse (Oglala), 233
Creek National Council, 125
Creeks ("Red Sticks"), 15,
48, 81. *see also individual
Creeks*
American settlers and,
116–17
ceremonies and, 16
Cherokees and, 25, 123
debt and, 114
Fort Jackson Treaty and, 118
Georgia and, 108
New York Treaty and, 107
Shawnees and, 86
Tahlequah conference and,
156
western, 139
Creek War, 117, 118
Crine (Mohawk), 93
Crockett, Davy, 132
Croghan, George, 14, 40, 45,
66
authority and, 9
character of, 57–58
Connolly and, 84
Fort Pitt negotiations and,
60, 64–65
Fort Stanwix Treaty and, 66,
68, 75–76, 77, 80
Franklin and, 60, 61
Indiana Company and, 66
Indian wars and, 89–90
Lydius and, 75
Mohawks and, 57
Montour and, 69
Peters on, 67
Revolutionary War and,
93–94

on settlers, 85, 87
as speculator, 88
on Teedyuscung, 39–40
trip to England, 58–59
Washington and, 83
western frontier and, 57
western tribes and, 88
Croghan, William, 58
Crook, George, 233, 234–35
cross-cultural diplomacy,
12–19
cross-cultural interaction
colonial era and, 15–19
the Crow (Kiowa), 191
Crows, 171, 226. *see also* Plains
Indians
Fort Laramie Treaty and,
174–75
Lone Horn and, 175–76
US sovereignty and, 170
Crow Treaty (1825), 171
Cuerno Verde (Green Horn)
(Comanche), 166
Culbertson, H., 175
Culloden, 67
Cumberland, William Duke
of, 67
Cumberland Gap, 67
Cumberland-Tennessee-
Kentucky region, 77
Curler, Arent van, 25
Currey, Benjamin Franklin,
140, 141, 142, 147
Custer, George Armstrong,
185, 188, 193, 218–19, 233
Custer Died for Your Sins
(Deloria), 239

Dagdoga (He Stands). *see*
Watie, Stand
Daily Alta California
(newspaper), 173
Dakotas, 174, xii. *see also*
Plains Indians
Dartmouth, Earl of, 82
Dartmouth College, 42, 52, 74
Davis, Edmund, 221
Dawes Act (General Allotment
Act) (1887), 234, 236
Dean, James, 42
debt, 114–15
debts, 119
deeds, 44
Deerfield (MA), 26
deerskins, white, 30

Deganawidah the
Peacemaker, 16
Delaware River, 38, 39, 77
Delawares (Lenni Lenapes). *see
also individual Delawares*
calumet and, 34
Cherokees and, 25, 76
Croghan and, 61, 64–65, 90
Detroit conference and, 105
Fort Pitt Treaty and, 96–97
Fort Stanwix Treaty and, 65,
68, 75
Fort Wayne Treaty and, 116
Hurons and, 25
Iroquois and, 25, 54
Jefferson and, 113–14
W. Johnson and, 76
Johnson Hall conference
and, 59–60
Mahicans and, 25
Morgan and, 96
Ojibwes and, 25
T. Penn and, 38
Pennsylvania and, 30, 38–39
Peters and, 68
reservations, 219
Susquehanna attack, 62
Tahlequah conference and,
156
treaty and, 47–48
wampum and, 30
White Eyes and, 97
women and, 18
Delaware State, 94
delegations to London, 15, 30
delegations to Washington,
98–99, 169, 175, 176, 221,
227, 231, 236–37
delegation to New York City,
231, *232*
delegation to Philadelphia, 15
Deloria, Jr., Vine, 239
DeMallie, Raymond, 16–17
Denny, William, 33, 39
dependence, Indian, 99, 100,
134, 229
dependence, mutual, 19
De Smet, Pierre-Jean, 175, 189
Devil's Horn. *see*
Schermerhorn, John F.
Diaquanda (Teyohaquende)
(Onondaga), 68, 71, 89
Dinwiddie, Robert, 42, 67
diplomacy. *see also*
negotiations; rituals

American, 98, 103, 227
cross-cultural, 12–19, 98–99
Iroquois, 24, 53
Lone Horn and, 175–76
Plains Indians and, 164–65,
171
power and, 164–65, 173
"dirt king," 104
diseases
Caddos and, 165
Cherokees and, 150, 152
germ warfare, 54, 58, 68
Iroquois League and, 1
Lone Wolf and, 224
Plains Indians and, 167, 174
power and, 13
treaty locations and, 15
venereal, 57
Dodge, Richard Irving,
221–22, 230
Doer of Justice
(Saorghweyoghsta)
(William Franklin), 70,
71, 77
Dog Soldiers (Cheyenne), 183,
193, 195, 209, 210–11,
222. *see also individual
Dog Soldiers*
Dohate (Owl Prophet)
(Maman-ti) (Touching the
Sky) (Kiowa), 223, 224
Donelson, John, 81
Doolittle, James R., 185
Doublehead (Cherokee), 123
Douglas, Stephen, 176
Douglass, Henry, 196
Downing, Lewis (Cherokee),
232
Dragging Canoe (Cherokee),
91, 92
dress. *see* clothing
Drew, John (Cherokee), 161
drinking. *see* liquor
Duane, James, 99
Dunlap, R. G., 137
Dunmore, Governor (Lord)
(James Murray), 90
Dunmore's War, 90
Dutch, 3, 4, 25, 26
Dutch language, 42
Dutch Reformed Church, 153
Duthu, N. Bruce
(Houma), 242
Duwali (Bowles) (Cherokee),
156

Eastern Woodland Indians,
46, 114
Ecueracapa (Leather Shirt)
(Iron Coat) (Comanche),
21
editing, 37
education, 125. *see also* schools
New Echota Treaty and, 145
Eel River tribes, 116
Eghnisera (Andrew Montour,
Sattelihu), 69
Egushawa (Augooshaway)
(Gushgushagwa)
(Ottawa), 106, 113, 244
Elliott, Joel, 193, 213–14, 218,
230
Emlen, James, 110
empire, 2, 4, 5, 6, 12
English. *see also specific
colonies*
calumet and, 32–33
captives and, 47
French and, 4, 36, 44
neutrality and, 2
wampum and, 31
western Indians and, 72
writing and, 35
English language, 42
Esopus Indians, 37, 295n125
ethnic cleansing, 9, 121
Texas and, 156
Europeans. *see also specific
nationalities*
colonial era and, 4
Indian culture and, 14
Osages and, 165
protocols and, 12
Evans, Lewis, 29
Evarts, Jeremiah ("William
Penn"), 131–32
Everett, Edward, 132
extermination, 186

Fairfax, Thomas Lord, 45
Fallen Timbers campaign, 113
Fallon, Benjamin, 170, 171
farming. *see* agriculture
"father," 24, 99
Fayel, William, 189, 192
feathers, 30, 34, 64, 102, 194,
197
*Federal Power Commission v.
Tuscarora Indian Nation*
(1960), 239
fences, 44, 47, 64, 87

Fenton, William, 67, 70, 79
Fetterman, William, 185
fictive kinship, 12–13, 18
Fillmore, Millard, 174, 175
First Nations tribes, 5, 10
Fishermore (Kiowa), 194,
    198, 205
fishing, 240
Fitzpatrick, Margaret (Adams)
    (Wilmarth) (Wilmott)
    (Walking Woman)
    (Arapaho), 184, 197, 198,
    210
Fitzpatrick, Thomas (Broken
    Hand), 174, 175, 184, 197
Five Nations, 1. *see also*
    Iroquois (Iroquois
    League) (Six Nations);
    specific tribes
flags, 167
Flatheads (Salish), 169, 171,
    179. *see also* Plains
    Indians
Florida, 98, 125, 223, 224
Forbes, John, 57, 114–15
Forbes, John and Company,
    114–15
force. *see* coercion;
    US military
Foreman, James, 157
Foreman, Tom (Cherokee), 138
Forks of the Ohio, 57, 58,
    75–76
Forsythe, Thomas, 293n90
Fort Bent, 184
Fort Chartres, 84
Fort Duquesne (Fort Pitt)
    (Fort Dunmore), 57,
    69, 84
Fort Johnson, 52
Fort Marion (FL), 224
Fort Niagara, 54, 68, 92, 93
Fort Pitt (Fort Duquesne)
    (Fort Dunmore), 57, 58,
    69, 84, 85. *see also* Treaty
    of Fort Pitt (1778)
Fort Randolph, 91
Fort Sill, 219, 222, 223
Fort Stanwix, 93. *see also*
    *Treaties of Fort Stanwix
    (1768, 1784)*
Fox Indians (Mesquakies), 34,
    115, 170, 235
France and Frenchmen. *see
    also* Paris, Peace of

(1763, 1783); *individual
    Frenchmen*
alliances, Indian, 1, 4, 57,
    165
Britain and, 20, 53, 76
calumet and, 32–33, 33–34
English and, 4, 36, 44
Indian culture and, 14
Indian support for, 37
as interpreters, 40
W. Johnson and, 53
Plains Indians and, 165–66
Texas and, 165
Virginia and, 81
wampum and, 29–30, 31, 32
*Frank Leslie's Illustrated
    Newspaper,* 189
Franklin, Benjamin, 6, 58,
    60–61, 62, 63, 82, 83, 94
Franklin, William
    (Doer of Justice)
    (Saorghweyoghsta),
    58, 66, 70, 71, 77, 81,
    94, 248
fraud
    Greenville Treaty and,
        309n51
    Henderson treaty (Sycamore
        Shoals Treaty) and, 104
    Indian Springs Treaty and,
        118
    New Echota Treaty and,
        148, 151
    Pennsylvania and, *38,* 39
    private, 2, 4
French and Indian Wars
    (1754–63), 4, 20, 22, 44,
    47–48, 58, 65–66, 67
Frightening Bear (Conquering
    Bear) (Sioux), 176
Frontenac, Count, 31

Gage, Thomas, 80–81, 86
Galagina (Buck Watie)
    (Cherokee). *see* Boudinot,
    Elias
Gap in the Woods (Howea)
    (Yamparika Comanche),
    236
Gardner, Alexander, *195*
Gatling guns, 192, 324n29
Gaustrax (Seneca), 77
General Allotment Act (Dawes
    Act) (1887), 234
George III, 54, 55, 63, 247

Georgia. *see also individual
    governors*
    Cherokee homelands and,
        122, 135, 137, 141
    Cherokees and, 118, 121,
        129, 131, 134–35, 136
    Corn Tassel and, 134
    Creeks and, 118
    Creeks and Cherokees and,
        108
    Hopewell Treaty and, 104
    Indian Removal Act and,
        133
    Jackson and, 117
    land claims by, 98
Georgia, Cherokee Nation v.,
    134
Georgia, Worcester v. (1832),
    134
Georgia Guard, 133, 134
German, John and Lydia,
    222–23
Germans, 5, 42, 57. *see also
    individual Germans*
germ warfare, 54
gifts. *see also specific gifts*
    Buffalo Chief on, 210
    captives as, 47, 167
    Cheyenne-Kiowa alliance
        and, 171–72
    colonial era and, 19–22,
        290n39
    Croghan and, 57, 58
    Fort Laramie Treaty, 175
    Fort Stanwix Treaty and, 66,
        71, 76, 77
    as inducements, 46
    W. Johnson and, 52, 89
    Lewis and Clark and, 167
    Medicine Lodge Treaty and,
        194, 202, 205–6, 327n66
    New Mexico and, 166
    treaty and, 167
    US commissioners and, 98
    writing *versus,* 35
Gillet, Ransom H., 119
Gilmer, George, 150
Girty, Simon, 108–9
Gist, George (Sequoyah), 128
Given, Joshua (Givens), 236
Glen, (governor of SC), 35
Godfrey, Edward, 202, 218,
    324n29
gold, 131, 133, 172, 185, 233
Gold, Harriet Ruggles, 126–27

Good Peter (Oneida), 93, 101, 102
goodwill, 16, 19, 175
gorgets, 21
governments, 17
Grand Ohio Company, 82, 83
Grant, Ulysses S., 219, 229, 231
Grattan, John, 176
Gray Head (Cheyenne Dog Soldier), 195
  Medicine Lodge Treaty and, 198
"Great Councillor of the Thirteen Fires." *see* Washington, George
Great Lakes land, 119, 139
Great Lakes tribes, 54, 61, 240. *see also specific tribes*
Great Mountain (Onontio) (Chevalier de Montmagny), 25
Great Peace of 1840, 5, 172, 197
Great Peace of Montreal (1701), 1–2, 8, 15, 49
"Great Warriors' Path," 63
Greenbrier Company, 67
Greene, David, 135
Green Horn (Cuerno Verde) (Comanche), 166
Grey Beard (Cheyenne Dog Soldier), 205, 222, 223–24
Griffin, Patrick, 88
Grinnell, George Bird, 332n26
Gros Ventres, 175
Guastrax (Genesee Seneca), 68, 248
Guerrier, Edmund, 196–97, *232*
Guerrier, Julia (Bent), 196, 197, 198
Guipahko (Lone Wolf) (Kiowa), 183
Gun Merchant (Upper Creek), 48
Gunter, John, 144
Gushgushagwa (Augooshaway) (Egushawa) (Ottawa), 106, 113, 244
Gus-Wen-Tah (Kaswentha). see wampum
Guyasuta (Kayusuta) (Seneca), 54

Haldimand, Frederick, 95
Half Town (Seneca), 100–101

Hall, S.F., 189
Hallowing King (Creek), 97–98
Hamilton, Louis, 218
Hancock, Winfield Scott, 185, 188, 189, 193, 194, 195, 196, 209
Harmar, Joseph, 108, 113
Harney, William S. (Winyan Wicakte) (Woman Killer)
  Brulé village destruction and, 176
  Fort Laramie Treaty (1867) and, 226, 227
  Fort Smith Treaty and, 162
  gifts and, 206, 209
  image, *187*
  life history and character of, 187–88
  Little Arkansas Treaty and, 184
  Medicine Lodge Treaty and, 186, 192, 194, 195, 200, 205, 264, 271, 272, 273, 275, 276, 282
  US Commission and, 229
Harper's Weekly (newspaper), 189, *198*
Harrison, William Henry, 114, 115–16, 157
Hauptman, Laurence, 161
Having Horns (Bao) (Cat) (Kiowa), 196
Hawkins, Benjamin, 103–4
healing, 243
Heap of Birds (Cheyenne), 223
Hears the Sunrise (Tananaica) (Voice of the Sunrise) (Yamparika Comanche), 222
Heckewelder, John, 25–26, 27, 30, 40
Heizer, Robert, 174
Henderson, James Youngblood, 242
Henderson, John B.
  on G. Bent, 184
  attitudes, 186, 193–94, 201
  on buffalo, 202
  Cheyennes and, 209
  Harney and, 187, 200, 205
  on Indians, 180
  Medicine Lodge Treaty and, 193–94, 198, 201, 202, 205, 209, 210–11, 226, 229
Henderson, Richard, 91, 104

Hendrick (Mohawk), 24, 44, 51, 52
Henry, Patrick, 89
Herring, Elbert, 143
He Stands (Dagdoga). *see* Watie, Stand
Hiawatha, 16
Hicks, Elijah, 157
Hidatsas, 172, 175. *see also* Plains Indians
Hillsborough, Lord, 63, 82, 86
Hitchcock, Ethan Allen, 237
Hitchcock, Lone Wolf v., 238
Hoag, Enoch, 214
Holton, Woody, 89
homelands
  Cherokee, *122,* 135, 137, 141
  Oneida, 110–11
  war and treaties and, 2
Honey Eaters (Peneteka Comanches), 183, 200, 204, 214–15
horses, 165–66, 167, 171, 172, 214, 222
hostages, 91, 100, 103
houses of elite Indians, 128
Howea (Gap in the Woods) (Yamparika Comanche), 236
Howland, John, 189, *198*
Howling Wolf (Cheyenne), *198,* 224
humanitarianism, 182
human rights, international, 243
Hunkpapas, 176
hunting. *see also* buffalos
  Cherokees and, 114–15, 122
  Fort Stanwix Treaty and, 91
  Iroquois and, 1
  Jefferson on, 114
  rights, 75
  settlers and, 87
  US expansion and, 107
Hurons, 15, 22, 25, *28,* 40, 105. *see also individual Hurons*
Hyde, George, 332n26

Idaho, 177
ideology, 42
Illinois, 60, 61, 105, 115, 119
"Indian" ("Native American"), xii
Indiana, 77, 105, 115, 153
Indiana Company, 66

Indian appropriations bill
(1871), 231, 233
Indian Claims Commission,
235, 238, 241
"Indian country," 172
Indian department (Britain), 56
Indian Industrial School (PA),
224
Indian negotiators, 7
Indian Office (Bureau of
Indian Affairs), 173, 229
Indian Removal Act of 1830,
9, 132, 133
Indian Rights Association, 237
Indian Territory
Boudinot and, 233
Medicine Lodge Treaty
and, 182
reservations, 183
US Civil War and, 161, 163
US Indian Peace
Commission and, 186
Indian Trade and Intercourse
Act (1790), 107, 241
Indian Trade and Intercourse
Act (1834), 172
Indian wars. *see also* violence
and retaliation; *specific
battles; specific massacres*
Auglaize River conference
and, 108
boundaries and, 99
Cherokees and, 91, 92
Croghan and, 58, 89–90
Fort Stanwix Treaty and, 86
Jefferson and, 114
Logan and, 88
Medicine Lodge Treaty and,
198–99, 217
military and, 229
misunderstandings and, 212
Revolutionary War and,
92, 93
right of conquest and, 105
Stanley on, 212
US Congress and, 105, 185
US power and, 108
western frontier and, 85, 111
industrial revolution, 180
intermarriages, 18, 103,
126–27, 167, 176, 184,
196–97. *see also* Métis
(mixed heritage people)
Internal Revenue Act of 1868,
233

interpretation, 238
interpreters and go-betweens
accuracy and, 37
bribery of, 108
Caddo, 165
colonial era and, 40–43
Comanche, 167
Fort Laramie Treaty and,
175
Fort Pitt Treaty and, 97
Fort Stanwix Treaty and, 68
Greenville Treaty and, 113
Lancaster Treaty and, 41
Lewis and Clark and, 169
mediators, 13
Pickering on, 111
Sandusky conference and,
108–9
Teedyuscung and, 39
Iowas, 156, 170, 174, 235
Irish traders, 9. *see also
individual Irish traders*
Iron Coat (Leather
Shirt) (Ecueracapa)
(Comanche), 21
Iroquoian languages, 41, 42
Iroquois Chain of Friendship,
24
Iroquois (Iroquois League) (Six
Nations). *see also member
nations; sub-tribes;
individual representatives*
Albany conference, 92
boundaries and, 72
British and, 49–50, 53, 54,
85–86
calumet and, 34
Canandaigua Treaty and,
110–11
Cherokees and, 25, 63–65
claims of, 9
Croghan and, 57, 90
cross-cultural interactions
and, 16
Detroit conference and, 105
diplomacy, 24, 53
elder/younger brothers of, 24
Fort Stanwix Treaty and, 45,
50, 66, 68, 74–80, 79–80,
85, 89, 100
gifts and, 20–21
government of, 17
Indiana Company and, 66
W. Johnson and, 51, 52, 56,
59, 62, 64, 88

Johnson Hall conference
and, 59–60
Kayaderosseras patent
and, 65
kinship and, 24–25
Lydius and, 75
memory and, 36
Montour and, 69
Morgan and, 96
names and, 25
negotiation and, 7
New York State and, 96,
101–2
19th century and, 119
Ohio country and, 54
Ohio Indians and, 77
other peoples' lands and,
49–50, 54, 60, 77, 80, 86
Peace of Montreal and, 1–2,
286n3
Peace of Paris and, 100
Pennsylvania and, 44–45, 62
Pickering and, 110
ratification and, 48
rights of, 43–44
Schermerhorn and, 139
settlers and, 119
stories and, 23
Susquehanna attack, 62
trade and, 12
treaty cloth and, 11
US and, 6
violence of, 1
Virginia and, 81
wampum and, 31, 32
women and, 18–19, 101–2
on writing, 40
Isawanhonhi, Nicolas Vincent
(Huron), *28*
I-See-O (Kiowa), 225
Isenberg, Andrew, 221

Jackson, Andrew
Cherokees and, 125, 129–30,
129–33, 135, 137, 138,
140, 148
Choctaws and, 118
Fort Jackson Treaty and, 117
Georgia and, 135
New Echota Treaty and, 148
on reservations, 144
Schermerhorn and, 139
on treaties, 132–33
Jacobites, 67
Jacobs, Wilbur, 86

James (King), 14
Jamestown, 13
Jefferson, Thomas. *see also*
    Clark, William; Lewis,
    Meriwether
  acquisition of Indian lands
    and, 113–14, 180
  Cherokees and, 133
  on Indians, 130
  Lewis and Clark and, 169
  Logan and, 88
  as speculator, 89
  Walker and, 67
  western tribes and, 164
Jemison, Jacob, 25, 31
Jerome, David H., 235, 236
Jerome Commission (Cherokee
    Commission), 235–37
John Forbes and Company,
    114–15
Johnson, Guy, 57, 65, 66, 68,
    78, 92, 93
Johnson, Molly (Mary)
    (Brant), 19, 51, 52, 57
Johnson, William (Sir William)
    (Warraghiyagey)
  authority of, 9
  Board of Trade and, 82
  British and, 60
  calumet and, 34
  calumet/Wampum and,
    30, 32
  captives and, 47
  Conoghquieson and, 46
  Croghan and, 59
  on Fort Stanwix Treaty, 88
  Fort Stanwix Treaty and,
    62–63, 65–66, 69–72, 76,
    77, 80, 246, 248
  Franklin and, 60–61
  on gifts, 22
  gifts and, 20
  Hudson Valley conference,
    37
  image, *50*
  Iroquois and, 9, 50, 52, 53,
    60, 64, 88
  Kayaderosseras patent
    and, 65
  kinship and, 57
  life history, 50–53
  Lydius and, 75
  Mohawk language and,
    68–69
  Mohawks and, 50–51, 65

New York lands of, 76
Niagara conference and, 55
Ohio nations and, 77
Oneidas and, 73–74
Onondagas and, 62
Senecas and, 54
on settlers, 89
on transactions with
    Indians, 12
wampum and, 10, 32
western frontier and, 56
women and, 19, 68
Johnson Hall, 92. *see also*
    conference, Johnson Hall
    (1762, '65, '68, '72)
Johnson v. McIntosh (1823),
    5, 109
Jones, Dorothy, 14, 84, 90, 98
Jones, Douglas, 194, 202, 210,
    213
Joseph, Chief (Nez Perce), 228
journalists. *see* newspapers
    (press); *individual
    journalists*
justice, 243
Justice, Daniel Heath, 144
Justice Department, 235, 241

Kagama, US v. (1886, 1903),
    237–38
Kahmungdaclageh (The Ridge)
    (Cherokee). *see* The Ridge
Kahnawake Mohawks, 26,
    34, 69
Kamiakin (Yakama), 179
Kanaghqweasea
    (Canaghquieson)
    (Kanaghwaes)
    (Kanongyweniyah)
    ("standing ears of
    corn") (Oneida). *see*
    Conoghquieson
Kanawha River, 62, 63, 66, 72,
    77, 81, 87, 90, 91
Kanien'kehaka (Mohawk), xii
Kansa Indians (Kaws), 170–71,
    216
Kansas
  Arapahos and Cheyennes
    and, 183
  Cherokee lands, 163
  Indian raids and, 183
  Little Arkansas Treaty and,
    184
  map, *215*

Medicine Lodge Treaty and,
    210–11, 216
  non-Indians and, 176
  reservations, 183
  Senecas and, 119
  violence and, 217
Kansas-Nebraska Act (1854),
    176
Kansas Pacific Railroad, 184,
    186
Kaswentha (Gus-Wen-Tah)
    (wampum belt), 3. *see also*
    wampum belts
Katsienkos (Koietsenkos)
    (Qóichégàus) (Real/
    Principal Dogs) (Sentinel
    Horses) (Kiowas), 191,
    197, *207*
Kaws (Kansa Indians), 170–71,
    216
Kayaderosseras patent, 65
Kayusuta (Guyasuta) (Seneca),
    54
Keeper of the Sacred Arrows
    (Medicine Arrows) (Stone
    Forehead) (Cheyenne),
    211, 216
Kendall, Amos, 125, 135, 158
Kentucky
  Boone and, 87
  Cherokees and, 91, *122*
  Fort Stanwix cession and, 90
  Henderson and, 104
  Shawnees and, 86, 91, 103
  Virginia and, 81, 84, 89, 98
Kentucky (Catawba) River, 81,
    303n129
Kickapoos, 60, 235
Kicking Bird (Teneangopte)
    (Tonaenko) (Kiowa)
  assassination of, 223
  gifts from, 206
  image, *203*
  medals and, 212
  Medicine Lodge Treaty
    and, 183, 194, 197, 198,
    202, 205
  Sheridan and, 218
  Warren Wagon Train
    Massacre and, 220
Killbuck (Delaware), 68, 85
King, Thomas (Oneida), 64
King George's War (1744–48),
    20, 24
kinship

boundaries and, 46–47
calumet and, 33
captives and, 47–48
Cherokees and, 123
Croghan and, 58
"fictive," 12–13, 18
French and, 287n9
Iroquois and, 24–25
W. Johnson and, 51, 57
metaphors, 99
Plains Indians and, 165
protests and, 120
trade and, 167
women and, 18
Kinzua Dam, 10–11
Kiowas. *see also* Plains
    Indians; *individual Kiowas*
additional compensation,
    238
alliances, 171
artists, 224
attacks south of Rio
    Grande, 172
Black Kettle and, 183
Cheyennes and, 5, 171, 197,
    210
Comanches and, 201, 210
Fort Atkinson Treaty and,
    176
Jerome Commission and,
    235–36, 237
Medicine Lodge Treaty and,
    182, 193, 194, 197, 201,
    205, 206, 209, 210, 215–16
as prisoners, 223
reservations, 163, 183, 203,
    205, 214, *215,* 219, 238
resistance by, 184
Texas and, 184
US Indian Peace
    Commission and, 186
violence of, 218–19, 220, 221
Kip, Lawrence, 177, 178, 179
Kirkland, Samuel, 74, 92, 102
Knell, David, 160
Knox, Henry, 98, 105, 109
Koietsenkos (Katsienkos)
    (Qóichégàus) (Real/
    Principal Dogs) (Sentinel
    Horses) (Kiowas), 191,
    197, *207*
Kondiaronk (the Rat) (Huron),
    15
Kutenais, 179
Kwahadi Comanches, 200, 216

labor, cheap, 173
La Chine massacre, 1
Lake Ontario, 1, 72
Lakotas (Sioux), xii. *see also*
    Plains Indians; *individual*
    Lakotas; specific Lakota
    subtribes
alliances, 171
Black Hills and, 234
calumet and, 35
Crows and, 171
Fort Laramie Treaty and,
    227
Harney and, 187
Oglalas, 35, 226, 239
Red Cloud War and,
    184–85
Sioux Act and, 234–35
Lamar, Mirabeau B., 156, 172
land. *see also* agriculture;
    buffalos; hunting;
    railroads; settlers,
    American; *specific treaties*
bounties, 58, 67, 84, 100,
    103, 111
colonial era and, 43–48
cultural understanding of, 44
Fort Stanwix Treaty and,
    48, 84
interpreters and, 42
ownership of, 5, 44
private (private property),
    93, 98, 204, 234
removal and, 118–19
land, sales of
    Black Hawk on, 115
    as capital offense, 118, 129
    Cherokees and, 123–24,
        133
    Croghan and, 58
    deceit and, 111
    Fort Stanwix Treaty and, 91
    prices, 116
    Red Jacket and, 113
    right of conquest *versus,* 105
    rights and, 65
    sales of, 4, 44, 56, 121
    Sandusky conference and,
        109
    speculators and, 55–56
    treaties and, 98, 113
    Wharton and, 84–85
    Wyandots on, 116
land companies, 4–5, 101. *see*
    also specific companies

languages of treaties, 196,
    197, 238, 240. *see*
    also interpreters and
    go-betweens
Latrobe, Charles, 118–19
Lawrence Tribune (newspaper),
    228
Lawyer (Nez Perce), 178, 227
leadership, Indian, 17, 19, 21,
    86, 129, 136, 149
Lean Bear (Cheyenne), 224
Leather Shirt (Ecueracapa)
    (Iron Coat) (Comanche),
    21
Leavenworth, Jesse, 184, 189,
    194, 201, 214, 216
Lee, Arthur, 100, 102
Lee, Richard Henry, 97–98
Lee, Williams v. (1959), 239
Left Hand (Arapaho), 197
legality, 3, 4, 14, 56, 58, 86,
    121, 145, 149, 229, 239,
    242. *see also* authority;
    rights of Indians;
    sovereignty; US authority;
    US courts; US Supreme
    Court
Lehigh Valley, 39
Le Jeune, Paul, 22
Lenni Lenapes. *see* Delawares
Leschi (Nisqually), 177
L'Etalie, François, 175
Lewis, Andrew, 66–67, 81,
    90, 94
Lewis, Charles, 90
Lewis, Meriwether, 5, 145, 164,
    167–71, 178, 228
The Life and Adventures of
    Joaquin Murieta, The
    Celebrated California
    Bandit (J. R. Ridge), 161
Lincoln, Abraham, 176, 194,
    200
Lindsay, William, 149
liquor
    Canasatego and, 23
    Chicago Treaty and, 119
    colonial era and, 45–46
    Conoghquieson on, 53–54
    Croghan and, 57
    Harrison and, 116
    Medicine Lodge Treaty and,
        197, 201, 216
    Montour and, 69
    Pickering on, 111

liquor (*Cont.*)
Satanta and, 192
Seneca treaty and, 119
Teedyuscung, 39, 46
Treaty of St. Louis and, 115
literacy, 111, 128, 129, 238. *see
also* written treaties
literature, treaties as, 8
Little Abraham. *see* Abraham
Little Carpenter
(Attakullakulla)
(Cherokee), 63, 81, 91
Little Man (Cheyenne Dog
Soldier), 210
Little Medicine (Cheyenne),
235
Little Mountain (Kiowa), 171,
172
Little Raven (Arapaho)
delegation to Washington
and, 231
Fort Larned conference
and, 191
image, *232*
Medicine Lodge Treaty and,
191, 205, 209–10, 211, 216
on Sand Creek massacre,
183
Sheridan and, 218
Stanley on, 198
on women, 18
Little Robe (Cheyenne), 183,
205, 209, 211, 212, 231,
232
Little Turkey (Cherokee), 95
Little Turtle (Miami), 112–13
Logan (Mingo), 88
London, delegations to, 15, 30
Lone Horn (Miniconjou
Sioux), 175–76
Lone Wolf (Guipahko)
(Kiowa), 176, 183, 198,
218–19, 220, 221, 224
Lone Wolf (Mamaydayte,
adopted son) (Kiowa),
225, 236, 237, 238
Lone Wolf v. Hitchcock, 237–38
Long, John, 17, 32, 33, 52
long knife (Assaryquoa)
(Assaraquoa) (sword),
25, 29
Looking Glass (Nez Perce),
179
Looney, John (Cherokee), 154
Lords of the Treasury, 82

Louisa River, 303n129
Louisiana, 40, 54, 166, 169
Louisiana Purchase, 170
Louisiana Territory, 5, 21,
34, 117
Louis XIV, 4
Lower Creeks, 116–17, 118
Lowery, George (Cherokee), 147
Loyal Land Company, 67
Lumpkin, Wilson, 137, 142,
148–49, 150, 155
Lydius, John Henry, 46, 75
Lyons, Scott, 2–3
Lyttleton, William, 48

Mackenzie, Ranald, 222
Magpie (Cheyenne), 190, *190,*
196, 218
Mahdabee, 10
Mahicans, 25, 108. *see also
individual Mahicans*
Maine Indian Claims
Settlement Act (1980),
241
Maman-ti (Touching the Sky)
(Dohate) (Owl Prophet)
(Kiowa), 223, 224
Mamaydayte (Lone Wolf,
adopted son) (Kiowa),
225, 236, 237, 238
Mandans, 167, 169, 170,
172, 175. *see also* Plains
Indians
Manifest Destiny, 172. *see also*
US expansion
Mann, Barbara, 309n51
Manypenny, George, 233–34
maps, 46–47, *78,* 175, *215*
Maquachake (Mekoche)
(Shawnee), 102, 103
Marquette, Jacques, 32
Marshall, John, 133, 134
Marshall, Peter, 63, 82
Marshe, Witham, 41, 46
Martin, Joseph, 103–4
Maryland, 41, 44
Mascoutens, 60
Mason-Dixon line, 83
Massachusetts, 241
Massachusetts Bay Colony, 4
Massasoit (Wampanoag),
13–14
matrilineal societies, 24
Mayetin (Woman's Heart)
(Kiowa), 221, 223, 224

McCusker, Philip, 196, 198,
206, 215, 231, *232*
McGillivray, Alexander, 107
McIlworth, Thomas, *50*
McIntosh, John, 157
McIntosh, Johnson v. (1823),
5, 109
McIntosh, Lachlan, 103–4
McIntosh, William (Creek),
118, 125, 129
McKay, William Cameron, 179
McKee, Alexander, 85
McKenney, Thomas, 99
Mdwekantons, 174
medals
allegiances and, 21
Hopewell Treaty and, 104
Kiowas and Comanches
and, 221
Lewis and Clark and, 167
Medicine Lodge Treaty
and, 212
peace medals, 99, 198, 206,
208, 212, 221
power and, 99
Wayne and, 112
mediators, 13. *see also*
interpreters and
go-betweens
Medicine Arrow ceremony, 205
Medicine Arrows (Keeper of
the Sacred Arrows) (Stone
Forehead) (Cheyenne),
211, 216
Meigs, Jane (Ross), 158
Meigs, Return J., 141–42
Meigs, Return J. (grandson),
158
Mekoche (Maquachake)
(Shawnee), 102, 103
Meldrum, Robert, 175
Memorial Peace Park
(Medicine Lodge), 225
memory
calumet and, 34
colonial era and, 35–40
Hopewell Treaty and, 104
US Supreme Court and, 238
wampum and, 27–29, 30, 32
writing and, 39
Menominees, 170
Merrell, James, 8, 57
Mesquakies (Fox Indians), 34,
115, 170, 235
metaphors, 14–15, 22, 24, 42

Métis (mixed heritage people), 32, 42–43
Mexican War (war of 1846–1848), 172
Mexico, 5, 138, 156, 165, 172
Miamis, 20, 25, 35, 105, 112–13, 116, 140
Michigan, 105, 115, 139
Mille Lacs (Ojibwe), 240
miners, 177
Mingos, 54, 77, 88
Miniconjou Sioux, 175
Minnesota, 174, 240
missionaries, 134. *see also individual missionaries*
Mississaugas, 32
Mississippi law, 118
Mississippi state, 98, 104–5, 115
Mississippi Valley, 4, 32
Missouri, 119, 169, 185
Missouri Democrat (newspaper), 188
Missouri Republican (newspaper), 189
Missouris, 167, 170
Mitchell, David D., 175
moccasins, 169
modern law, 241–42
modification of treaties, 48
Mohawk language, 68, 71
Mohawks. *see also* Iroquois (Iroquois League) (Six Nations); Kahnawake Mohawks; *individual Mohawks*
  abduction by, 26
  adoptions by, 41
  Croghan and, 58
  Dutch traders and, 3
  Fort Stanwix Treaty and, 75, 85, 246, 248
  Iroquois League and, 1, 24
  W. Johnson and, 50, 51, 52, 57, 65, 76
  Kayadoerosseras patent and, 65
  names for, xii
  neutrality and, 2
  post French and Indian War, 64
  Revolutionary War and, 92
  singing and, 31
  wampum and, 30–31
  women, 19

Mohawk Valley, 52, 69
Moluntha (Mekoche Shawnee), 103
Monongahela battle (1755), 57
Monroe, James, 170
Montagnais, 22
Montana, 171, 177
Montcalm, Marquis de, 20
Montmagny, Chevalier de (Great Mountain) (Onontio), 25
Montour, Andrew (Sattelihu, Eghnisera), 40, 41, 42, 68, 69, 88
Montour, Madam, 69
Montreal, Great Peace of (1701), 1–2, 8, 15, 49
Montreal surrender (1760), 54
Mooney, James, 196
morality, 242–43
Moravians, 25, 42, 47, 125, 142
Morgan, George, 58, 60, 61, 66, 90–91, 94, 96, 97
Morris, Robert Hunter, 16, 47
motives for treaties, 7–8
Mount Johnson, 52
multiculturalism, 14, 52–53
Murphy, Thomas, 184, 189, 217, 218
Murray, James (Governor (Lord) Dunmore), 90

names, 25
Napoleon Bonaparte, 5
Narragansetts, 13, 14, 19–20
National Party (Cherokee), 147, 153–54, 156, 160, 162. *see also* Ross, John (Cherokee)
nation-to-nation networks, 13
"Native American" ("Indian"), xii
Native American Rights Fund, 239
Navajos, 166, 227, 239
Nebraska, 183
negotiations. *see also* diplomacy; rituals
  Indians and, 3
  Iroquoian, 67
  power and, 7
neutrality, 2
Nevada, 172
New Corn (Potawatomi), 112
New France, 25, 47

New Jersey, 38, 49, 77, 94, 246
New Mexico, 21, 166, 172, *215,* 227
newspapers (press), 188, 189, 192, 193, 194, 196, 204–5, 206, 213. *see also individual reporters; specific newspapers*
New York City delegation, 231, *232*
New York Herald (newspaper), 188, 189, 212
New York State, 25, 31
  Canandaigua Treaty and, 111
  Fort Stanwix Treaty and, 49, 100, 101
  Iroquois and, 96, 101–2, 111
  Senecas and, 119
  shady deals, 101
  western lands and, 94
New York Times (newspaper), 230
New Zealand, 243
Nez Perces, 171, 177–78, *178, 179,* 227, 228. *see also* Plains Indians
Nicholls, Richard, 295n125, 295*n*125
Nickus (Mohawk), 57
Nimwha (Shawnee), 65
Nisquallys, 177
Norridgwocks, 26–27
North, Frank, 219
North American Review, 230
North Carolina, 98, 104, 118, 121, *122*
Northern Pacific Railroad, 177, 180
Northrup, Sarah Bird, 125, 126
Northwest Coast Indians, 240
Northwest Ordinance (1787), 94, 105
Norton, John, 25
Notes on the State of Virginia (Jefferson), 88

obligations
  gifts and, 19
  kinship and, 24–25
  wampum and, 27
Oconostota (Oconostata) (Oconostoto) (Cherokee), 63, 87, 91, 104
Ogden Land Company, 119

Oglala Lakotas (Sioux), 35, 226, 239
Ohio, 115
Ohio Company of Virginia, 44, 82
Ohio Indians
American diplomacy and, 103
Europeans and, 65, 72–73
Fort Stanwix Treaty and, 79, 80, 86
Iroquois League and, 54
W. Johnson and, 77
Revolutionary War and, 90
right of conquest and, 102
Washington and, 41–42
Ohio River and Valley
Auglaize River conference and, 108
as boundary, 95
British and, 45, 54, 65, 84
Cherokees and Iroquois and, 86
Croghan and, 57, 58, 60
Fort Harmar treaties and, 105–6
Fort Stanwix Treaty and, 49, 100
Indian wars and, 91
Lancaster Treaty and, 44
Pickering and, 110
right of conquest and, 102
Sandusky conference and, 109
settlers and, 87
Shawnees and, 103, 113
treaties and, 98
Ojibwes, 25, 105, 119–20, 170, 240
Oklahoma, 183, 201, *215,* 235
Old Settlers (Cherokees), 154, 156, 157, 159
Old Smoke (Sayenqueragtha) (Seneca), 68, 89, 92, 93
Omahas, 167, 170
Onas (feather/quill) (William Penn), 25, 30, 36, *38,* 131–32
Oneida country, 153
Oneidas. *see also* Iroquois (Iroquois League) (Six Nations); *individual Oneidas*
Canandaigua Treaty and, 110–11

Fort Stanwix Treaty and, 75, 248
homelands, 110–11
interpreters and, 42
Iroquois League and, 1, 24
W. Johnson and, 64, 73–74
missionaries and, 74
New York State and, 101, 111
Pickering and, 111
Revolutionary War and, 92
Oneyanha (Beech Tree) (Oneida), 101
Onondagas. *see also* Iroquois (Iroquois League) (Six Nations); *individual Onondagas*
calumet and, 34
Iroquois League and, 1, 24
W. Johnson and, 62, 70
Johnson Hall conference and, 60
New York State and, 101, 111
wampum and, 31–32
Wharton and, 299n44
Onondiyo (Captain John) (Oneida), 110–11
Onontio (Chevalier de Montmagny) (Great Mountain), 25
opportunism, 84. *see also* speculators
oral pacts, 5
oral tradition, 35–40
oratory, 7, 23, 43, 99, 209
Oregon, 172, 174, 177, 180
O'Reilly, Alejandro, 34–35
Osages, 156, 165, 169, 170–71, 183, 200, 216. *see also* Plains Indians
Ostler, Jeffrey, 175, 227
Otos, 167, 170
Otsinoghiyata (Bunt) (Onondaga), 77, 89, 248
Ottawas. *see also individual Ottawas*
calumet and, 34
Detroit conference and, 105
Great Lakes land and, 119
Mahicans and, 25
Prairie du Chien Treaty and, 170
trust and, 120
wampum and, 31, 32

Owl (Miami), 116
Owl Prophet (Dohate) (Maman-ti) (Touching the Sky) (Kiowa), 223, 224
Owl Woman (Bent) (Cheyenne), 184

Pacific Coast, 176. *see also specific states*
Pacific Northwest, 177. *see also specific states*
Pacific Railroad Acts (1862, 1864), 180
Painted Pole (Shawnee), 108
Palmer, Joel, 177, 178
Palo Duro Canyon, 222
panic of 1837, 151
Panis Indians, 47, 297n174
Panton, William, 114
Paris, Peace of (1763), 53, 54
Paris, Peace of (1783), 94–95, 97, 100, 105
Parker, Ely S. (Seneca), 162, 231
Parker, Quanah (Comanche), 237
Parsons, Samuel, 103
Paruasemena (Yamparika Comanche). *see* Ten Bears
Paschal, George, 318n151
Passamaquoddies, 241
passports, 34
patience, 110
patrilineal societies, 24
Pawnee Creek, 194
Pawnee Fork village, 195
Pawnees, 156, 170–71, 235. *see also* Plains Indians
Paxton Boys, 55
Payne, John Howard, 141, 142–43
peace
calumet and, 33, 34–35
Indian understanding of, 16
intertribal, 179
Medicine Lodge Treaty and, 213
Ross on, 229
peace ambassadors, 25–26
pen-and-ink witch-craft, 2, 36, 106, 244
Pend Oreilles, 179
Peneteka Comanches (Honey Eaters), 183, 200, 204, 214–15

Penn, John, 67, 93
Penn, Thomas, 38–39, 62
Penn, William (Onas) (feather)
    (quill), 25, 30, 36, *38,*
    131–32
Penn, William (pen name)
    (Jeremiah Everts), 131–32
Penn family, 85, 93
Pennsylvania. *see also* Paxton
    Boys; Treaty of Lancaster;
    individual Pennsylvanians
    Croghan and, 57
    Delawares and, 30, 38–39
    Fort Stanwix Treaty and, 49,
        70, 75–76, 83–84, 100, 246
    interpreters and, 41, 69
    Iroquois and, 44–45, 62
    Penn family and, 93
    unscrupulous practices, 37
    western lands and, 94
    written treaties and, 35, 36
    Wyoming Valley and, 61
Penobscots, 26–27, 37–38, 241
Perdue, Theda, 136, 316n100
Perrot, Nicholas, 34
Peters, Richard, 39, 67–68, 69,
    79, 93, 248
Philadelphia, delegation
    to, 15
Philbrick, Nathaniel, 188
Philips, Philip, 68, 69
Phoenix (Cherokee newspaper),
    9, 129, 131, 136, 142
Piankeshaws, 105
Pickens, Andrew, 103–4
Pickering, Timothy, 110–11
pictographs, 46
Piegans, 179
Pierce, Maris Bryant (Seneca),
    120
Pike, Albert, 161
pipes (calumets) and smoking.
    see also tobacco
    Caddos and, 165
    colonial era and, 14, 20,
        25–35
    Fort Finney conference
        and, 102
    Fort Laramie Treaty and,
        175
    Great Plains Indians and, 17
    W. Johnson and, 64
    Lewis and Clark and, 167,
        168–69
    Logstown Treaty and, 34

Medicine Lodge Treaty
    and, 209
New Mexico and, 166
truth and, 33
US commissioners and, 98
Wayne and, 111–12
Pitchlynn, John, 115
"Pittsylvania," 82
Pizelle, John (Poisal), 175, 197
Plains Indians. *see also* western
    lands and Indians; *specific
    tribes*
    alliances and, 171–72
    Cherokees and, 156
    diplomacy and, 164–65, 171
    diseases and, 167, 174
    Europeans and, 165–66
    Fort Atkinson Treaty and,
        176
    horses and, 165, 167
    intertribal alliances, 165
    leadership and, 16–17
    Medicine Lodge Treaty and,
        182, 196, 202
    reservations and, 9–10
    signatures, 46
    trade and, 167
    US Indian Peace
        Commission and, 186
    US military and, 177
    violence and, 172, 183,
        184–85, 216–17, 218–19,
        220, 221, 222
plenary power doctrine, 238
Plymouth Colony, 13–14, 19
Pocahontas (Powhatan), 13
Poinsett, Joel, 157
Point Pleasant battle, 90
Poisal, John (Pizelle), 175, 197
political savvy of Indians, 43,
    116, 119–20
Polk, James, 159, 173
Pomo tribe, 5
Poncas, 170–71, 235
Pontiac (Ottawa), 54
Pontiac's War, 47, 58, 66
Poor Bear (Plains Apache),
    176, 194, 198, 200
Porter, George, 139
Post, Christian Frederick, 47
Potawatomis. *see also individual
    Potawatomis*
    bribery and, 139–40
    Cherokee Commission and,
        235

Chicago Treaty, 118–19,
    139–40
Detroit conference and, 105
Fort Wayne Treaty and, 116
Mahicans and, 25
medals and, 112
number of treaties signed,
    5, 119
Prairie du Chien Treaty
    and, 170
Schermerhorn and, 139–40
trust and, 120
Wells and, 113
Powder Face (Arapaho), 216,
    231
Powell, William, 58
power
    American, 99
    diplomacy and, 164–65, 173
    Indian, 17
    Jackson and, 132–33
    liquor and, 45
    medals and, 21, 99
    Roman Nose on, 184
    treaties and, 228–29
    US and, 7, 108, 112
    US Supreme Court on, 238
    wars and, 13
    of words, 22–25
    writing and, 36, 38, 39–40
Powhatan, 13
Pratt, Richard Henry, 196,
    223–24
pre-contact Indians, 12–13
prewritten treaties, 170, 177
price of land, 144
Principal Dogs (Katsienko)
    (Koietsenko) (Qóichégàu)
    (Sentinel Horses), 191,
    197, *207*
prisoners, 92, 93, 94, *198,* 223,
    224
private meetings and
    agreements. *see also* secret
    articles
    chief salaries and, 107–8
    Fort Stanwix Treaty and,
        69–70, 75–76
    W. Johnson and, 69–70,
        72, 73
    Medicine Lodge Treaty
        and, 194
    Schermerhorn and, 140
    as standard practice, 40, 70
    Walla Walla Treaty and, 178

private property (land), 93, 98, 204, 234
Privy Council (Britain), 82, 84
Proclamation of 1763, 81, 89
promiscuity, 165
protests, 11, 104, 106, 120
protocols, 12, 14–15, 194
Prucha, Francis Paul, 172
Pueblos, 167
Puget Sound Basin, 177
Pumpshire, John, 39
Puyallups, 177

Qóichégàu (Katsienkos) (Koietsenkos) (Real/ Principal Dogs) (Sentinel Horses) (Kiowas), 191, 197, *207*
Quakers, 18, 42, 110, 111. *see also individual Quakers*
Quapaws, 33–34, 139
Quebec Act of 1774, 82–83
quill (feather) (Onas) (William Penn), 25, 30, 36, *38,* 131–32

racherías, 174
racism, 130
railroads. *see also specific railroad companies*
    attacks on, 183, 184, 198
    Boudinot and, 233
    buffalos and, 222
    Fort Laramie Treaty and, 226, 227
    Iroquois and, 119
    Jerome Commission and, 237
    Medicine Lodge Treaty and, 185, 204, 209, 210, 211, 219, 221
    Navajos and, 227
    Pacific Northwest and, 177, 180
    Plains Indians and, 186
    Stone Calf on, 231
the Rat (Kondiaronk) (Huron), 15
ratification, US Constitution and, 106–7
Raven of Chota, 91
Real Dogs (Katsienkos) (Koietsenkos) (Qóichégàus) (Sentinel

Horses) (Kiowas), 191, 197, *207*
Red Clay proclamation (1836), 148
Red Cloud (Oglala), 226–27
Red Cloud War, 184–85
Red Hawk (Shawnee), 86
Red Head (Onondaga), 34
Red Jacket (Seneca), 108, 110, 113
Red River War (Buffalo War), 221, 222–23
Red Sticks. *see* Creeks
religion. *see* Christianity
removal. *see also* Boudinot, Elias (Galagina) (Buck Watie) (Cherokee); The Ridge; Ridge, John; Ross, John (Cherokee); Treaty of New Echota (1835)
    Cherokees and, 120, 123–24, 129–30, 135–53
    Chicago Treaty and, 118–19
    W. Clark and, 170–71
    costs of, 152, 153–54, 160
    deadline, 151, 152
    depredations and, 152–53
    disease and, 150, 152
    Georgia and, 137
    Jackson and, 132–33, 135
    logistics and planning, 151–52
    New Echota Treaty and, 9
    numbers removed, 153
    opponents of, 129–32, 133
    Ross and Boudinot on, 149
    Scott and, 151
    timeline, 147
    US Civil War and, 163
    US Supreme Court and, 120, 133–34
Renan, Ernest, 225
reservations
    Arapahos and, 210
    California and, 173–74
    Cherokee Commission and, 236
    Cheyennes and, 211, 219
    Dawes Act and, 234
    Doolittle report and, 185
    extinction *versus,* 181, 182
    Fort Laramie Treaty and, 175, 226
    Fort Stanwix Treaty and, 84
    Grant and, 219

Indian Office and, 173
Indian opinions of, 222
Indian Trade and Intercourse Act of 1834 and, 172
Jerome Commission and, 237
Kiowas and, 238
Lakotas and, 235
Lapwai Valley Treaty and, 227
Little Arkansas Treaty and, 183, 184
Medicine Lodge Treaty and, 10, 182, 201–2, 203–4, 205, 210, 211, 214, 216
New Echota Treaty and, 144
railroads and, 186
settlers and, 230
Sheridan and, 219
Stevens and, 177
US Civil War and, 163
US Congress and, 230
US expansion and, 9–10
US Indian Peace Commission and, 186
resistance. *see also* violence and retaliation
    by Kiowas, 184
    New Echota Treaty and, 144
    by J. Ross, 156–57
    Sassaba and, 119–20
res judicata, 241
Revolutionary War
    Cherokee homelands and, *122*
    compensation for services, 111
    effects of, 96
    Fort Stanwix Treaty and, 90, 92
    land grants and, 100, 103, 111
    Sayenqueraghta on, 93
    Shawnees and, 103
    speculators and, 83
    Washington and, 100
Reynolds, Milton, 188–89
Richardville, Jean-Baptiste (Miami), 140
Rider, Ellis, 158
The Ridge (Major Ridge) (Kahmungdaclageh) (Cherokee). *see also* Treaty Party

death penalty and, 154
image, *124*
Jackson and, 148
life history, 123
New Echota Treaty and, 9,
143–45, 147
removal and, 124–26, 129,
131, 135–38, 150
wife, 125, 157
Ridge, Andrew Jackson, 140, 141
Ridge, John (Cherokee). *see
also* Treaty Party
Cherokee civil wars and, 155
death of, 154–55
family of, 318n151
image, *126*
Jackson and, 140, 148
life history, 125–28
New Echota Treaty and, 9,
141, 142, 147–48
removal and, 129, 135–38, 150
John Ross and, 135–38,
140–42, 145–46, 153
Schermerhorn and, 140,
141, 142
Ridge, John Rollin (Cherokee),
154, 157–58, 159, 160–61,
163
Ridge, Nancy, 125
Ridge, Susanna (Sehoya)
(Wickett) (Cherokee), 125
right of conquest, 100, 102,
105, 111
right of cultivation, 115
right of preemption, 95
rights, equal, 243–44
rights of discovery, 3–4, 5
rights of Indians, 3, 43, 129,
155–56, 231–32, 238–39,
242–43, 333n34. *see also*
legality
rights to buy, 4
rights to fish and to hunt, 75,
177, 217, 240
rights to sale of land, 65
rituals, 4, 12, 14–15, 16, 105,
167, 287n9; gifts; pipes
and smoking; wampum
belts; *(Gus-Wen-Tah)
(Kaswentha); specific
rituals*
roads, 179
Robinson, Alexander
(Chechebinquey)
(Potawatomi), 139–40

Robinson, Charles, 192
Rocky Mountains, 32
Rodgers, John (Cherokee), 154
Roman Nose (Cheyenne), 184,
193, 211, 216, 217, 219
Ross, Allen (Cherokee), 154
Ross, Andrew (Cherokee), 138,
144, 149
Ross, Edmond G., 188, 228
Ross, James (Cherokee), 162
Ross, Jane (Meigs), 158
Ross, John (Cherokee). *see
also* National Party
(Cherokee)
arrest of, 142–43
Bell and, 157
Cherokee civil wars and,
159–60
costs of removal and, 152,
160
death of, 163
image, *130*
Jackson and, 123, 135, 148
McIntosh and, 125
New Echota Treaty and,
141, 145–46, 149–50, 154,
156–57, 159, 160, 249
removal and, 129, 131,
136–38, 140–41, 151–52,
159
J. Ridge and, 135–38,
140–46, 153, 155
Schermerhorn and, 142,
145, 147
on sovereignty, 155, 158,
159, 162
Tahlequah conference and,
156
US Civil War and, 161–62
Stand Watie and, 154, 159,
162, 163
wives, 152, 159, 162
Ross, Mary, 162
Round Face (Seneca), 90
Rowlands, John. *see* Stanley,
Henry Morton
Rushforth, Brett, 47
Russia, 5

sachems, 17
Sac Indians (Sauks), 115, 170,
235
Sacred Arrows ceremony, 193,
211
Sadosky, Leonard, 117

Sakakawea (Charbonneau)
(Shoshoni), 169
Salish (Flatheads), 169, 171,
179
Sanborn, John B., 184, 186,
194, 226
Sand Creek massacre (1864),
183, 184, 186, 189, 190,
193, 195, 196, 197, 229
Santa Fe talks (1762), 166
Saorghweyoghsta (Doer
of Justice) (William
Franklin), 70, 71
sashes, 191, 197, 198, *207*
Sassaba (Ojibwe), 119–20
Satank (Sitting Bear)
(Kiowa)
description of, 197–98
horses and, 171
image, *207*
medals and, 212
Medicine Lodge Treaty and,
10, 183, 205
son of, 220, 236
speech by, 206–9
Warren Wagon Train
Massacre and, 220–21
Satanta (White Bear) (Kiowa)
Custer and, 218–19
death of, 223
description of, 191–92
image, *191*
medals and, 212
Medicine Lodge Treaty
and, 10, 183, 194, 197,
199–200, 201, 204, 205
violence of, 196, 209, 220,
221
Sattelihu (Andrew Montour,
Eghnisera), 69
Sauganash (Billy Caldwell)
(Potawatomi), 139–40
Sauguaarum, Loron
(Penobscot), 37–38
Sauks (Sacs), 115, 170, 235
Sault Ste. Marie, 3–4
Savery, William, 110
Sayenqueragtha (Old Smoke)
(Seneca), 68, 89, 92, 93
Scarouady (Oneida), 20, 57
Schermerhorn, John F. (Devil's
Horn)
Buffalo Creek Treaty and,
153
on Cherokee civil wars, 155

Schermerhorn, John F. (Devil's
    Horn) (*Cont.*)
  on New Echota Treaty, 145
  New Echota Treaty and,
    138–40, 141–42, 143, 144,
    145, 147, 152, 248
  Stockbridge Indians and,
    153
schools. *see also* education
  ABCFM and, 125, 127
  Bull Bear and, 219
  Carlisle (PA), 223, 224
  Fort Laramie Treaty and,
    226
  Medicine Lodge Treaty and,
    200, 201, 203, 204, 211
  Navajos and, 227
Schuyler, Philip, 96, 100, 111
Scioto River, 86
Scotsmen, 41, 129. *see also*
    individual Scotsmen
Scott, Winfield, 151
scribes, 37
seals, 35, 46, 48
secretaries, 37
secret articles, 107–8. *see also*
    private meetings and
    agreements
Sehoya (Susanna Wickett)
    (Ridge) (Cherokee), 125
Seminoles, 125, 139, 187
Senecas. *see also* Iroquois
    (Iroquois League) (Six
    Nations); Treaty of
    Buffalo Creek (1838);
    individual Senecas
  Auglaize River conference
    and, 108
  Big Tree Treaty and, 113
  British and, 54
  Canandaigua Treaty and,
    111
  Croghan and, 61, 64–65
  Fort Stanwix attacks, 93
  Fort Stanwix Treaty and,
    66, 68
  Iroquois League and, 1, 24
  Kinzua Dam and, 11
  Montour and, 69, 88
  New York State and, 101
  19th century treaties, 119
  Schermerhorn and, 139, 140
Sentinel Horses (Katsienkos)
    (Koietsenkos)
    (Qóichégàus) (Real/

Principal Dogs) (Kiowas),
    191, 197, *207*
Sequarusera (Tuscarora), 77,
    248
Sequoyah (George Gist), 128
settlers, American. *see also* US
    expansion
  Abraham on, 89
  British and, 92
  buffalos and, 221–22
  Cherokees and, 91
  Conoghquieson on, 88–89
  Creeks and, 116–17
  disease and, 174
  Fort Stanwix cessions and,
    90–91
  Fort Stanwix Treaty and, 89
  Iroquois and, 119
  Jerome Commission and,
    237
  W. Johnson on, 88, 89
  Kansas and, 211
  legal invasion and, 86
  Little Arkansas Treaty and,
    184
  Medicine Lodge Treaty and,
    200, 204
  Ohio River Valley and,
    85, 87
  Pacific Northwest and, 177
  railroads and, 180
  reservations and, 230
  Rio Grande, attacks south
    of, and, 172
  Sandusky conference and,
    109
  treaties and, 104
  US authority and, 107
  US v. Kagama and, 238
Seven Years' War, 44, 54
Shannon, Timothy, 51, 77, 84
Shawnees and Shawnee
    Confederacy. *see also*
    individual Shawnees;
    specific subtribes
  British and, 65–66, 88, 91
  Cherokees and, 92
  Croghan and, 61, 64–65
  Fort Finney conference and,
    102–3
  Fort Stanwix Treaty and,
    65–66, 68, 75, 77, 86,
    91–92
  Iroquois and, 54
  Jefferson and, 113–14

W. Johnson and, 76
Johnson Hall conference
    and, 60
  Mahicans and, 25
  Morgan and, 96
  Ohio River boundary and,
    108
  Oklahoma and, 235
  Schermerhorn and, 139–40
  settlers and, 87
  Tahlequah conference and,
    156
  treaty and, 47
  Virginia and, 89–90, 92
  wampum and, 31
Sheheke (Mandan), 169
Shelburne, Earl of, 61, 62, 63
Sheridan, Philip, 217–18, 220
Sherman, William Tecumseh
  image, *187*
  Kiowas and, 220, 221
  McCusker and, 196
  Medicine Lodge Treaty and,
    186–87, 212, 213
  Navajos and, 227
  reservations and, 214, 217
  starvation tactic of, 214
  US Commission and, 229
  violence of, 213
Shickellamy, John
    (Tachendorus) (Oneida),
    42
Shirley, William, 26–27
Shoshonis, 174, 175, 227. *see
    also* Plains Indians
signatures, 2–3, 46, 106–7, 171,
    211, 236
signing of treaties, Indian
    understanding of, 17
sign language, 196
Silver Brooch (Toshaway)
    (Peneteka Comanche)
    (Honey Eater), 183, 200,
    204, 214–15
Silver Horn (Kiowa), 205
singing, 31, 102, 175, 177
Sioux. *see also* Plains Indians;
    *individual Sioux; specific
    subtribes*
  Black Hills and, 234,
    240–41
  Custer and, 233
  Fort Laramie Treaty and,
    175, 176–77
  Lewis and Clark and, 167

Prairie du Chien Treaty and, 170
reservations, 226, 234–35
Traverse des Sioux Treaty/ Mendota Treaty and, 174
treaties with, 226
US Indian Peace Commission and, 186
US sovereignty and, 170
Sioux Act of 1888, 234–35
Sissetons, 174
Sitting Bear (Kiowa). *see* Satank
Sitting Bull (Sioux), 233
Six Nations. *see* Five Nations; Iroquois; *specific tribes*
Skenanadon (Oneida), 93
Skiagusta (Cherokee), 35
slavery, 147, 163, 166, 176
slaves, 47, 48, 52, 117, 122, 123, 128, 180, 297n174
Smallwood, Thomas, 58
Smith, Archilla (Cherokee), 144, 157
Smith, Frederick, 68, 248
Smith, Jack, 177, 197
Smith, John (colonist), 13
Smith, John Simpson, 175, 176–77, 184, 196, 197, 211, 231, *232*
Smith, Nathaniel, 148, 150
smoking. *see* pipes and smoking
Snake Woman (Blackfoot), 197
"sold," 44
Soule, W. S., *203, 207*
souls, 35
South Carolina, 35, 48, 92, 103, 108, 121, *122*
South Dakota, 226, 233
Southern Plains, *215*
Southwest, Old, 117
sovereignty. *see also* authority
cessions *versus,* 170
Cherokees and, 122, 128–29, 130–31, 132, 134, 155
Covenant Chain and, 24
Indian understanding of, 17
Iroquois and, 11, 49
Jackson on, 133
Massasoit and, 14
modern Indian, 239, 241, 242
removal and, 138
rights of discovery and, 4

John Ross on, 155, 158, 159, 162
treaties and, 5, 6, 230, 231, 239, 243, 333n37
US Constitution and, 134
Spain and Spaniards. *see also* Paris, Peace of (1763, 1783)
Comanches and, 166–67
Florida and, 98, 125
Louisiana and, 34
Plains Indians and, 165–66
Texas and, 165, 167
treaties and, 4, 5, 98
speculators. *see also* opportunism; *individual speculators; specific companies*
Britain and, 56, 82–83
Chicago Treaty (1833) and, 118
Fort Stanwix Treaty and, 66, 67, 68, 75–76, 77, 80, 82–83, 89
Indian, 113
treaties (1783–1786) and, 98
US authority and, 2, 5, 107
Spokanes, 180
Spotted Tail (Brulé Sioux), 226
Spotted Wolf (Arapaho), 216
Springer, William, 237
squatters, 56
Staked Plains, 200
Stambaugh, Samuel C., 125, 135, 158
Stamp Act, 63
"standing ears of corn" (Canaghquieson) (Kanaghwaes) (Kanaghqweasea) (Kanongyweniyah) (Oneida). *see* Conoghquieson
Stanley, Henry Morton (John Rowlands)
on Augur, 187
on Cheyennes, 211
on Fishermore, 194
J. Henderson's speech, 201
on Little Raven, 198
Medicine Lodge Treaty and, 10, 192–93, 194, 200, 205
on peace, 212
on Peace Commissioners, 186

on reporters, 189
Satank and, 206
on Satank's speech, 209
on Terry, 188
Stapler, Mary (Ross), 159
Star, Ellis, 158
Star, Thomas, 158
Star, Washington, 158
Starr, Ellis, 158
Starr, James, 137, 157, 158
starvation, 3, 142, 214–15, 217, 222, 224, 229
State Journal (newspaper), 188–89
Staten Island, 26
states, 5, 98, 122, 133, 137. *see also specific states*
St. Clair, Arthur, 105–6, 108, 113
Stevens, Isaac, 177–80, 227, 240
St. Germain, Jill, 185, 186, 330n3
St. Lawrence Valley, 32
Stockbridge Indians, 47, 111, 153
Stone Calf (Cheyenne), 231
Stone Forehead (Keeper of the Sacred Arrows) (Medicine Arrow) (Cheyenne), 211, 216
stories, 23, 27
Stuart, John, 51, 56, 72, 81, 82, 88
Stubbs, Mahlon, *232*
Stumbling Bear (Kiowa), 191, 205, 218, 221, 236
St. Vrain, Cerain, 184
Sullivan, John, 93
surveyors, 81
Susquehanna Company, 61–62
Susquehanna River and Valley, 46, 61

Tachendorus (John Shickellamy) (Oneida), 42
Tagawaron (Oneida), 68, 73
Taiaiake Alfred, xii
taimes, 218
Tall Bear (Cheyenne Dog Soldier), 184
Tall Bull (Cheyenne Dog Soldier), 195, 212, 219
Tanagharison (Seneca), 69

Tananaica (Hears the Sunrise)
(Voice of the Sunrise)
(Yamparika Comanche),
222
Tappan, Samuel F., 186, *187,*
194, 226, 227, 229
Tatum, Lawrie, 219, 221
taxes, 233, 239–40
Taylor, Alan, 57
Taylor, James E., 189
Taylor, Nathaniel G., 181, 186,
187, 194, 198, 212, 216,
227, 229
Tayorheasere. *see* Abraham
Tecumseh (Shawnee), 116
Teedyuscung (Delaware)
calumet and, 33
captives and, 47
death of, 62
drinking and, 39, 46
political savvy of, 43
protests by, 61
on wampum, 25
writing and, 38, 39–40
Tegaia (Cayuga), 77, 248
Teganissorens (Onondaga), 1
Teirhenhsere. *see* Abraham
Tejanos, 216
Ten Bears (Paruasemena)
(Yamparika Comanche)
death of, 221
delegation to Washington
and, 176, 194
image, *195*
on Leavenworth, 201
Little Arkansas Treaty and,
183
Medicine Lodge Treaty and,
194, 198, 200, 204–5
Teneangopte (Tonaenko)
(Kiowa). *see* Kicking Bird
Tennessee, 30, 90, 92, 98, 121,
122, 142, 143, 256. *see
also* Treaty of Sycamore
Shoals
Tennessee River, 63, 72,
77, 80
Terry, Alfred H., 186–87, *187,*
188, 194, 226, 227, 229–30
Texas
cattlemen and, 180
Cherokees and, 138, 156
Comanches and, 200, 201,
206, 216
France and, 165

Guadalupe Hidalgo Treaty
and, 172
Indian attacks on, 172
Kiowas and, 216, 218, 221
map, *215*
Plains Indians and,
166, 216
reservations, 183, 184
Spain and, 165, 167
treaties and, 5
women and, 18
Teyarhasere. *see* Abraham
Teyohaquende (Diaquanda)
(Onondaga), 68, 71, 89
Thacher, James, 15
theater, 63
Thomson, Charles, 37, 39
Tigoransera. *see* Abraham
Tilghman, James, 67, 248
Tilghman, Tench, 23–24, 36, 51
titles, 25
tobacco, 20, 45, 166, 167,
168, 178. *see also* pipes
(calumets) and smoking
Tonaenko (Teneangopte)
(Kiowa). *see* Kicking Bird
Tonawanda Senecas, 120
Tonkawas, 235
Toshaway (Silver Brooch)
(Peneteka Comanche)
(Honey Eater), 183, 200,
204, 214–15
Touching the Sky (Maman-ti)
(Dohate) (Owl Prophet)
(Kiowa), 223, 224
"town destroyer." *see*
Washington, George
trade and traders. *see also*
speculators; *individual
traders*
Choctaws and, 117
Fort Stanwix Treaty and,
75–76
intertribal alliances and, 165
Irish, 9
Jefferson and, 114–15
W. Johnson and, 52–53, 82
networks, 167
peace and, 12
Plains Indians and, 167, 170
sales of land and, 114
survival and, 13
Trade and Intercourse Act
and, 107
treaties and, 3, 119

The Trail of Broken Treaties
(march on Washington),
239
Trail of Tears, 9, 121, 153, 154
translators. *see* interpreters and
go-betweens
Transylvania Land Company,
91
treaties. *see also* conferences;
specific treaties
attacks on, 230
death and rebirth of,
226–44
empire and, 2
end of, 8, 186, 228–29, 230,
231–33
Indian-US relations and,
243–44
Indian views of, 228, 242–43
as literature, 8
Lumpkin on, 149
modern interpretations,
10–11, 239, 241–42
motives for, 7–8
number of, 5
power and, 228–29
pre-Revolutionary War, 100
rejection of, 48
removal and, 132
reprints of, 6
rights of Indians and,
238–39, 243
sale of lands and, 4–5, 98
sovereignty and, 230, 243
UN Declaration on the
Rights of Indigenous
Peoples and, 243
US expansion and, 10
treaty at Albany (Albany
Congress) (1754), 24, 31,
44–45, 65, 67
Treaty of Big Tree (1797), 113
Treaty, Blackfeet (Lame Bull's
Treaty) (Treaty of Fort
Benton) (1855), 179–80
Treaty of Buffalo Creek (1838),
119, 120, 153
Treaty of Canandaigua (1794),
5–6, 10–11, 110–11
Treaty of Casco Bay (1727),
37–38
Treaty of Charlestown (1756),
48
treaties with Cherokees (1817,
1819, 1866), 125, 163

Treaty of Chicago (1833), 118–19, 139–40
treaty, Comanche-Ute (1786), 5, 167
Treaty of Dancing Rabbit Creek (1830), 118, 120
Treaty of Doak's Stand (1820), 118
Treaty of Easton (1758), 37; (1756), 47
Treaty of Fort Atkinson (1853), 174, 176
Treaty of Fort Benton (Blackfeet Treaty) (Lame Bull's Treaty) (1855), 179–80
Treaty of Fort Bridger (1868), 227
Treaties of Fort Harmar (1788–89), 105–6
Treaty of Fort Herkimer (1785), 101
Treaty of Fort Jackson (1814), 117, 118
Treaty of Fort Laramie (Horse Creek encampment) (1851), 174–76
Treaty of Fort Laramie (1868), 226–27, 228, 233, 234, 239, 241, 330n3
Treaty of Fort McIntosh (1786), 102
Treaty of Fort Pitt (1778), 8, 94, 96–97
Treaty of Fort Smith (1865), 162
Treaty of Fort Stanwix (1768). *see also* Johnson, William (Sir William) (Warraghiyagey)
  boundaries and, 8, 9, 49–65, 71–77, *78*, 80–82, 83, 84, 86, 87, 88, 90, 95, 245, 247, 251
  cession struggles, 80–95
  Conoghquieson and, 54
  formal negotiations, 70–77, 100
  gifts, 21
  Greenville Treaty and, 113
  history of America and, 8–9, 10
  Iroquois and, 45, 50
  prenegotiation history, 49, 53–69

private agreements, 69, 75–76
  representation and, 48
  Tecumseh's death and, 116
  terms of, 77–80, 100
  text of, 245–48
Treaty of Fort Stanwix (1784), 100–101, 111
Treaty of Fort Wayne (1809), 116
Treaty of Fort Wise (1861), 176
Treaty of Greenville (1795), 8, 111–13, *112*, 164, 309n51
Treaty of Guadalupe Hidalgo (1848), 172
Treaty of Hard Labor (1768), 67, 81
Treaty of Hartford (1638), 14
Treaty of Hell Gate (1855), 179
treaty, Henderson (Treaty of Sycamore Shoals) (1775), 91, 104
treaty, Henry Bouquet's (1764), 47
Treaty of Holston (1791), 108
Treaty of Hopewell (1785–1786), 103–5
Treaty of Indian Springs (1825), 118, 125
treaty, Kiowa-Comanche (1867), 189, 205. *see also* Treaty of Medicine Lodge (1867)
Treaty, Lame Bull's (Blackfeet Treaty) (Treaty of Fort Benton) (1855), 179–80
Treaty of Lancaster (1744), 8, 23, 35, 41, 43–44, 45–46, 50, 81
Treaty of Lapwai Valley (1863), 227
Treaty of the Little Arkansas (1865), 183, 184, 186, 209, 238
Treaty of Lochaber (1770), 81, 90
Treaty of Logstown (1752), 27, 34, 41, 69
Treaty of Medicine Creek (1854), 177
Treaty of Medicine Lodge (1867)
  additional compensation, 238
  analysis of, 213

G. Bent and, 190
  buffalo hunting and, 221–22
  commemorations, 225
  commissioners and, 185–86, 189, 191, 192–93, 193–94, 196
  commissioner's report, 213–16
  Dog Soldiers and, 211
  end of treaties and, 228
  formal negotiations, 197–202, 205–12
  gifts, 205–6
  Grant and, 219
  Harney and, 162
  history of America and, 8–9, 10
  images, *198, 199*, 224
  Indian background, 196
  Indian negotiators, 189–92, 193, 194–95, 196–97
  Indian understanding of, 204–5
  Indian women and, 18, 197
  Jerome Commission and, 235, 237
  news coverage, 189, 194, 196, 204–5, 213
  prenegotiation history, 182–85, 189, 192–93
  prisoners and, 224–25
  reservations and, 10, 163, 201, 203–4, 216, 235
  Satank's speech, 206–9
  site and date of, 189
  Stone Calf on, 231
  terms of, 202–4, 211–12
  text of, 264–83
  US Congress and, 214
  US military and, 192–93, 213–14, 324n29
  US Peace Commission and, 182–97
  US Supreme Court and, 237
  violations of, 214–16
  violent responses, 216–24, 324n29
Treaty of Mendota (1851), 174
treaty, Montreal, Great Peace of (1701), 1–2, 8, 15, 49
Treaty of Mount Dexter (1805), 115
treaty with the Navajos (1868), 239

Treaty of New Echota (Ridge's Treaty) (1835). *see also* Red Clay proclamation (1836); removal; Treaty Party (Cherokee)
  Cherokees and, 9, 121–35
  civil wars and, 153–63
  corruption and fraud and, 148, 151
  costs of, 152, 153–54
  formal negotiations, 143–45
  history of America and, 8–9, 10
  income from, 160
  prenegotiation history, 121–40
  renegotiation of, 145–53, 157, 159
  Ridge *versus* Ross and, 135–38, 140–42, 145–46
  Schermerhorn and, 138–40, 141–42, 144, 147, 152, 248, 249
  text of, 248–64
  violations of, 153–54
Treaty of New York (1790), 107
treaty with Nez Perces (1868), 227
Treaty of Niagara (1764), 10–11, 55
treaty with Osages (1808), 169
Treaty of Paris (1763), 53, 54
Treaty of Paris (1783), 94–95, 97, 100, 105
Treaty of Portage des Sioux (1815), 170
Treaty of Prairie du Chien (1825), 170
Treaty, Ridge's. *see* Treaty of New Echota (1835)
treaty, Santa Fe (1785), 167
Treaty of Shackamaxon (1683), *38*
treaty, South Carolina (1721), 121
Treaty of St. Louis (1804), 115
Treaty of Sycamore Shoals (Henderson treaty) (1775), 91, 104
treaty, Texas (1785), 167
Treaty of Traverse des Sioux (1851), 174
Treaty of Walla Walla (1855), 177–79, *178*

treaties, Washington Territory (1854–1856), 177
treaty, Yakama (1855), 177–79
treaty cloth, 10
treaty federalism, 242
treaty locations, 15
Treaty Party (Cherokee). *see also* Boudinot, Elias; The Ridge; Ridge, John
  Cherokee civil wars and, 158
  Lumpkin on, 155
  members of, 136
  New Echota Treaty and, 144–45, 149
  Old Settlers and, 156
  removal of, 150, 158
  J. Ross on, 138
  on J. Ross Party, 147
  Ross-Watie conflict and, 153–54, 159–60
  US government and, 157
Trent, William, 54, 58, 61, 66, 68, 82
"tribe" ("nation"), xii
Trott, James, 144
trust by Indians, 119–20
Truteau, Jean Baptiste, 167
Tsosie, Rebecca, 242
Turle's Heart (Delaware), 68
Tuscarora Indian Nation, Federal Power Commission v. (1960), 239
Tuscaroras, 24, 77, 101, 111, 239, 248. *see also* Iroquois (Iroquois League) (Six Nations)
Tyearuruante, 73
Tyler, John, 157
Tyorhansera. *see* Abraham

Umatillas, 177
Union Pacific Railroad, 186
United Nations Declaration on the Rights of Indigenous Peoples, 243
United States government, 96–97, 98–100, 103–4. *see also entries beginning* US...
  UN Declaration on the Rights of Indigenous Peoples and, 243
Upper Creeks, 48
US, Winters v. (1908), 238

US authority, 2, 5, 107, 236. *see also* legality
US Bureau of Indian Affairs (Indian Office), 173
US citizenship, 114, 124, 134, 138, 182, 233, 237, 244
US Civil War, 5, 161–63, 180
US commissioners. *see also individual commissioners; specific treaties*
  coercion and, 115
  Fort Finney conference and, 102–3
  Hopewell Treaty and, 104
  US Constitution and, 106
  wampum and, 103
  after War of 1812, 170
  women and, 120
US Congress. *see also* US House of Representatives; US Senate; *specific legislation*
  1832 authorization, 173
  annuities and, 106
  authority of, 237–38
  Black Hills and, 241
  Cherokee removal and, 120, 131
  end of treaty system and, 231–32
  Fort Stanwix Treaty and, 100
  Indian wars and, 105, 185
  Jerome Commission and, 237
  Lakotas and, 234
  land transfers and, 241
  Medicine Lodge Treaty and, 202, 214
  New Echota Treaty and, 145, 147
  private land and, 98
  rights of Indians and, 333n34
  treaty making and, 5, 8
  treaty violations and, 132
  US Constitution and, 106, 242
US Constitution, 106, 107, 132, 134, 156, 230, 231, 241, 242
US Corps of Discovery, 164
US courts, 131, 133, 177, 212, 238, 240–41. *see also* legality; US Supreme Court

US Department of the Interior, 173, 231
US expansion. *see also* removal; settlers, American
boundaries and, 95, 174
British and, 55–57
Fort Stanwix Treaty and, 84
Harrison and, 115–16
Medicine Lodge Treaty and, 213
Northwest Ordinance and, 105
reservations and, 9–10
Supreme Court and, 5, 238
treaties and, 3, 113–14
US authority and, 107
US Indian Peace Commission and, 185–86
western lands and, 172–73, 180–81
US government. *see also other entries beginning US...; Revolutionary War; sovereignty; specific branches; specific treaties*
boundaries and, 98, 99, 100, 104, 105, 107, 109, 174
Cherokee civil wars and, 158–59
Cherokees and, 122, 146–47, 148
Forbes and Company and, 115
Fort Laramie Treaty (1868) and, 233
Georgia and, 142
New Echota Treaty and, 153
number of treaties made, 173
J. Ross and, 149–50, 156–57
states and, 133, 137
title to land and, 4
US House of Representatives, 159, 230–31
US Indian Peace Commission, 182, 185–89, *187,* 226, 229–30. *see also* Treaty of Medicine Lodge (1867); *individual commissioners*
US military. *see also individual leaders; specific actions*
Augur and, 187
Black Hills and, 233–34
blame by, 229

Fort Stanwix Treaty and, 100
Kiowas and, 221
Medicine Lodge Treaty and, 192–93, 324n29
New Echota Treaty and, 148, 155
Nez Perces and, 228
Plains Indians and, 177, 222
Red Cloud War and, 185
US Indian Peace Commission and, 186
US presidents, 106–7, 121, 132, 169, 185. *see also individual presidents*
US secretaries of war, 106. *see also individual secretaries*
US Senate
Buffalo Creek Treaty and, 119, 120
California treaties and, 174
Cherokee civil wars and, 159–60
Cherokees and, 138, 163
Indian Removal Act and, 132
Indian Springs Treaty and, 118
last treaty ratified, 227
Little Arkansas Treaty and, 184
New Echota Treaty and, 121, 147
Potawatomis and, 139–40
ratification and, 238
rule of law and, 242
US House and, 230
US sovereignty. *see* sovereignty
US statutes, 231–32
US Supreme Court, 5, 109, 120, 133–34, 233, 237–39, 239–40, 241, 333n34. *see also* legality; *specific cases*
US v. Kagama (1886, 1903), 237–38
US v. Winans (1905), 238
US War Department, 231
Utah, 172
Utes, 5, 166, 167, 218. *see also* Plains Indians

Van Buren, Martin, 120, 149–50, 151, 152
Vandalia proposal, 82–83

Vann, David (Cherokee), 138, 157
Vann, James (Cherokee), 123
Vaudreuil, Marquis de, 20
Vélez, Tomás, 20
victims, 243–44
Vimont, Barthélemy, 23
violence and retaliation. *see also* Indian wars; resistance; US military; wars; *specific battles; specific massacres*
Cherokee civil wars, 153–63
Dodge on, 230
Fort Stanwix Treaty and, 91
by Harney, 176
Kansas and, 217
Medicine Lodge Treaty and, 216–24, 324n29
by Oglalas, 226
on Osages, 216
Pennsylvania and, 55
Plains Indians and, 172, 183, 184–85, 216–17, 218–19, 220, 221, 222
Ross and, 159
of Satanta, 196, 209, 220, 221
settlers, American, and, 87
Sheridan and, 219
Virginia. *see also* Treaty of Lancaster (1744); *individual Virginians*
Cherokees and, 67, *122*
Fort Stanwix Treaty and, 49, 70, 83–84, 90, 246
Hard Labor Treaty and, 81
interpreters and, 41
Iroquois and, 23, 44
Kentucky and, 89, 98
Ohio River Valley and, 44, 98
Powhatan chiefdom and, 13
Shawnees and, 89–90, 92
smoking and, 34
speculators, 56
wampum and, 20, 27, 31
western lands and, 94
writing and, 35
Voice of the Sunrise (Hears the Sunrise) (Tananaica) (Yamparika Comanche), 222

Wabash nations, 60
wagon trains, 174

Wahpekutes, 174
Wahpetons, 174
Walker, Thomas, 66–67, 81, 90, 94, 248
"Walking Purchase" (1737), 39, 62
Walking Woman (Margaret Fitzpatrick) (Wilmarth) (Wilmott) (Adams) (Arapaho), 184, 197, 198, 210
Wallawallas, 177
Wallowa Valley, 228
Walpole, Richard, 82
Walpole, Thomas, 82
Walpole Associates, 82
Wampanoag tribe, 13–14
wampum belts. *see also (Gus-Wen-Tah) (Kaswentha)*
  Albany conference and, 34
  as atonement, 47
  Auglaize River conference and, 108
  colonial era and, 14, 25–32
  Conoghquieson and, 89
  Duane on, 99
  Fort Finney conference and, 102, 106
  Fort Pitt Treaty and, 97
  Fort Stanwix Treaty and, 62–63, 70, 71, 74, 75, 76
  Greenville Treaty and, 112
  image source, 292n70
  Indian wars and, 90
  meanings of, 3, 30, 293n90
  Montour and, 69
  preservation of, 37
  Revolutionary War and, 96
  rituals and, 16
  Shawnees and, 86, 88, 103
  Teedyuscung and, 39
  treaties and, 10
  US commissioners and, 98, 100, 106
  Virginia colony and, 20
  wars and, 91, 103
  Washington and, 42
  Wayne and, 111–12
  women and, 18
  written treaties *versus,* 35, 36
wampumpeag, 26
Ward, Edward, 58
War of 1812, 113, 117
war of 1846–1848 (Mexican War), 172

Warraghiyagey. *see* Johnson, William (Sir William)
Warren Trading Post Co. v. Arizona Tax Commission (1965), 239–40
Warren Wagon Train Massacre (1871), 220–21
warriors, Indian, 107, 109, 171, 183. *see also see also individual warriors*
wars, 1, 2, 13, 22, 31, 170. *see also* Indian wars; violence and retaliation; *specific wars*
Washburn, Cephas, 147
Washington, George ("Great Councillor of the Thirteen Fires") ("town destroyer")
  Cherokees and, 108
  on Greenville Treaty, 113
  Iroquois and, 100
  land bounties and, 67
  medals and, 112
  Monongahela battle, 57
  Montour and, 69
  Ohio country and, 42
  Pickering and, 111
  Quakers and, 110
  Senecas and, 100–101
  as speculator, 83, 84, 89
  on US authority, 107
Washington DC, delegations to, 169, 175, 176, 221, 227, 231, 236–37, 239
Washington state/territory, 177, 240
Watie, Buck (Galagina) (Cherokee). *see* Boudinot, Elias
Watie, Charlotte Jacqueline, 157, 163
Watie, Comiskey (Cumiskey), 157, 162
Watie, Ninnie Josephine, 157, 160, 163
Watie, Saladin Ridge, 157, 161, 162, 163
Watie, Sarah Caroline (Bell), 157, 162, 163
Watie, Solon Watica, 157
Watie, Stand (Dagdoga) (He Stands)
  businesses of, 153–54, 160
  Cherokee civil wars and, 158, 159–60

Cherokee Phoenix and, 142
  Christian name of, 125
  death of, 163
  death penalty and, 154
  family of, 147, 157, 158
  Foreman and, 157
  image, *146*
  Jackson and, 123
  New Echota Treaty and, 145, 154
  Paschal and, 318n151
  removal of, 150–51
  John Ross and, 154, 159, 162, 163
  A. Smith and, 157
  taxes and, 233
  US Civil War and, 161
  US government and, 163
Watie, Thomas, 158
Watie, Watica, 163
Watie party, 162
Watson, Blake, 85
Wayne, Anthony, 110, 111–13, 309n51
Weas, 105
Webster, Daniel, 132
Weisenberg, Catherine, 50, 57
Weiser, Conrad, 29, 40, 41, 45
Wells, William, 113
Welsh, 29
werowance, 13
West, Benjamin, *38*
West, Elliott, 180
West, Ellis, 158
West, George and Jacob, 157
western frontier
  British and, 55–57, 86
  English and, 72
  Indian unrest and, 85
  Indian wars and, 90
  Jefferson and, 114
  post 1834, 172–73
  US authority and, 107
western lands
  US expansion and, 172–73, 180–81
western lands and Indians.
  see also Clark, William; Lewis, Meriwether; Pacific Northwest; Plains Indians; Southwest, Old; *specific states and tribes*
  Canada and, 83
  Clark and, 169
  as commodities, 97

Croghan and, 88
Delaware State and, 94
New Echota Treaty and, 121
opportunism and, 84
post-Revolutionary War,
  97–98
southeastern ceded for,
  117–18
Tahlequah conference and,
  156
Wayne and, 111–12
West Virginia, 76, 81, *122*
Wharton, Samuel
British and, 58–59, 82
Fort Stanwix Treaty and,
  60–61, 66, 79, 84–85
B. Franklin and, 60–61, 83
on gifts, 77
image, *59*
Johnson and, 66, 71
Onondagas and, 299n44
Revolutionary War and, 83,
  94, 96
Wheelock, Eleazar, 51–52, 74
Whipple, Henry B., 230
Whitaker, A. A., 196
White Bear (Kiowa). *see*
  Satanta
White Eyes (Delaware), 91,
  96, 97
White Horse (Cimarron
  Cheyenne), 205, 211, 223
Wichita agency, 183
Wichitas, 167, 219, *232,* 235.
  see also Plains Indians
Wickett, Susanna (Sehoya)
  (Ridge) (Cherokee), 125
Wilkinson, Charles, 239,
  241–42
Williams, Eunice, 26
Williams, Joseph L., 152
Williams, Jr., Robert A., 243
Williams, Roger, 4

Williams v. Lee (1959), 239
Wills, George, 206
Wilmarth, Margaret (Adams)
  (Fitzpatrick) (Wilmott)
  (Walking Woman)
  (Arapaho), 184, 197, 198,
  210
Winans, US v. (1905), 238
Winnebagos, 170
Winters v. US (1908), 238
Winyan Wicakte (Woman
  Killer). *see* Harney,
  William S.
Wirt, William, 133–34
Wisconsin, 105, 119, 153
Wolcott, Oliver, 100
Wolf Slave (Arapaho), 191
Woman Killer (Winyan
  Wicakte). *see* Harney,
  William S.
Woman's Heart (Mayetin)
  (Kiowa), 221, 223, 224
women, Indian. *see also*
  intermarriages; *individual
  women*
Brulé, 167
Caddo, 165
Canandaigua Treaty and,
  110
Cherokee, 125
Cheyenne, 209, 223
clothes and, 202
Comanche, 167
Dancing Rabbit Creek
  Treaty and, 120
delegations to Washington
  and, 176
diplomatic roles of, 18–19
Fort Finney conference and,
  102, 103
as interpreters, 40
Iroquois, 101–2, 110
Johnson on, 51

Lewis and Clark and, 167
New Echota Treaty and, 143
removal and, 152
treaties and, 68
US Civil War and, 162
US Indian Peace
  Commission and, *187*
Walla Walla conference
  and, 178
wampum and, 27, 64
Wool, John, 148
Worcester, Samuel, 129, 134,
  154
Worcester v. Georgia (1832),
  134
words, power of, 19, 22–25
Wounded Knee, siege of
  (1973), 239
written treaties, 17, 35–40, 128.
  see also literacy
Wroth, Lawrence, 8, 14, 23
Wyandots, 32, 69, 96, 109,
  116, 156
Wynkoop, Edward,
  189, 196
Wyoming, 167, *215,* 227.
  *see also treaties of Fort
  Laramie*
Wyoming Valley, 61–62, 75

Yakamas, 177, 178. *see also
  individual Yakamas*
Yakama War, 179
Yamparika Comanches, 176,
  183, 194, 222, 236
Yanktons, 167. *see also* Plains
  Indians; Sioux
Yellow Bear (Arapaho), 191
Yellow Wolf (Nez Perce), 227
Yellow Woman (Bent)
  (Cheyenne), 184

Zacharias (Delaware), 62